The .NET and COM INTEROPERABILITY HANDBOOK

AF778004

ISBN 013046130-X

94999

9 780130 461308

The Integrated .NET Series from Object Innovations and Prentice Hall PTR

C#

- Introduction to C# Using .NET
  Oberg
- Application Development Using C# and .NET
  Stiefel/Oberg

INTEROPERABILITY AND MIGRATION

- XML Programming Using .NET and Java
  Chiang/Singh
- The .NET and COM Interoperability Handbook
  Gordon
- Migrating to .NET: A Pragmatic Path to VB.NET, Visual C++.NET, and ASP.NET
  Katre/Halari/Surapaneni/Gupta/Deshpande

PERL

- Programming Perl in the .NET Environment
  Menaker/Saltzman/Oberg

VISUAL BASIC

- Developing Windows Applications Using Visual Basic .NET
  Kanetkar/ Manickam/Wyatt
- Application Development Using Visual Basic and .NET
  Oberg/Thorsteinson/Wyatt
- Introduction to Visual Basic Using .NET
  Wyatt/Oberg

VISUAL C++

- .NET Architecture and Programming Using Visual C++
  Thorsteinson/Oberg

WEB APPLICATIONS

- Fundamentals of Web Applications Using .NET and XML
  Bell/Feng/Soong/Zhang/Zhu
- Mobile Application Development Using .NET
  Kumar/Maheshwari/Ramadurai
- .NET Security and Cryptography
  Thorsteinson
- Developing Web Applications Using ASP.NET and VB.NET
  Joshi/Ganesh/Kumar/Menaker

THE INTEGRATED .NET SERIES FROM OBJECT INNOVATIONS

The .NET and COM Interoperability Handbook

ALAN GORDON

PRENTICE HALL PTR

Prentice Hall PTR, Upper Saddle River, NJ 07458
www.phptr.com

Library of Congress Cataloging-in-Publication Data

A catalog record for this book can be obtained from the Library of Congress

Editorial/Production Supervision: *Nicholas Radhuber*
Acquisitions Editor: *Jill Harry*
Marketing Manager: *Dan DePasquale*
Manufacturing Buyer: *Maura Zaldivar*
Cover Design: *Anthony Gemmellaro*
Cover Design Direction: *Jerry Votta*
Interior Series Design: *Gail Cocker-Bogusz*

Publishing as Prentice Hall Professional Technical Reference
Upper Saddle River, NJ 07458

PRENTICE HALL PTR

Prentice Hall books are widely used by corporations and government agencies for training, marketing, and resale.

The publisher offers discounts on this book when ordered in bulk quantities. For more information, contact Corporate Sales Department, phone: 800-382-3419; fax: 201-236-7141; email: corpsales@pren-hall.com
Or write Corporate Sales Department, Prentice Hall PTR, One Lake Street, Upper Saddle River, NJ 07458.

Printed in the United States of America

10 9 8 7 6 5 4 3 2 1

ISBN 0-13-046130-X

Pearson Education LTD.
Pearson Education Australia PTY, Limited
Pearson Education Singapore, Pte. Ltd.
Pearson Education North Asia Ltd.
Pearson Education Canada, Ltd.
Pearson Educación de Mexico, S.A. de C.V.
Pearson Education — Japan
Pearson Education Malaysia, Pte. Ltd.

CONTENTS

About Prentice Hall Professional Technical Reference

With origins reaching back to the industry's first computer science publishing program in the 1960s, Prentice Hall Professional Technical Reference (PH PTR) has developed into the leading provider of technical books in the world today. Formally launched as its own imprint in 1986, our editors now publish over 200 books annually, authored by leaders in the fields of computing, engineering, and business.

Our roots are firmly planted in the soil that gave rise to the technological revolution. Our bookshelf contains many of the industry's computing and engineering classics: Kernighan and Ritchie's *C Programming Language*, Nemeth's *UNIX System Administration Handbook*, Horstmann's *Core Java*, and Johnson's *High-Speed Digital Design*.

PH PTR acknowledges its auspicious beginnings while it looks to the future for inspiration. We continue to evolve and break new ground in publishing by providing today's professionals with tomorrow's solutions.

PREFACE

At the company for which I work we have just begun the process of planning our migration to .NET. This process has been fraught with both political and technical challenges. The purpose of this book is to help you with the technical challenges of .NET migration, in particular using COM Interop. The only help I can give you on the political challenges is: Beware of people who want to use .NET just because it's "cool", because Microsoft says you should, or to pad their resume. Also, beware of people who don't want to use .NET because of personal biases against Microsoft. Decisions about what technologies should be used should be based on business objectives first, customer satisfaction second, and ease of development and maintenance third. Other agendas must be brushed aside.

But enough about politics, this is a technical book with a target audience of intermediate to advanced COM/COM+ programmers who are looking to make the move to .NET. I assume some knowledge of COM and COM+, but I don't assume any prior knowledge of .NET. This book also functions as a .NET tutorial for COM programmers. I start from first principles defining at an advanced level all of the technologies in the .NET Framework. I have included chapters on the CLR, a one-chapter tutorial on the C# programming language, and chapters on .NET Web Services, and .NET Remoting. All of these chapters are there to provide you with the foundational knowledge that you need to understand the meat of the book, which is the "pure" Interop material in chapters 6 through 9, 11 and chapter 12. Although these only chapters make up slightly more than 40% of the chapter count of the book, they make up about two-thirds of the page count. Chapters 7 and 8, which cover advanced topics in Interop, are particularly "beefy" chapters.

My pedagogical style in writing is similar to the teaching style that I have used at UCLA Extension. My approach when teaching new concepts is as follows:

1. Explain why it is important for the reader to learn the new concept? What problem does the new concept solve? Why should the reader care about it?
2. Explain the concept, in theory first, using copious analogies and diagrams.
3. Have the student use the concepts and theories they have just learned in a hands-on demonstration. The demonstration does not have to be complicated; it just has to illustrate the concept that the student is trying to learn.
4. Summarize what the reader should have just learned.
5. Along the way, point the reader to additional resources to consult for further information.

Most of the chapters start by explaining the problem that the .NET technology that you are about to learn about will solve. Next we discuss how this .NET-related technology works and how you will use it. You will find lots of analogies, diagrams and screen shots. Finally, in most of the chapters we will build a demonstration program. I don't think any of the demonstration programs are terribly sophisticated (they weren't meant to be). The example programs are designed to reinforce the topic in that chapter. I show you how to build the example program in enough detail that a beginning C# programmer should have no problem following along. I think you will learn the most by following along and building the example programs yourself, but if you don't want to go through the steps yourself, you can download the demonstration programs from the Web site for this book. The URL for the Web site is: *www.objectinnovations.com/dotnet.htm*. A link is provided at that Web site for downloading the sample programs for this book.

The sample programs are provided in a self-extracting file. When expanded, a directory structure is created, rooted in c:\OI\NetCom. The sample programs are in directories Chap01, Chap02, and so on. All the samples for a given chapter are in individual folders within the chapter directories. The names of the folders are clearly identified in the text. This book is part of the Integrated .NET Series. The sample programs for other books in the series are located in their own directories underneath c:\OI, so all the .NET examples from all books in the series will be located in a common area as you install them.

All of the source code examples in this book are in C#. I agonized for a long time over which .NET language to use for my source code examples. Although the .NET framework supports a wide variety of programming languages, the two languages that will be the most widely used are C# and VB.NET. Most of the source code examples in the .NET Framework documentation are implemented in both C# and VB.NET. I have seen some .NET books take this approach. After experimenting, I realized that since both languages share a common library, and VB.NET has been endowed with first-class object-oriented capability, there are few semantic differences between C# and VB.NET. The differences between the two languages are primarily syntactic. The choice of which language to use really comes down to which syntax you are most comfortable with. I decided, therefore, that it would be a waste of time—yours and mine—for me to try to write the examples in both languages. Therefore, I chose to do everything in C#. Don't despair if you are a VB programmer; my own experience has been that it is very simple to translate .NET code from VB.NET to C#, and vice versa.

The 12 chapters in this text are divided into three sections. The first five chapters contain introductory and foundational material. Chapter 1 is an executive overview of the names in the .NET namespace. Chapter 2 compares .NET to COM. Chapter 3 explains in detail how the CLR works. Chapter 4 is an introduction to C# and in Chapter 5 you will get the opportunity to build your first .NET component. If you are already familiar with .NET, you can skip some or all of these first chapters.

The meat of the book is in chapters 6, 7, and 8. In these chapters you'll learn all about COM Interop and PInvoke, too. In Chapter 6 I cover the basics of calling unmanaged code from a .NET component or application and calling a .NET component from an unmanaged client. I also cover the basics of Pinvoke. In Chapter 7 I dive into advanced aspects of .NET to COM Interop, that is, calling COM components from managed code. In this chapter I also cover some advanced aspects of Pinvoke. In Chapter 8 I cover advanced aspects of COM/Win32 to .NET Interop, that is, calling .NET components from unmanaged code.

The last four chapters are what I like to call "special topics". In Chapter 9, I discuss serviced components, which is the name in the .NET Framework for managed components that use the COM+ Services. In Chapter 10, I discuss XML Web Services. In this chapter I will give you some tips on exposing your existing COM+ applications as XML Web Services. In Chapter 11, I discuss .NET Remoting, which you can think of as the replacement for DCOM in the .NET Framework. In this chapter I also introduce you to the COM+ Web Services feature which is available in Windows XP and Windows .NET Server. This functionality allows you to expose any COM+ application as an XML Web Service simply by checking a box. Finally, in Chapter 12, I provide some best practices for incremental migrations.

A few words about my code listings: You will notice that there are two types of code listings. Some have numbered lines and some do not. Code that does not have a listing number is usually a short snippet that is included to illustrate a point. Usually I will not explain this code in any significant depth. An example is shown below

```
private void cmdAnnounce_Click(object sender,
System.EventArgs e)
    {
    PlayByPlayHandler microphone1=new
  PlayByPlayHandler(ReceivePlayByPlay);
    PlayByPlayHandler microphone2=new
      PlayByPlayHandler(ReceivePlayByPlay2);
    LakerAnnouncer chickHearn=new LakerAnnouncer();
    chickHearn.Microphone+=microphone1;
    chickHearn.Microphone+=microphone2;
    chickHearn.Announce(5);
}
```

Code which is important enough that I want to explain it line by line will have individually numbered lines, as shown here.

```
public delegate void PlayByPlayHandler(
   string strLines);
public class LakerAnnouncer
```

```
{
  public LakerAnnouncer()
  {
        mLines=new StringCollection();
        mLines.Add("It's in the refrigerator");
        mLines.Add("The butter's getting hard");
        mLines.Add("the jello is jigglin");
        mLines.Add("Slaaaam dunk!");
        mLines.Add("Since Hector was a pup");
        mLines.Add("Yo yoing up and down");
        mRandNumGen=new Random();
      }
      public void Announce(int numLines)
      {
        int r;
        string strLine;
        if (Microphone != null)
        {
          for (int i=0;i<numLines;i++)
          {
            r=mRandNumGen.Next();
            strLine=mLines[r % mNumLines];
            Microphone(strLine + "\r\n");
          }
        }
      }
      private StringCollection mLines;
      public PlayByPlayHandler Microphone;
      private Random mRandNumGen;
}
```

If you already understand the .NET Framework you can skip chapters 1, 3, 4 and 5. If you are not interested in writing code, you can skip the hands-on part in the chapters. If you just want Interop and nothing but Interop, read chapters 6–9, 11 and 12. Either way, have fun, and I hope that you find this book informative. Let's get started.

ACKNOWLEDGMENTS

My name may be listed as the sole author of this book, but it took the work of a team of people on both coasts to make this happen. Let me begin by thanking the people at Prentice Hall who were directly involved in the production of the book: my acquisitions editor, Jill Harry, my developmental editor, Jim Markham, and my technical reviewer, Duncan Mackenzie. I owe a special thanks to Duncan who did a fabulous job as a technical reviewer. Thanks also to Nicholas Radhuber, who did the final production work to turn my manuscript into the book you now hold in your hand.

I worked on this book during a tumultuous period of life. During the writing of this book (which took a year longer than expected) I switched publishers—twice, had a second child, and completely remodeled my house. I could not have made it through all of this without the unwavering support of my family. First, I would like to thank my parents, Agatha and Winston Gordon Sr., for always being there for me. When my first contractor abandoned my remodeling project after completely demolishing my house, my father was at my side every day helping me to get the project back on track. I could not have continued work on this project through that traumatic period without his help. I would also like to thank my older brother, Winston Gordon Jr., who inspired me to become a programmer. Next, I would like to thank my two children, Bria Almarie and Bryan Alan, for being a constant source of joy in my life. Finally, I would like to thank my wife of nine years, Tamber Lynn, for being a source of love and support during a very trying year. I promise, this is the last book. Of course, I said the same thing after I wrote the first one. To anyone I forgot, I'm sorry, I was well past my deadline when I wrote this.

The Integrated .NET Series from Object Innovations and Prentice Hall PTR

About this Series
Robert J. Oberg, Series Editor

Introduction

The Integrated .NET Series from Object Innovations and Prentice Hall PTR is a unique series of introductory to advanced books on Microsoft's important .NET technology. These books are based on proven industrial-strength course development and application development experience. The authors are expert practitioners, teachers and writers who combine subject matter expertise with years of experience in presenting complex programming technologies. These books *teach* in a systematic, step-by-step manner and are not merely summaries of the documentation. All the books come with a rich set of programming examples, and thematic case studies are woven through several of the books.

From the beginning, these books have been conceived as an *integrated whole* and not as independent efforts by a diverse group of authors. There are three broad categories:

- **NET Programming books.** These books cover both the languages themselves and surveys of the .NET Framework using a particular language.
- **NET Applications and Technology.** These books cover specific areas of .NET technology or application areas. In some cases a specific language is used and, in other cases, the book is about the technology or application without regard to a particular language.
- **.NET Interoperability and Migration.** These books cover fundamental technologies important to .NET's vision of strong interoperability across diverse platforms.

The diagram below gives the reader a broad overview of the entire series.

TITLES IN THE INTEGRATED .NET SERIES FROM OBJECT INNOVATIONS AND PRENTICE HALL PTR

.NET Programming Books	Programming Perl in the .NET Environment	Introduction to Visual Basic Using .NET	Introduction to C# Using .NET
	.NET Architecture and Programming Using Visual C++	Application Development Using Visual Basic and .NET	Application Development Using C# and .NET
.NET Applications and Technology	Fundamentals of Web Applications Using .NET and XML	.NET Security and Cryptography	Mobile Application Development Using .NET
	Developing Windows Applications Using Visual Basic .NET	Developing Web Applications Using ASP.NET and VB.NET	
.NET Interoperability and Migration	Migrating to .NET	The .NET and COM Interoperability Handbook	XML: Programming Using .NET and Java

PRENTICE HALL PTR

EXPERT PRACTITIONERS • .NET • SEASONED INSTRUCTORS

YOUR AUTHORS ARE EXPERT PRACTITIONERS AND SEASONED INSTRUCTORS

.NET Programming Books

These books cover important .NET programming languages. There are also surveys of the .NET Framework from the perspective of particular programming languages.

Introductory .NET Language Books

The first set of books teaches several of the important .NET languages. These books cover their language from the ground up and have no prerequisite other than programming experience in some language. Unlike many .NET language books, which are a mixture of the language and topics in the .NET Framework, these books are focused on the languages, with attention to important interactions between the language and the framework. By concentrating on the languages, these books have much more detail and many more practical examples than similar books.

The languages selected are the new language C#, the greatly changed VB.NET, and the open source language ported to the .NET environment, PerlNET. Visual C++ .NET is covered in our intermediate book, and JScript .NET is covered in *Fundamentals of Web Applications Using .NET and XML*.

Introduction to C# Using .NET

This book gives thorough coverage of the C# language from the ground up. The book is organized with a specific section covering the parts of C# common to other C-like languages. This section can be cleanly skipped by programmers with C experience or the equivalent, making for a good reading path for a diverse group of readers. The book gives thorough attention to the object-oriented aspects of C# and thus serves as an excellent book for programmers migrating to C# from Visual Basic or COBOL. Its gradual pace and many examples make the book an excellent candidate as a college textbook for adventurous professors looking to teach C# early in the language's life cycle.

Introduction to Visual Basic Using .NET

This book gives thorough coverage of the VB.NET language from the ground up. Like the companion book on C#, this book gives thorough attention to the object-oriented aspects of VB.NET. Thus the book is excellent for VB programmers migrating to the more sophisticated VB.NET, as well as programmers experienced in languages such as COBOL. This book would also be suitable as a college textbook.

Programming Perl in the .NET Environment

A very important part of the vision behind Microsoft .NET is that the platform is designed from to support multiple programming languages from many sources, and not just Microsoft languages. This book, like other books in the series, is rooted in long experience in industrial teaching. It covers the Perl language from the ground up. Although oriented toward the ActiveState PerlNET compiler, the book also provides excellent coverage of the Perl language suitable for other versions as well.

Intermediate .NET Framework Survey Books

The second set of books is focused on topics in the .NET Framework, rather than on programming languages. Three parallel books cover the .NET Framework using the important languages C#, VB.NET, and Visual C++. The C# and VB.NET books contain self-contained introductions to the languages suitable for experienced programmers, allowing them to rapidly come up to speed on the new languages without having to plow through an introductory book.

The design of the series makes these books much more targeted than many similar books. The language emphasis is cleanly broken out into introductory books, allowing the intermediate books to cover the important topics of the .NET Framework in greater depth. The series design also makes for flexible reading paths. Less experienced readers can read the language book followed by the intermediate framework book, while more experienced readers can go directly to the intermediate framework book.

Application Development Using C# and .NET

This book covers important topics in the .NET Framework for experienced programmers. The reader does not need prior experience in C#, because there is a self-contained treatment, but the reader should have experience in some object-oriented language such as C++ or Java. A seasoned Visual Basic programmer who has experience working with objects and components in VB could also read the book. A less experienced reader coming from the introductory C# book can skip the chapters on C# and proceed directly to a study of the Framework. The book is practical, with many examples and a major case study. The goal is to equip the reader to begin building significant applications using the .NET Framework.

Application Development Using Visual Basic and .NET

This book is for the experienced VB programmer who wishes to quickly learn the new VB.NET version of VB and then get on to learning the .NET Framework. It is also suitable for experienced enterprise programmers in other languages who wish to learn the powerful RAD-oriented Visual Basic language in its .NET incarnation and go on to build applications. Like the companion C# book, this book is very practical with many examples, and the same case study is implemented in VB.NET.

.NET Architecture and Programming Using Visual C++

This parallel book is for the experienced Visual C++ programmer who wishes to learn the .NET Framework to build high performing applications. Unlike the C# and VB.NET book, there is no coverage of the C++ language itself, because C++ is too complex to cover in a brief space. This book is specifically for experienced C++ programmers. Like the companion C# and VB.NET books, this book is very practical with many examples, and it uses the same case study implemented in Visual C++.

.NET Applications and Technology

These books cover specific areas of .NET technology or application areas. In some cases, a specific language is used and, in other cases, the book is about the technology or application without regard to a particular language.

Fundamentals of Web Applications Using .NET and XML

This book provides thorough coverage of building Web applications using .NET. Unlike other books about ASP.NET, this book gives attention to the whole process of Web application development. The book incorporates a review tutorial on classical Web programming, making the book accessible to the experienced programmer new to the Web world. The book contains significant coverage on ASP.NET Web Forms, Web services, SOAP and XML.

.NET Security and Cryptography

This book is intended to provide the reader with a practical and comprehensive tutorial on implementing both security and cryptography on the .NET platform. It is an effective tutorial, providing a large number of clear and focused code examples, with ample commentary on how the code examples work. Both C# and VB.NET code will be provided for all examples. The book is comprehensive, covering all of the most important concepts and techniques supported by the .NET platform. This book will also provide sufficient background information to enable the reader to clearly see why security and cryptography are critically important to modern software development. Important practical topics that are covered include Code Access Security, Role-based Security, ASP.NET Security, Digital Signatures and Certificate Authorities, as well as Symmetric and Asymmetric Cryptography using the .NET Framework.

Mobile Application Development Using .NET

This book covers the Mobile Internet Toolkit, the part of the .NET Framework used to build device-specific Mobile Applications. The book begins by familiarizing developers with the Mobile Internet Toolkit, Mobile Basic Controls, DataBound controls and Mobile Specific Controls. It includes extensive coverage of Style Sheets and Device Specific Controls, the Validation Control, Session State Management and Security features in Mobile Applications. In addition, the book includes information on J2ME, Mobile Information Server and the Compact.NET framework. The book also includes two case studies. The emphasis is on using Mobile controls that generate varying user interfaces depending upon the client device capability, which helps developers build single applications targeting multiple client devices without having to write separate programs for each device.

Developing Windows Applications Using Visual Basic .NET

This book teaches Windows programming and application development for the .NET platform using C#. It explains all necessary aspects of Windows programming including GUI, component development, accessing files, databases and printing. After building on the fundamentals, the book goes to the next level and explores the aspects of developing Windows applications. This book is organized into seven parts. Parts I and II introduce the essentials of the .NET Framework and VB.NET. Parts III and IV cover Windows Forms programming in depth. Part V covers ADO.NET programming. Part VI covers important topics for encapsulating the business layer, including multithreading, assemblies, remoting, Windows services and Web services. Part VII covers a wide range of topics such as file processing, printing, interoperability, networking, security and deployment, which are important in developing industrial strength Windows applications.

Developing Web Applications Using ASP.NET and VB.NET

This book is for experienced programmers familiar with Web development (possibly using ASP) and the .NET framework. We assume that the reader knows VB.NET language fundamentals. We also assume familiarity with XML and related technologies like XSLT. The book gives deeper insight into the topic of developing Web-based applications using ASP.NET and Visual Basic. NET. It covers Web Forms, Web server controls, database programming, handling XML data and documents, Web services, caching features, component development, configuration and deployment, and security.

.NET Interoperability and Migration

These books cover issues of fundamental technologies important to .NET's vision of strong interoperability across diverse platforms. They also address issues of migrating to .NET.

Migrating to .NET: A Pragmatic Path to VB.NET, Visual C++ .NET, and ASP.NET

This book gives an introduction to the Microsoft .NET platform and covers the basic concepts of migration. It contains a detailed look on various programming languages and technologies (VB.NET, Visual C++ .NET and ASP.NET) and key differences as well as advantages over their predecessors. The book has detailed steps involved in migration, and it also has a rich set of examples and case studies to cover important aspects of migration like Pre Migration and Post Migration. The last section of the book has coverage of issues related to component migration and interoperability.

The .NET and COM Interoperability Handbook

This book explains the .NET Framework from the perspective of a COM/COM+ programmer. It compares COM/COM+ and .NET. It also shows readers how to use their existing COM/COM+ components from .NET and how to call .NET components from their Win32/COM applications. This is not the kind of cursory coverage of COM interoperability that is found in most .NET Framework books. We delve deep into the subject, covering items such as the effect of the COM Apartment threading model, ActiveX controls, late binding and the impedance mismatch between reference counting in COM and garbage collection in .NET. The book also covers how to use the COM+ Services from a .NET application.

XML: Programming Using .NET and Java

This book is a concise and hands-on exploration of XML application for process interoperability using .NET and Java. With the advent of XML and Web services, the ubiquitous HTTP/HTML communication model has been greatly expanded. This book explores the process communication models using XML via HTTP, database connection, and SOAP/Web services. Along the way various powerful tools and programming techniques advanced by the .NET and Java runtime engines are discussed in detail. Sample code galore! This book offers a unique vista into the power of XML to bring the dream of easy process interoperability to reality.

ONE

What's in a Name?

This chapter is an executive summary of all the technologies in the .NET Framework. You will learn what .NET, the .NET Framework, and the .NET Framework Software Development Kit (SDK) are. You'll also learn how Visual Studio .NET fits into the picture. I define the key technologies in the .NET Framework: the Common Language Runtime (CLR), ASP.NET, ADO.NET, Extensible Markup Language (XML), Hypertext Transfer Protocol (HTTP), Simple Object Access Protocol (SOAP), and XML Web Services. You will also learn how Microsoft's older technologies like Component Object Model (COM), COM+, the Windows Distributed Internet Applications Architecture (Windows DNA), and ActiveX still fit into the picture, and I'll talk about how .NET compares to the Java programming language, runtime and libraries.

Microsoft .NET

Microsoft .NET is Microsoft's name for a technology initiative that is designed to make it simple to create and use a new class of Internet-enabled applications called XML Web services. XML Web services will transform the Internet from what it is now—isolated islands of information that present Hypertext Markup Language (HTML) pictures of data upon request--into a programmable platform, where information from XML Web services may be combined in value-adding ways before it arrives at a client device that is as likely to be a smart phone or a wirelessly connected Personal Digital Assistant (PDA) as it is to be a desktop Personal Computer (PC). With Microsoft.NET, Microsoft has—finally—truly embraced the Internet. Instead of "Windows Everywhere," Microsoft's new mission statement is to provide users with access to their information "anywhere, any time, and on any device." Figure 1–1 shows schematically the .NET vision of the Internet.

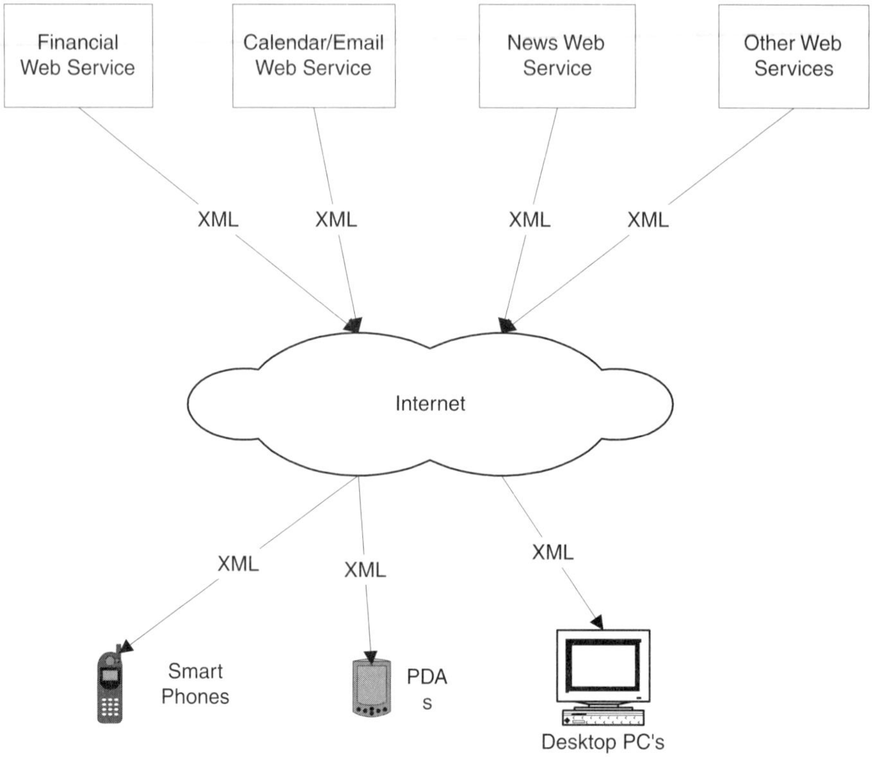

FIGURE 1–1 *The .NET vision.*

Before you start thinking that Microsoft.NET and XML Web services are just another thinly veiled attempt by Microsoft to take over the Internet, keep in mind that the technologies on which Microsoft.NET will be built, XML, HTTP, and SOAP, are all industry standards. In fact, some of Microsoft's fiercest competitors, including International Business Machines (IBM) and Sun Microsystems, are enthusiastically supporting XML Web services and SOAP even as they gear up to compete fiercely against all other aspects of Microsoft.NET. Therefore, although XML Web services are a key part of the Microsoft.NET strategy, the success of XML Web services as a concept is not tied to the success of Microsoft.NET. XML Web services will usher in the next generation of the Internet whether Microsoft.NET succeeds or fails.

Microsoft also wants to provide the preferred operating system that you will run your XML Web services on. Windows XP will be the first operating system with some .NET features. One of the .NET features of Windows XP is that it allows you to expose any COM+ application as a Web service by clicking a checkbox. Windows .NET Server, which is the replacement for Windows

2000 Advanced Server, will be the first operating system that was developed specifically for running .NET applications. It will ship with the runtime for the .NET Framework preinstalled and it will include SOAP Monikers that will make is easy to use XML Web Services even from unmanaged applications.

Microsoft will also be providing an entire family of .NET-enabled server applications that will make it easy to develop high-performance, scalable, secure, and highly available XML Web services. These servers are called the .NET Enterprise servers. They include SQL Server 2000, Exchange Server 2000, BizTalk Server 2002, Commerce Server 2002, Application Center 2000, Host Integration Server 2000, Internet Security and Acceleration Server 2000, and Microsoft Mobile Information Manager 2002. If these servers sound suspiciously like the server applications that were until recently part of the Windows DNA, you know that Microsoft is playing its usual maddening games with their technology names. Microsoft will also start building all of its applications, like Microsoft Office, to take advantage of .NET. It will create .NET-enabled device software that can be used to run devices ranging from cell phones to PDAs to gaming consoles. Microsoft may even create Internet-enabled kitchen appliances like refrigerators that can access recipes or even send an email to you when they need to be serviced.

In all, .NET has five main areas:

1. Developer tools (primarily the .NET Framework and Visual Studio. NET)
2. XML Web Services, this includes both the standards and infrastructure that you use to build your XML Web Services as well as "building block" XML Web Services like MapPoint.NET that you can leverage in your applications.
3. The .NET Enterprise servers.
4. Smart Client Software.
5. Smart Devices.

Whither .NET My Services?

Early in the release cycle of version 1.0 of the .NET Framework, Microsoft heavily promoted .NET My Services. .NET My Services (which was formerly known as Hailstorm and has since been renamed .NET Services) is a set of consumer-oriented XML Web Services that provides, among other things: calendaring, event notifications, email, contact management, profiles and preferences, document storage and electronic "wallets" for online purchasing. Microsoft's plan is to offer these services both directly to consumers and to developers who could customize the services and integrate them with their own Web service offerings to provide added value. These services are to be available on the Web, served up by high-speed and high-availability servers. Because these services are implemented as XML Web services, they can be used from any client: a smart phone, PDA, Windows desktop, UNIX workstation, or whatever.

Whither .NET My Services?

Unfortunately, industry and consumer acceptance of .NET My Services has not been what Microsoft hoped it would be. Right now, two Services are available: .NET Alerts, which implements notifications (see the following URL to learn more: www.microsoft.com/netservices/alerts) and .NET Passport (see the following URL to learn more: www.microsoft.com/netservices/passport). Microsoft is no longer promoting .NET Services very heavily and it is clear that they are backing away (at least in the near term) from their original vision of .NET My Services as one of the key components of .NET. The failure of .NET Passport to win wide acceptance has been particularly damaging to Microsoft's vision. .NET Passport is an authentication web service that allows users to identify themselves to service providers. It provides Single Sign In (SSI) capability allowing you to log in to any Passport-aware Web site or service with a single user name and password combination. Passport's market acceptance is key to realizing the rest of the vision because reliable authentication is required by all of the other services and the wallet capability also leverages .NET Passport. Acceptance of .NET Passport has been slow because many consumers and businesses are reluctant to entrust their sensitive information to a third-party. Despite Microsoft's assurance that the information will be stored in encrypted format, and that only the person who owns information can grant access to that information and despite their pledge not to "mine, sell, or rent" the information stored in these services, consumers are still wary of making their personal and financial information available on the Internet. Part of the problem is several recent high-profile virus and worm attacks, which have undermined confidence and trust in computer technology and the Internet in general, and Microsoft's technology in particular, because it is so often targeted. Another problem is the recent upsurge in identity theft and credit card fraud (I was a victim of both recently) that have made some people leery of eCommerce. Part of the problem is Microsoft itself. Whether it's fairly deserved or not, Microsoft has acquired a reputation for aggressive and predatory business practices. Many businesses and consumers these days are reluctant to "hitch their wagon" to products and services that would make them too dependent on Microsoft.

Regardless of the reasons for the slow industry and consumer acceptance of .NET Services, Microsoft has recently begun to "back-pedal" from their original .NET My Services vision. .NET My Services is no longer touted on the .NET homepage (www.microsoft/net) as one of the key components of Microsoft .NET as it was when Microsoft .NET was first announced. The homepage only mentions MapPoint .NET as an example of a "core set of XML Web Services – from authentication to calendaring" that Microsoft is developing with "others". Moreover, mention of .NET My Services has been conspicuous by its absence at recent developer conferences.

Microsoft is promoting XML Web Services primarily as an application integration technology for heterogeneous environments and less as a mechanism for delivering consumer-oriented services over the Web. I don't believe that they have given up on their original vision, they just realize that it is going to take much longer than they originally thought to realize it. See the following URL to learn more about .NET Services (www.microsoft.com/netservices/).

This book primarily covers the .NET Framework and Visual Studio. NET, however, in this chapter I will also give you an executive overview of the other areas of .NET like the .NET Enterprise Servers. You can find the latest general information about Microsoft.NET at the following Uniform Resource Locator (URL): *www.microsoft.com/net/*. You can find the latest developer-oriented information about the .NET Framework at msdn.microsoft.com/net.

Let's get started by defining the key technologies in Microsoft.NET: XML Web services, XML, and SOAP.

XML Web Services

An XML Web service is a programmable application component that is accessible through standard Internet protocols. If that definition doesn't make sense to you, perhaps you can understand XML Web services better by comparing how XML Web services work with the way the Web works today. Today, a web browser makes a request on a Web server using the HTTP. The Web server reads this request and responds with an HTML page that contains a visual representation of the requested data. In some cases, the Web server will use a technology like the Common Gateway Interface (CGI) or ASP to generate the HTML dynamically, perhaps using data from a database. In other cases, the Web server simply returns a static HTML page.

With XML Web services, a client application (the client application may or may not run in a browser) makes a request on a Web server using a network protocol called SOAP, which is essentially just XML encoded with HTTP. A listener application on the Web server parses this XML document, invokes a routine that performs some processing, and generates an XML document that contains the return value from the XML Web service. The listener then encodes this XML document into a SOAP response and sends it back to the client.

The main advantage of this approach is that it uses XML instead of HTML. An XML document contains both data and metadata (that is, it contains information that describes the structure and meaning of the data in the response document), whereas an HTML document only contains a visual representation of the data. Therefore, the document that you receive from a Web service can be easily sorted, searched, transformed, and combined with information from other Web services.

Note XML Web services aren't required to use SOAP. Notice that the definition of a Web service says that it can be accessed using "standard Web protocols," which does not preclude the use of other protocols. In fact, the .NET Web services infrastructure supports other network protocols in addition to SOAP. However, in practice, on the .NET platform, SOAP is the preferred approach.

Another huge advantage of this approach is that it is truly cross-platform. Any platform that can send and receive HTTP messages and parse XML can host an XML Web service or be a Web service client.

With XML Web services, it will be possible to deliver services that couldn't be dreamed of using HTML. For instance, imagine that you were injured while you were on the road on an important business trip. You may want to locate any doctor who will accept your insurance in the city that you are currently located in. You could go to the Web right now and search for the location of clinics in any city. However, you would have to search each link to know exactly where the clinic was located and what insurance they accepted. With Web services, it will be possible to create a directory Web service that returns the search results as XML. These search results will contain tags that identify the name, location, type of business—and in the case of a clinic—the insurance plans that they accept. You can filter the search results to show only those clinics that accept your insurance. You can then combine this information with information from a mapping and navigation Web service to quickly locate the closest clinic and to provide you with directions from your current location. Because this functionality is exposed as a Web service, you can access it from a PC, a PDA, or a smart phone. This is the essence of the "information anytime anywhere on any device" mantra of .NET. XML Web services are the key enabling technology behind the .NET vision.

Note Microsoft actually presented the use case for .NET mentioned previously in a hilarious video that it showed at several of its developer events.

Understanding XML Web services is also the key to understanding .NET. A substantial amount of the technology in .NET was developed to make it easy to create, use, and integrate XML Web services.

XML

XML is a computer language for describing information. XML, like HTML, is a subset of the Standard Generalized Markup Language (SGML). XML is similar to HTML, which is also a computer language for describing information, but HTML only allows you to specify how information will be displayed. For instance, the following HTML displays a table of information about books:

```
<HTML>
<HEAD>
<TITLE>Browse for a book by keyword</title>
</HEAD>
<BODY>
<TABLE BORDER="1">
    <TR>
```

```
      <TD><H4>Title</H4></TD>
      <TD><H4>Author Last</H4></TD>
      <TD><H4>Author First</H4></TD>
    </TR>
    <TR>
      <TD>The COM and COM+ Programming Primer</TD>
      <TD>Gordon</TD>
      <TD>Alan</TD>
    </TR>
    <TR>
      <TD>XML by Example</TD>
      <TD>McGrath</TD>
      <TD>Sean</TD>
    </TR>
</TABLE>
</BODY>
</HTML>
```

Lots of information is in this file that defines how the information will look when it is displayed, but no metainformation is carried with this HTML. There is nothing that tells us what the data *means*.

Now let's look at the same information displayed as XML:

```
<BOOKS>
    <BOOK>
      <TITLE>
 The COM and COM+ Programming Primer
      </TITLE>
      <AUTHORLAST>
 Gordon
      </AUTHORLAST>
      <AUTHORFIRST>
 Alan
      </AUTHORFIRST>
    </BOOK>
    <BOOK>
      <TITLE>
          XML by Example
      </TITLE>
      <AUTHORLAST>
          McGrath
      </AUTHORLAST>
      <AUTHORFIRST>
          Sean
      </AUTHORFIRST>
    </BOOK>
</BOOKS>
```

The two files contain the same information, and both can be displayed in Internet Explorer (IE) 5 or greater (try it), but that's where the similarities end. The XML file contains a great deal of metainformation that describes the meaning of the information in the file. This makes this file ideal for use as a medium for information exchange.

You can generate this XML file on any platform perhaps from data stored in a database. This file can be sent over the Internet and then parsed by another piece of software (that runs on a different platform) and imported into some other database. All the metainformation that describes the meaning of the data in the file travels with the file. So how is it displayed? However you want! A companion language called Extensible Style Language (XSL) can be used to format the XML file for display in any format you choose. I could go on like this for pages and pages. XML is a very exciting technology, but this is not a book about XML. If you would like to learn more about XML, I can recommend the following books: *Beginning XML*, by David Hunter et al., and *Professional XML* by Didier Martin et al. Wrox Press publishes both books.

SOAP

SOAP is a network protocol that allows you to make method calls across a network. Based on that description alone, nothing is particularly unique about SOAP. There are many other Remote Procedure Call (RPC) protocols out there already that can do the same thing, including Distributed Computing Environment (DCE) RPC; Distributed COM (DCOM), which is based on DCE RPC; and Internet Inter-ORB Protocol (IIOP), which is the protocol used by the Common Object Request Broker Architecture (CORBA). All of these protocols work essentially as shown in Figure 1–2.

To make a method call on a remote machine using RPC, you first call the desired method on some sort of proxy; this is Step 1 in Figure 1–2. The proxy usually presents an interface that looks exactly like the remote method. The proxy takes the method name and the parameters that the client is passing to the method and serializes them into a stream. If you are using an object-aware RPC implementation like DCOM or IIOP, the proxy also serializes an object identifier, and in the case of DCOM, an interface identifier, into the stream. In Step 2 of Figure 1–2, the proxy sends the stream to the server machine using a network protocol. Each of these RPC technologies uses a different protocol. DCOM, for instance, uses Transmission Control Protocol/Internet Protocol (TCP/IP) with a dynamically selected port in the range 1,024 to 65,535 (after an initial request is made on port 135).

Note You can configure the port that DCOM uses to be within a user-specified range. This is useful if you are trying to make DCOM requests across a firewall. You can simply open the ports that you have constrained DCOM to use. See Chapter 19 of the book *Inside COM+ Base Services* by Guy and Henry Eddon for more information on this.

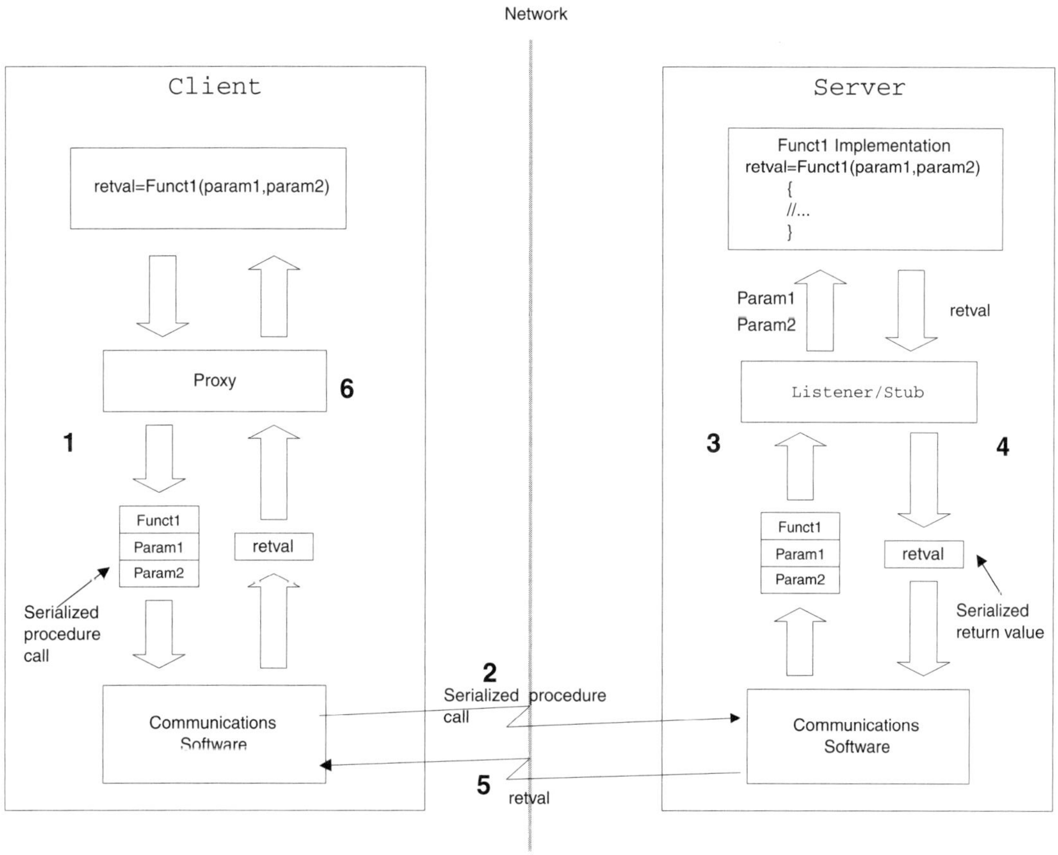

FIGURE 1–2 *Executing an RPC.*

In Step 3 of Figure 1–2, a stub that is listening on the prearranged port receives the message. The stub unpacks the message and calls the desired method.

Note With most RPC technologies, a separate piece of software is used to establish the connection between the proxy and the stub. Each RPC has a different name for this piece of software. In CORBA, it's called an Object Request Broker (ORB), and, in DCOM, it's called the Service Control Manager (SCM). With SOAP, a Web server typically performs this task.

After the method completes, the stub passes the return value of the method—and any output parameters—back to the client using the same communication mechanism used by the inbound request, as shown in Steps 4 and 5. On the client, the proxy receives this response message, extracts the return value, and returns the value to the client (Step 6). This process of serializing and deserializing a call stack is sometimes referred to as marshaling and unmarshaling, or sometimes the entire process (serializing and deserializing) is just referred to as marshaling. From the client's perspective, you make a method call, and a return value comes back. All of the underlying details of the communication are completely hidden.

Most RPC implementations have several problems. Let's consider DCOM because I know a lot more about it than CORBA. In order to use DCOM, several pieces of proprietary software must exist on both the client and server. Both the client and the server must have something called an SCM, which establishes the communication between the proxy and stub. In addition, a DCOM-compliant proxy must reside on the client, and a stub must reside on the server. You can create a proxy and stub in three ways: (1) You can use a language called Interface Definition Language (IDL) to describe your interfaces. You then use an IDL compiler called MIDL to generate the proxy and stub from the IDL. (2) You can use MIDL to create a binary meta file called a type library that describes the classes and objects in your server, and then you can use a system-provided proxy and stub. (3) You can use a system-provided interface called IDispatch to make your method call, in which case you can use a different system-provided proxy and stub. In either case, you are again dependent on a great deal of proprietary software. Although DCOM is available on several platforms, including Solaris, Linux, and Virtual Memory System (VMS), expect to have a lot of problems getting DCOM to work unless both your client and server are running some variant of Microsoft Windows. Expect to have even more problems if your DCOM server sits behind a firewall. I mentioned earlier that, by default DCOM uses TCP/IP with a dynamically selected port in the range 1,024 to 65,535. Most firewalls block this traffic by default. The solution is to configure DCOM to use a user-defined port range and then to convince your network administrator to allow traffic through on this port (good luck!).

Note You can also use a technology called the Remote Data Service (RDS) that allows a limited subset of DCOM functionality over HTTP on port 80. Most firewalls are configured to allow HTTP traffic on port 80 to go through.

What makes SOAP unique is that the proxy and stub are implemented using software that is universally available on every platform. To send or receive SOAP messages requires a Web server, a network library for sending and receiving HTTP messages and and an XML parser. Moreover, SOAP can use any of several Internet protocols, although usually HTTP on port 80 is used because it makes SOAP firewall friendly. No proprietary software is required to support SOAP on a particular platform.

With SOAP, the method call is serialized into an XML document using an XML schema that is defined in the SOAP specification.

Note Microsoft has submitted SOAP to the World Wide Web Consortium (W3C). At the time that I am writing this book, you can find the latest SOAP specification (1.1) at www.w3.org/TR/SOAP/. As I am writing this book, work on version 1.2 of the SOAP specification is underway see www.w3.org/TR/soap12-part1/ and www.w3.org/TR/soap12-part2/.

The XML document describes the method that the client wants to call as well as the name and (optionally) the type of each parameter. The following is an example SOAP request:

```
<?xml version="1.0"?>
<SOAP:Envelope
xmlns:SOAP="http://schemas.xmlsoap.org/soap/envelope/"
SOAP:encodingStyle="http://schemas.xmlsoap.org/soap/
encoding/">
<SOAP:Body>
<MonthlyPayment>
<numMonths>60</numMonths>
<interestRate>8</interestRate>
<loanAmt>10000</loanAmt>
</MonthlyPayment>
</SOAP:Body>
</SOAP:Envelope>
```

In this example, I am calling a method called MonthlyPayment that takes three parameters: numMonths, interestRate, and loadAmt.

Note Version 1.0 of the .NET Framework SDK and Visual Studio .NET are compliant with version 1.1 of the SOAP specification.

In practice, the XML document will be encoded into an HTTP post message, which is then sent to the server machine. The following code shows how the XML document can be encoded into an HTTP post message. This message is then sent to an HTTP server application on the server machine. This could be either the standard HTTP server on port 80 or a custom high-performance HTTP server that runs on a different port. Notice that there is a SOAPAction line in the HTTP post, which is so that a firewall can filter this message out if it wants to. However, if this message is sent on port 80, most firewalls will let it through.

```
POST /financialwebservice/TimeValue.asp HTTP/1.0
User-Agent: MSDNWS
Content-Type: text/xml
Content-Length: 325
SOAPAction: http://gordon1/financialwebservice/
TimeValue.asp#AmortizationTable

<?xml version="1.0"?>
<SOAP:Envelope
xmlns:SOAP="http://schemas.xmlsoap.org/soap/envelope/"
SOAP:encodingStyle="http://schemas.xmlsoap.org/soap/
encoding/">
<SOAP:Body>
<MonthlyPayment>
<numMonths>60</numMonths>
<interestRate>8</interestRate>
<loanAmt>10000</loanAmt>
</MonthlyPayment>
</SOAP:Body>
</SOAP:Envelope>
```

On the server machine, the stub (or listener as it's usually called in SOAP) simply has to parse the XML document to find the name of the method that it should call and the parameters that it should pass to the method. It then must find a piece of software that can handle this request. Notice that no implementation form is assumed or implied by this protocol. The MonthlyPayment method could be implemented in a COM object, a CORBA object, or no object at all. It could be implemented directly within the listener. After calling the method, the listener then serializes the return value into a SOAP response message, which is just another XML document, and sends it back to the client as the response to the HTTP post. The SOAP response to the request shown previously is shown here.

```
<?xml version="1.0"?>
<SOAP:Envelope
xmlns:SOAP="http://schemas.xmlsoap.org/soap/envelope/"
SOAP:encodingStyle="http://schemas.xmlsoap.org/soap/
encoding/">
<SOAP:Body>
<MonthlyPaymentResponse>
<return>202.76</return>
</MonthlyPaymentResponse>
</SOAP:Body>
</SOAP:Envelope>
```

If there is an error, you will see a message similar to this instead:

```
<?xml version="1.0"?>
<SOAP:Envelope
xmlns:SOAP="http://schemas.xmlsoap.org/soap/envelope/"
```

```
SOAP:encodingStyle="http://schemas.xmlsoap.org/soap/
encoding/">
<SOAP:Body>

<SOAP:Fault>
<faultcode>-2147221005</faultcode><faultstring>006~ASP
0177~Server.CreateObject Failed~Invalid ProgID.

For additional information specific to this message please
visit the Microsoft Online Support site located at: http://
www.microsoft.com/contentredirect.asp.
</faultstring><faultactor>-2147221005</
faultactor><detail>006~ASP 0177~Server.CreateObject
Failed~Invalid ProgID.

For additional information specific to this message please
visit the Microsoft Online Support site located at: http://
www.microsoft.com/contentredirect.asp.
</detail></SOAP:Fault>
</SOAP:Body>
</SOAP:Envelope>
```

Of course, SOAP isn't perfect. Its primary benefit—that it will work on any platform—is also its greatest weakness. SOAP implements a least-common denominator set of RPC features. SOAP does not address several issues that are crucial to building distributed systems. Issues like transactions, security and the ability to support the notion of a logical thread that spans multiple machines (DCOM calls this causality) are not addressed by SOAP. These technologies are not implemented uniformly on all platforms, so they were left out of the SOAP specification for now. SOAP does provide the ability for you to add additional information to your SOAP messages beyond that required by the SOAP specification, and you can even specify that the server must understand the additional information if it is to process the message. Thus, a message that requires a transaction will only be processed if the server can honor the transaction.

Note Shortly before the publication of this book, Microsoft announced the Global XML Web Services Architecture (GXA), which is an initiative to define open, standards-based protocols to provide infrastructure services such as transactions, security, and reliable messaging to XML Web Services. IBM and BEA Systems are participating in this effort. You can find out more about GXA at the following URL: msdn.microsoft.com/library/default.asp?url=/library/en-us/dngxa/html/understandgxa.asp.

SOAP also has relatively poor performance compared to other types of RPCs. My own benchmarking showed a SOAP method call to be about 10 times slower than an equivalent DCOM method call on a 100 megabyte per second (Mps) local area network (LAN). Part of the problem is HTTP, which is a relatively verbose, text-based protocol. Part of the problem is SOAP itself, which adds extra bytes in the form of XML tags. More bytes must be transferred across the network to make a method call using HTTP and SOAP than a comparable DCOM method call. The other overhead is the cost of parsing the XML and then creating a response XML document.

The numbers aren't as bad as they seem if you are using SOAP for the purposes for which it was intended. If the communication latency (the actual time to move the bytes across the wire from the client to the server through routers and so forth) is low—as it is on my home LAN—SOAP looks terrible next to DCOM because the additional overhead that SOAP causes is large compared to the network latency. However, on the Internet, network latency dwarfs the time to create and parse XML. Moreover, for a relatively small message size, the portion of the latency that is proportional to the size of the message is small compared to the fixed part of the network latency that you will incur regardless of whether you are sending a small message or a large message. The point is that, when used over the Internet, the performance difference between SOAP and DCOM will not look as bad as when it is used on a LAN. The comparison looks even better when you consider that, in many cases, you cannot use DCOM over the Internet at all because of firewall restrictions.

The .NET Framework

If you are a programmer, the most important element of the Microsoft.NET platform is the .NET Framework. You can think of the .NET Framework as the replacement for Win32. It comprises all the libraries, Application Programming Interfaces (APIs), and standards that you will use to create software for the .NET platform. Figure 1–3 shows all the major elements in the .NET Framework and how it relates to .NET overall.

If you're thinking that this looks nothing like the Windows API, you're starting to get the idea. The .NET Framework actually has a lot more in common with the Java programming language than it has with the Windows API.

The .NET Framework SDK

The .NET Framework SDK is a basic set of tools that includes libraries, compilers, debuggers, and other command-line tools that you can use to start building applications that leverage the .NET Framework. The .NET Frame-

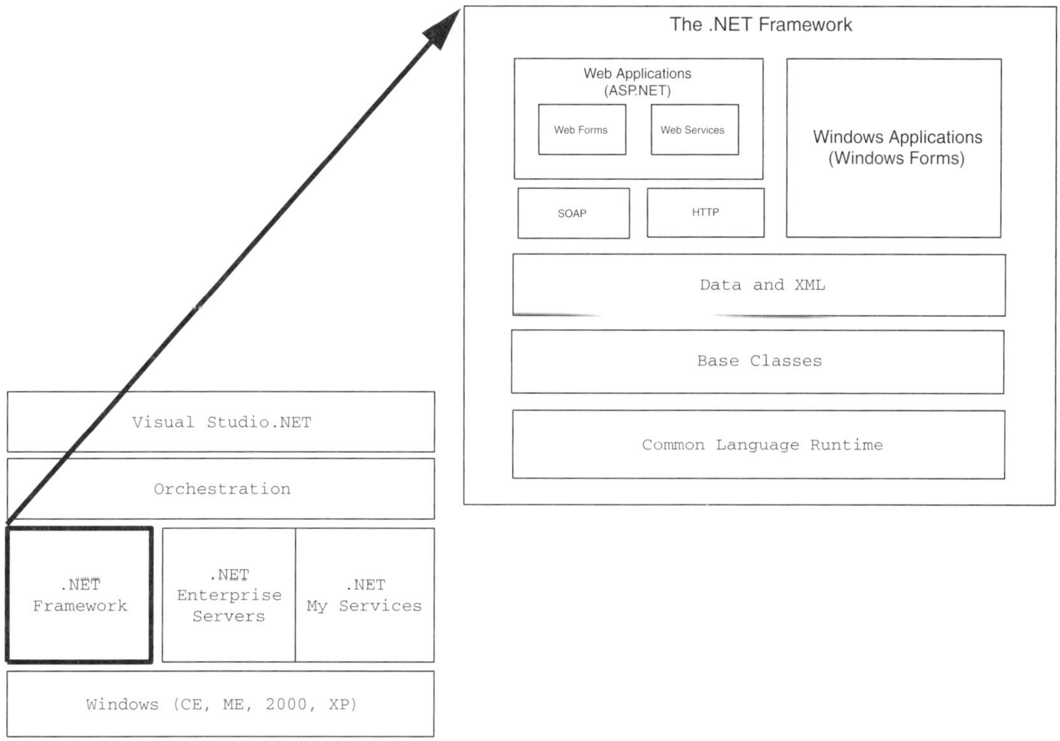

FIGURE 1–3 *The .NET Framework.*

work SDK is a free download that you can find on Microsoft's Web site at *msdn.microsoft.com/net*. You can install it on any variant of Windows XP or Windows 2000 and, of course, on Windows .NET Server. If you like doing things the hard way, the .NET Framework SDK is all you need. However, if you are like most people, you'll want an integrated development environment (IDE) with seamless editing, debugging, Intellisense, and programmability so you can automate common tasks. You will also want wizards and other tools that make the development process simpler and more enjoyable. These are all the things that Visual Studio .NET provides. Visual Studio .NET is not free, but I can tell you that it's an excellent tool and well worth the money. I start using Visual Studio .NET in Chapter 5 of this book. You can find out more about Visual Studio .NET at the following URL: *msdn.microsoft.com/vstudio*.

Because the .NET Framework (and the SDK) is the main focus of this book, I'll start at the bottom and work my way upward through the layers of the .NET Framework shown in Figure 1–3, starting with the CLR.

The CLR

At the heart of the .NET Framework is the Comman Languaage Runtime (CLR). The CLR is an execution environment that loads and executes code. Code that runs under the control of the CLR is called managed code. You can still create code that runs in the same way that Win32 executables and Dynamic Link Libraries (DLLs) run now, and this type of code is now called unmanaged code. Managed code will enjoy a number of benefits that aren't afforded to unmanaged code, including automatic memory management (garbage collection), type safety, security, a simple consistent programming model, simplified deployment, rich debugging support, consistent error handling, language independence, and even the possibility running on different platforms. All of these benefits are provided by the CLR.

How do you create managed code? Simple, you create source code using one of several languages, including C# (Microsoft's new "light" version of C++ that is very similar to the Java programming language); Visual Basic.NET (VB.NET, which is a vastly improved version of VB); an enhanced version of C++ called C++ with Managed Extensions; or a number of third-party languages, including COBOL, Eiffel, Smalltalk, and Pascal. Then you compile your code using one of many CLR-compliant compilers that are designed to emit managed code. Instead of emitting native code for your platform, the compiler generates code in a platform-independent, assembly-like language called Microsoft Intermediate Language (MSIL). This code is inserted into a binary (either an executable or DLL), along with a stub program that loads the CLR, and then begins executing the MSIL code in the managed code binary. The CLR compiles the MSIL into native code as it goes.

MSIL

A compiler that generates managed code has to do a few things differently than a standard, Win32 compiler. Figure 1–4 shows the difference between a managed code compiler and a Win32 compiler.

The Win32 compiler simply reads the source file and generates a Portable Executable (PE) file that contains x86 machine code.

Note The WIN32 PE file format is just the name for the file format that executable (EXE and DLL) files use on WIN32 operating systems (Windows NT, Windows ME/9x, Windows 2000, and so forth). This file format is "portable" in the sense that it runs on a number of WIN32 operating systems.

A managed code compiler also generates a PE file, but this file contains MSIL code and metadata. You can think of MSIL as a virtual assembly lan-

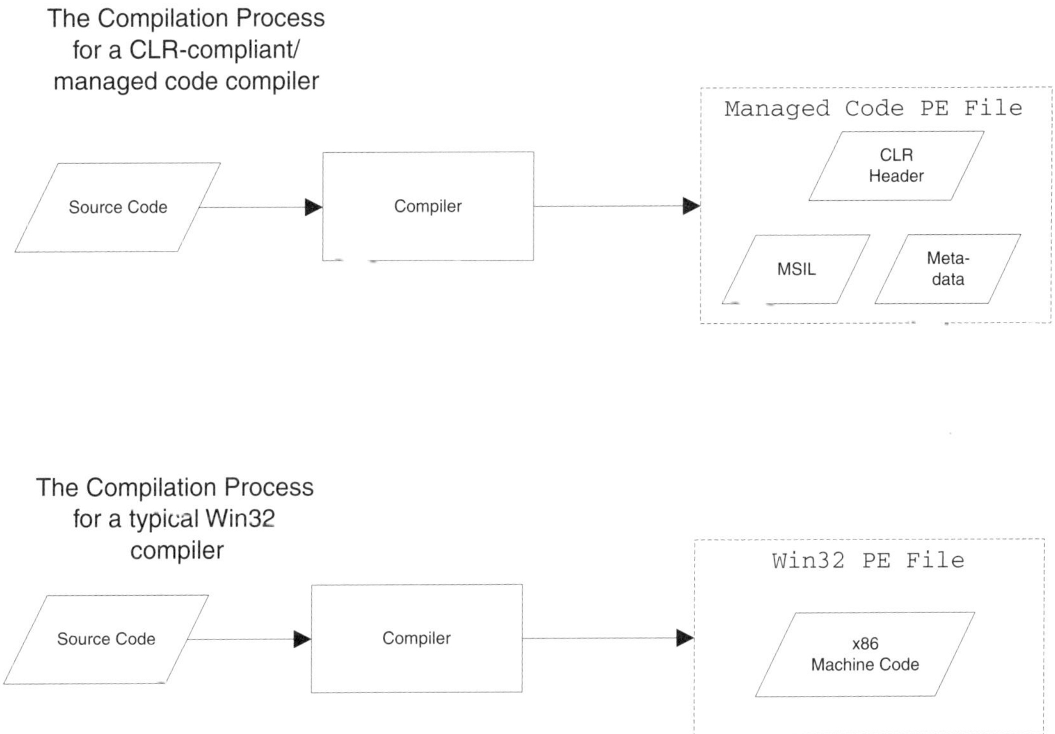

FIGURE 1–4 *The managed code compilation process.*

guage. It defines a set of assembly language-like operations that are easily translated into the native instruction set of most modern CPUs. The CLR uses the Virtual Execution System (VES) to compile the MSIL code into native code on the fly as you run a managed code executable. This process of converting MSIL code into native code is called just-in-time (JIT) compilation. The VES does not compile the code all at once; it compiles it method by method as the code is used. As soon as the MSIL for a method is compiled into native code, the MSIL code for that method is replaced with the compiled native code so that the next time the method is called it will run at native code speed. I can't emphasize this enough. The CLR is not an interpreter. If you know the Java programming language already, it would be very easy to think that MSIL is equivalent to Java bytecodes and that the CLR is equivalent to the Java runtime. Although MSIL is actually conceptually similar to Java bytecodes, which also define a virtual assembly language, the CLR does not interpret MSIL code as the Java runtime does. MSIL code is always compiled into native code and then executed. Just remember that MSIL is never interpreted, and the CLR is not an interpreter.

Note If you do not know what Java bytecodes and the Java runtime are, don't worry, I compare and contrast the Java programming language and the .NET Framework later in this chapter.

If you're still thinking that this "on-the-fly" compilation will be too slow, consider a few points. (1) The CLR compiles code—one function at a time—as you run a managed code executable. Therefore, it only compiles the code that you actually use. When you run most applications, you only use a fraction of the code in the executable. For instance, right now I'm using Microsoft Word to write this book. I consider myself to be an advanced user of Word, but still, in any given session with Word, I only use a tiny portion of the capability of Word. The larger an executable is means the more likely that a user will only use a small portion of the code in that executable in any given session. (2) Don't compare the amount of time that it takes to compile a C++ or VB application with the amount of time it takes to compile MSIL code. A source code compiler has to do basic syntax checking and lexical analysis. The process of converting MSIL code to native code is much faster than converting source code directly to native code, which is what Win32 compilers do. There is a much closer mapping between MSIL and the native instruction set of most CPUs than there is between high-level programming languages like C# and those instruction sets. Still, I have noticed with the beta versions of the .NET Framework that there is a noticeable lag when you first start using a .NET application. After a good portion of the code in the application has been compiled, though, it runs at least as quickly as a Win32 application.

Metadata

The metadata in a managed code executable is binary information that describes everything that you might want to know about the classes and other types that are implemented in an executable or DLL. This metadata is similar to, but far more complete than, the information in a COM-type library, and, unlike a type library, this metadata always resides in the executable or DLL that it describes. A managed code compiler must insert metadata into the binary files that it creates.

Note The .NET Framework provides services that make it easy for a managed code compiler to emit this metadata.

The metadata is used in a number of ways. Visual Studio.NET uses metadata to display Intellisense information to developers while they are creating a class. The metadata also enables compilers to do type-checking and method call signature checking to verify that you are calling a method with the correct number and types for the input parameters. Metadata is also used by compilers to lay out objects efficiently in memory and by system-level code to implement marshaling, that is, to allow code running in one process to use code that is executing in a different process.

Cross-Language Interoperability

The CLR enables an unprecedented level of cross-language interoperability. Whether you are using VB.NET or Microsoft's new Java-like language called C# (pronounced C-Sharp), or any of a dozen other CLR-compliant programming languages, you can mix code written in different programming languages with ease. You can instantiate classes created in one language from code written in a different language. You can throw exceptions from a method in a class written in one language and catch them in a method that was written in some other language. You can even—hold on to your hats—create a class in one language and then derive a subclass using a completely different language. The level of language interoperability afforded by the CLR is far beyond what was ever offered with COM. The key enabling technologies in the CLR that make that is possible—in addition to MSIL—are the Common Type System (CTS), the Common Language Specification (CLS), and the Virtual Object System (VOS). The CTS provides a common type representation for all CLR-compliant languages. The CLS defines the subset of the CTS that you must restrict yourself to and a set of rules that compiler and framework developers must follow to ensure that their software is usable by all CLR-compliant programming languages. The VOS defines an object model that is shared by all CLR-compliant programming languages I won't go into an in-depth summary of the CTS, the CLS, and the VOS in this chapter because it was intended to be an executive overview, but I discuss these important elements of the CLR in Chapter 3.

Available .NET Programming Languages

The following CLR-compliant languages are included with Visual Studio .NET: C#, Visual Basic, C++ with Managed Extensions, JScript (similar to Javascript), and FoxPro.

Microsoft is also shipping Visual J# (pronounced J-Sharp), which is Microsoft's, nonstandard, implementation of the Java programming language. Visual J# will not run on any Java virtual machines and Microsoft is not planning to implement the Java libraries. Their intention with this programming language is to provide an easy migration path for Visual J++ developers and Java programmers who want to switch to the .NET Framework. Microsoft will also provide conversion tools for these two groups of programmers as part of their Jump to the .NET strategy (see *msdn.microsoft.com/vjsharp/jump/*). You can find out more about Visual J# at the following URL: *msdn.microsoft.com/vjsharp/*.

Available .NET Programming Languages

In addition to the Microsoft languages, the following languages are being ported to the CLR by third parties and should be available now or in the near future: Eiffel, Cobol, Pascal, APL, Haskell, Mercury, Oberon, Perl, Python, Scheme, Smalltalk, ML, Ada, and Oz.

The .NET Framework Class Library

All programming languages contain a library of functions and/or classes that provide services to programmers developing software using that language. Examples of these services include string and memory manipulation, file and console Input/Output (I/O), mathematics, date and time manipulation, currency, collections, graphical user interface (GUI), threading, and networking. The need for these libraries can be expressed in one word: reuse. If programmers using a particular language do not have a library of commonly used routines to draw from, they would have to write their own code to implement all of the services, dramatically increasing the cost of developing applications using that language. The .NET Framework class library is a set of classes that provide all of the aforementioned services: string and memory manipulation, file and console I/O, etc. The .NET Framework class library also provides classes that handle security, configuration, diagnostics, messaging, globalization, and reflection (metadata inspection and generation). The .NET Framework class library is composed of several hundred classes. It would be difficult to get your arms around the classes if they weren't broken up into what are called namespaces. Namespaces are just a way of grouping related classes together into a common naming scope. Class names only need to be unique in their naming scope, although the classes in the .NET Framework class library are unique across all namespaces. Table 1–1 shows the list of namespaces in the .NET Framework class library and some of the key classes in each namespace.

The key advantage of the .NET Framework class library is that, because these classes are implemented using a CLR-compliant compiler (they are written in C#) and they adhere to the CLS, you can use them from any CLR-compliant programming language. You can even create your own subclasses by inheriting from classes in the .NET Framework class library regardless of what language you are using. If you are a Visual C++ programmer, you can imagine that the .NET Framework class library is a language-independent version of the Microsoft Foundation Classes (MFC).

The .NET Framework class library is implemented as a set of assemblies. You can find these assemblies beneath the **Framework** directory of your Microsoft .NET installation. On my machine, these files reside at **D:\WINNT\Microsoft.NET\Framework\v1.0.3705**. The leaf directory in

TABLE 1-1 *Namespaces and key classes in the .NET Framework class library.*

Namespace	Description	Key Classes
System	Contains all of the basic types	**Object**, **Array**, **String**
System.Collections	Contains classes for managing collections of objects	**Queue, Dictionary, Hashtable, SortedList, Stack**
System.IO	Contains classes for file-based I/O and reading and writing data streams	**File**, **FileStream**, **MemoryStream**, **StreamReader**, **StreamWriter**
System.Net	Contains types for network communication	**WebRequest**, **WebResponse**, **TcpClient**, **TcpListener**, **Sockets**
System.Security	Contains types that enable security features	**Permissions**, **Policy**, **Cryptography**
System.Globalization	Contains types that support internationalization	**Calendar**, **CultureInfo**
System.Runtime.Remoting	Contains types that allow for managing remote objects	**ChannelServices**, **Remoting Services**
System.Runtime.InteropServices	A collection of types that support using COM objects	**Marshal**, **COMException**
System.Data	The types that make up ADO.NET	**DataSet**, **DataTable**
System.Web	The types that support Web browser to server communications	**HttpApplication**, **HttpContext**, **HttpRequest**, **HttpResponse**
System.Web.UI	The types that support ASP.NET Web Forms	**Page**, **Control**, **UserControl**
System.Web.Services	The types that support ASP.NET Web services	**WebService**, **WebMethodAttribute**
System.Windows.Forms	Types that support the creation of Windows rich client applications	**Form**, **Control**, **TreeView**, **ListView**
System.EnterpriseServices	Types that support using COM+ services	**ServicedComponent**, **ContextUtil**, **TransactionAttribute**
System.XML	Types that provide support for processing XML	**XmlDataDocument**, **XmlReader**, **XmlWriter**

this path (**v1.0.3705**) is correct for the 1.0 release version of the .NET Framework, but your number may vary. A number of assemblies are in this directory, and most of them they have the same name as their namespace. For instance, the security classes can be found in System.Security.DLL, and the messaging classes can be found in System.Messaging.DLL. The classes in the System namespace are an exception to this naming convention; they can be found in mscorlib.dll.

ADO.NET

The .NET Framework class library contains a set of classes for data access. You can find these classes in the System.Data namespace. These classes are used primarily for accessing relational databases, but the classes are generic enough to allow you to use the technology to access other kinds of data stores (email, delimited text documents, Excel spreadsheets, and so forth). These classes are conceptually similar to ADO, which is Microsoft's popular data-access technology, so much so that Microsoft has called the classes in this namespace ADO.NET.

ADO.NET improves on ADO in three major ways: (1) It has vastly improved support for the disconnected programming model. (2) XML support is now a fundamental part of ADO.NET rather than a supported feature. (3) It has a vastly simpler driver model (the mechanism used to enable a particular data source to work with ADO.NET).

The Disconnected Programming Model

There are two types of client-server programming models: connected and disconnected. In the connected model, the client opens a connection to the server and maintains that open connection throughout its interaction with the server in a given session. In the disconnected programming model, the client opens a connection to the server, makes a request of the server, perhaps fetching a Web page or data from a table, and then immediately closes the connection. With each request on the server, the client creates and closes a new connection (although the client or server may pool and reuse connections). The connected model typically has higher performance—in terms of the latency of each request—because you don't have the overhead associated with creating a connection each time. The problem with the connected model is that it does not scale very well. If 10,000 clients are currently using a server, there will be 10,000 connections open on the server even though only a small percentage of those clients are actually making a request on the server at any instant in time. Each connection will consume some resources on the server. With the disconnected model, you may have 10,000 clients using a server, but you will only need as many connections as there are simultaneous requests. You could probably service these 10,000 clients with a few hundred connections. The Web uses a disconnected model The network protocol on which the Web is built, HTTP, uses a disconnected model. When you make a request on a Web server, your Web browser makes a connection to the server and then sends a request to the server. The server responds with the desired information (or possibly an error message). A new connection is used for each request/response pair.

ADO has had support for the disconnected programming model for some time now. With ADO, you can create a disconnected Recordset. The essential process is that you connect to some data source and perform some database operation (a query or a call to a stored procedure) that returns data. You then set the ActiveConnection property on the Recordset to null, and the Recordset, which functions as a database cursor in the connected usage scenario, now becomes a glorified collection object. You can sort, search, filter, and update the data in the Recordset even though you are not connected to its data source. When you are ready to update the database, you simply reconnect to the database by setting the ActiveConnection property to a valid connection and call the **UpdateBatch** method on the Recordset. The Recordset will then attempt to synchronize its updates with the database, that is, it will add any Recordsets to the database that have been added to the Recordset, it will attempt to modify any records that were updated in the Recordset, and it will delete any records that have been deleted in the Recordset. If there were conflicts, for example, a record was modified by some other user after you fetched the record, the Recordset will return a list of the conflicted records. You can then attempt either to resolve the conflict or return an error message to the user.

Unfortunately, there are several problems with ADO's support for the disconnected client-server model. One is that the disconnected programming model was kluged on to the ADO Recordset object, which was originally designed to model a database cursor (a mechanism for iterating through the results of a database query). In many cases, you will want to have a different schema in the disconnected representation of data from that which exists in the underlying data source. For example, you might have a table in a database called tblCustomer that has a primary key field called CstID. In your disconnected representation of the data, you might want to call the table Customer and the primary key field CustomerID. This was difficult to do with ADO Recordsets. Moreover, ADO Recordsets only contain data from a single table or query. This makes it difficult to use them with complex or hierarchical data.

Note With ADO, you could use hierarchical Recordsets to return data from multiple tables or queries, and you could even represent relationships. However, hierarchical Recordsets required nonstandard SQL, and they are complex to use.

ADO Recordsets also have limited support for XML. Starting with version 2.5, you could save a Recordset to a stream or file as XML and reconstitute the Recordset from the XML later. However, you had no control over the XML schema that the Recordset used when it wrote the XML document, and you could not create an ADO Recordset from an arbitrary XML document. With ADO.NET, all of these problems are solved thanks to a class called **DataSet**.

A **DataSet** in ADO.NET is somewhat similar to a Recordset in ADO.NET. One key similarity is that a **DataSet** will become a common mechanism for developers to pass data between the various tiers in a multitier .NET Framework application, just as the ADO Recordset became a common way to pass data amongst the multiple tiers in a Windows DNA application. One key difference is that a **DataSet** can contain multiple tables and can also easily model the relationships between those tables. The table names and field names in the **DataSet** do not have to be the same as the table and field names in the database. The **DataSet** class has a mechanism that you can use to map the schema in the underlying data source to a different schema supported by the **DataSet**. A **DataSet** also contains methods that you can use to synchronize the contents of the **DataSet** with the data in the underlying data store. ADO.NET also gives you more control over how this synchronization is done than ADO did.

Improved XML Support

ADO.NET also features vastly improved XML support than what was offered under ADO. With ADO.NET, you can turn the contents of a dataset into an XML document. You have the option of including just the XML data or the XML schema and the data. However, the biggest improvement in the XML support that ADO.NET offers over ADO is that ADO Recordsets have an XML schema that you can not alter. With ADO.NET, you have complete control of the XML schema that the **DataSet** uses to represent data, in other words, the layout and types of tags used in the document. You may define the XML schema for a **DataSet** programmatically by calling methods in the **DataSet** or by calling the **ReadXmlSchema** method on the **DataSet** and passing in an XSD schema file. You can also define the mapping between the elements and attributes in an XML document and the tables and fields in a database. After you have done this, you can move data seamlessly between a data source like a database and an XML document and vice-versa. This enables a number of usage scenarios that were not possible with ADO. For instance, you can set the XML schema for the **DataSet** to a Biztalk XML schema and then map the **DataSet** to a database schema, and you can move data seamlessly between a BizTalk document and a database. **DataSets** are also the preferred mechanism for passing data between processes in a distributed, .NET system, replacing disconnected Recordsets. Therefore, when your XML Web services need to return tabular data, you typically return that data as **DataSets** instead of disconnected Recordsets. The Web services infrastructure in the .NET Framework will automatically convert the **DataSet** to its XML representation and send it across the wire. You have complete control over the XML schema for this XML representation, so it's easy for this data to be interpreted by a client regardless of the platform that it runs on.

The ADO.NET Driver Model

Although ADO and ADO.NET have the same underlying purpose at their essence, that is, to make a data source available through some uniform interface, they are implemented in a very different way. In order to make a particular data source work with OLEDB, the vendor of the data source, a third-party, or in some cases Microsoft, had to create an OLEDB provider. An OLEDB provider is just a set of COM classes that implement the OLEDB interfaces. ADO is a set of Automation classes that hide the complexity of the OLEDB interfaces and provide a simpler way of using OLEDB. One way to think of it is that OLEDB is the low-level interface and that ADO is the high-level interface.

ADO.NET does not have separate high and low-level interfaces. In order to make a particular data source work with ADO.NET, the vendor of the data source, a third-party, or Microsoft has to create a managed provider. A managed provider consists of just the four classes shown in Figure 1–5.

The Connection and Command classes map to their counterparts in ADO. A Connection represents an open connection to a data store. It contains properties that allow you to specify the type of data store (SQL Server, Microsoft Access, Oracle, and so forth), as well as the location of the instance of the data store that you are using (the server name in the case of Oracle or SQL Server or a file name in the case of Access). It also allows you to open and close the connection, test if the connection is open, and set properties of the connection like the default timeout. The Command object is used to execute an operation against a data source, like executing a query or a stored procedure or performing an insert, update, or delete operation. A **DataReader** loosely corresponds to a forward-only, read-only Recordset, or what many database programmers refer to as a firehose cursor. The **DataAdapter** is used to build a **DataSet** from a Command; it is the link between the managed provider and the disconnected functionality provided by the **DataSet** class.

FIGURE 1–5 *The classes in an ADO.NET managed provider.*

What About the Other Cursor Types?

If you are a seasoned ADO programmer, you are probably wondering what happened to the other cursor types, such as scrollable and updateable cursors. ADO has always allowed you to create Recordsets that were scrollable, that is, you could move both forward and backward at will through the data. It also allowed you to create updateable cursors, which allowed you to alter data in the database. Supporting scrollable and updateable cursors is one of the main reasons that building an OLEDB provider is so complicated. In order to simplify the creation of a managed provider, Microsoft decided not to require this functionality in a .NET managed provider. If you are crying a river of tears because of the loss of this functionality, keep in mind that you can still use ADO in from .NET. through COM Interop.

The four classes implemented by a managed provider are exposed directly to the user, and they inherit from classes in the System.Data namespace in the .NET Framework class library. Each managed provider has unique names for these classes. For instance, Microsoft ships two managed providers with the .NET Framework SDK. One is a provider for Microsoft's client-server database, SQL Server, and the other is a managed provider that works with any OLEDB data source.

Note Version 1.0 of the .NET Framework SDK did ship with only the SQL Client and OLEDB managed providers. After the release of version 1.0 Microsoft released a managed provider for ODBC and one for Oracle. Both of these Managed providers will be included with the version 1.1 release of the .NET Framework, which should be released shortly after this book is released. In the beta, 1.1 version of the .NET Framework, the Oracle managed provider, which uses the Oracle Client Interface (OCI) can be found in the System.Data.OracleClient namespace. The ODBC managed provider can be found in the System.Data.Odbc namespace.

The SQL Server managed provider resides in the System.Data.SqlClient namespace, and the four managed provider classes have the following names: **SQLCommand**, **SQLConnection**, **SQLDataReader**, and **SQLDataAdapter**. The OLEDB provider resides in the System.Data.OleDb namespace, and the four managed provider classes have the following names: **OleDbCommand**, **OleDbConnection**, **OleDbDataReader**, and **OleDbDataAdapter**. Therefore, your client code may change slightly, depending on which data source and hence which managed provider, you decide to use. Obviously, this is a disadvantage relative to ADO, but keep in mind that the data source independence of applications written with ADO/OLEDB was always overstated. Unless you were writing a trivial data application, you had to architect your application specifically for data source independence if you wanted your application to work with multiple databases. For instance, you couldn't use stored procedures or nonstandard SQL features, and, of course, you have to test your application with each of your supported data sources and OLEDB providers. The reality is that every data source and every OLEDB provider have bugs and, unless your application is trivial, you will have a separate bug list, and potentially a different set of coding workarounds for each data source/OLEDB provider combination. In fact, at my previous company, we abandoned the use of a promising object-to-relational database-mapping tool because, although its vendor advertised that it worked with any data source, we ran into a number of very obvious problems when we tried to use it with Sybase Adaptive Server with a third-party OLEDB provider. Upon questioning the vendor, we found out that the product had only been tested with Microsoft SQL Server and Access using Microsoft's OLEDB providers.

Note At the risk of sounding like a Java basher and a Microsoft "shill," this illustrates the inherent problem with any technology that advertises itself as being platform independent. Unless every platform is bug free, you still have to test—and usually debug—each platform that your users may run on. This is why developers who wrote code with the Java often deride Sun Microsystem's "write once, run everywhere" mantra with one of their own: "write once, debug everywhere."

The main advantage of the managed provider approach is that it is much simpler to create a managed provider than it ever was to create an OLEDB provider, so you should see a proliferation of managed providers for a variety of data sources.

ASP.NET

Continuing my overview of the .NET framework, I have finally arrived at what might be the most important technology: ASP.NET. ASP.NET is a set of technologies in the .NET Framework that make it simple to create Web applications. These technologies are divided into two main areas: Web Forms and Web services.

Web Forms

Web Forms are a set of technologies that replace ASP and make it as easy to create HTML-based Web user interfaces as it is to build VB form applications. Because of the wild popularity of VB, the forms-based user interface (UI) programming paradigm has become the accepted standard in the industry. If you are a programmer, you know what I'm talking about. Most modern development tools present you with a form and a palette of available controls. To build your UI, you drag your desired controls onto the form. You then click the controls, and you are presented with a list of properties that you can set to customize the look and feel of the controls. Many of these properties, like the colors and fonts, have their own custom editors that make it simple to change the properties. You then double-click the control to add a handler for one of the events that the control fires. This paradigm started with VB, but now almost all modern development environments, including Visual C++, support it. Web Forms bring the forms-based development paradigm to Web application development. The secret is HTML server controls. These controls function just like the standard Windows controls do in traditional application development. In fact, many are analogous to the various different controls, such as edit boxes, labels, buttons, radio buttons, listboxes, and so forth, available in the Windows API. These controls have a design-time representation that allows you to drop them onto a Web Form and use them just like regular Windows controls in VB. At runtime, these controls run on the Web server and render platform-independent HTML to the client. This book does not cover ASP.NET extensively. I've found *Professional ASP.NET* by Richard Anderson et al. at Wrox Press to be a pretty good book. I build some of my example programs using ASP.NET, so you will get a flavor of how it works. You can then go to another book to learn more.

Web Services

The ASP.NET Web services infrastructure provides a high-level programming model for building XML Web services on the .NET Framework. You can build XML Web services without using the ASP.NET Web services infrastructure, but the infrastructure in the .NET Framework makes XML Web service development much simpler. For instance, turning a method in a class into an XML Web service can be done with a single line of code.

The classes in the System.Web and System.Web.Services namespace contain all the logic to receive and parse a SOAP request and turn it into a method call on a Web service implementation class that you provide. The ASP.NET Web services infrastructure then takes the return values (or exceptions) from your class methods and turns them into a SOAP response. The ASP.NET Web services infrastructure even contains logic to generate a Web Services Description Language (WSDL) file automatically for any Web service simply by calling it with a "?WSDL" parameter appended to its URL.

Note You can think of WSDL as the XML Web services equivalent of a C/C++ header .h file. If you are COM programmer, you can think of it as the XML Web services equivalent of a COM type library. A WSDL file contains the metadata for an XML Web service, that is, a description of the methods that the XML Web service exposes and the name and type of its parameters and return value. Software development tools can use a WSDL file to make it simpler to use XML Web services by automatically generating proxy classes, as the .NET Framework does.

The .NET Framework SDK contains a tool called the Web Services Description Language Tool (wsdl.exe) that you can use to build a client proxy class from this WSDL file. This proxy class handles all the low-level details to construct a SOAP request and sends it to the Web service using HTTP. To call the Web service, you only need to invoke methods on the proxy object.

The ASP.NET Web services infrastructure uses a stateless model. Each time that a service request is received, a new object is created, the request is converted into a method call on an object, and the object is destroyed. XML Web services can use the ASP.NET State Management services if they need to maintain state across requests. I cover Web services in this book starting in Chapter 10.

Windows Forms

Microsoft has not forgotten the needs of desktop application developers. The .NET Framework includes a set of classes in the System.Windows.Forms namespace that allows you to create rich, full-featured desktop GUI applications. These classes include support for Multiple Document Interface (MDI); menus; ActiveX control hosting; a new type of .NET control called a user control, which is the replacement for ActiveX controls; and Graphical Device Interface (GDI)+, which is the new graphics API in .NET (and the replacement for GDI in Windows). GDI+ includes support for fonts, brushes, two dimensional (2D), and three-dimensional (3D) line drawing, bitmaps, images, and pens. I do not cover Windows Forms extensively in this book, but I will build many of the examples that I use in this book using Windows Forms so that you will get the flavor of how they work.

Other Microsoft.NET Technologies

So far in this chapter, I have concentrated on the developer-related technologies in the .NET Framework SDK. Let's look at some other key Microsoft .NET technologies .

Windows and the .NET Enterprise Servers

Windows XP will be the first Microsoft operating system with some support for .NET built into it. With Windows XP, you will be able to turn any COM+ application into a Web service by clicking a checkbox (I talk about this capability more in Chapter 12). Even though Windows XP has some .NET features built into it, Windows .NET Server will be the first operating system that was built from the beginning with .NET in mind. The .NET runtime (primarily the CLR and the .NET Framework class library) will be included with Windows .NET Server. In order to run .NET applications on earlier versions of Windows, like Windows XP and 2000, you will need to install the .NET runtime.

Note Keep in mind that most of your .NET applications will only require you to have the .NET runtime on the server. On the client, most .NET applications will only require a standard browser and/or software that can receive HTTP messages and parse XML. Windows Forms applications (the new name for applications that use the Windows user interface) are a notable exception.

Microsoft has a complete suite of server applications that can be used to build enterprise-class distributed applications. These servers were previously part of Microsoft's DNA. They are now called the .NET Enterprise servers. The following sections give an overview of each of the .NET Enterprise servers.

HOST INTEGRATION SERVER 2000

Host Integration Server 2000 provides a variety of tools that can be used to integrate your Windows DNA applications with software that runs on other platforms, such as IBM mainframes, AS400, and UNIX. These tools can be divided into three categories: Network and Security Integration Services, Data Integration Services, and Application Integration Services.

NETWORK AND SECURITY INTEGRATION SERVICES • The Network and Security Integration Services include support for Systems Network Architecture (SNA) and LAN protocols, support for password synchronization and single sign-on, and support for Active Directory on other platforms.

DATA INTEGRATION SERVICES • Host Integration Server 2000 will also include a variety of tools that make it easier to share data across platforms, including bidirectional data replication tools that work between Microsoft SQL Server, IBM DB2, and Oracle. It will also include a wider range of Open Database Connectivity (ODBC) drivers and OLEDB providers than are currently available. Drivers and providers will be delivered for DB2, VSAM, AS400 file system, and Sybase, in addition to the popular ones on the PC platform that Microsoft always shipped. Host Integration Server 2000 will also include a facility that allows users of IBM DB2 to access Microsoft SQL Server as though it were a peer DB2 data source.

APPLICATION INTEGRATION SERVICES • The COM Transaction Integrator (COMTI) and the XML Transaction Integrator (XMLTI) highlight the Application Integration Services in Host Integration Server 2000. COMTI allows COM+ and Microsoft Transaction Server (MTS) applications to access mainframe applications built with the CICS or IMS transaction-processing environments. With COMTI, mainframe applications appear as COM+ or MTS components to a Windows application. XMLTI provides an XML interface to COMTI components; this allows XML-formatted documents and messages to initialize transactions. XMLTI will be particularly useful for business-to-business e-commerce, especially when used with BizTalk Server 2000 and BizTalk-compatible XML schemas.

Host Integration Server also includes a tool called the COMTI Component Builder that provides a graphical, drag-and-drop environment that developers can use to generate a COM+ component or an XML interface from existing business logic.

A bridge between the Microsoft Message Queuing (MSMQ) and Message Queuing (MQ) Series message-queuing products (MQ Series is available on a number of platforms) is also provided by Host Integration Server, as is an SDK that allows developers to extend Host Integration Server to work with any platform.

APPLICATION CENTER SERVER 2000

Application Center Server 2000 is a set of tools that simplifies the deployment and management of Web applications within farms of servers. Application Center Server 2000 makes it easy to configure and manage high-volume, high-availability server arrays.

BIZTALK SERVER 2002

BizTalk Server 2002 is a set of tools that enables companies to integrate, manage, and automate their business processes. The foundations of BizTalk Server 2002 are BizTalk Orchestration and BizTalk Messaging. Both technologies ship with BizTalk Server 2002, but they are independent enough that you can use one without the other.

BIZTALK ORCHESTRATION • BizTalk Orchestration is a set of tools that facilitates the modeling, implementing, and executing of complex business processes. The key to this technology is XLANG, which is an XML language for describing business processes. Using BizTalk Orchestration is simple; a business analyst creates a flow chart using the Biztalk Orchestration Designer (which is just Visio with a special template). A developer then creates COM objects, script components, and message queues that implement the business process. The developer connects these objects, script components, and message queues to the boxes on the flow chart. The developer then defines the data that flows between the objects, script components, and queues and compiles the Visio drawing into an XLANG file. The developer can now execute the XLANG file using the XLANG Scheduler Engine, which is included with BizTalk Server.

BIZTALK MESSAGING • BizTalk Messaging is a set of technologies that allow companies to exchange documents in a reliable and secure way. It supports a number of file formats, including Electronic Data Interchange (EDI), XML, and flat files. It includes a transformation engine and graphical tools that analysts and developers can use to transform documents from one format to another. BizTalk Messaging also supports a variety of transports, including SMTP, HTTP, and file transfer protocol (ftp). It also provides fault tolerance to ensure that documents are delivered, and it has mechanisms to ensure once-only delivery so that duplicate messages are not delivered. BizTalk Messaging also supports encryption and digital signatures so that documents can delivered with security and privacy.

COMMERCE SERVER 2002

Commerce Server 2002 is a software solution for creating e-commerce Web sites. It provides a tailorable application framework that you can use to create business-to-business or business-to-consumer Web sites, including fully functional out-of-the-box starter sites. Commerce Server 2002 has prepackaged solutions for customer profiling and targeting, product catalogs, and business process pipelines. Many third-party vendors provide add-on products that handle credit card validation, taxation, shipping and handling, content management, and business Internet analytics (which use data warehousing and Online Analytical Processing [OLAP] to collect, store, and analyze Web-click stream data).

MICROSOFT SQL SERVER 2000

Microsoft SQL Server 2000 is the latest version of Microsoft's Relational Database Management Server (RDBMS). Improvements over the previous versions include enhancements to performance, scalability, and support for XML. With SQL Server 2000, you can either return queries as XML or process updates using XML Update Grams. SQL Server 2000 will feature improved scalability and manageability. It will also have improved data warehousing and Online Analytical Processing (OLAP), as well as XML integration and improved data access through the Web.

EXCHANGE SERVER 2000

Microsoft Exchange Server 2000 is Microsoft's messaging and collaboration solution. Exchange Server 2000 is much more than just an email server. You can use it to manage and share all the resources and knowledge that your organization possesses, including everything from scheduling resources like conference rooms to public folders that function as either bulletin boards or repositories for company documents such as policies, procedures, and instruction manuals. Exchange Server 2000 features full integration with Active Directory and complete integration with the Internet, allowing company workers to access all the capabilities of exchange through any HTML Web browser.

INTERNET SECURITY AND ACCELERATION SERVER 2000

Internet Security and Acceleration Server 2000 is an integrated firewall and Web cache server.

MOBILE INFORMATION 2002 SERVER

Mobile Information 2002 Server is a reliable and scalable platform for wireless solutions that brings mobile users and information together—anytime, anywhere, and on any device.

Smart Client Software

Although I am a great admirer of Microsoft as an organization their constant need to rename and reclassify their technologies has always been something that I have found laughable at best, annoying at worst. And so with that as context, I can tell you that "Smart Client Software" is Microsoft's new name for their client operating systems. Since Microsoft .NET was designed to work with a wider array of client platforms, the implication is obviously that a client running a Microsoft operating system is "smart" and a client running some other operating system is not. Perhaps the reason for the creation of this name is that Microsoft is trying to market their client operating systems on the other platforms besides Personal Computers. Microsoft divides "smart clients" into 3 groups based on the class of targeted hardware: personal computers, small footprint devices, embedded devices.

FOR PERSONAL COMPUTERS

For personal computers (which includes laptops) Windows XP is Microsoft's Smart Client Software. Although you can obviously run code that is not built on .NET with Windows XP, Microsoft will over time add more .NET – related functionality to this platform to differentiate it from competing operating systems which can also function as clients for many .NET applications.

SMALL FOOTPRINT DEVICES

Windows CE .NET is Microsoft's "smart client" for small footprint devices, which includes Personal Digital Assistants (PDAs) and Smart Phones. Microsoft is making strong headway in this market as Palm has largely squandered their initial lead in this market by resting on their laurels and failing to innovate.

EMBEDDED DEVICES

Microsoft also makes a version of Windows XP for use as in embedded applications such as refrigerators, car stereos, TV set top boxes and retail kiosks. Windows XP Embedded is componentized so that developers and device makers can maintain a small footprint by only using the functionality that they need.

SMART DEVICES

A "smart" device is a device that has the ability to access XML Web Services. Example Smart devices are Pocket PC devices, Windows Powered Smartphone 2002, which are just starting to appear on the market and Microsoft's Xbox gaming console. There seems to be a lot of overlap between the definition of a Smart Client and a Smart Device. I wouldn't worry too much about understanding the difference, if past experience is any guide, the names or their meanings will likely change by the time you do understand.

Where Do Microsoft's Older Technologies Fit In?

So what happens to COM, COM+, ActiveX, Windows DNA, and the various other Windows technologies that Microsoft touted so heavily until it released .NET? The next section answers this question.

COM

COM is a specification and supporting system software that enables the creation of software components that are programming-language independent and location transparent. In the initial stages of the hype surrounding Microsoft's introduction of .NET and the .NET Framework, many people assumed that the .NET

Framework was the end of COM and COM+. It turns out that quite the opposite is true. Very few companies have the luxury of halting new work for several months—or years—while they migrate all of their code to the .NET Framework. At most organizations, .NET code and COM code will need to work together (interoperate) for some time to come. Microsoft's acceptance of this reality shows in the substantial amount of effort that it has put into .NET/COM interoperability. Any .NET components can be easily exposed as COM components to Win32/COM clients, and COM components can be exposed as .NET components to clients built with the .NET Framework. I cover .NET/COM interoperability extensively throughout this book.

DCOM

DCOM is that part of COM that is concerned with enabling COM-based software components to be used across a network. DCOM is for all intents and purposes dead in the .NET world. The problem is that DCOM was designed more for LANs than the Internet. It is not firewall friendly, and it is supported on only a limited number of platforms. It can also be difficult to configure. .NET Remoting can do everything that DCOM can d, and, because it can use XML and HTTP (SOAP) as its encoding format and transport protocol, it is (at least conceptually) cross-platform.

Note You can also use binary formatting and the TCP protocol with .NET Remoting for optimum performance.

Moreover, .NET Remoting is easier to configure and use than DCOM. DCOM never gained wide acceptance, so I doubt that it will be missed.

COM+

Contrary to popular opinion, the .NET Framework doesn't replace COM+. You still need COM+ services—such as distributed transactions, object pooling, Just In Time Activation, synchronization, and queued components—to build enterprise-class, distributed applications with .NET. The .NET Framework will not in its initial release offer a replacement for these services. If you want to use these services, you must still understand COM/COM+. Fortunately, the .NET Framework does include a set of types and attributes in the System.EnterpriseServices namespace that actually make it easier to use the COM+ Services with the .NET Framework than it was with Visual Studio 6. A .NET class that uses the COM+ services is called a Serviced Component, and I talk about Serviced Components in Chapter 9. Future releases of the .NET

Framework are expected to include a replacement for the COM+ Services that is built entirely on managed code.

Windows DNA

Windows DNA is a name that is dead and buried. If you go to the URL on Microsoft's Web site that contained all the information about Windows DNA, *microsoft.com/dna*, it redirects you to *microsoft.com/net/*.

ActiveX Controls

ActiveX is the consumer brandname for all Microsoft COM-based technologies. At least that is the last official definition that Microsoft had of this name. The reality is that the name ActiveX has been synonymous only with ActiveX controls, which are COM objects that support a special set of interfaces that make them easy to use in a Visual Development environment. Although Microsoft's attempt to promote ActiveX controls as a way to deliver dynamic content across the Internet was an abysmal failure, ActiveX controls are still a widely used technology, and a multibillion dollar industry of component vendors produce ActiveX controls. Microsoft realizes this, and, through COM interoperability, you can still use ActiveX controls in your .NET applications. Moreover, the .NET Framework does include two successors to ActiveX controls: Windows Forms User Controls and Web Forms User Controls. Windows Forms User Controls are for desktop applications, and they are very similar to ActiveX controls in concept. You can drag and drop them onto a form and set their properties in your designer to configure their appearance, and they store their state persistently. Web Forms user controls are the equivalent of ActiveX controls for Web applications. They allow you to take chunks of HTML and package them as a configurable control that you can reuse.

Stale .NET-Related Names

Microsoft has already changed the names of some .NET-related technologies. To help anyone who may be confused, I have summarized all of the already-obsolete .NET-related technology names that I know of in this section.

NGWS

Next Generation Windows Services (NGWS) was Microsoft's internal name for the .NET technologies before the marketing people got a hold of it and renamed it to .NET. Microsoft claims that it worked secretly on its .NET strategy for three and a half years before its introduction in the summer of 2000. It was probably known internally as NGWS for most of that time. Several Microsoft insiders wrote books about this technology prior to its introduction (and renaming to .NET), so the term NGWS did leak into the industry press.

Some examples of early .NET books that use the name NGWS include *Presenting C#* by Tony Goodhew and Sams Publishing, 2000, *A Preview of Active Server Pages+* by Richard Anderson et al. and Wrox Press, 2000, and *A Programmer's Introduction to C#* by Eric Gunnerson and APress, 2000. For that reason, I decided to define this acronym so you wouldn't be confused if you saw it. Just remember that NGWS is .NET, and you won't be confused.

Note One of the biggest leaks of information during this three-and-a-half-year period was a pair of articles written by Mary Kirtland (one of the COM leads at Microsoft) in the November and December 1997 issues of Microsoft Systems Journal. In those articles, she talked about Microsoft's plans for COM+, which was still in development at that time. She mentioned a universal runtime and other improvements that would make it as easy for Visual C++ programmers to develop COM objects as it is for Visual Basic programmers to develop COM objects. The article also talked about improved meta information that would replace type libraries and that the next version of COM+ would support implementation inheritance. Of course, none of these things came to pass for COM+ 1.0, which turned into a substantially improved version of MTS. Mary spent the next year telling everyone who would listen that the articles were based on initial plans and that they were no longer accurate. It's clear now that she was actually talking about the .NET Framework. The timing of her initial articles supports Microsoft's three-and-a-half-year timeline.

COOL

The Component Object Oriented Language (COOL) was Microsoft's internal name for C# prior to its renaming. Just like the term "NGWS," the name COOL leaked into the industry press on a number of occasions. One of the most famous leaks was in 1999 when Microsoft asked the judge in their now famous antitrust lawsuit if it would be in violation of their licensing agreement with Sun Microsystems if Microsoft created its own Java-like language. That set off a flurry of information in the industry press about COOL. At the Professional Developer's Conference (PDC), Developmentor (a famous COM think tank and training company [*www.develop.com*]) distributed a t-shirt that read: C# is COOL. If you can remember that, you shouldn't be confused by this name. What was previously known as COOL is now called C#. I even noticed that sample programs in the prebeta versions of the .NET Framework SDK contain references to cool in makefiles that are compiling C# code, as shown here from the master.mak makefile include file.

```
#default compiling cool files
#note: name.cs and name.exe must match
.cs.exe:
```

ADO+

This name was replaced by ADO.NET.

ASP+

This name was replaced with ASP.NET.

Comparing .NET to Java

If you know anything about Java, by the time you have reached this point in this chapter, you are probably thinking that .NET sounds like Microsoft just created its own version of Java. To some extent, that is an accurate assessment of .NET. There are some important differences though between the .NET architecture and Java. This sidebar summarizes the important similarities and differences.

Let's start by clearing up some misconceptions about Java. People often refer to Java as a single entity when it is really composed of three distinct (and largely independent) pieces of technology:

1. **The Java programming language**—Sun Microsystems defined a simple, object-oriented language that borrows most of the syntax of C++, but eschews most of C++'s more complex—and difficult to understand—features like pointers, operator overloading, and templates. Garbage collection and support for try/catch exception handling also makes this language a less error-prone and more productive language than C or C++.
2. **The Java libraries**—The Java SDK includes an object-oriented library that abstracts all the services that an operating system provides. In the Java libraries, which ship with the Java SDK, you will find classes for essential operating system services like basic GUI primitives (Windows, dialogs, message boxes, and standard controls like edit boxes and list boxes), more complex GUI elements (grids, trees, date/time pickers, and so forth), file and console I/O, 2D and 3D graphics, networking, and security. You will also find classes that provide you with the essential building blocks that you need to build any nontrivial application like collections, string manipulation, mathematics, database access, and more. You could use the Java programming language and not use the libraries. Microsoft created operating system specific APIs like J-Direct and the Windows Foundation Classes (WFC) for use with the Java programming language (precipitating the now-famous lawsuit against them). However,

having a common, platform-independent API to the operating system and other essential services is the key to the Java programming language running on all platforms, which is why Sun Microsystems sued Microsoft when it attempted to separate the Java programming language from the Java libraries. The Java libraries are absolutely key to the Java programming language's cross-platform potential.

3. **The Java runtime**—The Java programming language was designed to be an interpreted language. Java source code is compiled into platform-independent bytecodes. You can think of these bytecodes as a virtual assembly language. These bytescodes are executed using a Java interpreter—the Java runtime. This is the recommended way of executing Java code. You can use the Java language and the Java libraries without using the Java runtime. There are Java compilers available that can compile Java source to native executables for a particular platform. Some Java interpreters also use JIT compilation to convert the bytecodes into native code for a particular platform as it is running.

Microsoft's .NET Framework competes against each of these Java technologies. Let's consider each Java technology versus its .NET counterpart.

The Java Programming Language versus C#

To put it bluntly, C# is almost identical to the Java programming language. However, I don't think it's fair to say that C# is a Java programming language "ripoff" as I'm sure many people will say. Both languages have a common lineage. They are both simplified and more object-oriented variants of C++. The biggest difference between the Java programming language and C# is that, in order to use the Java libraries and the Java runtime, you must also use the Java programming language. You can, however, use all the features of the .NET Framework without using C#. The .NET Framework includes a CLR that allows you to use a variety of languages, including: Visual Basic, JScript, Cobol, Pascal, Smalltalk, and even the Java programming language, and you can still take advantage of the .NET Framework libraries and the .NET runtime environment.

Note Microsoft has released a .NET version of the Java programming language called J# (pronounced J-Sharp). You can find out more about J# at the following URL: http://msdn.microsoft.com/vjsharp/.

I can illustrate the similarity and some of the key differences between the Java programming language and C# using a simple program that I write in both languages. This program was carefully designed to illustrate the important differences between the two languages (see Listings 1.1 and 1.2).

LISTING 1.1 A SIMPLE PROGRAM WRITTEN IN THE JAVA PROGRAMMING LANGUAGE

```
import java.io.*;
import java.util.Date;
class Employee
{
  public Employee(String nm,Date hireDate)
  {
    m_name=nm;
    m_hireDate=hireDate;
  }
  public float getSalary()
  {
    return 50;
  }
  public String JobDescription()
  {
    return "Employee";
  }
  public String getName()
  {
    return m_name;
  }
  public void setName(String newName)
  {
    m_name=newName;
  }
  public void WriteToStream(PrintStream strm) throws IOException
  {
    strm.println(this.JobDescription());
    strm.print("Name = ");
    strm.println(this.getName());
    strm.print("Salary = ");
    strm.println(this.getSalary());
    strm.print("Hire date = ");
    strm.println(m_hireDate.toString());
  }
  private String m_name;
  private Date m_hireDate;
}
class Manager extends Employee
{
  public Manager(String nm,Date hireDate, int numStockOptions)
  {
```

```
    super(nm,hireDate);
    m_numStockOptions=numStockOptions;
  }
  public float getSalary()
  {
    return 500;
  }
  public String JobDescription()
  {
    return "Manager";
  }
  private int m_numStockOptions;
}
class HelloWorld
{
  public static void main(String[] args)
  {
    try
    {
      if (args.length == 2)
      {
        Employee emp=new Manager(args[0],new Date(),Integer.parseInt(args[1]));
        emp.WriteToStream(System.out);
      }
      else
      {
        System.err.println("Usage: HelloWorld Name #OfStockOptions");
      }
    }
    catch (IOException ex)
    {
      System.err.println(ex.getMessage());
    }
    catch (NumberFormatException ex)
    {
      System.err.println("The second argument must be a number");
    }
    catch (Exception ex)
    {
      System.err.println("The second argument must be a number");
    }
  }
}
```

If you run this program with the following command line:

```
HelloWorld "Alan Gordon" 5000
```

you will see the following output:

```
Employee:
Name = Alan Gordon
Salary = 500.0
Hire Date = Mon Oct 02 00:38:57 PDT 2000
```

Now consider the same program written in C#.

LISTING 1.2 A SIMPLE PROGRAM WRITTEN IN C#

```
using System;
using System.IO;
class Employee
{
  public Employee(string nm,DateTime hireDate)
  {
    m_name=nm;
    m_hireDate=hireDate;
  }
  virtual public float getSalary()
  {
    return 50;
  }
  virtual public string JobDescription()
  {
    return "Employee";
  }
  public string Name
  {
    get
    {
      return m_name;
    }
    set
    {
      m_name=value;
    }
  }
  public void WriteToStream(TextWriter strm)
  {
    strm.WriteLine(this.JobDescription());
    strm.Write("Name = ");
    strm.WriteLine(this.Name);
    strm.Write("Salary = ");
    strm.WriteLine(this.getSalary());
    strm.Write("Hire date = ");
    strm.WriteLine(m_hireDate.ToString());
  }
  private string m_name;
```

```
  private DateTime m_hireDate;
}
class Manager : Employee
{
  public Manager(String nm,DateTime hireDate, int numStockOptions) :
    base(nm,hireDate)
  {
    m_numStockOptions=numStockOptions;
  }
  override public float getSalary()
  {
    return 500;
  }
  override public string JobDescription()
  {
    return "Manager";
  }
  private int m_numStockOptions;
}

class HelloWorld
{
  public static void Main(String[] args)
  {
    try
    {
      if (args.Length == 2)
      {
        Employee emp=new Manager(args[0],DateTime.Now,args[1].ToInt32());
        emp.WriteToStream(Console.Out);
      }
      else
      {
        Console.Error.WriteLine("Usage: HelloWorld Name #OfStockOptions");
      }
    }
    catch (IOException ex)
    {
      Console.Error.WriteLine("IOException: {0}",ex.Message);
    }
    catch (FormatException ex)
    {
      Console.Error.WriteLine("FormatException: {0}",ex.Message);
    }
    catch (Exception ex)
```

```
85.         {
86.             Console.Error.WriteLine("Exception:
{0}",ex.Message);
87.         }
88.     }
89. }
```

At this point, it's not important that you understand every line of code in these two listings. The important point for you to grasp is how similar the two listings are. In fact, when I created these two programs, I coded the Java programming language version first. I then made less than five minutes worth of changes, and I had the C# version.

Notice that C# uses the keyword "using" to specify that the program will use unqualified names in a namespace (see Lines 1 and 2 of Listing 1.2). The Java programming language uses the import keyword for the same thing (see Lines 1 and 2 of Listing 1.1). The C# libraries contain a **DateTime** class to represent dates and times (see Lines 5, 37, and 40 in Listing 1.2). The Java programming language has an equivalent class called **Date**. Both languages support a generic mechanism to convert any object into a string representation of itself. The Java programming language supports a method called toString, and C# has a method called ToString. These differences are minor, and a Java-to-C# or C#-to-Java translator could easily resolve them.

Note As part of its Jump to .NET Strategy, Microsoft is creating both a Java-to-C# and a J++-to-J# converter. See the following URL: *msdn.microsoft.com/visualj/jump/default.asp.*

More significant differences, which would be harder for a translator to resolve, have to do with each language's support for runtime lookup of methods with object hierarchies. This is often referred to as virtual functions and relates to the language's implementation of polymorphism. If you're not sure what I mean by this, consider Line 68 of Listing 1.2:

```
Employee emp=new
Manager(args[0],DateTime.Now,args[1].ToInt32());
```

Notice that we have an **Employee** reference, emp, that points to a Manager object. **Employee** is a base class of **Manager**, so these types are assignment compatible in this way. If I call the getSalary method through the **Employee** reference, am I invoking the getSalary method associated with the type of the reference (**Employee**), in which case I will see $50.00, or am I invoking the getSalary method associated with the type of the object that the reference points to (**Manager**), in which case the method will return $500.00. The latter case is called runtime binding or sometimes a virtual function and is the correct implementation of polymorphism. The former case is an example of compile-time binding and is usually not the desired behavior, although in some cases you may want your methods to behave this way. The Java programming language always uses runtime binding (virtual functions). With C#, you can choose. Notice on Line 10 of Listing 1.2 that I declared the getSalary method in the **Employee** class using the virtual keyword:

```
virtual public float getSalary()
```

In C#, this is our way of indicating that we want the compiler to generate code that binds references to this method at runtime. When we derive a **Manager** class from **Employee**, we can now choose whether we want the base-class references to call the method in the derived class. You make this choice using either the new or override keyword. In the case of our **Manager** class, we used the override keyword as shown on Line 49.

```
override public float getSalary()
```

Note This is actually an interview question that I use quite often to see if an applicant really understands object-oriented concepts.

The Java Libraries versus the .NET Framework Libraries

The .NET libraries and the Java libraries are almost equivalent. Both the .NET libraries and the Java libraries are object-oriented libraries that contain classes that encapsulate all of the essential operating system services and building block components required to build applications. Both libraries have split the hundreds of classes that they contain into hierarchical namespaces. In the Java programming language, the main difference is that the Java libraries are designed to be cross-platform whereas the .NET Framework libraries are optimized for the Windows platform. For instance, the .NET libraries contain a set of classes in a namespace called system.runtime.interopservices that you can use to interoperate with COM components A set of classes are also in a namespace called System.EnterpriseServices that you can use to take advantage of the COM+ services. The data access classes in the System.Data namespace also have two sets of classes: system.data.OleDb to work with any database that is accessible through ADO/OLEDB and system.data.SqlClient for working with Microsoft SQL Server databases. The Java libraries eschew this kind of platform-specific functionality. You won't see any Sun.SolarisServices namespaces in the Java libraries. The Java library was designed from the ground up to be a platform-independent library. In addition, most of the APIs in the Java library (APIs are typically a group of classes in the same namespace) were designed with input from companies other than Sun Microsystems. The .NET libraries were designed for and optimized for the Windows platform. With that said, Microsoft seems to be hinting that it will port the .NET Framework to other platforms. My suspicion though is that .NET will always run best on Windows. Until Microsoft shows otherwise, you should assume that your .NET applications will run on Windows, but be easily integrated with other platforms through SOAP and Web services. If your applications themselves need to run on other platforms, you should consider using Java instead.

The Java Runtime versus the CLR

The Java runtime and the CLR could not be more different. A Java compiler compiles your Java source code into a virtual assembly language called Java bytecodes. Java bytescodes are conceptually similar to MSIL. In fact, the instruction set for Java bytecodes uses a stack-based architecture just like MSIL.

Note If you are not sure what I mean by an instruction set or a stack-based architecture, don't worry about it. You will understand after I discuss MSIL in-depth in Chapter 3.

The Java runtime includes an interpreter called the Java Virtual Machine (Java VM) that interprets Java bytecodes and executes them. In order to support Java applications on a given platform, Sun Microsystems (or a third party) only needs to provide an implementation of the Java VM for that platform.

A .NET compiler will compile your source code into a virtual assembly language—MSIL. However, the CLR is not an interpreter like the Java runtime. When you run a .NET application, the execution engine in the CLR will compile the MSIL into native code as it runs the application. It will compile the code method by method as each method is called, replacing the MSIL code in memory with the compiled code, so that it does not have to recompile the method again during that session. This process is called JIT compilation. Microsoft calls the entire process the VES. In order to support a .NET application on a give platform, Microsoft (or a third party) only needs to provide a JIT compiler that can compile MSIL code into the native code for that platform.

Which approach is better? The CLR (.NET) approach is faster in most circumstances. You will notice a slight delay at start-up with most .NET applications as the CLR compiles MSIL code into native code. However, with most applications, you will eventually reach a steady state where most of the code that you are going to use in that session has already been compiled into native code and your application will run nearly as fast as a "regular" executable. It may run faster in some circumstances because the JIT compiler is compiling the code on the same machine where the code will run. Therefore, it can take advantage of knowing the CPU speed, amount of available, and so forth to optimize the generated code. An interpreter will never approach the speed of native code despite Sun Microsystem's attempts to prove otherwise.

Note Some Java VMs do use JIT compilation.

It's no wonder that Microsoft boldly ported Sun Microsystem's performance benchmarking application for Java Enterprise Edition called J2EE (Java Pet Store) and showed .NET to be 28 times faster! See *gotdotnet.com/team/compare/* for more information.

At the end of the day, the best conclusion I can offer is that, if you can choose your server platform, use Windows and .NET. If you cannot control the server platform and the parties who do have control do not want Windows, or if your application must support several platforms on a single source base, the Java programming language is your best bet. The reality is that both platforms are here to stay. I don't expect .NET to replace the Java programming language or vice-versa. The Java programming language and the .NET Framework will likely coexist as the two dominant development platforms for new development work for the foreseeable future. Pick one and become an expert at it, and you will be gainfully employed for a long time. I don't recommend trying to become a master of both because there is too much to learn for that to be realistic.

Summary

This chapter has given you an executive overview of all the names in the .NET namespace. It has also explained how Microsoft's older technologies like COM, COM+, and ActiveX controls still fit into the picture. I concluded by comparing and contrasting the .NET Framework with the Java programming language. The next chapter compares COM and the .NET Framework as software component development technologies.

TWO

Comparing COM and .NET

If you understand COM already, understanding .NET will not be nearly as difficult as you might think. Both .NET and COM are enabling technologies that make it simple for you to create and use programming language-independent software components that can be used across process and machine boundaries. In my COM classes at the University of California at Los Angeles (UCLA), I would use the analogy of a software bus (the software equivalent of the hardware bus on most computers) to introduce this idea to my students. The idea behind this software bus is that you can "plug" software components into any machine on your network and those components are available for use (subject to security constraints) by any client application on any machine on your network.

The main difference between COM and .NET is that COM was designed primarily for use over LANs. COM uses a proprietary network protocol (DCOM), and, although there were some half-hearted attempts to port COM/DCOM to other platforms, it really only works on the Windows platform. The .NET software bus was designed with platform independence in mind; it was also designed for the Internet. The network protocol that .NET uses (SOAP) was built on the most widely used network protocol on the Internet (HTTP). The .NET software also improves on COM in areas where COM was notoriously weak, particularly in the areas of versioning, security, and ease of use.

What is a Software Component?

Before I talk about .NET as an enabling technology for creating and using software components, it makes sense to define what a software component is.

A software component is a binary, self-contained, *reusable*, and language-neutral piece of software that is used as a building block for applications. It's important to understand the distinction between an application and a software component. You can use Microsoft Word as an application to write letters or even a book (in fact, I am doing that right now), but Microsoft Word is also a software component. It has an API—that is exposed through COM—and, through this API, you can use Microsoft Word as a report writer. When you are writing a letter or a book with Word, you are using it as an application. When you use Word as a report writer, you are using it as a software component. The key distinction in the second case is that Word is being used as a building block for another application. I emphasized the word reusable in the definition of software component because it's the motivation for the other elements of the definition. In other words, software components are binary, language-neutral, and self-contained so that they are easy to *reuse*. With COM, a software component is deployed in an in-process server (a DLL) or an out-of-process server (an executable). With .NET, components are deployed in an assembly, which is just a DLL that contains MSIL code and metadata instead of native x86 code.

COM has only one physical realization of a software component. A software component is a COM class that is implemented in either an in-process or out-of-process server. With .NET, there are two physical realizations of a software component. First, a software component can be an externally accessible type (typically a class) that is deployed in an assembly. This type can then be used as a component by applications or other components on the same machine. The CLR is the integrating substrate that makes this possible. This usage scenario fits the definition that I gave earlier of a software component. The externally accessible types in an assembly are binary, language neutral, and self-contained, but .NET also allows us to expose some of the methods in our types as XML Web services. XML Web services are software components also. They use the Internet as their integration substrate. They also fit the definition that I gave earlier of a software component: They are binary, language neutral, and self-contained.

There are some fundamental differences in how the two types of .NET software components are used and integrated with client applications and other components. For instance, when used on a single machine, a .NET component may have a unique name that is created using a cryptographic key, but this unique name is not required. On the Internet, an XML Web service is identified by its URL. The cryptographic key associated with the component is not exposed in this scenario. Similarly, with life cycle management, a component used on a single machine will use the garbage collection in the CLR to manage its life cycle. However, on the Internet, an XML Web service will typically be stateless, and a new instance will be created to service each method call.

What Is a Software Bus?

In teaching my COM and COM+ classes at UCLA Extension, I found that thinking of COM as the software equivalent of the hardware bus that exists on all PCs really helped my students. Like the hardware bus on your computer, COM provides sockets that you can plug components into. However, when you build your software components for the COM software bus, you must—in addition to building the application-specific logic of your component—build a plug that fits into the socket that the software bus provides. In COM terms, this plug is the additional logic that you must write to enable your components to work with COM: implementing the IUnknown interface, creating a class factory, and creating and registering Globally Unique Identifiers (GUIDs) for your classes and interfaces. This is not unlike what a PC sound card manufacturer has to do if it is building a new sound card. It has to build the card in such a way that it plugs properly into the hardware bus of a PC. Building this plug is extra work, but, if you do the extra work, your software components are endowed with the attributes that the software bus provides. In the case of COM, this was location transparency and programming language independence. Figure 2–1 shows the COM software bus.

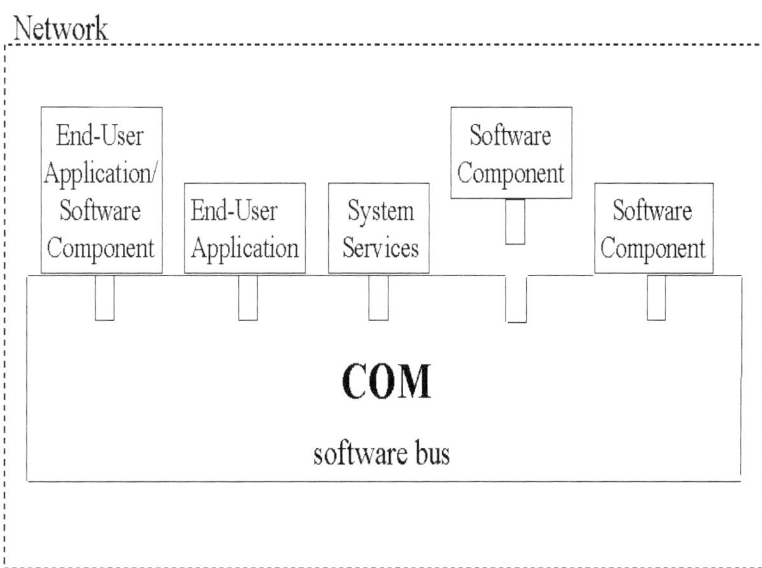

FIGURE 2–1 *The COM software bus.*

Notice that the software bus only encompasses a LAN. Also notice that the end-user applications that use COM software components are PC based.

Figure 2–2 shows the .NET software bus as it functions over the Internet.

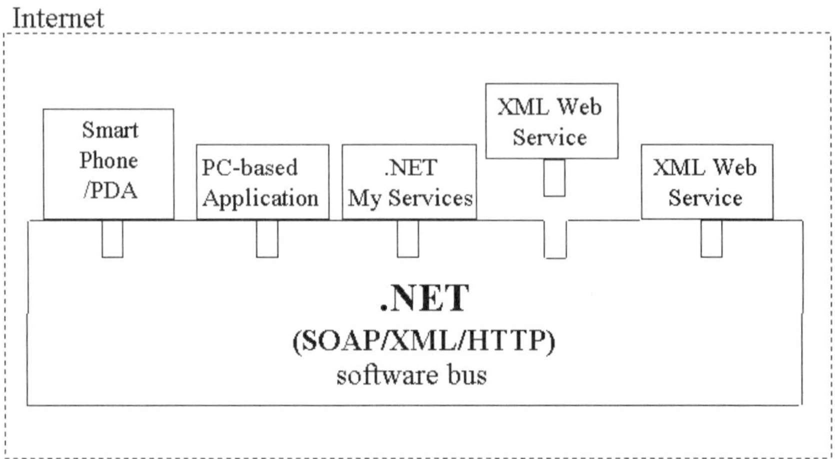

FIGURE 2–2 *The .NET Internet software bus.*

The differences here are that the software bus encompasses the entire Internet. The software components used on the .NET software bus are XML Web services. The network protocol that the .NET software bus uses is SOAP, which is platform independent because it requires no special software other than an HTTP server, client software that can send and receive HTTP messages, and an XML parser. Finally, and most important, the clients used with the .NET software bus are not just PC-based Windows applications. Smart phones and PDAs, as well as Windows-based PCs and even Unix workstations will be able to use the Web services that are plugged into the .NET software bus.

Figure 2–3 shows the .NET software bus as it functions within machines.

Notice in this case that the integration substrate is the CLR. By integrating with the CLR, a component automatically gains programming language independence and the other features provided by the CLR, including versioning, security, and tamper resistance.

The COM software bus enables a stronger notion of location transparency. The intramachine and intermachine integration substrates are the same; they are fundamentally built on RPC. DCOM is built on DCE RPC, so, when you are communicating across machines, you are using DCE RPC. When you are communicating between executable servers on the same machine, COM uses a lightweight variant of RPC called Local RPC (LRPC). In this way, DCOM

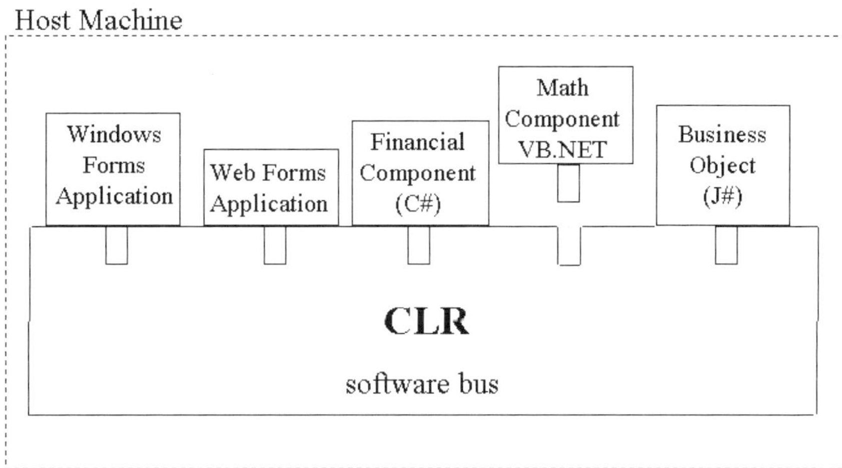

FIGURE 2–3 *The Intramachine .NET software bus.*

is essentially just COM with a longer wire. Thus, with COM, it really didn't make any sense to distinguish between an intramachine and intermachine software bus. With .NET, the intramachine integration technology—the CLR—is fundamentally different from the intermachine substrate, SOAP and XML Web services. As you will soon see, location transparency is not as strong a concept as it was under COM, but the advantages that .NET has over COM more than makes up for this shortcoming.

A number of key technical problems must be solved in order to implement a software bus. In order to be useful and robust, a software bus has to provide a solution for each of the following problems:

- Naming
- Life cycle management
- Programming language independence
- Location transparency
- Extensibility
- Security
- Versioning

COM used GUIDs to provide unique names for software components. It also used reference counting through the AddRef and Release methods of the IUnknown interface to implement life cycle management. COM also used a binary interface standard based on C++ vtables to provide programming language independence, and it used DCOM and LRPC to provide location transparency. Versioning was implemented by immutable interfaces, that is, requiring software components to continue to support old interfaces after they are released.

.NET offers an entirely different set of solutions to these problems. In the rest of this chapter, I explore these problems and the .NET solutions one by one, and, by doing this, you will understand .NET better.

Naming

A precise statement of the naming problem is simple. You need two things:

- A way to assign unique names to software components
- A way to discover the components that are currently installed on a host

The naming problem is slightly different when you are using components on a single machine as compared to when you are using components across the Internet. Consider first the intramachine case and what would happen if two companies created spell-checking software components (with completely different interfaces) and both decided to assign their components the imaginative name "SpellChecker." People would write software that used these components, and everything would work okay as long as only one of the company's spell checkers was installed on a particular host. What do you think would happen if both SpellCheckers were installed on the same machine? Client software that uses the SpellChecker and expects to get company A's component might instead receive company B's component with unpredictable results. Another question is how would I even know whether company A's, company B's, or any other SpellChecker is installed on the machine at all.

Now consider the Internet case. Eventually, the Internet and Corporate Intranets will contain thousands of XML Web services performing all sorts of services for end-users. How do I uniquely identify my XML Web service among the tens of thousands of other XML Web services out there so that someone half-way around the world can use it? Moreover, how can I promote my Web service so that someone half-way across the world can discover the capabilities of my Web service and build an application that uses it, hopefully paying me a fee in the process.

If you are a COM programmer, you are familiar with the COM solution to the naming problem: GUIDs. A GUID is a 16-byte (128-bit) integer that is used to identify COM classes and interfaces. When GUIDs are used to identify classes, they are called class IDs or CLSIDs. When they are used to identify interfaces, they are called interface IDs or IIDs. The following CLSIDs for two well-known COM classes are shown as they appear in the registry.

Microsoft Excel Worksheet:00020820-0000-0000-C000-000000000046

Microsoft Word Document:00020906-0000-0000-C000-000000000046

GUIDs are a sort of social security number for COM objects. The COM runtime includes a function called CoCreateGUID that creates GUIDs; this function uses an algorithm to generate these GUIDs that never generates the same sequence of numbers twice. COM's way of identifying COM objects is through GUIDs whether you are using a COM object on the same host, on another machine on your LAN, or on a machine half-way around the world that you are connected to by the Internet. Sure there are Programmers ID (ProgIDs), which are more user-friendly names for COM objects (such as "Word.Document"), but ProgIDs aren't guaranteed to be unique. They must also be turned into GUIDs before they can be used to identify a COM object anyway. GUIDs for COM objects are stored in the registry of their host machine. An application can discover which objects reside on a machine by interrogating the registry.

The naming solution is different with .NET. However, before I dive into those differences, I need to talk a little bit about the differences between the way that COM and .NET components are deployed. COM components are deployed in either an in-process (DLL) or out-of-process (executable) server. The server binary (exe or DLL) is the smallest enforceable unit of deployment, reuse, versioning, and—unless you are using COM+/MTS—security.

Note If you are using COM+/MTS, you can configure security on a per-interface or per-class basis.

A COM component may depend on other files, such as resources or other DLLs, but it was up to you—the developer—to make sure that the correct versions of all of the files that make up your component are deployed along with the server binary. In most cases it made sense to just bundle all of the code and resources that the component depends on into its server binary. This is the only way that you could be sure that the correct versions of all the constituent pieces of your COM component would be deployed. This complicated the use of COM components in a Web download deployment scenario because it tended to make COM binaries large.

.NET defined a notion of an assembly to solve all of these problems. An assembly is the smallest unit of deployment, versioning, and security in the .NET Framework. Logically, an assembly is a collection of related types (classes, interfaces, enumerations, and so forth) and their associated resources and data. Physically, an assembly consists of one or more modules as shown in Figure 2–4.

Each module may contain either a managed code file with MSIL code and metadata, or it may contain resources like JPEG or bitmap files. One of the code modules must contain a manifest, which is metadata that lists all the types exposed by the assembly and which module (file) that each type is

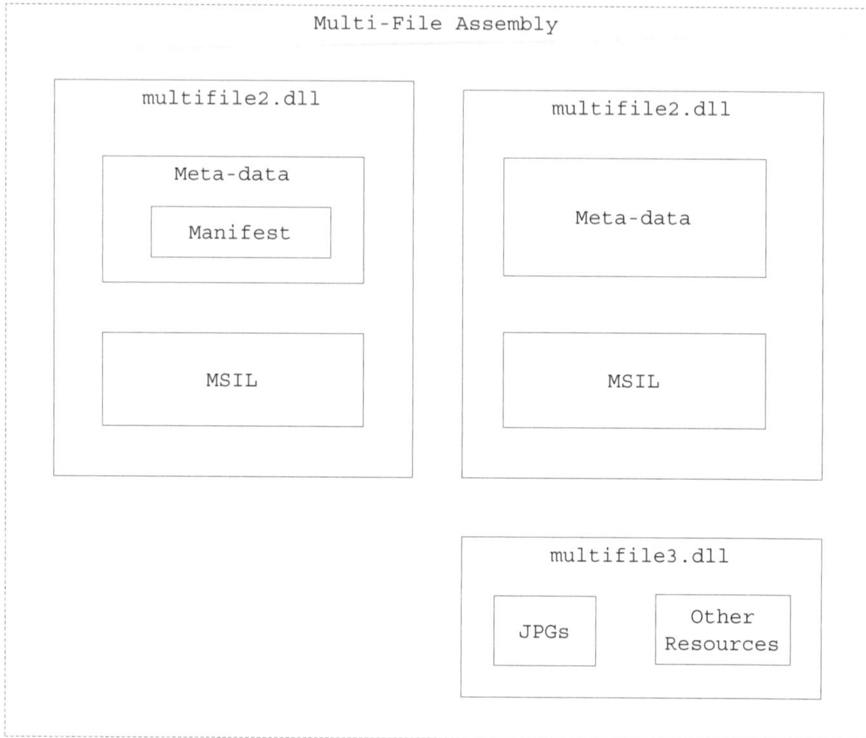

FIGURE 2–4 A .NET assembly.

located within. The CLR uses the manifest to create a single-file illusion for consumers of the assembly. The consumer only needs to reference a single file—the file that contains the manifest. The CLR takes care of loading the other modules as needed. The CLR also verifies that the version number and hash of the contents of each module match those that the assembly was built with. In other words, the CLR makes sure that the correct versions of all the files that make up the assembly are deployed. If they are not, it will throw an error.

.NET assemblies can be categorized into two groups: private and shared. Private assemblies are deployed within a subdirectory beneath the root directory of the application that uses them, and they are used only by that application. Shared assemblies are installed into the Global Assembly Cache (GAC) and may be used by several applications on a particular machine. Private assemblies aren't required to have a unique name because, at runtime, the CLR will search only subdirectories beneath the client application for the assembly. Moreover, there is no need to discover the private assemblies that are installed on a particular machine; indeed, these private assemblies are not supposed to be discovered. Shared assemblies have all of the naming problems that we associate with COM components. In other words, in the absence of a unique name, it would be possible for two companies to install two different assemblies with the same name into the GAC with unpredictable results. Microsoft's recommended approach is that you use private assemblies. I discuss why when I talk about versioning.

Before I discuss how you can assign unique names to a .NET assembly, I need to talk about .NET assembly naming in a more general sense. All .NET assemblies, whether they are private or shared, have a four-part name of the following form:

```
FileName,Version=version#,
Culture=[CultureName|Neutral],PublicKeyToken=KeyToken
```

The first part of the name contains the file name of the assembly without the .dll or .exe extension. The "Version" part of the name contains a four-part version number, the details of which I discuss in Chapter 3. The "Culture" part of the name contains an Request for Comments (RFC) 1766 culture name if the assembly contains culture-specific resources or "Neutral" if the assembly contains code. The PublicKeyToken contains the hash of a cryptographic key or null. If the PublicKeyToken is null, the name is a weak name and is not guaranteed to be unique. If the PublicKeyToken field contains a cryptographic key, the name is guaranteed to be unique, and it is called a strong name. Don't worry if you don't understand what a cryptographic key is. I'll explain this shortly.

Note RFC 1766 culture names contain both a language and a culture identifier. For instance, "en-US" identifies U.S. English whereas "en-GB" identifies United Kingdom English.

The following example shows a weak name for an assembly:

```
MyAssembly,Version=1.0.8.4,Culture=Neutral,
PublicKeyToken=null
```

Notice that the PublicKeyToken is equal to null.

The following example shows a strong name for an assembly:

```
MyAssembly,Version=1.1.0.0,Culture=Neutral,
PublicKeyToken=8a707be49fd7d8f4
```

In the second case, the PublicKeyToken part of the name contains a hash of the public key associated with the key pair that was used to digitally sign the assembly. The process for creating a cryptographic key pair and signing an assembly is simple. The .NET Framework SDK contains an application called the Shared Name Utility (sn.exe). To create a cryptographic key pair, run the Shared Name Utility with the following command line:

```
sn -k keyfilename
```

The Shared Name Utility will write the key pair to the file called **keyfilename**. You can then digitally sign an assembly using the key file that you just generated by adding the following attribute declaration to one of your source files:

```
[assembly: AssemblyKeyFile("keyfilename")]
```

Adding this code to your assembly will insert the public key from the file called **keyfilename** into the assembly, and it will use the private key to create a digital signature. A digital signature is just a hash of the contents of the assembly encrypted with the private key.

You will want to keep the private key secure. (For details about why you need to do this, see my sidebar in this chapter on public and private key cryptography.) The Shared Name Utility has a number of options that make it simple for you to use one key pair while you are developing your code and a second key pair (the official pair) when you are ready to ship. The .NET Framework supports an attribute called **AssemblyDelay** sign that allows you to reserve space in an assembly for a digital signature, but to not actually do the signing. The following code shows how you would do this:

```
[assembly: AssemblyDelaySign(false)]
```

You would then sign the assembly later using the Shared Name Utility. Most companies will allow only a select few individuals within the company to have access to their private key.

Now Microsoft could have stuck with GUIDs to provide uniqueness for their assembly names, but cryptographic keys have a huge advantage. They can also be used to verify the authenticity and integrity of an assembly, that is, to validate that the assembly that you are using was actually created by the person or organization that you think it was created by (authenticity) and that it has not been altered since it was created (integrity). I discuss how this is done and also how to sign your assembly with a cryptographic key in Chapter 3. The CLR cannot perform these validations unless you give your assembly a strong name, so it makes sense to give all of your assemblies strong (unique) names even if they will not be shared.

Public Key Cryptography

Public key cryptography uses encryption, which is a process whereby a piece of information is disguised so that it's original content is no longer recognizable to provide the following benefits:

- **Confidentiality**—The ability to transmit a message from one person to another across some medium while providing that only the person who is the intended recipient of the message can read it.
- **Authentication**—The ability to verify in an unsubvertible manner that people are who they claim to be or, in the case of .NET, that an assembly was created by a particular person or organization.
- **Integrity**—The ability to verify that a piece of information (or, in the case of .NET, an assembly) has not been modified since it was created.
- **Norepudiation**—A mechanism to ensure that the person who sent a message or, in the case of .NET, created an assembly cannot deny that they did it.

With public key cryptography, there are two keys: a public key and a private key. Information that is encrypted with the public key can only be decrypted using the private key and vice-versa; information that is encrypted with the private key can only be decrypted with the public key. You can make your public key available to anyone; your private key should be kept securely.

Let's consider the simplest use of public and private keys. Imagine that a beautiful teenage girl called Alice is going away on vacation. Her boyfriend Bob wants to send email to her, but fears that her mother, Eve, who doesn't care for Bob too much, will read his messages. Therefore, Bob creates a key pair (a public and private key) for Alice, and, before she leaves, Bob gives Alice a kiss and the private key and tells her to keep it (the key, not the kiss) near to her heart and away from her prying mother. When he wants to send an email message to her, he simply encrypts his message using Alice's public key. Only Alice will be able to decipher the message because only she has her private key. Notice that this protocol provides only confidentiality. Alice doesn't know that the message came from Bob because he is using her public key and someone else could get a hold of this key. In other words, the protocol that Alice and Bob are currently using does not provide nonrepudiation. If Alice becomes offended at one of Bob's letters, Bob could say that someone got a hold of Alice's public key and that the letter did not come from him.

If Alice or Bob are concerned that Eve's mother could get a hold of the public key and send an email encrypted with the key in such a way that it appears to have come from Bob, Bob could create another key pair, and this time he would keep the private key and give Alice the public key. With each email that he sent, he would create a hash of the contents of the message and then encrypt the hash using his private key. This is what is known as a digital signature, and it provides both nonrepudiation and integrity. Let's see how. After Alice receives the letter, she will decrypt the main body of the letter using her private key; this was to guarantee confidentiality as I discussed earlier. However, before reading it, she will use Bob's public key to decrypt the digital signature. She now has the hashed contents of the main body. She will then use the same algorithm that Bob used to hash the body of the letter. (Did I mention that Alice was a computer science major.) If the hash from the

Public Key Cryptography

decrypted digital signature and the hash of the received contents of the letter are identical, Alice knows two things: (1) The letter came from Bob because, if it can be decrypted successfully with Bob's public key, it must have been encrypted with Bob's private key. (2) The contents of the letter were not altered because it was encrypted and hashed. If it had been altered, the hash from the digital signature would not match the hash of the altered contents of the letter. .NET does not encrypt the contents of an assembly, but it does use digital signatures to ensure that unscrupulous people cannot insert viruses into assemblies. When you give an assembly a strong name, the Strong Name Utility will also create a hash of the contents of an assembly and sign it using the private key that you specify. At runtime when the CLR loads the assembly, it will decrypt this signature using the public key that is stored in the metadata of the referencing application. This will yield the hashed contents of the assembly at the time it was signed. The CLR will then rehash the contents of the assembly and compare it to the hash from the digital signature. If the hash values do not match, the assembly has been tampered with.

To learn more about public and private key cryptography, see the book entitled *Applied Cryptography* by Bruce Schneier and John Wiley & Sons.

You probably know that, when you instantiate a COM class by passing the GUID (CLSID) for the class to the CoCreateInstance (or similar method), the COM runtime looks up the entry for the GUID in the registry and loads the executable or DLL associated with the registry entry. The .NET Framework performs this name-to-implementation mapping in a different way.

In order to use a class in a .NET assembly from an application, you must reference the class's assembly at compile time. When you reference an assembly, your CLR-compliant compiler will store the full name of the assembly in the metadata of the referencing application. These entries tell the CLR which assembly to load when the application uses the class. At runtime, when your client application first uses a class from an assembly that is not already loaded, the CLR will use its search algorithm to locate an assembly that contains the class; it will search for the assembly using the full name, which is stored in the metadata of the referencing application. I discuss the full details of this algorithm in Chapter 3 when I do a drilldown into the CLR, but, for now, a grossly simplified way of looking at the CLR's search algorithm is that it searches the GAC first. It then searches a configurable codebase and then finally searches a configurable list of private directories. The GAC may contain multiple versions of the same assembly, so the CLR will use the version information that is cached in the referencing application to try to find the same version of the assembly that the application was built (and tested) with.

Referencing an Assembly

If you are using the C# command-line compiler, you can reference an assembly using the /r command-line parameter. For instance, the following command line for the C# compiler (csc) will build a Windows executable called loanclient.exe where the source code is contained in a file called FrmMain.cs:

```
csc /t:winexe /out:loanclient.exe FrmMain.cs  /
r:System.Xml.Serialization.dll /r:System.Windows.Forms.dll
```

The /t:winexe parameter means that you are building a Windows executable. The /out:loanclient.exe parameter specifies the name of the executable (loanclient.exe). The /r parameters specify that executable will use the XML Serialization and Windows Forms assemblies. With Visual Studio .NET, you can reference an assembly by selecting Project | Add Reference. This displays the dialog shown in Figure 2-5.

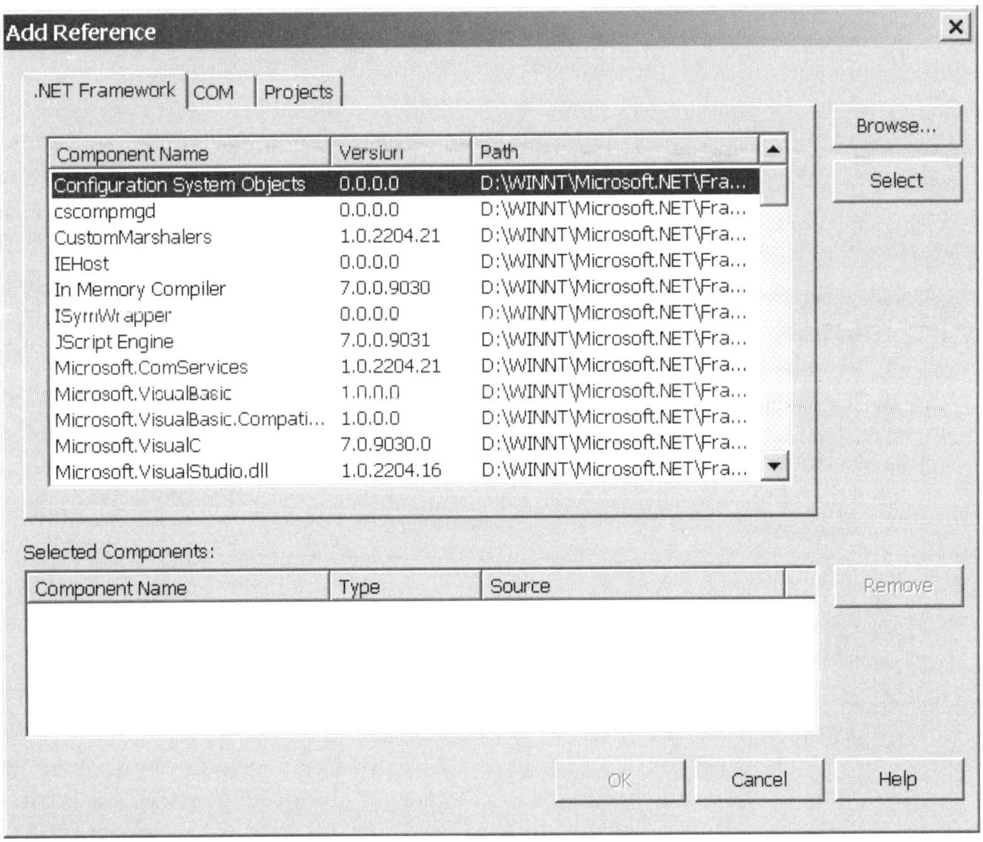

FIGURE 2–5 *The Add Reference Dialog in Visual Studio. NET.*

You can then select the assemblies you want to reference from the Component Name list, or you can click the Browse... button and select an assembly.

So far I have only talked about naming in the intramachine case, that is, uniquely identifying a component from among the other components installed on a particular machine. Developers also need a way to uniquely identify XML Web services. Fortunately, a unique naming scheme exists on the Internet already: URLs. An XML Web service's URL is its unique name on the Internet.

A URL has the following form:

```
Protocol://domain_name/pathname
```

The protocol identifies the communication mechanism that a client will use to exchange documents with the host server. Typically, this protocol will be HTTP when using XML Web services. Domain_name is the Domain Name Service (DNS) name of the server where the resource resides. The domain name is the part of the URL that guarantees uniqueness. Domain names are unique because they are handed out on a first-come, first-served basis by a centralized agency. After you have registered a domain name, this name is unique across the Internet because no one else is allowed to have that name.

The pathname portion of the URL identifies the relative path beneath the root directory of the server where the resource resides. Two example URLs are as follows:

```
http://strongbeach/financialwebservice/financial.asmx
http://localhost/DevDotNet/
```

The first is the URL for a Web service that I am running on my machine right now. Notice that the second URL does not contain a file name. This URL identifies the default resource in the specified directory. Usually, this will be a file called index.html or default.html or something similar.

To discover Web services on the Internet, you can use Universal Description, Discovery, and Integration (UDDI). UDDI defines a way to publish and discover information about XML Web services that other developers have created.

Life Cycle Management

In order to use an object, whether it's an instance of a .NET class or a COM class, the server for that object must be loaded into memory. In the case of COM, the COM runtime must load either an in-process server or an out-of-process server that contains the COM class into memory. In the case of .NET, the CLR must locate and load the assembly that contains the class. This is true in both the intra machine and inter machine (Internet) scenarios. After the CLR loads the assembly and creates an instance of the class, the class will likely acquire other resources on the system. The class instance (object) may open a file, allocate memory for a large string, or create a network or database connection.

If you created objects and never made any attempt to destroy objects that were no longer needed and hence reclaim the resources (memory, file handles, and so forth) that they use, eventually your software would consume all of its host's memory until the machine crashed. A software bus must provide a way for developers to keep alive only those objects that they currently need or may need in the future. If you no longer need an object, you should have some way of indicating this, and there should be a method for destroying the object, thereby reclaiming the resources used by the object. Therefore, the life cycle problem really distills down to three simple questions:

- How do you indicate that you are using an object or will use it in the future?
- How do you specify that an object is no longer needed?
- How do you reclaim the resources used by the object?

The COM Life Cycle Management Solution

COM's answer to these life cycle management questions is reference counting. Reference counting is a programming idiom that is fairly simple to understand. You associate an integer reference count with the resource that you want to manage. You increment this count any time that you assign some reference (usually a pointer) to the resource. When you decide that you will no longer access the resource through the reference or the reference goes out of scope, you decrement the reference count. When the reference count reaches zero, you can safely delete the resource because it can no longer be accessed by any references.

With COM, reference counting is done through the IUnknown interface. All COM objects are required to support this interface. Indeed, support for the IUnknown is part of the definition of a COM object. You can think of the IUnknown interface as part of the plug you have to build for your software components so that they will work with the COM software bus. The IUnknown interface supports two methods—AddRef and Release—that together implement reference counting. AddRef increments the reference count; Release decrements the reference count.

The COM specification stipulates that the Release method should delete an object when the reference count is zero, leading to the somewhat confusing (but legal) canonical implementation of the Release method in C++ that follows:

```
STDMETHODIMP_(ULONG) CSpellCheckImpl::Release(void)
{
    if (0L!=--m_ref)
        return m_ref;

    delete this;
    return 0;
}
```

Notice the call to delete "this" if the reference count is zero.

Unfortunately, there are a number of problems with reference counting and the IUnknown interface. It was actually fairly simple to implement the IUnknown interface, but not everyone even got this right. The following C++ code shows a common mistake:

```
STDMETHODIMP_(ULONG) CSpellCheckImpl::Release(void)
{
    if (0L!=--m_ref)
        return m_ref;

    delete this;
    return m_ref;
}
```

Did you spot the problem? If m_ref is a member variable of this implementation class, calling delete "this" will free the memory occupied by this object. The value of m_ref is therefore undefined.

The example that I just gave is only part of the problem. The biggest problem with reference counting is that you—the developer—must determine when to call Release. You must also be sure not to use an interface pointer after you have called Release on it because the Release method may delete the object if the reference count is zero. If you attempt to use an interface pointer after an object has deleted itself, you would get unpredictable results and most likely a General Protection Fault (GPF). You also have to be careful that you balance each call to AddRef with a corresponding call to Release. Not doing this will cause a resource leak. These unreleased resources will pile up in memory, degrading system performance and eventually causing the system to crash. Although it would seem simple to balance each call to AddRef with a call to Release, in practice it's actually quite difficult. Part of the problem is that not all calls to AddRef are explicit. If you acquire a COM interface pointer through a method call like CoCreateInstance, the method is responsible for calling AddRef. The client application that receives the interface pointer only needs to call Release when it is done with the interface pointer. There was another more insidious problem that could appear even if you had matched every call to AddRef with a corresponding call to Release: the so-called circular reference problem. This problem may occur if you have one object (Object A) that refers to another object (Object B) and Object B in turn has a reference back to object as shown in Figure 2–6.

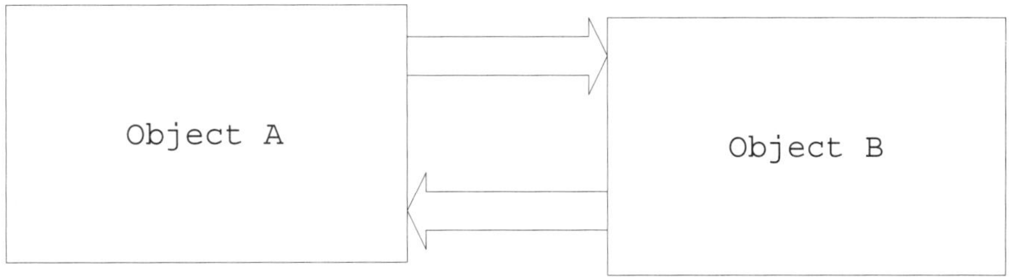

FIGURE 2–6 *The circular reference problem.*

The problem is that, in a scenario like this, you will probably implement the Release method in Object A so that it will release its reference to Object B when Object A's reference count goes to zero. You will probably also implement the Release method in Object B so that it will release its reference to Object A when Object B's reference count goes to zero. Therefore, Object A will not be deleted until Object B is deleted, and Object B will not be deleted until Object A is deleted. Both objects will wind up stuck in memory until you shut down the process.

Note The *Visual Basic Concepts* guide (in Visual Studio 6) has an excellent explanation of circular references and how to solve them. Find it on the web at the following URL: *msdn.microsoft.com/library/devprods/vs6/vbasic/vbcon98/vbcondealingwithcircularreferences.htm.*

No wonder that even Microsoft couldn't seem to use COM reference counting correctly. In the course of my own work on a recent project, we noticed a *fast* memory leak on the server portion of our application when we first ported it from Windows NT to Windows 2000. After several days of investigating, we determined that the problem was in the cross-context marshaling code in COM+. The problem was caused (in Microsoft's own words) by "improper release of objects passed as parameters between VB objects in the same apartment but in different COM+ contexts." Microsoft fixed this problem in Service Pack 1 of Windows 2000.

Note See article ID Q252934 in the Microsoft knowledgebase at *support.microsoft.com/support/kb/articles/Q252/9/34.asp* for more information about this memory leak problem.

We also encountered another problem that caused us to abandon using drag-and-drop with Windowless ActiveX controls. In the words of a Microsoft support engineer, the problem was "either VB or IE is calling Release on an interface pointer one too many times."

Even though I previously wrote a book extolling the virtues of COM and COM+, I must admit that the COM solution to life cycle management (reference counting) was simply too error prone. Thankfully life cycle management is much simpler in .NET

The .NET Life Cycle Management Solution

The problems with the COM reference counting can be distilled down to three main problems:

- Developers releasing objects that are still in use. This will likely lead to a GPF (a crash) if the call to Release caused the object to delete itself.
- Developers neglecting to call Release on an object when it is no longer needed. This will cause a memory (or other resource) leak.
- Developers misusing the reference counting functions (AddRef and Release) in other ways, that is, calling Release on an interface pointer too many times or not enough times.

The solution to all of these problems is to let the runtime environment determine when an object cannot be used any more. After the system determines that an object cannot be used, it can just go ahead and destroy it. The algorithms used to determine when an object is no longer in use and the mechanisms used to delete these objects is a well-studied topic in academic circles, and it is called Garbage Collection (GC).

A Garbage Collecting environment is the best of all possible worlds for developers. There is no need for special methods like AddRef and Release to control the life cycle of objects. Developers no longer have to track the life cycle of their objects. You simply instantiate objects as you need them using the new operator, and you do not have to concern yourself with when the object will be destroyed and its resources reclaimed. When your program can no longer access an object, the system will destroy it automatically. Think about it. No more memory leaks, and no more dangling references, which is what happens when you attempt to use an object that you have already deleted.

I explore how .NET GC works in Chapter 3 when I do the drilldown on the CLR. For now, a simple explanation is that, for an object to be accessible by a running instance of a program, a reference to the object must be stored in one of the following locations, or it must be in a tree of references that originates in one of these locations:

- A global or static variable
- A local or parameter variable on the stack
- A Central Processing Unit (CPU) register

These locations are called the application's roots. When the CLR senses that memory is low, it walks through every single object that a program has allocated starting at the roots. The CLR builds a graph of all the objects. Any objects not in the graph are no longer accessible by the program and can be deleted. Of course, the algorithm is far more complicated than I mention here, but this is enough for you to get the gist of how it works until I talk about it in more depth in Chapter 3.

Before the CLR deletes the object, it checks if the object contains a special method called a Finalize Destructor. If it does, the CLR will call the object's Finalize Destructor prior to reclaiming the object's memory. The Finalize Destructor is your opportunity to do any cleanup required by your object. This cleanup may include everything from closing a file to removing a list of items from a collection. It's tempting to think that the Finalize Destructor is the same as a C++ destructor, but it's not. A destructor is called in a deterministic manner. In other words, given a piece of code, it is fairly easy to determine when the destructor for an object will be called. If a C++ class contains a destructor, the destructor will be called for stack variables when the variable goes out of scope. The destructor will be called for heap variables (variables created with the new operator) only when you explicitly call the C++ delete operator.

The Finalize Destructor on an object will be called when (and if) the GC runs. The time when this occurs is nondeterministic. In many cases, it will not occur until the application closes down. Therefore, if your objects are holding a resource that is scarce or expensive to hold on to, such as a file handle, network, or database connection, you should implement a method that a client can call to free that resource explicitly. Relying on the Finalize Destructor will cause the resource to be held much longer than is otherwise necessary. By convention, this method should be called Close if it is possible to reopen the resource using the same object instance. This might be true of a file, for instance. The method should be called Dispose if the object should no longer be used after the method has been called. The preferred way to add a Dispose method to your object is to implement the IDisposable interface, which contains a Dispose method. There is no IClose interface, unfortunately.

Life Cycle Management on Remote Objects

So far I have discussed .NET life cycle management in the intra machine case. What about life cycle management when you are working with remote objects either on your LAN or across the Internet? In a distributed environment, the client communicates with a remote object on the server through a proxy object that runs on the client machine. This proxy appears to the client to be the remote object, but, in reality, the proxy turns requests on the proxy into a message that can be sent across the network to the actual remote object. System software on the server machine will unpack the message, call the requested method on the remote object and then send the return value and any output parameters back to the proxy object.

In a distributed environment, the client proxy and the server object reside on different machines and thus use different instances of the CLR. Therefore, their life cycles must be managed separately. Even if there are no longer any object pointers referencing the proxy object on the client, that doesn't automatically mean that the server object will be garbage collected. Ideally, when the proxy is garbage collected on the client, it should send a message to the remote object indicating to the CLR on the server machine that it may release its reference to the remote object. This should eventually cause the remote object to be garbage collected also. Unfortunately, this approach is not sufficient. Imagine what would happen if the client application crashed before the client could send a message to the server that the remote object was no longer needed. The remote object would continue to "live" on the server even though the client was no longer using it.

DCOM handled this problem by having each client ping its remote objects every 2 minutes. The server would delete an object if it did not receive a ping from any of its clients for 3 ping periods (6 minutes). Unfortunately, if there were enough clients and objects, this pinging could generate significant network traffic. Therefore, COM performed this pinging intelligently, grouping all the pings for a single machine into one message and sending only changes (deltas) to this group.

.NET remoting uses leased-based life cycle management. The .NET remoting infra-structure contains a Leasing Distributed Garbage Collector (LDGC), which associates a lease with each remote object. A lease is an object that implements the System.Runtime.Remoting.Lifetime.ILease interface, which has the properties shown in Table 2–1.

TABLE 2–1 *The members of the ILease interface*

Property	Description
CurrentLeaseTime	A read-only property that contains the amount of time remaining on the lease.
InitialLeaseTime	A read/write property that contains the amount of time initially assigned to the lease (default = 5 minutes)
RenewOnCallTime	A read/write property that contains the amount of time to add to the current lease time after each call (default = 2 minutes)
SponsorshipTimeout	A read/write property that contains the amount of time to wait for a sponsor to renew the lease (default = 2 minutes)
CurrentState	A read-only property that contains the current status of the lease. A lease can have the following states: Active, Expired, Initial, Renewing, Null. You can only set the properties of a lease when it is in the Initial state.

TABLE 2–1 *The members of the ILease interface (continued)*

Property	Description
Register	A method that you can call to register a sponsor for the lease.
Unregister	A method that you can call to unregister one of a lease's sponsors.
Renew	A method that you can call to renew a lease.

You can access the lease for a remote object by calling the GetLifetimeService method on the object as shown below

```
Company obj=new Company();
ILease lease=(ILease)obj.GetLifetimeService();
```

If you execute the code shown above from a client you will not be able to assign to the properties of the lease because the lease will already be active and you can only update the properties of a lease when it is in the initial state. You will see shortly how to set these properties.

Note The GetLifetimeService method is a member of the System.MarshalByRefObject class. An object that will be called from a remote AppDomain must inherit from this class either directly or indirectly.

Each lease starts out with a default, initial time of 5 minutes. All leases in an AppDomain (see the sidebar in this chapter to understand what an AppDomains is) are controlled by a lease manager as shown in Figure 2–7.

The lease manager periodically checks for expired leases in its AppDomain. The time period between these checks is determined by the LeaseManagerPollTime property on the System.Runtime.Remoting.Lifetime.LifeTimeServices class. The default polling time is 10 seconds. When an object's lease has expired, the lease manager, will remove all references to the object, thereby allowing the remote object to be garbage collected. A lease can be renewed 3 ways:

1. A lease is renewed whenever a client makes a call on the object. The lease is renewed for the amount of time specified by the RenewOnCallTime property. Specifically, the amount of time remaining on the lease is set to the Max(remaining time on the lease,RenewOnCallTime).
2. A lease can also be renewed by explicitly calling the Renew method on the ILease interface and passing in a TimeSpan object. A client can obtain an ILease interface by calling the GetLifetimeService method on the remote object.
3. You can also renew a lease by registering a sponsor. A sponsor is an object that implements the System.Runtime.Remoting.Lifetime.ISponsor interface.

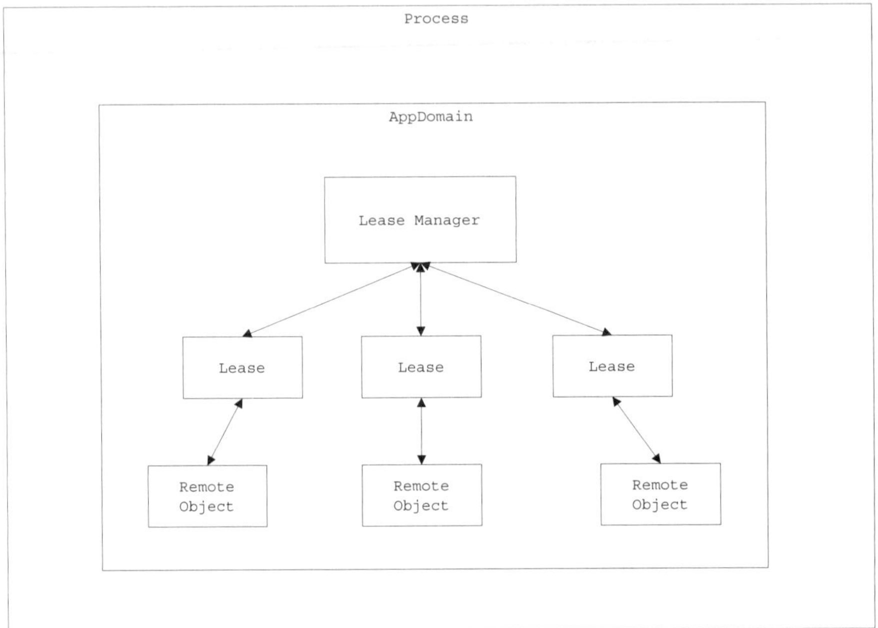

FIGURE 2–7 *Lease-based lifetime management.*

When an object's lease expires, the lease manager will contact all of the sponsors registered for the object and give them an opportunity to renew the lease. The lease manager will wait for the length of time specified by **ILease.SponsorshipTimeout** before marking the object for garbage collection. A client can register a sponsor by calling the GetLifetimeService method to retrieve an ILease interface and then calling the Register method passing in an object that implements the ISponsor interface.

A remote object can configure its leasing-related parameters in one of two ways: programmatically or with a configuration file. To set leasing parameters programmatically override the MarshalByRefObject.InitializeLifetimeService method on your remote object as shown here.

```
public class Company : MarshalByRefObject
{
 // code omitted for clarity…
public override object InitializeLifetimeService()
{
        ILease myLease=(ILease)
base.InitializeLifetimeService();
        if (myLease.CurrentState == LeaseState.Initial)
        {
myLease.InitialLeaseTime=
```

```
TimeSpan.FromSeconds(30);
          myLease.RenewOnCallTime=
TimeSpan.FromMilliseconds(100);
          myLease.SponsorshipTimeout=
TimeSpan.FromMilliseconds(100);
        }
        return myLease;
}
// code omitted for clarity…
}
```

or you can create a configuration file as shown here.

```
<configuration>
      <system.runtime.remoting>
        <application>
          <lifetime leaseTime="30S"
renewOnCallTime="100MS"
sponsorshipTimeOut="100MS"
leaseManagerPollTime="100MS" />
 // the rest of this config. file is omitted for clarity…
        </application>
      </system.runtime.remoting>
</configuration>
```

You can then read this configuration file from your remote host executable as shown here.

```
RemotingConfiguration.Configure("configfilename");
```

Or if you are using IIS as your host executable, you can simply add the "lifetime" element shown above to your web.config file.

If lease-based life cycle management sounds complicated, keep in mind that, in most cases, you won't have to concern yourself with it. The CLR and the .NET remoting infrastructure provide reasonable defaults for most parameters so there is no need to change anything. Moreover, in many cases when you are accessing .NET objects remotely, you will do so using Web services or Single Call objects. When you configure your remote object to be a single call object, the remoting or ASP.NET runtime will instantiate an object to service the request, call the desired method on the object, and then destroy the object. When you configure your remote object's to be singlecall objects, the runtime does not use lease-based lifecycle management.

Note I talk more about .NET remoting, which is the .NET name for accessing objects across process, machine, and AppDomain boundaries in Chapter 11. In that chapter, you will also learn more about lease-based life cycle management, the MarshalByRefObject class, configuration files and client versus server activation, well-known objects, and single-call versus singleton life cycles.

Understanding AppDomains

An AppDomain is an isolated sub-process within a process. A default AppDomain is created when the CLR initializes within a process and this AppDomain is not destroyed unti the process terminates. In addition a process that hosts the CLR can create additional AppDomains. The most important aspect of an AppDomain is its isolation. Code that is executing in one AppDomain cannot directly access memory or objects that reside in a different AppDomain. In order to access objects across AppDomains they must be either serialized into the calling AppDomain (marshal by value objects) or, if the type derive from the System.MarshalByRefObject class, they can be accessed across AppDomains via a proxy that resides in the calling AppDomain and forwards the request to the AppDomain where the object resides (these are called marshal by reference objects).

Programming Language Independence

In order to implement a programming language-independent software bus, you must satisfy two requirements:

- You need a way to describe your software components in a programming language-independent way.
- You need a programming language-independent interface that developers can use to make method calls between components that are implemented in different programming languages.

The first requirement exists to make our lives as developers easier. If compilers and other development tools can discover the capabilities of a software component prior to runtime, they can perform a variety of compile-time verifications that can both save you time and help you to make your software more robust. For instance, your compiler can verify that a method that is being called on an object actually exists in the object's class. It can also verify that the method is being called with the correct number and type of parameters. Many development tools go even further than this and provide an intelligent prompt that guides you through the construction of a method call. The prompt shows you the available methods on an object and then shows you the type, name, and even a description of each parameter as you enter it. Microsoft calls this Intellisense.

The COM solution for describing software components in a programming language-independent way is type libraries. COM includes a language called IDL that developers can use to describe the classes and interfaces that a COM server supports. You then use a compiler called MIDL to turn this IDL into a type library, which contains a standardized, binary representation of the classes, interfaces, and other declarations in the original IDL file. The COM API contains a set of methods that you may use to interrogate the contents of a type library. Many development environments eschew the need for IDL and simply generated the type library directly (VB does this). In most cases, there is a type library for each COM in-process or out-of-process server. Usually, the type library file is embedded within the server although this was not a requirement. COM type libraries can—and often are—distributed separately from the server that they describe.

The .NET Framework takes the idea of a type library and runs with it. In the .NET world, CLR-compliant compilers are required to generate copious metadata automatically and insert the metadata in the binary files that they generate. There is no separate language for declaring and creating metainformation like IDL. The compiler creates the metadata directly from the code, and, unlike COM, this metadata *must* reside in the assembly that it describes.

.NET metadata includes information that describes all of the types (classes or structures) in the assembly. In addition, the metadata describes the name and type of each field, property, method, and event in those types. For methods and events, the type and directionality (input, output, input and output) of each parameter is described in an assembly's metadata. So far all of the .NET metadata that I have talked about also existed in COM types. The biggest improvement that .NET metadata has over COM type libraries is that .NET metadata also includes important dependency and versioning information that was not stored in COM type libraries. The metadata for each assembly includes the full name of each assembly that it depends on. This means that the CLR can verify that the correct version of each dependent assembly is resident on a host machine at runtime. If the correct version is not present, it can throw an error that clearly indicates that a versioning problem exists. This solves a good portion of the DLL hell problem that plagued the Win32/COM platform.

The second programming language independence requirement—that there be a language-neutral interface for calling methods—derives from the fact that different programming languages have different ways of making method invocations. It's not enough to just describe our COM components in a programming language-independent way. We must also be able to call them in a language-independent way. This is complicated by the fact that most programming languages have different calling conventions. For instance, a C/C++ compiler will emit code to push the parameters on the stack in reverse order (from right to left), and the calling function is responsible for cleaning up the stack when the method is done. However, some programming languages push the parameters on the stack in the other order (left to right), and most other programming languages require the called function to clean up the stack.

COM solved this problem by defining a binary-level calling convention for COM objects. COM's binary-level calling standard specifies that all method invocations on a COM object be made through interfaces that the object supports. These COM interfaces are an array of function pointers. There is one pointer for each method in the interface. These functions must use the Pascal calling convention, which means that the called function cleans up the stack. Any compiler or development environment that wants either to create or consume COM objects must support this convention.

.NET takes a completely different approach. Instead of directly generating executable code, all CLR-compliant compilers generate MSIL code, which is a sort of virtual assembly language. MSIL also defines a standardized representation for objects, which Microsoft calls the VOS. The VOS defines an object model that is shared by all CLR-compliant programming languages. An object model specifies such things as the types of members that a class may have (in .NET, a class may have methods, properties, fields, and events), the possible visibilities of those members (public, private, and so forth), and whether single or multiple inheritance is supported (only single inheritance is supported in .NET).

Therefore, whether you're defining an object using Microsoft's Java-like language (C#) or its improved version of VB (VB.NET) or even Cobol or Haskell, a type implemented in any of these languages gets compiled into an equivalent form: a VOS object implemented in MSIL.

The advantages of this approach are numerous. Using MSIL and the VOS allows .NET to take programming language independence far beyond what was possible in COM. You can, for instance, create a type in VB.NET and create a subtype that inherits from this type using C#. You can create an exception object and throw it from code written in one language and catch it in code written in a different language.

The biggest disadvantage of this approach is that some programming languages (C++ in particular) that have a richer object model than the one supported by the VOS will have to be dumbed down to work with .NET. For example, C++ supports multiple inheritance, but, because the VOS only supports single inheritance, Microsoft's version of C++ for .NET, which is called C++ with Managed Extensions, only supports single inheritance. If you try to use multiple inheritance when you are using the C++ Managed Extensions, the compiler will generate a compilation error. This is not as big a deal as you might think (even though I'm sure some C++/object purists will decry this as a step back) because many people found multiple inheritance to be one of the most confusing aspects of C++. Moreover, although you can only inherit from a single type, you can inherit from multiple interfaces. I explore this more when I discuss the C# language in Chapter 4.

Note Keep in mind that you can use the C++ compiler in Visual Studio .NET with or without managed extensions. If you use managed extensions, the compiler generates managed code that runs under the control of the CLR, and you are limited to single inheritance. If you do not use the managed extensions, the compiler generates x86 native code, and you are free to use multiple inheritance to your hearts content.

Location Transparency

Location transparency is the ability to use a software component in the exact same way regardless of whether it is running in the same process as its client or whether the software component is running on the same machine as its client or on a remote machine. If a software component *does* reside in the same process as its client, making a method call is simple. A method call simply involves pushing the parameters that are being passed to the method along with the return address—the location where the flow of control should continue after the method call—onto the stack. The flow of control then jumps to the memory address in the process where the method resides. The method then pulls the parameters off the stack and executes its logic, and then the flow of control jumps to the return address. The return value from the method is either pulled off the stack or perhaps out of a CPU register. Any output parameters can be pulled off the stack also. Again, this is how it typically works; compilers are free to implement this logic in different ways.

The process that I just described will only work if the calling code and the method reside in the same process *and* share the same memory address space. If two pieces of code share the same memory address space, memory addresses that are valid for one piece of code are also valid for the other. This means that you can pass pointers between the two pieces of code and you can jump from one point in the code to another using the memory address of a routine.

If the calling code resides in a different process than the method or if the calling code does not share the same address space, you must use a process called marshalling.

Marshaling

Marshaling is a technique for making method calls across process and machine boundaries. The essential idea behind marshaling is that we want to take a stack frame that resides in one process and turn it into a data stream that we can pass to another process on the same machine or to a different machine on our network. At the receiving process (or machine), we will unpack the data stream, reconstruct the stack frame, make the method call, and then send any return values and output values back as a data stream to the caller, which can then put them on its own stack. To the caller, it appears that we made a method call normally, and the return values and output parameters came back.

The whole idea behind location transparency is to make this process as simple (to the developer) as possible. Ideally, making a call to a remote object or an object in another process should be as simple as making a direct method call to an object that resides in the same process.

Marshaling is usually implemented using a proxy that resides in the calling process. This proxy looks exactly like the object with the method that you are trying to call. It has the same methods, and those methods have the same parameters and return values. When you call the proxy, the proxy takes the method call and serializes it into a data stream. This message is sent by some network protocol (if the caller and callee reside on different machines) or by some form of Interprocess Communication (IPC) (if the caller and callee reside on the same machine) to the receiving process or machine. On the receiving process or machine, a piece of software, which is usually called a stub, receives the message, unpacks the message, calls the requested method, and then sends the return values back as a message. The proxy receives this message and updates the stack frame (return value and parameters) on the client. The network protocol and logic that connect the proxy and the stub are called a channel.

So far, I have talked about marshaling only in the context of making method calls across process and machine boundaries. If you are an experienced COM programmer, you know that marshaling was also required when you made method calls across Apartments in the same process. The .NET Framework and the CLR does not support Apartments, but it does support something called an AppDomain, which is a logical subprocess within a physical process. Method calls that are being made across AppDomains must also be marshaled, even if the caller and the calling code reside in the same process. The CLR is smart enough to optimize the marshaling process if the caller's AppDomain and the called object's AppDomain reside in the same process.

Marshaling is required when making method calls across AppDomains because two applications running in different AppDomains are completely isolated from one another, even if the two AppDomains are running in the same process. In other words, memory faults in one application won't bring the entire process down. The two applications can be independently stopped and debugged, and an application running in one AppDomain cannot directly access resources (memory, file handles, and so forth) held by an application in another AppDomain, even if the two applications share the same process. With COM, the only way to provide this sort of isolation between two applications was to separate them into different processes. However, with the .NET Framework, the CLR provides a level of type safety and code verification. These make it possible to provide this same level of isolation while avoiding the need for expensive (in terms of time) process switches.

Conceptually, COM and .NET implement marshaling in a very similar manner. They both use proxies, stubs, and channels. They differ substantially though in the following areas:

- How they construct the proxy and stub
- How method calls are serialized into a data stream
- What network protocol is used to send the stream across machines

CONSTRUCTING THE PROXY AND STUB

One of the main keys to making the marshaling process as seamless as possible is to hide the fact that the client is communicating with the server through a proxy. Ideally, the proxy should be created automatically by the operating system or runtime only when it is needed, and calling methods through the proxy should be as simple as making a direct method call. The underlying operating system or runtime code must therefore have complete meta information about the remote object. It must know the return type of each remotely callable method. It must know the type and size of each parameter, and it must know the directionality of each parameter, that is, which parameters are inputs, which are outputs, and which are both input and output. With COM, there were two ways to provide this information to the COM runtime:

- You could use COM IDL and MIDL compiler to create a custom marshalling/proxy-stub DLL that contains all of the logic needed to create the proxies and stubs for one or more COM classes.
- If your COM classes only used automation types for parameters and return values, you could use the type library marshaler in the COM runtime. In this case, all you needed to do was to register a type library for your server.

Figure 2–8 shows how you would generate a custom marshaling/proxy-stub DLL using IDL and the MIDL compiler.

You (or your development environment) would generate the IDL file. You then compile this IDL file using MIDL. MIDL will generate several source files. You then compile and link these source files with a few system libraries to create your marshaling/proxy-stub DLL. You then had to install and register this DLL on both the client and server machine. The COM runtime then automatically uses this DLL whenever you make a cross-process, remote (or inter-Apartment) method call on an object for which the DLL can provide a proxy and stub.

Using type library marshaling was much simpler, and this is why it eventually became the preferred approach. With this approach, all you had to do was to generate a type library for each COM server. You could generate this type library using an IDL description of the classes and interfaces in a COM server. Many development environments, VB for example, generated a type library automatically and embedded it within the DLL or executable that they generated. After you registered this type library, the type library marshaler that was included with the COM runtime would use the type library to get all the meta information it needed to construct a proxy for a remote or cross-process method call.

With .NET, creating the proxy and stub is much easier. Once again, the copious metadata that is embedded in every assembly comes to your aid. This metadata contains all the information that the Remoting infrastructure in the .NET Framework needs to create a proxy for any class within an assembly.

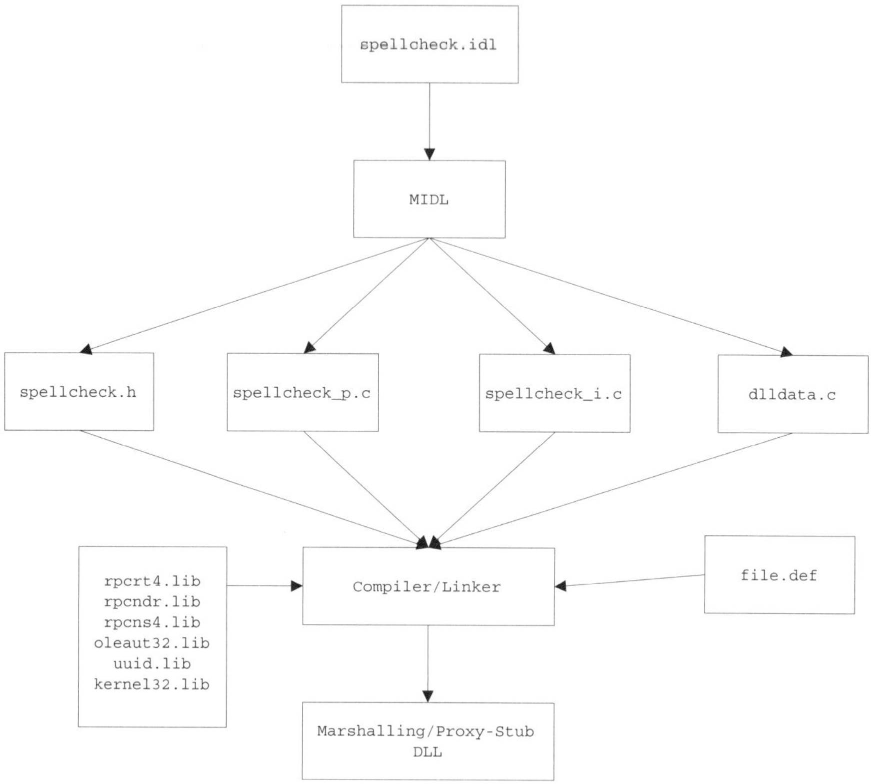

FIGURE 2–8 *Using MIDL in COM to generate a marshalling/proxy-stub DLL.*

There's no need to create a separate description of your classes and interfaces in IDL and no need for a separate proxy/stub DLL.

In order to be remotable, a class must instead inherit from a base class called **System.MarshalByRefObject** as shown in the following:

```
Class MyRemotableClass : MarshalByRefObject
{
}
```

After you have done this, the CLR is smart enough to create a proxy automatically whenever a reference to an object is passed out of the AppDomain in which the object resides.

An object can be passed out of its own host AppDomain as a parameter or a return value of a remote method call. A reference is also passed out of its AppDomain when you instantiate a remote object in a different AppDomain using .NET Remoting. A remote object in this context means that it can be located in any of the following locations relative to its client:

- On a different machine
- In a different process on the same machine
- In a different AppDomain in the same process

If you wanted to be a stickler for details, you could argue that the mere fact that you must inherit from a different class (**System.MarshalByRefObject** instead of **System.Object**) to create a **Remotable** class is a violation of location transparency. It's hard to argue with that, but, considering how much easier it is to use .NET remoting than DCOM (as you will see in chapter 11), I think that this is a small price to pay.

What About Marshal by Value Objects?

In some cases, when you access a remote object (that is, an object in a different process or AppDomain), you do not want the object to remain in its host process or AppDomain while you access it through a proxy. Instead, you may want the object to marshal its entire state across the process or AppDomain boundary so that all further interaction with the object can take place within the calling process or AppDomain; this is sometimes referred to as Marshal-by-Value. ADO Recordsets are the most commonly used marshal-by-value COM object. Marshal-by-Value objects do not need to inherit from MarshalByRefObject; they only need to inherit from System.Object. They must be serializable, however, so that the CLR can stream the state of the object across AppDomains. The simplest way to make a class serializable is to use the Serializable attribute as follows:

```
[serializable]
class MySerializableClass
{
//...
}
```

SERIALIZING METHOD CALLS INTO A DATA STREAM

When you are accessing a remote object, the proxy will take the method calls that you make on the object and serialize all the information needed to make the method call (an identifier for the method, the parameters, and so forth). The proxy then serializes it into a data stream that can be sent across processes or across the network. COM uses a format called Network Data Representation (NDR).

.NET gives you more choices. For a start, the .NET Remoting architecture includes the notion of a Formatter and a Channel. Formatters are responsible for serializing method calls into a data stream; Channels are responsible for transporting the data stream across the network (or between processes on the same machine). There are two available channels in the .NET Remoting infrastructure: an HTTP Channel (see System.Runtime.Remoting.Channels.HTTP) and a TCP channel (see System.Runtime.Remoting.Channels.TCP). There are also two types of Formatters: a SOAP formatter (see System.Runtime.Serialization.Formatters.Soap) and a binary formatter (see System.Runtime.Serialization.Formatters.Binary). Both formatters use the metadata in the remote object's assembly to convert a method call into an XML-based SOAP message in the case of the SOAP formatter and to a proprietary binary format in the case of the binary formatter. By default, the HTTP channel uses the SOAP formatter, and the TCP channel uses the binary formatter. However, you can change this if you like and use the binary formatter with the HTTP channel, for instance. Using the TCP channel with the binary formatter is in some ways equivalent to using DCOM. The key difference between .NET Remoting and DCOM is the availability of the HTTP Channel and the SOAP formatter. Both of which make it easier to make method calls across the Internet.

COMPARING THE NETWORK PROTOCOLS

Both COM and DCOM gave you some flexibility in the network protocol that you used when making method calls across a network. With DCOM, you could use the dcomcnfg tool to choose the network protocols that DCOM would use and the order that the protocols would be chosen in as shown in Figure 2–9.

With DCOM, TCP and User Datagram Protocol (UDP) were the most commonly used protocols although you could select others. With .NET, HTTP will be the most commonly used protocol. Rather than using a tool like dcomcnfg, you will select the protocol—and even the port—that you will use when you select your channel. You can select a channel either programmatically using the RegisterWellKnownType or RegisterActivatedType methods on the **RemotingServices** class or using a configuration file.

You can see that, with regard to location transparency, .NET is just as capable as COM/DCOM (although it's not quite as transparent). The copious metadata that managed code compilers generate obviates the need for IDL and for IDL-generated proxy-stub marshalling DLLs. With .NET's formatter and channel architecture, you have far more choices in how method calls are serialized into a network-transportable message and how those messages are transmitted across the network.

Extensibility

No matter how feature-rich your software components are, your users will always want more. A software bus must support some means for developers to extend the functionality of their software components. When I talk about extensibility here, I am really talking about clients (usually other developers) who buy a software component and then want to extend the functionality of those components in some way. If developers who created a software com-

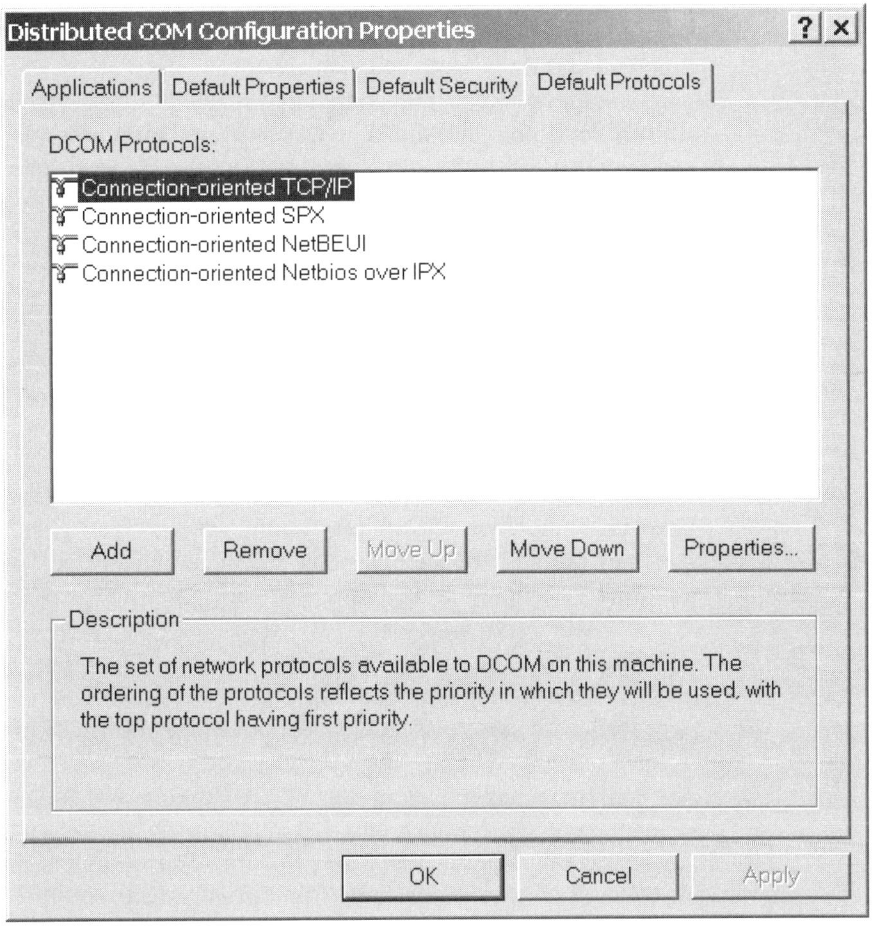

FIGURE 2–9 *Available network protocols with DCOM.*

ponent want to extend the functionality of a component, they face a versioning, not an extensibility, problem. The developers of a software component have the source code for the component, so enhancing the component is easy. Their biggest concern is not breaking existing software that uses the component (versioning). Developers who buy the software component will likely not have the source code for the component. Therefore, they need extensibility at the binary level, or the ability to inherit from a software component for which they do not have the source code.

If you talk to software developers who know anything about object-oriented design and programming and you mention extensibility, the first word out of their mouths will likely be inheritance. One of the central ideas in object-oriented design and programming is that, given a type (a class), I should be able to create a subtype that inherits the state of its base class. This subtype should be able to either inherit the operations in its base class as-is, or override some of the operations in the base class and provide its own implementation. Unfortunately, COM did not support implementation inheritance. The COM software bus gives you two choices for extending a COM object: aggregation and containment. In both cases, you create an outer class that contains all of the interfaces that the extended COM class will support. In other words, the interfaces that the base class supports and any new interfaces that the extended object will add to the base class. The base class was called an inner class. The outer object will typically create an instance of the inner class on initialization and hold onto a reference to the inner object for as long as it lives. The main difference between containment and aggregation is the manner in which the outer object uses the inner object.

If you used containment to extend a COM class, the outer class would provide its own implementation of the interfaces in the base/inner class. This implementation would delegate to the implementation in the inner object. The key point is that the inner object is never directly exposed to a user of the outer object. Figure 2–10 shows schematically what containment looks like.

If you used aggregation to extend a COM class, you directly expose interfaces from the inner object. When a user of the outer object requests an interface that is implemented in the inner object, the outer object would simply fetch and return an interface pointer on the inner object. Figure 2–11 shows a schematic view of aggregation.

Although aggregation seems simpler and certainly more elegant than containment, conceptually, it is actually quite complicated. For a start, one of the basic rules of COM is that all of the interfaces that are supported by a COM class should be available from any interface. In other words, if a COM

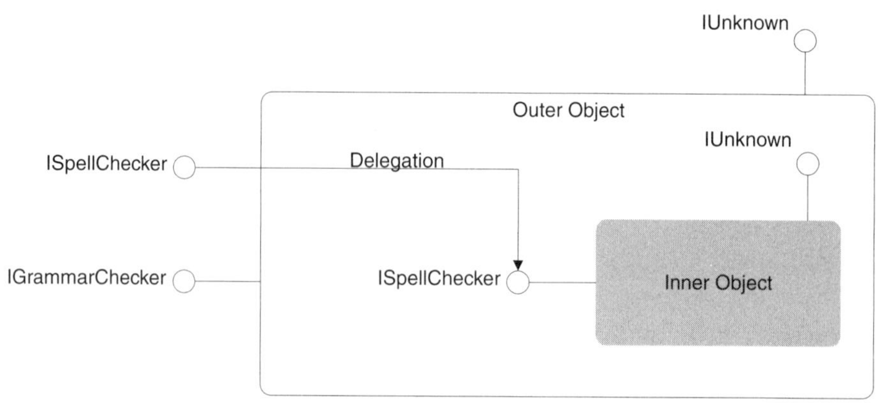

FIGURE 2–10 *Extending a COM software component using containment.*

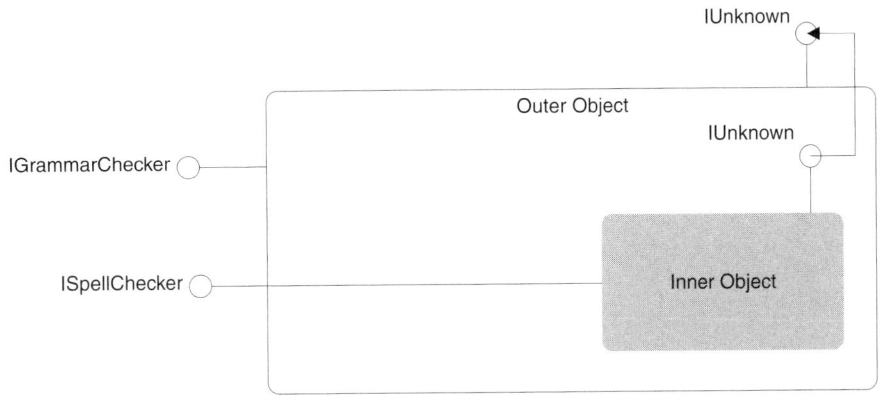

FIGURE 2–11 *Extend a COM software component using aggregation.*

class supports interfaces A, B, and C, you should be able to obtain interfaces A and B given a pointer to interface C. Similarly, given a pointer to interface B, you should be able to obtain pointers to interfaces A and C. Unfortunately, if A and B are the interfaces supported by the inner object and C is the interface supported by the outer object, there is no way for a pointer to interface A to return a pointer to interface C because the implementation of the inner object knows nothing about interface C. The solution is for the inner object to delegate its implementation of the IUnknown interface to the outer object. The inner object of course has to be implemented in such a way that it knows when it is part of an aggregate. Confused? A lot of people were, and I always encouraged my COM students not to get discouraged if they did not understand aggregation right away. It was very complex, especially when compared to the elegant simplicity of implementation inheritance.

Publicly, Microsoft stated that the reason that COM did not support implementation inheritance was because of the "fragile base-class problem." This basically means that, when you use implementation inheritance, it is possible for a subclass to break its base class by overriding its methods with an unsuitable or incomplete implementation, perhaps failing to call the base class method to perform some necessary work. They also stated that polymorphism was the real goal and that implementation inheritance was only one way to achieve that goal.

They obviously thought otherwise privately because the .NET Framework supports binary-level, programming language-independent implementation inheritance. Given a managed type in an assembly, you can create a subtype using any programming language that supports .NET. Therefore, you can create a base class in C# and inherit from it using VB.NET. You are limited by the CLR to single inheritance, but still this is a huge step forward from COM. Has the "fragile base-class problem" suddenly gone away in .NET? In a word...No. You can still get yourself into trouble in a hurry using implementation inheritance. Before you inherit from a class, make sure you understand the base class well enough that you understand the ramifications of overriding a method in the base class. In many cases, you will need to call the base class's implementation of the method in your override. If you do not have the source code for a base class, it can be difficult to know when it is safe to override a method. Fortunately, the CLR provides some help with this problem. First, the CLR allows for both virtual (overridable) and nonvirtual methods in a class. If overriding a particular method in one of your classes may cause problems, make sure you declare it as nonvirtual. With C#, methods in a class are nonvirtual by default; you have to use the virtual keyword explicitly to make a method overridable.

The CLR also supports the notion of sealed classes, that is, classes that cannot be subtyped. The following code shows how you would create a sealed class in C#:

```
sealed class MyClass
{
//...
}
// This will cause a compiler error
class NoCanDo : MyClass
{
//...
}
```

You should get in the habit of declaring a class as sealed if you know that inheriting from the class may cause problems.

Versioning

Any environment that uses binary software components must address the software component versioning problem. This problem occurs when you install an application, and suddenly some other application stops working. The culprit is usually DLLs that are shared by several applications. The MFC runtime DLL, mfc42.dll, is a good example of a shared DLL. It is used by all applications that are built with Visual C++. If you install an application that was built with Visual C++ (and therefore depends on mfc42.dll) and then later install some other application that uses an earlier version of mfc42.dll, the first application will likely cease to work if the second application installs the older version of the DLL. If the second application senses that a newer DLL is already resident on the system and does not install the older version (a correctly written setup program should do this), it is possible that the second application will not work. The second application is now using a different version of the MFC runtime DLL than it was built with. Usually, newer DLLs are backward compatible with old ones, but there are no guarantees. So how do you fix this problem?

COM's solution was immutable interfaces. The basic idea is that, after you published an interface in a COM class, you should never change that interface. If you want to add new functionality to a component, you should add additional interfaces to the component, preserving the older interfaces unchanged. This should—in theory—guarantee that client software that was built using a particular interface will always work. My own experience is that the COM solution worked better than most people gave it credit for. Most of the versioning problems that I encountered weren't caused by COM components. When these problems were caused by COM components, it was because developers were not following the rules. There were some problems with the COM approach, though.

One problem is that it is possible for the behavior of a method to change even though the signature of the method (the number and type of its parameters and its return value) is the same. Perhaps using zero for the first parameter means one thing for version 1 and something totally different for version 2. Indeed, the COM specification said that new versions of software components should preserve both the signature and the semantics of its interfaces, but in practice it was easy for subtle behavior changes to creep in, especially over many new versions. Speaking of many new versions, another problem with the COM approach to versioning is the sheer proliferation of interfaces that tend to occur as you maintain and enhance a component over many years. For instance, in my COM class that I taught at UCLA, I used the Microsoft Active Movie Control for an in-class exercise on building applications using ActiveX controls. It made for a very visual and fun exercise. I noticed as the years went by the proliferation of IActiveMovie interfaces in the ActiveX control. By the time I stopped teaching the class, after 3 years, there were three IActiveMovie interfaces: IActiveMovie, IActiveMovie2, and IActiveMovie3. Each of these interfaces was only slightly different from the others, but, as Microsoft added new features to the Active Movie control, it was forced to add new interfaces in order to obey COM's immutable interfaces rule. Therefore, although it is possible to maintain backward compatibility from version to version with COM, in practice, it was difficult and a lot of work.

.NET takes a completely different approach to versioning. The solution can really be summed up with three concepts: private assemblies, metadata, and side-by-side execution.

Private Assemblies

A private assembly exists (on a particular machine) solely for the use of a single application. That assembly will not be shared by any other applications on the machine. Microsoft recommends that you use private assemblies as much as possible. Each application should be distributed with the versions of the assemblies that it was built and tested, with and those assemblies should be deployed into a directory that is private to that application. Obviously, this fixes the notorious versioning problems (DLL hell) that COM and regular Win32 DLLs were always afflicted with. If an application does not share its assemblies with another application, there is no danger that one application will install a version of an assembly that will break another application on the same machine. The only down side to this approach is that you will use up more disk space. If you have a dozen applications on your machine that depend on a particular assembly there will be a dozen potentially different versions of the assembly resident on your hard drive if you use private assemblies,. However, nowadays this isn't a problem; hard disk space and RAM are cheap. At the time when Win32 and COM were architected, both RAM and hard disk space were far more scarce and expensive than they are now. It is far cheaper to buy a larger hard disk so that each application can use the version of the assembly that it was built and tested with than it is to have a highly paid system administrator or developer tracking down a problem that was caused by an incompatible version of a shared DLL.

Metadata

Although Microsoft recommends that you use private assemblies, obviously, they are not suitable in all situations. The assemblies that comprise the .NET Framework class library are a good example of assemblies that must be shared by many applications. The .NET Framework class library is therefore implemented as a set of shared assemblies that are deployed in the GAC. There will be situations where you will need to create shared assemblies also. Thankfully, even in this situation, .NET provides technologies that should improve the versioning problem. Every .NET assembly stores not just metadata describing the types that are implemented *within* the assembly, but they also store copious metadata describing all of the assemblies that the assembly is *dependent* on. This metadata stores the name of each dependent assembly. This name includes a cryptographic key, if the assembly has a strong name, culture information, and, most important (at least for this discussion), the version # of the dependent assembly. This version number contains four parts.

```
[major version].[minor version].[build number].[revision]
e.g.
1.2.52.123
```

Let's say I have assembly #1, which uses types from assembly # 2. When developers build assembly #1, they will reference assembly #2, and the metadata for assembly #1 will contain, the name, the version #, culture information, and the public key of assembly #2 as shown in Figure 2–12.

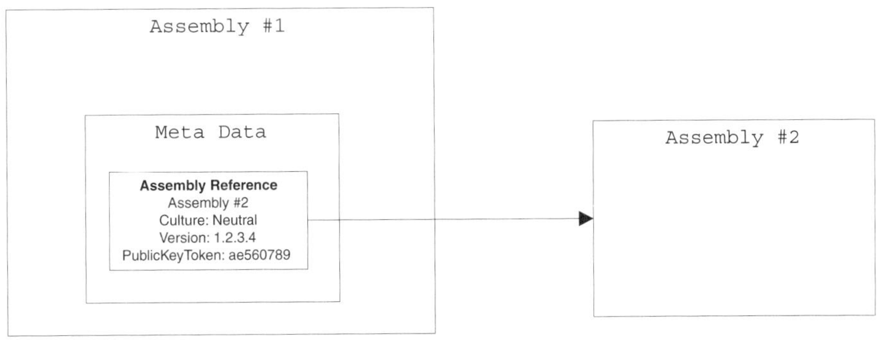

FIGURE 2–12 *An assembly reference.*

When code that resides in assembly #1 first uses a type from assembly #2, the CLR will attempt to locate assembly #2. By default, the CLR will search for the same version of assembly #2 that assembly #1 was built with. In Chapter 3, you will see that there are a number of ways that you can redirect assembly #1 to a different version of assembly #2. However, you would only do this if you knew that the version of assembly #2 that you are redirecting assembly #1 to use is compatible with the version of assembly #2 that assembly #1 was built with.

Note Each application may have a configuration file where a developer or administrator can specify such things as the assembly binding settings, which affect how the CLR resolves references to assemblies. You can use these assembly binding settings to redirect all references to one version of an assembly to a different version. You will learn more about configuration files in Chapter 3. The .NET Framework also supports publisher policies, which allow the publisher of a component to redirect references to one version of an assembly to a different version. You will learn more about publisher policies in Chapter 3. System administrators on a host machine can turn off publisher policies if they want to.

Side-by-Side Execution

Side-by-side execution is the ability of the CLR to run multiple versions of the same assembly simultaneously. The CLR can even run multiple versions of the same assembly in different AppDomains within a single process (for example, if a Web server is running multiple applications that use different versions of an assembly). Side-by-side execution is probably the most important element of the .NET solution to the versioning problem. It means that each application can run with the same version of the components that it was built and tested with. Components in .NET no longer have to maintain backward compatibility. Backward compatibility—or the lack of it—was the main cause of the DLL hell problems in Win32/COM.

COM's versioning scheme required you to make newer versions of a component backward compatible with older ones so that all the applications on a box could then share the same version of the component. Unfortunately, it was difficult and time consuming to maintain backward compatibility. As time went by, you simply had too many versions to maintain compatibility with, and it is easy for subtle differences to creep in. The .NET solution of having each application deploy the version of its components that it was built and tested with and then having the CLR support side-by-side executions of multiple versions of the same component should banish the problem of DLL hell forever.

Summary

In this chapter, I compared .NET and COM using the analogy of a software bus. I compared their solutions to the software bus problems of naming, life cycle management, programming language independence, location transparency, extensibility, and versioning. You have seen that, although .NET and COM use very different approaches, they are solving many of the same problems. At their essence, both COM and .NET are about creating binary, programming language-independent software components that can be easily used across process and machine boundaries. .NET has more of an Internet focus whereas COM was designed more for LANs, but many of the technical problems in both environments are the same.

Much of the knowledge that you have of COM will simply map to .NET. For instance, COM uses GUIDs for naming, and .NET uses cryptographic keys. However, the problem is the same: creating a unique name for a software component. Hopefully, this chapter has also allowed you to begin mapping the knowledge that you have of COM to .NET.

In the next chapter, I take a closer look at a piece of technology in the .NET Framework that does not have an analogy in COM: the CLR.

THREE

Exploring the CLR

In this chapter, I dig a little deeper into the CLR. In the .NET overview in Chapter 1, I briefly discussed metadata, MSIL, CTS, CLS, VOS, and VES. In this chapter, I dive deeper into all of these concepts. You will also understand what an assembly is and how the CLR locates assemblies, executes managed code, and enforces security. You'll learn how the CLR implements automatic memory management (garbage collection) and what changes you need to make to your programming style to take advantage of it. As I go through this material, keep in mind that, just as you didn't have to understand all the low-level details of the Win32 API to program on the Windows platform, you don't have to be an expert on the CLR to use .NET. Understanding how the CLR works will make you a better programmer though, and this knowledge will help you to be a true .NET expert.

Describing The CLR

The CLR is an execution environment that loads and executes code. All Win32 operating systems (and indeed all other operating systems) have facilities to load and run binary files. However, no operating systems that I know of have a mechanism for verifying that the code they are running has not been tampered with or that the code does not violate type safety or access memory that it should not. This sort of security checking is particularly necessary in the Internet era when executable code may be received as an attachment to an email or downloaded automatically from a Web site. It's also not usually the goal of most operating systems to make it easy for people to port software written for one operating system to other operating systems. Moreover, most operating systems don't provide system-level support for features desired by today's software developers (garbage collection, stack walking, metadata, programming language independence, and so forth). Some programming languages, like VB, provide support for some of these features in their language-specific runtimes. However, no operating system currently provides all of these features at the system level so that the features are available to any programming language that targets that operating system. Also, few operating systems have features specifically designed to make it easy to deploy and version software. DLL hell was becoming a sad fact of life with Windows applications and a huge waste of time. Enhanced security, portability, and ease of development and deployment are just some of the goals of the CLR.

The CLR is system-level code that subsumes some of the functionality of a traditional compiler (because it compiles MSIL code into native code). It also subsumes some of the functionality of the code loader in the operating system (because it reads PE format binary files and loads them into memory), and of language runtimes like the C runtime or the VB runtime (because it manages heap memory and provides services that make it easier to write software). The CLR is implemented as a set of DLLs. The most important of these is the runtime execution engine. The runtime execution engine is the part of the CLR that executes code; it can be found in a DLL called mscoree.dll that resides in your **System32** directory. Other files required by the runtime, such as the file that contains the core pieces of the class library, mscorlib.dll, can be found in a directory called **WINNT\Microsoft.NET\Framework\v1.0.3705**. Your version number may vary. The binary files for the CLR are installed when you install the .NET Framework SDK or Visual Studio .NET. You will have to redistribute these files when you deploy a .NET Framework application. Microsoft provides a merge module that you can add to your setup to simplify this. With Microsoft's newer operating systems, like Windows .NET Server, these files will be bundled with the operating system. However, even if the target platform has the .NET Framework installed, you may still need to distribute the specific version of the Framework that you built your application with.

Defining Managed Code and Managed Data

Code that runs under the control of the CLR is called managed code. By targeting the CLR, managed code enjoys all the benefits that I discussed in the previous section, enhanced security, portability, and so forth.

The Official Definition of Managed Code

The "official" definition of managed code from Partition 1 (Architecture) of the Tool Developers Guide in the .NET Framework SDK Documentation is as follows:

Managed code is simply code that provides enough information to allow the CLR to provide a set of core services, including:

- Given an address inside the code for a method, locate the metadata describing the method
- Walk the stack
- Handle exceptions
- Store and retrieve security information

You can find the Tool Developer's Guide at: [Visual Studio .NET Install Directory]\ FrameworkSDK\Tool Developers Guide\docs. On my machine, the full path is: C:\Program Files\Microsoft Visual Studio .NET\FrameworkSDK\Tool Developers Guide\docs.

Only managed code can access managed data. Managed data is a special memory heap that is allocated and released automatically by the CLR through a process called garbage collection.

You can still create unmanaged code (which is the new name for the standard Win32 code you wrote before .NET) with Visual Studio .NET by creating an MFC or Active Template Library (ATL) project in the latest version of Visual C++, which is included with Visual Studio .NET.

Note You can also create managed code with Visual C++ thanks to something called C++ with Managed Extensions. There is also talk that Microsoft will support VB 6.0 for some time to come. Because the .NET Framework represents such a fundamental shift from Win32/COM, the two platforms will likely coexist for a number of years.

Unmanaged code cannot use managed data, and it will not enjoy the benefits afforded by the CLR: garbage collection, enhanced security, simplified deployment, rich debugging support, consistent error handling, language independence, and even the possibility of running on different platforms.

I will begin our tour of the CLR by looking at types. I then talk about assemblies. In the section on assemblies, you build a multifile assembly that we will use as a running example to illustrate other concepts throughout the chapter. After I talk about assemblies at a conceptual level, I discuss the two major constituents of an assembly: metadata and MSIL. I next discuss how the CLR locates assemblies. I end the chapter by discussing garbage collection and code access security.

Types

The .NET Framework is built around types. A type in .NET is a class, structure, interface, enumeration, or delegate. Every piece of code that you write in .NET, even the main program for your application, must be a member of some type.

The following code shows the simplest "hello world" application that you can write.

```
class TestClass
{
  static void Main(string[] args)
  {
    System.Console.WriteLine("Hello World");
  }
}
```

Notice that the Main method in this case is a static member of a class called **TestClass**. Not only will all of the code that you write be contained within some type, but all of the code that you use, both the classes in the .NET Framework base class library and any third-party class libraries, are all implemented as types. There are no global functions in .NET.

What Is a Type?

In the software world, a type is a just a set of operations, and, optionally, some state that all instances of that type have in common. Most programming languages have intrinsic types like the int, float, char, and long types in C/C++ (and C#) and the Integer, Single and String types in VB. Each of these types has some state representation associated with it. For instance, an int in C is either a 16- or 32-bit block of memory depending on the platform. A C float is a 32-bit block of memory on most platforms. Each of these types has a set of operators that can be applied to them, and "+", "-", "/" are just a few of these operators. The main difference between these types is how they represent their state. The bits in a 32-bit int represent a base 2 number, and the bits in a 32-bit float represent a real number that is encoded using one of several formats, such as Institute of Electrical and Electronic Engineers (IEEE) 754.

What Is a Type? *(continued)*

Most programming languages also allow developers to create user-defined types that are conglomerates of the intrinsic types and other user-defined types, such as an Employee structure in C that contains an int ID member, a float salary member, and a string name member that is a null-terminated char array. Object-oriented programming languages introduced the notion of a class type that stores its state as a conglomerate of other types. Classes also support a set of methods that operate on the state; this is sometimes called the behavior of the class.

So what's the advantage of this approach? That's simple. It means that your code is easier to verify. If all of your code is a member of a type, as long as you can guarantee type safety—in other words, as long as you can guarantee that it is impossible to coerce an object of one type into behaving like another type that it is not assignment compatible with (in other words, that is not in its inheritance tree)—you can go a long way toward guaranteeing that the code is safe. Indeed, one of the most common types of security attacks these days, buffer overflows, can be at least partially avoided through the use of type-safe code. To understand buffer overflows, imagine that you have a 50-element array. If you can create a piece of code that treats that 50-element array as though it were a 250-element array, you can gain access to memory that would not normally be accessed by application code. This memory may contain system-level information, or it might contain a handle that someone can use to write to the file system. If you can enforce type safety, that is, guarantee that a 50-element array can only be accessed as a 50-element array; you can eliminate an entire class of security problems. Type-safe code also has the additional benefit of being less error-prone and easier to debug.

CTS

In addition to making it easy to write code that is more secure, less error prone, and easier to debug, Microsoft also wants to enable an unprecedented level of cross-language interoperability in the .NET Framework. One of the key enabling technologies in the .NET Framework that makes this possible is the Common Type System (CTS). The CTS provides a common set of types for all CLR-compliant languages. One of the most difficult problems that you tend to encounter when trying to mix code from different programming languages is mapping the types in one language to the types in another language. For instance, strings in Visual Basic (BSTRs) are length prefixed, Unicode character arrays. Strings in C/C++ are null-terminated, single-byte character arrays. One solution to this problem is to create a set of functions that map one type to another. For instance, the MFC **CString** class contains a method called AllocSysString that converts an MFC string to a BSTR. Another approach is to create a type system that is independent of any programming language and then map language-specific types to this type system. Microsoft's first attempt at a common type system was the so-called Automation types: Variant, BSTR (strings), Currency, Date, Short, and Long. Unfortunately, the automation types weren't as language independent as they first seemed. All of the Automation types are simply the VB representation of that type. Some automation types, particularly the Integral types, like Short, Long, and so forth, mapped neatly to types in other programming languages. Other types like BSTR, Variant, and Currency didn't map so well and were difficult to use in other languages, such as C++, requiring a special set of functions and extra work to manipulate them. In the end, you had a choice. Your interfaces could either be easy to use from C++, in which case you eschewed the Automation types. Or you could use the automation types, and your interfaces would be easy to use from high-level languages like VB, but difficult to use for C++ programmers.

The CTS simply takes the idea of Automation types one step further. With the CTS, Microsoft has created a type system that all CLR-compliant programming languages share. Table 3–1 shows a list of the types supported by the CTS. The definitions of all of these types can be found in the System namespace in the Framework libraries, which I describe shortly. Don't worry about the column labeled CLS Type for now. I will explain what the CLS is in the next section.

TABLE 3–1 *CTS types*

Type Name	CLS Type	Description
System.Boolean	Yes	True/False Value
System.Code	Yes	16-bit, Unicode character
System.Object	Yes	Generic object or boxed value type (I explain what a boxed type is later in this chapter). You can think of this type as being the .NET equivalent of a variant.
System.String	Yes	Unicode string
System.Single	Yes	IEEE 32-bit floating point
System.Double	Yes	IEEE 64-bit floating point
System.SByte	No	Signed 8-bit integer
System.Byte	Yes	Unsigned 8-bit integer
System.IntPtr	Yes	Signed integer of native size
System.UintPtr	No	Unsigned integer of native size
System.Int16	Yes	Signed 16-bit integer
System.Uint16	No	Unsigned 16-bit integer
System.Int32	Yes	Signed 32-bit integer

TABLE 3–1 *CTS types (continued)*

Type Name	CLS Type	Description
System.Uint32	No	Unsigned 32-bit integer
System.Int64	Yes	Signed 64-bit integer
System.Uint64	No	Unsigned 64-bit integer
System.TypedReference	No	Pointer plus runtime type

You don't have to worry about converting from your language's native types to the CTS types. In order for a programming language to work with the CLR, the language must use the CTS types as its native types. Internally, most programming languages will have aliases for these types that map to the expected, primitive types of the language. Table 3-2 shows a mapping of C# types (which were designed to closely resemble the C/C++ types) to CTS types.

TABLE 3–2 *A mapping of native C# types to CTS types*

C# Type	Equivalent CTS Type
bool	System.Boolean
byte	System.Byte
char	System.Char
System.DateTime	System.DateTime
decimal	System.Decimal
double	System.Double
int	System.Int32
long	System.Int64
object	System.Object
short	System.Int16
float	System.Single
string	System.String

Table 3–3 shows the mapping of VB types to CTS types.

TABLE 3–3 *A mapping of native VB types to CTS types*

VB Type	Equivalent CTS Type
Boolean	System.Boolean
Byte	System.Byte
Char	System.Char
Date	System.DateTime
Decimal	System.Decimal
Double	System.Double
Integer	System.Int32
Long	System.Int64
Object	System.Object
Short	System.Int16
Single	System.Single
String	System.String
User-Defined Type	System.ValueType

C/C++ and C# programmers are used to dealing with a type called int that is usually a 32-bit integer. VB programmers have an equivalent type called Integer. Each type maps to a CTS type called System.Int32, and you can declare a variable of type System.Int32 in each programming language if you really want to. However, each programming language also contains an alias for the CTS type that has the name that developers who use that language are used to seeing. For C# programmers, the System.Int32 can also be called an int, and, for VB programmers, the System.Int32 can also be called an Integer.

The beauty of the CTS is that, if you are writing a VB client that calls a component written in C#, there is no need to do type conversions. The VB representation of a string, for instance, is exactly the same as the C# representation of a string. They both use the **System.String** class from the CTS to represent a string.

Microsoft bashers (and there are lots of them) will probably say that the CTS—and the CLR—are just another example of Microsoft forcing other vendors to do things their way. This time, Microsoft is using its control of the operating system platform to coerce compiler vendors into building their compilers with a type system that they (Microsoft) have specified. Actually, the opposite is true. Most compiler vendors have eagerly embraced the CLR and hence the CTS. By targeting the CLR and using the CTS, a programming language instantly becomes a first-class player in the .NET world. Classes written in any programming language can inherit from classes in the .NET Framework, and they can serve as base classes to classes written using other CLR-compliant languages. Moreover, any CLR-compliant programming language can use the exception handling, deployment, versioning, debugging, and profiling features built into the CLR; they also instantly gain support for garbage collection. The CLR and the CTS is actually a tremendous win for compiler vendors. The CLR does a lot of work that they had to do themselves in the past. That's why far from viewing this as Microsoft once again asserting its hegemony, dozens of third-party compiler vendors have rushed to support the CLR.

CLS

Even though the CLR attempts to make all languages equal, the reality is that they are not. For instance, some languages have the notion of an unsigned integer, and some do not. The CTS (and hence the CLR) does support unsigned integers. Microsoft did not want to require all CLR-compliant programming language to support all the features and types in the CLR, because this would require compiler vendors to change the expected behavior of some programming languages. Instead, Microsoft has defined a subset of the CTS and features supported by the CLR that all languages must support as a minimum. This subset is known as the Common Language Specification (CLS). For compiler vendors, supporting the CLS means that your language can use any CLS-compliant class library or framework. Moreover, the types created by your programming language can be used and extended by any other programming language that is compliant with the CLS. For class library and framework developers, making sure that your library or framework is CLS compliant means that your software will be usable by the greatest number of .NET programming languages.

The distinction between the CTS and CLS is a little confusing. Think of it this way: the CTS defines the full set of types supported by the CLR and available internally to any .NET programming language, the CLS defines the subset of the CTS that you must restrict yourself to and a set of rules that compiler and framework developers must adhere to, in order to ensure that their software is usable by all CLR-compliant programming languages. The second column of Table 3–1 shows which of the CTS types are also CLS compliant. Some examples of the rules in the CLS are as follows:

- A type is CLS compliant if its public interfaces, methods, fields, properties, and events contain only CLS-compliant types or are marked explicitly as not CLS compliant.
- A CLS Consumer can completely use any CLS-compliant type.
- A CLS Extender is a CLS consumer tool, and it can also extend (inherit from) any CLS-compliant base class, implement any CLS-compliant interface, and use any CLS-compliant custom attribute on any type, method, field, parameter, property, or event.

You can find a complete description of the CLS in Partition 1 of the Tool Developers Guide.

VOS

The Virtual Object System (VOS) is the object model used by all CLR-compliant programming languages. The VOS specifies how classes are defined; it enables the unprecedented level of cross-language interoperability that the CLR provides. For instance, with the .NET Framework, you can create a class in one programming language and then derive a subclass from it in a different programming language. You could not do this unless both programming languages shared a common representation of what a class is. The VOS provides that common representation.

The VOS is essentially just a set of rules that describe how classes are represented in the CLR. Some of the rules in the VOS are as follows:

- A class may contain zero or more members.
- The members of a class can be one of the following: Field, Method Property, or Event.
- Members of a type may have one of the following visibilities:
  - **Public**—The member can be called or accessed by code in any assembly.
  - **Private**—The member can be called or accessed only by methods in the same type.
  - **Family**—The member can be called or accessed only by methods in the same type or derived types in any assembly.
  - **Assembly**—The member can be called or accessed only by methods in the same assembly.
  - **Family and Assembly**—The member can be called or accessed by methods in the same type or derived types only if the type is in the same assembly.
  - **Family or Assembly**—The member can be called or accessed by methods in the same type or derived types in any assembly. It can also be accessed by any type in the same assembly.
- Class supports only single inheritance.
- Classes must inherit (directly or indirectly) from a class called **System.Object**.

Just as you don't have to be an MSIL expert to use the .NET Framework, you don't have to be a VOS expert to create and use classes and objects in the .NET Framework. Your programming language will be integrated with the VOS, and you will use the native object constructs of your programming language. These constructs will map to the VOS. For instance, even though C++ supports multiple inheritance, if you use C++ with Managed Extensions (which is just a variant of C++ that uses the CLR), you are limited to single inheritance.

The key point here is that, whether you create your classes using C#, VB, or C++ with Managed Extensions—thanks to the VOS—after the code is compiled into MSIL, these classes are equivalent.

Reference Types

The .NET Framework supports the notion of reference types and value types. Reference types are always allocated on the managed heap, and they can only be accessed through a reference (a reference is the managed code equivalent of a pointer). Arrays, pointer types, interfaces, and delegates are all reference types. (If you are not sure what delegates are, you'll learn in Chapter 4). The garbage collector tracks instances of reference types, and they are automatically freed when your program is no longer using them. Because the garbage collector does not run immediately, an instance of a reference type will likely remain in memory after the method in which it was created has returned. In C#, reference types are created using the class keyword, so the following code defines an Employee reference type:

```
public class Employee
{
public Employee(int id,string name,decimal salary)
    {
      this.mName=name;
      this.mID=id;
      this.mSalary=salary;
    }
    public int ID
    {
      get { return mID; }
      set { mID=value; }
    }
    public string Name
    {
      get { return mName; }
      set { mName=value; }
    }
    public virtual decimal GetSalary()
    {
      return mSalary;
    }
    private int mID;
    private string mName;
    private decimal mSalary;
}
```

All reference types must derive from **System.Object** either directly or indirectly. Even though I have not specified a base class for the **Employee** class, it still derives from **System.Object**.

When you assign a reference to some other reference, you are performing a shallow copy. In other words, you are making a copy of the reference, not a copy of the object that the reference points to. The following code should make this clear:

```
static void Main(string[] args)
{
    Employee emp1, emp2;
    emp1=new Employee(1,"Alan Gordon",500);
    emp2=emp1; // assign emp2 to emp1 (shallow copy)
    emp1.Name="Tamber Gordon";
    System.Console.WriteLine(
        "Emp1 name = {0}",emp1.Name);
    System.Console.WriteLine(
        "Emp2 name = {0}",emp2.Name);
}
```

This program will write the following output to the console:

```
Emp1 name = Tamber Gordon
Emp2 name = Tamber Gordon
```

In this program, I have defined two Employee references: emp1 and emp2.

```
Employee emp1, emp2;
```

I create a single Employee object using the C# new operator. Because the **Employee** class is a reference type, the new operator creates the variable on the managed heap:

```
emp1=new Employee(1,"Alan Gordon",500);
```

The next line is the key line in this example:

```
emp2=emp1;
```

In this line, I assign emp2 to the reference emp1. Emp2 now points to the same object that emp1 points to. Emp2 does not contain a copy of that object. Therefore, if I change the name property of the object pointed to by emp1, emp2 will reflect the change also. There is only one object; any change made through one reference will immediately be reflected in the other reference. Figure 3–1 should make this clear.

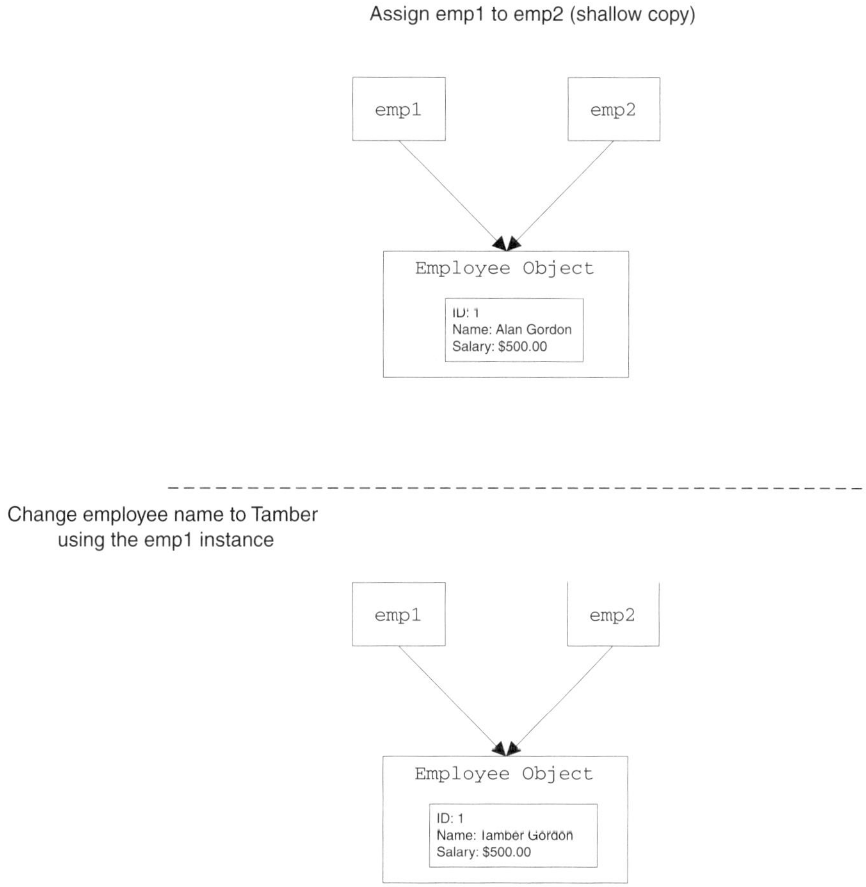

FIGURE 3–1 *Two instances of a reference type pointing to the same object.*

Value Types

Value types in .NET are allocated on the stack. The built-in types, such as int, float, and so forth, and enumerations are value types, and you can create user-defined values types. They are not garbage collected. Like all stack variables, an instance of a value type lives—at most—as long as the method in which it was created lives. Value types are always accessed directly; you cannot create a reference to a value type.

When you assign to an instance of a value type, you create a deep copy of the variable that is being assigned. An example will make this clear. I change the definition of the Employee type to look as follows:

```
public struct Employee
{
    public Employee(int id,string name,decimal salary)
    {
      this.mName=name;
      this.mID=id;
      this.mSalary=salary;
    }
    public int ID
    {
      get { return mID; }
      set { mID=value; }
    }
    public string Name
    {
      get { return mName; }
      set { mName=value; }
    }
    public decimal GetSalary()
    {
      return mSalary;
    }
    private int mID;
    private string mName;
    private decimal mSalary;
}
```

I have now changed Employee to be a value type. Notice that I use the keyword struct instead of class to define this type. You use the struct keyword to declare user-defined value types in C#. Notice also that I removed the virtual keyword from the GetSalary method. Value classes are sealed, which means you cannot inherit from them. It therefore makes no sense to have virtual functions, so the compiler rejects a virtual function in a value type. If you now run the following code shown, which is exactly the same code that I ran for the reference version of Employee, you'll notice that, if I assign emp1 to emp2 and then change one of the fields of emp1, emp2 still reflects the original value:

```
static void Main(string[] args)
{
    Employee emp1, emp2;
    emp1=new Employee(1,"Alan Gordon",500);
    emp2=emp1;
    emp1.Name="Tamber Gordon";
    System.Console.WriteLine(
        "Emp1 name = {0}",emp1.Name);
    System.Console.WriteLine(
        "Emp2 name = {0}",emp2.Name);
}
```

The code shown previously will write the following output to the console:

```
Emp1 name = Tamber Gordon
Emp2 name = Alan Gordon
```

This indicates that emp1 and emp2 are different objects. Therefore, the runtime made a deep copy of emp1 when you assigned it to emp2. Figure 3–2 should make this clear.

All value types derive either directly or indirectly from a class called **ValueType**. **ValueType** derives from **System.Object** and overrides the methods in **System.Object** to provide an appropriate implementation for a value type.

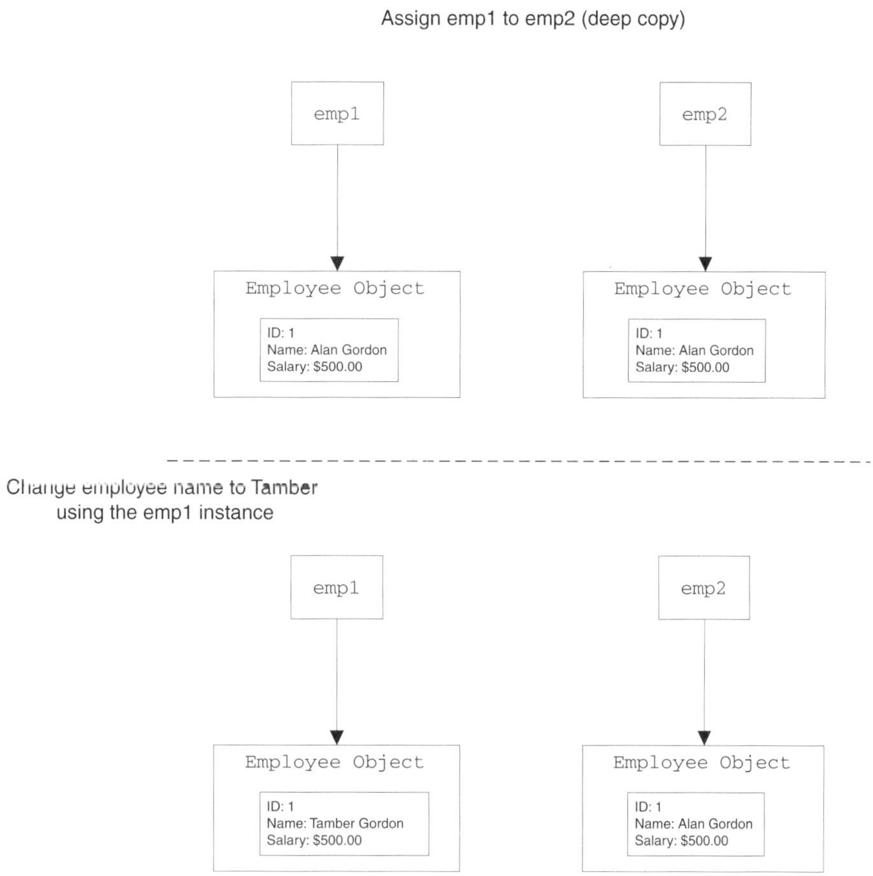

FIGURE 3–2 *Two instances of a value type.*

Boxing and Unboxing

There will be times that you will want a value type object to behave like a reference type object and vice versa. For example, all of the collection classes in the **System.Collections** store instances of **System.Object**. But there will be times when you will need to store value types in a collection. Consider the following code that pushes two Employee value type objects onto a Stack and then pops them off:

```
using System;
using System.Collections;
namespace TestApp
{
static void Main(string[] args)
{
      Employee emp1, emp2;
      emp1=new Employee(1,"Alan Gordon",500);
      emp2=new Employee(2,"Tamber Gordon",600);
      Stack myStack;
      myStack=new Stack(10);
      myStack.Push(emp1);
      myStack.Push(emp2);
      emp1=(Employee)myStack.Pop();
      emp2=(Employee)myStack.Pop();
}
}
```

The Push and Pop methods in the **System.Collections.Stack** class are declared as follows:

```
public virtual void Push(System.Object obj);
public virtual System.Object Pop();
```

Therefore, when you push the two Employee objects onto the Stack, the CLR has to perform some "magic" to convert the two value type objects to System.Object reference type objects. Similarly, when you pop the two Employees off the Stack, the CLR has to convert the reference type objects on the Stack back to value type objects. The process of converting value type instances to reference type instances (the Push case) is called boxing. When the CLR needs to box a value type instance, it allocates a reference object on the heap and then copies the value type's data into it. The wrapper is marked as a boxed object so that the system knows that it contains a boxed representation of a value type. The reverse process is called unboxing. When the CLR unboxes a reference type object, it first checks that the object is in fact a boxed value type, and then it copies the data in the reference type object into the value type object you are assigning to. Although we are jumping ahead of ourselves a little bit, take a look at a portion of the MSIL code that the C# compiler will generate for the preceding example code. Notice that there is a "box" call prior to each "Push" on to the Stack and an "unbox" call after each "Pop" off the Stack.

```
IL_0038:  box        TestApp.Employee
IL_003d:  callvirt   instance void Stack::Push(object)
IL_0042:  ldloc.2
IL_0043:  ldloc.1
IL_0044:  box        TestApp.Employee
IL_0049:  callvirt   instance void Stack::Push(object)
IL_004e:  ldloc.2
IL_004f:  callvirt   instance object Stack::Pop()
IL_0054:  unbox      TestApp.Employee
IL_0059:  ldobj      TestApp.Employee
IL_005e:  stloc.0
IL_005f:  ldloc.2
IL_0060:  callvirt   instance object Stack::Pop()
IL_0065:  unbox      TestApp.Employee
```

You must unbox a reference object back to its pre-boxed type. Therefore, the following code, where Manager is also a value type, will cause a runtime error because I boxed an Employee object and then I am trying to unbox it as a Manager:

```
static void Main(string[] args)
{
    Employee emp;
    Manager mgr;
    emp=new Employee(1,"Alan Gordon",500);
    Stack myStack;
    myStack=new Stack(10);
    myStack.Push(emp);
    mgr=(Manager)myStack.Pop(); // Runtime error here!
}
```

The semantics of value types and reference types are a fundamental part of the behavior of the CLR, not the C# language. Therefore, another programming language may not use the keyword "class" to declare a reference type or the keyword "struct" to declare a value type, but the behavior of these different categories of types as well as boxing and unboxing will be the same.

Assemblies

You deploy .NET types in Assemblies. A .NET assembly is the unit of deployment, reuse, versioning, and security in the .NET Framework. An assembly consists of one or more modules. Each module may contain either a managed code PE file with MSIL code and metadata, or it may contain resources like JPEG or

BMP files. One of the managed code PE files must contain a manifest. The manifest is part of an assembly's metadata, it contains the following information:

- Versioning information about the assembly, such as its version number, culture information, the publisher's public key, and some additional flags.
- An entry for each file that constitutes the assembly that contains the file name, but not the path, of each file in the assembly, a hash value of the file's contents, and some additional flags.
- An entry for each publicly exported type in the assembly that tells the runtime which file in the assembly contains the type.
- An entry for each resource that tells the runtime which resource file in the assembly contains a particular resource.

Figure 3–3 shows a schematic view of a single file assembly and a multifile assembly.

In the single file case, the header, the metadata—including the manifest—and the MSIL code are all contained in a file called singlefile.dll. In the multi file case, there are a total of 3 files: multifile1.dll, multifile2.dll, and multifile3.dll. Multifile1.dll is the most important file in the assembly because it contains the manifest for the assembly; it also contains MSIL code and metadata. Multifile2.dll contains MSIL code and metadata also, but notice that it does not contain a manifest. The last file in the multi file assembly, multifile3.dll, contains images and other resources.

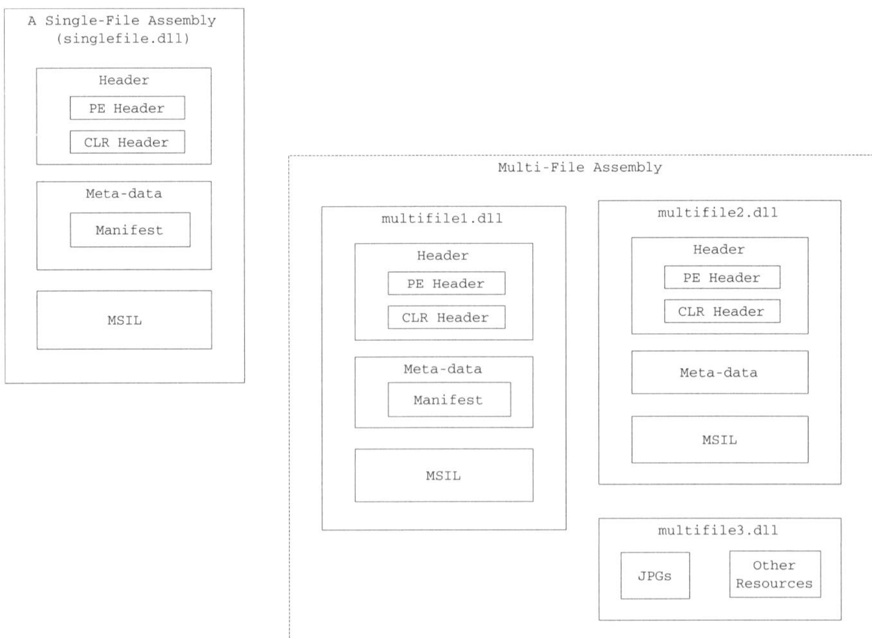

FIGURE 3–3 *A multifile assembly.*

To a client that is using an assembly, the fact that the assembly may consist of multiple files is completely hidden. The CLR uses information in the assembly's metadata to create a logical single-file illusion for the consumers of the assembly. Only the developer of the assembly needs to be aware that the physical implementation of the assembly consists of multiple files. When you want to use the types in an assembly, you simply reference the file that contains the manifest. (You can consider this to be the main module of the assembly although it isn't officially labeled as such.) When you first use a type or resource that is not contained in the main file, the CLR will use the information in the manifest to load the module that contains the type or resource. Before it loads the file, the CLR will verify that the module that it is loading is exactly the same as the module that the assembly was built with. It does this using information in the manifest. For each module in the assembly, the manifest stores the file name and a hash value that is generated from the contents of the file. The CLR will regenerate the hash value from the module that resides on disk and compare it to the hash value that is stored in the manifest for that module. If the two hash values do not match, the module that currently resides on disk is not the same as the module that the assembly was originally built with, and the CLR will throw an error. This process guarantees the atomicity of the assembly. In other words, it guarantees that the assembly is deployed and versioned as an indivisible whole. You cannot, for instance, fix a bug by deploying a new version of just one of the modules in an assembly. If you want to make a change to any part of an assembly, you must rebuild and redeploy the entire assembly.

You are hopefully starting to get the idea that an assembly has two views: (1) a logical view and (2) a physical view. The physical view of an assembly is a collection of files that are either managed code module files that contain metadata and MSIL code or resources files that contain JPEGs, Graphic Interchange Formats (GIFs), or other graphical elements like menus or icons. One of these managed code files contains a manifest. The logical view of an assembly is a collection of types in one or more namespaces. In this logical view, the assembly is a single, atomic whole.

By now you're probably asking why Microsoft decided to create this new assembly concept. What advantages does it have over the Win32 approach in which the unit of deployment, versioning, and security is a single executable (DLL or EXE) file? The major advantage of the assembly concept is that it is far more efficient in the scenario where code is downloaded across the Internet. The assembly concept allows you to take rarely used types and resources and package them into separate files that will only be downloaded from the Internet if they are needed. Whether you are dealing with a code library or a functional application, it is very rare for someone to use all of the capabilities of a piece of code during each use.

If you are still confused about the whole concept of an assembly, keep in mind that most assemblies that you create will consist of a single file. In fact, Visual Studio .NET only supports the creation of a single-file assembly. If you want to create a multi file assembly, you have to use the command-line tools in the .NET Framework SDK.

An Example: Building an Assembly

In order for you to gain a better understanding of assemblies, let's build a very simple example that shows you how to create a multi-file assembly. The example is a simple assembly that contains two main types: an **Employee** class and a **Manager** class that derives from the **Employee** class. Each of these types will reside in its own module. The third file will contain only the manifest for the assembly. A schematic of the assembly is shown in Figure 3–4.

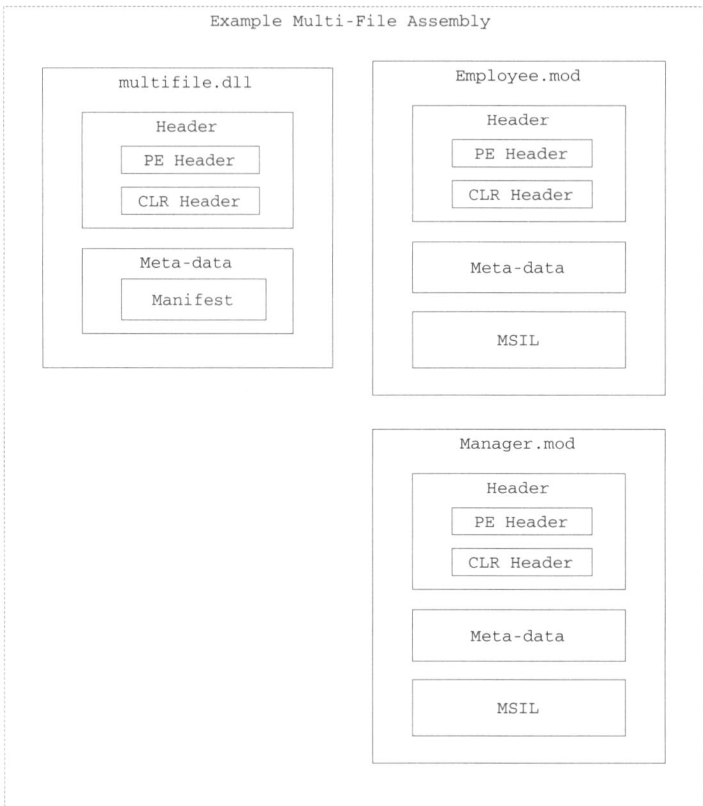

FIGURE 3–4 *An example multifile assembly.*

Because Visual Studio .NET does not support multi-file assemblies, you will build this assembly using the command-line tools in the .NET Framework SDK. You will also use this assembly as a running example throughout the chapter to discuss other topics like metadata and MSIL.

A SUMMARY OF THE STEPS

To build an assembly, you will perform the following steps:

1. Declare an **Employee** class.
2. Declare a **Manager** class.
3. Compile the **Employee** class into a module.
4. Compile the **Manager** class into a module.
5. Compile the modules with an assembly info file (that contains metadata for the assembly) into an assembly.
6. Create a client application that uses the assembly.

DECLARE AN EMPLOYEE CLASS

The **Employee** class is declared as follows:

```
using System;
namespace metadatademo
{
    public class Employee
    {
      public Employee(int id,string name,
            decimal salary)
      {
        this.mName=name;
        this.mID=id;
        this.mSalary=salary;
      }
      public int ID
      {
        get { return mID; }
        set { mID=value; }
      }
      public string Name
      {
        get { return mName; }
        set { mName=value; }
      }
      public virtual decimal GetSalary()
      {
        return mSalary;
      }
    private int mID;
    private string mName;
    private decimal mSalary;
```

```
        }
    }
```

This class is very simple. It's essentially the same definition that I used earlier when I talked about reference types, so I won't go into an in-depth discussion of this class here. If there are things that you don't understand about this definition like the use of the "using" and "namespace" keywords or the declaration of the "Name" property, don't worry about it. These things will be clearer later after I talk about C# in Chapter 4. Save this code in a file called **Employee.cs**.

DECLARE A MANAGER CLASS

The **Manager** class is declared as follows:

```
using System;
namespace metadatademo
{

    public class Manager : Employee
    {
      public Manager(int id,string name,
            decimal salary,decimal bonus) :
            base(id,name,salary)
      {
        this.mBonus=bonus;
      }
      public override decimal GetSalary()
      {
        return base.GetSalary()+mBonus;
      }
      private decimal mBonus;
    }
}
```

Again, this is a very simple class. Don't worry about the syntax, such as the use of the "base" and "override" keywords; their use will be clear after Chapter 4. Save this code in a file called **Manager.cs**.

COMPILE THE EMPLOYEE CLASS INTO A MODULE

To compile the **Employee** class into a module, open up a command prompt. If you have Visual Studio .NET installed, select Start | Programs | Microsoft Visual Studio .NET | Visual Studio .NET Tools | Visual Studio .NET Command Prompt. This creates a command prompt session that is guaranteed to have the environment (path and so forth) configured properly for using the command-line tools in the .NET Framework SDK. Now change directories to the directory where you saved the **Employee.cs** and **Manager.cs** files and enter the following command at the prompt:

```
csc /out:Employee.mod /t:module Employee.cs
```

This command will run the C# compiler (csc). The /out parameter allows you to specify the name of the output file, which in this case is **Employee.mod**. There is nothing significant about the .mod extension; you could give this file any extension you want. The /t parameter is short for "target," and it's how you specify the type of output you want the compiler to produce. In this case, I want a module file to be produced, which is a file that will be combined with other files to create an assembly. Some of the other possible values for the /t parameter to the C# compiler are the following:

- **exe**—Creates a console executable assembly.
- **winexe**—Creates a windows executable assembly.
- **library**—Creates a DLL assembly.
- **module**—Creates a module that must be combined with other files to create an asssembly.

COMPILE THE MANAGER CLASS INTO A MODULE

To compile the **Manager** class into module, run the following command in the same command prompt that you used to compile the **Employee** class:

```
csc /out:Manager.mod /t:module /addmodule:Employee.mod
Manager.cs
```

Notice that, in this case, I specified that the output file is called **Manager.mod** and that the output type is a module. The /addmodule parameter requires some explanation though. You cannot compile the **Manager** class without referring to the module that contains the **Employee** class. The compiler must have access to the definition of the **Employee** class because the **Manager** derives from the **Employee** class. You use the /addmodule parameter when you want to create modules that are dependant on types in other modules or when you are combining modules into an assembly. In this case, if you did not use the /addmodule:Employee.mod parameter, you would receive the following error at compile time:

```
Manager.cs (5,25): error CS0246: The type of namespace name
'Employee' could not be found.
```

COMPILE THE MODULES INTO AN ASSEMBLY

We now have our Employee and Manager types compiled into modules, but, at this point, they are still not usable. In order to use these types, they must be built into an assembly with a manifest. To create an assembly, I use the C# compiler to create a third file that contains a manifest that refers to the Employee and Manager modules. To do this, run the following command in the same command prompt that you used to compile the **Employee** and **Manager** classes:

```
csc /out:multifile.dll /t:library /addmodule:employee.mod /
addmodule:manager.mod assemblyinfo.cs
```

In this case, I specify the name of the assembly as **multifile.dll** and the type of the output as library, which means I am creating a DLL-based assembly. I then use the /addmodule parameter to link the employee and manager modules into the assembly.

Before you can understand the other source file that appears in this command, **assemblyinfo.cs**, I have to discuss attributes first.

ATTRIBUTES

Managed code compilers automatically add various metadata elements without you, the developer, having to specify explicitly that the metadata should be added or without having to specify what the value of that metadata element should be. An example of this is the hash value that is stored for each module in an assembly. There are other kinds of metadata for which developers must have some explicit control. Some examples of this type of metadata include:

- Whether a class requires a transaction when it runs
- Whether a method in a class is exposed through a Web service or the version number of an assembly
- Whether an input parameter to a method is an input, an output, or both.

You can explicitly declare and set the values for certain kinds of metadata using attributes. There are pre-defined attributes that you can set values for. You can also create user-defined attributes. Some of the pre-defined attributes provide information that may be used by client code or code generators. Other attributes influence the behavior of the CLR, such as the AssemblyFlagsAttribute that you can use to specify the allowable side-by-side execution behavior of an assembly. Some attributes influence the way a class behaves. For instance, when a class is adorned with the Transaction attribute and the TransactionOption parameter for this attribute is TransactionOption.Required, the CLR and the COM+ runtime will make sure that a Distributed Transaction Coordinator (DTC) transaction is started whenever you call a method on an instance of the class.

In addition, you can create your own attributes. Users can apply your user-defined attributes to your types, and then, at runtime, your code can query for the values that the user has assigned to the attribute and take appropriate action.

Attributes provide support for the declarative programming style that was first popularized with COM (in the way it supports threading models using the ThreadingModel registry key) and MTS. You can support and configure functionality simply by setting an attribute that is associated with a type.

To specify a value for an attribute in C#, you use the following syntax:

```
[attributename]
```

An example is shown here:

```
[Transaction]
public class Books : ServicedComponent
{
//...
}
```

This code is using the Transaction attribute from the System.EnterpriseServices namespace. You use this attribute to specify that a class requires transaction support from the COM+ runtime infrastructure.

Note You will learn more about the Transaction Attribute, serviced components, and COM+ integration in Chapter 9.

Each attribute is a class that derives from the **Attribute** class in the System namespace. In this case, the Transaction attribute is a class called **TransactionAttribute**, which resides in the System.EnterpriseServices namespace. An attribute may have parameters on its constructor that allow you to specify how the attribute behaves. An example of this is the TransactionOption parameter of the Transaction attribute. This parameter may be set to one of the four possible values of the TransactionOption enumeration shown in Table 3–4.

TABLE 3–4 *Possible values for the TransactionOption parameter of the transaction attribute*

TransactionOption Value	Description
Disabled	Ignores any transactions in the current context.
NotSupported	Will neither start a transaction nor participate in its caller's transaction.
Supported	Will not start a transaction, but will share its caller's transaction if it has one.
Required	Will share its caller's transaction if it has one; starts a new transaction if the caller does not have a transaction.
RequiresNew	Always starts a new transaction.

The default value of this parameter is Required, so the code I showed with the **Books** class could have been written—equivalently—as follows:

```
[Transaction(TransactionOption.Required)]
public class Books : ServicedComponent
{
//…
}
```

If you want to set the TransactionOption parameter to Supported, you could use the following code:

```
[Transaction(TransactionOption.Supported)]
public class Books : ServicedComponent
{
//…
}
```

Attributes can also have named parameters. For instance, the Transaction attribute has Timeout and Isolation parameters. You can use the Timeout parameter to specify the maximum duration of the transaction before it times out. The Isolation parameter allows you to specify the isolation level for the transaction.

Note I will discuss transactions and isolation levels in Chapter 9.

In the following example, I have set the timeout to 45 seconds and the isolation level to Repeatable Read.

```
[Transaction(TransactionOption.Required,
  Isolation=TransactionIsolationLevel.RepeatableRead,
  Timeout=45)]
public class Books : ServicedComponent
{
//…
}
```

The generalized form of an attribute declaration in C# is as follows:

```
[attributename(param1,param2,…,paramN,prop1=val1,
prop2=val2,…, propN=valN)]
```

Where param[N] is the specified value for a parameter and prop[N] is the name of a property and val[N] is the value assigned to that property.

Attributes can be applied to an assembly; a module; or any type, such as a class, structure, enum, or delegate; they can also be applied to any member of a type, such as a field, property, method, and so forth. All attributes have a usage attribute that specifies which elements the attribute can be applied to.

The Transaction attribute can only be applied to a class. The following code uses the WebMethod attribute from the System.Web.Services namespace to specify that a method will be exposed using a Web service. The WebMethod attribute can only be applied to a method.

```
[WebMethod]
public DataSet GetBooksByTitle(string title)
{
//…
}
```

If you tried to apply the WebMethod attribute to a class as shown here:

```
[WebMethod]
public class Books : ServicedComponent
{
//…
}
```

you will receive the following compiler error:

```
Attribute 'WebMethod' is not valid on this declaration
type. It is valid on 'method' declarations only.
```

The .NET Framework contains a special set of attributes called assembly attributes that were developed to provide information about an assembly as opposed to types or members of a type. These assembly attributes are divided into four groups: identify attributes, informational attributes, manifest attributes, and strong name attributes. The assembly identity attributes are shown in Table 3-5.

TABLE 3–5 *The assembly identity attributes*

Identity Attribute	Description
AssemblyVersion	This is a numerical version number in the format major.minor.build.revision.
AssemblyCulture	If this attribute is set to something other than the empty string (""),it indicates that this is a satellite assembly that contains culture-specific resources.
AssemblyFlags	This is used to specify whether an assembly supports side-by-side execution on the same machine, in the same process, or in the same application domain.

The assembly informational attributes are shown in Table 3–6.

TABLE 3–6 *The assembly informational attributes*

Informational Attribute	Description
AssemblyCompany	Specifies the name of the company that produced the assembly.
AssemblyCopyright	Specifies copyright information for the assembly.
AssemblyFileVersion	Specifies the version number that will appear in the Win32 file version resource. It defaults to the assembly version, but does not have to be the same.
AssemblyInformationalVersion	Specifies version number information that is not used by the runtime.
AssemblyProduct	Specifies product information.
AssemblyTrademark	Specifies trademark information.

The assembly manifest attributes are shown in Table 3–7.

TABLE 3–7 *The assembly manifest attributes*

Manifest Attribute	Description
AssemblyConfiguration	Specifies the configuration of the resource, for example, retail or debug.
AssemblyDefaultAlias	Specifies a friendly name to use for the assembly if the name of the resource is not friendly.
AssemblyDescription	Specifies a short description of the purpose and description of the assembly.
AssemblyTitle	Specifies another friendly name for the assembly.

The strong name attributes are shown in Table 3–8.

TABLE 3–8 *The assembly strong name attributes*

Identity Attribute	Description
AssemblyDelaySign	A Boolean value that indicates whether you want to reserve space in the assembly for a signature, but delay actual signing until later (true) or whether you will be signing the assembly with the private key immediately (false). Using this attribute makes it easier for a company to safeguard its private key by not requiring all developers to have it.
AssemblyKeyFile	Specifies the name of the file that contains the public (or public and private) key.
AssemblyKeyName	Specifies the key container that contains the key pair.

You can assign these assembly attributes to an assembly using the standard attribute declaration prefixed with assembly: as follows:

```
[assembly: AttributeName(param1,param2,…,paramN,prop1=val1,
prop2=val2,…, propN=valN)]
```

You can create an assembly without using any of these attributes. However, the assembly will not have a strong name, description, or title, and its version number will be 0.0.0.0. Therefore, in most cases, you will want to use at least some of these attributes when you create your assemblies. You can declare these attributes in any source file of the assembly that you want, but a good convention (and the convention used by Visual Studio .NET) is to create an assembly info file that contains all the assembly-level attribute declarations. You then compile this source code file into your assembly.

With that, I can move the discussion back to the assembly info file in the example. I created a file called **assemblyinfo.cs** for the example, and this file will contain the assembly attributes for the assembly. The contents of this file are as follows:

```
using System.Reflection;
[assembly: AssemblyDescription("A test multifile
assembly")]
[assembly: AssemblyVersion("1.2.3.4")]
[assembly: AssemblyDelaySign(false)]
[assembly: AssemblyKeyFile("mykey.snk")]
```

In this file, I start by adding a using statement for the Reflection namespace in the System assembly because all of the assembly attributes are declared in that namespace. I use the AssemblyDescription attribute to add a description for the assembly. The description is "A test multifile assembly". I use the AssemblyVersion attribute to set the version number of the assembly to "1.2.3.4". These four numbers are the major, minor, build, and revision number, respectively. Before I talk about the AssemblyDelaySign and AssemblyKeyFile attributes I first need to discuss how to create a cryptographic key pair.

The .NET Framework SDK contains a tool called the Strong Name Tool (sn.exe) that you can use to create a cryptographic key pair. To use the Strong Name Tool, open a Visual Studio .NET command prompt by selecting Programs | Microsoft Visual Studio .NET | Visual Studio .NET Tools | Visual Studio .NET Command Prompt from the Start menu, change directories to the location where you created the assemblyinfo.cs file and then enter the following command.

```
sn -k mykey.snk
```

This command will create a file called "mykey.snk" that contains both the public and private key of a key pair. Notice that we specified the "mykey.snk" file in the AssemblyKeyFile attribute to indicate that we wish to sign the assembly with this key pair. We also use the AssemblyDelaySign attribute to indicate that we are signing the assembly immediately with the private key specified in the AssemblyKeyFile attribute.

CREATE A CLIENT APPLICATION THAT USES THE ASSEMBLY

To test the assembly, I create a very simple console application that uses the **Manager** and **Employee** classes. The code for this test application is as follows:

```
using System;
using metadatademo;
class TestClass
{
    static void Main(string[] args)
    {
      Employee emp1, emp2;
      emp1=new Employee(1,"Alan Gordon",500);
      emp2=new Manager(2,"Tamber Gordon",800,200);
      System.Console.WriteLine(
            "Emp1 name = {0}",emp1.Name);
      System.Console.WriteLine(
            "Emp2 name = {0}",emp2.Name);
    }
}
```

To compile this code into an executable application, save the preceding code into a file called **testclass.cs** and execute the following command at the same command prompt that you used previously to build the multifile assembly:

```
csc /out:testmultifile.exe /t:exe /r:multifile.dll
testclass.cs
```

To build an application or module that uses types in an assembly, you must use the /reference parameter on the C# compiler, which is usually abbreviated /r, to reference the assembly. The compiler uses the metadata in the referenced assembly to do compile-time validation; it also inserts metadata in the client application that tells the CLR the name, version number, strong name, and so forth of the assembly that the application was built against. The CLR will use this information when you run the application to make sure that it uses the same, or a compatible, version of the assembly.

Try running the client application. It will print the names of two employees: Alan Gordon and Tamber Gordon. You might want to add more code to test the Employee and Manager types further. Another good exercise is to attempt to recompile one of the files in the multifile assembly without rebuilding the entire assembly. This is a definite "no-no" because the CLR will enforce the atomicity of the assembly. If the hash of one of the files that constitutes the assembly is not exactly the same as the hash in the assembly's manifest, the CLR will fail to load the file. I got the following error when I rebuilt the Employee module alone without recompiling the assembly:

```
System.IO.FileLoadException: The check of the module's hash
failed for Employee.mod
```

Metadata

Now that you understand types, assemblies, and attributes, we are ready to begin an in-depth discussion of .NET metadata. Metadata is key to making software development manageable. Metadata is descriptive information about the types in an executable file or software library. This descriptive information includes the name of each type and the name and type of each member (fields, methods, events, and so forth) of each type. For method and events, this metadata should also include the name and type of each parameter to the method or event as well as the return type of the method or event.

Metadata is not a new concept. A header (".h") file in C/C++ is an example of metadata. If you are a COM programmer, you are probably familiar with type libraries, which are the metadata format for COM.

Metadata is used for lots of purposes. Compilers or runtime environments use it to lay out objects in memory. An example of this is a C++ compiler using the definition of a class in a header file to create the vtable for the class in memory. Metadata is also used by system-level code to implement marshaling, for example, to allow code running in one process to use code that is executing in a different process. An example of this is type-library marshaling in COM. Type library marshaling uses metadata in the type library to serialize method calls into a stream that can be sent across processes or machines. Code generators use metadata to create code. An example of this is the COM support in MFC that includes a Visual C++ code generator that allows you to create a set of ColeDispatchDriver-derived wrapper classes for a COM server from the type definitions in its type library. Metadata is also used by compilers to do compile-time error checking that would have to be deferred until runtime if metadata was not available. This error checking includes verifying that a method that you are calling on an object is actually a member of the object's class with the appropriate access and that the method is being called with the right number and types of arguments. Most programmers also use metadata as their first level of documentation. This is especially true now that most IDEs support Intellisense technology. Intellisense uses metadata to automatically display, in the programmer's editor, the complete list of available methods that may be called on an object as soon as the developer types in the method invocation symbol ("." or "->") after a variable name. Intellisense works by interrogating the metadata associated with the types that you are using.

There are a number of problems with COM type libraries that .NET metadata rectifies. First, a type library may or may not be embedded within the executable code that it describes. Most ActiveX controls have their type library embedded as a resource in their .ocx file, but the type library for Office applications (Excel, Word, and so forth) resides in a separate file. If the metadata is in a separate file, there is always a danger that it will become separated from the code that it describes or that someone will accidentally ship version X of the type library with version Y of a COM server. Another problem with COM type libraries is that they aren't guaranteed to be present. Most COM components that I have seen ship with a type library, but the COM specification does not require it.

.NET metadata fixes all of these problems. The metadata for a .NET assembly is always embedded within the assembly. A managed code compiler must generate both MSIL code and metadata. There is no danger that the assembly and its metadata will be separated or that the assembly will be shipped with the wrong version of its metadata.

The metadata in an assembly consists of a manifest and a set of metadata tables that contain the bulk of the type-specific metadata of the assembly, including descriptive information about each type and each field in each type. Regardless of how many files an assembly contains, it will only have one manifest, which may be embedded in one of the modules that comprise the assembly or it may reside in its own file.

The manifest is probably the most important single piece of metadata. The manifest is the only assembly file that a consumer of the assembly has to reference. The manifest contains a directory or index that contains all the information that the CLR needs to locate all the types that are implemented within an assembly, regardless of which module they reside in. The other files in the assembly are loaded on demand only when you use a type that is implemented in one of those files. A high-level listing of the contents of a manifest is the following:

- Versioning information about the assembly, such as its version number, culture information, the publisher's public key, and some additional flags
- An entry for each file that makes up the assembly that contains the file name, but not the path, of each file in the assembly and a hash value of the file's contents
- An entry for each publicly exported type in the assembly that tells the runtime which module in the assembly contains the implementation of the type
- An entry for each resource that tells the runtime which file in the assembly contains a particular resource
- An entry for each external assembly on which the assembly depends that contains the name, version number, public key, and hash value of the referenced assembly

Let's look at the manifest in the multifile assembly that you created earlier. In this case, the manifest is the sole contents of the file called **multifile.dll**. You can view the manifest for an assembly and all the other metadata for a .NET assembly using the MSIL disassembler (ILDasm). See the sidebar on ILDASM to learn more about this powerful tool.

The MSIL Disassembler (ILDASM)

ILDASM is a tool that is bundled with the .NET Framework that allows you to view both the compiled MSIL code and the metadata within an assembly. After you have installed Visual Studio .NET, the easiest way to use ILDASM is to select Programs | Microsoft Visual Studio .NET | Visual Studio .NET Tools | Visual Studio .NET Command Prompt. This gives you a command prompt that is configured with the environment that you need to run any of the command-line tools in the .NET Framework SDK. Now you can run ILDASM by typing "ildasm [space] assemblyname". You can also fire up ILDASM without loading an assembly and then choose File | Open. ILDASM also supports drag and drop. Use the command line "ildasm /?" to view the command-line options for ILDASM. You can also find documentation about ILDASM in the .NET Framework SDK documentation at **\Tools and Debuggers\.NET Framework Tools**. Curiously, neither this documentation or the /? command say anything about the /adv argument for ILDASM, which makes the tool display more verbose information. To find out about this option, you have to go to a rather small Word file in the Tool Developers Guide documentation, which you can find at **[Root directory for Visual Studio .NET installation]\FrameworkSDK\Tool Developers Guide\docs\ILDasmAdvancedOptions.doc**. If you run ILDASM with the "/adv" parameter as follows:

```
Ildasm /adv assemblyname
```

It will add three new items to the View menu:

1. COR Header, which displays the header for an assembly. The header contains both the PE header and the CLR header.
2. Statistics, which allow you to see the sizes of the various portions of the assembly, such as the PE header, the CLR header, the metadata, and the managed code.
3. Metainfo, which contains several submenu items, the most important of which is the Show! Item, which allows you to view the metadata tables in their "raw" form

The main window of ILDASM is shown in Figure 3-5.

FIGURE 3–5 *The main window of ILDASM.*

John Robbins has an excellent article in the May, 2001 edition of MSDN magazine that will explain more than you probably want to know about ILDASM and MSIL. See his bugslayer column in that issue.

To view the manifest for the multifile assembly, execute the following command at a Visual Studio .NET command prompt:

```
ildasm multifile.dll
```

The manifest of the multifile assembly follows. I have cleaned up the code a little for clarity.

```
.assembly extern mscorlib
{
  .publickeytoken = (B7 7A 5C 56 19 34 E0 89 )
   .hash = (6D A2 04 14 10 73 D7 37 A6 59 AB 4A 1B F2 DF 1E
AD 04 EC 1D )
   .ver 1:0:3300:0
}
.assembly multifile
{
   .custom instance void
[mscorlib]System.Reflection.AssemblyKeyFileAttribute::.ctor
(string) =
( 01 00 09 6D 79 6B 65 79 2E 73 6E 6B 00 00 )        //
...mykey.snk..
   .custom instance void
[mscorlib]System.Reflection.AssemblyDelaySignAttribute::.ct
or(bool) =
```

```
( 01 00 00 00 00 )
  .custom instance void
[mscorlib]System.Reflection.AssemblyDescriptionAttribute::.
ctor(string) =
( … )    // A test multi-file assembly..
  .publickey = ( … )
  .hash algorithm 0x00008004
  .ver 1:2:3:4
}
.file Employee.mod
    .hash =
(2D 9E 4C 0A FF 28 9C AA 9D AA 25 66 AA DD C5 18 B5 3F 93
67 )
.file Manager.mod
    .hash =
(E1 14 BA FB 2F 43 B3 FB 86 FB A8 E0 FF 35 E4 EF E0 34 83
FB )
.class extern public AssemblyDemo.TerminationReason
{
  .file Employee.mod
  .class 0x02000002
}
.class extern public AssemblyDemo.Employee
{
  .file Employee.mod
  .class 0x02000003
}
.class extern public AssemblyDemo.Manager
{
  .file Manager.mod
  .class 0x02000002
}
.module multifile.dll
// MVID: {8F84316B-55AC-475D-A0E3-BA1C6941B5BA}
.imagebase 0x00400000
.subsystem 0x00000003
.file alignment 512
.corflags 0x00000009
// Image base: 0x031a0000
```

The first section of the manifest contains the assembly extern entries that contain information about the only other assemblies that this assembly is dependent on.

```
.assembly extern mscorlib
{
  .publickeytoken = (B7 7A 5C 56 19 34 E0 89 )
  .hash = (6D A2 04 14 10 73 D7 37 A6 59 AB 4A 1B F2 DF 1E
AD 04 EC 1D )
  .ver 1:0:3300:0
}
```

This assembly is only dependent on the core system library (mscorlib). If this assembly were dependent on other assemblies besides mscorlib, you would see one entry similar to this for each assembly on which the assembly depends. Notice that the entry contains the public key of the referenced assembly, the hash of the assembly, and the version number of the assembly. The public key and the hash value of the referenced assembly will only be there if the referenced assembly was signed with a strong name. The C# compiler (or any other managed code compiler) will insert the public key token and hash of the referenced assembly into the metadata when you build the assembly.

Note The public key token is a hash of the public key. The token is used in the metadata instead of the public key to conserve space.

When the CLR loads an assembly, it will use the public key token to unsign the digital signature in the referenced assembly. The digital signature in the referenced assembly contains the hash of the contents of the assembly, encrypted with the assembly creator's private key. Therefore, unsigning the assembly will yield the hash of the assembly. The CLR will then compare the unsigned hash from the assembly to the hash in the assembly extern entry, and, if they are the same, it knows that the assembly that it is loading is the same as the assembly that the client was built against (or at least the creator has the same private key). It also knows that the assembly was not tampered with because the hash values match.

The next section of the manifest contains the assembly attributes for the multifile assembly:

```
.assembly multifile
{
  .custom instance void
[mscorlib]System.Reflection.AssemblyKeyFileAttribute::.ctor
(string) =
( 01 00 09 6D 79 6B 65 79 2E 73 6E 6B 00 00 )        //
...mykey.snk..
  .custom instance void
[mscorlib]System.Reflection.AssemblyDelaySignAttribute::.ct
or(bool) =
( 01 00 00 00 00 )
  .custom instance void
[mscorlib]System.Reflection.AssemblyDescriptionAttribute::.
ctor(string) =
( … )    // A test multi-file assembly..
  .publickey = ( … )
  .hash algorithm 0x00008004
  .ver 1:2:3:4
}
```

You can clearly see the information that was contained in the assembly info file. In this case, I had specified a key file called **mykey.snk**. The hex numbers are just an encoded version of the string "mykey.snk". I also used the DelaySign attribute and specified false. The hex numbers are just the encoded false Boolean. The AssemblyDescription attribute was quite long, so I elided it. The next few lines show the hex encoding of the public key, which I also elited because it is long. The next line contains an identifier for the hash algorithm that was used to generate the hash values that are stored in the assembly:

```
.hash algorithm 0x00008004
```

The final line shows the version number that I specified in the assembly info file with the AssemblyVersion attribute:

```
.ver 1:2:3:4
```

The next section of the manifest contains an entry for each module in the assembly that is separate from the file that contains the manifest. The following metadata is the entry for the Employee.mod module.

```
.file Employee.mod
    .hash =
(2D 9E 4C 0A FF 28 9C AA 9D AA 25 66 AA DD C5 18 B5 3F 93
67 )
```

Each of these entries lists the name of the file, without the path, and the hash of the file.

The next section of the manifest contains location information (an index) for all types declared in an external file, that is, a file other than the file that contains the manifest.

```
.class extern public AssemblyDemo.Employee
{
  .file Employee.mod
  .class 0x02000003
}
```

Types declared in the same file as the manifest don't require one of these entries because the CLR does not have to load another file in order to find the metadata or implementation for the class. Each of these extern entries contains the name of the file where the class is implemented and the class token, which is 0x2000003 in this case. The entry shown above is for the **AssemblyDemo.Employee** class; it informs the CLR that this class resides in a module called Employee.mod.

The last section of the manifest contains information that is used by the CLR loader when it loads the assembly into memory and initializes it. This section contains a Module Version Identifier (MVID) and other information as shown here:

```
.module multifile.dll
// MVID: {8F84316B-55AC-475D-A0E3-BA1C6941B5BA}
.imagebase 0x00400000
.subsystem 0x00000003
.file alignment 512
.corflags 0x00000009
// Image base: 0x031a0000
```

An MVID is a unique identifier (a GUID) that is associated with each compilation of a module. The CLR uses the MVID when you precompile code, which is just .NET Framework-speak for compiling the MSIL in an assembly into native code ahead of time and caching it before it runs. The usual practice with the .NET Framework is that the CLR will compile code as it executes the code. If you do precompile, the CLR will store the MVID of the MSIL code that it compiles with the native code. Whenever you run the native code, the CLR loader will compare the MVID of the cached native code with the MVID of the MSIL code that the native code was generated from. If they are different, the source assembly has been recompiled, which means that the cached native code will need to be regenerated. The CLR will then revert to the MSIL assembly instead of using the out-of-date native code. The subsystem, imagebase, file alignment, and corflags entries are information used by the CLR to lay out the module in memory after it loads it.

Note You can find out more about precompiling, which is also called pre-JITing, by looking up the Native Image Generator (Ngen.exe) in the .NET Framework tools help.

Although it is vitally important, the manifest is only a small part of the metadata in a .NET assembly. The bulk of the metadata consists of tables that contain descriptive information about every module, type, method, field, property, event, enumeration, and delegate in an assembly. This metadata is spread out through all the modules of an assembly. Each module contains the metadata for the types in that module. This metadata consists of definition or Def metadata tables that describe the types, methods, fields, parameters, and so forth declared in an assembly and reference or Ref metadata tables that describe the external assemblies, modules, types, and members used by an assembly.

There are seven definition (def) metadata tables that describe modules, types, methods, fields, parameters, and events defined in the current assembly:

- **ModuleDef**—Contains the name and a unique identifier (a GUID) for each module in the assembly.
- **TypeDef**—Contains the name, base type, accessibility (private, public, and so forth) of each type in the assembly. Each entry contains a pointer to the MethodDef, FieldDef, PropertyDef, and Event entries

for each method, field, property, or event that is a member of the type.

- **MethodDef**—Contains the name, flags (public, private, virtual, abstract, final, and so forth) for each method in the assembly as well as the offset within the assembly where the MSIL code for the method can be found. Each method also contains tokens pointing to entries in the ParamDef table for each parameter of the method.
- **FieldDef**—Contains the name, type, and flags (public, private, and so forth) for each field defined in the assembly. A field is just a member variable of a class or structure.
- **ParamDef**—Contains the name and flags (in, out, retval, and so forth) for each method parameter defined in the assembly.
- **PropertyDef**—Contains the name, flags, type, and underlying field (if used) for each property defined in the assembly.
- **EventDef**—Contains the name and flags for each event defined in the assembly. Events in .NET are analogous to connection point events in COM.

There are four main reference (Ref) metadata tables that contain references to "def" entries:

- **AssemblyRef**—Contains the name (without path and extension), version number, public key token, and hash for each assembly that the current assembly references.
- **ModuleRef**—Contains the file name and extension (without path) for each module that comprises the assembly.
- **TypeRef**—Contains the name and location information (either an AssemblyRef token or a ModuleRef token) for each type referenced by the current module.
- **MemberRef**—Contains the name, signature, and a TypeRef for each member (field, method, property, and event) referenced by the current assembly.

These Reference metadata tables are one of the main improvements that .NET metadata has over COM type libraries. Type libraries provide fairly detailed information about the type defined within a COM server. However, they do not provide any information about other COM servers or types that the COM server is dependent upon. Reference metadata does that in the .NET Framework.

The metadata for each element (type, method, field, and so forth) resides in a single place—in the module where its enclosing type is implemented. Each element has a token associated with it, which is just an index into the table for that element. The token is used whenever the element is referenced from some other place in the assembly. For instance, earlier I looked at the .extern entries for each class that appears in the manifest. The entry for the **Employee** class, which is implemented in a module called Employee.mod is as follows:

```
.class extern public AssemblyDemo.Employee
{
  .file Employee.mod
  .class 0x02000003
}
```

The value 0x02000003 is the token for the **Employee** class. With the module name and the token, the CLR can perform a very fast lookup of the metadata for the class. It can go straight to the file where the class is implemented and then do an index lookup into the metadata tables to find the metadata for the class.

Let's look at these metadata tables in the multifile assembly. To do that, I'll use the MSIL Disassembler (ildasm) with the (undocumented) advanced option. Execute the following command at a Visual Studio .NET command prompt:

```
ildasm /adv manager.mod
```

After ildasm appears, select View | MetaInfo/Show!. The following text shows the metadata for the **Manager** class:

```
TypeDef #3
-------------------------------------------------------
TypDefName: metadatademo.Manager  (02000004)
Flags     : [Public] [AutoLayout] [Class] [AnsiClass]
(00100001)
Extends   : 02000003 [TypeDef] metadatademo.Employee
Field #1
-------------------------------------------------------
    Field Name: mBonus (04000008)
    Flags     : [Private]  (00000001)
    CallCnvntn: [FIELD]
    Field type:  ValueClass System.Decimal

Method #1
-------------------------------------------------------
    MethodName: .ctor (06000009)
    Flags     : [Private] [HideBySig] [ReuseSlot]
[SpecialName] [RTSpecialName] [.ctor]  (00001881)
    RVA       : 0x00002108
    ImplFlags : [IL] [Managed]  (00000000)
    CallCnvntn: [DEFAULT]
    hasThis
    ReturnType: Void
    4 Arguments
      Argument #1:  I4
      Argument #2:  String
      Argument #3:  ValueClass System.Decimal
      Argument #4:  ValueClass System.Decimal
```

```
    4 Parameters
      (1) ParamToken : (0800000a) Name : id flags: [none]
(00000000)
      (2) ParamToken : (0800000b) Name : name flags:
[none] (00000000)
      (3) ParamToken : (0800000c) Name : salary flags:
[none] (00000000)
      (4) ParamToken : (0800000d) Name : bonus flags:
[none] (00000000)

Method #2
-------------------------------------------------------
    MethodName: GetSalary (0600000A)
    Flags     : [Public] [Virtual] [HideBySig] [ReuseSlot]
(000000c6)
    RVA       : 0x00002128
    ImplFlags : [IL] [Managed]  (00000000)
    CallCnvntn: [DEFAULT]
    hasThis
    ReturnType: ValueClass System.Decimal
    No arguments.
```

The first section of the metadata, which follows, contains the token for the **Manager** class, which is just its address in the TypeDef table (02000004). The flags for the class show that it is public, that the CLR should lay out the class in memory as it sees fit (AutoLayout), that the type is a Class (all types whether they are structures or enumerations show "Class" actually), and that strings should be interpreted using Ansi conventions (AnsiClass). The extends entry shows that the **Manager** class inherits from the class with token 02000003, which is the **Employee** class.

```
TypDefName: metadatademo.Manager  (02000004)
Flags     : [Public] [AutoLayout] [Class] [AnsiClass]
(00100001)
    Extends   : 02000003 [TypeDef] metadatademo.Employee
```

The next section of the metadata is for the mBonus field in the **Manager** class:

```
    Field Name: mBonus (04000008)
    Flags     : [Private]  (00000001)
    CallCnvntn: [FIELD]
    Field type:  ValueClass System.Decimal
```

Notice that this section of the metadata contains the token for the mBonus field (04000008). The flags for this field indicate that it is private and the type of the field is System.Decimal.

The next section of code contains the metadata for the **Manager** class' constructor:

```
MethodName: .ctor (06000009)
Flags     : [Private] [HideBySig] [ReuseSlot] [SpecialName]
[RTSpecialName] [.ctor]  (00001881)
RVA       : 0x00002108
ImplFlags : [IL] [Managed]  (00000000)
CallCnvntn: [DEFAULT]
hasThis ReturnType: Void
4 Arguments
    Argument #1:  I4
    Argument #2:  String
    Argument #3:  ValueClass System.Decimal
    Argument #4:  ValueClass System.Decimal
4 Parameters
    (1) ParamToken : (0800000a) Name : id flags: [none]
(00000000)
    (2) ParamToken : (0800000b) Name : name flags: [none]
(00000000)
    (3) ParamToken : (0800000c) Name : salary flags:
[none] (00000000)
    (4) ParamToken : (0800000d) Name : bonus flags: [none]
(00000000)
```

The token for the constructor (its address in the MethodDef table) is 06000009. The location in memory of the MSIL that implements this method, which is called a Relevant Virtual Address (RVA), is 0x00002108. The tokens for the id, name, salary, and bonus parameters, which are the addresses of these parameters in the ParamDef table, are 0800000a, 0800000b, 0800000c and 0800000d, respectively. Notice that the metadata lists the type and name for each of these parameters.

Viewing Metadata Programmatically

You can use two APIs to query and use .NET metadata from your programs. There is an unmanaged API, which is implemented as a set of COM interfaces. The only documentation I have seen on this API is a document called **Assembly Metadata Unmanaged API.doc** and a file called **Metadata Unmanaged API.doc**, which you can find in the Tool Developer's guide area of the documentation at **[Root directory for Visual Studio.NET installation]\FrameworkSDK\Tool Developers Guide\docs**. The documentation in this directory is for compiler vendors or people implementing the Common Language Infrastructure (CLI). There is also an excellent article written by Matt Pietrek in the October, 2000 edition of MSDN magazine. A detailed discussion of this interface is outside the scope of this book. The other API is a managed API called the reflection API. This API is very easy to use. There are two main entry points to this API. One is the GetType method of the **Object** class in the System Namespace, which is the base type for all other types that you declare in the .NET Framework. The GetType method returns a Type object. The Type object contains a set of methods that you can use to query the metadata associated with a particular type. Another entry point is to use the static Load method in the **Assembly** class, which can be found in

Viewing Metadata Programmatically *(continued)*

the System.Reflection namespace. The **Assembly** class contains methods that you can use to query and view the modules and types in an assembly. The demonstrations for this chapter contain a simple application called the AssemblyViewer that uses the Reflection API to display the metadata for an assembly. To use this application, you type in the name of an assembly. The application will then locate the assembly and display a list of all the types in the assembly. You can then double-click on a type, and it will show a list of the members of the type. I won't show the code for this example here in the text of this chapter, but you can download the code for this book and view the code for yourself at your leisure and see how easy it is to query and use .NET metadata.

MSIL

I mentioned earlier that the two major contents of a .NET assembly are metadata and MSIL code. Now that I have beaten the subject of .NET metadata to death, let's move the discussion along to MSIL. You can think of MSIL as a virtual assembly language. It defines a set of assembly language-like operations that are easily translated into the native instruction set of most modern CPUs.

Common Intermediate Language (CIL)

In the documentation for the .NET Framework SDK, you will see MSIL referred to as CIL. You may also hear the CLR referred to as the CLI. The difference between these names is that the CLI and CIL (as well as the CTS) are part of a specification that Microsoft has submitted to the European Computer Manufacturer's Association (ECMA) for ratification as a standardized platform. The CLR and MSIL are Microsoft's proprietary implementation of the CLI and CIL, respectively. Other vendors are now free to implement the CLI or CIL although it remains to be seen if any will actually do so. You can find out everything you want to know about MSIL in Partition III of the CLI documentation, which you can find in the Tool Developer's Guide documentation.

The CLR uses the VES to compile the MSIL code into native code on the fly as you run a managed code executable. This process of converting MSIL code into native code is called JIT compilation. The VES does not compile the code all at once; it compiles it method by method as the code is used. As soon as the MSIL for a method is compiled into native code, the CLR replaces the MSIL code for that method with the compiled native code so that the CLR can simply run the native code the next time the method is called.

Note It would be very easy to think that MSIL is equivalent to Java byte codes and that the CLR is equivalent to the Java runtime. Although MSIL is actually conceptually similar to Java bytecodes, which also define a virtual assembly language, the CLR does not interpret MSIL code as the Java runtime does. MSIL code is always compiled into native and then executed. Just remember that MSIL is never interpreted, and the CLR is not an interpreter.

MSIL implements a stack-based instruction set. What this means is that you execute an instruction by first loading the arguments into a Last In First Out (LIFO) data structure. This data structure is called a stack, and loading arguments into this data structure is usually referred to as pushing arguments onto the stack. You then execute an instruction, which will pop the arguments off the stack and replace the item at the top of the stack with the result of the operation. The CIL documentation uses the following stack transition diagram to illustrate this type of operation.

```
value1, value2 ➠ …, result
```

This diagram indicates that two values (value1 and value2) must be pushed onto the stack prior to executing this operation. The values are pushed left to right in this notation so value2 is at the top of the stack. The instruction will then perform some operation on the stack operands, pop the operands off the stack and leave the result on the top of the stack. An example of an operation that would have a stack transition diagram like this is the multiplication (mul) instruction. Here is the stack transition diagram for a unary instruction (one that only requires a single operand). The neg instruction, which simply negates a number, is an example of such an instruction.

```
value ➠ …, result
```

Notice that I only push one argument on the stack and then the operation will pop the argument off the stack and leave the result at the top of the stack. Some instructions require no stack operand. The best examples of this are the push and pop operations themselves. Here is the stack transition diagram for the ldarg function, which you will use to push method arguments onto the stack.

```
➠ …, value
```

This simply indicates that no arguments need to be pushed onto the stack prior to executing the instruction, and the result of the operation is that the specified value will reside on the top of the stack.

There are two major categories of instructions in MSIL: (1) base instructions and (2) object model instructions. The base instructions are the instructions that you use to move data on and off the stack; perform essential arithmetic like add, subtract, multiply, divide; and perform bitwise operations like AND, OR, NOT, XOR, and left and right shifts. The base instructions also include branching operations that are used by most programming language to implement flow of control, such as branch on false, branch on not false, branch if equal, branch if greater than, unconditional branch, and so forth. The basic instruction set also includes comparison instructions like compare equal, compare greater than, and compare less than and functions for copying and initializing memory blocks and calling and returning from methods. The base instruction set forms a Turing Complete set of operations, meaning that, with these instructions, you can perform all the calculations expected of a modern computer. The MSIL instruction set closely mirrors the instruction set of a modern microprocessor. This makes it simple to implement an MSIL-to-native-code compiler.

Table 3-9 lists some of the instructions in the base instruction set for moving data on and off the stack.

TABLE 3–9 *Instructions for moving data on and off the stack*

Instruction	Description
ldarg num	Pushes argument num onto the stack.
ldarg.0, ldarg.1, ldarg.2, ldarg.3	Is the short form for pushing arguments 0, 1, 2, or 3 on to the stack.
ldarga num	Pushes the address of argument num on to the stack. The ldarga instruction should only be used for by-ref parameter passing. In most cases, you should use ldarg.
ldloc indx	Pushes the local variable identified by index (indx) on to the stack.
ldloc.0, ldloc.1, ldloc.2, ldloc.3	Is the short form for pushing local variable with index 0, 1, 2, or 3.
ldloca indx	Pushes the address of the local variable identified by index (indx) on to the stack.
ldc.<type> value	Pushes the numeric constant value of type <type> on to the stack, e.g. idc.i4 5 will push the value 5 onto the stack as a 4-byte integer, idc.i8 3 will push the value 3 onto the stack as an 8-byte integer, ldc.r4 3.5 will push the value 4-byte float 3.5 onto the stack, ldc.r8 4.8 will push the 8-byte float (double) value 4.8 on to the stack.
starg num	Stores the item at the top of the stack (pops the stack) into argument num.
stloc indx	Pops the stack into the local variable identified by index (indx).
stloc.0, stloc.1, stloc.2, stloc.3	Is the short form for popping the stack into local variable with index 0, 1, 2, or 3.

TABLE 3–9 *Instructions for moving data on and off the stack (continued)*

stind.<type>	The stack transition diagram for this instruction is as follows: addr, val ➡ … This instruction stores the value val of type <type> into the address identified by addr. stind.i4 will store a 4-byte integer at the specified address.
Pop	Removes the top element on the stack.

Table 3–10 lists some of the instructions in the base instruction set for performing arithmetic operations on data.

TABLE 3–10 *Instructions for performing arithmetic operations*

Instruction	Description	Stack Transition Diagram
add	Adds value1 and value2.	value1, value2 ➡ …, result
sub	Subtracts value2 from value1.	value1, value2 ➡ …, result
mul	Multiplies two values.	value1, value2 ➡ …, result
div	Divides two values and returns a quotient or floating point result.	value1, value2 ➡ …, result
rem	Calculates the remainder of value1 divided by value2.	value1, value2 ➡ …, result

Table 3–11 lists some of the branching and flow control instructions in the base instruction set.

TABLE 3–11 *Branching and flow control instructions*

Instruction	Description	Stack Transition Diagram
beq target	Branch to instruction (target) if value1 = value2.	value1, value2 ➡ …
bne.un target	Branch to instruction (target) if value1 <> value2 or is unordered.	value1, value2 ➡ …
bge target	Branch to instruction (target) if value1 >= value2.	value1, value2 ➡ …
bgt target	Branch to instruction (target) if value1 > value2.	value1, value2 ➡ …
ble target	Branch to instruction (target) if value1 <= value2.	value1, value2 ➡ …
brfalse target	Branch to instruction (target) if value = false, null, zero.	value ➡ …

TABLE 3–11 *Branching and flow control instructions (continued)*

Instruction	Description	Stack Transition Diagram
brtrue target	Branch to instruction (target) if value = non-false, non-null.	value ➠ …
br target	Unconditional branch.	➠ …
call method	Calls the method identified by method.	…, arg1, arg2 … argn ➠ …, retVal (not always returned)
ret	Return from a method The methods stack must be empty except for the return value (if there is one). This return value will be copied from the method's stack to the stack of its caller.	Return value on method's stack (not always present) ➠…, return value on callers stack (not always present)

Table 3-12 contains some of the bitwise instructions in the base instruction set.

TABLE 3–12 *Bit manipulation instructions*

Instruction	Description	Stack Transition Diagram
or	Computes the bitwise OR of value1 and value2.	value1, value2 ➠ …, result
and	Computes the bitwise AND of value1 and value2.	value1, value2 ➠ …, result
xor	Computes the bitwise XOR of value1 and value2.	value1, value2 ➠ …, result
not	Computes the bitwise complement of the value on the top of the stack.	value ➠ …, result

The object model instructions are built on the base instructions, and they provide a common set of services to high-level, object-oriented programming languages. Let's take a look at some of the object model instructions. These instructions provide a set of services that simplify the development of high-level, object-oriented languages. These services include accessing and updating the fields of an object, making late-bound (virtual) method calls, boxing and unboxing objects, creating arrays and accessing and updating the elements of an array, instantiating and type-casting objects, and throwing exceptions. Table 3–13 contains a partial list of the instructions in the object model instruction set.

TABLE 3–13 *object model instructions*

Instruction	Description	Stack Transition Diagram
newobj ctor	Create a new, uninitialized object or value type and call its constructor.	*arg1, … argN* ➠ *…, obj*
ldfld field	Push a field of an object onto the stack.	obj ➠ …, value
callvirt method	Calls a late-bound method on an object.	obj, arg1, … argN ➠ …, return value (optional)
stfld field	Updates the value of a field of a specified object with a new value.	*obj, value* ➠ …,
box valueTypeToken	Converts a value type object to a reference type object.	valueObj ➠ …, refObj
unbox valueTypeToken	Converts the boxed (reference type) representation of a value type back to its value type form.	refObj ➠ …, valueObj
castclass class	Casts an object to a specified class.	obj ➠ …, obj2
initobj classtoken	Initializes all the fields of the value object to null or a 0 of the specified type.	addrOfValueObj ➠ …,
cpobj classtoken	Copies a value object of type indicated by classtoken from sourceObj to destObj.	*destValueObj, srcValueObj* ➠ …,
ldobj classtoken	Loads an instance of the value type indicated by classtoken onto the stack.	addrOfValueObj ➠ …, valueObj
stobj classtoken	Copies an instance of the type indicated by classtoken from the stack into memory.	addr, valueObj ➠ …,
newarr *etype*	Creates a new array of the type indicated by etype.	*numElems* ➠ *…, array*
ldelem.<type>	Pushes the element of type <type> onto the stack. ldelem.i4 will push the element as 4-byte integer, ldelem.i8 will push the element as an 8-byte integer, and so forth	array, index ➠ …, value
stelem.<type>	Stores the value on the stack of type <type> into the array element indicated by index.	*array, index, value* ➠ …,
ldlen	Pushes the number of elements of an array on to the stack.	array ➠ …, length

Now that you know more about MSIL than you probably wanted to know, let's take a look at some MSIL code. I'll start by taking a look at the MSIL code for the GetSalary method in the **Manager** class. To view the MSIL, perform the following steps:

1. Open a Visual Studio .NET command prompt by making the following selection from the Start menu: Programs | Microsoft Visual Studio .NET | Visual Studio .NET Tools | Visual Studio .NET Command Prompt.
2. Change directories to the location where you built the multifile assembly that you have been using throughout this chapter.
3. Enter the following command at the Visual Studio .NET command prompt:

```
ildasm Manager.mod
```

It's important that you run ildasm on the Manager.mod module because this is the file that contains the implementation of the **Manager** class. In the ildasm main window, find the GetSalary method in the **Manager** class as shown in Figure 3–6.

Now double-click the GetSalary method, and you should see a window that contains the following code. I did clean up the code slightly to make it a little more readable.

```
.method public hidebysig virtual instance valuetype
[mscorlib]System.Decimal GetSalary() cil managed
{
  // Code size       22 (0x16)
  .maxstack  2
  .locals init (valuetype [mscorlib]System.Decimal V_0)
  IL_0000:  ldarg.0
  IL_0001:  call       instance valuetype System.Decimal
```

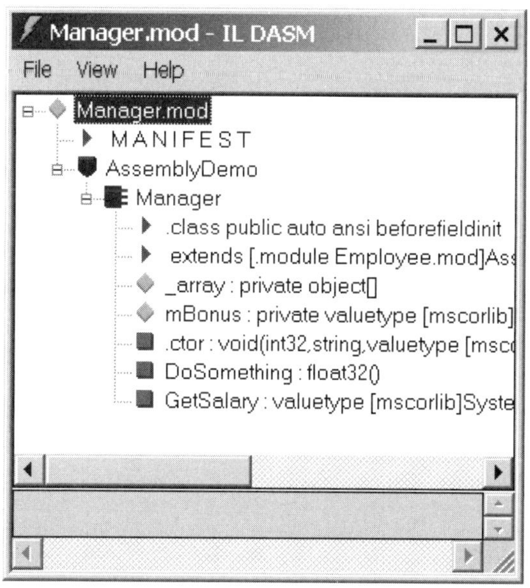

FIGURE 3–6 *The Manager class as viewed in ildasm.*

```
[.module Employee.mod]Employee::GetSalary()
  IL_0006:  ldarg.0
  IL_0007:  ldfld  valuetype System.Decimal Manager::mBonus
  IL_000c:  call   valuetype System.Decimal
System.Decimal::op_Addition(
valuetype System.Decimal,
        valuetype System.Decimal)
  IL_0011:  stloc.0
  IL_0012:  br.s       IL_0014
  IL_0014:  ldloc.0
  IL_0015:  ret
} // end of method Manager::GetSalary
```

The C# source code for this method is as follows:

```
public override decimal GetSalary()
{
    return base.GetSalary()+mBonus;
}
```

The first two lines in the MSIL code declare the maximum stack size for the method and initialize a local variable for the method:

```
.maxstack  2
  .locals init (valuetype [mscorlib]System.Decimal V_0)
```

You don't explicitly declare a local variable in this method, but the compiler has to create one in the generated MSIL to store the return value of this method temporarily before you return it. To understand the next few lines, you have to first know that every nonstatic method of a class has an implied zeroth argument that contains the "this" pointer for the current instance:

```
IL_0000:  ldarg.0
  IL_0001:  call       instance valuetype System.Decimal
[.module Employee.mod]Employee::GetSalary()
```

Therefore, the previous code pushes the "this" pointer on the stack and then calls the GetSalary method of the base class of **Manager (Employee)**. This method returns the Salary (without the Manager's bonus) of the Employee. The return value of the method will be left on the top of the stack. This is the convention that MSIL uses for return values of methods.

On the next three lines, you load the "this" pointer for the current object and then use the ldfld instruction from the Object Model instruction set to load the mBonus field from the Manager instance:

```
IL_0006:  ldarg.0
IL_0007:  ldfld      valuetype System.Decimal
Manager::mBonus
IL_000c:  call       valuetype System.Decimal
System.Decimal::op_Addition(
```

```
valuetype System.Decimal,
valuetype System.Decimal)
```

The ldfld instruction will pop the "this" pointer off the stack. Therefore, after the ldfld instruction, the top two items on the stack will be the Salary for the current instance (without Manager's bonus) and the bonus amount (in the mBonus) field for the current Manager instance. The next line of code calls the op_Addition method in the **System.Decimal** class to add these two values together, yielding the total salary for the Manager. Remember a Decimal is a valuetype object that is declared in the Base class library; the regular add instruction will not work for this type. After the op_Addition method call, the result will be at the top of the stack.

The next four lines store the return value from the op_Addition method in the local variable for this method:

```
IL_0011:  stloc.0
IL_0012:  br.s        IL_0014
IL_0014:  ldloc.0
IL_0015:  ret
```

I'll just have to come clean and admit that I have no idea why the compiler generated the line of code labeled IL_0012. Notice that this line of code is just an unconditional branch to the next line. The next line after this oddity simply loads a local variable on to the stack. This line is pushing the return value on to the stack. You must push the return value of a method on to the stack (if there is one) before you return. The final line is a call of the ret instruction, which will return from the method and put the return value at the top of the stack of the calling method.

Do you see how simple it is to read MSIL after you understand the base and object model instruction sets? Let's try out your newly acquired knowledge on some system code. The base class library in the .NET Framework contains a full-featured set of collection classes. The collection classes include stack, queue, hashtable, arraylist, and sorted list classes. You can learn a lot about how the stack collection class is implemented by examining the implementation of the push method.

To do this, navigate to the latest version of your .NET Framework directory. On my machine, the directory is **D:\WINNT\Microsoft.NET\Framework\v1.0.3705**. The collection classes are found in an assembly called mscorlib.dll. Enter the following command at a command prompt in this directory:

```
ildasm mscorlib.dll
```

Now find the stack class as shown in Figure 3-7 and double-click the push method within this class.

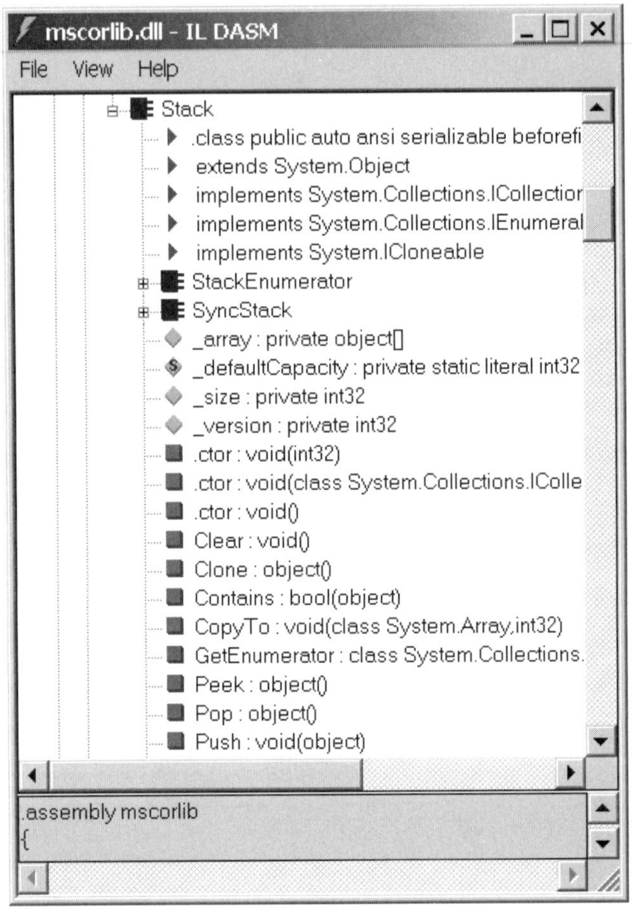

FIGURE 3–7 *The System.Collection.Stack class as viewed in ildasm.*

The following code shows the MSIL code for the push method in the **System.Collection.Stack** class. Once again, I did clean up the code a little to enhance its readability. Let's break down this code section by section.

```
.method public hidebysig newslot virtual
        instance void  Push(object obj) cil managed
{
  // Code size       100 (0x64)
  .maxstack  5
  .locals (object[] V_0, int32 V_1)
  IL_0000:  ldarg.0
  IL_0001:  ldfld      int32 Stack::_size
  IL_0006:  ldarg.0
  IL_0007:  ldfld      object[] Stack::_array
```

```
  IL_000c:  ldlen
  IL_000d:  conv.i4
  IL_000e:  bne.un.s   IL_003c
  IL_0010:  ldc.i4.2
  IL_0011:  ldarg.0
  IL_0012:  ldfld      object[] Stack::_array
  IL_0017:  ldlen
  IL_0018:  conv.i4
  IL_0019:  mul
  IL_001a:  conv.ovf.u4
  IL_001b:  newarr     System.Object
  IL_0020:  stloc.0
  IL_0021:  ldarg.0
  IL_0022:  ldfld      object[] Stack::_array
  IL_0027:  ldc.i4.0
  IL_0028:  ldloc.0
  IL_0029:  ldc.i4.0
  IL_002a:  ldarg.0
  IL_002b:  ldfld      int32 .Stack::_size
  IL_0030:  call       void System.Array::Copy(
class System.Array,int32,
class System.Array,int32,int32)
  IL_0035:  ldarg.0
  IL_0036:  ldloc.0
  IL_0037:  stfld      object[] Stack::_array
  IL_003c:  ldarg.0
  IL_003d:  ldfld      object[] Stack::_array
  IL_0042:  ldarg.0
  IL_0043:  dup
  IL_0044:  ldfld      int32 Stack::_size
  IL_0049:  dup
  IL_004a:  stloc.1
  IL_004b:  ldc.i4.1
  IL_004c:  add
  IL_004d:  stfld      int32 Stack::_size
  IL_0052:  ldloc.1
  IL_0053:  ldarg.1
  IL_0054:  stelem.ref
  IL_0055:  ldarg.0
  IL_0056:  dup
  IL_0057:  ldfld      int32 Stack::_version
  IL_005c:  ldc.i4.1
  IL_005d:  add
  IL_005e:  stfld      int32 Stack::_version
  IL_0063:  ret
} // end of method Stack::Push
```

The first line of code declares two local variables called V_0, and V_1, which are typed as an object array and a 4-byte integer, respectively.

```
.locals (object[] V_0, int32 V_1)
```

I will call these two local variables newArray and curSize. You will see why shortly. The next seven lines of code are simply an "if" statement.

```
IL_0000:  ldarg.0
IL_0001:  ldfld      int32 Stack::_size
IL_0006:  ldarg.0
IL_0007:  ldfld      object[] Stack::_array
IL_000c:  ldlen
IL_000d:  conv.i4
IL_000e:  bne.un.s   IL_003c
```

If you recall that the instruction ldarg.0 loads the "this" pointer for the current object and that the ldfld instruction loads a field of an object, you can see that lines (IL_0000 thru IL_007) are simply loading two private variables of the stack object onto the execution stack: (1) the current number of elements in the stack collection (_size) and (2) an object array (_array) that holds the contents of the stack collection. The next two lines (IL_000C and IL_000D) will replace the top item on the execution stack with the declared length of the internal array and convert the length to a 4-byte integer. Line IL_000e will branch to line IL_003C if the top two items in the execution stack are not equal to each other, in other words, if the number of elements in the stack collection is not equal to the declared length of the internal array. If I was to convert this MSIL code into C#, it would look as follows.

```
If ( this._size == this._array.Length)
{
// Lines IL_0010 thru IL_0037 go here
}
```

Therefore, the lines of MSIL code shown previously (IL_0000 thru IL_000e) are testing to see if the internal storage that was allocated for the stack contents is full. Let's look at lines IL_0010 through IL_0037 to see how the stack collection expands its internal storage if there are too many elements to fit within the current storage buffer. In other words, you are looking to see what happens when the "if" statement evaluates to true. These lines are as follows:

```
IL_0010:  ldc.i4.2
IL_0011:  ldarg.0
IL_0012:  ldfld      object[] Stack::_array
IL_0017:  ldlen
IL_0018:  conv.i4
IL_0019:  mul
IL_001a:  conv.ovf.u4
IL_001b:  newarr     System.Object
IL_0020:  stloc.0
IL_0021:  ldarg.0
```

```
  IL_0022:  ldfld       object[] Stack::_array
  IL_0027:  ldc.i4.0
  IL_0028:  ldloc.0
  IL_0029:  ldc.i4.0
  IL_002a:  ldarg.0
  IL_002b:  ldfld       int32 Stack::_size
  IL_0030:  call        void System.Array::Copy(
class System.Array,
                int32,class System.Array,
                int32,int32)
  IL_0035:  ldarg.0
  IL_0036:  ldloc.0
  IL_0037:  stfld       object[] Stack::_array
```

Line IL_0010 loads the number 2 onto the stack. Lines IL_0011 through IL_0018 load the current length of the array that contains the stored elements of the stack. Line IL_0019 multiplies this length by 2, and line IL_001a converts the multiplication result to an unsigned integer. Line IL_001b instantiates a new array of System.Object instances whose length is the multiplication result, and line IL_0020 stores this new array in the local variable with index zero. Remember I had called this local variable newArray earlier. Do you see why? This local variable is used to store the new expanded array. So now, if you converted lines IL_0010 through IL_0020 into C#, you would get the following code:

```
newArray=new System.Object[(uint)(2*this._array.Length)];
```

In other words, if the internal storage array for a stack collection is full, when you attempt to add a new item to the stack collection, the stack collection will create a new array that is double the size of the existing array. On lines IL_0021 through IL_0030, the MSIL is setting up a call to the Copy method in the **Array** class to copy the contents of the existing array (_array) into the new larger array (newArray). The copy function takes five parameters in order from left to right: (1) the source array, (2) the starting index in the source array to copy from, (3) the destination array, (4) the starting index in the destination array to copy to, and (5) the number of elements to copy from the source to the destination array. You must push all of these arguments, in order from left to right, onto the execution stack before calling the Copy method. In other words, you push the first argument (the source array) first and the last argument (the number of elements to copy) last. Lines IL_0021 and IL_0022 push the _array field of the stack collection instance onto the execution stack; this is the source array. Line IL_0027 pushes 0 for the starting index in the source array. Line IL_0028 pushes the destination array onto the execution stack; remember this array is stored in the local variable at index 0. Line IL_0029 pushes the starting index in the destination array onto the stack, and lines IL_002a and IL_002b push the current size of the stack collection onto the stack, which is the number of elements that you want to copy from the source to the destination. Line IL_0030 makes the actual call to the copy function.

The next three lines push the this pointer and the newArray local variable onto the execution stack and then store the newArray into the _array local variable.

```
IL_0035:  ldarg.0
IL_0036:  ldloc.0
IL_0037:  stfld      object[] Stack::_array
```

This will remove the only outstanding reference to the _array environment variable and thereby free it to be garbage-collected the next time the garbage collection algorithm runs.

So far, the code that you have looked at is the code that will be executed only if the internal storage for the stack needs to be expanded. The next section of code is the instructions in the push method of the stack collection class that actually places the new element on to the stack. Let's take a look at this code, which runs from IL_003c to IL_0063:

```
IL_003c:  ldarg.0
IL_003d:  ldfld      object[] Stack::_array
IL_0042:  ldarg.0
IL_0043:  dup
IL_0044:  ldfld      int32 Stack::_size
IL_0049:  dup
IL_004a:  stloc.1
IL_004b:  ldc.i4.1
IL_004c:  add
IL_004d:  stfld      int32 Stack::_size
IL_0052:  ldloc.1
IL_0053:  ldarg.1
IL_0054:  stelem.ref
IL_0055:  ldarg.0
IL_0056:  dup
IL_0057:  ldfld      int32 Stack::_version
IL_005c:  ldc.i4.1
IL_005d:  add
IL_005e:  stfld      int32 Stack::_version
IL_0063:  ret
```

The lines from IL_003c to IL_004c are difficult to understand unless you understand how the stack works. Just keep in mind that most instructions require one, two, or three arguments to be on the stack. The instruction will use the arguments on the execution stack and then pop them off the stack when it is done and replace the arguments with the result of the operation if there is one. Line IL_003c pushes the "this" pointer for the Stack collection on to the execution stack. Line IL_003d pushes the _array member field of the Stack collection onto the execution stack; it also pops the "this" pointer off the

FIGURE 3–8 *The execution stack after Instruction IL_0049.*

execution stack. Line IL_0042 pushes the "this" pointer onto the execution stack, and the next line, IL_0043, duplicates the top element on the stack. The next two lines load the _size field on to the stack and duplicate it. The ldfld instruction also uses one of the "this" pointers on the stack. Therefore, after line IL_0049, the execution stack will look like Figure 3–8.

Line IL_004a will store the top item on the execution stack into the local variable with index 1. Remember that I called this variable currSize. This instruction will also pop one of the _size values off the execution stack (see Figure 3–8). Line IL_004b pushes the literal value 1 on to the execution stack, and line IL_004c will add the value 1 to the remaining _size value on the top of the execution stack (and also pop the remaining _size value off the execution stack, replacing it with the result of the operation). The top of the execution stack will now contain the value _size + 1. Line IL_004d will store this value into the _size field and pop the remaining "this" pointer off the execution stack. The top of the execution stack will now contain the _array field. Line IL_0052 will push the currSize local variable, which contains the size of the array, on to the execution stack. This value will be used as the index position for the new element in the stack collection. Line IL_0053 will load the argument to this method on to the execution stack. In this case, the argument is the object that you are pushing on to the stack collection.

Note Remember argument 0 is the "this" pointer. Argument 1 is the first real argument.

Line IL_0054 will store the object into the internal array at the index specified on line IL_0052. It will also pop the _array field, the currSize field, and the object (argument 1) off the execution stack. Lines IL_0055 and IL_0056 load the "this" pointer onto the stack and duplicate it. Line IL_0057 will push the _version field onto the execution stack (and pop one of the "this" pointers off the stack). Line IL_005c will load the literal value 1 on to the stack, and line IL_005d will add 1 to _version, and line IL_005e stores this new value back to the _version field. In other words, lines IL_0055 through IL_005e are equivalent to the following C# code:

```
this._version = this._version + 1;
```

It's not clear to me what the _version field is used for. I looked at the code for the Pop method in the stack collection class, and the _version field is incremented each time you call the pop method also. The _version field appears to track the number of times you perform an operation on the stack collection. It's not clear why this is necessary because I could not find any properties or methods that return or use this information. The final line of MSIL code, IL_0063, is obviously just a return instruction. The push method in the **System.Collections.Stack** class has no return value (it's typed as a void), so the execution stack is left empty when you return. Therefore, now I can show you the complete, decompiled C# code for the Push method in the **System.Collections.Stack** class.

```
public void Push(System.Object arg1)
{
    System.Object[] newArray;
    int currSize;
    if ( this._size == this._array.Length)
{
      newArray=new System.Object
        [(uint)(2*this._array.Length)];
      System.Array.Copy(_array,0,newArray,0,this._size);
      _array=newArray;
    }
    currSize=this._size;
    this._size=this._size+1;
    this._array[currSize]=arg1;
    this._version=this._version+1;
}
```

I think you can see how easy that was. The key difference between a .NET assembly and a regular Win32 DLL is that the Win32 DLL contains machine code, an almost unintelligible encoding of 0s and 1s. Sure, you can disassemble this code into x86 assembly language code, but native, x86 assembly language still does not contain the kind of high-level instructions (particularly the object model instructions) that make MSIL so easy to decipher. Moreover, it is much easier to read assembly language code if it uses only stack-based instructions like MSIL does. When an instruction set has lots of CPU registers, it is harder to figure out what's going on because different compilers will use these registers in different ways.

The fact that MSIL code is so easy to read is both good news and bad news. The good news is that you can always understand exactly how a class or method is implemented, even if you do not have the source code for the class. I have used my ability to decipher MSIL code a number of times while writing this book to gain insight into how certain aspects of the .NET Framework's class library are implemented.

Note Now that you know how the push method in the stack collection class is implemented, you can be smarter about how you use it. Because you know that the push method will double the size of the internal storage every time it has to grow the stack, you know that it is important to try to initialize the stack to the largest size that you think you might need. One of the constructors for the stack collection class allows you to specify the initial size for the stack's internal storage.

The bad news, of course, is that, if you write your code and ship it as a .NET assembly, other people will be able to decipher *your* code. Your competitors can easily gain access to your intellectual property, and a savvy programmer can easily steal your proprietary algorithms. At first, when I realized this, I was horrified, and I questioned whether this fact alone would cause people to avoid using the .NET Framework. After thinking about it more, I realized that it's probably not a big deal as long as you know that this issue exists. For a start, obfuscation technology already exists that makes it nearly impossible for someone to decipher the MSIL code in your .NET assemblies.

Note Some of the .NET obfuscation products that are available include Salamander, which is made by a company called Remote Soft (see *www.remotesoft.com* for more information), DotFuscator, from preEmptive Solutions (see *www.preemptive.com*), and Demeanor from Wise Owl (see *www.wiseowl.com*). Unfortunately, these obfuscators cost anywhere from a few hundred to more than a thousand dollars. Desaware makes an open source obfuscator called QND-Obfuscator, which is available for "free" if you purchase an e-book for $39.95. See *www.desaware.com* for more information.

If you're worried that determined intellectual property thieves may someday find a way to subvert these obfuscators (a valid concern), you can still hide your most sensitive intellectual property by implementing key algorithms as an unmanaged COM server using Visual C++ or VB6 and then use COM Interop (which I discuss extensively in this book) to call the methods in this COM server.

How the Runtime Locates Assemblies

Now that I have discussed the contents of an assembly (metadata and MSIL), I can turn my attention to how the CLR locates assemblies prior to running them. One of the key differences between the .NET Framework and COM is the notion of side-by-side execution. In a nutshell, this is the idea that two completely different versions of a component may be resident and even executing at the same time on a single machine. With COM, each COM class (CLSID) on a machine has entries in the registry under the HKEY_CLASSES_ROOT key that identifies the complete path to the DLL or executable that implements the type. There can only be one path for any given CLSID, so there can only be one implementation of a particular type on a given machine. All clients that use the type are limited to using this one implementation of the type, even if those clients were actually built with a different version of the type than is currently resident on this machine.

Things are completely different with the .NET Framework. When you compile a piece of software that uses a type that resides in an external assembly (I'll call this software "the client" not because it has to be UI code, but because it is a consumer of an external assembly), your managed code compiler will insert TypeRef entries into the metadata for the client that identify the assembly that contains that type. For instance, if you look at the client application that you built earlier to test the **Employee** and **Manager** classes from our multifile assembly using the advanced parameter on ILDASM (I won't repeat the steps to do this because I have done it several times before), you can find the TypeRef for the **Employee** class by scrolling down and looking for the TypeRefName called AssemblyDemo.Employee as follows:

```
TypeRef #6 (01000006)
-------------------------------------------------------
Token:                0x01000006
ResolutionScope:      0x23000002
TypeRefName:          AssemblyDemo.Employee
```

The ResolutionScope (0x23000002) identifies the assembly that this type can be found in. This resolution scope corresponds to an AssemblyRef. If you scroll down further in the ILDASM window, you should be able to find the AssemblyRef with a token=0x23000002 as follows:

```
AssemblyRef #2
-------------------------------------------------------
    Token: 0x23000002
    Public Key or Token: ef 41 b5 08 ea 1c fb 8b
    Name: multifile
    Major Version: 0x00000001
    Minor Version: 0x00000002
    Build Number: 0x00000003
```

```
    Revision Number: 0x00000004
Locale: <null>
    HashValue Blob:
```

Notice that this AssemblyRef identifies the name of the assembly (multifile); the public key token for the assembly (which is just a statistically unique hashed representation of the public key); the major, minor, build, and revision numbers for the assembly, which are 1, 2, 3, and 4, respectively; and the locale for the assembly. However, the AssemblyRef does not identify the path to the assembly. When the client application first uses a type that resides in the assembly, the CLR will use the Assembly Resolver to find the assembly identified by the AssemblyRef, that is, version 1.2.3.4 of the assembly called multifile with a public key token of ef41b508ea1cfb8b.

The Assembly Resolver

The Assembly Resolver is an internal component within the CLR that is responsible for taking assembly names and finding the requested assembly. It does not load the assembly; there is another module within the CLR called the Assembly Loader that does that. The Assembly Resolver's job is simply to map an assembly name (which includes the version number and [optionally] public key information) to a file on disk that contains the requested version of the assembly. The Assembly Resolver is exposed to developers through the Load method in the **System.Reflection.Assembly** class.

Every assembly has a four-part name. This four part name consists of the friendly name for the assembly, the version number (which is the the concatenation of the major, minor, build, and revision numbers), the locale, and the public key token. Here is the full name for the multifile assembly:

```
Multifile,Version=1.2.3.4,Culture=Neutral,PublicKeyToken=8a
707be49fd7d8f4
```

The Assembly Resolver can use either the full name for an assembly, or it can use a partial name, which will contain the assembly name but may be missing any of the other three elements of the full name.

The Algorithm for Locating an Assembly

To find an assembly, the Assembly Resolver takes the name and executes the algorithm shown in Figure 3–9.

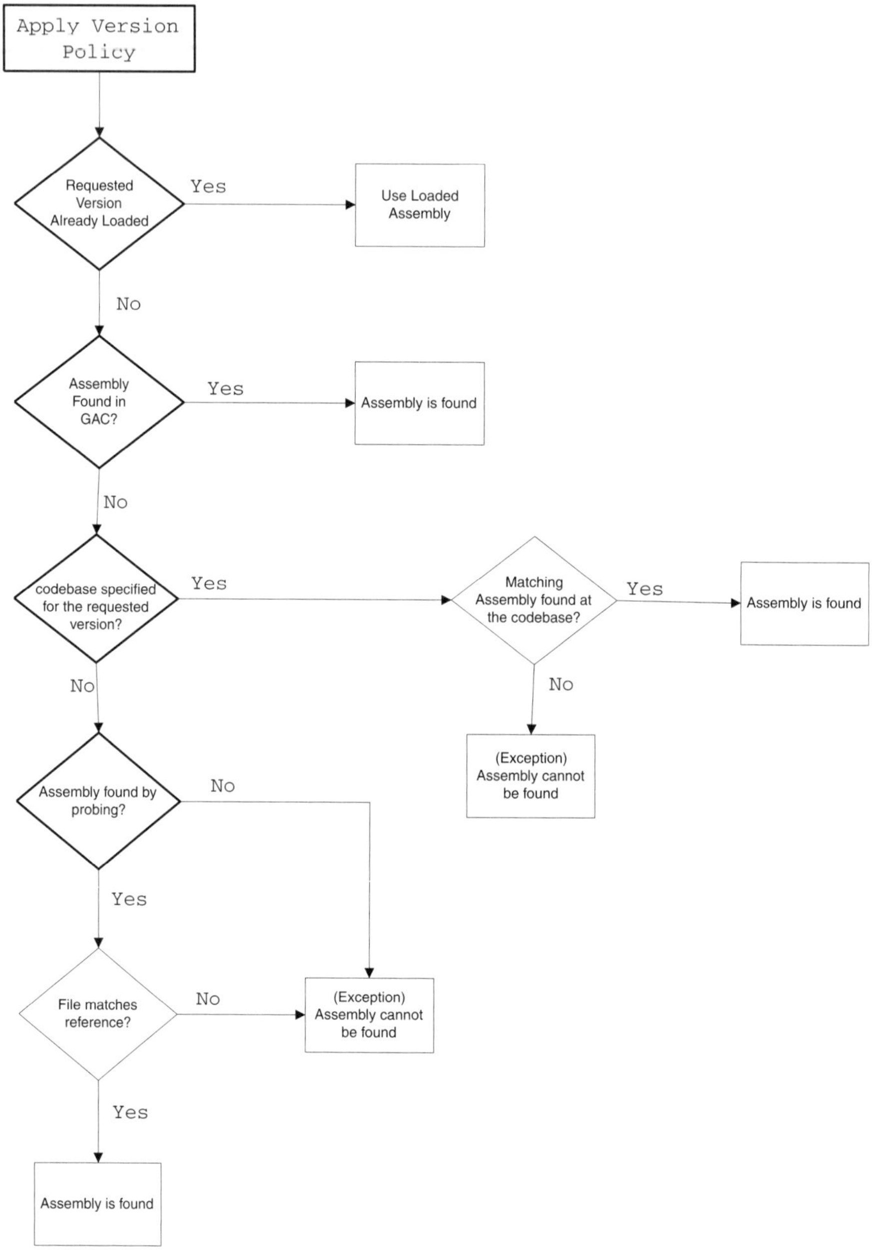

FIGURE 3–9 *The assembly binding algorithm.*

There are five main steps to this algorithm, and I have outlined those steps in bold on the flowchart.

1. Apply versioning policy.
2. Check if the desired version is loaded already.
3. Check the GAC.
4. Look in the codebase specified in the configuration file.
5. Probe.

Let's look at each of these steps.

VERSIONING POLICY

With the .NET Framework, you can use multiple versions of the same assembly on a single machine. By default, the Assembly Resolver will attempt to use the same version of an assembly that the client application was built with. However administrators or users of a machine can redirect a particular client application--or all client applications on the machine--to use a different version of an assembly than the one they were built with. This is called version redirection

An administrator or user may choose to use version redirection if they know that a newer version of a component has substantial improvements that client applications can use, and they know that the new version of the assembly will not break any of these client applications. The beauty of the .NET approach is that users and administrators have choice. They can choose to use a newer version of an assembly or not and if they attempt to use a newer version and run into problems, they can quickly roll back to the previous version by changing one entry in a configuration file. Version redirection can be done at three levels:

1. **Machine**—All applications on a machine that use a version of an assembly are redirected to use a different version.
2. **Application**—A particular application is redirected to a different version of a dependent assembly.
3. **Publisher policies**—The vender of a software component publishes a special, shared assembly that contains only a configuration file that instructs all clients who use a particular version of an assembly to use a different version. You can turn off support for publisher policies if you want in your application-level configuration file.

Version policies are specified using configuration files. These configuration files are XML documents that obey the schema shown in Figure 3-10.

The mechanisms that you use to perform version redirection are the same; the only difference between doing version redirection at the machine, application or publisher policy level is which configuration file you use to specify the redirection. Machine, Application, and Publisher Policy configura-

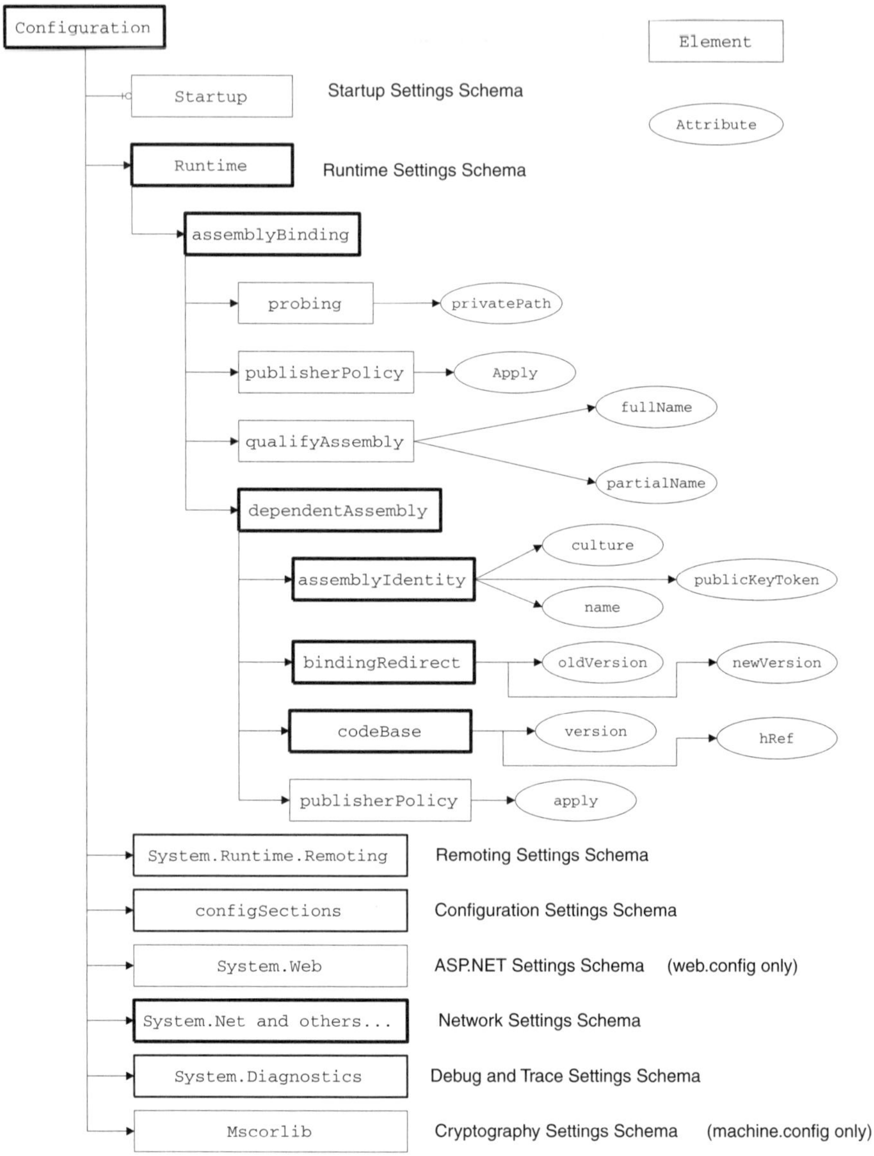

FIGURE 3–10 *The XML schema for .NET configuration files.*

tion files all use the same XML schema, but not all of the elements can be used in each type of file. I used line thickness on elements in Figure 3–10 to show which elements can be applied where. The thinnest lines, probing for instance, indicate that the element can only be used in an Application configuration file. The medium thickness lines, System.Runtime.Remoting for instance, indicates that the element can be used on either Application or Machine configuration files. The thickest lines, Runtime for instance, indicate that the element can be used on Application, Machine, or Publisher Policy configuration files.

Assembly binding is controlled by the assemblyBinding element (and its subelements) in the configuration file. This element can be used in an Application, Machine, or Publisher Policy configuration file. Versioning policy is controlled by the bindingRedirect subelement and the publisherPolicy element. The bindingRedirect element appears beneath the dependentAssembly element, and it allows you to redirect a client that is trying to bind to one version of a dependent assembly to a different version. The publisherPolicy element, which appears both directly beneath the assemblyBinding element and also as a subelement of the dependentAssembly element, allows you to turn on or off support for publisherPolicies. You can do this either for all dependent assemblies used by the current application, in which case you would use the publisherPolicies element directly beneath the assemblyBinding key, or you can turn on or off support for publisherPolicies just for a particular assembly, in which you would use the publisherPolicies element directly beneath the dependentAssembly element. You can probably understand how these elements work by looking at some examples using the multifile assembly that you built earlier.

```
<configuration xmlns:asm="urn:schemas-microsoft-
com:asm.v1">
<runtime>
<asm:assemblyBinding>
<asm:dependentAssembly>
<asm:assemblyIdentity name="multifile"
publicKeyToken="8a707be49fd7d8f4" />
<asm:bindingRedirect oldVersion="1.2.3.4"
newVersion="2.0.0.0" />
<asm:codeBase version="2.0.0.0" href="file://C:/Alan/books/
dotnetbook/demos/chapter3/multifileassembly/
multifileassembly_2_0/multifile.dll" />
</asm:dependentAssembly>
</asm:assemblyBinding>
</runtime>
</configuration>
```

The configuration file shown previously will redirect a client that was using version 1.2.3.4 of the assembly to use version 2.0.0.0. Notice that in addition to using the “asm:bindingRedirect” key to redirect the assembly reference to version 2.0.0.0 of the assembly, I also use the “asm:codeBase” key to specify where version 2.0.0.0 of the assembly can be found. Of course, to make this redirection work, you will need to save this document to the same directory as the client executable using the filename of the client with .config appended to it. For example, if the name of the application is myapp.exe, then you should name the configuration file myapp.exe.config.

If you want to redirect all clients on a machine from version 1.2.3.4 to version 2.0.0.0 of an assembly, you will need to add the entries shown above to your machine configuration file. You can find the machine configuration file in the config directory of your .NET Framework installation (for example, **D:\WINNT\Microsoft.NET\Framework\v1.0.3705\CONFIG**).

Another way to redirect references from one version of an assembly to another is with a Publisher Policy file. Publisher Policy files are used by component vendors to state which versions of their components are backward compatible with each other. A Publisher Policy file is just a configuration file that is embedded in a digitally signed, shared assembly and then installed into the GAC. The naming convention for this assembly is as follows:

```
policy.major.minor.assemblyname.dll
```

"Major" and "minor" are the major and minor version number of the assembly that the Publisher Policy should be applied to. A Publisher Policy file that would redirect version 1.2.3.4 to version 1.3.0.0 of the multifile assembly would have the following file name:

```
policy.1.2.multifile.dll
```

It would also contain the following contents:

```
<configuration xmlns:asm="urn:schemas-microsoft-
com:asm.v1">
<runtime>
<asm:assemblyBinding>
<asm:dependentAssembly>
<asm:assemblyIdentity name="multifile"
publicKeyToken="8a707be49fd7d8f4" />
<asm:bindingRedirect oldVersion="1.2.3.4"
newVersion="1.3.0.0" />
<asm:codeBase version="1.3.0.0" href="file://C:/Alan/books/
dotnetbook/demos/chapter3/multifileassembly/
multifileassembly_1_3/multifile.dll" />
</asm:dependentAssembly>
</asm:assemblyBinding>
</runtime>
</configuration>
```

Notice that there is no difference in terms of the XML schema and content between this configuration file and the application and machine configuration files that I showed you before. The only difference between this file and the application and machine configuration files is the way that they are deployed. To deploy a Publisher Policy file, you must build an assembly with this configuration file embedded into it and then register this file in the GAC. To do this, I saved the configuration file into a file called **multifileassembly.config**. I then ran the following command to create the assembly:

```
al /link:multifileassembly.config /
out:policy.1.2.multifile.dll
/keyf:mykey.snk /v:1.3.0.0
```

I then installed this assembly into the GAC using the gacutil command-line tool in the .NET Framework SDK:

```
gacutil -I policy.1.2.multifile.dll
```

The fact that you can only specify the major and minor version numbers in the name of the Publisher Policy file means that you can have only one Publisher Policy for each major/minor number combination. Therefore, you cannot redirect versions 1.2.3.4 and 1.2.4.0 to different new versions.

Now that you have seen three different ways to redirect an assembly reference from one version of an assembly to another (Application Configuration file, Machine Configuration file, or Publisher Policy file), the obvious question is how do the three forms of version redirection interact with each other? In other words, if I have an Application Configuration file, a Machine Configuration file, and a Publisher Policy file all in place for an assembly, which version number will I eventually get?

Version redirects in Application Configuration, Publisher Policy, and Machine Configuration files are applied serially as shown in Figure 3–11.

The original assembly reference (version 1.2.3.4) is first run through any version redirects in the Application Configuration file. This may lead to a change in the requested version (perhaps to version 1.3.0.0). This updated version number is then run through the Publisher Policy file, which may again change the requested version number. Keep in mind that the search for the Publisher Policy file in the GAC will be based on the major and minor version numbers of the request after it has been run through the Application Configuration file. Therefore, in this case, the Assembly Resolver will look for a Publisher Policy file called **policy.1.3.multifile.dll** because the requested version number after it has been run through application configuration file is 1.3.0.0.

FIGURE 3–11 *How versioning policies are applied.*

A machine configuration file is the last step in the versioning policy chain. After the requested version of the assembly is (potentially) altered by the Application Configuration file and a Publisher Policy, the resulting version number is then run through the Machine Configuration file, which may alter the version number one more time. The Machine Configuration file is usually controlled by a system administrator, and it allows the system administrator final control over which version of an assembly is used to satisfy a particular request. More important, the Machine Configuration file is applied for all binding requests to a particular assembly, regardless of which client application the request came from, unlike Application Configuration files that only affect the assembly binding for a particular application. The example shown in Figure 3–11 has an initial version number of 1.2.3.4 that is redirected through the application configuration file to version 1.3.0.0. A Publisher Policy for major.minor version number 1.3 will then redirect the request to version 2.0.0.0. Finally, the Machine Configuration file will redirect the request to version 2.1.0.0. Let's test your understanding of how the process works. Refer back to Figure 3–11. Let's say that the Publisher Policy file redirects version 1.3.0.0 to version 1.4.0.0 instead of 2.0.0.0. What version number will the client application bind to? The answer is 1.4.0.0. Why? Because after the Publisher Policy file is processed, the requested version number is 1.4.0.0. Therefore, the version redirect in the machine configuration file from version 2.0.0.0 to version 2.1.0.0 will not be processed.

You can turn off support for Publisher Policy files in the Application Configuration file using the publisherPolicy key. You can do this on a per-assembly basis using the publisherPolicy element as a subelement of the dependentAssembly element as follows:

```
<configuration xmlns:asm="urn:schemas-microsoft-
com:asm.v1">
<runtime>
<asm:assemblyBinding>
<asm:dependentAssembly>
<asm:assemblyIdentity name="multifile"
publicKeyToken="8a707be49fd7d8f4" />
<asm:publisherPolicy apply="no" />
</asm:dependentAssembly>
</asm:assemblyBinding>
</runtime>
</configuration>
```

You can also turn off Publisher Policies for all assemblies used by an application using the publisherPolicy element as a subelement of assemblyBinding as follows:

```
<configuration xmlns:asm="urn:schemas-microsoft-
com:asm.v1">
<runtime>
<asm:assemblyBinding>
<asm:publisherPolicy apply="no" />
<asm:dependentAssembly>
<asm:assemblyIdentity name="multifile"
publicKeyToken="8a707be49fd7d8f4" />
</asm:dependentAssembly>
</asm:assemblyBinding>
</runtime>
</configuration>
```

The ability to turn off Publisher Policies is a key improvement over COM provided by .NET. With COM, after you installed a new version of a component, all clients on that machine that use the component will automatically start using the new version of the component. This was a main cause of DLL hell and the brittleness of some COM-based systems. If the new version was not backward compatible with the version that the clients were built against, the system would break. The way that COM worked was essentially equivalent to having publisherPolicies files for a component that redirect every past version to the latest version. The advantage of .NET is that you have the option of overriding the component vendor's backward compatibility matrix as expressed in the Publisher Policy file and either forcing a client to use the version of the component that it was built with or explicitly specifying some other version using a version redirect.

CHECK IF THE DESIRED VERSION IS LOADED ALREADY

The next step in the assembly binding process—checking to see if the desired version of the assembly is already loaded—should be fairly simple to understand. After the Assembly Resolver has determined the final version number of the requested assembly, it checks to see if the requested version of the assembly has already been loaded by the application. If it has, the binding process is successful, and the assembly-binding process stops. If the assembly has not been loaded, the binding process continues.

CHECK THE GAC

The next step in the assembly-binding process is to check the GAC. The GAC stores assemblies that are shared by several applications. To be installed in the GAC, an assembly must have a strong name. You can install assemblies in the GAC by dragging and dropping an assembly into the **WinNT\Assembly** directory, using the gacutil command-line tool in the .NET Framework SDK, or using Windows Installer 2.0 or later. To install an assembly into the GAC using gacutil, run the following command:

```
gacutil -i assembly.dll
```

To remove an assembly from the GAC, execute the following command:

```
gacutil -u assembly.dll
```

In most cases, you will not want to install your assemblies into the GAC. Microsoft recommends that you use private assemblies that are installed in a subdirectory of their client application. Only this approach is absolutely guaranteed to never cause versioning problems. Still, there are good reasons for creating shared assemblies. The assemblies in the .NET Framework class library are all deployed as shared assemblies. These assemblies are fairly large, and they will be used by every .NET application on a particular machine. It would be impractical to install a version of these assemblies for each application, although there is nothing stopping you from doing this if you want to.

In most cases, you will not be creating shared assemblies, so, if the assembly is not found in the GAC, the Assembly Resolver next searches through a configurable set of directories for the assembly. This search is called probing.

PROBING

The probing process starts at an application's AppBase. The AppBase is the directory that contains the configuration file for an application. For an executable, the AppBase is the directory where the executable was started. For a Web application, the AppBase is a little harder to pin down because each directory beneath the root of the virtual directory structure of the application can have a configuration file. Therefore, the AppBase may be different for each page, but, in general, the AppBase will be at the root of the virtual directory structure. Secure Web sites will likely put the pages that need to be protected in a separate directory, and the secure pages will likely have a different configuration file in that secure directory. Therefore, if you went to a nonsecure page, the AppBase will be the root of the virtual directory structure. If you went to a secure page, the AppBase would be the root of the secure part of the virtual directory structure.

The probing process first looks for the assembly in the AppBase itself. If it does not find it there, it looks for a directory beneath the AppBase that has the same name as the assembly. Therefore, with the multifile assembly, and a client that resides at **c:\myclient\myclient.exe**, the Assembly Resolver will look in the following directories:

```
C:\myclient\
C:\myclient\multifile\
```

Within these directories, the CLR will look first for a file with the name **multifile.dll** and then for a file with the name **multifile.exe**. Therefore, the Assembly Resolver will look for an assembly that can satisfy the bind request at the following paths in the order shown:

```
C:\myclient\multifile.dll
C:\myclient\multifile\multifile.dll
C:\myclient\multifile.exe
C:\myclient\multifile\multifile.exe
```

The Assembly Resolver is not smart enough to continue looking if it finds a file with the correct file name and strong name, but the incorrect version number. Therefore, if a client application that resides at **c:\myclient\myclient.exe** requests version 1.3.0.0 of an assembly, and version 1.2.3.4 resides in **c:\myclient** and version 1.3.0.0 resides in **c:\myclient\multifile**\, the Assembly Resolver will fail and throw version mismatch exception back to the client because it will find version 1.2.3.4 first. If you deleted version 1.2.3.4 from the **c:\myclient directory**, the bind would succeed because the Assembly Resolver will eventually find version 1.3.0.0 in **c:\myclient\multifile**\.

In addition to the default probing locations, you can instruct the Assembly Resolver to probe into additional subdirectories beneath the AppBase using the privatePath element in the configuration file as follows:

```
<configuration xmlns:asm="urn:schemas-microsoft-
com:asm.v1">
<runtime>
<asm:assemblyBinding>
<asm:probing privatePath="bin;assemblies" />
<asm:dependentAssembly>
<asm:assemblyIdentity name="multifile"
publicKeyToken="8a707be49fd7d8f4" />
<asm:bindingRedirect oldVersion="1.2.3.4"
newVersion="1.3.0.0" />
</asm:dependentAssembly>
</asm:assemblyBinding>
</runtime>
</configuration>
```

Notice that this configuration file adds the **bin** and **assemblies** subdirectories to the search path, so now the list of directories searched is as follows:

```
C:\myclient\multifile.dll
C:\myclient\multifile\multifile.dll
C:\myclient\bin\multifile.dll
C:\myclient\bin\multifile\multifile.dll
C:\myclient\assemblies\multifile.dll
C:\myclient\assemblies\multifile\multifile.dll
```

```
C:\myclient\multifile.exe
C:\myclient\multifile\multifile.exe
C:\myclient\bin\multifile.exe
C:\myclient\bin\multifile\multifile.exe
C:\myclient\assemblies\multifile.exe
C:\myclient\assemblies\multifile\multifile.exe
```

Notice how the additional subdirectories that I added through the privatePath element (**bin** and **assemblies** in this case) are interpreted by the Assembly Resolver to be subdirectories beneath the AppBase (**C:\myclient** in this case).

The search paths that you have seen so far are the paths that the Assembly Resolver will use if the requested assembly has a neutral culture, which will be true of all code assemblies. If the Assembly Resolver is probing to find a culture-specific assembly (these are called satellite assemblies) that contains localized strings or other resources, the probing sequence is a little different. The Assembly Resolver will append the culture name to the search path.

Note Culture names in .NET use the RFC 1766 standard, which uses the following format: <2-letter language code> – < country/region code>
The lower-case language code is derived from International Organization for Standardization (ISO) 639-1 and the upper-case country/region codes are derived from ISO 3166. Some example culture names are as follows:

Culture Name	Country/Region
en-US	English – United States
en-GB	English – United Kingdom
fr-FR	French – France
fr-CA	French – Canada
es-ES	Spanish – Spain
es-MX	Spanish – Mexico
zh-CHS	Chinese (Simplified)
zh-CHT	Chinese (Traditional)

To see a complete list of culture names, see the documentation for the System.Globalization.CultureInfo class.

Therefore, if I am on a machine where the local culture setting is Spanish – Mexico, the Assembly Resolver will search the following directories for a satellite assembly that contains localized resources:

```
C:\myclient\es-MX\multifile.dll
C:\myclient\es-MX\multifile\multifile.dll
C:\myclient\bin\es-MX\multifile.dll
C:\myclient\bin\es-MX\multifile\multifile.dll
C:\myclient\assemblies\es-MX\multifile.dll
```

```
C:\myclient\assemblies\es-MX\multifile\multifile.dll
C:\myclient\es-MX\multifile.exe
C:\myclient\es-MX\multifile\multifile.exe
C:\myclient\bin\es-MX\multifile.exe
C:\myclient\bin\es-MX\multifile\multifile.exe
C:\myclient\assemblies\es-MX\multifile.exe
C:\myclient\assemblies\es-MX\multifile\multifile.exe
```

ASSEMBLY BINDING IN DEVELOPMENT MODE

The assembly-binding process makes it complicated to develop shared assemblies. When you compile a new version of a shared assembly, you will need to remember to remove the old version from the GAC and install the new version into the GAC. This is obviously time consuming and error prone. To make development of shared assemblies easier, you can use the CLR's development mode. In this mode, the CLR will first look for assemblies in the directory specified by the DEVPATH environment variable. You can set this environment variable to point to the directory where your development tool writes your compiled assemblies. You must also tell the CLR to run in development mode. You do this by adding the developmentMode tag to your machine configuration file. Simply add the following element to your machine.config file:

```
<configuration>
//… the rest of the configuration file is omitted.
<runtime>
      <developmentMode developerInstallation="true" />
   </runtime>
</configuration>
```

Because this setting is configured in **machine.config**, after it is set, it will apply to all applications currently running on that machine. Remember that this mode should only be used during development. The CLR does not do version checking when you are running in development mode.

DEBUGGING THE ASSEMBLY-BINDING PROCESS

Now that you understand the assembly-binding process, you are probably thinking that it must be difficult to debug. Fortunately, the .NET Framework SDK comes with a command-line tool called the Assembly Binding Log Viewer, which has the rather odd executable file name of **fuslogvw.exe**. You can find this tool in the “bin” directory of your .NET Framework SDK installation. On my machine it resides at:

```
D:\Program Files\Microsoft Visual Studio
.NET\FrameworkSDK\Bin
```

If you run this tool, you will see the window shown in Figure 3–12.

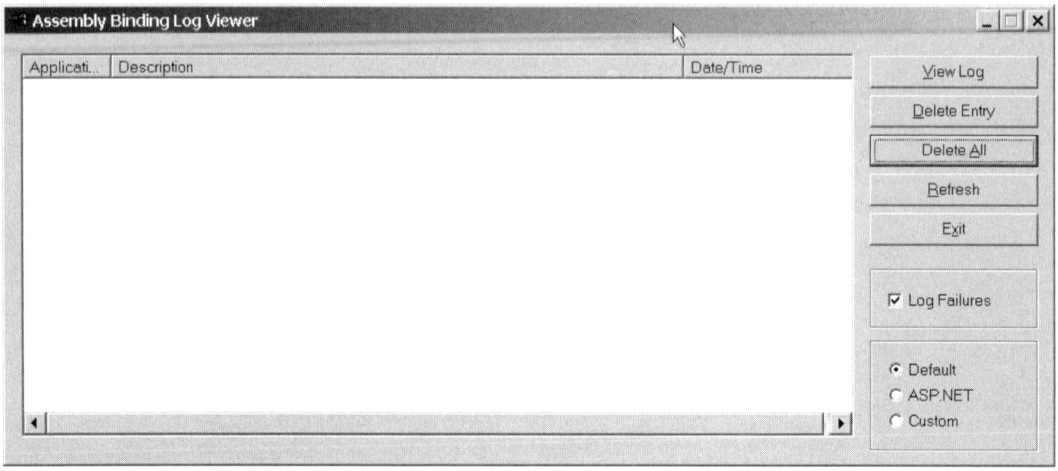

FIGURE 3–12 The Assembly Binding Log Viewer.

As long as the Log Failures checkbox is set, this tool will log all binding failures. Figure 3–13 shows the entry that you will see when a binding error occurs.

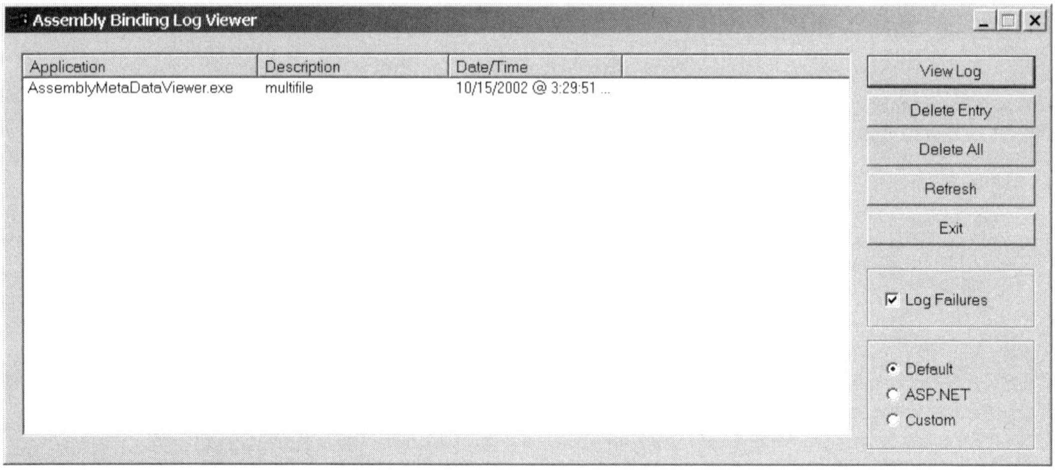

FIGURE 3–13 The Assembly Binding Log Viewer.

If you either double-click the entry that appears in the Assembly Binding Log Viewer or select the entry and click the View Log button, you will see detailed binding error information similar to the following (assuming the bind failed, of course):

```
*** Assembly Binder Log Entry  (1/16/2002 @ 12:33:01 AM)
***

The operation failed.
Bind result: hr = 0x80131040. No description available.

Assembly manager loaded from:
D:\WINNT\Microsoft.NET\Framework\v1.0.3328\fusion.dll
Running under executable
C:\Alan\books\dotnetbook\demos\chapter3\TestVersioningPolic
y\bin\Debug\TestVersioningPolicy.exe
--- A detailed error log follows.

=== Pre-bind state information ===
LOG: DisplayName = multifile, Version=1.2.3.4,
Culture=neutral, PublicKeyToken=8a707be49fd7d8f4
 (Fully-specified)
LOG: Appbase =
C:\Alan\books\dotnetbook\demos\chapter3\TestVersioningPolic
y\bin\Debug\
LOG: Initial PrivatePath = NULL
LOG: Dynamic Base = NULL
LOG: Cache Base = NULL
LOG: AppName = NULL
Calling assembly : TestVersioningPolicy,
Version=1.0.737.3124, Culture=neutral, PublicKeyToken=null.
---
LOG: Processing DEVPATH.
LOG: DEVPATH is not set. Falling through to regular bind.
LOG: Private path hint found in configuration file:
bin;assemblies.
LOG: Host configuration file not found.
LOG: Redirect found in application configuration file
1.2.3.4 -> 1.3.0.0.
LOG: Publisher policy file is not found.
LOG: Using machine configuration file from
D:\WINNT\Microsoft.NET\Framework\v1.0.3328\config\machine.c
onfig.
LOG: Post-policy reference: multifile, Version=1.3.0.0,
Culture=neutral, PublicKeyToken=8a707be49fd7d8f4
LOG: Cache Lookup was unsuccessful.
LOG: Attempting download of new URL file:///C:/Alan/books/
dotnetbook/demos/chapter3/TestVersioningPolicy/bin/Debug/
multifile.DLL.
LOG: Attempting download of new URL file:///C:/Alan/books/
dotnetbook/demos/chapter3/TestVersioningPolicy/bin/Debug/
multifile/multifile.DLL.
LOG: Assembly download was successful. Attempting setup of
file:
C:\Alan\books\dotnetbook\demos\chapter3\TestVersioningPolic
```

```
y\bin\Debug\multifile\multifile.DLL
LOG: Entering run-from-source setup phase.
WRN: Comparing the assembly name resulted in the mismatch:
Minor Version
ERR: The assembly reference did not match the assembly
definition found.
ERR: Failed to complete setup of assembly (hr =
0x80131040). Probing terminated.
```

This particular binding log shows the error that you will see when the assembly resolver finds an assembly with the wrong version number. In this case, the application configuration file contained a redirect from version 1.2.3.4 to version 1.3.0.0, but the application's directory contained version 1.2.3.4 of the assembly. By default, the Assembly Binding Log Viewer will not display any information if the bind was successful. You can get the Assembly Binding Log Viewer to display information even for successful binds by adding the following key to the registry and then setting its value equal to 1:

```
HKEY_LOCAL_MACHINE\SOFTWARE\Microsoft\Fusion\ForceLog
```

This will cause the Assembly Binding Log Viewer to display information for all assembly binds. The following output shows the result of a successful bind:

```
*** Assembly Binder Log Entry  (1/16/2002 @ 12:28:18 AM)
***

The operation was successful.
Bind result: hr = 0x0. The operation completed
successfully.

Assembly manager loaded from:
D:\WINNT\Microsoft.NET\Framework\v1.0.3328\fusion.dll
Running under executable
C:\Alan\books\dotnetbook\demos\chapter3\TestVersioningPolic
y\bin\Debug\TestVersioningPolicy.exe
--- A detailed error log follows.

=== Pre-bind state information ===
LOG: DisplayName = multifile, Version=1.2.3.4,
Culture=neutral, PublicKeyToken=8a707be49fd7d8f4
 (Fully-specified)
LOG: Appbase =
C:\Alan\books\dotnetbook\demos\chapter3\TestVersioningPolic
y\bin\Debug\
LOG: Initial PrivatePath = NULL
LOG: Dynamic Base = NULL
LOG: Cache Base = NULL
LOG: AppName = NULL
Calling assembly : TestVersioningPolicy,
```

```
Version=1.0.737.3124, Culture=neutral, PublicKeyToken=null.
===

LOG: Processing DEVPATH.
LOG: DEVPATH is not set. Falling through to regular bind.
LOG: Private path hint found in configuration file:
bin;assemblies.
LOG: Host configuration file not found.
LOG: Redirect found in application configuration file
1.2.3.4 -> 1.3.0.0.
LOG: Publisher policy file is not found.
LOG: Using machine configuration file from
D:\WINNT\Microsoft.NET\Framework\v1.0.3328\config\machine.c
onfig.
LOG: Post-policy reference: multifile, Version=1.3.0.0,
Culture=neutral, PublicKeyToken=8a707be49fd7d8f4
LOG: Cache Lookup was unsuccessful.
LOG: Attempting download of new URL file:///C:/Alan/books/
dotnetbook/demos/chapter3/TestVersioningPolicy/bin/Debug/
multifile.DLL.
LOG: Attempting download of new URL file:///C:/Alan/books/
dotnetbook/demos/chapter3/TestVersioningPolicy/bin/Debug/
multifile/multifile.DLL.
LOG: Assembly download was successful. Attempting setup of
file:
C:\Alan\books\dotnetbook\demos\chapter3\TestVersioningPolic
y\bin\Debug\multifile\multifile.DLL
LOG: Entering run-from-source setup phase.
```

You can interface with the assembly-binding process programmatically through the Load method in the **System.Reflection.Assembly** class. This method takes an assembly name. The assembly name can be a full name like the following:

```
multifile, Version=1.3.0.0, Culture=neutral,
PublicKeyToken=8a707be49fd7d8f4
```

or it can be a partial name like the following:

```
multifile
```

With either name, it will load the requested assembly. The source code for this book includes an example program in the Chapter 3 directory called the AssemblyMetaDataViewer that shows you how to call the Load method in **System.Reflection.Assembly**. If you download and run the AssemblyMetaDataViewer application, you will see the window shown in Figure 3–14.

You can then type in either a full or partial name and click the Load button. Assuming the application is able to bind to the assembly, it will display the metadata for the assembly and the location where it loaded the assembly from. The code behind the Load button is as follows:

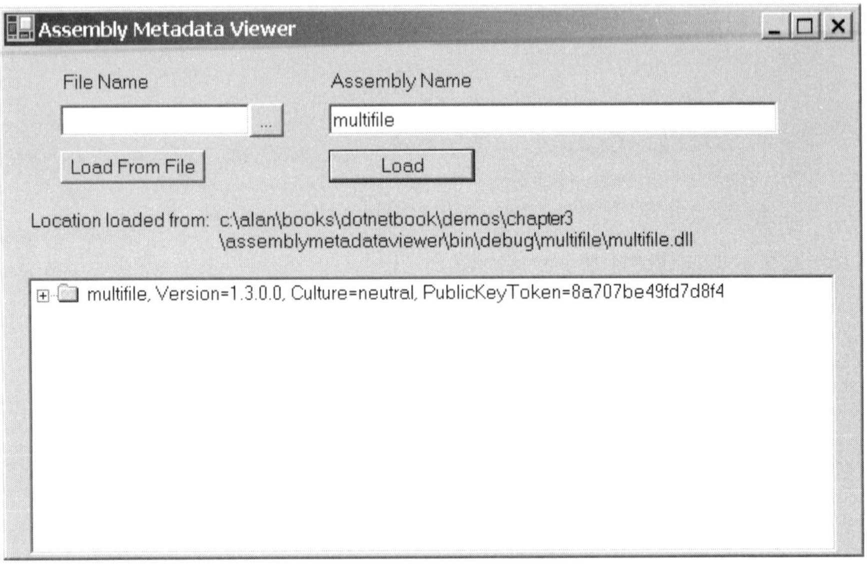

FIGURE 3–14 *The Assembly Metadata Viewer.*

```
private void cmdLoad_Click(object sender,
    System.EventArgs e)
{
    System.Reflection.Assembly anAssembly;
    try
    {
        anAssembly=Assembly.Load(txtAssemblyName.Text);
        lblLocation.Text=anAssembly.Location;
    // The LoadMetadata method populates the tree view
    // with the meta-data for the assembly.
        LoadMetadata(anAssembly);
    }
    catch (Exception ex)
    {
        MessageBox.Show(ex.Message);
    }
}
```

The Assembly Metadata Viewer together with the Assembly Binding Log Viewer are the only tools that you need to understand the assembly-binding process. You can type in an assembly name in the Assembly Metadata Viewer and then see the location where the application found the assembly. You can play around with configuration files, publisher policies, GAC, and probing paths and see how the chosen assembly changes. This is how I understood the assembly-binding process. If the bind fails, you can then use the Assembly Binding Log Viewer to see why.

Loading the Code in an Assembly

The Assembly Resolver takes either a full or partial assembly name and turns it into a physical path where an assembly that can satisfy the binding request resides. The Assembly Loader is responsible for actually loading this assembly into memory. You can interface with the Assembly Loader using the LoadFrom method in the **System.Reflection.Assembly** class. The AssemblyMetaDataViewer example in this chapter also allows you to test the LoadFrom method. To test the method, enter a path into the File Name edit box (See Figure 3–14) or click the Browse... button, choose a file, and then click the Load From File button. The code behind this button is shown here:

```
private void cmdLoadFromFile_Click(object sender,
    System.EventArgs e)
{
    try
    {
        mSelectedAssembly=
            Assembly.LoadFrom(txtFileName.Text);
        LoadMetadata(mSelectedAssembly);
    }
    catch (Exception ex)
    {
        MessageBox.Show(ex.Message);
    }
}
```

Executing the Code in an Assembly

After the assembly is loaded, the CLR's next job is to execute the code in the assembly. With native x86 code, the execution process was almost exclusively the job of the CPU. With managed code modules, things become a lot more complicated because the code in an assembly is MSIL code that will not execute on any CPU. The code must be compiled into x86 code before it can execute. One approach to this problem would be for the CLR to invoke a compiler, which would compile all the code into native x86 before it executed anything. There are a number of problems with this approach. The first problem is that, in most cases, you would compile a lot of code that was never used. Typically, when you use an application, you only use a small amount of the code in the application. Think about Microsoft Word for instance. Microsoft Word has several hundred commands and (probably) several million lines of code. In any given session, you will most likely use only a few dozen commands and a small fraction of the code in the application. Compiling all of the code in this application would be wasteful if you only use a small portion of the code at any time. A better solution is to compile only the code that you need when you need it. The execution process for .NET assemblies, which is called the VES, compiles the MSIL code in the assembly as it is needed. This process is called JIT compilation.

The process begins when you run a managed code executable. Each managed code executable will contain a small, unmanaged stub function that is the entry point for the executable. This stub function loads the execution engine of the CLR (**MSCorEE.dll**) and calls a method called _CorExeMain in the execution engine. This function will initialize the runtime and then call the managed code entry point of the executable. Remember that the managed code entry point will be a static member function called main in a class. Therefore, before the runtime can execute the managed code entry point, it must load the class that contains the main method.

Note You can only have one main method in a managed code executable. If you try to compile an executable that has more than one static class method called main, you will receive an error that tells you that the executable has more than one entry point defined.

The class loader in the CLR will lay out the class in memory and insert a small stub function for each of the methods of the class. This stub method invokes the JIT compiler to compile the MSIL code for the method. After the compiler has compiled the method, the CLR will replace the stub method with the compiled native code. Therefore, the next time the CLR calls the method, there is no need to compile the method again. The CLR can simply start executing the native code.

As it runs, the main method will call other methods in the class or instantiate other classes. The CLR will load these classes and lay them out in memory with stub functions that compile the MSIL code for the method when they are called. The metadata in the executable will contain a reference to any assemblies that the executable was built with, and, as soon as you use a class that resides in an external assembly, the CLR will load that assembly and then load the class, and the process repeats. More and more code is compiled as you run the executable.

On resource-constrained platforms, the CLR will support code pitching. If the host machine does not have enough memory to hold all of the compiled code that it needs in memory, it can simply toss the compiled native code by replacing it with the stub function, which is more compact. The next time the CLR calls the method, the stub function will compile the MSIL back to native code again.

You're probably thinking that this JIT compilation process must be slow. It's actually much faster than you might think for a number of reasons. First, the JIT compiler is converting MSIL code (not source code) to native code.

The MSIL code has already been compiled and checked for correct syntax by your language compiler. Second, MSIL code is structurally similar to native machine language, so the compilation process is extremely fast. Also, consider that you are only going to pay a penalty with JIT compilation on startup. On interactive applications, you will very quickly reach a steady state where all of the code that you are currently using has been compiled. Users will only notice a slight delay when they use a new feature for the first time in their session.

Of course, there are still going to be some times when startup is critical. For these situations, there is the Native Image Generator.

The Native Image Generator

The Native Image Generator (ngen.exe) is a command-line tool that is included with the .NET Framework SDK. It allows you to precompile .NET assemblies so that you will not incur the performance penalty of JIT –compilation. The Native Image Generator stores the compiled code in the native image cache. The CLR searches this cache for precompiled code before it compiles the MSIL code in an assembly. Even if you use the Native Image Generator, the original assembly with the MSIL still has to be present on disk. If the compiled code in the Native Image Cache differs from the requested assembly in any way, the CLR will revert back to JIT compiling the MSIL code in the assembly. Ngen will store a unique identifier called a MVID along with the code that it compiled in the native image cache. When the CLR fetches compiled code from the native image cache, it will check the MVID of the cached code against the MVID of the assembly that resides on disk. If they do not match, that means that the compiled code in the native image cache was not generated from the assembly that the CLR tried to bind to. In this case, the CLR will fall back to JIT compiling the code in the assembly. When you precompile an assembly using Ngen, you have the option of specifying whether the code that it creates has debugging or profiling information included. If the CLR is running in a debugging or profiling mode, it will fall back to using JIT compilation unless the code in the native image cache also has debugging and profiling information included. You can include debugging and/or profiling information in an assembly that is compiled with Ngen using the /debug, /debugopt, and /prof options.

Garbage Collection

Dynamically allocated memory is the bane of most programmers' existence. Although you need heap memory to write most non-trivial applications, managing this memory correctly is an error-prone nightmare. Only the most careful and diligent programmers get it right, and failure to do so results in applications that leak memory (because the programmer forgot to free memory that is no longer being used) or that crash sporadically because the programmers have deallocated memory that is still needed by their application. These two bugs are the two biggest time-wasters in software development for programmers and for testers who spend countless hours finding and documenting these bugs. They also take a huge toll on the productivity of end-users who waste countless hours dealing with the results of such bugs: brittle software that crashes or gradually eats up all the memory on a client until it or some other application crashes.

The basic idea of garbage collection is that programmers should be able to allocate as much memory as they see fit (within reason of course), and, when they are not using a block of memory, the system should simply reclaim it. In this model, there is no need for delete, dealloc, or release functions.

The managed heap in the CLR uses garbage collection to automatically free memory that is no longer being used. As a programmer using the .NET Framework, you don't have to do anything special to use the managed heap. You simply allocate instances of objects from the managed heap using the new operator in your language of choice. When a request for more memory cannot be satisfied with the available memory, the CLR's garbage collection algorithm will run (or you can explicitly run the garbage collection algorithm by calling the Collect method on the **System.GC** class). The garbage collector figures out which blocks of memory are no longer being used by your application, frees that memory, and compacts the used memory into a contiguous block. The rest of this section explains how the .NET Framework's garbage collection algorithm works.

The first premise that you must accept before you can understand garbage collection is that, in order for a block of memory to be used (now or in the future) by an application, that memory must be reachable through a pointer/reference, that is, at least one pointer/reference must point to it. If there are no pointers/references pointing to a block of memory, it can no longer be used by an application. COM took advantage of this fact to implement its life cycle management scheme. With COM, each object was responsible for maintaining a count of the references that currently point to it by implementing the AddRef and Release methods in the IUnknown interface. Consumers of a COM object use the AddRef method in IUknown to increment the reference count and the Release method to decrement the reference count. The object is supposed to delete itself when its reference count goes to zero. The problem with this approach is that it is manual. In order for COM reference counting to work correctly, component developers must implement the IUnknown interface correctly, and consumers of those components must use the interface correctly.

Garbage collection takes us error-prone developers out of the memory management process. The CLR determines if a block of memory can still be used or not by first assuming that all memory is garbage. It then starts at the roots of the application and builds a graph of all the objects that are reachable from the roots. The roots of an application include static and global pointers, local variables, method parameters on the stack, and even CPU registers. If an object is not part of this graph, it is unreachable from any reference/pointer within the application and is therefore garbage. The garbage collector then compacts all the nongarbage objects by shifting them down in memory using the memcpy function so that no gaps are in the heap.

This process is best illustrated by Figure 3–15. In the scenario illustrated by this picture, Object 1 is currently loaded in a CPU register and contains a pointer to Object 7. Objects 3 and 4 are pointed to by stack pointers (either parameters to a method or local variables to a method). Object 5 is referenced by a static object pointer. Object 5 also contains a pointer to Object 3. Objects 2 and 6 are not currently pointed to by any of the roots or any objects reachable from the roots, so they are garbage. The garbage collector will start at the roots and build a graph. Objects 2 and 6 will obviously not be in the graph because they are not referenced by the roots or any objects reachable from the roots. The garbage collector will then remove all the gaps in memory and position the next object pointer that contains the address of the next available block of memory after Object 7, as shown in Figure 3–16.

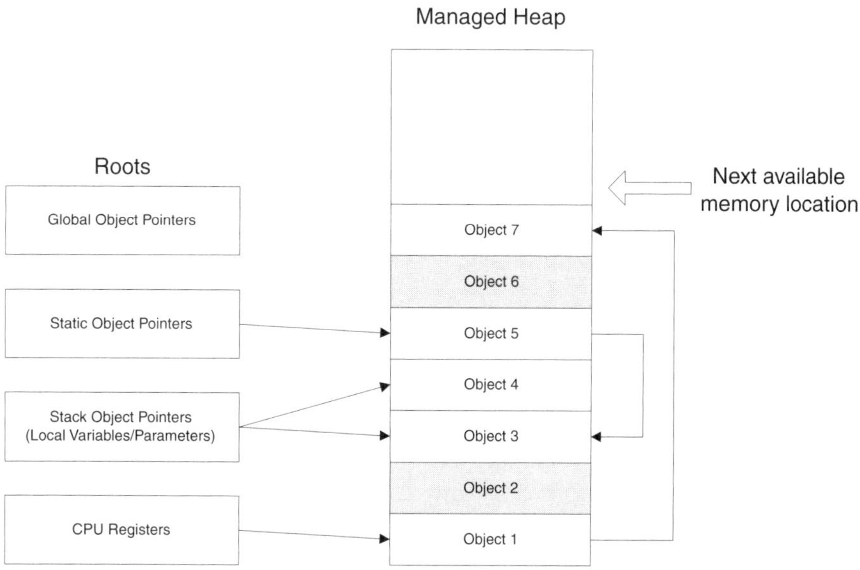

FIGURE 3–15 *The heap prior to garbage collection.*

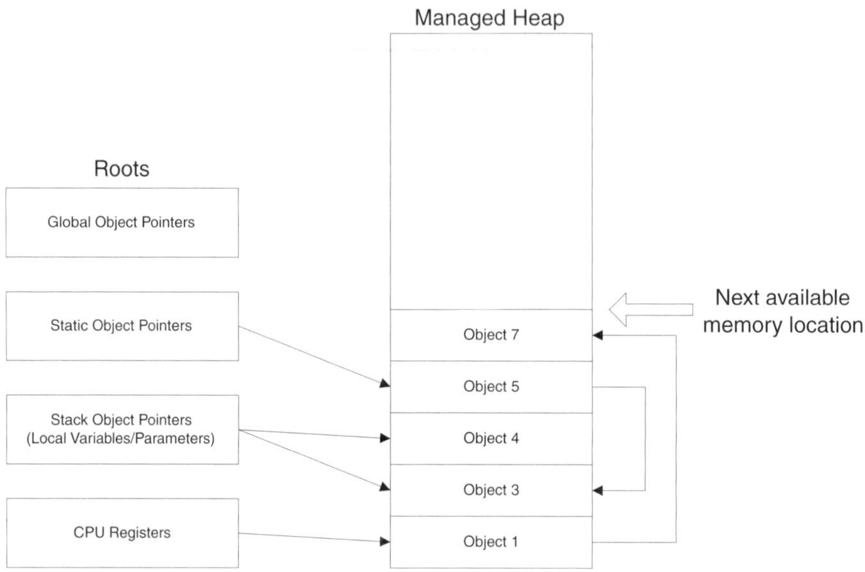

FIGURE 3–16 *After garbage collection.*

For performance reasons, the garbage collector may elect not to compact memory if most of the objects survive the collection. The CLR also maintains, for performance reasons, a separate managed heap for large objects. Objects in this heap are garbage collected like the regular heap, but, to avoid copying large objects, the CLR does not compact this heap.

So far so good, but there's actually a lot more to the garbage collection algorithm than this simple explanation. First, many objects contain cleanup logic that must be run when the object is destroyed. For instance, if a business object holds a connection to a database, you may want the connection to be closed when the object is destroyed. Most object-oriented programming languages support the notion of a destructor, which is a method that gets called automatically when the object is destroyed. Cleanup logic, such as closing a database connection or freeing any other resource used by the object, is usually placed in this method. The cleanup method in the .NET Framework is called Finalize, and the process is called Finalization. Curiously, the C# language uses the same destructor syntax as C++, and it also refers to its cleanup method as a destructor. C# destructors also will automatically call the destructor of their base class. The Finalize method in other .NET programming languages does not do this. The destructor for a C# class is declared as follows:

```
public class Manager : Employee
{
```

```
    public Manager(int id,string name,decimal salary,
        decimal bonus) : base(id,name,salary)
    {
        this.mBonus=bonus;
    }
    public override decimal GetSalary()
    {
        return base.GetSalary()+mBonus;
    }
    ~Manager()
    {
        // This destructor will also call the destructor
        // in its base class.
        MessageBox.Show(
            "Finalize method called in Manager.");
    }
    private decimal mBonus;
}
```

Therefore, in this case, where I have a **Manager** class that inherits from an **Employee** class, the destructor for the **Employee** class will be called immediately after the destructor for the **Manager** class.

You can use this new knowledge of MSIL and ildasm to see what is really going on behind the scenes when you create a destructor. Here is the (slightly simplified) MSIL code for the destructor in the **Manager** class:

```
void Finalize()
{
  .try
  {
    IL_0000:  ldstr   "Finalize method called in Manager."
    IL_0005:  call    MessageBox::Show(string)
    IL_000a:  pop
    IL_000b:  leave.s    IL_0014
  }  // end .try
  finally
  {
    IL_000d:  ldarg.0
    IL_000e:  call    gctest.Employee::Finalize()
    IL_0013:  endfinally
  }  // end handler
  IL_0014:  ret
} // end of method Manager::Finalize
```

Notice that the method is actually called Finalize in the generated MSIL code. The logic in the Manager destructor displays a message box, and then it calls the Finalize in the **Employee** base class of the **Manager** class. In beta 1 and 2 of the .NET Framework, you had to override the Finalize method in the **System.Object** class to implement a cleanup method in C#. The destructor syntax and terminology is unique to the release version of C#. Visual Basic .NET still uses a Finalize method in the release version of the .NET Framework. The following code shows how you would implement a Finalize method in Visual Basic .NET:

```
Public Class Class1
    Sub New()
        MessageBox.Show("Constructor called")
    End Sub
    Protected Overrides Sub Finalize()
        MessageBox.Show("Destructor called")
    End Sub
End Class
```

Note Even though Microsoft in the release version of .NET decided to use the term destructor with C#, I prefer a term that I saw in the .NET Framework SDK docs, finalize destructor, and this is the term that I will use throughout the rest of this chapter.

In order to implement finalize destructors, the CLR maintains a pair of queues called the Finalization and the Freachable queue. The Finalization queue contains a list of all nongarbage objects that have Finalize destructors. The Freachable queue contains a list of garbage objects that are waiting for a special runtime thread to execute their finalize destructors. When an object that has a Finalize destructor is instantiated, a pointer to that object is inserted into the Finalization queue; this indicates to the CLR that this object will require Finalization when it is destroyed. If an object that has a destructor is determined to be garbage when the garbage collector runs, the pointer to the object is removed from the Finalization queue and appended to the Freachable queue; this indicates that the object is no longer being used and is waiting for a special thread to run its finalize destructor. The CLR does not run the Finalize destructor immediately because poorly written Finalize destructors may take a long time to execute and cause the garbage collection process to take an unacceptably long period of time. An object that has a Finalize destructor will actually survive a garbage collection in a sort of zombie state, even if the garbage collector determined that the object is garbage. After the garbage collector runs, the object will be referenced by the Freachable queue which is considered to be a root. At some point, a special thread in the CLR will wake up and start calling the Finalize destructors on all of the objects in the Freachable queue. After this thread calls the Finalize destructor on an object, it will remove the reference to the object from the Freachable queue. Now the object is truly garbage, and, the next time the garbage collector runs, the memory occupied by the object will be reclaimed.

There are a few key points to glean from this explanation: (1) Finalize destructors are expensive. A class that has a Finalize destructor will actually require two garbage collections before its memory can be reclaimed. Therefore, think carefully before you add one to your classes. (2) You should not make any assumptions about the thread that your Finalize destructor will run on. It will run on a unique thread provided by the CLR, so you will need to avoid accessing thread-local resources in a Finalize destructor. (3) The actual time when a Finalize destructor will run is indeterminate. The CLR will not call the Finalize destructor on a class until (a) the garbage collector runs, (b) the object is determined to be garbage, and (c) the special thread assigned to executing Finalize destructors completes its work. The Finalize destructor may run any time from when the last reference to the object is removed to when the application shuts down. This is totally different than what most developers are used to. With languages like C++, the destructor is called for a stack object as soon as it goes out of scope; the destructor is called for a heap object when you use the "delete" operator on the object. Because you cannot know when a Finalize destructor will run, it is unwise to leave the cleanup or reclamation of scarce resources to a Finalize destructor. For instance, in most cases in the .NET Framework, it is a bad idea to close a database connection in a Finalize destructor. This is a common thing that people (myself included) did in C++. If your object uses scarce resources like database connections, you should instead put the logic to close the database connection in a Dispose or Close method. By convention, you should use a Close method if the object may be used again after the call to the Close method. You should use Dispose if the object will not be used again. There actually is an IDisposable interface in the System namespace that contains a Dispose method. You should implement this interface to provide your Dispose method. The recommended semantics for this method are as follows: A Dispose method should release all resources that the object on which it was called owns. It should also remove the object from the Finalization queue so its destructor will not get called. Therefore, if you had an **Employee** class that used a database connection, you would implement the IDisposable interface as follows:

```
public class Employee : IDisposable
{
    public Employee(int id,string name,decimal salary)
    {
      this.mName=name;
      this.mID=id;
      this.mSalary=salary;
    }
    public int ID
    {
      get { return mID; }
      set { mID=value; }
    }
    public virtual void Dispose()
    {
```

```
        Dispose(true);
        GC.SuppressFinalize(this);
    }
    protected virtual void Dispose(bool disposing)
    {
        if(!disposed)
        {
        // if disposing = true cleanup
// managed resources

// Close database connection here...

        }
        disposed = true;
    }
    public string Name
    {
        get { return mName; }
        set { mName=value; }
    }
    public virtual decimal GetSalary()
    {
        return mSalary;
    }
    ~Employee()
    {
        Dispose(false);
    }
    private string mName;
    int mID;
    decimal mSalary;
    private bool disposed = false;
}
```

This code shows the recommended design pattern for implementing the IDisposable interface. There are a number of reasons why this code is so complicated. First, remember that once you implement the IDisposable interface, your class must be able to handle 2 different "cleanup" scenarios. One is where the finalize destructor is called by the garbage collector, in this case you will need to close the database connection (or free any other unmanaged [non-garbage collected] resources) there is no need to cleanup managed resources, the garbage collector will do that for you. The other scenario is where the user has explicitly called the Dispose method. In this scenario you should close the database connection (or free any other unmanaged resources) and cleanup any managed resources—if necessary. Microsoft recommends that you put both the managed and unmanaged cleanup logic in a protected, virtual method called Dispose that takes a boolean parameter; this method is an overload of the Dispose method from the IDisposable interface.

If you call this method with "true" specified for the parameter it should cleanup both the managed and unmanaged resources, if you pass in "false" it should cleanup just the unmanaged resources. You should call this method with "false" specified for the parameter from the destructor (the garbage collector will handle the cleanup of managed resources). You should call this method from the IDisposable.Dispose method with "true" specified for the parameter, because the method call there is not made within the context of a garbage collection. The IDisposable.Dispose method should also call the SuppressFinalize method on the **GC** class. The SuppressFinalize method will remove the object from the Finalization queue, so its Finalization method will not be called. The Finalization call is no longer necessary because I have already disposed of the object.

The **GC** class in the System namespace contains methods for interacting with the garbage collector, and it includes methods for removing an object from the Finalization list (SuppressFinalize) and re-adding an object to the Finalization queue (ReRegisterForFinalize). You will typically only call ReRegisterForFinalize if you decide to resurrect an object during its Finalize method. Remember I mentioned that an object with a Finalize destructor will exist in a zombie state after the garbage collector has determined that it is garbage. The garbage collector will remove the object's entry from the Finalization queue, and add it to the Freachable queue. After the runtime thread in the CLR executes the Finalize destructor, it is possible that the Finalize destructor could resurrect the object by assigning the object's "this" pointer to a global or static variable. The garbage collector will not collect the object the next time it runs because it will be reachable from a root. Of course, the object is in a weird state now because its Finalize destructor has been called. Even if you reinitialize the object's state, you still have a problem, because its entry has been removed from the Finalization queue, Finalization will not be called again. You can remedy this situation by calling ReRegisterForFinalize, which will add the object's entry back to the Finalization queue. In almost all cases, resurrecting an object like this is a bad idea, and it should be avoided.

The CLR will determine when to run the garbage collector, but if you want to explicitly start a garbage collection, the **GC** class contains a method called Collect that allows you to explicitly cause the garbage collector to run at a particular time. There are two forms of this method: one takes no parameters as follows:

```
GC.Collect();
```

The other form of the method takes an integer parameter, which is the generation that you want to collect:

```
int gen=0;
GC.Collect(gen);
```

Note The .NET garbage collector is highly optimized and in most cases you are better off letting it decide when to perform a garbage collection rather than trying to do it manually.

Generations are a technique that the garbage collector uses to optimize the garbage collector for speed. The basic ideas underlying generations are that (1) it is faster to compact a portion of the managed heap instead of the entire heap, (2) newer objects will have shorter lifetimes, and (3) older objects will have longer lifetimes. Of course, these three points aren't always true, but they have been found through research to be true for most applications. To take advantage of these ideas, the garbage collector in the CLR assumes that all new objects are in generation 0. When the garbage collector runs, any objects that survive the collection are considered to be in generation 1. Any new objects that are created after the garbage collection go into generation 0. When another garbage collection needs to occur, the garbage collector has two choices: (1) It can collect only generation 0, or (2) it can collect generations 0 and 1 (actually, there are three choices because there is also a generation 2, which I will talk about shortly). In most circumstances, the garbage collector will only attempt to garbage-collect generation 0. The exact algorithm that the garbage collector uses to determine whether to garbage-collect only generation 0 or 0 and 1 is obviously a Microsoft secret, but, in general, the garbage collector will only collect generation 1 If performing a garbage collection on generation 0 does not free up enough memory to satisfy a memory allocation request. Any objects that survive a collection on generation 0 and 1 are promoted to generation 2. There are again more heuristics built into the garbage collector that determine when it will run a collection on all three generations. Any objects that survive a collection on all 3 generations will remain in generation 2 because the garbage collector currently only supports three generations (0,1, and 2). Microsoft does seem to be leaving the door open to support more generations in the future because the **GC** class in the System namespace does support a MaxGeneration property that you can use to determine the highest generation number. This method currently returns 2 but this may change in the future.

The last garbage collector-related topic that I will discuss is weak references. Weak references give you a way to maintain a reference to an object, while allowing the garbage collector to collect the object if a collection occurs. Normal references are called strong references because, if the garbage collector runs while you are holding a strong reference to an object, the object will not be collected. In order to use the object pointed to by a weak reference, you must first obtain a strong reference from the weak reference. If the garbage collector has collected the object, the conversion from a weak reference to a strong reference will fail, so you will have to re-create the object. Weak references are good for objects that take up a lot of memory, but are easy to re-create. A good example is a directory tree for a file system. A directory tree can be extremely large and therefore may take a lot of time to re-create. For performance reasons, you may like to keep this tree in memory, but requiring the system to keep this tree in memory will put a lot of memory pressure on your system. So you may choose to keep the directory tree in memory, but still allow the garbage collector to reclaim the memory used by the tree if it needs to. Let's look at some code that should make this much clearer.

You can create a weak reference on an object using the code shown in the cmdCreateWeak_Click method that follows. Notice that I first check to see that the object has not been collected using the IsAlive property on the **WeakReference** class before I attempt to use the Manager object.

```
public class Form1 : System.Windows.Forms.Form
{
    private WeakReference wkRef;
    // Other code omitted from this class.
    //...
    private void cmdCreateWeak_Click(object sender,
        System.EventArgs e)
    {
        Manager mgr=new Manager(1,"Alan Gordon",500,100);
        wkRef=new WeakReference(mgr);
    }
    private void cmdUseWeak_Click(object sender,
        System.EventArgs e)
    {
        if (wkRef.IsAlive)
        {
            aManager=(Manager)wkRef.Target;
            MessageBox.Show("The object is alive");
            // Use the manager object
            // ...
        }
        else
            MessageBox.Show(
                "The manager has been collected");
    }
}
```

You can specify a Boolean trackResurrection parameter in the WeakReference constructor as follows:

```
wkRef=new WeakReference(mgr,true);
```

If you specify false for this second parameter (the default), the WeakReference will not track the underlying object (that is, the IsAlive property will return false) after its Finalize Destructor has run. This is called a short weak reference. If you specify true for the trackResurrection parameter, the WeakReference will continue to track the object while it exists in the zombie state after its Finalize Destructor has run, but before a second garbage collection has finished off the object. This is called a long weak reference. Essentially, specifying true for the trackResurrection property allows you to specify whether you can use the WeakReference to resurrect an object whose Finalize method has been run.

Code Access Security

In the modern computing environment, you may receive code from several different sources: from your local hard drive, from your corporate intranet, from a network drive, from email, or from the Internet. Depending on where the code originates from and other properties of the code, such as who authored the code, you may want to assign different permissions to the code. For instance, if the code originated from your hard drive, you may want to allow it to do just about anything. If it originated from your local intranet or from a network drive on your corporate intranet, you may not want to prevent the code from writing to your local files, but you may allow it to read your files. If the code came from the Internet, you probably would want to prevent it from doing most things.

The Code Access Security functionality in .NET provides you with the capability to define, in a very precise way, the permissions that code will be granted based on evidence that includes (among other things) the location where the code originated from. The basic idea is that certain code groups with membership conditions are based on evidence that the CLR can gather about the assembly. This evidence includes the zone, site, or URL where the assembly originated from, who published the assembly, the strong name of the assembly, the hash of the assembly, or whether the assembly came from the same directory or a child directory of its client application. Each code group has a permission set associated with it. A permission set is a named set of permissions that you can grant as a single unit to a code group. Some of the individual permissions that comprise a permission set include the following:

- Whether the code can read or write files
- Whether the code can read or write environment variables
- Whether the code can access isolated storage, or access the local DNS server, or open a window on the user interface of the client
- Whether the code is allowed to print

If an assembly matches the membership condition for a code group, it is granted all of the permissions in the permission set associated with that code group.

When the CLR loads an assembly, it gathers the evidence associated with the assembly, that is, where the code originated from (local hard disk, intranet, Internet, and so forth), its publisher, hash and strong name, and so forth and presents this evidence to the security policy in effect on the machine. The security policy is the set of rules that the CLR uses to determine which permissions to grant to an assembly based on its presented evidence as shown in Figure 3–17.

The steps that the CLR performs to determine the permissions that it will grant to an assembly are as follows:

1. Gather the evidence associated with the assembly.
2. Present this evidence to the security policy that is in effect on the machine.
3. The security policy determines the list of matching code groups for the assembly and, from that, determines the list of permission sets to grant to the assembly.

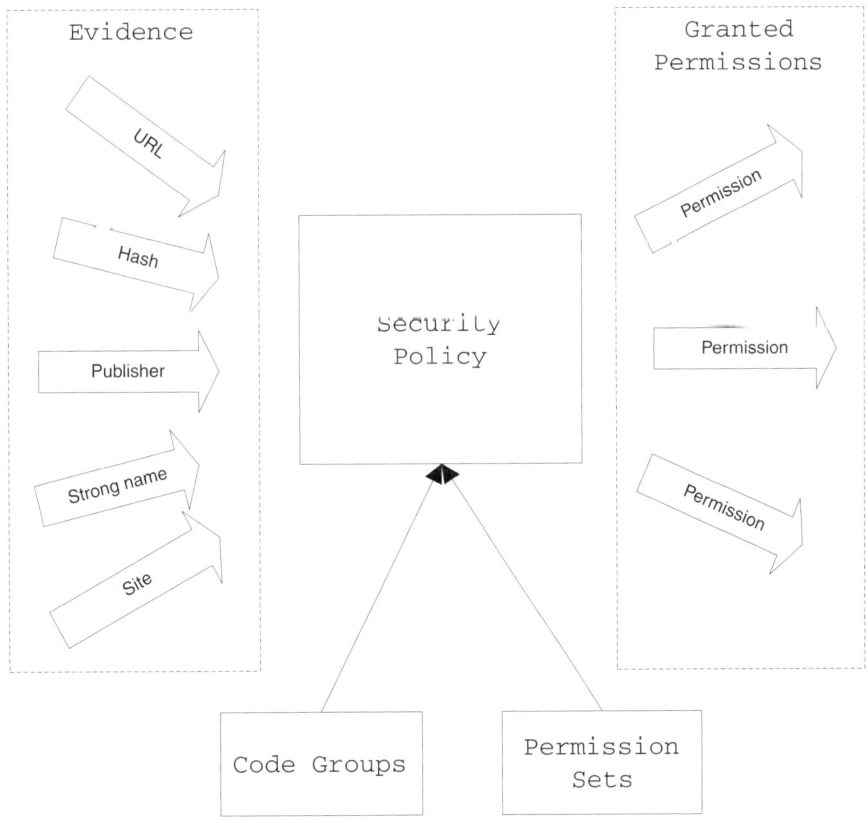

FIGURE 3–17 *Security policy.*

4. The CLR grants the union of the permissions in the matched permission sets to the assembly.

The assembly may affect this final set of granted permissions by refusing certain permissions and requesting minimum and optional permissions, but I discuss this more when I drill-down deeper into security policy later in this chapter.

Now that you have a high-level idea of how permissions are granted to an assembly, let's discuss how those permissions used? All of the .NET Framework class library methods that access protected resources demand permission to use the resource before they actually use it. For instance, before it executes any of the code in an assembly, the CLR demands permission to execute code. When you open a disk file, the class library method that you use will demand FileIO permission. Any action that may have security implications, such as attempting to read or write environment variables or the registry, to open a UI window, or to execute unmanaged code will lead to a permission demand. Each type of permission has a class associated with it in the System.Security namespace. Each of these permission classes derives from a class called **System.Security.CodeAccessPermission**. The **CodeAccessPermission** class contains a method called Demand. This is the method that the CLR and the .NET Framework class library call to demand a particular permission. When you demand a permission, the CLR will walk upward through the current call stack, and, if any of the callers in the stack have not been granted the requested permission, it will throw a security exception. This stack walk is a critical part of code access security. It prevents a "Trojan horse" attack, where an assembly that has not been granted a particular permission can cause damage simply by loading another piece of code that does the damage on its behalf. If the Trojan horse assembly calls a method in a dangerous assembly, the stack walk will wind its way back up to the original caller (the Trojan horse), and, if this assembly was not granted the permission to perform the operation, the CLR will throw a security exception. One exception to this behavior (which is important given that this book talks about COM Interop and using unmanaged code) is that code access security does not affect managed code. Therefore, a Trojan horse assembly can simply call unmanaged code (either a Windows API method or a COM object) to do its dirty work. Fortunately, before the CLR makes a call to unmanaged code, it will demand the permission to execute unmanaged code. If this permission has not been granted, a security exception will be thrown. Therefore, if you are worried about Trojan horse programs like this, you can simply not grant the execute unmanaged code permission to any assemblies. In fact, by default, only code that originates from your local hard drive is allowed to execute unmanaged code anyway. Code that comes from either the Internet or your local intranet will not be able to execute unmanaged code unless you explicitly allow it to.

The preceding explanation was a very high-level view. Let's look at code groups and permission sets and security policies at a slightly lower level, and then I will conclude with an example.

Code Groups

A code group is comprised of a membership condition and a permission set. If an assembly matches the membership condition for the code group, it is granted the permissions in the code group's associated permission set. When you install the .NET Framework, a number of code groups are defined for you already, and you can create additional ones. To see the code groups that currently reside on your machine, we'll use the .NET Framework Configuration Tool, which is a convenient snap-in for the Microsoft Management Console (MMC).

Note You can also view and edit the code groups on your machine using the Code Access Security Policy tool (caspol.exe), which is a command-line tool that is included with the .NET Framework SDK. The .NET Framework Configuration Tool is much easier to use, so I have used it throughout this chapter.

To view the code groups on your machine in the .NET Framework Configuration Tool, perform the following steps:

1. Select Programs | Administrative Tools | Microsoft .NET Framework Configuration from the Start menu. (You will see the window shown in Figure 3–18.)
2. Open the Code Groups node under Runtime Security Policy | Machine | Code Groups as shown in Figure 3–19.

Notice that three levels of code groups are displayed in the .NET Framework Configuration Tool: Enterprise, Machine, and User. I discuss these various levels and the hierarchical structuring of the code groups more when I talk about security policy. For now, let's looks at the machine node. The root of the code group tree contains a code group called All_Code that all assemblies will match. If you want to apply a set of permissions to all assemblies (for a given policy level), you can put the permission in the permission set associated with the All_Code code group. Notice that all of the code groups directly beneath the All_Code code group are based on zones. In other words, the membership condition for the code group is that the assembly must have originated from the specified zone. (See the sidebar in this chapter about zones to learn how zones are created and edited.) The Intranet_Same_Site_Access, Intranet_Same_Directory_Access, and Trusted_Same_Site_Access code groups are custom code groups with custom permission sets that allow a component downloaded from a trusted or intra-

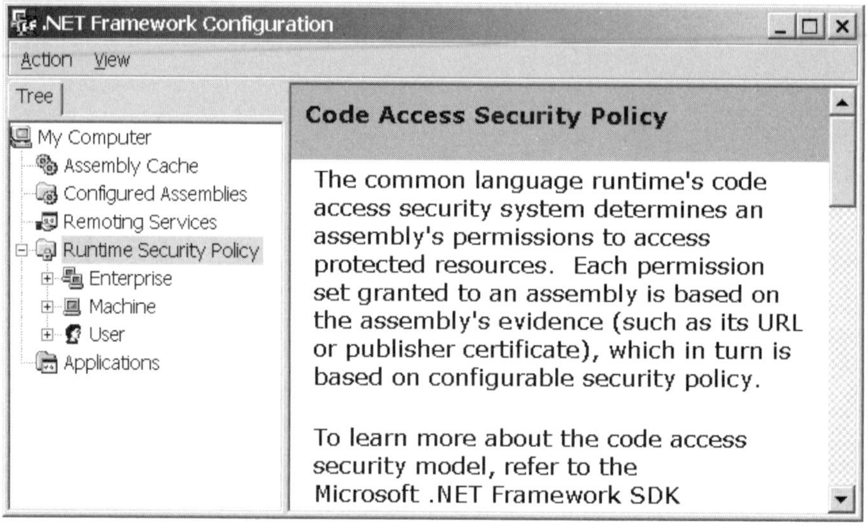

FIGURE 3–18 *The .NET Framework Configuration Tool.*

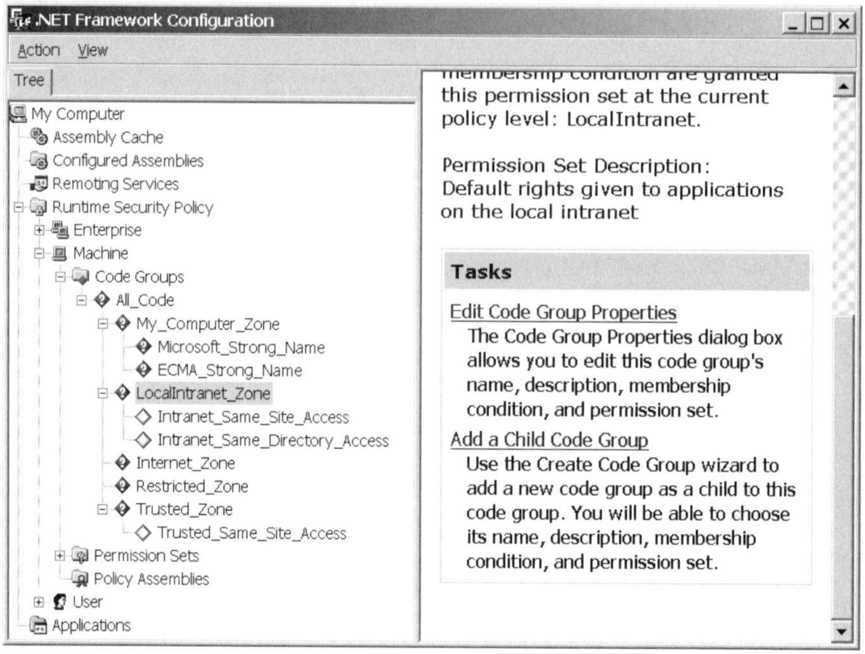

FIGURE 3–19 *Viewing code groups.*

net site to connect back to the Web site where it originated from (Intranet_Same_Site_Access and Trusted_Same_Site_Access) and allow a component downloaded from an intranet site to access the directory that it originated from (Intranet_Same_Directory_Access). You cannot edit these code groups with the .NET Framework Configuration Tool, but, fortunately, you can edit all the others.

Zones

Zones are managed within Internet Explorer. To view the zones that currently reside on your machine, perform the following steps:

1. Start Internet Explorer.
2. Select Tools | Internet Options. The Internet Options dialog will appear.
3. Click the Security tab. Your window should look as shown in Figure 3–20.

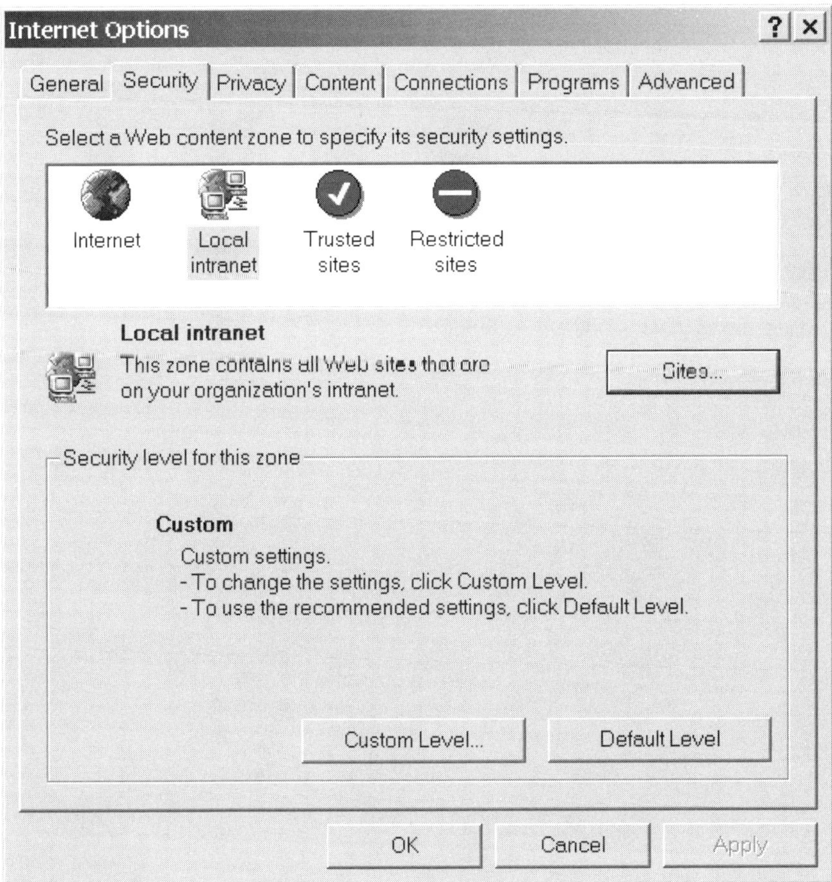

FIGURE 3–20 *The Internet Options Dialog.*

For all zones except the Internet zone, you can select the zone and then click the Sites... button to add or remove sites from that site. If you use the Intranet zone, you can choose which sites you consider to be on your Intranet. The Trusted and Restricted zones are simply lists that you can add sites to. If you trust that a site will not damage your computer you can add it to the Trusted list. Or if you believe that a site may damage your computer you can add it to the Restricted list. The Internet zone consists of all sites that are not in any of the other zones. You can assign permissions to web sites in each of these zones.

You can view and edit the membership condition and permission sets associated with a code group by right-clicking the code group and selecting Context | Properties. You will then see the code properties dialog as shown in Figure 3–21 for the Local Intranet. Zone.

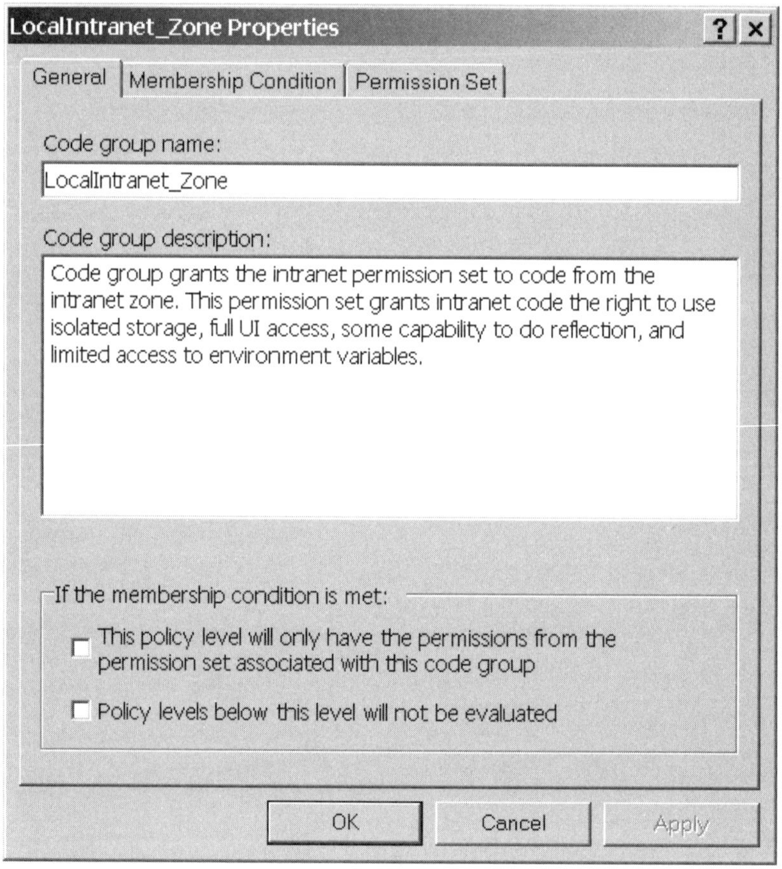

FIGURE 3–21 *The General tab of the code group properties dialog.*

On the General tab, notice that each code group has a name and a description. I will explain the two checkboxes on this page when I talk about security policy later in this chapter. The Membership Condition tab is how you specify the criterion that the CLR should use to determine if an assembly is a member of the code group. The Membership Condition tab of the properties dialog is shown in Figure 3–22.

The controls that you see on this window are a function of the condition type that you select for the code group. The default condition type is Zone, and, when you select this condition type, you will be presented with a dropdown that allows you to select the zone for the code group as shown in Figure 3–22. If you selected Publisher as your condition type instead, you will see controls that allow you to enter a digital signature for a publisher as shown in Figure 3–23.

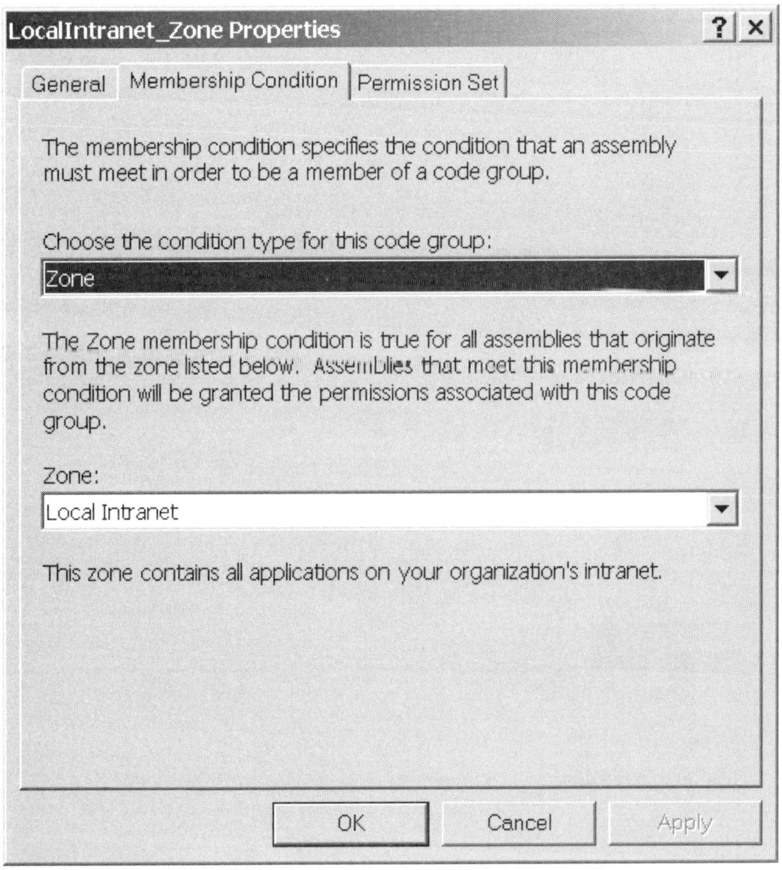

FIGURE 3–22 *The Membership Condition tab of the code group properties dialog.*

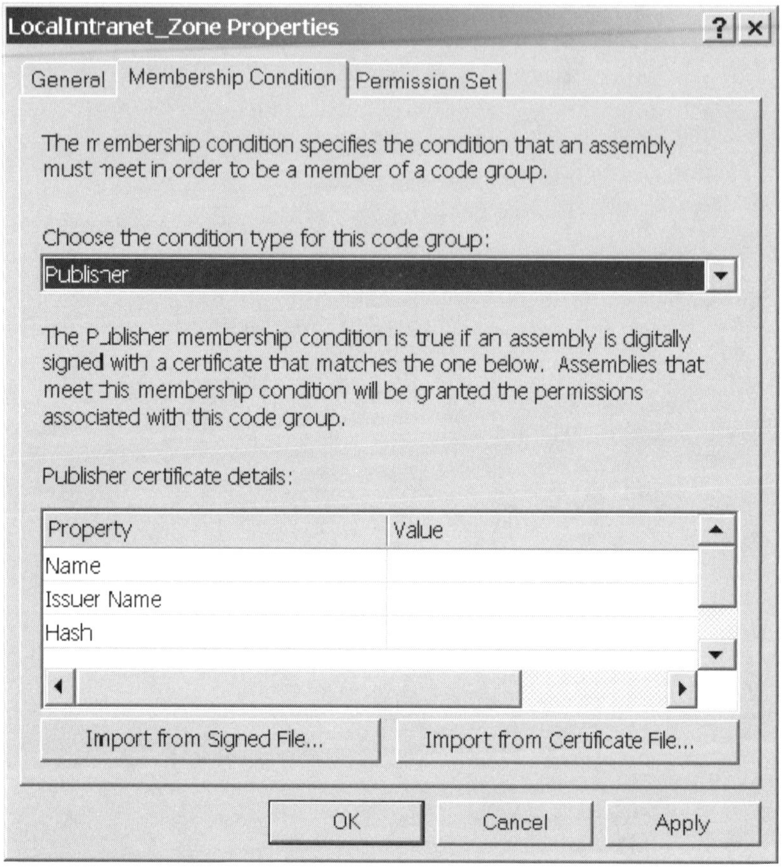

FIGURE 3–23 *The Membership Condition tab of the code group properties dialog with Publisher selected for the condition type.*

You can choose the condition type from the top-most dropdown. The possible options are shown in Table 3–14:

TABLE 3–14 *Available condition types for code group membership conditions*

Condition Type	Returns True if . . .
All	For all assemblies
Application Directory	If an assembly originates from the same directory or a child directory of the running application
Hash	If the hash of the assembly matches the one specified
Publisher	If the digital signature matches the one specified

TABLE 3–14 *Available condition types for code group membership conditions (continued)*

Condition Type	Returns True if . . .
Site	If the assembly comes from the specified site
Strong Name	If the assembly matches the one specified
URL	If the assembly originates from the specified URL
Zone	If the assembly originates from the selected zone
Custom	If the assembly matches the custom membership condition specified. You cannot add code groups with custom membership conditions with the graphical tool.

Permission Sets

After an assembly matches the membership condition for a code group, it is granted the permissions in the permission set associated with the code group. Permission sets allow you to group permissions together so that you can add them as a single unit to a code group. When you install the .NET Framework, it will create the permission sets shown in Figure 3–24 on your machine.

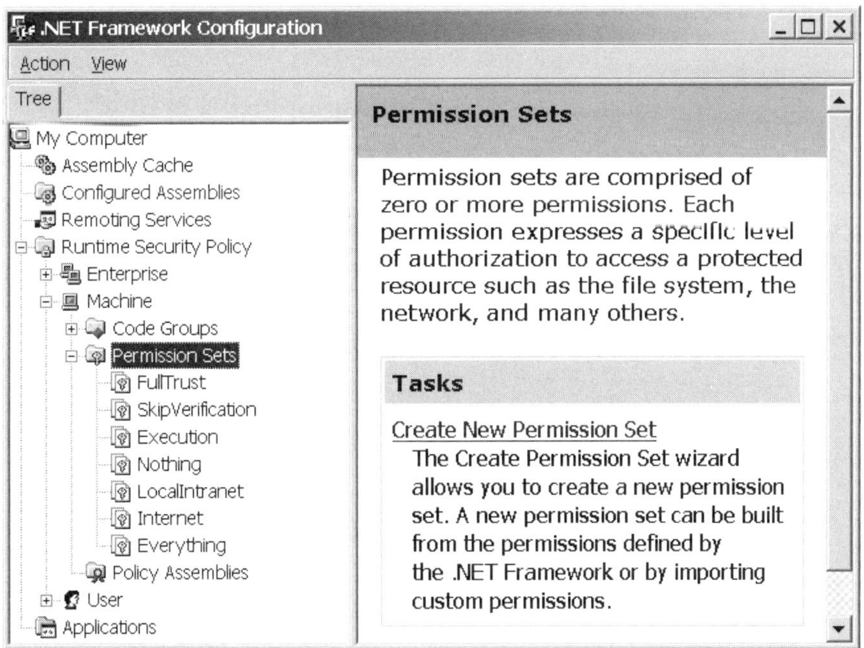

FIGURE 3–24 *Permission sets.*

You can also add your own permission sets. Each permission set contains a list of permissions. The set of individual permissions that permission sets are built from is shown in Table 3–15.

TABLE 3–15 *Available permissions to add to a permission set*

Permission	Description
Directory Services	A list of active directory paths. For each path, you can specify whether you can just browse or also write to the directory, or you can specify unrestricted access.
DNS	You can choose whether an assembly has unrestricted access to DNS or no access whatsoever to DNS.
Event Logs	You can grant Browse, Instrument, or Audit permissions for the Event Logs on a list of machines, or you can specify unrestricted access.
Environment Variables	You can grant read and/or write access to a list of environment variables, or you can specify unrestricted access.
File IO	You can grant read, write, and append privileges to a list of directory paths, or you can specify unrestricted access.
File Dialog	You can grant access to the Open, Save, or Open and Save dialogs, or you can specify unrestricted access.
Isolated Storage	You can grant access to file-based isolated storage with a specified disk quota and usage, or you can grant unrestricted access to file-based storage.
MessageQueue	You can grant access to a specific queue or to all queues.
Custom	You can grant access to a custom permission that you must specify using an XML schema. You cannot add custom code groups with the .NET Framework Configuration Tool.
OLEDB	You can grant access to specific OLEDB providers or unrestricted access to all OLEDB providers.
Performance Counters	You can grant browse or instrument access to a list of performance counters or unrestricted access to all performance counters.
Printing	You can specify All Printing, Safe Printing, Default Printing, or unrestricted access to printing.
Registry	You can specify Read, Write, or Create access to a list or registry keys or unrestricted access to the registry.
Reflection	You can specify that an assembly can read member (methods, properties, and so forth) and/or type (classes) information and/or that the assembly is allowed to emit metadata, or you can specify unrestricted access to reflection.

TABLE 3–15 *Available permissions to add to a permission set (continued)*

Permission	Description
Security	You can specify whether an assembly should (or should not) be granted any of a number of permissions including: Enable Assembly Execution Allow Calls to Unmanaged assemblies Skip Verification Enable Thread Control Enable Remoting Configuration
Service Controller	You can specify browse or control access to a list of services on specified machines or unrestricted access to all services.
Socket Access	You can allow access to a particular end point, that is, host/port/direction using TCP or UDP or unrestricted access to all sockets.
SQL Client	You can allow access to Microsoft SQL Servers through ADO.NET or unrestricted access to Microsoft SQL Server.
Web Access	You can grant accept or connect privileges to a list of hosts or unrestricted access to all Web sites.
User Interface	You can grant access to UI windows and/or the clipboard, or you may grant unrestricted access to all user interface elements.

The Security permission is perhaps the most interesting because you must grant the Enable Assembly Execution permission for an assembly to run at all, and you must grant the Allow Calls to Unmanaged assemblies permission in order to use unmanaged code through COM Interop.

Permission Sets are a convenience that frees you from the need to add each of these permissions individually to your code groups. You simply compile these permissions into permission sets, and then you can assign these permission sets to a code group.

Security Policy

Simply saying that an assembly is granted the permissions in the permission sets associated with the code groups that it matches is actually an oversimplification. In reality, the mapping from a set of matched code groups to a list of permissions that the assembly is granted is quite complicated. This mapping of matched code groups to permissions is called security policy.

I mentioned earlier that there are four levels of code groups. Three of these levels are visible in the .NET Framework Configuration Tool: Enterprise, Machine, and User. You can see these in Figure 3–25.

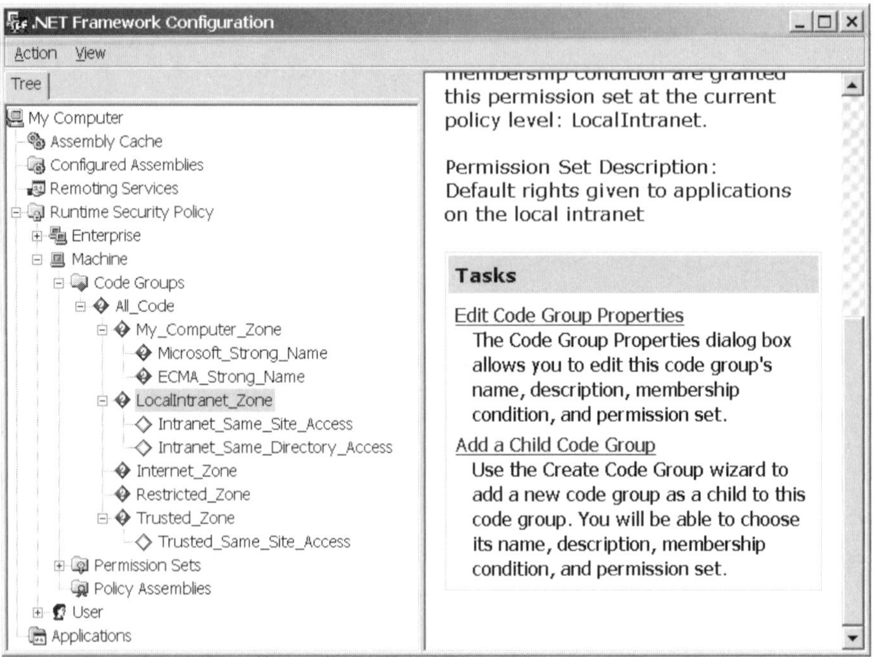

FIGURE 3–25 *The three code group levels visible in the .NET Framework Configuration Tool.*

The fourth level is the Application Domain level, which you can set programmatically. In Figure 3–25, you can also see that, within each level, the code groups are laid out in a hierarchy as shown in Figure 3–26.

When the CLR loads an assembly, it will walk the code group hierarchy once for each of the four levels. It determines the set of permissions at each level as the union of the permissions in the permission sets associated with the matched code groups at that level. After the CLR determines the permissions granted for a particular level, it then calculates the permissions granted from security policy as the intersection of the permissions granted at each level as shown in Figure 3–27.

If you are not familiar with set theory, this means that, in order for a particular permission, let's say File IO, to be granted to an assembly, it must be a part of the calculated permissions for each level. Therefore, by default, only the Machine level is relevant because the Enterprise and User levels initially have the All_Code code group associated with them, and the permission set associated with the All_Code code group is Full Trust, that is, all permissions are granted. A system administrator can use the Enterprise or User Permissions then to prevent certain permissions from being granted even if they

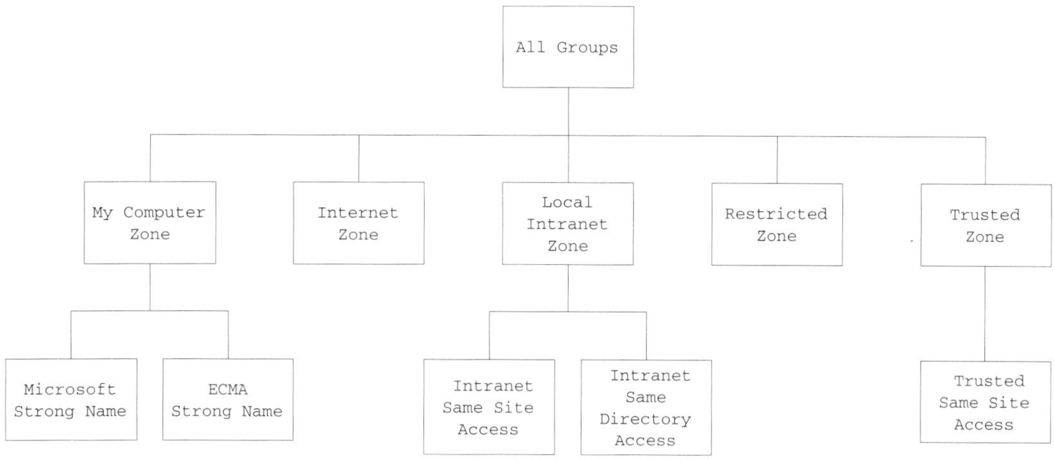

FIGURE 3–26 Code group hierarchy.

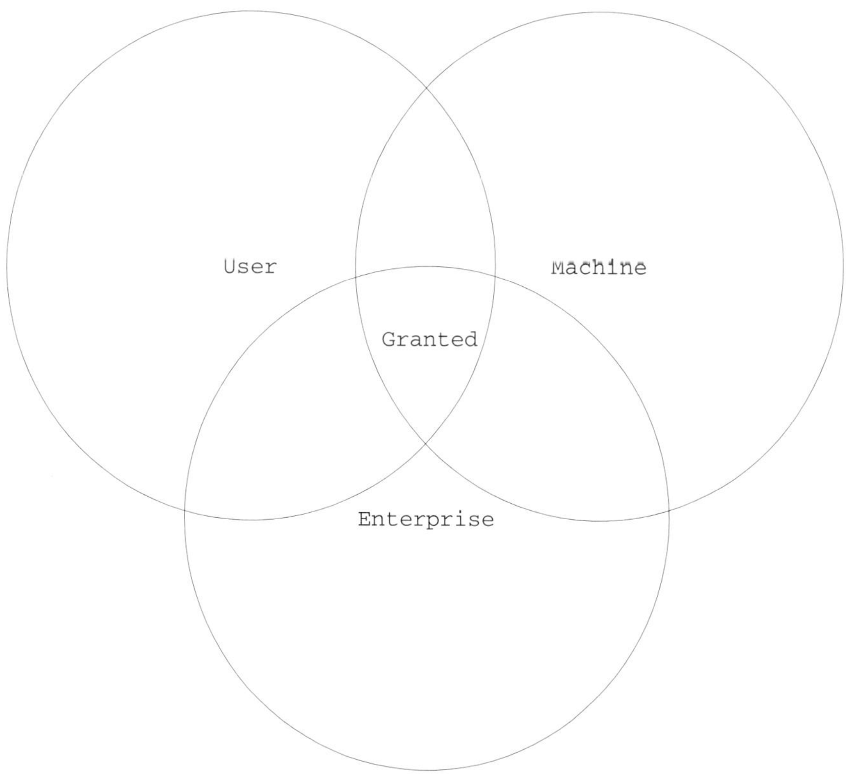

FIGURE 3–27 Granted permissions.

would ordinarily be granted based on the code groups and permission sets at one of the other levels.

At each level, the walk of the code group hierarchy begins at the All_Code code group, which matches every assembly.

Note The All_Code code group is a convenient place to put permissions that you would like every assembly to have. By default, this code group does not have a permission set associated with it.

If an assembly's evidence matches the membership condition for a code group, the CLR will also check the children of the code group for matches. For example, consider that I modified the default hierarchy shown in Figure 3–26 so that I added two custom code groups. The membership condition for each of these code groups uses the Site condition with the specified site for one of the code groups being the Human Resources (HR) server and other site being the Accounting server on the corporate LAN. The code group hierarchy at the Machine level will now look as shown in Figure 3–28.

Based on this hierarchy, a Microsoft .NET-based application loaded from your local hard drive will match the following code groups at the Machine Level: All Code, My Computer zone, and Microsoft strong name. A .NET application downloaded from the HR server on your corporate intranet will match the following code groups: All Code, Local intranet zone, HR server, Intranet same site access, and Intranet same directory access.

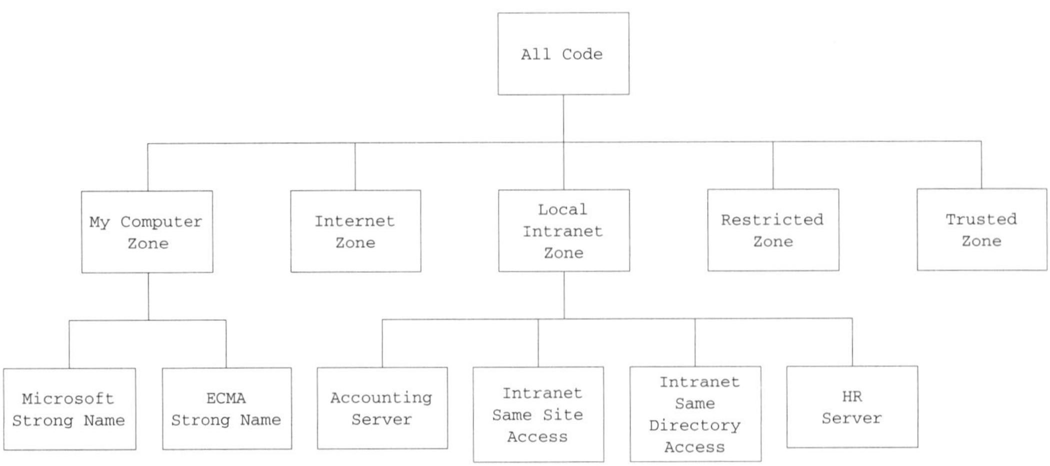

FIGURE 3–28 *A modified code group hierarchy.*

Note You can alter the way the tree is traversed. You can do this using the Exclusive and LevelFinal attributes on a code group. If the Exclusive attribute is applied to a code group at a policy level, the CLR will grant the permissions in that code group for the policy level and ignore the other code groups at that policy level. You can obviously only have one code group at a given policy level with the Exclusive attribute. The policy levels are arranged in a hierarchy with Enterprise at the highest level, following by machine, user, and then AppDomain. If the LevelFinal attribute is applied to a code group at a policy level, as long as the assembly matches a code group at that policy level, no code groups at a lower level will be checked.

After the CLR determines the permissions at each level by traversing the code group hierarchy at each level, it calculates the granted permissions by taking the intersection of the permissions granted at each of the four levels. This total is called the permissions from policy and is still not the final set of permissions that the CLR will grant to the assembly. An assembly is allowed to refuse permissions. In general, an assembly should not accept more permissions than it needs. An assembly can also request the minimum set of permissions that it requires to run. If the assembly is not granted at least the minimum set of permissions, it will fail to load. This prevents the CLR from loading an assembly and then failing with a security exception every time the assembly tries to do anything. An assembly can also request optional permissions. These are permissions that the assembly can run without, but can take advantage of if they are available. The CLR will not grant more privileges than the set of minimum plus optional permissions. The final formula for the set of granted permissions is as follows:

$$P_{granted}=P_{min} + (P_{optional} \cap P_{policy}) - P_{refused}$$

If you are not familiar with set theory, this formula reads in English: the set of granted permissions $P_{granted}$ equals the minimum requested permissions (P_{min}) plus the set of permissions that are both declared optional permissions by the assembly ($P_{optional}$) and granted by policy (P_{policy}), minus the list of permissions that are explicitly refused by the assembly ($P_{refused}$).

Example

I think a lot of these concepts can be made clearer with an example. Earlier in this chapter when I talked about assembly binding, I showed you an example application, which you can download from the Web site, called the Assembly-MetaDataViewer, which you can see here in Figure 3–29.

This application loads assembly files, so it will call .NET Framework class library methods that will demand the file IO permission. Make sure the multifile assembly that you built in this chapter is loaded into the GAC by performing the following steps:

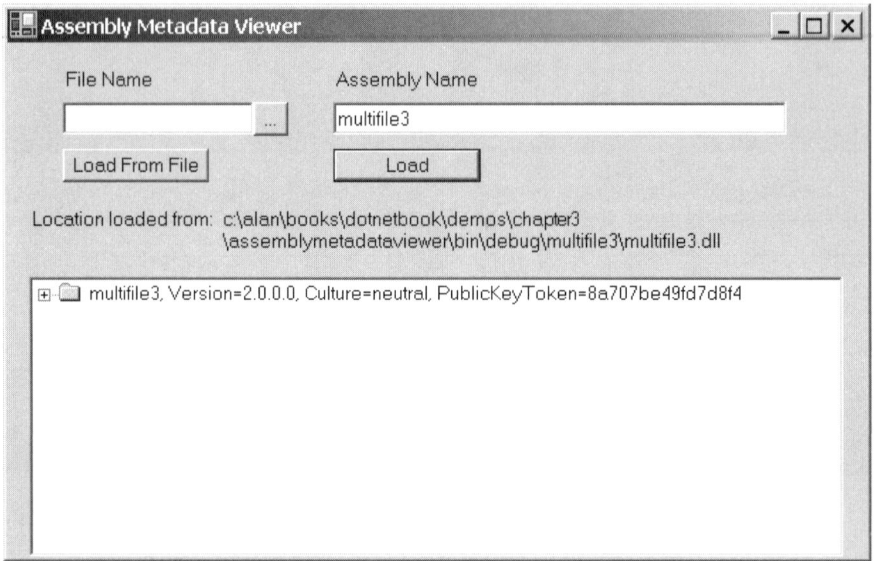

FIGURE 3–29 *The assembly metadata viewer.*

1. Open a Visual Studio .NET command prompt by selecting Programs | Microsoft Visual Studio .NET | Visual Studio .NET Tools | Visual Studio .NET Command Prompt from the Start menu.
2. Navigate to where you built the multifile assembly.
3. Enter "gacutil –i multifile.dll" at the command prompt.

Now run the AssemblyMetaDataViewer application. Enter "multifile" into the Assembly Name textbox and click the Load button. The tool calls the Load method in the **System.Reflection.Assembly** class, and then it displays the location that it loaded the assembly from. Running the tool from your hard drive verifies that the AssemblyMetaDataViewer is allowed to open and read an assembly file when you run it from your local machine.

Let's try running the AssemblyMetaDataViewer application by downloading it from the intranet. First, create an IIS virtual directory by performing the following steps:

1. Select Programs | Administrative Tools | Computer Management from the Start menu. The computer management MMC console will appear.
2. Open the Services and Applications node.
3. Open the Internet Information Services node.
4. Right-click on Default Web site.
5. Select New | Virtual Directory from the console. You should see Step 1 of the Virtual Directory Creation Wizard.

6. Click the Next button. You should see Step 2 of the Virtual Directory Creation Wizard.
7. Enter "TestSecurity" in the Alias field.
8. Click the Next button. You should see Step 3 of the Virtual Directory Creation Wizard, which allows you to specify where the physical directory is.
9. Click the Browse... button and navigate to where the AssemblyMetaDataViewer executable resides on your hard drive.
10. Click the Next button. You should see the access permissions step of the Virtual Directory Creation Wizard.
11. Accept the defaults for the access permissions and click the Next button.
12. Click Finish on the last page of the wizard.

Now, open Internet Explorer and navigate to the following URL:

```
http://localhost/testsecurity/assemblymetadataviewer.exe
```

The assemblymetadataviewer application should appear. Now enter “multifile” again and click the Load button. You should see the error message shown in Figure 3–30.

What happened? First, let’s go back to the .NET Framework Configuration Tool and see if we can figure out which code groups the assembly will match when we access it from the intranet. The .NET Framework Configuration Tool is shown in Figure 3–31.

At the machine level (remember this is the only level that matters by default because the other levels grant everything), the assembly will match the All Code and Intranet zone groups. The All Code code group has the Nothing permission set associated with it, and the LocalIntranet_Zone code group has the Local Intranet permission set associated with it. Figure 3–32 shows the list of permissions in the Local Intranet permission set.

FIGURE 3–30 *The security error when running over the intranet.*

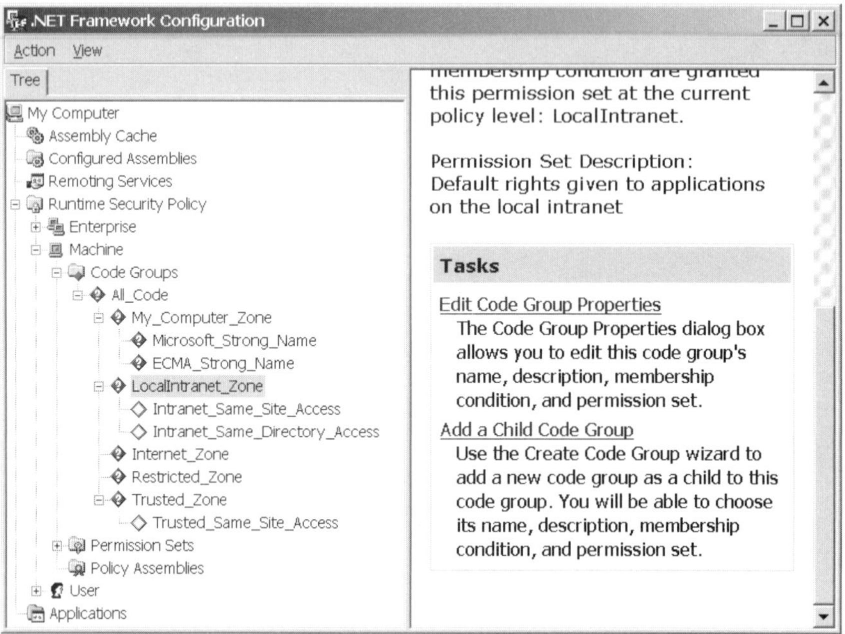

FIGURE 3–31 The three code group levels visible in the .NET Framework Configuration Tool.

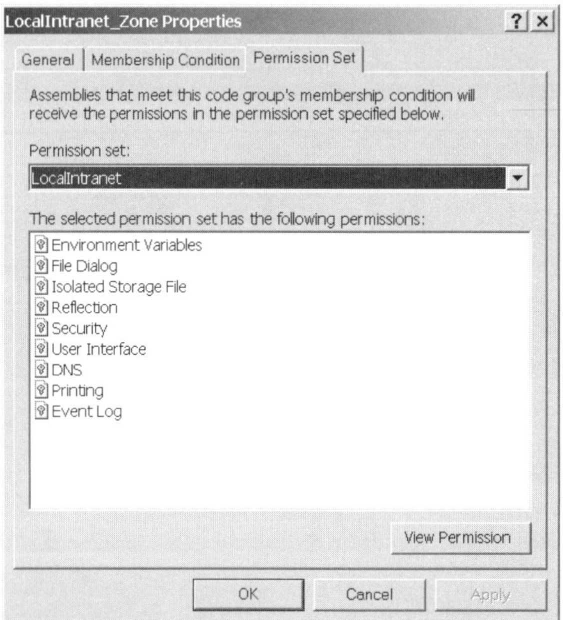

FIGURE 3–32 Permissions in the Local intranet permission set.

Notice that this permission set does not include the FileIO permission that you need to use the AssemblyMetaDataViewer. So how do you fix this? To state this more specifically, how can you allow the assemblymetadata-viewer application to run in an Intranet environment? You have a number of choices. You could add the FileIO permission to the Local intranet permission set. This has the side effect of granting the FileIO permission to all assemblies that originate from you Intranet. A better choice would be to add a new code group beneath the Local intranet code group with a URL membership condition. We can set the granted permissions associated with this code group to allow the FileIO permission only to assemblies that originate from the URL of the metadataviewer application. Using this approach also allows me to demonstrate how to create a new code group and a new permission set. To add the code group and new permission set, perform the following steps:

1. In the .NET Framework Configuration Tool, right-click the LocalIntranet_Zone code group (a context menu will appear) as shown in Figure 3–33.

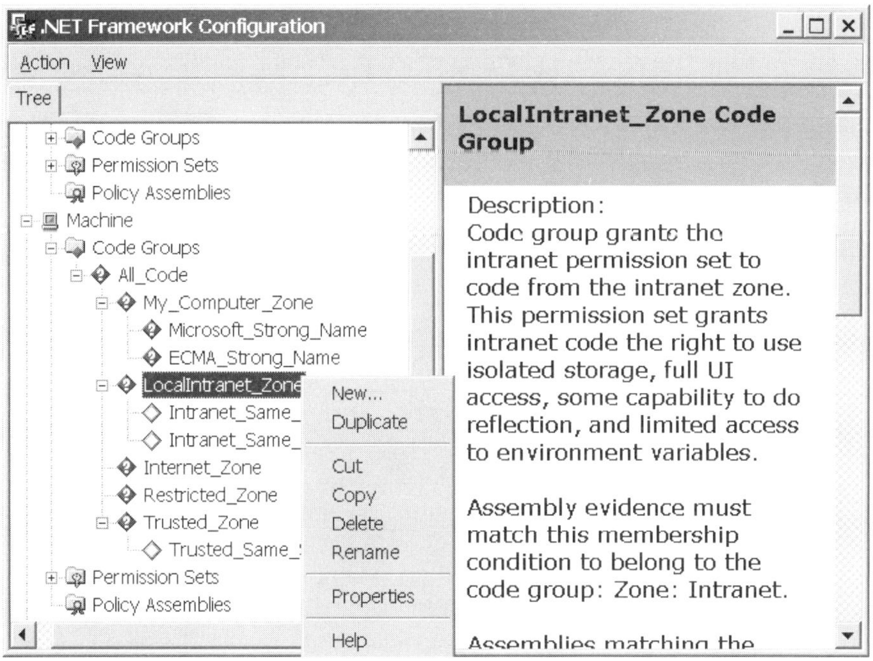

FIGURE 3–33 *The context menu for a code group.*

2. Select New... from the context menu. The first page of the Create Code Group wizard will appear as shown in Figure 3–34.

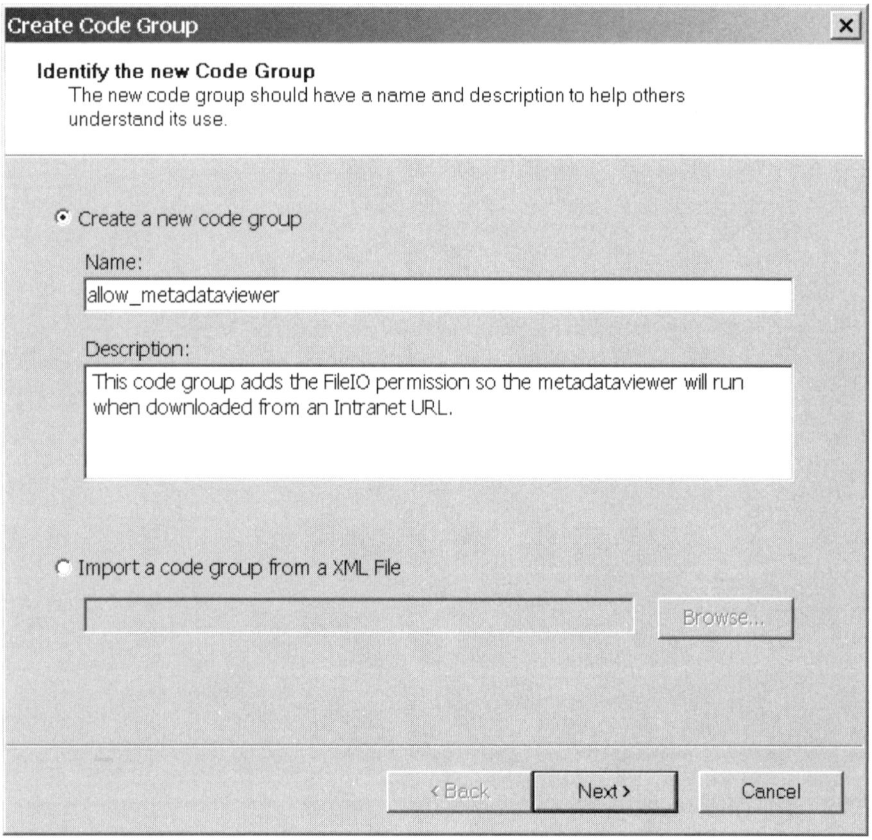

FIGURE 3–34 *The first page of the Create Code Group wizard.*

3. Enter the name "allow_metadataviewer" (or any name you want) for the code group, enter a description (if you want to, this is not required), and click the Next button. The second page of the Create Code Group wizard will appear as shown in Figure 3–35.
4. Select URL for the Condition Type, enter "http://localhost/testsecurity/assemblymetadataviewer.exe" for the URL (or whatever is the URL where you deployed the metadataviewer), and click the Next button. The third page of the Create Code Group wizard will appear as shown in Figure 3–36.

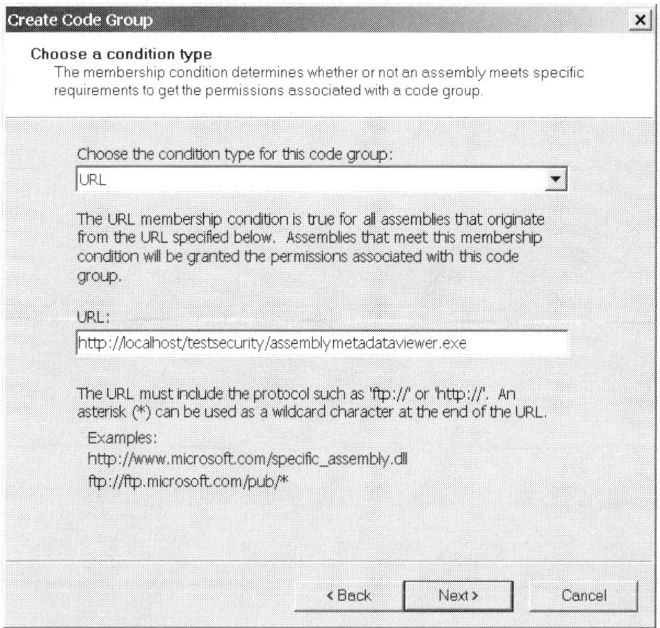

FIGURE 3–35 *The second page of the Create Code Group wizard.*

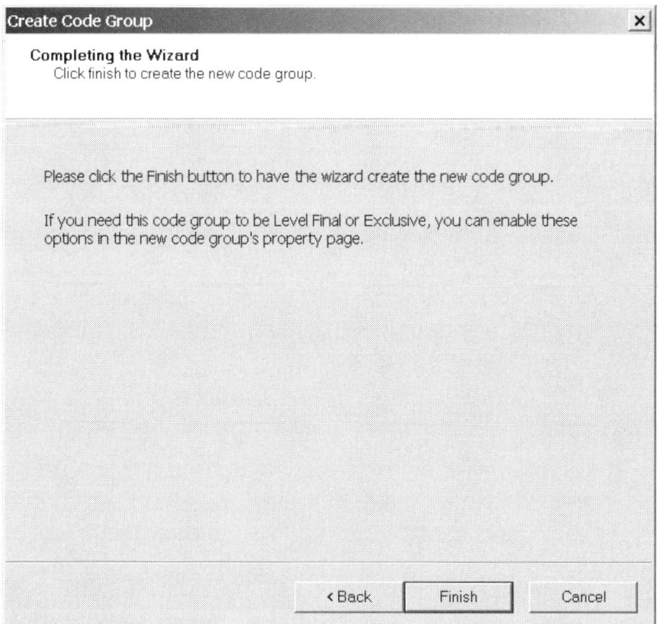

FIGURE 3–36 *The third page of the Create Code Group wizard.*

5. Click the Create a new permission set radio button and click the Next button. The first page of the Create Permission Set wizard will appear as shown in Figure 3–37.

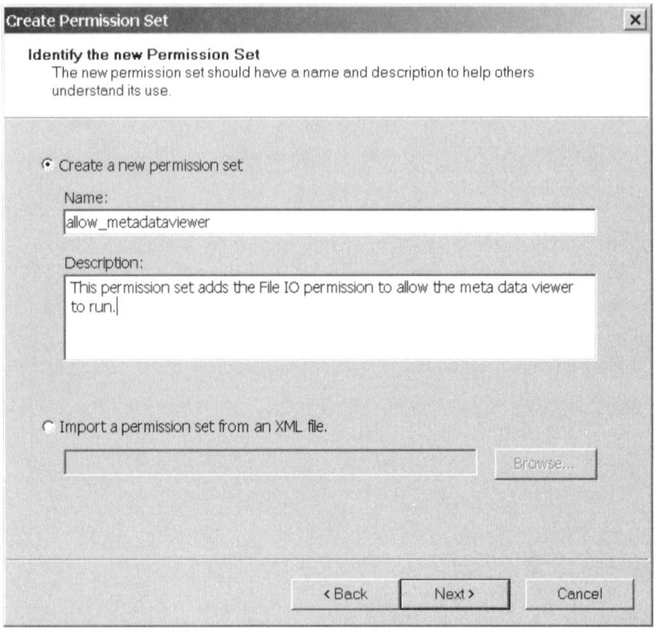

FIGURE 3–37 *The first page of the Create Permission Set wizard.*

6. Enter the name "allow_metadataviewer" (or any name you want), (optionally) add a description, and then click the Next button. The second page of the Create Permission Set wizard will appear as shown in Figure 3–38.
7. Select File IO from the list of available permissions and click the Add >> button. The configuration dialog for the File IO permission will appear as shown in Figure 3–39.
8. We'll keep things simple and just click the Grant assemblies unrestricted access to the filesystem checkbox and then click the OK button.
9. You should now be back on the second page of the Create Permission Set wizard (see Figure 3–38). Click the Next button on this page and then click the Finish button on the final page of the Wizard.

The membership condition for the allow_metadataviewer code group is: all assemblies that originate from URL *http://localhost/testsecurity/assemblymetadataviewer.exe*, and the permission set granted to an assembly that matches this membership condition contains the File IO permission. The

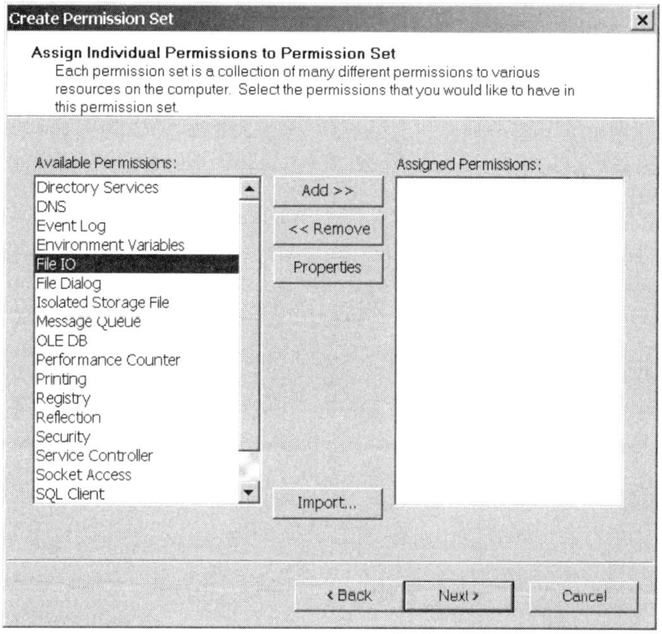

FIGURE 3–38 *The second page of the Create Permission Set wizard.*

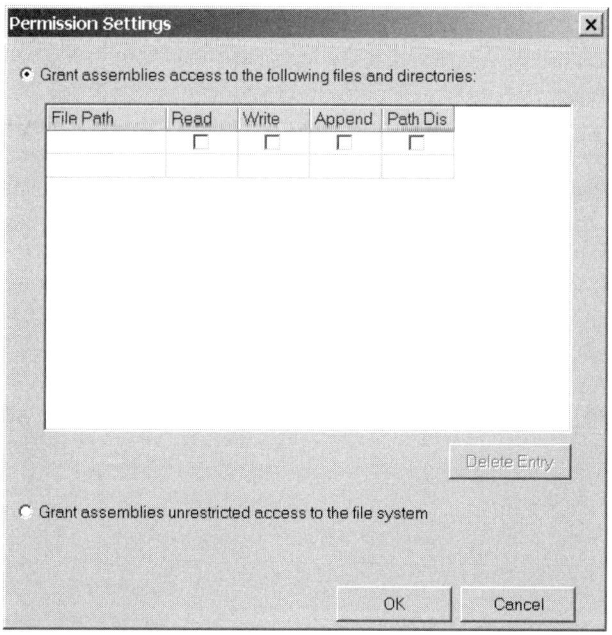

FIGURE 3–39 *The configuration dialog for the File IO permission.*

metadataviewer will obviously match the membership condition for this group and therefore will be granted the permission. Try running the metadataviewer again by pointing Internet Explorer at the following URL:

```
http://localhost/testsecurity/assemblymetadataviewer.exe
```

You should now be able to enter "multifile" (or any other assembly name for that matter) and load the assembly without problem.

Now if you are following along with this example, you are probably thinking that it would be too much trouble for someone to perform these steps manually for each machine on a corporate LAN that needs to use an application. That's where the Code Access Security Policy tool (caspol.exe) comes in handy. Caspol.exe is a command-line tool that is included with the .NET Framework SDK that allows you to perform all the steps I just performed with the .NET Framework Configuration Tool in a command-line environment. You can create scripts that perform the same steps that I did manually and then run the caspol.exe utility on those scripts to apply your Code Access Security Settings to a machine. You could even do this automatically when a user logs in. See the .NET Framework SDK documentation to learn more about the Code Access Security Policy tool..

Summary

In this chapter, you have learned more than you probably ever wanted to know about the CLR. It's particularly important to understand these ideas if you are a component developer on the .NET platform. Some of the ideas that you learned in this chapter, such as how the CLR locates and loads assemblies, how you can affect the version of an assembly that an application will attempt to bind to, and how garbage collection will affect how you write software for the .NET Framework, are critical things for you to learn if you are going to be a productive component developer on the .NET platform. In the next chapter, I drill-down into the C# language.

FOUR

A Quick Introduction to C#

All of the examples that you will do in this book will be written using Microsoft's new language called C#. C# is syntactically very similar to C++, but it is a much simpler language, and it has better support for object-oriented programming even though it does not support multiple inheritance. In this chapter, I give you a quick introduction to C# to better enable you to follow the source code examples that you will build in subsequent chapters. This chapter is by no means a comprehensive introduction to C#. That will require an entire book. Because a number of excellent books have already been written on the subject (I recommend *A Programmer's Introduction to C#* by Eric Gunnerson and APress or *Professional C#* by Simon Robinson et. al. and Wrox Press), there is no need for me to cover that ground. My only intention with this chapter is to give you enough to get started.

Getting Started with C#

Assuming that you are an experienced programmer in some programming language you need a few key questions answered before you are ready to start programming in a new language. After you have the answers to these questions, learning the rest of the language is essentially just "filling in the gaps" and learning how to use the various libraries associated with the language. Here are the questions as I see them:

- How do I create a simple "hello world" application in the language? A "hello world" application shows you how to structure a simple program, how to do I/O, and how to use the standard libraries provided by the language. It also shows you how to create the entry point for an application.

- How do I compile, link, and run an application written in the programming language, including how to link with both standard and third-party libraries.
- What is the basic set of operators that are available in the language, including assignment, test for equality, comparison (less than, greater than, and so forth), and mathematical operations.
- What is the basic set of primitive types available in the language?
- How do I create and manipulate a string in the language?
- How do I create and use arrays in the language?
- How do I declare classes? This includes how to declare static and nonstatic members of a class and how to assign accessibility (private, public, protected, and so forth) to the members of a class.
- How do I declare and use instances of a class? What operator or method is used to create a new instance of a class? Are both stack and heap-resident instances supported? and how do I create instances of each type? What operator is used to call methods and properties on an instance of class?
- How do I use inheritance? and how to I override a function in a subclass? Also, how do I call the base class implementation of a method in my override?
- What are the available flow-of-control constructs? How do you use the standard if, elseif, and else constructs as well as switch statements, that is, selecting one possibility from among many based on a condition and iteration statements such as for, while, and do loops?
- How do I implement exception handling?

If an experienced developer knows the answers to these questions about a language, they are ready to start programming in the language, and they can gradually learn the rest that they need to know—the nuances, gotchas, and idioms of the language—in time.

Creating a Simple Hello World Application

A simple hello world application written in C# follows:

```
namespace HelloWorld
{
    using System;
    public class Hello
    {
        public Hello()
        {
```

```
            // Constructor logic goes here
        }
        public static int Main(string[] args)
        {
      Console.WriteLine("Hello: ");
         if (args.Length==0)
        Console.WriteLine("who ever you are!");
      else
         for (int i=0;i<args.Length;i++)
        Console.Write(" {0} ", args[i]);
            return 0;
        }
    }
}
```

Let's examine the code a little deeper. First, notice that the code is enclosed within a namespace called HelloWorld

```
namespace HelloWorld
{
//...
}
```

The class name is **Hello**, therefore, the full name of the class that I have declared here is called **HelloWorld.Hello**, that is, the name is **[Namespace-Name].[ClassName]**.

Note The fact that I even need to declare a class to write my hello world program is a key difference between C++ and C#. C# does not have any global functions. Even the Main function that you write to be the entry point for your application must be a member of a class.

You can declare an instance of this class using the full class name as follows:

```
HelloWorld.Hello helloApp;
```

or, you can add a "using" statement to enable you to use the classes in the namespace without prepending the namespace name to the class name as follows:

```
using HelloWorld;
//...
Hello helloApp;
```

The next statement in the main listing is a using statement for the System namespace. This statement allows us to use the **Console** class, which is in the System namespace, without having to use the name of its namespace. If you did not add the "using" statement for the System namespace, you would have to substitute **System.Console** everywhere that you used the **Console** typename.

Namespaces are just a way to assign a longer (and thus more likely, unique) name to a class so that you avoid naming clashes. Namespaces can be nested, and Microsoft recommends that you use at least two nested layers of namespaces with your company name followed by the technology name and optionally the feature and design as follows:

```
CompanyName.TechnologyName[.Feature][.Design]
```

Some example names for namespaces are the following:

```
Microsoft.Office
Microsoft.Office.Charting
Microsoft.Office.Charting.Design
```

Using this naming convention prevents two published namespaces from having the same name. The first two parts of the namespace name, the CompanyName and the TechnologyName, should be enough to guarantee uniqueness in most cases, particularly if you use your Internet domain name for the company name. The CompanyName and TechnologyName are the only parts of the namespace name that are required. The "Feature" part of the name is optional and can be used to provide an extra hierarchy layer for complex technologies with multiple, related groups of classes. If a library or framework contains types that support design-time functionality, you should enclose the Design-related types in a namespace with "Design" as the innermost name.

Therefore, if you worked for ACME Software in the business objects group, you would probably use ACME as the CompanyName portion of your namespace name and BusinessObjects as the TechnologyName portion of your namespace name as shown here:

```
namespace ACME
{
    namespace BusinessObjects
    {
    // Your types and other code goes here…

     }
}
```

A short, and better, form for declaring a two-level nested namespace is the following.

```
namespace ACME.BusinessObjects
{
// Your types and other code goes here…

}
```

The rest of the code in the "hello world" example contains the declaration of a class called **Hello**. I won't dwell on this definition because there is another section in this chapter that talks about declaring classes in C#. I will talk about the "Main" method in the **Hello** class though. Much like C and C++, all C# programs will have a "Main" method. This method is the entry point for the application, that is, it's the first user-defined code that the operating system will execute when you run a program. In C#, this method must be declared as a static method that returns an integer. The method takes a string array as its only argument. The CLR will fill this array with the command-line arguments that were passed to the program when it was started. As you can see in the program, you can find out how many arguments were passed to the program using the Length property of the array, and you can access the arguments using the index operator, [].

The "hello world" program also shows you how to do console I/O using the Write and WriteLine methods on the **Console** class.

Compiling and Linking the Hello World Application

Compiling the "hello world" application is simple, and you do not need Visual Studio .NET to do it. If you are a glutton for punishment and don't mind using a text editor and a debugger that is not integrated with your editor, the Microsoft.NET Framework SDK is all you need to create a simple application with .NET.

The following compilation instructions will work if you have Visual Studio .NET or just the .NET Framework SDK installed:

```
csc out:/Hello.exe /t:exe Hello.cs
```

Tip If you get an error that says "csc is not recognized as an internal or external command, operable program or batch file", make sure that you have your environment configured correctly. There are a few environment variables that you need to set, and your path should include the bin directory for the .NET Framework SDK. See the .NET Framework SDK for more detailed information. If you have Visual Studio .NET, you can select Programs | Microsoft Visual Studio .NET | Visual Studio .NET Tools | Visual Studio .NET Command Prompt from the Start menu, and this will create a command prompt that has a fully configured environment.

The csc command invokes the C# compiler. The /out parameter specifies the name that you want to give the assembly that the compiler generates. Remember that the output of this compilation is not a traditional x86 executable. The output of any compilation with the C# compiler will either be a complete assembly, which includes metadata, MSIL code, and a manifest or it will be a module, which contains metadata and MSIL code that you can subsequently link using the csc command or the assembly linker (al) to create an assembly. The "/t" parameter, which is a short form for "/target", specifies the type of binary file that the compiler will generate. Using /t:exe, as specified here will generate a console executable assembly. Using /t:winexe will generate an executable assembly with a GUI. Using /t:library will create an assembly that is a DLL, and using /t:module will create a module that must be linked into a multifile assembly before it will be usable.

Like most programming languages, if you use types from libraries, even the standard ones, you will need to specify which libraries those types came from. With languages like C and C++, you had the choice between static and dynamic linking. If you used static linking, the code that you referenced from the external library would be embedded into your generated executable so that the resulting application was not dependent on the library file at runtime. In other words, you did not have to redistribute a DLL with your executable. With dynamic linking, your linker simply inserted a reference to the DLL. Your executable was smaller because it did not include the code that you used from the DLL, but now you have to redistribute the library with your application. The linking process with .NET is similar to dynamic linking. In .NET, linking to an assembly is called referencing the assembly. If you are using a multifile assembly, you will only reference the file that contains the manifest for the assembly. With the C# compiler, you reference an assembly using the "/reference" command-line option, which can be abbreviated to "/ r". For instance, the hello world example that I did before used the **Console** class, which resides in the core, system assembly (mscorlib.dll). You do not have to reference this assembly explicitly because the C# compiler always implicitly references it. However, if you did want to explicitly reference the mscorlib assembly, you would do so as follows.

```
csc /out:Hello.exe /t:exe /r:mscorlib.dll Hello.cs
```

Note

You can prevent the compiler from automatically referencing this assembly using the nostdlib parameter as shown here: csc out:/Hello.exe /t:exe /nostdlib /r:mscorlib.dll Hello.cs. If you do use the nostdlib parameter, you must explicitly reference mscorlib.dll.

Of course, in most cases, you will not use the command-line tools in the .NET Framework SDK to compile your applications. You will compile your applications using Visual Studio .NET, which is much simpler. Because you will be using Visual Studio extensively starting in the next chapter, I will not cover it here.

The Basic Operators in C#

The basic set of operators supported by the C# language is essentially the same as those supported by C and C++. You can group the available operators into the following categories: arithmetic, relational, logical assignment, and type operators. The conditional operator is in a category by itself.

Arithmetic Operators

Table 4–1 shows the list of available arithmetic operators.

TABLE 4–1 *C# Arithmetic operators*

Operator	Usage Example	Description
Unary Plus	res = +x;	Returns the value of x.
Unary Minus	res = -x	Returns zero minus x.
Addition	res = x + y	Adds x and y. Also used for string concatenation.
Subtraction	res=x - y	Subtracts y from x. When checked, will throw an OverflowException if the result is outside the range of the result type.
Multiplication	res=x*y	Multiplies y times x. When checked, will throw an OverflowException if the result is outside the range of the result type.
Division	res = x / y	Divides the x by x. Will throw a DivideByZeroException if y is zero.
Remainder	res = x % y	Returns the remainder of x/y. When checked, will throw a DivideByZeroException if y is zero.
Left shift	res = x << y;	Left shifts the bits in x by y positions. High-order bits are discarded, and empty, low-order bits are set to zero.
Right shift	res = x >> y;	Right shifts the bits in x by y positions. Low-order bits are discarded, and empty, high-order bits are set to zero.
Increment and Decrement (postfix)	res = x++ res = x--	Increments (++) or decrements the (--) x by 1. The increment is performed after the read, so if x =2, res will equal 2 after res=x++.
Increment and Decrement (prefix)	res = ++x res = --x	Increments (++) or decrements the (--) x by 1. The increment is performed before the read, so, if x =2, res will equal 3 after res=x++.

Most of the arithmetic operators (the shift and increment/decrement operators are exceptions) are only defined for the int, uint, long, ulong, float, double, and decimal types. If you use one of these operators on a type smaller than int, like short or byte, the compiler will perform an implicit conversion to the int type. You will then receive a compiler error if you try to assign the result of the arithmetic operation, which is an int, to a byte or a short because the conversion from an int to a short or byte is a narrowing conversion that may cause data loss. In other words, the following code will not compile.

```
short res, x=5, y=3;  // this code will not compile. Cannot
res = x + y;    // implicitly convert type int to short.
```

To compile this code, you must explicitly convert the result of the addition to a short as follows:

```
short res, x=5, y=3;
res = (short)(x + y);
```

If you perform multiplication or addition on two large int values, the result will likely be too large to store in an int result. By default, the operation will overflow silently without throwing an exception. You can instruct the C# compiler to generate code that will throw an exception if it detects overflow using the /checked argument. The following command line causes the compiler to generate code that checks for overflow:

```
csc /checked+ myfile.cs
```

You do pay a slight performance penalty for this extra checking, which is probably why the default for both the C# command line and Visual Studio .NET is not to perform overflow checking.

Note If you are using Visual Studio .NET, you can turn on overflow checking by changing the Checked for overflow setting from false (the default) to true on the property pages for your project (See chapter 5).

If you explicitly want to specify that you do *not* want overflow checking, you can use the following command line for the C# compiler:

```
csc /checked- myfile.cs
```

This is an unnecessary step, however, because overflow checking is off by default. Even if you have not enabled overflow checking globally using the compiler command-line switch, you can instruct the compiler to perform overflow checking for a particular set of operations using the checked operator as follows:

```
checked
{
    int res, x=32000000, y=32000000;
    res = x * y;  // this line will cause an exception
          Console.WriteLine("res={0}",res);
}
```

Relational Operators

Table 4–2 lists the available relational operators in C#.

TABLE 4–2 *C# Relational operators*

Operator	Usage Example	Description
Equals	x == y	Returns true if x is equal to y.
Not Equals	x != y	Returns true if x is not equal to y.
Less than	x < y	Returns true if x is less than y.
Less than or equal	x <= y	Returns true if x is less than or equal to y.
Greater than	x > y	Returns true if x is greater than y.
Greater than or equal	x >= y	Returns true if x is greater than or equal to y.

These operators are straightforward and are exactly the same as the C/C++ relational operators, so I won't dwell on them.

Logical Operators

Table 4–3 lists the available logical operators in C#.

TABLE 4–3 *C# Relational operators*

Operator	Usage Example	Description
Bitwise AND	x & y	Returns the bitwise AND of x and y.
Bitwise OR	x | y	Returns the bitwise OR of x and y.
Bitwise XOR	x ^ y	Returns the bitwise XOR of x and y.
Logical AND	x && y	Returns the logical AND of x and y.
Logical OR	x || y	Returns the logical OR of x and y.
Logical negation	!(x [op] y)	Returns the negation of a Boolean expression.

Once again, these operators are straightforward and are exactly the same as the C/C++ relational operators, so I won't dwell on them.

Assignment Operators

C# uses a single equals (=) for assignment. Just like C and C++, C# also supports a variety of shortcut assignment operators that allow you to perform an operation on two operands and assign the result to the left operand. In all of these cases, you are essentially abbreviating the following statement:

```
x = x [op] y
```

as this:

```
x [shortcut op] y
```

In other words,

```
x = x + y
```

can be abbreviated to:

```
x += y
```

C# supports the following shortcut operations: +=, -=, *=, /=, &=, %=, ^=, >>=, <<=. I have already explained the long form of each of these operators, so I won't give a detailed explanation of each operator when used in the shortcut form.

Type Operators

C# supports three operators, typeof, is, and as, which deal with types instead of values.

TYPEOF

The typeof operator returns the System.Type object for a particular type. You can also get the System.Type object associated with a type by calling the GetType method on an instance of the type.

Note The GetType method is implemented in the **System.Object** class, which is the root base class for all other types.

However, using the typeof operator, you can get the System.Type object without having to create an instance of the type. The following code uses the typeof operator to obtain the System.Type object associated with the **Manager** class and then prints out a list of the methods in the class:

```
Type mgrType=typeof(Manager);
foreach (MethodInfo method in mgrType.GetMethods())
{
    Console.WriteLine(method.Name);
}
```

IS

You use the "is" operator to determine if an object reference can be converted to a specified type. For instance, if the **Manager** class is a subtype of an **Employee** class, a Manager object reference can be converted to an Employee object reference. However, an Employee object reference can only be converted to a Manager object reference if the Employee object reference actually points to a Manager object.

Note If you are having problems understanding the last point, just remember that a Manager is an Employee, so you can always perform the conversion from Manager to Employee. However, all Employees are not Managers, so the conversion from Employee to Manager may not always work.

The "is" operator allows you to test if an Employee object can be converted to a Manager. The following code will print the bonus of the Manager because the empMgr, Employee object reference points to a Manager object.

```
Employee empMgr=new Manager(1,"Tamber Gordon",800,200);
if (empMgr is Manager)
{
    Manager mgr=(Manager)empMgr;
    Console.WriteLine("Bonus = {0}",mgr.Bonus);
}
else
      Console.WriteLine("Not a manager!");
```

The following code will print "Not a Manager!" because the empEmp, Employee object reference points to an Employee object:

```
Employee empEmp=new Employee(2,"Alan Gordon",500);
if (empEmp is Manager)
{
    Manager mgr=(Manager)empEmp;
    Console.WriteLine("Bonus = {0}",mgr.Bonus);
}
else
      Console.WriteLine("Not a manager!");
```

AS

The "as" operator tests to see if an object reference can be converted to a specified type just like the "is" operator. The difference is that the "as" operator also performs the conversion if it is valid. If the object reference cannot be converted to the specified type, the "as" operator returns null. The following code demonstrates how to use the "as" operator:

```
Employee empMgr=new Manager(1,"Tamber Gordon",800,200);
Manager mgr = empMgr as Manager;
if (mgr != null)
    Console.WriteLine("Bonus = {0}",mgr.Bonus);
else
      Console.WriteLine("Not a manager!");
```

THE CONDITIONAL OPERATOR

I'll end our discussion of C# operators by talking about the conditional operator, which doesn't fit neatly into any of our categories. The conditional operator selects from two expressions based on the result of a Boolean expression as follows:

```
(boolean_exp) ? exp1 : exp2
```

If the Boolean expression evaluates to true, the conditional operator will return the result of exp1; if the Boolean expression evaluates to false, the conditional operator will return the result of exp2. The following code demonstrates how to use the conditional operator:

```
static string GetSalaryDescription(Manager mgr)
{
    return (mgr.Salary > 1000) ? "overpaid" : "underpaid";
}
```

The Primitive Types Available in C#

The list of primitive types available in C# is very similar to C and C++. One of the major reasons for the cross-language interoperability of the .NET Framework is that all languages share a common type system: the CTS. The primitive types in C# are just aliases for CTS types. Table 4–4 shows the primitive types available in C#.

TABLE 4–4 *A Mapping of C# types to CTS types*

C# Types	CLS Compliant	Equivalent CTS Type	Description
bool	Yes	System.Boolean	True or false
byte	Yes	System.SByte	Unsigned 8-bit number
sbyte	No	System.Byte	Signed 8-bit number
char	Yes	System.Char	16-bit Unicode character
int	Yes	System.Int32	Signed 32-bit number
uint	No	System.UInt32	Unsigned 32-bit number

TABLE 4–4 *A Mapping of C# types to CTS types (continued)*

C# Types	CLS Compliant	Equivalent CTS Type	Description
long	Yes	System.Int64	Signed 64-bit number
ulong	No	System.UInt64	Unsigned 64-bit number
short	Yes	System.Int16	Signed 32-bit number
ushort	No	System.UInt16	Unsigned 32-bit number
float	Yes	System.Single	32-bit floating point number
double	Yes	System.Double	64-bit floating point number
system.DateTime	Yes	System.DateTime	Date time
decimal	Yes	System.Decimal	Signed 96-bit number
string	Yes	System.String	Unicode character string.
object	Yes	System.Object	Base class for all types

Most of the familiar primitive types from C and C++ like int, long, short, char, float, and double are present in C#. C# also supports unsigned types like uint, ushort, and unlong, but keep in mind that these unsigned types are not CLS compliant. Therefore, if you do expose types from your libraries that use these unsigned types in their interface, those libraries will not be usable from many managed code languages including VB.NET. Avoid unsigned types in your interfaces if you want to write components that may be consumed by languages other than C#.

Note The CLS specifies the features that *all* managed code languages must support as a minimum.

With C#, as in most managed-code languages, you can use either the language-specific alias or the CTS type name freely and interchangeably. In other words, declaring a variable to be of type "int" is exactly the same as declaring it to be of type "System.Int32". In addition, a function that accepts a parameter of type float will also accept a parameter that is typed as System.Single.

Creating and Manipulating a String in C#

One of the most fundamental things that you will need to do as a computer programmer in any programming language is to work with strings: creating them, comparing them, searching them for subvalues, concatenating them, and parsing them. The biggest problem with string manipulation in C and C++ on the Windows platform is that there are so many ways to manipulate strings. The Windows platform supports strings with single-byte characters or wide characters or you can write code that is portable to both. There is a different set of string manipulation functions in the C and C++ runtime library for each of these character types. Of course, if you are using the MFC, it makes sense for you to use the **CString** class. However, if you do this, you will probably have to do many conversions to the BSTR string type if you are also using ActiveX controls or other COM objects. ATL has a string class called CComBSTR that wraps the BSTR string type. The native COM support in Visual C++ has its own class that wraps BSTR called _bstr_t. If you decide to use the Standard Template Library (STL), there is yet another string class called string, which is a generic (template) class that will work with both wide and single-byte characters. Each of these string classes has a completely different set of capabilities. The situation is an absolute mess!

With the .NET Framework, this problem is fixed. All programming languages that target the CLR will use the CTS string type called System.String. The **System.String** class stores its internal string using Unicode characters. It has a rich set of methods for manipulating a string. Table 4–5 shows a small sample of these methods. For a complete list and description of all the methods and properties in the string class, see the .NET Framework class library reference.

TABLE 4–5 *A Sample of the methods in System.String*

Method Name	Description
Clone	Returns a reference to the current string (shallow copy).
Compare	Compares two strings with or without case sensitivity. Returns -1 if the first string is less (lexically) than the second string, 0 if the two strings contain the same value, 1 if the first string is greater than the second string.
CompareOrdinal	Similar to the Compare function, but performs its comparison without regard to local language or culture.
CompareTo	Similar to the Compare method, but unlike Compare, which is a static method, CompareTo compares the instance on which it is called against a specified string.
Concat	Concatenates two, three, or an array of strings into a single string.

TABLE 4–5 *A Sample of the methods in System.String (continued)*

Method Name	Description
Copy	Copies the contents of one string to another string.
Equals	Determines if two strings contain the same contents. The comparison is case sensitive.
Format	Replaces each format specification with the textual representation of an object's value. Similar to sprintf.
Indexof	Returns the index of the first occurrence of the specified string, character, or array of characters.
LastIndexof	Returns the index of the last occurrence of the specified string, character, or array of characters
Join	Joins an array of strings together with a specified separator between the strings.
Split	Creates an array of strings by splitting a string using a specified array of separators. This method is used for tokenization.
PadLeft	Right-aligns the characters in a string by padding on the left with a specified number of spaces or a character.
PadRight	Left-aligns the characters in a string by padding on the right with a specified number of spaces or a character.
Replace	Replaces all occurrences of a character with a specified replacement.
Substring	Returns a portion of a string starting at a specified index and continuing either to the end of the original string or to a specified length
ToLower	Returns a copy of the string with all characters in lower-case.
ToUpper	Returns a copy of the string with all characters in upper-case.

Any type can be converted to a string using the toString function, which is defined on the **System.Object** class from which all other classes ultimately derive. Calling the toString method on many objects will return the name of the object's class, but some objects have a type-specific implementation of this method. For instance, most of the numerical types will return a textual representation of their underlying number. You can override the toString method in your types to return something else.

The string class also supports a Length property that returns the number of characters in a string and an equality operator "==" that allows you to test if two strings contain the same value; the equality operator is built on the Equals method, which is described in Table 4–5. The string class also contains an indexer method that allows you to return the individual characters in the string as follows:

```
namespace StringApp
{
    using System;
    public class TestStr
    {
    public static int Main(string[] args)
    {
      string str="Bria and Bryan";
      for (int i=0;i<str.Length;i++)
      {
        Console.WriteLine(str[i]);
      }
         return 0;
    }
  }
}
```

However, strings are immutable, so don't try to execute the following code, which will cause an error:

```
namespace StringApp
{
  using System;
  public class TestStr
  {
    public static int Main(string[] args)
    {
      string str="Bria and Bryan";
      str[5]='t';// compiler error
      return 0;
    }
  }
}
```

You cannot modify a string after it has been created (I'll discuss this point in greater detail later). The string class also supports an addition operator, which you could use to concatenate two strings together as follows:

```
namespace StringApp
{
  using System;
  public class TestStr
  {
    public static int Main(string[] args)
    {
      string str;
      str="Bria and Bryan" + " are playing";
      Console.WriteLine(str);
      return 0;
    }
  }
}
```

Later in this chapter, you will see why in some situations you are better off using the **StringBuilder** class instead.

The following code shows a sample program that demonstrates the use of some of these string functions. This program demonstrates some of the comparison functions like Compare, CompareTo, and Equals.

```
namespace StringApp
{
  using System;
  public class TestStr
  {
    public static int Main(string[] args)
    {
      string str1, str2;
      int compResult;
      bool equalsResult;
      str1="Bria";
      str2="Bryan";
      // Code below returns -1.
      // Bria is lexically less than Bryan
      compResult=String.Compare(str1,str2);
      Console.WriteLine("{0}",compResult);
      // This will give the same result
      // as the code shown above
      compResult=str1.CompareTo(str2);
      // Code below returns -1.
      // Bria is lexically less than BRIA
      compResult=String.Compare(str1,"BRIA");
      Console.WriteLine("{0}",compResult);
      // Code below returns 0, because the
      // third parameter, "true", indicates
      // that this is a case insensitive comparison
      compResult=String.Compare(str1,"BRIA",true);
      Console.WriteLine("{0}",compResult);
      // Code below returns true
      equalsResult=String.Equals(str2,"Bryan");
      Console.WriteLine("{0}",equalsResult);
      // Code below returns false
      equalsResult=str2.Equals(str1);
      Console.WriteLine("{0}",equalsResult);
      // Code below returns false
      equalsResult=(str1 == str2);
      Console.WriteLine("{0}",equalsResult);
      return 0;
    }
  }
}
```

The next example program demonstrates some of the searching and indexing methods supported by the string class as well as the use of the Format method.

```
namespace StringApp
{
  using System;
  public class TestStr
  {
    public static int Main(string[] args)
    {
      string str;
      int indexResult;
      bool searchResult;
      str="Bria and Bryan are playing";
    // The code below returns true
      searchResult=str.EndsWith("ing");
      Console.WriteLine("{0}",searchResult);
    // The code below changes the string to:
    // Bria and Bryan are laughing and playing
      str=str.Insert(19,"laughing and ");
      Console.WriteLine(str);
    // The code below will return 5
      indexResult=str.IndexOf("and");
      Console.WriteLine("{0}",indexResult);
    // The code below will return 28
      indexResult=str.LastIndexOf("and");
      Console.WriteLine("{0}",indexResult);
    // The code below will return "laughing"
      Console.WriteLine(str.Substring(19,8));
    // The code below will print 3.433E+002
      str=String.Format("The string is: {0:E3}",343.34);
      Console.WriteLine(str);
    // The code below will print 343.34
      str=String.Format("The string is: {0:##.###}",343.34);
      Console.WriteLine(str);
    // The code below will print 343.340
      str=String.Format("The string is: {0:##.000}",343.34);
      Console.WriteLine(str);
      return 0;
    }
  }
}
```

The last example program exercises the Join, Split, and Concat function.

```
namespace StringApp
{
  using System;
  public class TestStr
  {
    public static int Main(string[] args)
    {
```

```
        string str;
        string str2Split1, str2Split2;
        string[] strArray=new string[6];
        string[] strSplitArray;
        strArray[0]="A";
        strArray[1]=".NET";
        strArray[2]="Primer";
        strArray[3]="For";
        strArray[4]="COM+";
        strArray[5]="Programmers";
        str2Split1="The COM and COM+ ";
        str2Split2="Programming Primer";
        str=string.Join(" ",strArray);
// Prints the string: "A .NET Primer For COM+ Programmers"
        Console.WriteLine(str);
        str=string.Concat(str2Split1,str2Split2);
// Prints the string: "The COM and COM+ Programming Primer"
        Console.WriteLine(str);
        strSplitArray=str.Split(new char[] {' '});
        foreach (string strSplitItem in strSplitArray)
        {
          Console.WriteLine(strSplitItem);
          }
        return 0;
      }
  }
}
```

Strings are immutable. In other words, after a string has been created, its contents cannot subsequently be changed. All of the **string** methods that appear to modify a string actually return a new instance of the string that contains the modification. For instance, on first glance, you would probably think that the following code would print the string “Bria and Bryan are laughing and playing”.

```
namespace StringApp
{
  using System;
  public class TestStr
  {
    public static int Main(string[] args)
    {
      string str;
      str="Bria and Bryan are playing";
      str.Insert(19,"laughing and ");
      Console.WriteLine(str);
      return 0;
    }
  }
}
```

Well, you are wrong. If you compile and run this program, you will see that it prints the string "Bria and Bryan are playing". The call to Insert does not modify the string on which it is called; it returns a completely new string. Because we did not assign the return value of the Insert function to a variable, the result of the Insert function is lost. The correct way to write this program would be as follows:

```
namespace StringApp
{
  using System;
  public class TestStr
  {
    public static int Main(string[] args)
    {
      string str1, str2;
      str1="Bria and Bryan are playing";
      str2=str1.Insert(19,"laughing and ");
      Console.WriteLine(str2);
      return 0;
    }
  }
}
```

Creating new strings all the time will obviously degrade the performance of most applications. This is why Microsoft created the **StringBuilder** class. The **StringBuilder** class can be found in the System.Text namespace; it provides a string-like class that is more efficient to use when you are constructing a string by concatenating other strings together. The operations on the **StringBuilder** class operate on the current instance rather than generating a new string after each method call. The basic idea is that you assemble your string using the **StringBuilder** class and then you convert the string to a regular string when its contents are complete. The **StringBuilder** class contains the methods shown in Table 4–6:

TABLE 4–6 *A sample of the methods in System.Text.StringBuilder*

Method Name	Description
Append	Appends the string representation of an object to the StringBuilder instance on which it is called.
AppendFormat	Appends the string representation of an object to the StringBuilder instance on which it is called using a specified format string.
EnsureCapacity	Ensures that the capacity of the string is at least a specified integer value.
Insert	Inserts the string representation of an object at a specified location.

TABLE 4–6 *A sample of the methods in System.Text.StringBuilder (continued)*

Method Name	Description
Remove	Removes the specified characters from the StringBuilder.
Replace	Replaces all occurrences of a character with a specified new character.

It also contains the properties listed in Table 4–7.

TABLE 4–7 *A Sample of the Properties in System.Text.StringBuilder*

Property Name	Description
Capacity	Sets or gets the number of characters that this StringBuilder can hold.
Chars	Gets or sets the character at the specified index in the string. This property performs the same function as the StringBuilder indexer directly below.
[ ]	The StringBuilder indexer. Unlike the String object, you can use this indexer to get or set a specific character in a StringBuilder instance.
Length	Gets or sets the length of the current StringBuilder.
MaxCapacity	Gets the maximum allowed capacity for the current StringBuilder (read-only).

The following example program demonstrates how to use the **StringBuilder** class to build up a string. If you had simply used the "+" operator on the string class to concatenate these strings, you would be creating a new string each time you used the "+" operator. In this example I built up a string using a single StringBuilder instance and then converted it to a string when I was done.

```
namespace StringApp
{
  using System;
  using System.Text;
  public class TestStr
  {
    public static int Main(string[] args)
    {
      StringBuilder stb;
      string str;
      int orderID=12345;
      decimal cost=4.54m;
      stb=new StringBuilder(
```

```
            "The total cost for order: ");
        stb.AppendFormat("{0}", orderID);
        stb.Append(" = ");
        stb.AppendFormat("{0:C}",cost);
        str=stb.ToString();
    // Will print the following:
    // The total cost for order: 12345 = $4.54
        Console.WriteLine(str);
        return 0;
      }
    }
  }
```

The best thing about the **System.String** class is that all CLR-compliant programming languages share it. Therefore, whether you are using C#, VB.NET, JScript.NET, or any of a dozen other third-party languages that should be introduced around the same time as .NET, the way that you work with strings will be the same.

Creating and Using an Array in C#

Working with Arrays in C# is simpler and less error-prone than C and C++. Arrays in C# are objects that support the properties shown in Table 4–8.

TABLE 4–8 *A sample of the properties in System.Array*

Property Name	Description
Length	Returns the number of elements in the array. If the array is multidimensional, it returns the total number of elements in all dimensions.
Rank	Returns the number of dimensions of the array, that is, the rank will be 2 for a 2D array.

The C# array class contains the methods shown in Table 4–9.

TABLE 4–9 *A sample of the methods in System.Array*

Method Name	Description
Clear	Sets a range of elements in the array to zero or a null reference.
Copy	Copies a portion of one array to another (deep copy).
Clone	Returns another reference to the array (a shallow copy).
GetLowerBound	Returns the lower bound of a specified dimension of the array.
GetUpperBound	Returns the upper bound of a specified dimension of the array.
GetValue	Returns the value at a specified index (or indexes in a multidimensional array) in an array. You can also use the index [] operator for this.
SetValue	Sets the value at a specified index (indices) you can also use the index "[]" operator for this
IndexOf	Returns the first occurrence of a specified value in a one-dimensional array.
LastIndexOf	Returns the last occurrence of a specified value in a one-dimensional array.
Reverse	Reverses the order of the elements in a one-dimensional array.
Sort	Sorts the elements in a one-dimensional array. (Each element must support the IComparable interface.)

As you can see from looking at the methods and properties supported by the array class, arrays are full-featured collections in C#. You can perform a shallow or deep copy, search for the first or last occurrence of a specified value, reverse the order of the elements in the array, or sort the elements in the array. Using an array is similar to the way that you would use an array in C++. The following code demonstrates how to use arrays in C#:

```
namespace ArrayApp
{
  using System;
  using System.Text;
  internal class Employee
  {
    public Employee(string name)
    {
      this.name=name;
    }
    public string name;
  }
  public class TestArray
  {
```

```
    public static int Main(string[] args)
    {
      // An array of value types
      int[] intArray=new int[20];
      // An array of reference types
      Employee[] empArray=new Employee[2];
      // An initialized array
      string[] strArray= {"A", ".NET","Primer"};
      int i;

      for (i=0;i<20;i++)
        intArray[i]=i;

      empArray[0]=new Employee("Alan Gordon");
      empArray[1]=new Employee("Tamber Gordon");

      Console.WriteLine(intArray[1]);
      Console.WriteLine(strArray[1]);
      Console.WriteLine(empArray[1].name);
      return 0;
    }
  }
}
```

You can also create multidimensional arrays in C#. The following example program demonstrates how to declare and use multidimensional arrays:

```
namespace ArrayApp
{
  using System;
  using System.Text;
  internal class Employee
  {
    public Employee(string name)
    {
      this.name=name;
    }
    public string name;
    }
  public class TestArray
  {
    public static int Main(string[] args)
     {
      float[,,] fltArray=new float[2,3,4];
      Employee[,] empArray=new Employee[2,3];
      string[,] strArray= {
        {"A", ".NET","Primer"},
        {"COM","COM+","Primer"}};
      int i, j, k;
```

```
        for (i=0;i<2;i++)
          for (j=0;j<3;j++)
            for (k=0;k<3;k++)
              fltArray[i,j,k]=
                i*1.5f+2.5f*j+3.5f*k;

        empArray[0,1]=new Employee("Alan Gordon");
        empArray[1,1]=new Employee("Tamber Gordon");

        Console.WriteLine(fltArray[1,1,1]);
        Console.WriteLine(strArray[1,2]);
        Console.WriteLine(empArray[1,1].name);
        return 0;
      }
    }
  }
```

Declaring classes in C#

The syntax for declaring classes is a major point of departure between C# and C++. With C#, the entire definition of a class lives in a single file. In C++, you would typically have both a header file that contains a declaration of the class (and may optionally contain the inline declaration of some of the simpler methods) and an implementation file usually with the extension .c or .cpp that contains the bulk of the implementation of the class. You typically distribute the header file to users of your class along with a compiled ".dll" or ".lib" file. The header file functions as a sort of metadata for the classes in the ".dll" or ".lib" file. The following program shows how you would declare and use a class in C#:

```
namespace ClassApp
{
  using System;
  public class Employee
  {
    public Employee(int id,string name)
    {
      this.name=name;
      this.ID=id;
    }
    public decimal GetSalary()
    {
      return 500.00m;
    }
    int ID;
    public string name;
```

```
    }
    public class TestClass
    {
      public static int Main(string[] args)
      {
        Employee emp=new Employee(80,"Alan Gordon");
        Console.WriteLine(emp.name);
        return 0;
      }
    }
}
```

Let's examine the code more closely. You begin the class declaration by specifying the accessibility level for the class (public in this case), the keyword class, and then the class name as follows:

```
public class Employee
```

The public accessibility qualifier means that the class is exposed to the outside world. In other words, it is visible to clients outside of its own assembly. The top-level types declared within an assembly can either have the public or internal accessibility level. If you wanted to declare a class so that it is only usable from within the assembly where it was defined you would declare it as internal instead.

```
internal class Employee
```

A complete list of the accessibility levels supported by types and members (fields, methods, properties, and) of a type is shown in Table 4–10.

TABLE 4–10 *Accessibility levels*

Accessibility Level	Description
public	Access is not restricted in any way.
internal	Access is limited to the assembly where the type or member is defined.
private	Access is limited to the containing type (can only be applied to members of a class or nested classes).
protected	Access is limited to the containing class or subclasses of the containing class type (can only be applied to members of a class or nested classes).
protected internal	Access is limited to the current assembly or subclasses of the containing class type (can only be applied to members of a class or nested classes).

Notice that only two of these accessibility levels (public and internal) may be applied to a top-level type in a namespace. A top-level type is a type that is defined directly beneath its namespace as the **Employee** class was defined within the ClassApp namespace previously. This is as opposed to a nested class as follows:

```
namespace AccessTest
{
  public class Outerclass
  {
    // …
    protected class InnerClass
    {
    // …
    }
  }
}
```

In this case, the class called **OuterClass** is a top-level class in the AccessTest namespace, so it can only have either the public or internal accessibility levels assigned to it. However, the class called **InnerClass** is not a top-level class; it is defined within **OuterClass**, so it can have any of the five accessibility levels shown previously.

The next section of code in the Employee class contains the constructor for the class.

```
public Employee(int id,string name)
{
    this.name=name;
    this.ID=id;
}
```

The constructors have the same name as their class, and they can be overloaded. Therefore, if you wanted to create another constructor for the **Employee** class that only took a name as a parameter and generated an ID for the employee internally, you would write the following code:

```
public Employee(string name)
{
    this.name=name;
    this.ID=550;
}
```

The compiler automatically generates a call to the constructor whenever you create a new instance of a particular class. It chooses the correct constructor from the overloads based on the parameters that you use when you call new. Therefore, the following call will generate a call to the first constructor:

```
Employee emp=new Employee(80,"Alan Gordon");
```

And the following code will generate a call to the second constructor:

```
Employee emp=new Employee("Tamber Gordon");
```

Constructors are usually public, but you can define a private constructor to prevent someone from creating an instance of a class if, for instance, the class only contains static members or should only be used as a base class.

Classes are reference types only. In other words, you can only create instances of classes on the heap using the new operator. This is unlike C++ where you can create classes on the heap or stack as follows:

```
// C++ code
// emp1 resides on the stack
Employee emp1(80,"Alan Gordon");
// emp2 resides on the heap
Employee *emp2=new Employee(90,"Tamber Gordon");
```

If you want to create user-defined types that reside on the stack in C#, you must declare them as value types using the struct keyword instead of class.

The next section of code declares a public method of the **Employee** class called GetSalary that returns a hard-coded amount of $500.00.

```
public decimal GetSalary()
{
    return 500.00m;
}
```

Note In the .NET Framework, the decimal type is typically used to store currency (monetary) values.

The final section of code in this class declaration contains a declaration of two member fields in this class: an int that contains the ID for the employee and a string that contains the name of the employee.

```
int ID;
public string name;
```

The name field has a public accessibility level, but notice that the ID field has no accessibility level specified. What's its level? It turns out that, in this case, the accessibility level is private because the default accessibility level for a class is private. Each of the categories of types that you can declare in .NET: enum, class, interface, and struct has a default accessibility level as shown in Table 4–11.

TABLE 4-11 *Default accessibility levels*

Type	Default Accessibility Level
Enum	public
Class	private
Interface	public
Struct	private

One significant difference between C# and C++ is C#'s support for properties. You can think of properties as a method (or more typically a pair of methods) that behaves like a field. The public name field in **Employee** could be converted to a property as follows:

```
public class Employee
{
//...
  public decimal Name
  {
    get { return name; }
    set { name=value; }
  }
  private string name;
}
```

To declare a property, you declare its accessibility, type, and name. Next you define the get and set logic for the property. The logic in the get block is executed whenever someone reads the property as follows:

```
Employee emp1=new Employee(80,"Alan Gordon");
Console.WriteLine(emp1.Name);
```

The logic in the set block is executed whenever someone writes to the property as follows:

```
Employee emp1=new Employee(80,"Alan Gordon");
emp2.Name="Bryan Gordon";
```

Notice that I changed the accessibility of the name field in the **Employee** class to private after I changed the name field to a property. This is good object-oriented practice. In most cases, it is a bad idea to expose a field of a class directly because it will make it difficult if you need to change the internal implementation of the class later because clients will be written that depend on the field. With properties, you get the convenient syntax of a field with the encapsulation of accessor methods. If you look at the generated MSIL for the **Employee** class, you will see that, behind the scenes, the C# compiler actually generated two hidden methods called get_Name and set_Name that are called whenever you use the Name property as follows:

```
.method public hidebysig specialname
  instance string  get_Name() cil managed
{
  // Code size       11 (0xb)
  .maxstack  1
  .locals init (string V_0)
  IL_0000:  ldarg.0
  IL_0001:  ldfld      string
    ACME.BusinessObjects.Employee::mName
  IL_0006:  stloc.0
  IL_0007:  br.s       IL_0009

  IL_0009:  ldloc.0
  IL_000a:  ret
} // end of method Employee::get_Name

.method public hidebysig specialname
  instance void  set_Name(string 'value') cil managed
{
  // Code size       8 (0x8)
  .maxstack  2
  IL_0000:  ldarg.0
  IL_0001:  ldarg.1
  IL_0002:  stfld      string
    ACME.BusinessObjects.Employee::mName
  IL_0007:  ret
} // end of method Employee::set_Name
```

You can create a read-only property by omitting the set block in your property declaration. Although they are unusual, you can also create a write-only property by omitting the get block.

I can't leave the subject of class declarations without talking about static fields and methods. So far, I have only declared per-instance fields and methods in the classes, but occasionally you will have the need for class-level fields and methods that are shared by all instances of a class. C#, like C++, uses the keyword static for declaring class-level fields. You can call static methods and access static fields and properties on a class without declaring an instance of the class. You access static members of a class using the class name instead of an object reference. This is in contrast with C++ that allowed you to access static members using the class name or an instance variable.

As an example, you could declare a variable that maintains a count of the currently extant employees as follows:

```
public class Employee
{
  public Employee(int id,string name,decimal salary)
  {
    mID=id;
    mName=name;
    mSalary=salary;
```

```
    mNumEmployees++;
  }
  ~Employee()
  {
    mNumEmployees--;
  }
  //… the rest of the Employee class is
//  omitted for clarity
  static public int GetNumEmployees()
  {
    return mNumEmployees;
  }
  private int mID;
  private string mName;
  private decimal mSalary;
  static private int mNumEmployees=0;
}
```

Notice that you use the static keyword to declare a field to hold the current number of Employees (mNumEmployees). You then increment the count of Employees in the constructor and decrement the count in the destructor. I also declared a static method called GetNumEmployees that returns the count of Employees. You can now call the GetNumEmployees method using the following syntax:

```
Console.WriteLine(Employee.GetNumEmployees());
```

Notice that I specified the class name **Employee** to the left of the . instead of an Employee instance. You can access static fields from per-instance (nonstatic) methods, but you cannot access nonstatic fields from static methods. Static methods are not associated with an instance of the class, so no instance data ("this" pointer) is available when a static method is called.

C# also supports static properties, so, instead of having a static GetNumEmployees method, you can declare a static NumEmployees property as follows:

```
static public int NumEmployees
{
    get { return mNumEmployees; }
}
```

You can now use this property as follows:

```
Console.WriteLine(Employee.NumEmployees);
```

C# also supports static constructors. Static constructors are useful when you have static fields that require initialization. Static constructors are called automatically by the CLR before the first instance of the class is created. They are declared without access modifiers (public, private, and so forth), and they cannot have arguments. As an example, let's say that, instead of maintaining a count of the number of extant Employees, you want to maintain a static collection that contains references to every employee. To do this, you would change the declaration of the **Employee** class as follows:

```
public class Employee
{
  public Employee(int id,string name,decimal salary)
  {
    mName=name;
    mID=id;
    mEmployees.Add(mID,this);
  }
  static Employee()
  {
    mEmployees=new Hashtable(50);
  }
  ~Employee()
  {
    mEmployees.Remove(mID);
  }
  //… the rest of the Employee class is
  //  omitted for clarity
  static public Hashtable Employees
  {
    get { return mEmployees; }
  }
  private int mID;
  private string mName;
  private decimal mSalary;
  static private Hashtable mEmployees;
}
```

Notice that I declared a private Hashtable field to hold the references to all of the Employee objects. I then declare a static constructor, and, in that constructor, I assign the Hashtable field to a new instance of the **Hashtable** class. I then alter the per-instance constructor and destructor to add and remove items from the Hashtable.

Using Inheritance in C#

With object-oriented design and programming, you design and build your applications by discovering (through analysis and design) and then implementing the key abstractions in the problem domain as well as implementing (or buying) key-implementation abstractions, such as collections, GUI classes, and so forth. One of the key pillars of object orientation is inheritance. Inheritance is how you express an “is-a” relationship between two abstractions (classes). In other words, inheritance is how you model and implement a relationship where two or more types are generalizations/specializations of each other. For instance, if you are building a payroll application, you would likely need an **Employee** class to model the employees that will be paid through our system. However, most companies have various different kinds of employees. There are the general "rank-and-file" employees who are paid only a salary; managers who receive a salary plus a bonus that is tied to the performance of their department; and executives who receive a salary, a bonus, and stock options. Even though the employee, manager, and executive types have lots of things in common, each type has certain things that are unique to that type. For instance, managers have a bonus amount, and they also have a list of employees that they manage. Executives have all the things that a manager has, but they also have stock options. Although managers and executives have state and operations that are unique to those types, they are also employees and have all of the characteristics of a "rank-and-file" employee, such as a name and an employee ID. That's what I mean by an "is-a" relationship. An executive is a manager, and a manager is a employee.

Inheritance allows us to create types that inherit the interface and implementation of their base type. However, you can also add additional state and operations and even override certain methods from your base types to provide a more appropriate implementation for the specialized version of the class. This last point—the ability to override certain methods from the base class—is key. It means that variables that are typed as a base class may actually reference instances of a subtype of the base class and operations that you call on these base classes may actually invoke different methods depending on what type of object the variable references. This is known as polymorphism, and it is closely related to dynamic binding (also called virtual functions), which I discuss shortly.

Enough with the conceptual discussion. Let's see how to use inheritance and polymorphism in C#. The following code shows a slightly more realistic (but still simple) **Employee** class.

```
public class Employee
{
  public Employee(int id,
    string name,
    decimal salary)
  {
    this.mName=name;
    this.mID=id;
    this.mSalary=salary;
  }
  public int ID
  {
    get { return mID; }
```

```
    set { mID=value; }
  }
  public string Name
  {
    get { return mName; }
    set { mName=value; }
  }
  public decimal Salary
  {
    get { return mSalary; }
    set { mSalary=value; }
  }
  public decimal GetPay()
  {
    return mSalary;
  }
  private int mID;
  private string mName;
  private decimal mSalary;
}
```

Notice that this class has three private variables, mID, mName, and mSalary, that contain the state that I am storing for an employee.

```
private int mID;
private string mName;
private decimal mSalary;
```

The class also contains a constructor that initializes the state from arguments that you pass in.

```
public Employee(int id,
          string name,
          decimal salary)

{
    this.mName=name;
    this.mID=id;
    this.mSalary=salary;
}
```

In the constructor, you refer to the state variables using the this pointer. C# is just like C++ in that each nonstatic method of a class has an implicit argument called a this pointer, which contains a pointer to the object on which this method is being called. In this case, the use of the keyword this is optional. I could just as easily have defined the constructor as follows:

```
public Employee(int id,string name,decimal salary)
{
  mName=name;
  mID=id;
```

```
  mSalary=salary;
}
```

You are not limited to one constructor. You can have several constructors with different argument lists. The C# compiler will pick the appropriate constructor based on the argument list that you pass in when you instantiate an Employee instance.

This **Employee** class also uses properties to expose the ID, name, and salary of an employee as follows for name:

```
public string Name
{
    get { return mName; }
    set { mName=value; }
}
```

The following code shows a **Manager** class that inherits from **Employee**:

```
public class Manager : Employee
{
  public Manager(int id,string name,
    decimal salary,decimal bonus) : base(id,name,salary)
  {
    this.mBonus=bonus;
    mSubordinates=new Hashtable(50);
  }
  ~Manager()
  {
    RemoveAllSubordinates();
  }
  public void AddSubordinate(Employee emp)
  {
    mSubordinates.Add(emp.ID,emp);
  }
  public void RemoveSubordinate(int ID)
  {
    mSubordinates.Remove(ID);
  }
  public void RemoveAllSubordinates()
  {
    mSubordinates.Clear();
  }
  public Hashtable Subordinates
  {
    get { return mSubordinates; }
  }
  public new decimal GetPay()
  {
    return base.Salary+mBonus;
```

```
  }
  private decimal mBonus;
  private Hashtable mSubordinates;
}
```

The syntax for deriving a subclass from a base class is shown here:

```
public class Manager : Employee
```

In this case, I am creating a public class called **Manager** that inherits from a class called **Employee**. C# only allows single inheritance, so there can only be one base class. The **Employee** class must either be a class that is defined in the same assembly (as it is in this case), or it must be defined in an assembly that the current assembly references. You can access the public methods, fields, and properties in the base class using the base keyword. I used this during the definition of the constructor as shown here:

```
public Manager(int id,string name,decimal salary,decimal
bonus) : base(id,name,salary)
{
    this.mBonus=bonus;
    mSubordinates=new Hashtable(50);
}
```

In this case, you pass the ID, name, and salary through to the constructor for the **Employee** class so that the **Employee** part of the Managers state can be initialized. You also use the Salary property in the **Employee** base class to implement the GetPay method as follows:

```
public new decimal GetPay()
{
    return base.Salary+mBonus;
}
```

The GetPay method in the **Manager** class uses the Salary property from the **Employee** class to fetch the manager's salary and then adds on her bonus.

Note Don't worry about the use of the new keyword in the declaration of the GetPay method. I discuss that shortly when I talk about polymorphism.

Only members with a public or protected accessibility level are callable from a derived class. If the **Employee** class contained the following method:

```
public class Employee
{
    // code elided for clarity …
    private void GiveRaise(decimal amt)
    {
```

```
      mSalary+=amt;
    }
    // code elided for clarity…
}
```

the following code in the **Manager** class would not compile:

```
public class Manager : Employee
{
    // code omitted for clarity…
    public void IncreaseCompensation(
        decimal salary,
        decimal bonus)
    {
        mBonus+=bonus;
        base.GiveRaise(salary);  // compiler error!
    }
    // code omitted for clarity…
}
```

You will receive the following error from the C# compiler when you attempt to compile the **Manager** class:

```
Employee.GiveRaise is inaccessible due to its protection
level
```

If you changed the definition of the GiveRaise method in the **Employee** class to the following:

```
public class Employee
{
    // code elided for clarity …
    protected void GiveRaise(decimal amt)
    {
      mSalary+=amt;
    }
    // code elided for clarity…
}
```

The IncreaseCompensation method in the **Manager** class will compile; this behavior is exactly the same as C++.

Polymorphism

No discussion of inheritance would be complete without a discussion of polymorphism. Consider the following client code that was written using the current definition of the **Employee** and **Manager** classes.

```
class TestClass
{
    static void Main(string[] args)
    {
```

```
            Employee emp;
            emp=new Manager(2,"Tamber Gordon",800,200);
            System.Console.WriteLine("Pay = {0}",
            emp.GetPay());
        }
    }
```

Notice that I have declared an Employee reference and then assigned it to a new Manager object. The manager has a salary of $800 and a bonus of $200. The question is what will the GetPay method return when it is called through an Employee reference as it is here. The GetPay method will return $800 if it uses the Employee implementation of GetPay, and it will return $1,000 if it uses the Manager implementation of GetPay. With the current definitions of **Employee** and **Manager**, the correct answer is $800. To understand why, let's go back to the definition of the GetPay method in the **Employee** class.

```
// The implementation of GetPay in the Employee class
public decimal GetPay()
{
    return mSalary;
}
```

This method is not declared as a virtual method. With a nonvirtual method, the compiler will bind to the GetPay method at compile time, and it will use the GetPay method associated with the type of the reference (Employee in this case), not the type of the object that the reference points to (a Manager in this case). When a virtual method is called through an object reference, the CLR will use runtime lookup to bind to the method associated with the type of the object that the reference points to. This runtime lookup will start at the type of the object (Manager in this case) and look for a method that matches the requested virtual method. If the CLR does not find a matching method in the **Manager** class, it will search the base classes in order until it finds a matching method. That way, if the derived class overrides a method, the method in the derived class will be called. If the derived class does not override a method, the version of the method in the base class will be called. This behavior is the very essence of polymorphism.

To make the GetPay method virtual, you simply need to change its definition in the **Employee** class to look as follows:

```
public virtual decimal GetPay()
{
    return mSalary;
}
```

Now, if you run the following code again, what do you think the result will be?

```
class TestClass
{
    static void Main(string[] args)
    {
      Employee emp;
      emp=new Manager(2,"Tamber Gordon",800,200);
      System.Console.WriteLine("Pay = {0}",
      emp.GetPay());
    }
}
```

If you said $1,000 (which would indicate that the Manager version of GetPay was called), you are still wrong. The code will return $800, indicating that the Employee version of GetPay was used. So what gives?

OVERRIDING METHODS

One major difference between C++ and C# is that the C# compiler does not automatically assume that you want to override a virtual method in a base class if you declare a method by the same name in a derived class. C++ tended to create fragile base classes because it was very easy to override a method when you didn't intend to. With C#, you must explicitly choose whether you want to hide or override a base class method using the new and override keywords. If you do not use one of these keywords, the compiler will assume that you want to hide the base class method, and it will issue the following warning:

```
warning CS0114: [derivedclassname.methodname] hides
inherited
member [baseclassname.methodname].
To make the current member override that implementation,
add the override keyword.
Otherwise add the new keyword.
```

If you explicitly use the new keyword in the redeclaration of a virtual method in a derived class (as I have done), the method hides the method with the same name in the base class.

```
public new decimal GetPay()
{
    return base.Salary+mBonus;
}
```

Hiding means that, if you call the Manager object through a Manager reference, you will get the Manager's version of GetPay. However, if you call the GetPay method on a Manager object method through an Employee reference, you will get the Employee's version of GetPay.

If you want the version of GetPay in the **Manager** class to override the GetPay method in the **Employee** class, you must use the override keyword as follows:

```
public override decimal GetPay()
{
    return base.Salary+mBonus;
}
```

If you use the override keyword in the declaration of the GetPay method in the **Manager** class, our test code will return $1,000.00, indicating that the GetPay method associated with the **Manager** class was called.

```
class TestClass
{
    static void Main(string[] args)
    {
      Employee emp;
      emp=new Manager(2,"Tamber Gordon",800,200);
      System.Console.WriteLine("Pay = {0}",
      emp.GetPay()); // now returns $1000.00
    }
}
```

The key advantage of the C# approach is that it provides better support for versioning and makes for less fragile base classes. Let's say I decided to add a Pontificate method to my **Manager** class (we all know that most managers are prone to such behavior).

```
public class Manager : Employee
{
//… I elided the code in the Manager class for clarity
  public virtual string Pontificate()
  {
    return "blah blah blah";
  }
}
```

I can write code that uses the Pontificate method using a Manager reference as shown here:

```
Manager mgr;
mgr=new Manager(2,"Alan Gordon",800,200);
System.Console.WriteLine(mgr.Pontificate());
```

Now let's say that the **Employee** class came from a third-party library, and, in version 2 of their library, they decide to implement a Pontificate method in the **Employee** class as shown here:

```
public class Employee
{
//… I elided the rest of the code in the Employee class
//  for clarity
  public virtual string Pontificate()
  {
    return "When I started at this company…"";
  }
}
```

It was probably not your intention to override the Pontificate method in the **Employee** class when you created a Pontificate method in the **Manager** class. Indeed, it couldn't have been your intention because the **Employee** class did not have a Pontificate method when you created the **Manager** class. The decision to override a method in a base class should always be a carefully considered one. You should always consider whether you need to call the base classes' implementation of the method. Failure to do so could cause the base class to break. With C#, the Pontificate method in the **Manager** class cannot accidentally override the Pontificate method in the **Employee** class.

ABSTRACT CLASSES

Like C++, C# supports abstract classes. An abstract class is a class where one or more of the methods in the class is left unspecified. Abstract classes make sense when you want to define a signature for a method in a class so that all classes that inherit from the class must support the method. However, the base class in which you want to define the method is so generic that you cannot provide a suitable implementation of the method in that class. You cannot create an instance of an abstract class. To create an instantiatable class, you must derive a class from the abstract class and provide an implementation for all of the abstract methods in the class. This derived class is now called a concrete class. Even though you cannot create an instance of an abstract class, you can declare a reference that is typed to the abstract class and then point that reference to an object that is typed as a concrete class that derives from the abstract class.

I can probably make this clearer using an example from the **Employee** class. With its current design, this class will only support salaried employees. Ideally, you would like to support hourly employees as well as contractors, and consultants who may be paid hourly or a lump sum. The best way to support a wide variety of compensation algorithms is to redesign the **Employee** class and make it more generic. I will remove the Salary property and the mSalary member from the **Employee** class. I will then create **SalariedEmployee** and **HourlyEmployee** classes that derived from the **Employee** class. I will leave the declaration of GetPay method in the **Employee** class. However, given the wide variety of compensation schemes that may be applied to an Employee, it is impossible to provide an implementation for the GetPay method in the **Employee** class, so we will turn it into an abstract class as follows:

```
    public abstract class  Employee
  {
    public Employee(int id,string name)
    {
      mName=name;
      mID=id;
    }
    ~Employee()
    {
      MessageBox.Show("Destructor called");
    }
    public int ID
    {
      get { return mID; }
      set { mID=value; }
    }
    public string Name
    {
      get { return mName; }
      set { mName=value; }
    }
    public abstract decimal GetPay();
    private int mID;
    private string mName;
    }
```

Notice that I used the abstract keyword both on the GetPay method and the class itself. Also notice that I have not provided an implementation of the GetPay method. The following code shows how you would create a **SalariedEmployee** class that inherits from the **Employee** class and provides an implementation for the GetPay method.

```
public class SalariedEmployee : Employee
{
  public SalariedEmployee(int id,string name,
    decimal salary) :
      base(id,name)
  {
      mSalary=salary;
  }
  public decimal Salary
  {
      get { return mSalary; }
      set { mSalary=value; }
  }
  public override decimal GetPay()
  {
      return mSalary;
  }
  private decimal mSalary;
}
```

The **SalariedEmployee** class is now a concrete class. The following code will succeed:

```
SalariedEmployee salEmp=new SalariedEmployee(5,"Alan
Gordon",500);
```

As will this:

```
Employee emp=new SalariedEmployee(5,"Alan Gordon",500);
```

However, the following code will not compile because you are trying to create an instance of an abstract class.

```
Employee emp=new Employee(5,"Alan Gordon");
```

INTERFACES

Somewhat related to abstract classes are interfaces. An interface is a set of related methods that together define some behavior. An interface has no associated implementation for any of its methods; it just defines the prototype for the methods. You can almost think of an interface as an abstract class where *all* of the methods in the class are left abstract. In fact, people usually implement interfaces in C++ as abstract classes that contain only abstract (unimplemented) methods. To use an interface, you simply add a comma-delimited list of the interfaces that your class will implement using the same syntax that you use for inheritance as follows:

```
public class SalariedEmployee : Employee, IDisposable,
IMyInteface
{
//… the rest of the class definition is omitted for clarity
}
```

Notice that the **Employee** base class is listed first. If your class inherits from a base class and implements one or more interfaces, the base class must appear first in the comma-delimited list of base classes and interfaces. One key difference, though, between inheritance and implementing interfaces is that a class can implement multiple interfaces, but it can only inherit from one base class.

If you wanted to turn the **Employee** abstract class into an interface, you would write the following code.

```
public interface IEmployee
{
    void Work(int numHours);
    decimal GetPay();
    void Terminate();
}
```

An acid test of whether inheritance makes sense or not is that the sentence "a [**derivedclassname**] is a [**baseclassname**]" should make intuitive sense. For example, "a manager is a employee." Interfaces, however, are used to model a "has the behavior of" or a "behaves like" relationship. In other words, the sentence "a [**implementingclassname**] behaves like a [interface-name]" should make intuitive sense. In many cases, both sentences will make sense.

In an object hierarchy like the one that I have created, interfaces are useful when you find yourself needing to implement the same behavior in a number of classes. It's a good tipoff that you need to create an interface when you find yourself implementing the same set of methods over and over again in many classes. By factoring these methods into an interface and then implementing those interfaces in your classes, you gain a commonality of expression that you can exploit. You can create reference variables typed to that interface and then point those variables at an instance of any class that implements the interface.

Once again, let's create an example using the **Employee** classes. After I split the hierarchy into salaried and hourly employees, I have a problem. Which of these classes should the **Manager** class derive from? I could have managers who were either salaried or paid hourly. This means that we will need 2 Manager classes, SalariedManager and HourlyManager, but both of those classes will share similar functionality. For example, a manager has subordinates and does performance reviews. Additionally, I would like to be able to write code that operates on all managers whether they are salaried or paid hourly. You can accomplish this using an IManager interface as follows:

```
public interface IManager
{
    void AddSubordinate(Employee emp);
    void RemoveSubordinate(int ID);
    void RemoveAllSubordinates();
    Hashtable Subordinates();
    decimal GetBonus();
}
```

You can then create a **SalariedManager** class that implements the IManager interface as follows:

```
public class SalariedManager : SalariedEmployee, IManager
{
  public SalariedManager(int id,string name,
    decimal salary,decimal bonus) :
    base(id,name,salary)
  {
    this.mBonus=bonus;
    mSubordinates=new Hashtable(50);
  }
  ~SalariedManager()
  {
    RemoveAllSubordinates();
```

```
  }
  public decimal GetBonus()
  {
    return mBonus;
  }
  public void AddSubordinate(Employee emp)
  {
    mSubordinates.Add(emp.ID,emp);
  }
  public void RemoveSubordinate(int ID)
  {
    mSubordinates.Remove(ID);
  }
  public void RemoveAllSubordinates()
  {
    mSubordinates.Clear();
  }
  public Hashtable GetSubordinates()
  {
    return mSubordinates;
  }
  public override decimal GetPay()
  {
    return base.Salary+mBonus;
  }
  private decimal mBonus;
  private Hashtable mSubordinates;
}
```

The following code shows how you would use the **SalariedManager** class and the IManager interface:

```
1.  static void Main(string[] args)
2.  {
3.  Decimal decBonus;
4.  Employee empMgr=new
5.      SalariedManager(1,"Tamber Gordon",1800,200);
6.  Employee empEmp=new
7.      SalariedEmployee(2,"Alan Gordon",500);
8.  IManager mgr = empMgr as IManager;
9.  if (mgr != null)
10. {
11.   decBonus=mgr.GetBonus();
12.   mgr.AddSubordinate(empEmp);
13. }
14. else
15.   Console.WriteLine("Not a manager!");
16. }
```

The key line of code here is line 8 where you cast the empMgr Employee reference (which actually points to a SalariedManager object) to a

IManager interface reference using the as operator. If the Employee reference can be cast to an IManager interface reference, you then call the GetBonus and AddSubordinate methods on the IManager interface on lines 11 and 12.

Flow of Control Constructs

C# supports the same flow of control statements that you are familiar with from C and C++. The structure of an if statement is almost exactly the same as C and C++. C# also supports switch statements and adds the very useful ability to switch on a string. There are for, do, and while loops and a new loop called the foreach loop that you will probably find yourself using more than any other type of loop.

Let's start by looking at the if statement. The following code shows an example of a simple if statement in C#:

```
int x=0, y=1;
if (x > y)
    System.Console.WriteLine("x is greater than y");
```

You can also use else if and else clauses as follows:

```
int x=0, y=1;
if (x > y)
    System.Console.WriteLine("x is greater than y");
else if (y > x)
    System.Console.WriteLine("x is less than y");
else
      System.Console.WriteLine("x and y are equal");
```

If you want to have multiple statements within your if block, you use curly braces just like C and C++.

```
int x=0, y=1;
if (x > y)
{
    System.Console.WriteLine("X is greater than y");
    System.Console.WriteLine("And I am so happy");
}
```

Switch statements in C# are very similar to switch statements in C and C++. The following code shows a simple switch statement in C#:

```
int intInputValue;
string strInput;
strInput=Console.ReadLine();
try
{
```

```
    intInputValue=int.Parse(strInput);
    switch (intInputValue)
    {
      case 1:
        Console.WriteLine("You entered 1");
        break;
      case 2:
        goto case 3;
      case 3:
        Console.WriteLine("You entered 2 or 3");
        break;
      case 4:
        goto default;
      default:
        Console.WriteLine(
        "You entered a number > than 3 or < 1");
        break;
    }
}
catch
{
    System.Console.WriteLine("Please enter a number");
}
```

Rather than using "goto case 3" on case 2, you can combine case 2 and 3 as follows:

```
switch (intInputValue)
{
    case 1:
      Console.WriteLine("You entered 1");
      break;
    case 2:
    case 3:
      Console.WriteLine("You entered 2 or 3");
      break;
    case 4:
      goto default;
    default:
      Console.WriteLine(
      "You entered a number > 3 or < 1");
      break;
}
```

There are some differences between C# and C and C++ switch statements. First, the endpoint of each case within the switch statement must not be reachable. There must be either a break or a goto to another case. This eliminates a common source of bugs in C and C++: the unintended fallthrough from one case to another as follows:

```
// C++ code
switch (intInputValue)
{
    case 1:
      Console.WriteLine("You entered 1");
      // falls through to case 2
    case 2:
      Console.WriteLine("You entered 2");
      break;
    default:
      Console.WriteLine(
      "You entered a number > than 2");
      break;
}
```

Notice that there is no break at the end of case 1. With C and C++, case 1 would fall through to case 2. With C#, this code will not compile. If you tried to compile this code with the C# compiler, you will receive the following error:

```
        Control cannot fall through from one case label
('case 1:') to another
```

Another key difference between C# and C and C++ switch statements is that, with C#, you can switch on strings as follows:

```
string strInput;
Console.WriteLine("Enter a color");
strInput=Console.ReadLine();
switch (strInput)
{
    case "red":
      Console.WriteLine("You entered RED");
      break;
    case "green":
      Console.WriteLine("You entered GREEN");
      break;
    case "blue":
      Console.WriteLine("You entered BLUE");
      break;
    default:
      Console.WriteLine("You entered a non-primary color");
      break;
}
```

The previous code will only work if the user enters the color string in all lower-case characters. You can solve this problem and create a case-insensitive switch statement using the ToLower function on the string that you are switching on.

```
switch (strInput.ToLower())
{
    case "red":
      Console.WriteLine("You entered RED");
      break;
    case "green":
      Console.WriteLine("You entered GREEN");
      break;
    case "blue":
      Console.WriteLine("You entered BLUE");
      break;
    default:
      Console.WriteLine("You entered a non-primary color");
      break;
}
```

C# has very similar looping constructs to C and C++. C# supports while loops, do loops, and for loops. A while loop loops while a condition is true. The condition is evaluated at the beginning of the loop as follows:

```
int i=0;
while (i < 10)
{
    Console.WriteLine("i = {0}",i);
    i++;
}
```

A do loop is very similar to a while loop except the condition is evaluated at the end of the loop.

```
int i=0;
do
{
    Console.WriteLine("i = {0}",i);
    i++;
} while (i < 10);
```

The for loop gives you a convenient way of looping over a range of values. It is often used for looping through arrays. In this example, I use a for loop to iterate through the array of command-line arguments that the user has passed to a console application.

```
public static int Main(string[] args)
{
    for (int i=0;i<args.Length;i++)
```

```
        Console.Write(" {0} ", args[i]);
      return 0;
}
```

A better way to iterate over all the elements of a collection or array is to use the foreach loop. Using a for loop to iterate over all the elements of a collection or array is a little more error prone (even though most competent programmers get it right). In order for it to work, you have to set up the initial condition and increment the count correctly. The foreach loop is also syntactically more terse and elegant. You can change the code shown previously to use a foreach loop as follows:

```
foreach (string arg in args)
{
    Console.Write(" {0} ", arg);
}
```

As you can see, the code here is shorter and more elegant.

With each of the aforementioned looping statements, you can use jump statements. C# supports the following jump statements: continue, break, and goto. A continue statement allows you to skip the portion of the loop after the continue statement for the current iteration. You can think of it as a jump to the end of the loop. The loop will continue if the looping condition is still met, however. The following code demonstrates the use of a continue statement with a foreach loop.

```
foreach (string arg in args)
{
    if (arg=="skip")
      continue;
    Console.Write(" {0} ", arg);
}
```

The break statement will exit the loop completely. The flow of control will continue on the first line after the loop. The following code shows a break statement with a for loop:

```
for (int i=0; i < 10; i++ )
{
    if (i==2)
      break;
    Console.WriteLine("i = {0}",i);
}
```

Break statements are also used with switch statements to jump out of each case.

Although its use is widely disparaged, the goto statement is a part of almost every computer language. You use the goto statement to jump directly to a label as follows:

```
int[,] a={{1,2,3},{4,5,6},{7,8,9}};
for (int i=0; i < 3; i++ )
{
  for (int j=0; j < 3; j++ )
  {
    if (i==1 && j==1)
      goto after_loop;
    Console.WriteLine(
      "i = {0}, j= {1}, a={2}",i,j,a[i,j]);
  }
}
after_loop:
```

This code actually shows one of the few legitimate uses of a goto: to jump completely out of a nested series of loops. If you used a break statement here instead of a goto, you will only get out of the innermost loop. Gotos can also be used in switch statements as follows:

```
switch (intInputValue)
{
    case 1:
      Console.WriteLine("You entered 1");
      break;
    case 2:
      goto case 3;
    case 3:
      Console.WriteLine("You entered 2 or 3");
      break;
    case 4:
      goto default;
    default:
      Console.WriteLine(
          "You entered a number greater than 3 or less
          than 1");
      break;
}
```

You cannot use a goto in C# to jump into the middle of a statement. For example, you cannot jump into the middle of a for loop.

Exception Handling in C#

One area where both C# and the .NET Framework significantly improve on C++ and COM/Win32 is in the area of exception handling. C# supports the same structured try/catch statements for exception handling that C++ has, but it adds a few key improvements. To use C# exception handling, simply enclose the code that may throw an exception inside a try block and then add catch blocks for each type of exception that you would like to handle. An example is as follows:

```
try
{
    Console.WriteLine("Enter the numerator");
    string strNumerator=Console.ReadLine();
    int intNumerator=int.Parse(strNumerator);
    Console.WriteLine("Enter the denominator");
    string strDenominator=Console.ReadLine();
    int intDenominator=int.Parse(strDenominator);
    int intResult=intNumerator/intDenominator;
    Console.WriteLine("The result is: {0}", intResult);
}
catch (Exception e)
{
    Console.WriteLine(
      "The exception type is: {0}",e.GetType());
    Console.WriteLine(
      "The exception message is: {0}",e.Message);
    Console.WriteLine(
      "The stack trace is: {0}",e.StackTrace);
}
```

The code here reads a numerator and a denominator from the console, converts the two inputs into integer numbers, and then divides the numerator by the denominator. There are a number of things that can go wrong with this code. The user could type in a value for the numerator or denominator that is not a number. Users could also enter zero for the denominator. If anything does go wrong with the code in a try block, the flow of control will jump to the catch block immediately following the try block. In this example, I print out the type of the exception, the message associated with the exception, and a stack trace.

The object that is thrown and caught in an exception statement is just an instance of a class that derives from **System.Exception**. The base class library contains a number of Exception classes, and you can also define you own by deriving a new class from **System.Exception**.

In most cases, you will not just want to return the message associated with the exception to the reader. You probably will want to present a user-friendly message to the user and perhaps perform some special processing in response to each particular type of exception. You can have a separate catch block for each type of exception that your code may throw. The code that follows has a catch block for the DivideByZeroException and another for FormatException (which is the exception that the code will throw if the user does not enter a number). Notice that I also still have a handler for the generic **Exception** class. The handler for the generic Exception class will catch any errors other than the divide by zero and format errors.

```
try
{
    Console.WriteLine("Enter the numerator");
    string strNumerator=Console.ReadLine();
    int intNumerator=int.Parse(strNumerator);
    Console.WriteLine("Enter the denominator");
    string strDenominator=Console.ReadLine();

    int intDenominator=int.Parse(strDenominator);
    int intResult=intNumerator/intDenominator;
    Console.WriteLine("The result is: {0}", intResult);
}
catch (DivideByZeroException e)
{
    Console.WriteLine("You attempted to divide by zero");
    Console.WriteLine("The exception message is: {0}",
        e.Message);
}
catch (FormatException e)
{
    Console.WriteLine("You must enter a number");
    Console.WriteLine("The exception message is: {0}",
        e.Message);
}
catch (Exception e)
{
    Console.WriteLine("The exception type is: {0}",
        e.GetType());
    Console.WriteLine("The exception message is: {0}",
        e.Message);
    Console.WriteLine("The stack trace is: {0}",
        e.StackTrace);
}
```

You must define your exception handlers with the handlers for the more specific exceptions first and the most generic handler last. If you attempt to put the handler for a more generic exception class ahead of one of its derived types, the compiler will print the following error:

```
A previous catch clause already catches all exceptions of
this or a super type
```

In some cases, you will want to handle an exception by performing some processing and then throwing the error again so that the method above the current method in the call stack can handle the error too. You can do this with the following code:

```
try
{
//… code omitted for clarity
}
```

```
catch (Exception e)
{
    Console.WriteLine(e.Message);
    throw e;
}
```

However, a better way to write this code is as follows:

```
try
{
//… code omitted for clarity
}
catch (Exception e)
{
    Console.WriteLine(e.Message);
    throw;
}
```

The difference has to do with the stack trace. When you write "throw e", the compiler treats this as if you are throwing the exception identified by "e" for the first time. Therefore, the stack trace looks as though the exception originated at the method that contains the "throw e" statement. Using the throw statement without an exception object means to rethrow the *current* exception. An example will make this clearer, so consider the following code:

```
class TestClass
{
    static void Main(string[] args)
    {
        try
        {
            OuterMethod();
        }
        catch(Exception e)
        {
            Console.WriteLine(e.StackTrace);
        }
    }
    static void OuterMethod()
    {
        try
        {
            GenException();
        }
        catch(Exception e)
        {
            throw e;
        }
    }
    static void GenException()
    {
```

```
            try
            {
            //… code that generates an exception
            }
            catch (Exception e)
            {
                Console.WriteLine(e.Message);
                Throw e;
            }
        }
    }
```

Here I have a method call GenException that contains some logic that may throw an exception. GenException is called by a method called OuterMethod, which is called from the main routine. If you run this program, you will see that the stack trace from the catch block in the main method will look as follows:

```
OuterMethod
  Main
```

The stack trace does not include the GenException method, which is where the exception actually originated. The problem is that the "throw e" call in OuterMethod created a new exception. If you changed the definition of OuterMethod to the following:

```
static void OuterMethod()
{
    try
    {
      GenException();
    }
    catch(Exception e)
    {
      throw;
    }
}
```

you will now get the following—correct—stack trace:

```
GenException
  OuterMethod
    Main
```

So far, I have looked at catching (and rethrowing exceptions). Throwing exceptions from within your own code is also quite simple in C#. First, you have to decide what exception class to use for the exception that you will be throwing. You can use one of the predefined exception classes, or you can create your own exception class. The System namespace contains a number of exception classes that are generic enough to use in your own code. Table 4–12 lists just a few of them.

TABLE 4–12 *Useful exception classes*

Class Name	Description
ApplicationException	Thrown when a nonfatal application error occurs. Use this class as the base class for your custom, nonfatal exception classes.
ArgumentException	Thrown when an invalid argument is passed to a method.
ArgumentNullException	Thrown when a null argument is passed to a method. This exception class derives from **ArgumentException**.
ArgumentOutOfRangeException	Thrown when an argument to a method is not within the allowable range. This exception class derives from **ArgumentException**.
InvalidOperationException	Thrown when a method call is not valid for the current state of an object.
NotImplementedException	Thrown when a method that is called on an object has not been implemented.

You can use one of these classes or derive your own class from one of these or the other exception classes in the System namespace.

Regardless of whether you are using a built-in exception class or an exception class that you created, you throw an exception by creating a new instance of the **Exception** class and then using the throw keyword with the new instance as an argument. The following code shows how you would create a new **Exception** class:

```
public enum RejectionReasons
{
    IncomeTooLow,
    PaymentsTooHigh,
    CreditScoreTooLow,
}
class LoanException : ApplicationException
{
    public LoanException(RejectionReasons aReason) :
        base("You loan was rejected")
    {
        mReason=aReason;
    }
    public override string Message
    {
```

```
            get
            {
                string strRetval;
                switch (mReason)
                {
                case RejectionReasons.IncomeTooLow:
                    strRetval=
                        "Your income is too low";
                    break;
                case RejectionReasons.PaymentsTooHigh:
                    strRetval=
                        "Too much debt";
                    break;
                case RejectionReasons.CreditScoreTooLow:
                    strRetval=
                        "Your credit score too low";
                    break;
                default:
                    strRetval="Unknown reason";
                    break;
                }
                return strRetval;
            }
        }
        private RejectionReasons mReason;
}
```

Notice that I overrode the Message property to display a string that is consistent with the rejection reason. The following code shows how to use this exception from within your code:

```
float fltIncome, fltLoanAmt;
string strIncome, strLoanAmt;
Console.WriteLine("Enter your requested loan amount");
strLoanAmt=Console.ReadLine();
fltLoanAmt=float.Parse(strLoanAmt);
Console.WriteLine("Enter your annual income");
strIncome=Console.ReadLine();
fltIncome=float.Parse(strIncome);
if (fltLoanAmt/fltIncome > 3)
      throw new
LoanException(RejectionReasons.IncomeTooLow);
```

Summary

This chapter has given you a high-level introduction to C#. At this point, you should know enough about C# to follow along with the examples that I will be developing later in this book. There are still plenty of things about the C# language that I have not covered in this chapter, such as delegates, events, and XML documentation. The .NET Framework documentation and *A Programmer's Introduction to C#* by Eric Gunnerson and APress are excellent sources of information if you would like to know more. In the next section, I talk about Visual Studio .NET and build an example program using this world-class development tool.

F I V E

Using Visual Studio .NET

So far, I have built all of the examples using the command-line tools in the .NET Framework SDK. Unless you are a luddite or a glutton for punishment, you will probably not write software for the .NET Framework using these primitive tools. Most people will use Visual Studio .NET, or some other IDE to write software for the .NET Platform. Visual Studio .NET is the latest version of Microsoft's Visual Studio product that was specifically designed for the .NET Framework. It contains integrated form designers, code and image editors, an integrated debugger, and new design tools for creating XML schemas and database queries. It also contains a design tool called the server explorer that allows you to view all of the server resources (SQL Servers, message queues, performance counters, services, and so forth) that are currently available on your network.

In this chapter, I will build an assembly that contains a spell-checker component. I also build a Windows Forms client and a Web Forms client. Along the way, you will learn how to use Visual Studio .NET to create and implement a project. As a bonus, you will also learn about XML code documentation, which (particularly when used with Visual Studio .NET) makes it easy for you to create code comments that can be extracted as an XML document and then transformed into an easily readable HTML form using an Extensible Style Language Transformation (XSLT).

Introduction

If you have used Visual Studio 6 or any of its constituent products, such as VB, Visual C++, and Visual InterDev, you are going to love Visual Studio

.NET. Visual Studio 6, like all previous versions of Visual Studio, consisted of a set of separate and independent development environments that were bundled together for marketing purposes. The development tools in Visual Studio 6 were very different from each other. VB, Visual InterDev and Visual C++ have completely different GUI designers, debuggers, and code editors. The default keyboard bindings are different across these tools as are the standard libraries that are available to you in each tool. Cross-language development and debugging was difficult in this environment. Visual Studio .NET has finally delivered on the promise that Microsoft has been making for years—to have all of its development tools share a common development environment. Because all .NET programming languages share the base class library from the .NET Framework, you also get the additional benefit of having a common standard library for all the development tools in Visual Studio .NET. Visual Studio .NET is so simple and easy to use that, in most cases, it is much better to use it than the command-line tools in the .NET Framework SDK even for simple projects. The only time you will likely still need to use the command-line compiler is to build multifile assemblies (which Visual Studio .NET does not support). Because Visual Studio .NET is such a time saver, I will use it for most of the remaining examples in this book. Because of this, I wanted to end this introductory section of the book by introducing you to Visual Studio .NET. I build a simple spell-checker component and two clients that use the component. The following is a high-level summary of the steps I will follow in this chapter:

1. Create a spell-checker component.
2. Create a Windows Forms client.
3. Create a Web Forms client.

Creating a Spell-Checker Component

To create the spell-checker component, I perform the following steps:

1. Create a Visual C# class library project.
2. Implement the **SpellChecker** class.
3. Add a strong name to the project.
4. Compile the assembly.

Creating a Visual C# Class Library Project

Start Visual Studio .NET and then execute the following steps:

1. Select File | New | Project. The New Project dialog will appear as shown in Figure 5–1.
2. Select Visual C# Projects under Project Types and then choose Class Library under Templates.

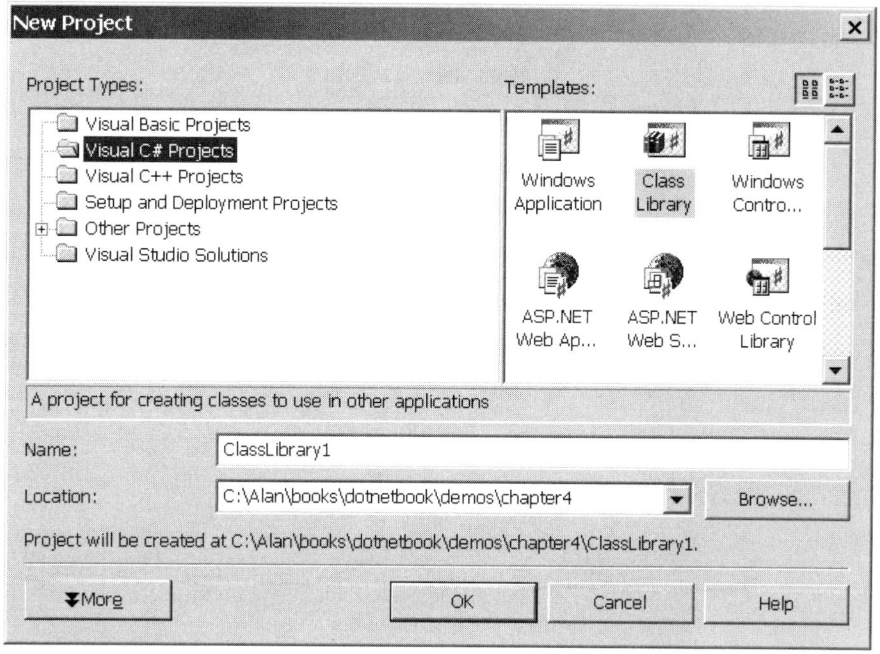

FIGURE 5–1 *The New Project dialog.*

3. Change the name of the project to WritersTools.
4. Select the location where you would like to save the project.
5. Click OK.

Visual Studio .NET will create a new project. The project will contain two files: **Class1.cs** and **AssemblyInfo.cs**. AssemblyInfo.cs contains the assembly-level attributes for the WritersTools assembly. The contents of AssemblyInfo.cs are as follows:

```
using System.Reflection;
using System.Runtime.CompilerServices;

[assembly: AssemblyTitle("")]
[assembly: AssemblyDescription("")]
[assembly: AssemblyConfiguration("")]
[assembly: AssemblyCompany("")]
[assembly: AssemblyProduct("")]
[assembly: AssemblyCopyright("")]
[assembly: AssemblyTrademark("")]
[assembly: AssemblyCulture("")]
[assembly: AssemblyVersion("1.0.*")]
[assembly: AssemblyDelaySign(false)]
[assembly: AssemblyKeyFile("")]
[assembly: AssemblyKeyName("")]
```

The Class1.cs contains an empty class declaration as follows:

```
using System;

namespace WritersTools
{
    /// <summary>
    /// Summary description for Class1.
    /// </summary>
    public class Class1
    {
      public Class1()
      {
        //
        // TODO: Add constructor logic here
        //
      }
    }
}
```

Notice that Visual Studio .NET has added a using statement for the System namespace and has enclosed the generated class in a namespace that has the same name as the name that I gave the project WritersTools. The comments marked with three slashes (///) are XML code documentation comments. The C# compiler allows you to embed the documentation for your classes into your code using the special, three slash (///) syntax as shown previously. You can put any well-formed XML in your documentation comments, but Microsoft has defined an XML schema that contains XML tags for most things that you need. There are tags to specify summary information about a type and the fields, properties, methods, and events of the type. There are also tags for documenting the exceptions that a type may throw and the parameters and return values for methods. There are also tags for embedding example code in your documentation comments and for adding see also cross-references. Table 5–1 summarizes the tags in Microsoft's XML code documentation schema.

TABLE 5–1 *Tags in the documentation comments XML schema*

Tag Name	Description	Usage
remarks	Used to document overview information about a class or type.	<remarks> description </remarks>
summary	Used to document overview information about a member of a class or type. Visual Studio .NET uses the summary tag to document the class or type, although the .NET Framework SDK documentation recommends that you use the remarks tag for this.	<summary> description </summary>

TABLE 5–1 *Tags in the documentation comments XML schema (continued)*

Tag Name	Description	Usage
param	Used to describe the parameters for a method.	<param name="name"> description </param>
returns	Used to describe the return value for a method.	<returns> description </returns>
value	Used to describe properties in a type.	<value> description </value>
exception	Used to document the exceptions that a class may throw.	<exception cref="member"> description </exception>
seealso	Used to create cross-references to other information in the documentation.	<seealso cref="member" />
example	Used to create examples of how to use types and methods. This tag is usually used with the code tag.	<example> description <code> source code for example. </code> </example>
code	Used to create multiline code examples in your documentation.	See above.
c	Used to indicate that text within a description (for a summary, remark, and so forth) contains code.	<summary> description <c> code </c> description </summary>

The C# compiler includes a parameter called /doc parameter that will extract the comments from your code and generate an XML document that contains your documentation. The following command line will generate an XML document that contains the documentation for the **Class1** class:

```
csc /doc:mydocs.xml Class1.cs
```

If you are using Visual Studio .NET, you can specify a file name for the XML documentation on the project property pages. To do this, perform the following steps:

1. Select View | Property Pages. The Project property pages dialog will appear as shown in Figure 5–2.
2. Select Build in the Configuration Properties folder.

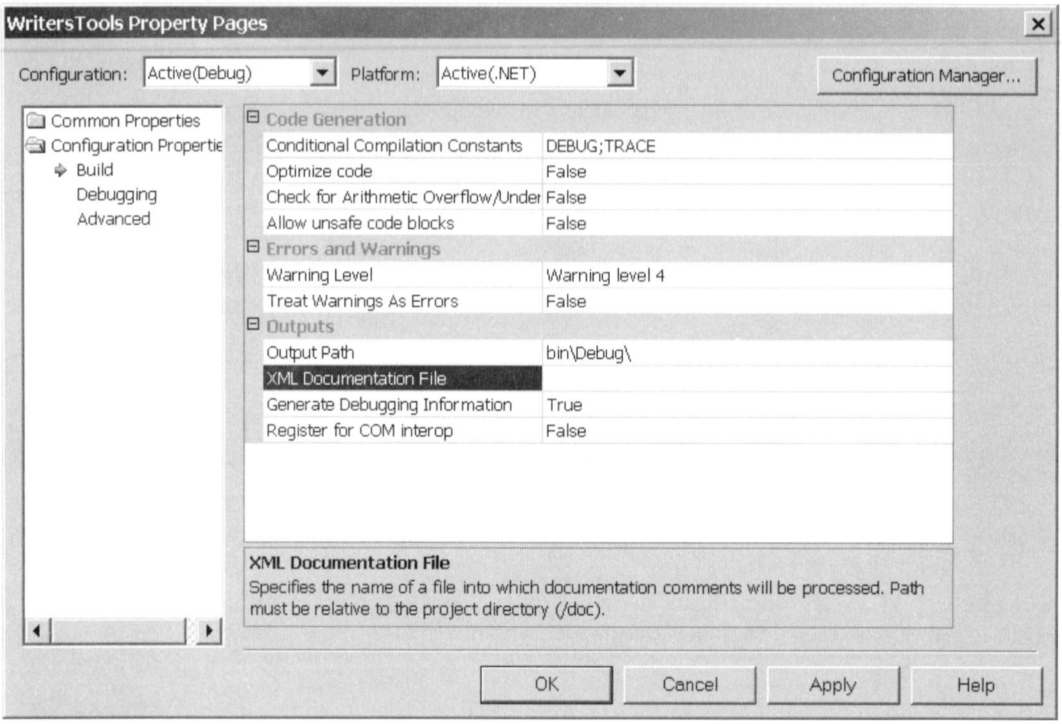

FIGURE 5–2 *The Project property pages dialog.*

3. Enter a file name in the XML Documentation File field.
4. Click OK.

Although you can use the XML documentation feature with the command-line tools in the .NET Framework SDK, Visual Studio .NET contains some very nice features that make it easy to use XML documentation. Visual Studio .NET does an excellent job of thinking ahead and filling in most XML tags for you; you simply have to type in the information describing your types and members. For instance, if you type in the prototype for a new method in a class (the name, parameter list, and return value of the method) and then place your cursor right above the method and type the triple slashes (///) for an XML documentation comment, Visual Studio .NET will create the summary, param, and returns tags for the method. For instance, if you add the following method to your class in the Visual Studio .NET editor:

```
public float TestDocs(int arg1,string arg2)
{
//… implementation omitted
}
```

and then type the triple slashes above the method, Visual Studio .NET will add the following text to your file:

```
/// <summary>
///
/// </summary>
/// <param name="arg1"></param>
/// <param name="arg2"></param>
/// <returns></returns>
```

All you have to do is to fill in the summary and add a description for each parameter and the return value. The Intellisense feature of Visual Studio .NET is also fully integrated with XML documentation comments. Therefore, if you are on a line that starts with triple slashes and you type the less than symbol (<) to open an XML tag, Visual Studio .NET will present a list of the available XML documentation tags. When you select one, it will fill in the closing tag and place your cursor between the opening and closing tag. You truly have no excuse for not documenting your code properly now.

Implementing the SpellChecker Class

I'll now replace the **Class1** class that Visual Studio .NET generated with the implementation of a **SpellChecker** class. Change the code in Class1.cs to look as follows:

```
using System;
using System.Collections.Specialized;
using System.IO;
namespace WritersTools
{
/// <remarks>
/// A class that performs "simple-minded" spellchecking
/// </remarks>
public class SpellChecker
{
/// <summary>
/// The dictionary for the spell checker
/// </summary>
  private StringCollection mDictionary;
/// <summary>
/// The path to the dictionary file
/// </summary>
  private string mDictionaryPath;
/// <summary>
/// This constructor reads the initial dictionary
/// from the default location, dictionary.txt
/// </summary>
  public SpellChecker()
  {
    mDictionary=new StringCollection();
```

```
  mDictionaryPath="dictionary.txt";
  StreamReader dictionaryReader=
  new StreamReader(mDictionaryPath,
    System.Text.Encoding.ASCII);
  ReadDictionary(dictionaryReader);
  dictionaryReader.Close();
 }
/// <summary>
/// This constructor reads the initial dictionary
/// for the spellchecker from the specified path.
/// </summary>
/// <param name="dictionaryPath">The path from
/// where spell checker should read its
/// dictionary
/// </param>
 public SpellChecker(string dictionaryPath)
 {
   mDictionary=new StringCollection();
   mDictionaryPath=dictionaryPath;
   StreamReader dictionaryReader=
   new StreamReader(mDictionaryPath,
     System.Text.Encoding.ASCII);
   ReadDictionary(dictionaryReader);
   dictionaryReader.Close();
 }
 /// <summary>
 /// A private method that populates the
 /// dictionary from a stream reader that
 /// is passed in as a parameter.
 /// </summary>
 /// <param name="dictionaryReader">
 /// The stream that contains the dictionary
 /// for the spellchecker
 /// </param>
 /// <returns></returns>
 private int ReadDictionary(
   StreamReader dictionaryReader)
 {
   int numWordsRead=0;
   string aWord;
   aWord=dictionaryReader.ReadLine();
   while (aWord != null)
   {
     mDictionary.Add(aWord);
   aWord=dictionaryReader.ReadLine();
     numWordsRead++;
   }
   return numWordsRead;
 }
/// <summary>
```

```
/// Checks if a word resides in the spellcheckers
/// dictionary
/// </summary>
/// <param name="aWord">
/// the word to be spellchecked
/// </param>
/// <returns>
/// true if the word resides in the dictionary
/// </returns>
  public Boolean CheckSpelling(String aWord)
  {
    Boolean bRetval=false;
    if (mDictionary.Contains(
        aWord.ToLower()))
      bRetval=true;
    return bRetval;
  }
/// <summary>
/// Adds a word to the spellcheckers dictionary
/// </summary>
/// <param name="aWord">
/// The word to add to the dictionary
/// </param>
/// <exception cref="System.ArgumentException">
  /// Thrown when you attempt to add a word to the
  /// dictionary that is already in the dictionary
  /// </exception>
    public void AddToDictionary(String aWord)
    {
    string lwrCaseWord=aWord.ToLower();
    if (!mDictionary.Contains(
      lwrCaseWord))
    {
      mDictionary.Add(lwrCaseWord);
      StreamWriter dictWriter=
         new StreamWriter(
         mDictionaryPath,
         true,
         System.Text.Encoding.ASCII);
      dictWriter.WriteLine(
      lwrCaseWord);
        dictWriter.Close();
    }
    else
      throw new ArgumentException(
        aWord +
     " already exists in the dictionary",
        "aWord");
    }
  }
}
```

On line 2 and 3, I added using statements for the System.Collections.Specialized and System.IO namespaces. Both of these namespaces are implemented in the core system assembly mscorlib.dll. System.Collections.Specialized contains the definition of some specialized collection classes, such as the **StringCollection** class that I use to hold the dictionary for the spell checker. System.IO contains the definition of the **StreamReader** class that I use to read the spell checker's dictionary from a disk file and the **StreamWriter** class that I use to write new entries to the dictionary.

On lines 8 and 9, I declare the class, which I call **SpellChecker**. Right above the declaration of the class, I have the remarks XML comment that contains a description of the class. On lines 11 through 13, the summary XML comment describes the mDictionary private field of the class (which is declared on line 14) that contains the dictionary of the spell checker. Lines 15 through 18 contain the summary comments and declaration of a field called mDictionaryPath that holds the path to the spell checker's dictionary file. Lines 23 through 32 contain one of the constructors for the **SpellChecker** class. This constructor has no arguments, and it instantiates a new StringCollection object and then fills it with the contents of the default dictionary file, which is called **dictionary.txt** and resides in the default directory for the component. Lines 41 through 50 contain the declaration of a second constructor that allows you to specify the path to the dictionary file. This constructor is needed if you are going to use this component on a Web application because you will probably want to locate the dictionary file somewhere beneath the virtual directory for the application. Lines 61 through 74 contain the declaration of a private method called ReadDictionary that populates the mDictionary string collection with the contents from a StreamReader. This method exists to factor out code that is used by both constructors. Lines 85 through 92 contain the declaration of the CheckSpelling method. The implementation of this method is really simple. It converts the specified word to lower-case and then checks if the mDictionary string collection contains the word. If it does, the CheckSpelling method returns true, indicating that the word is correctly spelled. If the word does not exist in the dictionary, the CheckSpelling method returns false, indicating that the word was probably misspelled.

Note This is obviously a hopelessly simplistic implementation of a spell checker that would be too slow and memory intensive if you had a dictionary of realistic size. If you were implementing a real spell checker, you would probably use a simple database engine to store your dictionary.

Lines 103 through 124 contain the declaration of the AddToDictionary method. This method converts the specified word to lower-case and then checks if the word already resides in the dictionary. If it does, it throws an exception; if it does not, it adds the word to the dictionary. Now that I have implemented the **SpellChecker** class, the next step is to create a strong name for the assembly.

Adding a Strong Name to the Project

Although it's not a requirement, it's a good idea to give every assembly a strong name. Giving an assembly a strong name allows the CLR to perform more stringent consistency checking, and it allows the eventual consumer of the assembly to put the assembly in the GAC if it wants to. To give an assembly a strong name, you must create a cryptogramic key pair (a public and private key) and then digitally sign your assembly with the private key. Digitally signing an assembly involves creating a hash of the contents of the assembly and then encrypting the hash with the private key from the key pair. When you sign an assembly, you will also insert the public key into the assembly. When you reference an assembly from a client application or component, your compiler will insert this public key into the referencing code. At runtime, the CLR will use the public key to unsign (decrypt) the digital signature. The unsigned digital signature contains the hashed contents of the assembly. The CLR will then rehash the contents of the assembly and compare it to the hash from the digital signature. If the hashes do not match, the assembly was altered since it was built. Assuming the hashes do match, you now know two things: (1) The assembly on disk was authored by the same person who created the assembly that you referenced when you built the client application or component (or at least they have the same private key), and (2) the contents of the assembly were not tampered with after they were compiled. The CLR can only perform these important validity checks if you sign (add a strong name) to the assembly.

You must follow two steps to add a strong name to an assembly:

1. Create a cryptographic key pair.
2. Sign the assembly with the key pair.

CREATING A CRYPTOGRAPHIC KEY PAIR

The .NET Framework SDK contains a utility called the Strong Name Tool that you can use to create a cryptographic key pair. The following command line will create a key pair and store it in a file called **mykey.snk**:

```
sn -k mykeypair.snk
```

The -k option tells the Strong Name Tool to write both the public and private key to the specified file.

Many people may use an organization's public key, but the private key represents the identity of an organization. If it is compromised, other people can do great harm to the organization by doing mischievous or even criminal acts while using the organization's identity. A private key is so sensitive that there are typically only a few people who will ever have it in their possession. Because of this, you may want to separate the public key from the key pair. You can do this using the -p option on the Strong Name Tool. The following command line will extract the public key from the key pair, **mykeypair.snk**, and save it to a file called **publickey.snk**:

```
sn -p mykeypair.snk publickey.snk
```

You cannot use a public key alone to "properly" sign an assembly. You must have the private key to create a digital signature. You can use the public key to delay-sign an assembly. I talk about delay signing shortly.

Note In practice, you won't have to create a new key pair whenever you build a new component. Your company will have a digital key, probably from a Certification Authority (CA) like Verisign.

SIGNING THE ASSEMBLY

You can sign an assembly in two ways: immediately or with delay signing. In order to sign an assembly immediately, you must have both the private and public key. You can sign the assembly at compile time using the AssemblyKeyFile attribute. Usually, you add this attribute to an assemblyinfo file that contains all of your assembly-level attributes as follows:

```
[assembly: AssemblyDelaySign(false)]
[assembly: AssemblyKeyFile("..\\..\\mykey.snk")]
```

The parameter for the AssemblyKeyFile attribute specifies the name and location of the file that contains the key pair. The directory for the file is relative to the output location for the compiler, which with Visual Studio .NET is **[project directory]\bin\[configuration]**, for example, **c:\demos\writerstools\bin\debug**. If you would like to store the key in your root project directory, you would specify "..\\..\\keyfilename" as shown previously. Notice that I have also specified false for the AssemblyDelaySign attribute. Visual Studio .NET uses immediate signing by default, that is, if you do not use the AssemblyDelaySign attribute.

You can also sign an assembly using the assembly linker (al.exe), which is yet another tool in the .NET Framework SDK. To use this approach, you must first use the command-line C# compiler to compile the **SpellChecker** class into a module and then use the assembly linker to build and digitally sign your assembly. The following command line will create a module from the **spellchecker.cs** file:

```
csc /target:module /out:writerstools.mod spellchecker.cs
```

The following command line will build and sign this assembly using the assembly linker and the **mykey.snk** file that contains the key pair:

```
al /out:writerstools.dll writerstools.mod /
keyfile:mykey.snk
```

If you wish to delay sign your assembly, you will specify true for the parameter to the AssemblyDelaySign attribute as follows:

```
[assembly: AssemblyDelaySign(true)]
[assembly: AssemblyKeyFile("..\\..\\publickey.snk")]
```

In this case, the specified key file needs only to contain the public key. Remember that the whole purpose of delay signing is to restrict the number of people who have access to the private key of the company. Delay signing inserts the public key into the assembly, which allows developers to write client code that references the assembly. The referencing application or component stores a copy of the public key, which it uses to unsign the digital signature when the application or component runs later. Because a delayed-signed assembly does not have a digital signature, the CLR cannot perform the usual verification (unsigning the digital signature, verifying the hash, and so forth). If you attempt to use an assembly that has been delayed-signed, you will get the following error on your system:

```
Strong name validation failed for assembly '[AssemblyName]'
```

To use a delay-signed assembly, you must register the assembly for verification skipping on your machine. This lets the CLR know that it should not attempt to perform validation on the assembly. To register your assembly for verification skipping, use the Strong Name Tool with the following command line:

```
sn -Vr writerstools.dll
```

You can now use the assembly on your machine. You must do this for each machine that you want to use the assembly on. When you are ready to ship the assembly, a person who has the private key can use the following command line to sign the assembly properly:

```
sn -R writerstools.dll mykey.snk
```

In this case, **mykey.snk** is a file that contains both the public and private keys. Now that the assembly is signed, you should unregister the assembly for verification skipping using the following command line:

```
sn  -Vu writerstools.dll
```

Creating a Windows Forms Client

I'll start using our spell-checker component by creating a Windows Forms client. To create a Windows Forms client, I will perform the following steps:

1. Create a Visual C# Windows application project.
2. Draw the UI.

3. Reference the WritersTools assembly.
4. Implement the UI.
5. Compile the application.
6. Create a dictionary file.
7. Test.

CREATING A VISUAL C# WINDOWS APPLICATION PROJECT

Start Visual Studio .NET and then execute the following steps:

1. Select File | New | Project. The New Project dialog will appear as shown in Figure 5–1.
2. Select Visual C# Projects under Project Types and then choose Windows Application under Templates.
3. Change the name of the project to SpellCheckClient.
4. Select the location where you would like to save the project.
5. Click OK.

Visual Studio .NET will create a project that initially contains a single form that is the main window of your application. You can drag and drop controls onto this form and then double-click the controls to add handlers for any of the events that the control fires. If you are familiar with VB, you will feel right at home. Before I actually build the UI of the application, let's reference the spell-checker component.

DRAWING THE UI

Using the toolbox in Visual Studio .NET, draw the UI shown in Figure 5–3 on your form.

Give the textbox control the following Name: txtWordToCheck. Give the Check Spelling and Add to Dictionary buttons the names cmdCheckSpelling and cmdAddToDictionary, respectively.

REFERENCING THE WRITERSTOOLS ASSEMBLY

With Visual Studio .NET, it's easy to reference and use .NET assemblies. To do this, perform the following steps:

1. Select Add Reference... from the Project menu. The Add Reference dialog will appear as shown in Figure 5–4.
2. Click the Browse... button (the Select Component dialog will appear) and navigate to where the spell-checker component resides on your system.
3. Click the Open button.
4. Click OK on the Add Reference dialog.

You can now use the spell-checker component to implement the UI.

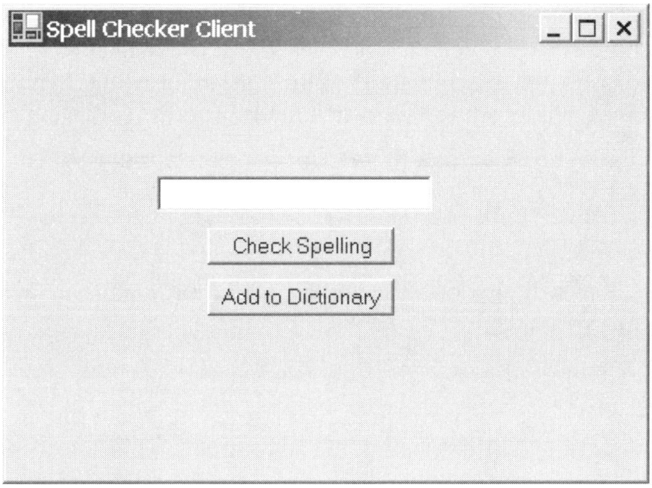

FIGURE 5–3 *The UI for the Windows Forms client.*

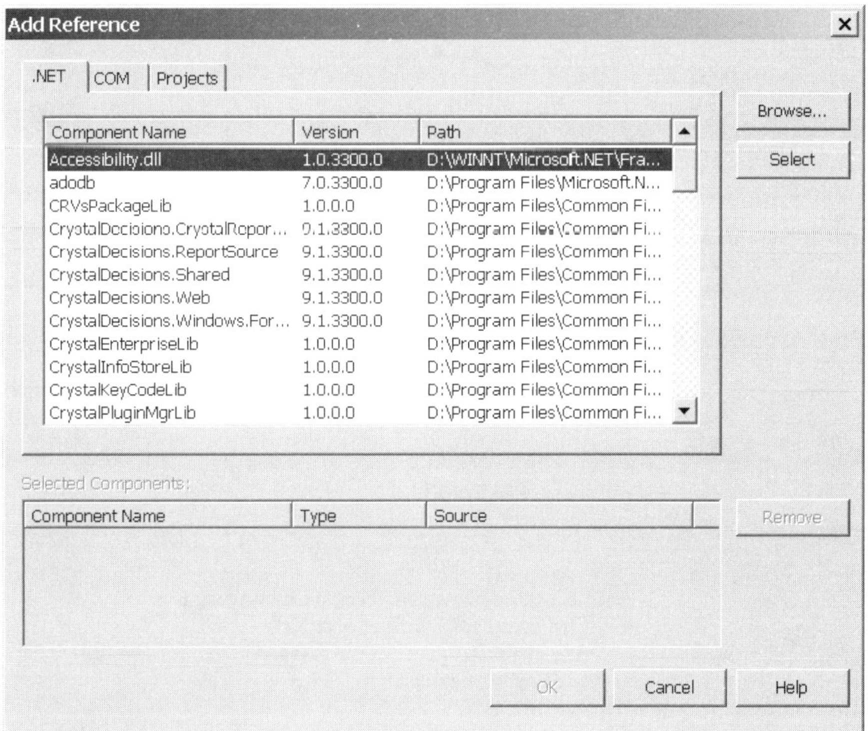

FIGURE 5–4 *The Add Reference dialog.*

IMPLEMENTING THE UI

In the form designer, double-click the form, which should take you to the handler for the Load method of the form, that is, the method that gets called automatically when the form first loads. Add the following code to this form:

```
private void Form1_Load(object sender, System.EventArgs e)
{
    mSpellChecker=new WritersTools.SpellChecker();
}
```

You will also need to add a declaration for the mSpellChecker component to your form class as shown here:

```
public class Form1 : System.Windows.Forms.Form
{
//… code is omitted here for clarity
    private WritersTools.SpellChecker mSpellChecker;
    public Form1()
    {
    }
//… code is omitted here for clarity
}
```

Back in the form designer, double-click the CheckSpelling button to add a Click event handler and add the following code:

```
private void cmdCheckSpelling_Click(object sender,
  System.EventArgs e)
{
  if (mSpellChecker.CheckSpelling(txtWordToCheck.Text))
    MessageBox.Show("Spellcheck complete");
  else
    MessageBox.Show(txtWordToCheck.Text +
      " is misspelled");
}
```

Next double-click the Add to Dictionary button and add the following code:

```
private void cmdAddToDictionary_Click(object sender,
  System.EventArgs e)
{
  try
  {
    mSpellChecker.AddToDictionary(
      txtWordToCheck.Text);
  }
  catch (Exception ex)
  {
    MessageBox.Show(ex.Message);
  }
}
```

Since the AddToDictionary method in the SpellChecker object will throw an exception if you attempt to add a work to the dictionary that is already present, we enclose our call to the AddToDictonary method in a try/catch statement.

CREATING A DICTIONARY FILE

The spell-checker component depends on a dictionary file that must reside in the same directory as its client. Create a text file that contains the following commonly misspelled words (or any words you like) and save it as a text file with the name **dictionary.txt** in the same directory where you will run the client, for example, **C:\DEMOS\CHAP5\SPELLCHECKCLIENT\BIN\DEBUG**.

```
License
Lieutenant
Obedient
Parliament
Surprise
Misspelled
```

Make sure you put each word on its own line and put a carriage return at the end of each line.

TEST

Congratulations, you have now built your first .NET component and client application using Visual Studio .NET. You can test the application by running the executable. Type in one of the words that is currently in the dictionary, and you will see a message box that says "Spell check complete". Type in any other word, and you will see a message box that says "[word] is misspelled". If you click the button that says "Add to dictionary", the word will be added to the dictionary. The next time that you check spelling on that word, you will see the Spell check complete dialog. Next, I create a Web Forms client.

Creating a Web Forms Client

Web Forms is a .NET technology that makes it as easy to create Web-based UIs as it is to create forms-based Windows applications using VB. Web Forms are a part of Microsoft's ASP.NET technology, which also encompasses the infrastructure for Web services. The key to Web Forms is server controls, which are components that typically have both a runtime and a design time visual representation. You place these controls on a form, set their properties, and handle their events to determine how they will look and behave. At runtime when a user makes a request, the ASP.NET runtime renders an HTML representation of the server control to the client. Server controls are smart enough to render HTML that is browser independent, that is, a Web Forms application that will run on Internet Explorer, Netscape, or another other browser that supports HTML 3.2 as a minimum. Server controls are also smart enough to take advantage of the capabilities of up-level browsers, like scripting. Let's see how simple it is to build a client application for the spell-checker component using Web Forms. To build the application, I will perform the following steps:

1. Create a Visual C# ASP.NET Web application project.
2. Draw the UI.
3. Reference the WritersTools assembly.
4. Implement the UI.
5. Create a dictionary file.
6. Test the application.

CREATING A VISUAL C# ASP.NET WEB APPLICATION PROJECT

Start Visual Studio .NET and then execute the following steps:

1. Select File | New | Project. The New Project dialog will appear as shown in Figure 5–1.
2. Select Visual C# Projects under Project Types and then choose ASP.NET Web Application under Templates.
3. Change the location of the project to *http://localhost/SpellCheckWebClient.*
4. Click OK.

Visual Studio .NET will create a new virtual directory for the application at the location that you specified. The physical location of the virtual directory is the following:

```
[Inetpub]\wwwroot\SpellCheckWebClient
```

Visual Studio .NET will create a project at this location that contains a single form that is the main window of your application. The difference is that now this form is an ASP.NET Web page with the name **WebForm1.aspx** as shown in Figure 5–5. You can drag and drop controls onto this form and then double-click the controls to add handlers for any of the events that the control fires, just as you did with the Windows Forms application. Once again, if you are familiar with VB, you will feel right at home.

DRAWING THE UI

Using the toolbox in Visual Studio .NET, draw the UI shown in Figure 5–6 on your form.

Give the text box the name txtWordToCheck. The red "lblResponse" text that you see in Figure 5–6 is a label with the name lblResponse and the forecolor property set to red. As before, give the Check Spelling button the name cmdCheckSpelling and use cmdAddToDictionary for the name of the Add to

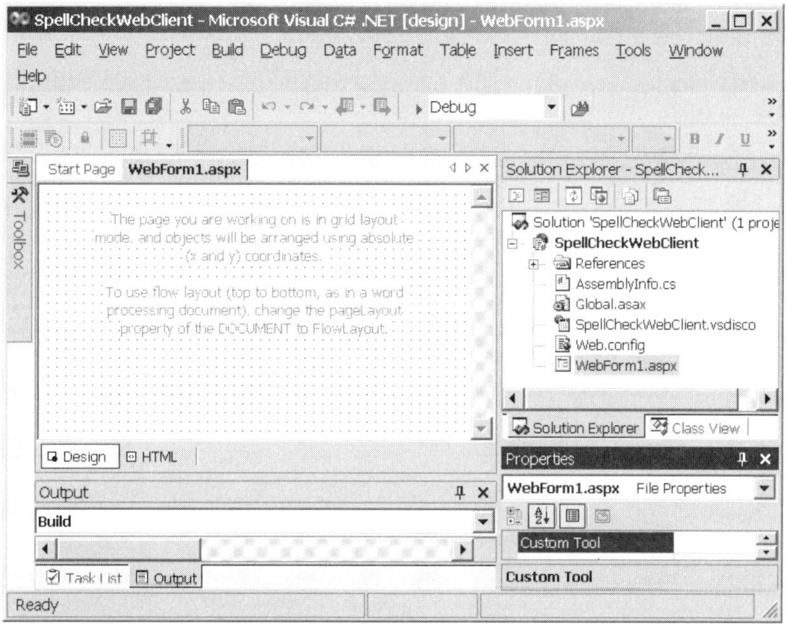

FIGURE 5–5 *An ASP.NET Web application project in Visual Studio.NET.*

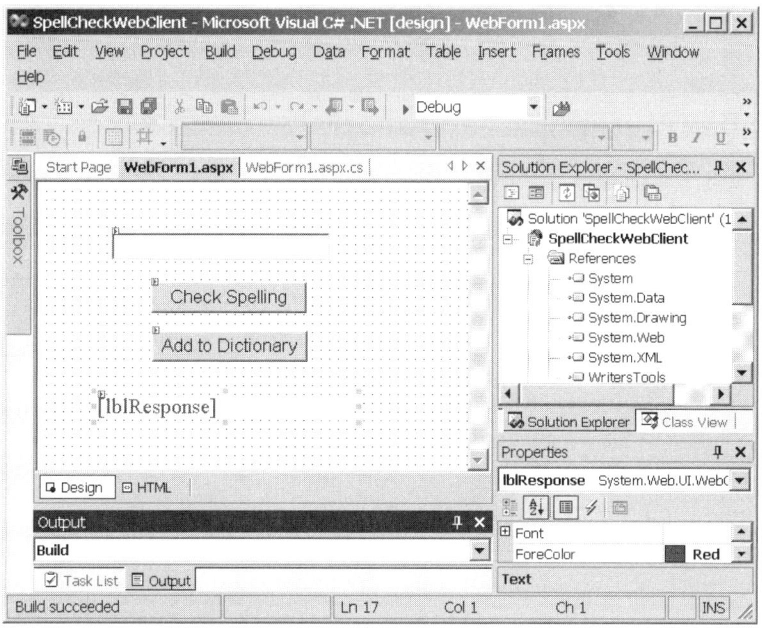

FIGURE 5–6 *The UI for the Web Forms client in Visual Studio .NET.*

Dictionary button. Before I implement the UI of the application, let's reference the spell-checker component.

REFERENCING THE WRITERSTOOLS ASSEMBLY

The steps to reference a .NET assembly from a Web Forms application are exactly the same as the steps for a Windows Forms application, so I won't repeat them here. Refer back to the section with the same name in the steps for building a Windows Forms application.

IMPLEMENTING THE UI

Implement the UI for the Web Forms client by double-clicking the Check Spelling button on the main form of the application. This will create an empty click event handler for the button. Add the following code to the event handler:

```
private void cmdCheckSpelling_Click(object sender,
  System.EventArgs e)
{
  WritersTools.SpellChecker spellChecker;
  string strDictionaryPath=
    Request.PhysicalApplicationPath +
    "dictionary.txt";
  spellChecker=new WritersTools.SpellChecker
    (strDictionaryPath);
  if (spellChecker.CheckSpelling(txtWordToCheck.Text))
    lblResponse.Text="Spellcheck complete";
  else
    lblResponse.Text=txtWordToCheck.Text +
      " is misspelled";
}
```

Notice that I create a new instance of the SpellChecker component each time the user clicks the Check Spelling button. With ASP.NET Web Forms, a new instance of the page class is created to service each request, so we must create a SpellChecker object each time. An alternative is to cache the SpellChecker in the ASP.NET session object.

Next double-click the Add to dictionary button on the main form and add the following code to the click event handler for that button:

```
private void cmdAddToDictionary_Click(object sender,
  System.EventArgs e)
{
  try
  {
    WritersTools.SpellChecker spellChecker;
    string strDictionaryPath=
      Request.PhysicalApplicationPath +
```

```
        "dictionary.txt";
      spellChecker=new WritersTools.SpellChecker
        (strDictionaryPath);
      spellChecker.AddToDictionary(
        txtWordToCheck.Text);
      lblResponse.Text=txtWordToCheck.Text +
        " has been added to the dictionary";
    }
    catch(ArgumentException argEx)
    {
      lblResponse.Text=txtWordToCheck.Text +
        " already exists in the dictionary";
    }
    catch(Exception ex)
    {
      lblResponse.Text=
        "The following error occurred: " +
        ex.Message;
    }
  }
```

CREATING A DICTIONARY FILE

You will also need to create a dictionary file and copy it to the virtual directory for the application. The easiest thing to do is to just copy the **dictionary.txt** file that you built for the Windows Forms client earlier. Copy this text file to the root directory of your Web application. On my machine, this was **D:\Inetpub\wwwroot\SpellCheckWebClient**.

TESTING THE APPLICATION

To test the application, open up Internet Explorer and type the following URL into your browser: *http://localhost/SpellCheckWebClient/WebForm1.aspx*.

> **Note** This URL assumes that you did not rename your initial Web Form, which has the name WebForm1.aspx.

You should see the UI in Figure 5–7 in Internet Explorer.

You can enter a word to spell check and click the Check Spelling button. If a word is not found in the dictionary, you can click the Add to Dictionary button, and it will add the word to the dictionary so that, the next time you spell check the word, it will find it.

FIGURE 5–7 *The Web Forms client in Internet Explorer.*

Summary

In this chapter, you learned how to use Visual Studio .NET to build a simple .NET assembly. You also learned how to build both a Windows Forms and a Web Forms client. You now have the necessary background to dive into the main topic of this book: COM Interop.

SIX

An Introduction to COM Interop

No matter how good the .NET Framework is as a standalone technology, it could not possibly be successful if it did not integrate seamlessly with Microsoft's existing suite of technologies: Win32, COM/COM+/MTS, that is, the technologies formerly known as the DNA architecture. Microsoft has been touting these technologies for years and thousands of organizations and individuals have written millions of lines of code using these technologies. Few organizations have the luxury of halting functional development for six months to a year or more to completely rearchitect their applications to use .NET. Most organizations therefore will take a gradual migration approach, either integrating .NET technologies into their existing architecture, gradually replacing Win32/COM/COM+ (unmanaged) components and subsystems with software written with .NET or building an infrastructure around .NET while continuing to use unmanaged components to implement core functionality. Either of these approaches requires interoperation (Interop), which is Microsoft's word for allowing .NET (managed) applications and components to use unmanaged components and applications and unmanaged components to use managed components. Interoperation in both directions is needed to accommodate different migration strategies.

Note I will discuss migration strategies in Chapter 12.

Introduction

Microsoft has two major Interop technologies: COM Interop and Platform Invocation Services (PInvoke). COM Interop has tools and technologies that allow .NET components and applications to use COM/DCOM/COM+ components and that allow Win32 applications and COM/DCOM/COM+ components to use .NET components. PInvoke allows .NET applications and components to call Win32, that is, non-COM DLLs. PInvoke is particularly useful for calling Win32 API functions, although you can also use it to call non-COM DLLs that you created yourself. All of these technologies are designed to be as seamless as possible. In other words, using a COM component from managed code feels just the same as using a managed component, and using a .NET component from unmanaged code feels just like using any other COM object.

COM Interop

COM Interop is used in two scenarios: (1) When you want a managed code (.NET) application or component to consume a COM component or (2) when you want an unmanaged (Win32/COM) application or component to consume a .NET component. Both of these scenarios are shown in Figure 6–1.

Scenario 1 will probably be the most widely used initially because most people who start using the .NET Framework will have a large existing code base of unmanaged code that they will want to reuse. However, don't underestimate the importance of scenario 2. Let's say that you have two COM objects, object A and object B, and let's say that object B uses the services of object A in its implementation as shown in Figure 6–2.

The only way that you can migrate object A to .NET without also migrating object B at the same time is for the new .NET implementation of object A to continue to expose itself as a COM object through COM Interop to object B.

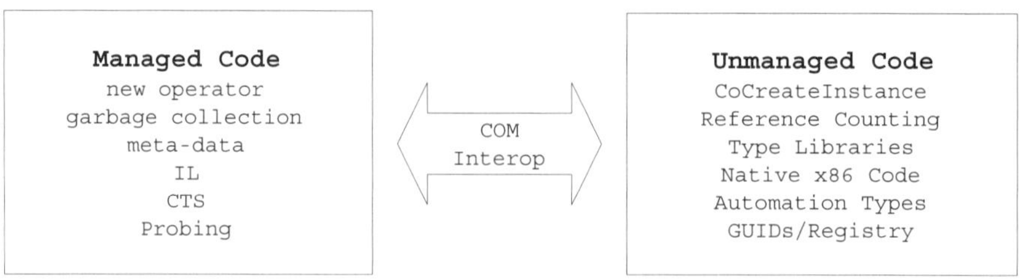

FIGURE 6–1 *The two COM Interop scenarios.*

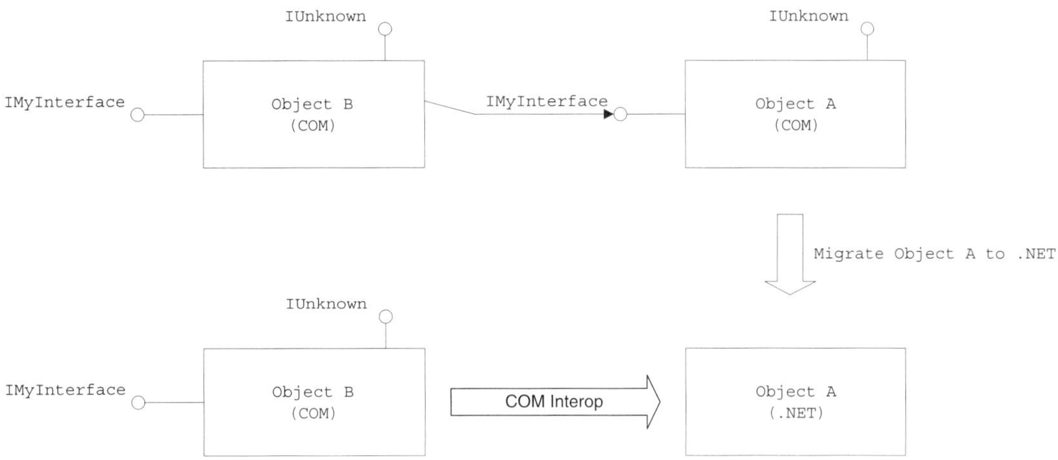

FIGURE 6–2 *The importance of COM to .NET Interop.*

One of the key goals of COM Interop is to make interoperation between COM and .NET as transparent as possible. In other words, when you are using a COM object from a .NET client, the COM object should appear to the .NET client to be just another .NET component. You should be able to instantiate it using the new operator, and you should not have to manage the object's lifetime manually using the AddRef and Release methods. Ideally, the object should have the same metadata associated with it that you would have with a regular .NET object. Similarly, if you use a .NET component from a COM or Win32 client, the .NET component should appear to be just like any other COM object. You should instantiate it with CoCreateInstance (or one of the other COM activation functions). You should use reference counting through the IUnknown interface to control the life cycle of the object.

In Chapter 2, I compared the .NET Framework to COM. In that chapter, you saw that that COM and the .NET Framework implement naming, object lifetime management, runtime type information inspection, location transparency, and versioning in very different ways. In order to have seamless interoperation between .NET and COM, there needs to be a piece of software that sits between the .NET consumer and the COM object or the Win32/COM consumer and the .NET object. This software bridges the large gap between these two completely different object infrastructures. This software is called a Runtime Callable Wrapper (RCW) in the case of a .NET consumer using a COM object and a COM Callable Wrapper (CCW) in the case of a Win32/COM consumer using a .NET object. RCWs and CCWs are the key to the seamless interoperation between COM and .NET. Let's see how it works.

Using COM Objects from .NET Clients

Using COM objects from .NET clients is sure to be the most widely used COM Interop scenario. In this section, I discuss the infrastructure and tools that the .NET Framework provides to make it easy for you to use COM object from within managed code clients. The two important pieces are the RCW that sits between the managed code client and the COM object and performs all the magic required to make the COM object appear to be just another managed code object and the Type Library Importer (**tlbimp.exe**) that allows you to generate .NET metadata from a COM type library. I'll conclude this section by building a simple example application that uses a COM object through Interop.

RCW

The CLR automatically creates a RCW for you whenever you instantiate a COM object from a managed code application. There is one RCW for each COM object regardless of how many managed code clients the object has. The RCW holds all the COM interface pointers that the managed code client is using as shown in Figure 6-3.

FIGURE 6–3 *The relationship between a RCW, a COM object, and managed code clients.*

The RCW holds all outstanding interface pointers on the COM object. Managed code clients call methods on the RCW and the RCW forwards those method calls to the COM object through the interface pointers it holds on the COM object. The RCW handles marshaling of parameters and return values between the managed code client and the COM object. The RCW also handles life cycle management for the COM object, and consumes all of the system-level interfaces that the COM object exposes to support rich error handling (ISupportsErrorInfo), connection point events (IConnectionPointContainer and IConnectionPoint), and late binding and metadata inspection (IDispatch and ITypeInfo). The RCW converts COM error objects into exceptions that can be caught using the try/catch statements in managed code. The RCW presents connection point events to managed code clients using the standard delegate-based event-handling mechanism supported by the CLR. Late binding is handled using the CreateInstance method on the **System.Activator** class and the InvokeMember function on the **System.Type** class. Metadata inspection is handled using the standard Reflection mechanisms in .NET, which use the methods in the **System.Type** class and the types in the System.Reflection namespace, especially the **Assembly** class.

The RCW is a managed code object, so it is garbage-collected just like any other managed code object. When the RCW is garbage-collected, it will release all of the interface pointers that it is holding on the COM object and the COM object will delete itself. This does mean that the life cycle semantics of a COM object are different when it is called from a managed code client. Typically, when you use a COM object, you will delete it by calling Release on the interface pointer as soon as you are done with it. When you are calling a COM object from a managed code client, the RCW will not call Release on the interface pointers it is holding until the garbage collector runs, which may not be until the application shuts down. In many cases this change in the life cycle semantics of a COM object won't make a difference, but, if this distinction is important, you can call the System.Runtime.InteropServices.Marshal.ReleaseComObject method from your managed code to release a COM object immediately as shown here:

```
private void cmdCalcPayment_Click(object sender,
System.EventArgs e)
{
    double pmt;
    financialdotnet.CFinancial objFinancial;
    try
    {
      objFinancial=new financialdotnet.CFinancial();
      pmt=objFinancial.MonthlyPayment(
        short.Parse(txtNumMonths.Text),
        double.Parse(txtAPR.Text),
        double.Parse(txtLoanAmt.Text));
      txtPmtResult.Text=String.Format("{0:C}",pmt);
```

```
            System.Runtime.InteropServices.
              Marshal.ReleaseComObject(objFinancial);
        }
        catch (Exception ex)
        {
            MessageBox.Show(ex.Message);
        }
    }
```

I talk about the ReleaseComObject method more when I discuss advanced aspects of COM Interop in the next two chapters.

One of the most important things that the RCW does is marshaling. The RCW implements a default mapping between COM types and .NET types. For instance, a managed code client can simply pass an instance of the **System.String** class to a COM object method that expects a BSTR (a typical COM representation of a string). The RCW will automatically handle all the steps required to marshal a System.String object into a BSTR.

Note There is a performance penalty to pay with COM Interop. The overhead of marshaling managed types into unmanaged types and vice versa is a big part of that penalty.

Table 6–1 shows the default mapping between COM types and CTS and C# types, that is, how COM types are marshaled to managed types and vice versa. This is only the default mapping; I will show that you can change this mapping in the next chapter.

TABLE 6–1 *Mapping COM types to .NET types*

COM Type	CTS Type	C# Type
char, small	System.SByte	sbyte
unsigned char, byte	System.Byte	byte
short	System.Int16	short
unsighed short, wchar_t	System.Uint16	ushort
long, int, bool	System.Int32	int
unsigned long, unsigned int	System.Uint32	uint
hyper	System.Int64	long
unsigned hyper	System.UInt64	ulong
single	System.Single	float
double	System.Double	double
VARIANT_BOOL	System.Boolean	bool

TABLE 6–1 *Mapping COM types to .NET types (continued)*

COM Type	CTS Type	C# Type
HRESULT	System.Int16 (can be System.IntPtr also)	short
BSTR	System.String	System.String
DATE	System.DateTime	System.DateTime
VARIANT	System.Object	System.Object
DECIMAL	System.Decimal	System.Decimal
CURRENCY	System.Decimal	System.Decimal
IUnknown *	System.Object	System.Object
IDispatch *	System.Object	System.Object
GUID	System.Guid	System.Guid

When using COM Interop, you can choose either to use early binding or late binding. The late-bound approach is similar to using the IDispatch interface in COM. To use the late-bound approach, first call either the GetType FromProgID or the GetTypeFromCLSID methods on the **System.Type** class to obtain a System.Type. You pass a string that contains the ProgID of the COM object to the GetTypeFromProgID method, and you pass an instance of the **System.Guid** class to the GetTypeFromCLSID method. Both of these methods have an overload that allows you to pass the name of a server on which to instantiate a remote object. After you have a System.Type object, you can call the CreateInstance method on the **System.Activator** class to create an instance of your COM object. To call a method on the object, you call the InvokeMember method on the **System.Type** class. This is actually harder than it sounds because InvokeMember is the managed code equivalent of the Invoke method in IDispatch. To call this method, you pass the name and type (Method, Property, and so forth) of the member that you are trying to call. You then declare an array of System.Objects that will hold the parameters for the method and then populate this array in the same order that they appear in the method that you are calling, that is, the item at the zero index in the object array should correspond to the first parameter in the method that you are trying to call. The following code shows how you would call a COM object from a managed code client using late binding:

```
private void cmdGetLoanAmt_Click(object sender,
  System.EventArgs e)
{
  System.Type typFinancial;
  System.Object objFinancial;
  Object[] objParams=new Object[3];
  Object objResult;
```

```
8.     string strTypeName;
9.     try
10.    {
11.      typFinancial=
12.      System.Type.GetTypeFromProgID
13.          ("Financialcomponent.CFinancial");
14.      objFinancial=
15.          Activator.CreateInstance(typFinancial);
16.      objParams[0]=float.Parse(txtMonths.Text);
17.      objParams[1]=
18.          float.Parse(txtInterestRate.Text);
19.      objParams[2]=
20.          float.Parse(txtMonthlyPmt.Text);
21.      objResult=
22.      typFinancial.InvokeMember("LoanAmount",
23.      System.Reflection.BindingFlags.InvokeMethod,
24.      null,objFinancial,objParams);
25.      lblLoanAmt.Text=
26.          String.Format("{0:C}",objResult);
27.    }
28.    catch(System.Exception ex)
29.    {
30.      MessageBox.Show(ex.Message);
31.    }
32. }
```

The code here is using a simple COM object that performs time value of money calculations (that is, given an amortized loan amount, a specified term, and an interest rate, calculate the corresponding monthly payment or given the monthly payment calculate the loan amount). The COM object implements an interface called ITimeValue that has two methods.

1. **LoanAmount**—Takes a number of months, an annual interest rate, and a monthly payment and returns the equivalent loan amount.
2. **MonthlyPayment**—Takes a number of months, an annual interest rate, and a loan amount and calculates the equivalent monthly payment.

Note The LoanAmount and MonthlyPayment methods are accurate. The formulas were taken from *Engineering Economy* by DeGarmo et al., MacMillan 1984, which was the textbook for an economics class that I took while I was a student at UCLA. The code for this COM object is available on the Web site for this book. For detailed instructions on how to build the object, see Chapter 7 of my first book, *The COM and COM+ Programming Primer*, Prentice Hall 1999.

On line 12 of the example code, I call the GetTypeFromProgID method on **System.Type** to get a System.Type object that I can use to instantiate a late-bound object. On lines 14 and 15, I call the CreateInstance method on the

System.Activator class to create an instance of the COM object using the System.Type object that we obtained on line 12. The CreateInstance method returns an instance of an undocumented class called **System.__ComObject**. On lines 16 through 20, I populate the parameters array with the data the user entered on the UI. On lines 21 through 24, I call the InvokeMember method on the **System.Type** object. Notice that I pass to InvokeMember the name of the method on the object that I want to call (LoanAmount), a flag that indicates that the member I am calling is a method (as opposed to a property), the null third parameter is an optional System.Binder object that you can use to specify custom type conversions, the fourth parameter is the object instance on which I am invoking the method, and the fifth parameter is the array of arguments for the method. Lines 25 and 26 display the result on the UI.

In addition to being somewhat complex, late binding to a COM object is slow (because all parameter validation must be done at runtime) and error-prone because you give up the compiler's ability to perform type-checking on parameters and return values. You also do not get the advantage of Visual Studio's Intellisense feature when you use late binding. It is much nicer when working with any object to have a strongly typed interface and to early bind to your COM object. To get a strongly typed interface, you will need metadata. You can generate .NET metadata for your COM objects using the Type Library Importer.

The Type Library Importer (tlbimp)

The closest thing to .NET metadata in the COM world is a type library. The .NET Framework SDK includes a tool called the Type Library Importer (**tlbimp.exe**) that converts the type information found in a COM type library into a .NET assembly that contains equivalent metadata as shown in Figure 6–4.

The assembly that the Type Library Importer generates is called an Interop assembly. Interop assemblies contain strongly typed classes that sit on top of the RCW and provide a strongly typed interface to the RCW's underlying COM object. You can generate an Interop assembly by entering the following command at a Visual Studio .NET command prompt:

```
tlbimp typelibraryfile [options]
```

You can either specify a type library file (with a .tlb) extension or the name of a DLL or executable that has an embedded type library for the typelibraryfile parameter. Table 6–2 lists the command-line options for tlbimp.

To use **tlbimp.exe** to generate an Interop assembly for the financial COM component, perform the following steps:

1. Start a Visual Studio.NET command prompt (select Programs | Microsoft Visual Studio .NET | Visual Studio .NET tools | Visual Studio .NET Command Prompt from the Start menu).

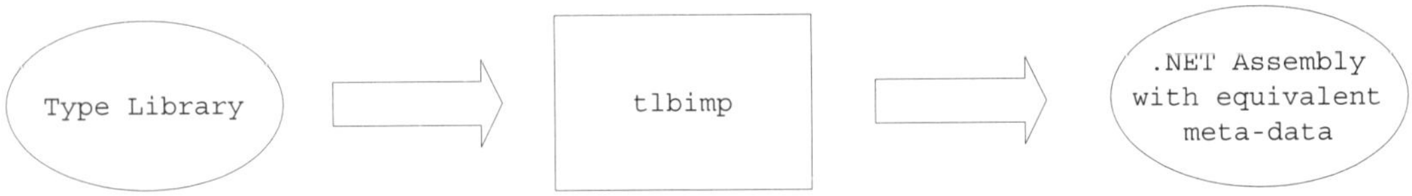

FIGURE 6–4 *The Type Library Importer.*

TABLE 6–2 *Available command-line parameters for tlbimp*

Parameter	Description
out	File name for the generated Interop assembly. Also sets the default name for the namespace that the Interop types will reside in. If you do not specify this parameter, the Interop assembly and the generated namespace will default to the name of the type library.
namespace	Allows you to explicitly specify the name of the Interop assembly's namespace.
asmversion	Allows you to specify the version number of the generated assembly.
reference	Allows you to specify the file name of the assembly to use to resolve references.
keyfile	Allows you to specify the file that contains the key pair that should be used to sign the Interop assembly.
delaysign	Used to specify that the Interop assembly will be delay-signed.
publickey	Allows you to specify the file that contains the public key that should be used to delay-sign the Interop assembly.
unsafe	Produce interfaces without runtime security checks.
nologo	Prevents tlbimp from displaying the Microsoft logo.
silent	Suppresses all output except errors.
verbose	Display extra diagnostic output information.
primary	Produces a primary Interop assembly.
sysarray	Import SAFEARRAY as System.Array.
strictref	Only use assemblies specified with /reference to resolve references.

2. Change directory to the location where the financial component resides on your disk. You can download the financial component from the Web site for the book.
3. Enter the following command at the command prompt: tblimp financial-component.dll /out financial.dll.

The following code shows the type library for the TimeValue COM object that I used in the previous code example:

```
[
  uuid(EB47FA01-22EE-11D3-998A-E0EC08C10000),
  version(1.0)
]
library FINANCIALCOMPONENTLib
{
    importlib("stdole2.tlb");
    interface ITimeValue;
    interface ITaxCalculator;
    [
      odl,
      uuid(EB47FA0D-22EE-11D3-998A-E0EC08C10000),
      dual,
      oleautomation
    ]
    interface ITimeValue : IDispatch {
        [id(0x00000001)]
        HRESULT MonthlyPayment(
                    [in] short numMonths,
                    [in] double interestRate,
                    [in] double loanAmt,
                    [out, retval] double* result);
        [id(0x00000002)]
        HRESULT LoanAmount(
                    [in] short numMonths,
                    [in] double interestRate,
                    [in] double monthlyPmt,
                    [out, retval] double* result);
    };

    [
      odl,
      uuid(1C208680-22F2-11D3-998A-E0EC08C10000),
      dual,
      oleautomation
    ]
    interface ITaxCalculator : IDispatch {
        [id(0x00000001)]
        HRESULT CalculateTax(
                    [in] double earnings,
                    [out, retval] double* tax);
    };

    [
      uuid(EB47FA0E-22EE-11D3-998A-E0EC08C10000)
    ]
    coclass CFinancial {
        [default] interface ITimeValue;
        interface ITaxCalculator;
    };
};
```

For those who are more visually oriented, a COM diagram of this component will look as shown in Figure 6–5.

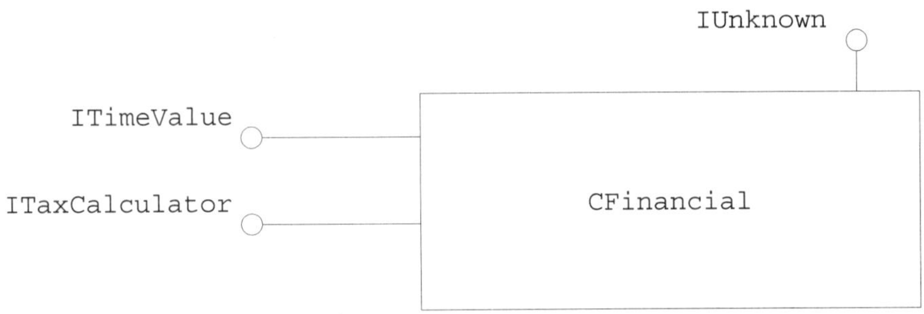

FIGURE 6–5 *The financial COM component.*

The type library importer will generate a .NET assembly from the contents of this type library. By default, the types in this assembly will reside in a namespace that has the same name as the type library (FinancialComponentLib in this case). A general mapping between types in a COM type library and types in a generated Interop assembly is shown in Table 6–3.

TABLE 6–3 *Mapping between entities in the COM type library and the Interop assembly*

COM Type Library Type	.NET Assembly Type
Library Name	A .NET namespace with the same name as the library name, or, if you specify a /out parameter to tlbimp, the same name as the specified output assembly.
Interface	.NET Interface with GUID and TypeLibType attributes.
CoClass	**CoClass Interface—**An interface with same name as the CoClass in the type library that derives from the default interface of the COM CoClass and has the same GUID attribute as the default interface. This interface also uses the CoClass and TypeLibType attributes. The CoClass attribute references the type object associated with the RCW class, which is explained next. **RCW Class—**A .NET class with the same name as the COM coclass, but with Class appended to it. This class wraps the RCW and uses the same GUID as the CoClass. This class implements all of the interfaces supported by the COM class, so it contains the union of all the methods supported by the COM class.
Source Interfaces (events)	This is so complicated that I'll cover it in the next chapter when I talk about advanced aspects of Interop.
Structures	.NET values types (structs in C#, structures in VB .NET).
Enumerations	.NET enumeration.

TABLE 6–3 *Mapping between entities in the COM type library and the Interop assembly (continued)*

COM Type Library Type	.NET Assembly Type
Unions	.NET values types with explicit memory layout using the StructLayout and FieldOffset attributes.
Typedefs	Converts to the underlying type with the ComAliasName attribute.
Parameter and Return Values Types	See the type transformation in Table 6-1.

Notice that most of the .NET types that are generated are marked with the GUID and TypeLibType attributes. The GUID attribute stores the GUID of the COM type that the equivalent .NET type was generated from. The TypeLibType attribute records that the .NET type originated from the transformation of a COM type library.

In the case of the financial component, the Interop assembly will contain the types shown in Table 6–4.

TABLE 6–4 *The types in the Interop assembly for the financial COM component*

COM Type	COM Name	Interop Assembly Type	.NET Name
Type Library	FINANCIALCOMPONENTLib	Namespace	FinancialAssembly
Coclass	CFinancial	RCW Class	CFinancialClass
		CoClass Interface	CFinancial
Default Interface	ITimeValue	Interface	ITimeValue
Interface	ITaxCalculator	Interface	ITimeValue

A UML class diagram of these types is shown in Figure 6–6.

Certain aspects of the COM-to-.NET transformation may seem counterintuitive. For instance, why would a COM coclass map to both a CoClass interface and an RCW class? The reason has to do with VB and the way that it attempts to hide the COM interface-based programming style. C++ programmers who use COM are used to using a COM object through interface pointers. Most programmers who program with other languages like VB or other object-based systems like Java are used to instantiating an object and then calling methods on the object directly. I have found from my teaching experience that VB programmers in particular seem to have a great deal of trouble with interface-based programming. Perhaps because of this, VB attempts to hide the presence of interfaces in COM by mapping each VB class to both a COM coclass and a default interface that has the same name as the class with an underscore prepended to the name. You create instances of the class and

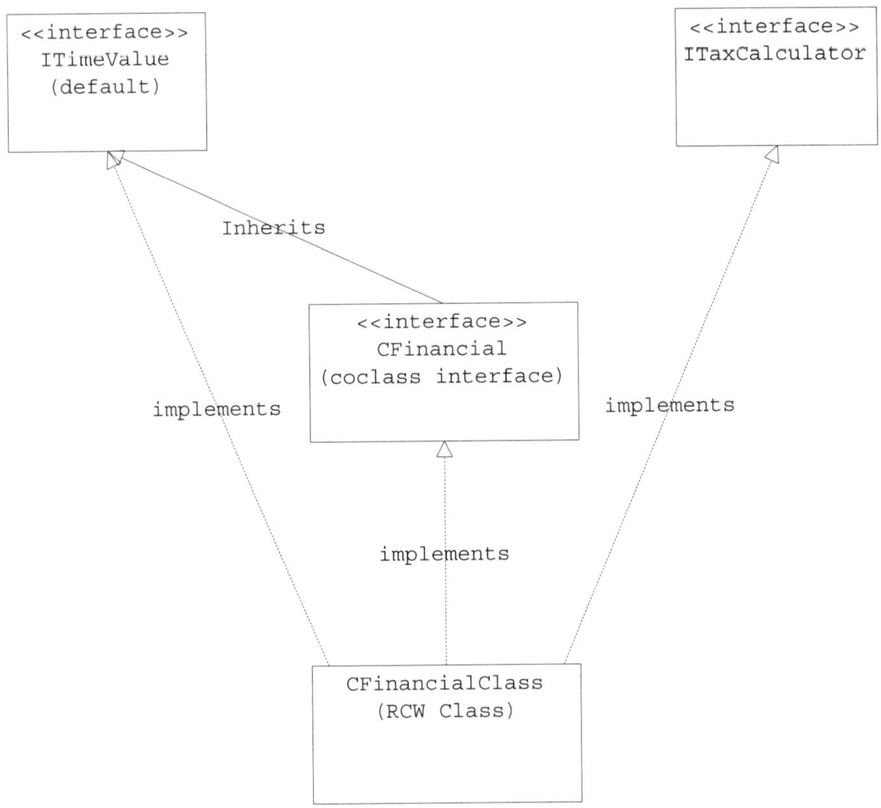

FIGURE 6–6 *A Unified Model Language (UML) diagram of the Interop assembly for the financial component.*

call methods on it, and the VB runtime uses the default interface behind the scenes. Therefore, if you created a VB class called CFinancial, you would see in the COM type library a coclass called CFinancial with a default interface called _CFinancial. When you call methods on an instance of the **CFinancial** class, the VB runtime knows to call the corresponding method on the default interface of the **CFinancial** class (_CFinancial). Tlbimp tries to duplicate this functionality. For instance, in the case of the Financial COM component, tlbimp will generate a class called **CFinancialClass**; this is the RCW class shown in Table 6–3. The RCW class implements all of the interfaces supported by the COM class (ITimeValue and ITaxCalculator in this case). Tlbimp will also generate an interface called CFinancial (this is the coclass interface shown in Table 6–3) that inherits from the default interface of the COM class. The CLR will create an instance of the RCW class (CFinancialClass) automatically when you attempt to create an instance of the coclass interface (CFinancial). The end result of these transformations is that, from your .NET client, you can create an object reference using the same type name as the COM class (**CFinancial**) and call all the methods supported by its default interface. If you want to call methods in the nondefault interfaces, you must instantiate an instance of the RCW class directly (CFinancialClass in this case). For example, you can use the following code to call any of the methods in the ITime-Value interface:

```
Double dblResult;
CFinancial objFinancial=new CFinancial();
dblResult=objFinancial.LoanAmount(360,6.75,2000.0);
```

CFinancial is an interface, and, normally, you cannot instantiate interfaces this way. However, the C# compiler looks at the coclass attribute on the CFinancial interface and instantiates the class identified in the coclass attribute instead (**CFinancialClass** in this case). Hence the code shown previously is equivalent to the following code, and you can write the code either way.

```
Double dblResult;
CFinancial objFinancial=new CFinancialClass();
dblResult=objFinancial.LoanAmount(360,6.75,2000.0);
```

Regardless of how you write this code, you can only call methods in the default interface as it is currently written. The following code will not compile:

```
Double dblResult, dblTaxes;
CFinancial objFinancial=new CFinancialClass();
dblResult=objFinancial.LoanAmount(360,6.75,2000.0);
dblTaxes=objFinancial.CalculateTax(70000.0); // error!!!
```

The CalculateTax method is in the ITaxCalculator interface, which is a non-default interface on the Cfinancial coclass. To call the CalculateTax method, you should write the following code:

```
Double dblResult, dblTaxes;
CFinancial objFinancial=new CFinancialClass();
dblResult=objFinancial.LoanAmount(360,6.75,2000.0);
ITaxCalculator objTaxes=(ITaxCalculator)objFinancial;
dblTaxes=objTaxes.CalculateTax(70000);
```

Notice that, in this case, I cast the object reference to an ITaxCalculator interface reference before I can call the CalculateTax method. Another way to access the CalculateTax method is to type the original object reference as a CFinancialClass, which contains all the methods supported by the COM class.

```
Double dblResult, dblTaxes;
CFinancialClass objFinancial=new CFinancialClass();
dblResult=objFinancial.LoanAmount(360,6.75,2000.0);
dblTaxes=objFinancial.CalculateTax(70000.0);
```

After you have generated the Interop assembly, you can reference and use it from a client the same way that you would any other .NET assembly. You can compile a C# client that uses the Interop assembly for the financial component using the following command line:

```
csc /out:interoptest1.exe /r:financial.dll form1.cs
assemblyinfo.cs
```

Notice that I reference the Interop assembly (**financial.dll**) using the /r argument to the compiler. The following listing shows client-side code that uses the Interop assembly:

```
using FINANCIALCOMPONENTLib;
private void cmdGetLoanAmt_Click(object sender,
    System.EventArgs e)
{
    short shtNumMonths;
    Double dblInterestRate, dblMonthlyPmt, dblResult;
    try
    {
        TimeValue objFinancial=new TimeValue();
        shtNumMonths=short.Parse(txtMonths.Text);
        dblInterestRate=
        Double.Parse(txtInterestRate.Text);
        dblMonthlyPmt=Double.Parse(txtMonthlyPmt.Text);
        dblResult=objFinancial.LoanAmount(shtNumMonths,
        dblInterestRate,dblMonthlyPmt);
        lblLoanAmt.Text=String.Format("{0:C}",dblResult);
    }
    catch(System.Exception ex)
    {
        MessageBox.Show(ex.Message);
    }
}
```

Notice that the code here is much simpler than the late-bound client code that I showed you before. Instead of instantiating an object using the CreateInstance method on the **System.Activator** class and then calling the InvokeMember method on the **System.Type** class, I simply create an instance of the **TimeValue** class and call the LoanAmount method. I will also get a compiler error, instead of a runtime error, if I pass the wrong parameters to the method or attempt to assign the return value to something other than a double.

If you are using Visual Studio .NET, it's even easier to generate an Interop assembly for a COM object. To generate an Interop assembly in Visual Studio .NET, perform the following steps:

1. Select Add Reference… from the Project menu.
2. Select the COM tab (as shown in Figure 6–7).
3. Highlight the COM component(s) that you want to use and click the select button. If the type library for the component is not registered, you can click the Browse… button and select the component.

4. Repeat Step 3 for as many COM components that you like.
5. Click OK.

Visual Studio .NET will create an assembly with the following name:

```
Interop.[typelibraryname].dll
```

This assembly will reside in your build directory. For a Windows application project, the build directory is **[project rootdir]\bin\debug**. For an ASP.NET project, the build directory is **[virtualdirpath]\bin** where virtualdirpath is the physical directory underlying the virtual directory for the project. The Interop assembly that Visual Studio .NET generated for the financial component is called **Interop.FinancialComponentLib.dll**. The generated namespace is called FinancialComponentLib.

So far, we have looked at only the most basic elements of using a COM object from a managed code client. There are a number of issues that make using COM object from .NET a little more difficult than what you see here. One of the issues is that not all types that you can represent in COM are representable in .NET. There is also the issue of Apartments, advanced marshaling support, events, and exceptions. I discuss all of these issues in greater depth when I discuss advanced aspects of Interop in Chapters 7 and 8.

Using .NET Objects from COM Clients

Now that you understand how to use COM objects from your managed code clients, let's look at the other side of the same coin: using a .NET object from a COM client. Once again, you face the problem of trying to bridge two very different object models (COM and .NET). In this case, you want a .NET object to be exposed to a COM/Win32 client as a COM object, and, once again, your interface should be as natural as possible. In other words, the .NET object should appear to the COM/Win32 client (for better or worse) to be just like any other COM object. You should be able to create the object using CoCreateInstance or one of the other COM activation functions. The object should expose the IUnknown interface that you use to manage the life cycle of the object. The object should also have a type library and store information in the registry just like any other COM object. And just as it was when I used COM objects from managed code, the marshaling from unmanaged types to managed types—and vice versa—for parameters and return values should be handled automatically. The CLR provides both a runtime wrapper object called a CCW and a tool that you can use to convert your .NET metadata into a COM type library and add the necessary entries to the registry (regasm.exe).

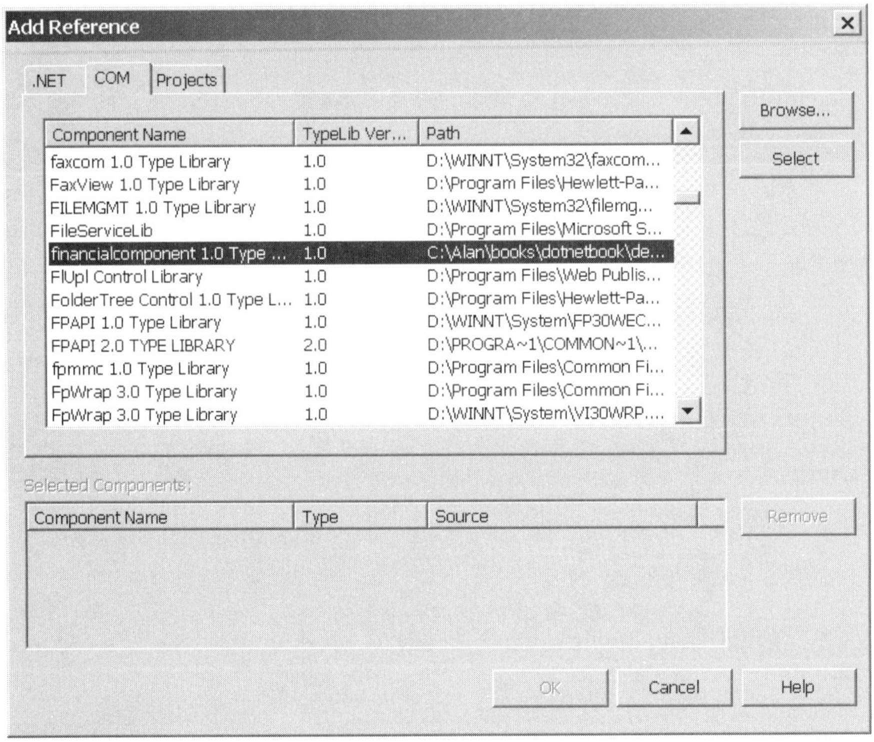

FIGURE 6–7 *The COM tab on the References dialog.*

CCW

When you instantiate a .NET object from a Win32 application or a COM component, the CLR will automatically create a CCW that transparently handles all of the mapping issues between a Win32/COM client and a .NET component as shown in Figure 6–8.

A CCW provides the opposite functionality to an RCW. It handles marshaling of unmanaged types on the client to managed types in the object and vice versa. The CCW is a COM object. It holds a reference to the managed object and exposes the managed object to unmanaged clients. When the client releases all of the interfaces it holds on the CCW, the CCW removes its reference to the underlying managed object, and it then becomes eligible for garbage collection. Notice in Figure 6–8 that, in addition to IDispatch and IUnknown, which the CCW always supports, the CCW also may expose generated class interfaces. It will also expose COM equivalents of any managed code interfaces that the underlying managed code object implements. Because the COM runtime interrogates the registry for location information

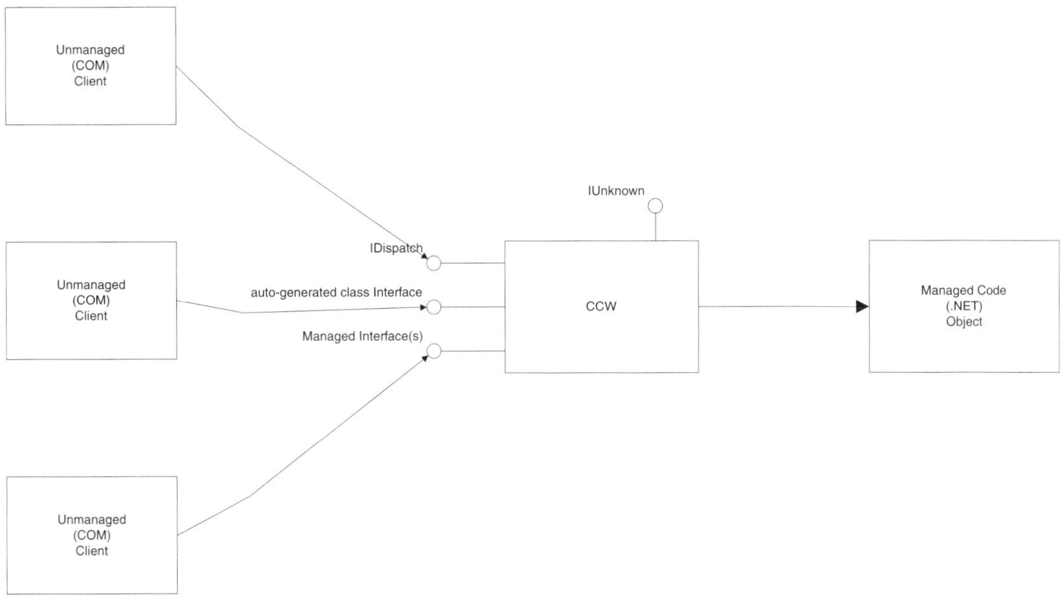

FIGURE 6–8 *A CCW.*

when you instantiate an object, you must first insert a few entries in the registry before you can use a .NET object from an unmanaged client. Also, because type libraries are such a fundamental part of COM, you will also need to have a type library before you can use the .NET object from your managed code client.

Fortunately, the .NET Framework SDK provides you with three ways to generate the registry entries that you need and two ways to generate a type library. You can generate the registry entries in one of the following ways:

- Using the command-line Assembly Registration Tool (regasm.exe) in the .NET Framework SDK
- Using the Register for COM Interop option under Configuration Properties | Build on the project properties page in Visual Studio .NET
- Using the RegisterAssembly or RegisterTypeForComClients methods in the **System.Runtime.InteropServices.RegistrationServices** class

I explore using the Assembly Registration Tool (regasm.exe) and the Register for COM Interop option in this chapter.

Assembly Registration Tool (regasm.exe)

The Assembly Registration Tool uses the metadata in an assembly to generate registry entries and (optionally) a type library, which allow COM clients to use .NET objects. Figure 6–9 shows a conceptual view of this process.

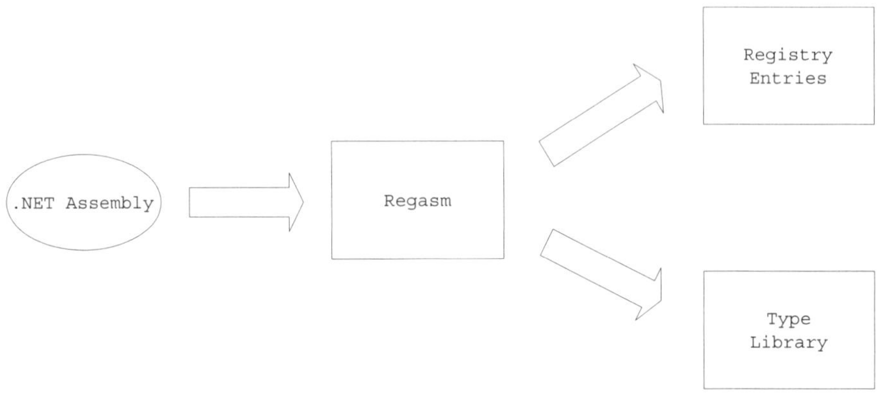

FIGURE 6–9 *The Assembly Registration Tool.*

The regasm is a command-line tool, and the basic syntax for using it is as follows:

```
regasm assemblyfilename [options]
```

The list of command-line options for regasm is shown in Table 6–5.

TABLE 6–5 *Available options for regasm*

Parameter	Description
tlb:[filename]	Allows you to specify the name for the type library file.
regfile:[filename]	Generates a reg. file instead of registering the types.
codebase	Sets the codebase in the registry.
registered	Only refers to registered type libraries.
nologo	Removes the types in the registry.
silent	Suppresses all output except errors.
verbose	Displays extra diagnostic output information.

Run regasm with the simplest command line as follows:

```
regasm [assemblyname]
```

Running this command will add entries to the registry that allow all the types in the assembly to be used by unmanaged clients as though they were COM types. If you want to generate a type library too, use the /tlb option on regasm. If you do not want to add the registry entries immediately, you can use the regfile option to generate a registry (.reg) file that you can use to add the registry entries later. You will need to use the registry editor (regedit) to add the contents of this file to the registry as shown here:

```
regedit [registryfilename]
```

Curiously, you cannot use the regfile option with the /tlb option. Another important optional parameter for regasm is the codebase option. The regasm tool inserts the full assembly name into registry (that is, the friendly name, version number, public key token if there is one, and culture). The CLR uses its regular search rules (which were explained in Chapter 3) to locate the assembly. This means that the assembly that contains the managed object must reside in a subdirectory beneath the unmanaged client application or in the GAC. The codebase option on regasm sets the codebase in the registry equal to the path of the assembly that you originally passed to regasm. The CLR will check the codebase after it checks the GAC, but before it starts probing beneath the directory structure of the client executable. This option is useful if you do not want to put the .NET assembly into the GAC or into a subdirectory of the managed application. Some example command lines for regasm are as follows:

```
regasm dotnetfinancial.dll
regasm dotnetfinancial.dll /tlb:dotnetfinancial.tlb
regasm dotnetfinancial.dll /reg:dotnetfinancial.reg
regasm dotnetfinancial.dll /codebase
```

The first command line will insert the required entries into the registry for a .NET assembly called dotnetfinancial. The second command line will insert the required registry entries into the registry and create and register a type library called **dotnetfinancial.tlb**. The third command will generate the registry entries, but it won't add them to the registry. It will instead create a registry file called **dotnetfinancial.reg** that contains the registry entries. You can run the regedit command to add these entries to the registry later. The fourth command line will insert the required entries into the registry and add a codebase to the registry that the CLR will search for the assembly after it searches the GAC.

The Type Library Exporter (tlbexp.exe)

You can also generate a type library using the Type Library Exporter (tlbexp), which is yet another command-line tool in the .NET Framework SDK. The Type Library Exporter only generates type libraries. Unlike the /tlb option on regasm, tlbexp does not also register the assembly. You have to do that separately. The syntax for using tlbexp is as follows:

```
tlbexp assemblyfilename [options]
```

The list of available options for tlbexp is shown in Table 6–6.

TABLE 6–6 *Available options for tlbexp*

Parameter	Description
out:[filename]	Allows you to specify the name for the type library file.
nologo	Prevents tlbimp from displaying the Microsoft logo.
silent	Suppresses all output except errors.
verbose	Displays extra diagnostic output information.
names:[FileName]	A file where each line specifies the capitalization to use for each name in the generated type library.

An example command line for tlbexp is as follows:

```
tlbexp dotnetfinancial.dll /out:dotnetfinancial.tlb
```

Using Visual Studio .NET

If you have Visual Studio .NET, you do not have to resort to the command-line tools to register your .NET assemblies for use by unmanaged clients using COM Interop. With your managed code project open, perform the following steps to register your assembly for use by COM and to create a type library:

1. Right-click the project name in the solution explorer window in Visual Studio .NET. A context menu will appear. (See Figure 6–10.)
2. Select Properties from the context menu. The project property pages dialog will appear. (See Figure 6–11.)
3. Select True from the dropdown list next to Register for COM Interop.
4. Click the OK button.

An Example

To show you how to use regasm to make a .NET assembly accessible from COM, I created a .NET version of the financial component. I won't go into a series of step-by-step instructions for building this component. Creating the project for this assembly is very similar to the spell-checker example that I built in Chapter 5. The assembly has a namespace called DotNetFinancial that contains a single class called **TimeValue**, which follows:

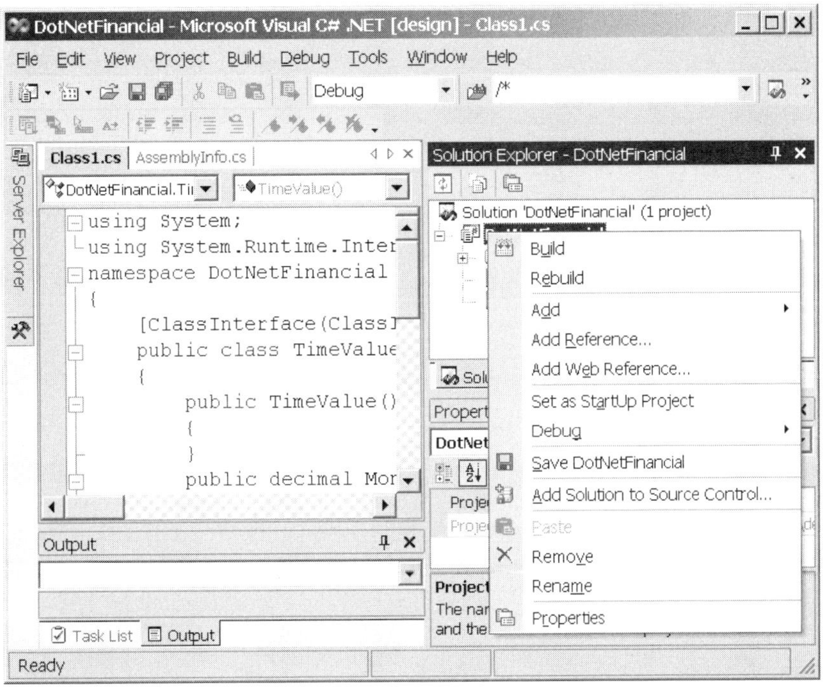

FIGURE 6–10 *The Solution Explorer window in Visual Studio .NET.*

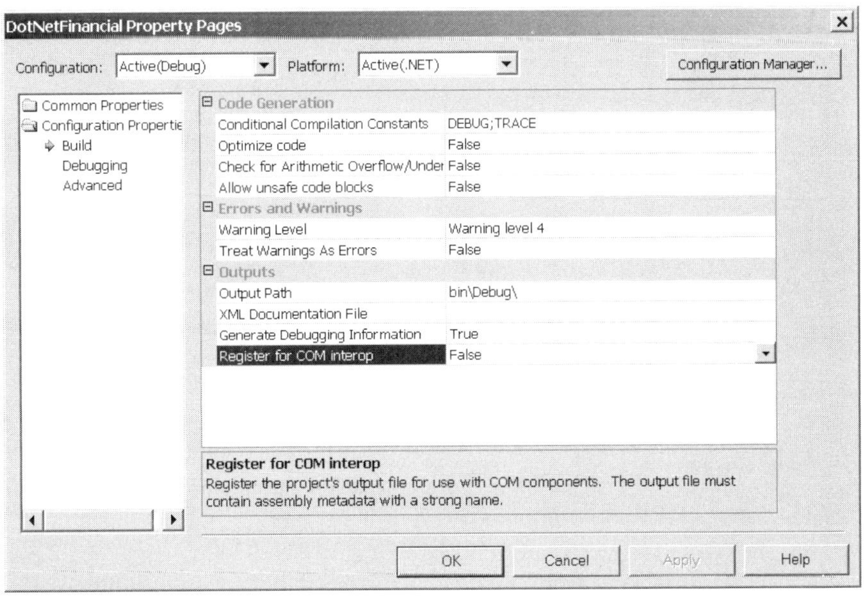

FIGURE 6–11 *The project property pages dialog in Visual Studio .NET.*

```
namespace DotNetFinancial
{
    public class TimeValue
    {
        public TimeValue()
        {
        }
        public decimal MonthlyPayment(
            short numMonths,
            double interestRate,
            decimal loanAmt)
        {
            double monthlyRate, tempVal;
            decimal unRoundedAmt;
            monthlyRate=interestRate/1200;
            tempVal=Math.Pow((1+monthlyRate),
                (double)numMonths);
            unRoundedAmt=(decimal)((double)loanAmt*
                (monthlyRate*tempVal/(tempVal-1)));
            return decimal.Round(unRoundedAmt,2);
        }
        public decimal LoanAmount(
            short numMonths,
            double interestRate,
            decimal monthlyPmt)
        {
            double monthlyRate, tempVal;
            decimal unRoundedAmt;
            monthlyRate=interestRate/1200;
            tempVal=
                Math.Pow((1+monthlyRate),
                (double)numMonths);
            unRoundedAmt=
                (decimal)((double)monthlyPmt*
                (tempVal-1)/(monthlyRate*tempVal));
            return decimal.Round(unRoundedAmt,2);
        }
    }
}
```

I also added a strong name to the assembly by creating a key pair using the Strong Name Tool (**sn.exe**) and then referencing the key file in the AssemblyKeyFile attribute in the Assemblyinfo file of my project. If you are not sure how to do this, see the example project that I built in Chapter 5. The process is exactly the same for this assembly. You can also download the code for this book and look at the DotNetFinancial server project in the code for Chapter 6.

The DotNetFinancial assembly resides in a file called **DotNetFinancial.dll**. You can register the assembly for use by an unmanaged client using the following command line:

```
regasm dotnetfinancial.dll /tlb:dotnetfinancial.tlb
```

This command line will generate a type library and insert the following entries into the registry for the assembly:

```
[HKEY_CLASSES_ROOT\DotNetFinancial.TimeValue]
@="DotNetFinancial.TimeValue"

[HKEY_CLASSES_ROOT\DotNetFinancial.TimeValue\CLSID]
@="{311F0CBD-FB08-3DB4-A87C-96EA3C30DA0D}"

[HKEY_CLASSES_ROOT\CLSID\
{311F0CBD-FB08-3DB4-A87C-96EA3C30DA0D}]
@="DotNetFinancial.TimeValue"

[HKEY_CLASSES_ROOT\CLSID\
{311F0CBD-FB08-3DB4-A87C-96EA3C30DA0D}\InprocServer32]
@="D:\WINNT\System32\mscoree.dll"
"ThreadingModel"="Both"
"Class"="DotNetFinancial.TimeValue"
"Assembly"="DotNetFinancial, Version=1.0.814.40736,
Culture=neutral, PublicKeyToken=null"
"RuntimeVersion"="v1.0.3328"


[HKEY_CLASSES_ROOT\CLSID\
{311F0CBD-FB08-3DB4-A87C-96EA3C30DA0D}\ProgId]
@="DotNetFinancial.TimeValue"

[HKEY_CLASSES_ROOT\CLSID\
{311F0CBD-FB08-3DB4-A87C-96EA3C30DA0D}\
Implemented Categories\
{62C8FE65-4EBB-45E7-B440-6E39B2CDBF29}]
```

It will also generate the following registry entries for the type library:

```
[HKEY_CLASSES_ROOT\TypeLib\{1D726C13-12E6-32A3-95F0-
E30D9286344B}]

[HKEY_CLASSES_ROOT\TypeLib\{1D726C13-12E6-32A3-95F0-
E30D9286344B}\1.0]
@="DotNetFinancial"

[HKEY_CLASSES_ROOT\TypeLib\{1D726C13-12E6-32A3-95F0-
E30D9286344B}\1.0\0]

[HKEY_CLASSES_ROOT\TypeLib\{1D726C13-12E6-32A3-95F0-
E30D9286344B}\1.0\0\win32]
@="C:\\demos\\chap6\\bin\\dotnetfinancial.tlb"

[HKEY_CLASSES_ROOT\TypeLib\{1D726C13-12E6-32A3-95F0-
E30D9286344B}\1.0\FLAGS]
@="0"
```

```
[HKEY_CLASSES_ROOT\TypeLib\{1D726C13-12E6-32A3-95F0-
E30D9286344B}\1.0\HELPDIR]
@="C:\\demos\\chap6\\bin\\"
```

Let's look first at the registry entries that regasm generated for the assembly. The first two entries contain the progID key for the **DotNetFinancial.TimeValue** class as shown here:

```
[HKEY_CLASSES_ROOT\DotNetFinancial.TimeValue]
@="DotNetFinancial.TimeValue"

[HKEY_CLASSES_ROOT\DotNetFinancial.TimeValue\CLSID]
@="{311F0CBD-FB08-3DB4-A87C-96EA3C30DA0D}"
```

The value at the first key contains the name of the managed class that implements the ProgID (**DotNetFinancial.TimeValue**). The second key contains the usual pointer from the ProgID to its associated CLSID. Notice that the generated progID has the form assemblyname.classname. Once again, this is a default that you can affect using the ProgID attribute in System.Runtime.InteropServices. You change the definition of the managed TimeValue class to be as follows:

```
using System.Runtime.InteropServices;
namespace DotNetFinancial
{
    [Guid("8D37CFCB-1C0E-45bb-B1D6-FE21C07237B8")]
    [ProgId("Financials.AlansFunkyClass")]
    public class TimeValue
{
//...
}
}
```

Regasm will use Financials.AlansFunkyClass as the ProgID, and the first two registry entries will now look as follows:

```
[HKEY_CLASSES_ROOT\Financials.AlansFunkyClass]
@="DotNetFinancial.TimeValue"

[HKEY_CLASSES_ROOT\Financials.AlansFunkyClass\CLSID]
@="{8D37CFCB-1C0E-45BB-B1D6-FE21C07237B8}"
```

The rest of the assembly entries define the CLSID information for the TimeValue type beneath the HKEY_CLASSES_ROOT\CLSID key. Regasm synthesizes a CLSID from the full name of the assembly, that is, the friendly name (DotNetFinancial in this case), the version number, the public key token (if the assembly has a strong name), and the culture. You will need to keep this in mind because, unless you explicitly specify the CLSID that regasm should generate (you'll see how to do this shortly), the CLSID for the **TimeValue** class will change whenever you change the version number of the assembly.

Note To guarantee that the generated GUID is unique to your organization, it is always a good idea to add a strong name to any managed code assemblies that you intend to use through COM Interop. When you get right down to it, it's a good idea to always add a strong name to your assemblies anyway.

In this case, regasm generated the following CLSID for the **TimeValue** class in the DotNetFinancial assembly:

```
{311F0CBD-FB08-3DB4-A87C-96EA3C30DA0D}
```

If you have a specific CLSID that you would like regasm to use, or if you would like to guarantee that the generated GUID will never change, you can use the GUID attribute in the System.Runtime.InteropServices namespace to associate a CLSID with the managed **TimeValue** class. For instance, if you change the C# class definition of the **TimeValue** class to look as follows:

```
using System.Runtime.InteropServices;
namespace DotNetFinancial
{
[Guid("8D37CFCB-1C0E-45bb-B1D6-FE21C07237B8")]
    public class TimeValue
    {
    //...
    }
}
```

then the CLSID generated by regasm for the **TimeValue** class will always be {8D37CFCB-1C0E-45bb-B1D6-FE21C07237B8} regardless of the version number of the DotNetFinancial assembly.

The CLSID key that regasm generated for the **DotNetFinancial.TimeValue** class in this case is shown here:

```
[HKEY_CLASSES_ROOT\CLSID\
{311F0CBD-FB08-3DB4-A87C-96EA3C30DA0D}]
@="DotNetFinancial.TimeValue"
```

The default value at this key DotNetFinancial.TimeValue is the name of the managed class that implements the CLSID. The next registry entry is the most important one for any COM object, the InProcServer32 key, which is shown here:

```
[HKEY_CLASSES_ROOT\CLSID\
{311F0CBD-FB08-3DB4-A87C-96EA3C30DA0D}\InprocServer32]
@="D:\WINNT\System32\mscoree.dll"
"ThreadingModel"="Both"
```

```
"Class"="DotNetFinancial.TimeValue"
"Assembly"="DotNetFinancial, Version=1.0.814.40736,
Culture=neutral, PublicKeyToken=null"
"RuntimeVersion"="v1.0.3328"
```

This key will contain five values:

- The default value for the key contains the path to the piece of software that implements the class identified by this CLSID. The specified path in this case points to the CLR's execution engine: **D:\WINNT\System32\mscoree.dll**. The execution engine does not implement the TimeValue object, but it does implement the CoGetClassObject entry point that the COM runtime will look for and call after it loads the execution engine. The execution engine will then load the managed class specified in the Class value beneath the InProcServer32 subkey (see the third bullet).
- The ThreadingModel value specifies which COM Apartments this object may run in. All managed classes that are called through COM Interop use the Both threading model, which really means that the object can run in either a Single Threaded Apartment (STA) or a Multithreaded Apartment (MTA). The object will always run in the same Apartment as its client.
- The Class value contains the name of the managed class that implements the CLSID, that is, the name of the managed class that the CLR should load when you call the object through a CCW.
- The Assembly value contains the full name, that is, the friendly name, four-part version number, public key token, and culture of the assembly that implements the managed class identified in the previous Class value.
- The RuntimeVersion value identifies the version of the CLR that the managed class will work with.

The next key contains the back-pointer from the CLSID to the ProgID.

```
{311F0CBD-FB08-3DB4-A87C-96EA3C30DA0D}\ProgId]
@="DotNetFinancial.TimeValue"
```

The final key, which follows, contains the component categories for this COM class:

```
[HKEY_CLASSES_ROOT\CLSID\
{311F0CBD-FB08-3DB4-A87C-96EA3C30DA0D}\
Implemented Categories\
{62C8FE65-4EBB-45E7-B440-6E39B2CDBF29}]
```

Component categories provide a way to group related COM classes together. For instance, there is a component category that you can use to specify that a COM object is an ActiveX control. There is another component category that you can use to specify that a COM object is an embeddable object. Each component category has a GUID associated with it: a CATID. The CATID for the ActiveX control component category is {40FC6ED4-2438-11CF-A3DB-080036F12502}, and the one for an embeddable object is {40FC6ED3-2438-11CF-A3DB-080036F12502}. You can find all of the component categories on your system by looking under the HKEY_CLASSES_ROOT\Component Categories\ key on your machine. An object indicates that it is part of a category by adding a subkey with the desired CATID beneath its Implemented Categories under the object's CLSID subkey. The registry entries for a managed code object include a component category called .NET Category with GUID {62C8FE65-4EBB-45e7-B440-6E39B2CDBF29}.

The Type Library

The Assembly Registration Tool (regasm) also created a type library when I ran it. The IDL in the generated type library is as follows:

```
[
  uuid(1D726C13-12E6-32A3-95F0-E30D9286344B),
  version(1.2)
]
library DotNetFinancial
{
    importlib("mscorlib.tlb");
    importlib("stdole2.tlb");

    interface _TimeValue;
    [
      uuid(311F0CBD-FB08-3DB4-A87C-96EA3C30DA0D),
      version(1.0),
        custom({0F21F359-AB84-41E8-9A78-36D110E6D2F9},
        "DotNetFinancial.TimeValue")
    ]
    coclass TimeValue {
        [default] interface _TimeValue;
        interface _Object;
    };

    [
      odl,
      uuid(F00794BD-914A-3411-A633-6FABAD549E80),
      hidden,
      dual,
        oleautomation,
        custom({0F21F359-AB84-41E8-9A78-36D110E6D2F9},
        "DotNetFinancial.TimeValue")
    ]
    interface _TimeValue : IDispatch {
  };
};
```

The GUID for the type library (the LIBID), which you can see on line 2, is generated from the full assembly name just like the CLSID for the **TimeValue** class. The version number on line 3 is the major and minor version number of the managed code assembly. On line 7, you can see that the type library imports the type library for the **mscorlib.dll** assembly, which contains many of the types in the System namespace. The type library has to do this because it uses the _Object interface, which contains all of the methods that reside in the **System.Object** class that is the base class for all other types in .NET. The _Object contains such methods as ToString, GetType, GethashCode, and Equals. Line 10 is a forward declaration for the _TimeValue class interface. Lines 11 through 20 contain a declaration of the TimeValue coclass, which maps to the **TimeValue** class that I defined in the .NET assembly. The **TimeValue** class implements the _TimeValue and _Object interfaces with _TimeValue as the default. Lines 22 through 32 contain the declaration of the _TimeValue class interface.

In COM, you can only call methods on an interface. Coclasses simply group interfaces. If your managed class does not implement any managed interfaces, regasm will automatically create a COM interface that has the same name as the managed class (**TimeValue** in this case) prefixed with an underscore. This automatically generated interface is called a Class Interface. It would seem logical that this interface would contain all of the methods that are declared in the managed **TimeValue** class, that is, LoanAmount and MonthlyPayment, but you will notice that it does not. Instead, the _TimeValue interface is an empty dual interface that derives from IDispatch. You have to use late binding through the Invoke method IDispatch to call the methods in the class interface.

The reason that regasm defines the class interface this way has to do with the way clients bind to methods in COM and the differences between the way that COM and .NET implement versioning. A COM object's interfaces form a binary-level contract between the COM object and its clients. COM interfaces are implemented as C++ style vtables, that is, an array of function pointers. When a COM-enabled compiler sets up an early-bound call to a COM object, it generates code to invoke the method pointed to by a specified index in the vtable. If this interface changes in any way (even if you just add a method), you can potentially break clients. This is why COM enforced its rule of immutable interfaces, that is, that an interface, after it is published, should never be changed. The problem is that there is no such immutable class rule for .NET. The .NET clients bind to classes dynamically at runtime, so it is permissible to add a method to a class without breaking a managed code client. Unfortunately, if you create a .NET object, early bind to it from an unmanaged client through COM Interop, and then alter the .NET class, you will probably break your early bound unmanaged clients because they are dependent on the vtable index of each method. The solution to this problem is not to allow early binding by default and require you to use late binding.

You can get regasm to generate a dual interface with methods that you can early bind to using the ClassInterface attribute. The ClassInterface attribute, which resides in the System.Runtime.InteropServices namespace, has three possible values:

- **AutoDispatch**—This is the default and indicates that an empty IDispatch class interface will be created at runtime that only supports the methods in IDispatch. Hence, it can only be late bound. You should always call GetIDsOfNames from your unmanaged client to fetch the DispIDs for your methods. You should not cache the DispIDs in a wrapper class like the ColeDispatchDriver-derived classes do in MFC.
- **AutoDual**—Indicates that the runtime (and regasm when you run it) should generate a dual class interface that both derives from IDispatch and contains all of the methods that you declared in your managed class. You can thus either early bind or late bind to this interface. Early binding is discouraged because it does not version well.
- **None**—No class interface is generated. The only COM interfaces supported by the CCW (besides the system interfaces like IDispatch and ISupportsErrorInfo) are COM equivalents of the managed interfaces that are explicitly implemented by the object.

AutoDispatch is the default value for the ClassInterface attribute, so, if you do not specify a value for this attribute on your managed class, the COM interface that the CLR creates at runtime will contain only an empty IDispatch interface. If you specify AutoDual for the class interface attribute as follows:

```
using System;
using System.Runtime.InteropServices;
namespace DotNetFinancial
{
    [ClassInterface(ClassInterfaceType.AutoDual)]
    public class TimeValue
    {
    // implementation omitted for clarity…
    }
}
```

Then the generated COM interface for your class in the CCW will contain all of the methods that you declared in your managed code class as follows:

```
[
  uuid(F26CCE1C-A2DC-3C16-B2B2-350FDA238CEE),
  version(1.2)
]
library DotNetFinancial
{
    importlib("mscorlib.tlb");
```

```
        importlib("stdole2.tlb");

        interface _TimeValue;

        [
          uuid(50D80C16-B2A3-35B4-8A67-DBD4940781C5),
          version(1.0),
            custom({0F21F359-AB84-41E8-9A78-36D110E6D2F9},
            "DotNetFinancial.TimeValue")
        ]
        coclass TimeValue {
            [default] interface _TimeValue;
            interface _Object;
        };

        [
          odl,
          uuid(8C14F750-B657-3ACA-B95D-14B9733A5F29),
          hidden,
          dual,
          nonextensible,
          oleautomation,
            custom({0F21F359-AB84-41E8-9A78-36D110E6D2F9},
            "DotNetFinancial.TimeValue")

        ]
        interface _TimeValue : IDispatch {
            [id(00000000), propget,
           custom({54FC8F55-38DE-4703-9C4E-250351302B1C}, "1")]
            HRESULT ToString([out, retval] BSTR* pRetVal);
            [id(0x60020001)]
            HRESULT Equals(
                        [in] VARIANT obj,
                        [out, retval] VARIANT_BOOL* pRetVal);
            [id(0x60020002)]
            HRESULT GetHashCode([out, retval] long* pRetVal);
            [id(0x60020003)]
            HRESULT GetType([out, retval] _Type** pRetVal);
            [id(0x60020004)]
            HRESULT MonthlyPayment(
                        [in] short numMonths,
                        [in] double interestRate,
                        [in] wchar_t loanAmt,
                        [out, retval] wchar_t* pRetVal);
            [id(0x60020005)]
            HRESULT LoanAmount(
                        [in] short numMonths,
                        [in] double interestRate,
                        [in] wchar_t monthlyPmt,
                        [out, retval] wchar_t* pRetVal);
        };
    };
```

Notice that the **_TimeValue** class interface contains declarations for the LoanAmount and MonthlyPayment methods that were defined in the managed code class as well as the ToString, GetHashCode, GetType, and Equals methods from **System.Object**. Even though it might seem like AutoDual is a better choice than AutoDispatch, Microsoft does not recommend this approach because the layout of the automatically generated _TimeValue interface will change if you change the managed class. The best approach is either to stick with the AutoDispatch default and let your COM clients late bind to your managed code classes. Better yet, if you know that your managed code classes will be used by COM clients, you should implement managed interfaces in those classes to expose their functionality. COM equivalents of these managed code interfaces will be exposed to COM clients. I talk about this more in Chapter 8 when I talk about advanced aspects of .NET object to unmanaged client Interop.

Before I conclude this chapter, let's take a look at some unmanaged VB 6 and Visual C++ code that uses the managed **DotNetFinancial.TimeValue** class through COM Interop. Because it is so much easier to use, let's start with the VB 6 code.

The following code shows the key portion of the code for a VB 6 standard executable client that uses the **DotNetFinancial.TimeValue** class:

```
Private Sub cmdPayment_Click()
    On Error GoTo errHandler
    Dim objFinancial As Object
    Set objFinancial =
        CreateObject("DotNetFinancial.TimeValue")
    lblPayment.Caption =
        objFinancial.MonthlyPayment(txtNumMonths.Text,
        txtInterestRate, txtLoanAmount)
    Exit Sub
errHandler:
    MsgBox Err.Description
End Sub
```

I am using late binding here, so I declare my object variable to be of type object (which maps to the IDispatch interface). I then instantiate the object using the CreateObject function, passing in the ProgID for the managed class. Unfortunately, unless you were prescient enough to have run regasm with the /codebase parameter or you installed the DotNetFinancial assembly in the GAC, you will probably receive the error shown in Figure 6–12 if you attempt to run this executable either from within the VB IDE or by compiling and then running the executable.

This is the error that you get when the CLR cannot locate an assembly. If you refer back to the registry entries that regasm added, you can probably figure out why this didn't work. For a regular COM object, the default value of the InprocServer32 registry key contains the path to the DLL or executable

FIGURE 6–12 *The CLR cannot locate the referenced assembly.*

that implements a CLSID. For a .NET class that is being used through COM Interop, the default value at the InprocServer32 key contains the path to the CLR's execution engine (**mscoree.dll**). Additional values beneath this registry key contain the full name of the assembly that implements the CLSID. By default, there is no path information, so the CLR must be able to locate the assembly using its usual search rules. That means that, in order for the client to work, the DotNetFinancial assembly must reside in one of the following areas:

- In the same directory as the client's executable
- In a bin or DotNetFinancial directory beneath the client executable's directory
- In the GAC

If you cannot put the assembly in one of these locations, you must set the codebase for the assembly using regasm.

Note When you run an executable within the VB 6 environment, the client executable is actually the VB IDE, that is, D:\Program Files\Microsoft Visual Studio\VB98\vb6.exe. Therefore, if you don't want to put the DotNetFinancial assembly in the GAC or use the codebase parameter on regasm, you must put the DotNetFinancial assembly in the same directory as vb6.exe.

To put the DotNetFinancial assembly in the GAC, run the following command at a Visual Studio .NET command prompt:

```
gacutil -i dotnetfinancial.dll
```

Remember that, if you want to put the assembly in the GAC, you must sign it with a strong name first.

If you would rather use the /codebase option on regasm, just run regasm again with the following command line:

```
regasm dotnetfinancial.dll /tlb:dotnetfinancial.tlb /
codebase
```

Regasm will add the following value beneath the InprocServer32 registry subkey for the CLSID:

```
"CodeBase"=file:///C:/demos/chap6/bin/DotNetFinancial.DLL
```

The CLR will search the codebase location for the assembly after it checks the GAC, but before it starts probing. Either using the GAC or the codebase parameter will cause the error shown in Figure 6–12 to go away. Microsoft recommends that you put the assembly in a directory beneath the client, but, if you can't do this, the GAC is a good second choice. Using the codebase parameter on regasm should be a last resort.

I'll conclude this chapter by looking at an unmanaged Visual C++ (MFC) client. I included this mainly so you can see clearly that using a managed code object through COM is exactly the same from the client side as using a regular COM object.

```
void CVcppclientDlg::OnCalculatePaymentButton()
{
  HRESULT hRes;
  DISPID dispid;
  float fltResult;
  IDispatch *pDisp;
  OLECHAR *methodName=L"MonthlyPayment";
  CLSID clsID;
  EXCEPINFO errorInfo;
  UINT intArg;
  VARIANT vntArgs[3], vntResult;
  DISPPARAMS param;
  param.cArgs=3;
  param.rgvarg=vntArgs;
  param.cNamedArgs=0;
  param.rgdispidNamedArgs=NULL;
  vntResult.vt=VT_R4;
  vntArgs[0].vt=VT_R4;
  vntArgs[0].fltVal=m_loanAmount;
  vntArgs[1].vt=VT_R4;
  vntArgs[1].fltVal=m_apr;
  vntArgs[2].vt=VT_I2;
  vntArgs[2].iVal=m_numMonths;

  UpdateData(TRUE);
  hRes=::CLSIDFromProgID(
    L"DotNetFinancial.TimeValue",&clsID);
  hRes=CoCreateInstance(clsID,NULL,CLSCTX_ALL,
    IID_IDispatch,(void**)&pDisp);
  hRes=pDisp->GetIDsOfNames(IID_NULL,&methodName,1,
    GetUserDefaultLCID(),&dispid);
  hRes=pDisp->Invoke(dispid,IID_NULL,
    GetUserDefaultLCID(),DISPATCH_METHOD,
    &param,&vntResult,&errorInfo,&intArg);
```

```
35.     VarR4FromDec(&vntResult.decVal, &fltResult);
36.     m_payment.Format("%.2f",fltResult);
37.     UpdateData(FALSE);
38.     pDisp->Release();
39. }
```

The code in this example is much longer than the VB code, but it is functionally equivalent. On lines 3 through 23, I declare all the variables that I need to make an Invoke call on an IDispatch interface pointer. The important lines are line 7 where I declare a string that holds the name of the method that I plan to call and lines 11 through 23 where I set up the DISPPARAMS structure that will contain the parameters that I pass to the method. Keep in mind that, when using Invoke on a method that has more than one parameter, you must pass the parameters in the reverse order, that is, the parameter that appears last in the parameter list for the method will be at index zero in your parameter array. The UpdateData call on line 25 is for MFC UI processing. On line 26, I use the CLSIDFromProgID COM API method to fetch the CLSID for the managed class. On line 28, I call CoCreateInstance, passing in the CLSID that I received on line 26 and specifying that I want to obtain an IDispatch interface on the object. On line 30, I call GetIDsOfNames to fetch the Dispatch ID (DispID) of the MonthlyPayment method. Lines 32 through 34 are probably the most important lines in this example because this is where I actually call the Invoke method on the IDispatch pointer. On lines 35 thru 37 we process the results for display, and on line 38 we release the IDispatch interface pointer. Note that I have completely ignored error checking in this function for the sake of clarity. The code that I just showed is exactly the same as the code that you would write for any COM object regardless of how it was implemented.

Platform Invoke

Although the focus of this book is COM Interop, I would be remiss if I didn't discuss Platform Invocation Service (PInvoke), which allows you to call non-COM DLLs, Windows API and System functions. To use PInvoke perform the following steps:

- Declare a function in your managed code that has an equivalent parameter list and return value to the unmanaged function. You will need to use the static and extern keyword in your function declaration.
- Use the System.Runtime.InteropServices.DllImport attribute on your function declaration to (among other things) indicate which unmanaged DLL the implementation of the method resides in.

- Optionally specify custom marshaling attributes for the parameters and return values if necessary.
- Call the declared function the same way you would call any managed code.

We'll explore the first two steps in this chapter and we'll talk about the third step in Chapter 7. Let's look at the simplest example using PInvoke. In this example we'll call the GetCurrentThreadId function which resides in the Kernel system DLL (kernel32.dll). The GetCurrentThreadId method is defined as follows:

```
DWORD GetCurrentThreadId(VOID);
```

The following code shows the function declaration you would need to call the GetCurrentThreadId Windows API function from managed code. This declaration should go in the same managed source file from which you will call the GetCurrentThreadId function.

```
using System.Runtime.InteropServices;
[DllImport("kernel32.dll")]
public static extern uint GetCurrentThreadId();
```

On the first line we have a "using" statement for the System.Runtime.InteropServices namespace. On the next two lines we declare the managed equivalent for the GetCurrentThreadId function. Notice that we use the static and extern keywords to indicate that the method is contained in an external DLL. On line 2 we use the DllImport attribute to indicate that the GetCurrentThreadId resides in the kernel32.dll system DLL. You can find out which System DLL a Windows API function is implemented in using the Platform SDK documentation.

One of the biggest challenges when using PInvoke is mapping the types of the parameters and return values of the original, unmanaged function to the correct managed type. Fortunately, the mapping that I showed you in Table 6–1 applies to PInvoke as well as COM. The GetCurrentThreadId method returns a DWORD, which is actually a typedef for unsigned long. For your convenience, Table 6–7 shows the mapping from some common Win32 types to CTS and C# types.

TABLE 6–7 *Mapping Win32 types to .NET types*

Win32 API (wtypes.h)	CTS Type	C# Type
HANDLE/INT/LONG/BOOL	System.Int32	int
UINT/ULONG/DWORD	System.Uint32	uint
BYTE	System.Byte	byte
SHORT	System.UInt16	ushort
WORD	System.Int16	short

TABLE 6–7 *Mapping Win32 types to .NET types (continued)*

Win32 API (wtypes.h)	CTS Type	C# Type
BOOL	System.Boolean	int
CHAR	System.Sbyte	sbyte
LPSTR/LPWSTR	System.String in, System.Text.StringBuilder out	string in, System.Text.StringBuilder out
LPCSTR/LPCWSTR	System.String	string
FLOAT	System.Single	float
DOUBLE	System.Double	double

Looking at Table 6–7 you can see that a DWORD maps to the CTS type System.Uint32 or simply uint in C#, this is why the managed declaration of the function returns a uint.

The following snippet shows how we would call the GetCurrentThreadId method from managed code.

```
private void Test_Thread(object sender,
      System.EventArgs e)
{
     lblThreadID.Text=GetCurrentThreadId().ToString();
}
```

Notice that there is nothing special about the calling code. We call the GetCurrentThreadId function the same way we would call any function.

Let's look at a slightly more complicated example. We'll call the MessageBox Win32 API function. The MessageBox function displays a message box; it is defined as follows in the Win32 API:

```
int MessageBox(HWND hWnd,LPCTSTR lpText,
LPCTSTR lpCaption,UINT uType);
```

This function is implemented in the system DLL called User32.dll. Like many Windows functions that deal with strings there are actually 2 versions of this function in User32.dll. There is a function called MessageBoxA that is used with ANSI (single-byte) strings and a method called MessageBoxW that is used with Unicode (multi-byte) strings. You can call the MessageBoxA and MessageBoxW functions explicitly if you want to, but in most cases when you are writing code in C/C++ you can just call the MessageBox function, your compiler and linker will figure out which function to use depending on whether you choose to do a Unicode or ANSI build.

The simplest code that you can write to declare the MessageBox function for use by managed code is shown below.

```
using System.Runtime.InteropServices;
[DllImport("User32.dll")]
```

```
public static extern int MessageBox(int hWnd,string pText,
          string pCaption,uint uType);
```

Managed code that calls this function is shown below.

```
private void cmdPInvoke_Click(object sender,
System.EventArgs e)
{
  string strText="Hello VS Live!";
  string strCaption="PInvoke Demo";
  MessageBox(0,strText,strCaption,0);
}
```

The MessageBox function has 2 strings in its parameter list: the caption and the text that is displayed in the message box. The CLR will call either MessageBoxA (for Ansi strings) or MessageBoxW (for Unicode strings) depending on how you choose to marshal the strings. You can choose to marshal the string as an ANSI or Unicode string using the CharSet property on the DllImport attribute as shown here.

```
[DllImport("User32.dll",CharSet=CharSet.Unicode)]
public static extern int MessageBox(int hWnd,string pText,
          string pCaption,uint uType);
```

In this case we are specifying that the strings should be marshaled as Unicode, so the CLR will pass the text and caption strings in Unicode format to the MessageBoxW function. There are 4 possible values for the CharSet field as shown in Table 6-8.

TABLE 6-8 *Values for the CharSet enumeration*

Value	Description
Ansi	Strings are marshaled in single byte Ansi format
None	Obsolete (same as Ansi)
Unicode	Strings are marshaled in 2-byte, Unicode format
Auto	Unicode on Win NT and 2K, Ansi on Windows 9x

If you don't want the CLR to determine which function to call, you can set the ExactSpelling property on the DllImport attribute to true. This will tell the CLR to interpret the specified function name literally. If you change the function declaration to look as follows:

```
[DllImport("User32.dll",ExactSpelling=true,
CharSet=CharSet.Unicode)]
public static extern int MessageBox(int hWnd,string pText,
  string pCaption,uint uType);
```

you will receive a runtime error that says that the runtime could not find an entry point called MessageBox. You will now have to explicitly specify which MessageBox function you want to use as follows:

```
[DllImport("User32.dll", ExactSpelling = true,
CharSet=CharSet.Unicode)]
public static extern int MessageBoxW(int hWnd,string pText,
    string pCaption,uint uType);
```

You will also have to change your calling code to use MessageBoxW instead of MessageBox.

```
private void cmdPInvoke_Click(object sender,
    System.EventArgs e)
{
    string strText="Hello VS Live!";
    string strCaption="PInvoke Demo";
    MessageBoxW(0,strText,strCaption,0);
}
```

If you don't like having to use the name MessageBoxW in your calling code, you can use the EntryPoint property to specify a different name for the function when it is called from managed code. The following function declaration will allow you to call the MessageBox function as ShowPopup from managed code.

```
[DllImport("User32.dll", ExactSpelling = true,
CharSet=CharSet.Unicode,
  EntryPoint="MessageBoxW")]
public static extern int ShowPopup(int hWnd,string pText,
      string pCaption,uint uType);
```

Here is managed code that calls the ShowPopup function (which is actually calling MessageBoxW).

```
private void cmdPInvoke_Click(object sender,
System.EventArgs e)
{
  string strText="Hello VS Live!";
  string strCaption="PInvoke Demo";
  ShowPopup(0,strText,strCaption,0);
}
```

Note Calling the Show method on the System.Windows.Forms.MessageBox is the recommended way to display a message box in the .NET Framework. I show you how to call the MessageBox API function as an example of what you could do, and not what you should do.

The last DllImport property that we will look at in this chapter is the SetLastError property. Set this property to true to tell the CLR that the unmanaged function that you are calling will call the Win32 API SetLastError function before returning. If SetLastError is true, the CLR will call GetLastError and cache the return value. You can access the error value by calling Marshal.GetLastWin32Error. The following code demonstrates how to use SetLastError and Marshal.GetLastWin32Error with the CreateFile Win32 API function:

```
1.  const uint GENERIC_READ = 0x80000000;
2.  const uint OPEN_EXISTING = 3;
3.  [DllImport("Kernel32.dll", SetLastError=true)]
4.  static extern int CreateFile(string filename,
5.    uint desiredAccess,uint shareMode,
6.    uint attributes,uint creationDisposition,
7.    uint flagsAndAttributes,uint templateFile);
8.  [DllImport("Kernel32.dll")]
9.  static extern bool CloseHandle(int hFile);
10. private void cmdCreateFile_Click(object sender,
11.   System.EventArgs e)
12. {
13.   int error, handle, nRead;
14.   byte[] buffer;
15.   bool bIsOkay;
16.   ASCIIEncoding encoding=new ASCIIEncoding();
17.   buffer=new Byte[256];
18.   handle=CreateFile(txtFileName.Text,
19.     GENERIC_READ,
20.     0,0,OPEN_EXISTING,0,0);
21.   error=Marshal.GetLastWin32Error();
22.   if (error != 0)
23.     System.Windows.Forms.MessageBox.Show(
24.       "The error number is: " +
25.       error.ToString());
26. //
27. // Do something with the file…
28. //
29.   CloseHandle(handle);
30. }
```

Lines 1 and 2 contain declarations of constants that we need to use the CreateFile Win32 API function. Lines 3 thru 7 contain a managed code declaration of the CreateFile function. Notice that we set the SetLastError property on DllImport to true on line 3. Lines 8 and 9 contain a managed code declaration for the CloseHandle function. On line 18 we open a file. Because we set the SetLastError property to true in our managed code declaration for the CreateFile function we can call Marshal.GetLastWin32Error() to retrieve any errors from the call to CreateFile. On lines 22 thru 25 we display the error if there is one, and on line 29 we close the file.

We will talk about advanced aspects of PInvoke in Chapter 7, including how to deal with: pointers, callback functions, structures, and custom marshaling.

Summary

In this chapter, you learned the basics of using .NET COM Interop, both to use a COM object from managed code and also to use a .NET object from unmanaged code. I have just begun to scratch the surface of COM Interop, however. In real-world use, COM Interop is much more complicated than what you have seen so far. The next chapter will look at more advanced aspects of using a COM object from managed code.

SEVEN

Advanced .NET to COM Interop

In the last chapter, you learned the basic essentials of COM Interop. You learned how to use a simple COM object from a managed code (.NET) client and how to use a simple managed code (.NET) component from an unmanaged client. However, everything that you learned in Chapter 6 is really just the tip of the iceberg. I did not discuss a number of issues in that chapter that make using COM Interop more complicated than you have seen so far. In this chapter, I concentrate on advanced aspects of .NET to COM Interop, that is, using COM components from a managed code client. Some of the issues that I discuss in this chapter are object life cycle differences between reference counting and garbage collection, handling COM connection point events and rich error information, the effect of COM Apartments, advanced marshaling considerations, use of ActiveX controls, and performance. By the time you are done with this chapter, you will be ready to use .NET to COM Interop in most real-world scenarios.

Object Life Cycle Implications

There is a variety of ways to instantiate an object with COM, the typical way being to call CoCreateInstance. With COM, any function that activates an object will also initialize the reference count to one. When you are done with the object, you must remember to call Release on the object. When you decide to call Release is entirely up to you. In some cases, you will instantiate an object, call methods on one or more of its interfaces, and then immediately release the interface pointer. In other cases, you may instantiate your COM object when the application starts and hold the interface pointer until the application shuts down. In this latter model, you will likely use the same object again and again. Which approach you choose is entirely up to you, but it will likely be strongly driven by (a) the cost (in terms of time) to instantiate an object and (b) the cost in terms of memory and or other resources, like database connections or locks to maintain an extant object. In other words, if it does not take much time to instantiate an object, but the object consumes a lot of resources while it exists, you are better off instantiating the object only when you need it and then releasing it immediately. If the reverse is true, that is, it takes a long time to instantiate the object, but, after it is created, it does not consume a great deal of resources, you are better off keeping the object around until the application shuts down. Of course, many COM objects do not fall strongly into either camp; they neither take an excessively long time to instantiate nor consume a great deal of resources while they are extant. In those cases, you are better off taking the approach of instantiating the object when your application starts and then holding until your application shuts down. With this approach, you save the overhead associated with instantiating and destroying your objects.

If the resource consumption or initialization time of a COM object does favor one or the other life cycle approaches, be aware that using a COM object from a managed code client dramatically changes its life cycle semantics. All managed code objects are garbage collected. A managed code object only becomes eligible for garbage collection when it is no longer reachable through a reference. When you are using a COM object through COM Interop, the RCW, which is a managed code object, holds all the Interface pointers on the underlying COM object. The Finalize method in the RCW will release all of these interface pointers when the RCW is garbage collected. Unfortunately, because it's a managed object, the RCW won't be garbage collected until the garbage collector runs, which, if memory is not in short supply on your system, will likely not be until the application shuts down.

Fortunately, you can immediately release a COM object using the ReleaseCOMObject method on the **System.Runtime.InteropServices.Marshal** class. Calling this method will immediately call the Release method on the underlying COM object.

Let's look at an example that illustrates this point using the COM financial component that I introduced in Chapter 6. To make the example more useful for the subject matter of this section, I will override the FinalRelease method in the ATL **CComObjectRootEx** class and have it display a message box when the financial object's reference count goes to 0.

Note A COM object built with ATL will call the FinalRelease method when its reference count goes to 0, but before it is destroyed.

Add the following code to the **TimeValue.h** file in the Visual C++ project:

```
class ATL_NO_VTABLE CTimeValue : …
{
public:
        CTimeValue()
        {
        }
// … code omitted for clarity
        void FinalRelease();
private
        double mInterestRate;
};
```

I omitted the code before the FinalRelease method to show only those parts that are relevant to this discussion. I then added the following code to the .cpp file for the **TimeValue** class.

```
void CTimeValue::FinalRelease()
{
        ::MessageBox(0,"Object is Released",
            "Object Released",0);
}
```

I first built an unmanaged VB 6 client for this object with the following code in a click handler:

```
Private Sub Command1_Click()
    Dim objFinancial As TimeValue
    Set objFinancial = New TimeValue
    Label1.Caption = objFinancial.MonthlyPayment(
        360, 6.75, 350000)
    Set objFinancial = Nothing
End Sub
```

Notice that I set the reference to the object to "Nothing" before I leave the method. With VB6, setting an object reference to nothing will cause the VB runtime to generate a call to the Release method on the object that the reference was previously pointing to. Since there is only one reference pointing to the object, this will cause the object's reference count to go to zero. Therefore, each time that the objFinancial object reference goes out of scope, it will call Release on the underlying COM object, so you will see a message box like the one shown in Figure 7–1 each time you pushed the button.

This is the expected life cycle behavior for an unmanaged client. Let's take a quick look at the code that you wrote for the managed client in Chapter 6 so that you can understand the expected life cycle for the object when it is called from a managed client.

FIGURE 7–1 *The message box showing that the object is released.*

```
1.  private void cmdGetLoanAmt_Click(object sender,
2.        System.EventArgs e)
3.  {
4.    short shtNumMonths;
5.    double dblInterestRate, dblMonthlyPmt, dblResult;
6.    try
7.    {
8.      TimeValue objFinancial=new TimeValue();
9.              shtNumMonths=short.Parse(txtMonths.Text);
10.             dblInterestRate=
11.     Double.Parse(txtInterestRate.Text);
12.     dblMonthlyPmt=
13.       Double.Parse(txtMonthlyPmt.Text);
14.     dblResult=
15.       objFinancial.loanAmount(shtNumMonths,
16.       dblInterestRate,dblMonthlyPmt);
17.     lblLoanAmt.Text=
18.         String.Format("{0:C}",dblResult);
19.   }
20.   catch(System.Exception ex)
21.   {
22.     MessageBox.Show(ex.Message);
23.   }
24. }
```

The code that you are looking at is the Click handler for the Get Loan Amount button; this is the logic that gets executed each time you click the Get Loan Amount button. Notice that I instantiate the object as a local variable on line 8. The objFinancial object reference will go out of scope on line 19. Therefore, the object that I instantiated on line 8 is actually eligible for collection after I pass line 19. If you run the client, though, you will notice that the Object is Released message box never shows up. In fact, you'll notice that, even if you click the button several times, you'll never see the message box. If you shut down the managed client (by clicking the X button in the upper right-hand corner, for instance), the message box pops up as many times as you clicked the Get Loan Amount button. This indicates that all of the objects were deleted when you shut down the application.

The life cycle behavior of this COM object is very different when it is used from a managed client as compared to an unmanaged client. To make the COM object behave the same when it is called from a managed code client as it would when it is called from an unmanaged code client—that is, the object is created and released each time you click the button—add the following line of code at the end of the try block, that is, after line 18 in the previous listing.

```
System.Runtime.InteropServices.
Marshal.ReleaseComObject(objFinancial);
```

The ReleaseComObject method immediately decrements the reference count of the COM object that you pass to it. Now you will see the Object is Released message box each time you click the button indicating that the object is being released immediately. If you attempt to use an object after you have called the ReleaseComObject method, the RCW will throw an error of type System.Runtime.InteropServices.InvalidComObjectException that contains the following message:

```
COM object that has been separated from its underlying RCW
can not be used.
```

Using COM Events in Managed Code

One of the most complicated aspects of using COM Interop is its support for connection point events. The Type Library Importer generates a rather complex Interop assembly if your COM server uses connection points. The reason for this complex Interop assembly is the rather convoluted mapping that occurs between delegate-based events in the managed world and connection point events in the COM world. I'm going to assume that you already know about connection points (if you don't, see Chapter 8 of my book, *The COM and COM+ Programming Primer*), but, before I get started on handling COM events using Interop, let's talk about .NET delegates and events.

In some cases, the typical client/server model where a server component or application waits passively for a client to make requests on it is not sufficient. In some cases, you need to enable two-way communication between the client and server. In these cases, you usually implement a callback that allows the server to notify the client when some event of interest to the client occurs. This may be anything from notifying the client that an asynchronous operation that the client initiated earlier has succeeded or that a stock has changed price or that a user has pressed a button on a user interface. The basic idea with callbacks is that the client implements a method that performs the logic that the client wants to have performed in response to the event from the server. The client then passes some sort of pointer to this method to the server. The server holds on to this method pointer and calls the method whenever it wants to notify the client that the event occurs. This is exactly how COM connection points work.

Understanding Delegates

With .NET, you use delegates to implement the callbacks that I just described. You can think of a delegate as a type-safe function pointer. After you have declared a delegate, you can point it to any static or per-instance method that matches the argument list and return value of the delegate. For instance, the following code defines a delegate called PlayByPlayHandler:

```
public delegate void PlayByPlayHandler(string strLines);
```

You can point an instance of this delegate to any method that has a single, string parameter and returns void. I can create an instance of this delegate as shown here:

```
PlayByPlayHandler microphone=new
        PlayByPlayHandler(ReceivePlayByPlay);
```

Where ReceivePlayByPlay is a method that matches the prototype of the delegate as follows:

```
void ReceivePlayByPlay(string str)
{
  //...
}
```

Now that I have created an instance of this delegate, I can pass it to an object that uses a delegate of this type to issue callbacks. As an example, I created a class called **LakerAnnouncer**, which issues callbacks using a PlayByPlayHandler delegate:

```
public delegate void PlayByPlayHandler(
    string strLines);
public class LakerAnnouncer
{
  public LakerAnnouncer()
  {
    mLines=new StringCollection();
    mLines.Add("It's in the refrigerator");
    mLines.Add("The butter's getting hard");
      mLines.Add("the jello is jigglin");
      mLines.Add("Slaaaam dunk!");
    mLines.Add("Since Hector was a pup");
    mLines.Add("Yo yoing up and down");
    mRandNumGen=new Random();
  }
  public void Announce(int numLines)
```

```
17.    {
18.      int r;
19.      string strLine;
20.      if (Microphone != null)
21.      {
22.        for (int i=0;i<numLines;i++)
23.        {
24.          r=mRandNumGen.Next();
25.          strLine=mLines[r % mNumLines];
26.          Microphone(strLine + "\r\n");
27.        }
28.      }
29.    }
30.    private StringCollection mLines;
31.    public PlayByPlayHandler Microphone;
32.    private Random mRandNumGen;
33. }
```

This class stores some of the most famous signature lines of Los Angeles Lakers play-by-play announcer Francis "Chick" Hearn, such as "It's in the refrigerator" and "The Jell-O's jiggling." The constructor for this class, which is shown on lines 5 through 15, creates a collection that's typed as a StringCollection and then adds six of Chick Hearn's most famous lines to the collection. It then initializes a counter that stores the number of lines in the collection. The Announce method on lines 16 through 29 takes an integer parameter called numLines that contains the number of play-by-play lines that you want to send to the client. If the Microphone delegate is not null, this method will loop numLines times, and it will generate a random number between 0 and 5 (inclusive), use that number to extract one of Chick Hearn's famous lines from the collection, and then call the Microphone delegate, passing in the selected line. On the client, this will invoke the method that the client assigned to the delegate. Notice also that I defined a public field called Microphone on line 32 that holds the instance of the delegate that the LakerAnnouncer object will call back on. I could have defined this class so that the client passed its delegate as a second parameter to the Announce method. However, with this way, the client is freed from having to maintain a pointer to the delegate if it wants to call the Announce method several times.

Note The **StringCollection** class is defined in the System.Collection.Specialized namespace.

When a client wants to receive play-by-play commentary from the LakerAnnouncer, it first has to create a method that takes a string parameter and returns void, which is the prototype that matches the PlayByPlayHandler delegate. This method can be either static or a per-instance method. The client must then create a new PlayByPlayHandler delegate instance and set the

Microphone member in the **LakerAnnouncer** class equal to this new delegate. The client then calls the Announce method specifying the number of lines it would like to receive, and the LakerAnnouncer instance will call back on the method specified in the delegate.

Note This example is my personal tribute to long-time Los Angeles Lakers play-by-play announcer Chick Hearn who died on August 5, 2002. Chick Hearn is acknowledged by most people to be the best play-by-play announcer of all time, and perhaps the greatest announcer in any sport. He is the creator of such phrases as "slam dunk," "air ball," and "dribble drive." Before he underwent heart surgery in 2002, Chick also had an improbably long streak of 3,338 consecutive games broadcasted. To appreciate how staggering a feat Chick's consecutive games streak is, imagine not missing a day of work since 1965. Some of Chick's other signature lines are putting a game "in the refrigerator," when a team builds up an insurmountable lead. This is usually followed by "the butter's getting hard" and "the Jell-O's jiggling."

The following code shows what this client code will look like:

```
1.  public class Form1 : System.Windows.Forms.Form
2.  {
3.  //… additional code in this class is omitted
4.    void ReceivePlayByPlay(string str)
5.    {
6.      txtLines.AppendText(str + "\r\n");
7.    }
8.    private void cmdAnnounce_Click(object sender,
9.    System.EventArgs e)
10.   {
11.     PlayByPlayHandler microphone1=new
12.       PlayByPlayHandler(ReceivePlayByPlay);
13.     LakerAnnouncer chickHearn=new
14.       LakerAnnouncer();
15.     chickHearn.Microphone=microphone1;
16.     chickHearn.Announce(5);
17.   }
```

Notice that on lines 4 through 7 I declare the ReceivePlayByPlay method, which will just append the play-by-play text to a multiline text box. The key piece of code is on lines 8 through 17. On lines 11 and 12, I declare a delegate called microphone1 that points to the ReceivePlayByPlay method. On lines 13 and 14, I declare an instance of the **LakerAnnouncer** class. On line 15, I assign the Microphone member of the **LakerAnnouncer** class to the delegate that I created on lines 11 and 12. Finally, on line 16, I call the Announce method with a parameter of 5, meaning that the LakerAnnouncer instance will call the ReceivePlayByPlay method with five randomly selected Chick Hearn quotes. In this example, the LakerAnnouncer object will call back on the ReceivePlayByPlay method five times.

So far, I have only shown the case where the server calls back on a single method, but a delegate can actually point to several methods. All of these methods will be called when the server calls back on the delegate, which is called multicasting.

Note If you look at the MSIL code that the C# compiler generated when I declared the PlayByPlayHandler, you will see that the generated **PlayByPlayHandler** class derives from a class called **MulticastDelegate**. This class provides all the logic that you need to support multicasting.

A client can add multiple callbacks by using the "+=" operator to add multiple delegates to the Microphone member of the **LakerAnnouncer** class. The following code shows how you would add two callbacks to a LakerAnnouncer, one that appends to a multiline textbox and another that displays a message box:

```
1.  void ReceivePlayByPlay(string str)
2.  {
3.    txtLines.AppendText(str + "\r\n");
4.  }
5.  void ReceivePlayByPlay2(string str)
6.  {
7.    MessageBox.Show(str);
8.  }
9.  private void cmdAnnounce_Click(object sender,
10. System.EventArgs e)
11. {
12.   PlayByPlayHandler microphone1=new
13.     PlayByPlayHandler(ReceivePlayByPlay);
14.   PlayByPlayHandler microphone2=new
15.     PlayByPlayHandler(ReceivePlayByPlay2);
16.   LakerAnnouncer chickHearn=new LakerAnnouncer();
17.   chickHearn.Microphone+=microphone1;
18.   chickHearn.Microphone+=microphone2;
19.   chickHearn.Announce(5);
20. }
```

On lines 1 through 4, I declare a method called ReceivePlayByPlay, which has a prototype that matches the PlayByPlayHandler delegate. On lines 5 through 8, I declare a second method called ReceivePlayByPlay2 that also matches the PlayByPlayHandler delegate. On lines 12 and 13, I create a PlayByPlayHandler delegate called microphone1 that points to ReceivePlayByPlay, and, on lines 14 and 15, I create a PlayByPlayHandler delegate called microphone2 that points to ReceivePlayByPlay2. On line 16, I create a new LakerAnnouncer instance, and, on line 17, I add the microphone1 delegate to the delegate member in the LakerAnnouncer instance using the "+=" operator.

On line 18, I use the "+=" operator again to add the microphone2 delegate to the Microphone delegate in the **LakerAnnouncer** class. Now, both the ReceivePlayByPlay and ReceivePlayByPlay2 methods will be called when the **LakerAnnouncer** class calls back on the Microphone delegate.

Understanding Events

Of course, you can probably see that there are a lot of problems with .NET delegates as I have presented them so far. The first problem is that there is no standardized way for the client to pass its delegate to the server. In the previous case, I simply exposed a public delegate field, and the client accessed this field directly. If you find exposing a public field from a class deplorable (and you should), you could have declared the delegate field to be private and exposed a public property instead. You could even have declared the field to be private and added an AddConsumer method for a client to pass its delegate to the server and a RemoveConsumer method for halting further notifications from the server.

Another big problem with delegates is that it is very easy to make a critical mistake when using multicasting. Using the "=" operator on a delegate will assign the delegate on the right side of the equals sign to the one on the left side of the "=" sign. Any previous assignments will be lost. The "+=" operator will add (combine is the official lingo) the delegates on the left and right side of the equals and then assign the result to the delegate on the left. Therefore, if you plan to use multicasting, but accidentally use the "=" operator instead of the "+=" operator, you will wind up with a delegate that contains only the last delegate that you added. As an example, the following code will not display the result that you would expect:

```
private void cmdAnnounce_Click(object sender,
System.EventArgs e)
{
      PlayByPlayHandler microphone1=new
      PlayByPlayHandler(ReceivePlayByPlay);
      PlayByPlayHandler microphone2=new
        PlayByPlayHandler(ReceivePlayByPlay2);
      LakerAnnouncer chickHearn=new LakerAnnouncer();
      chickHearn.Microphone=microphone1;
      chickHearn.Microphone=microphone2;
      chickHearn.Announce(5);
}
```

If you ran this client code, you will notice that only the second delegate microphone2 will be called. The problem is that I assigned the microphone2 instance to the delegate in the LakerAnnouncer instance using the "=" operator instead of using the "+=" operator. Therefore, the second assignment to the Microphone delegate will overwrite the first. If I changed the code to look as shown here, both the microphone1 and microphone2 delegates will be called.

```
private void cmdAnnounce_Click(object sender,
System.EventArgs e)
{
      PlayByPlayHandler microphone1=new
      PlayByPlayHandler(ReceivePlayByPlay);
      PlayByPlayHandler microphone2=new
        PlayByPlayHandler(ReceivePlayByPlay2);
      LakerAnnouncer chickHearn=new LakerAnnouncer();
      chickHearn.Microphone+=microphone1;
      chickHearn.Microphone+=microphone2;
      chickHearn.Announce(5);
}
```

To prevent someone from making this mistake, I could make the Microphone delegate field in the **LakerAnnouncer** class private and use a pair of methods (like AddConsumer and RemoveConsumer) that would always use the correct operator internally. Of course, this is extra code that I would have to write every time I wanted to use delegates. Fortunately, there is a better way to do this using .NET events.

To use events in the LakerAnnouncer class, you would still begin by declaring a delegate that defines the prototype for the callback function that the client must create.

```
public delegate void PlayByPlayHandler(string strLines);
```

The definition of the delegate is the same as the one I used earlier. However, instead of defining a public field to hold the delegate, I simply declare an event that uses the PlayByPlayHandler delegate as follows:

```
public event PlayByPlayHandler PlayByPlay;
```

The complete definition of the **LakerAnnouncer** class will now look as follows:

```
using System;
using System.Collections.Specialized;
namespace EventServer
{
      public delegate void PlayByPlayHandler(
          string strLines);
      public class LakerAnnouncer
      {
        public LakerAnnouncer()
        {
        //… same as before
        }
        public void Announce(int numLines)
        {
```

```
                int r;
                int strLine;
                for (int i=0;i<numLines;i++)
                {
                    r=randomNumberGenerator.Next();
                    strLine=mTrademarkLines[r % numEntries];
                    PlayByPlay(strLine + "\r\n");
                }
            }
            public event PlayByPlayHandler PlayByPlay;
            private StringCollection mTrademarkLines;
            private Random randomNumberGenerator;
            private int numEntries;
        }
}
```

The only change in the source code is the line where I declare the PlayByPlayHandler event. You can understand better how making this change alters the code by looking at the MSIL code that the C# compiler generated for the altered **LakerAnnouncer** class using ILDASM.

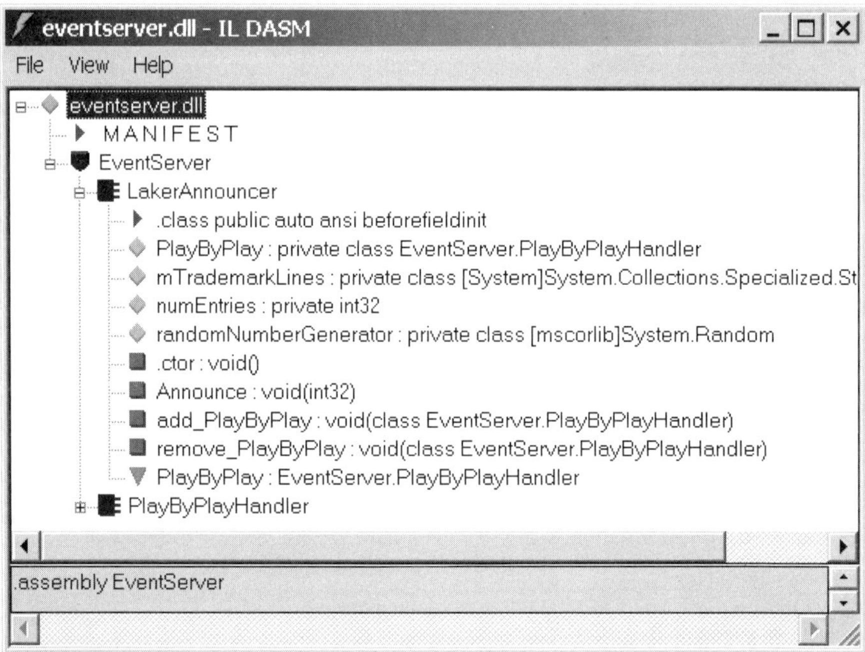

FIGURE 7–2 *Events displayed in ILDASM.*

You'll notice that the event declaration caused the C# compiler to add three new members to the class:

- A private member variable called PlayByPlay that holds an instance of the PlayByPlayHandler delegate
- An add_PlayByPlay method that a client can use to register a delegate to receive callbacks
- A remove_PlayByPlay method that a client can call when it no longer wants to receive callbacks

A cleaned-up version of the MSIL code showing the members that the compiler adds is as follows:

```
public class LakerAnnouncer
{
  public LakerAnnouncer()
  {
  //… same as before
  }
  public void Announce(int numLines)
  {
  //… same as before
  }
  [hidebysig specialname]
  void add_PlayByPlay(PlayByPlayHandler aDelegate)
  {
  //… implementation omitted
  }
  [hidebysig specialname]
  void remove_PlayByPlay(PlayByPlayHandler aDelegate)
  {
  //… implementation omitted
  }
  private PlayByPlayHandler PlayByPlay;
  private StringCollection mTrademarkLines;
  private Random randomNumberGenerator;
  private int numEntries;
  .event PlayByPlayHandler PlayByPlay
  {
     .addon instance void add_PlayByPlay(
    class PlayByPlayHandler)
     .removeon instance void remove_PlayByPlay(
    class PlayByPlayHandler)
  }
}
```

The bolded lines are actually snippets of MSIL code that I got from ILDASM. The compiler did what I proposed to do earlier to prevent people from accidentally using the wrong operator when using delegates, that is, the compiler added a private PlayByPlayHandler delegate instance and then added public methods that a client can use to add and remove its delegates to this internal instance. The add_PlayByPlay and remove_PlayByPlay methods have special attributes, hidebysig and specialname, that cause them to be hidden (see lines 11 and 16). Lines 25 through 31 have an .event declaration for the PlayByPlayHandler event, which specifies addon and removeon methods. These are assigned to add_PlayByPlay and remove_PlayByPlay, respectively. All of this code is hidden from you. The CLR will automatically call the addon method when you use the "+=" operator on the event, and it will call the removeon method when you call the "-=" operator on the event. Another key advantage of .NET events over using plain delegates is that the Visual Studio .NET IDE recognizes events. Therefore, it presents a class' events to you in an easy-to-use way and allows you to add handlers for those events with point-and-click ease.

The following code shows client-side code that uses these events:

```
void ReceivePlayByPlay(string str)
{
       txtLines.AppendText(str + "\r\n");
}
void ReceivePlayByPlay2(string str)
{
       MessageBox.Show(str);
}
private void cmdAnnounce_Click(object sender,
       System.EventArgs e)
{
       PlayByPlayHandler microphone1=new
         PlayByPlayHandler(ReceivePlayByPlay);
       PlayByPlayHandler microphone2=new
         PlayByPlayHandler(ReceivePlayByPlay2);
       LakerAnnouncer chickHearn=new LakerAnnouncer();
       chickHearn.PlayByPlay+=microphone1;
       chickHearn.PlayByPlay+=microphone2;
       chickHearn.Announce(5);
}
```

Notice that this code looks very similar to the code that I wrote before that did not use events. The main difference is that, if you attempt to assign a delegate to the PlayByPlay event by (incorrectly) using the "=" operator, you will receive the following error from the compiler:

```
The event 'LakerAnnouncer.PlayByPlay' can only appear on
the left hand side of += or -=
```

Events are the mechanism that UI controls use to fire events back to their container, for example, to fire a click event when you click a button. UI controls always use the following prototype for their delegate:

```
Public delegate void MyDelegate(object sender, EventArgs e)
```

The first parameter to the delegate is the object that is sending the event. The second parameter is an instance of the **EventArgs** class. **EventsArgs** is a class that resides in the System namespace. When you define a delegate that will be used with an event, you should also create a class that derives from **Event-Args** and add the member variables that your event needs to pass to the code that receives the event. For instance, the MouseDown event on the System.Windows.Forms has the following delegate:

```
Public delegate void MouseEventHandler(object sender,
    MouseEventArgs e)
```

The **MouseEventArgs** class inherits from **EventArgs** and adds X, Y, Button, Clicks, and Delta properties, which respectively store the x coordinate, y coordinate, button state, number of button clicks, and the amount of wheel rotation for the mouse.

I would be remiss if I left the subject of events and did not discuss Microsoft's recommended design pattern for events. Microsoft's recommendation is that you create all events in a manner similar to UI events, that is, the delegate for the event should return void and have two parameters, one of which should contain the object that generated the event and the other should be an EventArgs object that contains the data that the event will pass to its client. You should try to follow this pattern as much as possible in the new .NET code that you write. When you are using COM Interop, however, the delegate that the type library importer generates will match the signature of the equivalent COM event.

Note I discuss the .NET guidelines for defining events in much more detail in Chapter 8.

Let's quickly review COM connection points before I discuss how they map to .NET events and delegates. A COM object indicates that it supports events by publishing one or more source interfaces as shown here:

```
[ uuid(4506CE8F-2A84-11D3-998A-E0EC08C10000) ]
dispinterface _IStockMonitorEvents
{
methods:
    [id(0x00000001)]
    HRESULT PriceChange([in] BSTR ticker,
        [in] single newPrice, [in] single oldPrice);
    [id(0x00000002)]
    HRESULT MonitorInitiated([in] BSTR ticker,
        [in] single currentPrice);
};
[uuid(4506CE8E-2A84-11D3-998A-E0EC08C10000)]
coclass StockMonitor
{
```

```
    [default] interface IStockMonitor;
    [default, source] dispinterface _IStockMonitorEvents;
};
```

In this case, the _IStockMonitorEvents interface is a source interface. If a COM object includes a source interface in its type library, that means that the interface is not implemented by the object. Instead, the COM object is advertising that a client can receive callbacks from the object if the client implements the source interface and then passes its implementation of the source interface—through the Advise method in the IConnectionPoint interface—to the COM object. In the language of COM connection points, the object is indicating that it is a source for events, that is, it produces connection point events. An object that sources events is sometimes called a connectable object. If a client implements the source interface and then passes its implementation of the interface to the connectable object, it becomes a sink, that is, it consumes the events.

A COM object that supports connection points must implement two interfaces: IConnectionPoint and IConnectionPointContainer. These interfaces provide the means for a client to pass its sink object to the server. The client uses the FindConnectionPoint or EnumConnectionPoints methods on the IConnectionPointContainer interface to find the IConnectionPoint interfaces supported by the connectable object. There should be one IConnectionPoint implementation for each source interface. The client then passes the IUnknown pointer of the Sink object to the Advise method on IConnectionPoint. The COM specification requires that the connectable object immediately do a QueryInterface on the Sink object to verify that the sink object implements the interfaces that the IConnectionPoint implementation is associated with. Assuming that the sink object does implement the source interface, the connectable object will cache the interface pointer on the sink object and use it to call back on the source interface when an event of interest occurs on the client.

Now that I have beaten the subject of .NET delegates and events and COM connection points to death, let's bring the discussion back to the topic at hand: how COM connection point events are mapped to managed code. Before I dive into this, let me warn you that this mapping is quite complicated and very hard to understand. You will most likely have to read this section a few times before it makes sense to you. It is absolutely critical that you understand how .NET events and delegates and COM connection points work independent of COM Interop before you dive in here. The good news is that, even though understanding the mapping of COM connection point events to .NET managed events is difficult, using the resulting Interop assembly is really simple, assuming you understand managed events. All you have to remember is that each method in the source (event) interfaces in your COM component will map to a managed event. In order to receive those events from a managed client, you only need to add a method that has the same prototype as the delegate associated with the managed event and then use the "+=" operator to add your method as a callback for the event. Because of this, I will start by doing an example, and then I'll peek behind the scenes and explore how it works.

Because you are probably getting sick of calculating monthly payments and loan amounts, let's do something a little different this time. For this example, I am going to use a stock monitoring application that I built in Chapter 8 of my first book: *The COM and COM+ Programming Primer* (Prentice Hall). The code for this example is available on the Web site for the book that you are now holding. This example is an out-of-process server that monitors stock prices and sends an event when a stock's price changes. I won't go into any details on how I built this COM component; there are step-by-step instructions for how to build this component in my first book.

Note The stock monitor component obviously does not really monitor stock prices. The component loops continuously, and, each time through its loop, it will use a random number generator to pick a stock whose price it will change. It then uses a factor, which I call the propensity, to determine whether the price will go up or down. The stock monitor component will change the price of the stock and then sleep for 3 seconds before looping again.

The IDL for the stock monitor component is the following:

```
 [ uuid(4506CE81-2A84-11D3-998A-E0EC08C10000)]
library STOCKSERVERLib {
    [ uuid(4506CE8F-2A84-11D3-998A-E0EC08C10000) ]
    dispinterface _IStockMonitorEvents {
        properties:
        methods:
            [id(0x00000001)]
            HRESULT PriceChange([in] BSTR ticker,
               [in] single newPrice,
               [in] single oldPrice);
            [id(0x00000002)]
            HRESULT MonitorInitiated([in] BSTR ticker,
               [in] single currentPrice);
    };
    [uuid(4506CE8E-2A84-11D3-998A-E0EC08C10000)]
    coclass StockMonitor {
        [default] interface IStockMonitor;
        [default, source] dispinterface
                _IStockMonitorEvents;
    };
    [ uuid(4506CE8D-2A84-11D3-998A-E0EC08C10000),dual]
    interface IStockMonitor : IDispatch {
        [id(0x00000001)]
```

```
        HRESULT GetPrice([in] BSTR ticker,
               [out, retval] single* price);
        [id(0x00000002)]
        HRESULT AddNewStock([in] BSTR ticker,
               [in] single price,
               [in] short propensityToRise);
    };
};
```

Notice that it has a source interface called IStockMonitorEvents, which has two callback methods: (1) MonitorInitiated, which the object will call whenever you register a new stock for monitoring, and (2) PriceChange, which is called whenever the price of a stock changes. Let's run the Type Library Importer on this COM component to generate an Interop Assembly. The Stock Server is an executable, so I ran the following command:

```
tlbimp stockserver.exe /out:stockserver.dll
```

This command will save the Interop Assembly to a file called **stockserver.dll**.

When you run tlbimp on a COM type library, it will generate a managed code equivalent of each regular COM interface in the type library. It will also generate a coclass interface and an RCW class (see Chapter 6 for a reminder of what these are) for each coclass in the type library. If COM classes in the type library support source interfaces (COM events), the Type Library Importer will also generate a delegate for each event, that is, there will be one Delegate for each method in the original source interface. The Type Library Importer will also generate a managed code equivalent of the source interface, and it will generate the following three types for each source interface (there's usually only one source interface):

- A managed code interface that has the following name: **[SourceInterfaceName]_Event** that is very similar to the source interface, but has add_[MethodName] and remove_[MethodName] methods for each method in the source interface.
- A class called **[SourceInterfaceName]_EventProvider** that implements the interface described in the previous bullet. The CLR will call the add_ and remove_ methods on this class when you add or remove a delegate from the events exposed by this class. This class is hidden and is only used internally within the Interop assembly.
- A class called **[SourceInterfaceName_SinkHelper]** that the class described in the previous bullet uses to implement the add_ and remove_ methods. This class is a sink object for the original COM event. The provider will pass an instance of this class to the Advise method of IConnectionPoint, and, when the COM object calls back on this sink object, it will forward the method call to the managed

code delegate. This class is hidden and is only used internally within the Interop assembly.

If you examine the Interop assembly that ILDASM generated for the StockServer, you will see the types shown in Figure 7–3.

There is a total of nine types in this assembly. IStockMonitor, StockMontior, and StockMonitorClass are the default interface, coclass interface, and RCW class respectively. The StockServer COM component has two events: PriceChange and MonitorInitiated. Therefore, the interop assembly also contains two delegates: PriceChangeEventHandler and MonitorInitiatedEventHandler. _IStockMonitorEvents is the managed code equivalent of the source interface in the Stock Server, and _IStockMonitorEvents_Event, _IStockMonitorEvents_EventProvider, and _IStockMonitorEvents_SinkHelper are the three types described previously that are generated for the default source interface in the COM component. Table 7-1 summarizes these types.

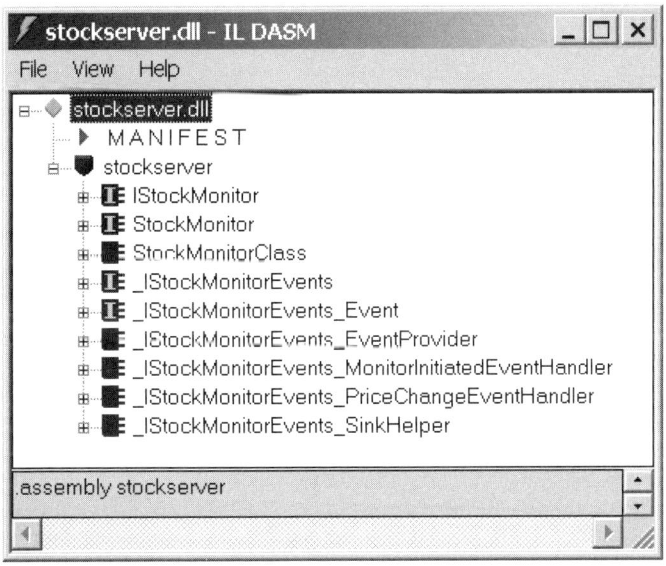

FIGURE 7–3 *The Interop assembly for the StockServer.*

TABLE 7–1 *Managed types in the Interop assembly for a COM component that has connection point events*

Type Name	Description
IStockMonitor	The default interface from the Stock Server COM class.
StockMonitor	The coclass interface that implements IStockMonitor and _IStockMonitorEvents_Event.
StockMonitorClass	The RCW class that implements IStockMonitor, StockMonitor, and _IStockMonitorEvents_Event. Also contains every method implemented by the class, including hidden add_ and remove_ methods for each interface.
PriceChangeEventHandler	A delegate that maps to the PriceChange event.
MonitorInitiatedEventHandler	A delegate that maps to the MonitorInitiated event.
_IStockMonitorEvents	The outgoing (event) interface from the Stock Server COM class.
_IStockMonitorEvents_Event	An interface that is the managed code equivalent of the _IStockMonitorEvents interface but also includes add_ and remove_ methods for each method in the event interface.
_IStockMonitorEvents_EventProvider	A class that implements _IStockMonitorEvents. The CLR will call the add_ and remove_ methods on this class when you add or remove a delegate from the events exposed by this class. This class is hidden and is only used internally within the Interop assembly.
_IStockMonitorEvents_SinkHelper	A helper class that implements the _StockMonitorEvents interface and stores public PriceChange and MonitorInitiated delegate instances and does null checking, that is, if the delegates are not set, it simply returns without doing anything. If the delegates are set, it passes the call through to the underlying delegate. This class is hidden and is only used internally within the Interop assembly.

Only seven of these types are visible outside of the Interop Assembly; _IStockMonitorEvents_EventProvider and _IStockMonitorEvents_SinkHelper are hidden classes. The first three classes, IStockMonitor, StockMonitor, and StockMonitorClass, would have been generated even if the COM server did not have any source interfaces. The other six classes are event related. This is the complicated part that I warned you about earlier. I will explain how these six classes work shortly, but, because using the Interop assembly is easy, let me show you that first. Let's build a managed code client using Windows Forms.

Create a Windows Forms Client

To create a Windows Forms client, you perform the following steps:

1. Create a Visual C# Windows application project.
2. Draw the UI.

3. Reference the StockServer assembly.
4. Implement the UI.
5. Compile the application.
6. Test.

CREATE A VISUAL C# WINDOWS APPLICATION PROJECT

Start Visual Studio .NET and then execute the following steps:

1. Select File | New | Project. The New Project dialog appears.
2. Select Visual C# Projects under Project Types and then choose Windows Application under Templates.
3. Change the name of the project to StockClient.
4. Select the location where you would like to save the project.
5. Click OK.

Visual Studio .NET will create a project that initially contains a single form that will be the main window of your application.

DRAW THE UI

Using the toolbox in Visual Studio .NET, draw the UI shown in Figure 7–4 on your form.

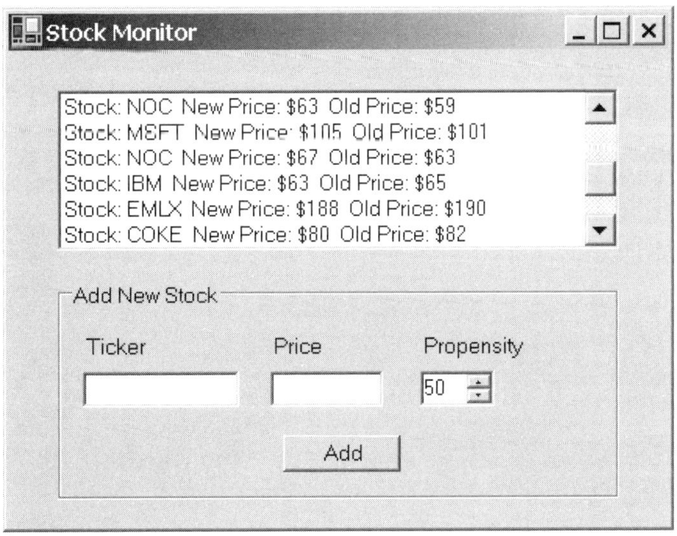

FIGURE 7–4 *The UI for the Windows Forms client.*

Name the controls on this form according to Table 7–2.

TABLE 7–2 *Control names for the stock server client*

Control Description	Control Name
Events list box in the upper half of the window.	lstEvents
Ticker edit box	txtTicker
Price edit box	txtPrice
Add button	cmdAdd
Propensity spinner	updPropensity

REFERENCE THE STOCKSERVER ASSEMBLY

With Visual Studio .NET, it's easy to reference and use .NET assemblies. To do this, perform the following steps:

1. Select Project | Add Reference. The Add Reference dialog appears.
2. Click the Browse... button. The Select Component dialog will appear. Navigate to where you saved the stockserver Interop assembly. This assembly was generated when you ran tlbimp on the **stockserver** COM component.
3. Click the Open button.
4. Click OK on the Add Reference dialog.

In this case, I am using the Interop assembly that I manually generated at the start of this example. You could also generate the Interop assembly in Visual Studio .NET by performing the following steps:

1. Select Project | Add Reference.
2. Select the COM tab.
3. Highlight the COM component with the name "stock server 1.0 Type Library" and click the Select button. If you do not see this item in the list, you need to register the stock server by running the following command at a command prompt: stockserver /regserver.
4. Click OK.

If you use the Add Reference command in Visual Studio .NET, it will create an Interop assembly with the name **Interop.STOCKSERVERLib.dll** in the build directory for your current configuration. If you are currently working on the debug configuration, you will find the Interop assembly in the **bin\debug** directory beneath your project directory. Visual Studio .NET will use the type library name as the namespace, so all of the types from the Stock Server assembly will reside in a namespace called StockServerLib. You will probably want to add a using statement like the following somewhere in the client code:

```
using STOCKSERVERLib;
```

If you manually generated the Interop assembly, that is, you used the Type Library Importer (tlbimp.exe) directly instead of using the Add References… dialog in Visual Studio .NET, the assembly will have the name, StockServer, and you would have a using statement similar to the following:

```
using stockserver;
```

IMPLEMENT THE UI

In the form designer, double-click the form, which should take you to the handler for the Load event of the form, which gets called automatically when the form first loads. The Load handler and all the other code in the file is part of a class called **Form1** that represents the main Windows of this application. Add the code shown in bold to this class:

```
// Add the using statement to the top of the file
using stockerserver // or… using STOCKSERVERLib
public class Form1 : System.Windows.Forms.Form
{
//… code is omitted here for clarity
   private StockMonitor mStockServer;

   private void MonitorInitiated(string ticker,
   float currentPrice)
   {
     string strMsg;
     strMsg="Monitor initiated for " + ticker +
       ", Current price $" +
       currentPrice.ToString();
     MessageBox.Show(strMsg,"Monitor Started");
   }
   public void PriceChange(string ticker,
     float newPrice, float oldPrice)
   {
     string strMsg;
     strMsg = "Stock: " + ticker +
     "  New Price: $" + newPrice.ToString() +
     "  Old Price: $" +
     oldPrice.ToString();
     lstEvents.Items.Add(strMessage);
   }
   private void Form1_Load(object sender,
   System.EventArgs e)
   {
     mStockServer = new StockMonitor();
     mStockServer.PriceChange+=new
_IStockMonitorEvents_PriceChangeEventHandler(PriceChange);
     mStockServer.MonitorInitiated+=new
_IStockMonitorEvents_MonitorInitiatedEventHandler(MonitorInitiated);
   }
}
```

On line 2, I add a using statement for the Interop assembly. If you generated your Interop Assembly yourself on the command line (and used the name **stockserver.dll** for the Interop assembly name), you will use stockserver for the namespace name, or you'll use STOCKSERVERLib if you generated the Interop assembly using Visual Studio .NET.

On line 6, I will declare a StockMonitor instance. On lines 8 through 26, I declare two methods, MonitorInitiated and PriceChange, that I will use to receive the callbacks. Notice that the MonitorInitiated method returns a void and takes a string, which contains the name of the new stock, and a float, which contains the price of the stock. This matches the prototype of the MonitorInitiated event from the COM object. The PriceChange method returns void and takes a string that contains the name of the stock and two floats, which contain the old and new price. This matches the prototype of the PriceChange event from the COM object.

The Form Load method is defined on lines 27 through 34. On line 30, I create a new instance of the StockMonitor. On line 31, I create a new instance of the PriceChangeEventHandler delegate and add this delegate to the PriceChange event on the StockMonitor instance. On line 33, I create a new instance of the MonitorInitiatedEventHandler delegate, and I add this delegate to the MonitorInitiated event on the StockMonitor instance.

Back in the form designer, double-click the Add button to add a Click event handler and add the following code:

```
private void cmdAdd_Click(object sender, System.EventArgs
e)
{
        mStockServer.AddNewStock(txtTicker.Text,
             float.Parse(txtPrice.Text),
             (short)updPropensity.Value);
}
```

This method adds a new stock for monitoring. If you run the application, you will almost immediately begin seeing price change events showing up in the event list. The Stock Server has an initial list of stock monitors that includes the following stocks: Microsoft (MSFT), Northrop Grumman (NOC), IBM (IBM), Coca Cola (COKE), Emulex (EMLX). You can also add additional stock monitors by filling in the name, price, and propensity to rise for a new stock and then click the Add button. Now that you've seen how easy it is to use COM events from a managed client, let's explore how the mapping of COM events to managed delegates is accomplished.

As you learned earlier, when a .NET client wants to receive events from a managed code object, the client will instantiate a delegate using a callback method that has the same prototype as the delegate associated with the event. The client will then use the "+=" operator to add the delegate to the event. To link connection point events and .NET events, I will need a sink object that implements the source interface that the COM object exposes. When the con-

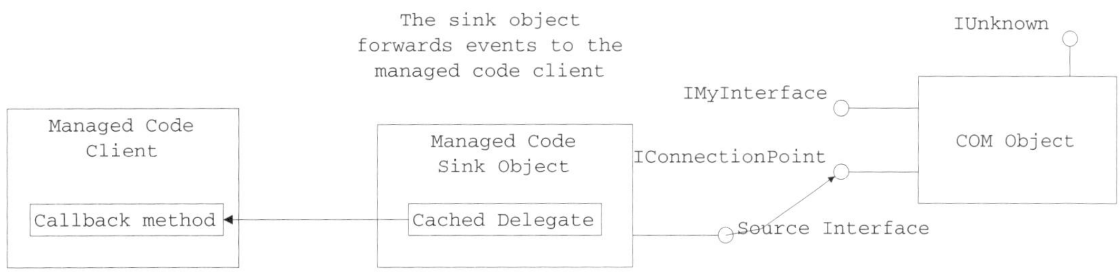

FIGURE 7–5 *Linking COM connection points and .NET events.*

nectable object calls this sink object, it should forward the method call to the delegate, which will then call the callback method that the .NET client specified (see Figure 7-5).

The problem is, how do you pass this sink object from the client to the server? What you essentially need is a custom implementation of the "+=" and "-=" operators for each event. When you add a callback for an event, this implementation should get the IConnectionPoint interface associated with the event from the COM object and pass the special sink object to the Advise method of IConnectionPoint. The implementation of the "+=" operator should cache the cookie that the Advise method returns. When you no longer want to receive events, the "-=" operator should use the cached cookie to call the Unadvise method in the IConnectionPoint.

The **_IStockMonitorEvents_EventProvider** class (see Table 7–1) contains the "+=" and "-=" methods that I described earlier. Remember from my discussion of events that declaring an event adds an add_ [EventName] and a remove_[EventName] method to your class. The implementation of these methods delegates to the methods with similar names in the **[SourceInterfaceName]_EventProvider** class. You can actually see the implementation of these methods (in MSIL code) if you run ILDASM on the Interop assembly. To view the implementation of the add_PriceChange method in the StockServer Interop assembly, perform the following steps:

1. Bring up the MSIL Disassembler by entering the following command at a Visual Studio .NET command prompt: ildasm StockServer.dll (or Interop.StockServerLib.dll if you used the Add Reference command in Visual Studio .NET to create your interop assembly).
2. Click the "+" symbol next to the class called **_IStockMonitorEvents_EventProvider**.
3. Double-click the purple box (which is the symbol for a method) labeled add_PriceChange.
4. The MSIL code for the add_PriceChange method will appear in a Window.

Rather than showing you the IDL for this method and the related methods in the **_IStockMonitorEvents_EventProvider** class, I translated the code for the add_PriceChange, remove_PriceChange, and Init methods into the C# code that follows.

Note The ease with which I was able to do this should serve as a reminder to be careful about the unobfuscated assemblies that you ship. See my note in Chapter 3 about available obfuscation technologies.

```
private sealed class
_IStockMonitorEvents_EventProvider
{
private ArrayList m_aEventSinkHelpers;
private UCOMIConnectionPoint m_connPt;
private UCOMIConnectionPointContainer m_connPtCtr;
void add_PriceChange(
_IStockMonitorEvents_PriceChangeEventHandler aDeleg)
{
    _IStockMonitorEvents_SinkHelper objSink;
    int aCookie;
    lock(this)
    {
      if (m_connPt==null)
        Init();
      objSink =new
        _IStockMonitorEvents_SinkHelper();
      aCookie=0;
      m_connPt.Advise(objSink,&aCookie);
      objSink.m_dwCookie=aCookie;
      objSink. m_PriceChangeDelegate=aDeleg;
      m_aEventSinkHelpers.Add(objSink);
    }
}
private void init()
{
    System.Guid aGuid;
    byte[] guidValue= new byte[16];
//…initialize array with the GUID for the
// StockServer's default, source interface.
    AGuid=new System.Guid(guidValue);
    m_ConnPtCtr.FindConnectionPoint(aGuid,&mconnPt);
    m_aEventSinkHelpers=new ArrayList();
}
void  remove_PriceChange(
   _IStockMonitorEvents_PriceChangeEventHandler aDeleg)
{
    int numSinks, i;
```

```
38.     _IStockMonitorEvents_SinkHelper objSink;
39.     lock(this)
40.     {
41.       i=0;
42.      numSinks=m_aEventSinkHelpers.get_Count();
43.      if (numSinks > 0)
44.      {
45.          do
46.          {
47.        objSink = m_aEventSinkHelpers.get_Item(i);
48.        if (objSink.m_PriceChangeDelegate != null)
49.        {
if (aDeleg.Equals(
    objSink.m_PriceChangeDelegate)
52.              {
53.          aEventSinkHelpers.RemoveAt(i);
54.             m_connPt.UnAdvise(objSink.m_dwCookie);
55.          if (numSinks <= 1)
56.          {
57.              m_connPoint=null;
58.              _aEventSinkHelpers=null;
59.              break;
60.          }
61.          break;
62.            }
63.        }
64.        i++;
65.          } while (i < numSinks);
66.      }
67.     }
68.  }
69. }
```

On lines 3 through 5, I show the declarations of three private variables in the _IStockMonitorEvents_EventProvider:

- **m_aEventSinkHelpers**—Contains a list of the sink objects that are currently attached to the underlying COM object.
- **m_connPt**—Contains an IConnectionPoint interface pointer for the default source interface. This variable is actually called m_ConnectionPoint in the MSIL code. I shortened the name to improve the formatting and readability of the source code.
- **m_connPtrCtr**—Contains an IconnectionPointContainer interface pointer for the underlying COM object. This variable is actually called m_ConnectionPointContainer in the MSIL code.

Lines 7 through 23 contain the definition of the add_PriceChange method. This method takes a single parameter, which is a delegate that will receive the events from the COM object. On lines 9 and 10 are the declarations of a sink object and a variable to hold the cookie for the connection to the COM object. The lock(this) statement on line 11 ensures that this method is thread safe. On lines 13 and 14, the code checks to see if the IConnection-Point interface pointer (m_connPt) has been initialized. If it has not, the code calls the Init method, which calls the FindConnectionPoint method on the IConnectionPointContainer interface pointer (m_connPtCtr) to initialize the connection point. The Init method also initializes the m_aEventSinkHelpers ArrayList. On lines 15 and 16, the code creates a new sink object, and, on line 18, the code calls the Advise method on the interface pointer, passing in the sink object. The cookie for this connection is returned in the second parameter to the Advise method. On line 19, I assign the cookie that was returned from the Advise method to the m_dwCookie field of the sink object, and, on line 20, I assign the delegatė that was passed into the add_PriceChange method to the m_PriceChangeDelegate field of the sink object. Finally, on line 21, I add the sink object to the list of sinks that you currently have on the COM object. Lines 24 through 33 contain the implementation of the Init method that I mentioned earlier. The implementation is fairly simple. It calls FindConnectionPoint on the IConnectionPointContainer interface that is exposed by the COM object and requests the default source interface. On line 32, this method also creates the ArrayList that will hold the list of sink objects. The remove_ method for the PriceChange event is shown on lines 34 through 68. On line 39, I see the lock statement to make the method thread safe. On line 42, the code gets the number "sink" objects in the list of sink objects (m_aEventSinkHelpers). If the number of sink objects is greater than zero, the code loops through the items in the list until it finds the one that that is equal to the delegate that was passed to the method as a parameter (see line 50). The code then removes this sink object from the list calls the Unadvise method on the connection point, passing in the cookie from the sink object that it found. The code on lines 55 through 60 will release the connection point, and the list that holds the sink objects if the sink object that the remove_PriceChange just removed was the only one on the list. Again, it's not critical that you understand all of this logic. I included it in case you were interested in how the mapping between COM events and managed events works. Even though the implementation of the mapping is quite complicated, as you saw earlier, using the mapping is very simple.

Using COM-Rich Error Information in Managed Code

COM objects use HRESULTs and error objects to return error information to their clients. .NET objects always use exceptions to return error information to their client. The mapping between these two is fairly straightforward. Before I go into that mapping, let's review COM HRESULTs and error objects because

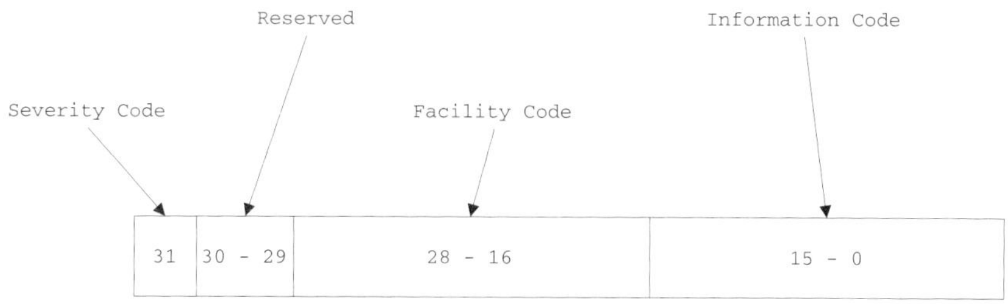

FIGURE 7-6 *A COM HRESULT.*

it is possible—particularly if you are a VB programmer—to use HRESULTs and error objects without understanding what they are and how they work.

The usual way to return an error in COM is to return a 32-bit error number that is typed as an HRESULT. In fact, all methods defined in a COM interface should return an HRESULT even if they succeed. HRESULTS are partitioned into four bit fields as shown in Figure 7-6: (1) The high-order bit is a severity code where 0 indicates success and 1 indicates an error, (2) the next 2 bits are reserved, (3) the next 13 bits make up a facility code, and (4) the final 16 bits make up a description code that uniquely identifies the error or warning if there is one.

Some example facility codes are FACILITY_DISPATCH, which is used for IDispatch errors; FACILITY_RPC, which is used for RPC errors; and FACILITY_ITF, which is used for errors that are returned from Interface methods. All user-defined HRESULTS should use FACILITY_ITF.

A method should return S_OK to indicate that it returned successfully. The COM runtime will fill the HRESULT return value if the method call fails for a system-level instead of an application-level problem. For instance, if a DCOM call fails because of a network problem, you will probably get a RPC_E_COMM_FAILURE. Similarly, if the security subsystem determines that a user is not authorized to use a server, it will fill the HRESULT with an E_ACCESSDENIED error. If an application-level error occurs in your code (that is, the client attempts to add a stock to be monitored that is already being monitored), you can either return one of many precanned HRESULTS, or you can create your own. The precanned HRESULTS include (among many others) E_FAIL, which indicates that an unspecified error has occurred; E_E_INVALIDARG, which is used to indicate that an argument passed to the method is invalid; or E_UNEXPECTED, which is used to indicate that some unexpected, catastrophic error has occurred (as if any catastrophic error is expected). The definitions of these HRESULTS from **winerror.h** are as follows:

```
#define E_FAIL
_HRESULT_TYPEDEF_(0x80004005L)
#define E_INVALIDARG
_HRESULT_TYPEDEF_(0x80000003L)
#define E_UNEXPECTED
        _HRESULT_TYPEDEF_(0x8000FFFFL)
```

Of course, these errors are so generic that they give the client little useful information with which to fix the problem, so most COM servers define custom HRESULT values that they can return to the client. The following code shows a definition of two custom HRESULTS in the **StockMonitor** class:

```
const E_STOCKNOTFOUND=
    MAKE_HRESULT(SEVERITY_ERROR,FACILITY_ITF,0x200+103);
const E_STOCKALREADYMONITORED=
    MAKE_HRESULT(SEVERITY_ERROR,FACILITY_ITF,0x200+104);
```

You create customer HRESULTs using the MAKE_HRESULT macro, which is also declared in the **winerror.h** file. The GetPrice method on the IStockMonitor interface will return the E_STOCKNOTFOUND HRESULT if you try to get the price of a stock that does not exist. The AddNewStock method will return the E_STOCKALREADYMONITORED HRESULT if you attempt to add a stock to the StockMonitor that is already being monitored. You can return a custom or standard HRESULT from your methods as shown in schematic form here:

```
STDMETHODIMP CMyObject::GetPrice(BSTR ticker,float *price)
{
      if (MethodSuccessful())
        return S_OK;
      else
        return E_STOCKNOTFOUND;
}
```

In most cases, though, you will want to return more information than just an error code to your client. You probably will want to send along a textual description of the error as well as information about the source of the error. You might even want to send along the path to a help file and a context ID that identifies the location in the help file where the user can go to read more about the error. To facilitate all of this, COM supports error objects. A COM error object is a COM object that implements the IErrorInfo interface. The IErrorInfo interface contains the methods shown in Table 7-3.

TABLE 7–3 *Methods in the IErrorInfo interface*

Method Name	Description
GetDescription	Returns a textual description of the error.
GetSource	Returns the ProgID of the class that returned the error.
GetGUID	Returns the GUID of the interface that generated the error.
GetHelpFile	Returns the path of the help file that describes the error.
GetHelpContext	Returns the help context ID for the error, which identifies a location within the help file.

Notice that there are no Set methods on this interface to initialize the information in the error object. To create an error object and to populate it with information, you must call the CreateErrorInfo COM API function, which returns an ICreateErrorInfo interface pointer. The ICreateErrorInfo interface contains the Set equivalents for all of the methods described in Table 7–3. After you have used the CreateErrorInfo function and the Set methods to build the error object, you call the SetErrorInfo method to set the object as an error for the current logical thread. The COM runtime will take care of marshaling the error object appropriately if the client resides in a different process or on another machine. The following code shows how you create, populate, and then send a COM error object to a client:

```
STDMETHODIMP CStockMonitor::AddNewStock(BSTR ticker, float
      price, short propensityToRise)
{
      map<CComBSTR,float>::iterator iter;
      ObjectLock lock(this);
      iter=m_StockPriceList.find(ticker);
      if (iter==m_StockPriceList.end())
      {
        m_StockPriceList[ticker]=price;
        m_StockPropensityList[ticker]=propensityToRise;
        m_StockTickerList.push_back(ticker);
        Fire_MonitorInitiated(ticker,price);
        return S_OK;
      }
      else
      {
          IErrorInfo *pErrorInfo;
          ICreateErrorInfo *pCreateErrorInfo;
        HRESULT hr=CreateErrorInfo(&pCreateErrorInfo);
        hr=pCreateErrorInfo->SetGUID(IID_IStockMonitor);
        hr=pCreateErrorInfo->SetDescription(
           OLESTR("This stock exists already"));
        hr=pCreateErrorInfo->QueryInterface(
```

```
                IID_IErrorInfo,(void**)&pErrorInfo);
            hr=SetErrorInfo(0,pErrorInfo);
            pCreateErrorInfo->Release();
            pErrorInfo->Release();
            return E_STOCKALREADYMONITORED;
        }
}
```

The following code shows how you would catch the error on a client:

```
void CStockserverclientDlg::OnAddstockButton()
{
        HRESULT hRes;
        BSTR bstrTicker;
        UpdateData(TRUE);
        IErrorInfo *pErrorInfo;
        BSTR bstrErrorMsg;
        if (m_serverOK)
        {
          bstrTicker=m_ticker.AllocSysString();
          hRes=m_pIStockMonitor->AddNewStock
               (bstrTicker,m_price,m_propensity);
          if (FAILED(hRes))
          {
            hRes=GetErrorInfo(0,&pErrorInfo);
            if (SUCCEEDED(hRes))
            {
              pErrorInfo->GetDescription
                    (&bstrErrorMsg);
              AfxMessageBox(CString(bstrErrorMsg));
            }
            else
              AfxMessageBox("Everything Failed");
          }
          ::SysFreeString(bstrTicker);
        }
        else
          AfxMessageBox("The server failed to start.");
}
```

Fortunately, it is much easier to use COM errors in practice than you have seen here. ATL includes an Error function that encapsulates all of the logic required to create, populate, and send an error object. Using this function, I could rewrite the function shown previously as follows:

```
STDMETHODIMP CStockMonitor::AddNewStock(BSTR ticker,
    float price,short propensityToRise)
{
    map<CComBSTR,float>::iterator iter;
    ObjectLock lock(this);
    iter=m_StockPriceList.find(ticker);
    if (iter==m_StockPriceList.end())
    {
        m_StockPriceList[ticker]=price;
        m_StockPropensityList[ticker]=propensityToRise;
        m_StockTickerList.push_back(ticker);
        Fire_MonitorInitiated(ticker,price);
        return S_OK;
    }
    else
        return Error(
          _T("This stock exists already"),
          IID_IStockMonitor,
          E_STOCKALREADYMONITORED);
}
```

COM error objects are much easier to use from VB 6. You can use the raise method in the global err object to populate and return an error object to a client. The parameters to the raise function allow you to specify the source, description, help file, and so forth for the error object. The following code shows schematically how you would raise errors from VB code:

```
Public Property Let CustomDictionary(ByVal vData As String)
  On Error GoTo HandleErr
    'The logic for this routine goes here...

    Exit Property
    'If an error occurs you will jump to here

HandleErr:
    'we specify the error number, Source, and description
    Err.Raise errDictionaryFileProblem, _
        "SpellChecker.CustomDictionary", _
        "Dictionary not found or could not be read"
End Property
```

In comparison to COM error handling, .NET exception handling is simple. With .NET, when you want to tell your client that an error has occurred, you simply create an instance of an exception object, populate the fields in the object with information that is relevant to the error, and throw the object to your client. An example is shown here.

```
void TestExceptions(float arg1)
{
      if (arg1 >= 0)
```

```
        {
        //... perform some processing
        }
        else
          throw new ArgumentOutOfRangeException
              ("arg1",arg1,"Argument cannot be negative");
}
```

In this case, I throw an instance of the **ArgumentOutOfRangeException** class. Exception classes are customized to allow you to easily pass all the information that a client may need about the type of error that the exception class represents. In this case, the constructor for the **ArgumentOutOfRangeException** class has three arguments. The first argument is a string that contains the name of the argument that is out of range, the second argument contains the value of the offending argument, and the third argument contains a textual description of the error.

You can write the following code to catch the exception:

```
private void cmdTestException_Click(object sender,
      System.EventArgs e)
{
      try
      {
        TestExceptions(float.Parse(textBox1.Text));
      }
      catch (ArgumentOutOfRangeException ex)
      {
        MessageBox.Show("Out of range error: " +
              ex.Message);
      }
      catch (Exception ex)
      {
        MessageBox.Show("Generic error: " + ex.Message);
      }
}
```

Notice that I can write multiple catch statements for a single try block. If I do this, I must start with the most derived class and then have my base exception classes at the end. The CLR will only execute the try block that is closest to the actual type of the exception object. For instance, in this case, if the server threw an exception object of type ArgumentOutOfRangeException, the client would execute the catch statement associated with the **ArgumentOutOfRangeException** class. If the client threw any other exception, the client would execute the catch statement associated with the base Exception class.

Note The ArgumentOutOfRangeException class, like most exception classes, has a number of overrides, but all of them allow you to construct an exception object with the same basic information: an argument name, its value, and a textual description.

You can use one of the many exception classes that the .NET Framework base class library provides for you, or you can create our own custom exception classes that derive from **System.Exception** or from another class that derives from **System.Exception**. The main reason for creating your own class is if there is information that you want to return to the client that is not provided by one of the standard classes. Table 7–4 lists just a few of the exception classes that the .NET Framework base class library provides.

TABLE 7–4 *Useful exception classes*

Method Name	Description
ApplicationException	Thrown when a nonfatal application error occurs. Use this class as the base class for your custom, nonfatal exception classes.
ArgumentException	Thrown when an invalid argument is passed to a method.
ArgumentNullException	Thrown when a null argument is passed to a method and derives from **ArgumentException**.
ArgumentOutOfRangeException	Thrown when an argument to a method is not within the allowable range and derives from **ArgumentException**.
InvalidOperationException	Thrown when a method call is not valid for the current state of an object.
NotImplementedException	Thrown when a method that is called on an object has not been implemented.
COMException	Thrown when an unrecognized or user-defined HRESULT is returned from a COM method call.

Note I presented an introduction to exception handling in the .NET Framework in Chapter 4. In that chapter, I showed an example of creating a custom exception class.

All exception classes inherit from **System.Exception**, so it defines the set of methods and properties that are universally supported by all exceptions. The members supported by the **System.Exception** class are shown in Table 7–5. I ignored the standard System.Object methods.

TABLE 7–5 *Members of the System.Exception class*

Member Name	Type of Member	Description
Message	Property	Gets or sets the textual description of the exception.
Source	Property	Gets or sets the name of the application that caused the exception.
StackTrace	Property	Gets a stack trace at the time the exception occurred.
TargetSite	Property	Gets the name of the method that caused the exception.
InnerException	Property	Gets the exception that caused the current exception.
HelpLink	Property	Gets or sets a link to a help file that describes the exception.
HResult	Property	Gets or sets the HRESULT associated with this exception and is a protected property.

After you have a basic understanding of how COM error objects work, understanding the mapping between COM error objects and .NET exceptions is fairly simple. When a COM object returns an error (that is, an HRESULT with an error severity code such as E_NOINTERFACE), the CLR will convert the HRESULT to a managed exception and throw it to the client. The mapping is seamlessly handled by the CLR. The exception object will contain the HRESULT, but notice from Table 7–5 that it is a protected property. In most cases, you will not need to manipulate HRESULTs directly in your managed code. You can tell what type of error occurred by examining the type of the exception class that you receive. You can then write type-specific Catch statements with potentially different logic for each exception type. For many errors, especially those that originate in unmanaged code, you may still want to examine the HRESULT associated with the error. That's why some exception classes like **System.Runtime.InteropServices.SEHException**, **System.Data.OleDb.OleDbException**, **System.Messaging.MessageQueueException**, **System.ComponentModel.Win32Exception**, **System.Web.HttpException**, and (most important for this discussion) **System.Runtime.InteropServices.COMException** expose the underlying HRESULT as a public property called ErrorCode.

Note The classes that expose the public ErrorCode property all derive from an exception class called System.Runtime.InteropServices.ExternalException. The ErrorCode property is declared in this class.

Some of the predefined HRESULTS like E_NOINTERFACE, E_NOTIMPL, and E_ACCESSDENIED map directly to exception classes. Table 7–6 shows the mapping between the most common predefined HRESULTS and .NET exception classes. The right-hand column in the table shows the .NET exception class you will see on a managed code client when a COM object returns the HRESULT in the left column. Notice that many of these exceptions simply map to an instance of **System.Runtime.InteropServices.COMException** with a customized message. In each of those cases, I show the custom message in parentheses

TABLE 7–6 *Mapping between HRESULTS and exception classes*

HRESULT	.NET Exception Class
E_FAIL	**System.Runtime.InteropServices.COMException** (Unspecified Error)
E_NOINTERFACE	System.InvalidCastException
E_ACCESSDENIED	System.UnauthorizedAccessException
E_NOTIMPL	System.NotImplementedException
E_INVALIDARG	System.ArgumentException
E_POINTER	System.NullReferenceException
E_OUTOFMEMORY	System.OutOfMemoryException
DISP_E_EXCEPTION	**System.Runtime.InteropServices.COMException** (Exception occurred)
DISP_E_PARAMNOTOPTIONAL	**System.Runtime.InteropServices.COMException** (Parameter not optional)
DISP_E_BADPARAMCOUNT	System.Reflection.TargetParameterCountException
DISP_E_DIVBYZERO	System.DivideByZeroException
DISP_E_UNKNOWNINTERFACE	**System.Runtime.InteropServices.COMException** (Unknown interface)
DISP_E_MEMBERNOTFOUND	**System.Runtime.InteropServices.COMException** (Member not found)

If, instead of using one of the predefined HRESULTs, you create a user-defined HRESULT as shown here and return it to the client, the CLR will convert the HRESULT to an exception of type **System.Runtime.InteropServices.COMException**.

```
const E_STOCKALREADYMONITORED=
      MAKE_HRESULT(SEVERITY_ERROR,FACILITY_ITF,0x200+104);
```

Regardless of whether you are using one of the predefined HRESULTs or a user-defined one, the exact contents of the exception object that the CLR will throw when the error originates in unmanaged code depends on whether the unmanaged code sets an error object or not. If the unmanaged code sets an error object by calling the Error function in ATL or by calling err.Raise in VB, the fields of the managed code exception object will be populated from the COM error object as shown in Table 7-7.

TABLE 7–7 *The mapping between fields in a COM error object and .NET exception classes when you populate the fields of the COM error object*

Where the Information Comes From in the COM Error Object	.NET Exception Field
IErrorInfo->GetDescription()	Message
IErrorInfo->GetSource()	Source
The top of the stack is the unmanaged code (COM) method that generated the error. The bottom of the stack is the managed code method that caught the error.	StackTrace
The name of the unmanaged code method that generated the exception	TargetSite
The HRESULT returned by the COM method	ErrorCode (available on **COMException** and other exception classes that derive from **System.Runtime.InteropServices. ExternalException**)
Null	InnerException

if (IErrorInfo->GetHelpContext() != 0)
IErrorInfo->GetHelpFile() +"#" +
IErrorInfo->GetHelpContext()
Else
IErrorInfo->GetHelpFile()
	HelpLink

If you return an HRESULT from your COM object, but do not populate the rich error information (COM error object) as follows, the .NET exception object will be populated by the CLR as shown in Table 7-8.

```
const E_STOCKALREADYMONITORED=
      MAKE_HRESULT(SEVERITY_ERROR,FACILITY_ITF,0x200+104);
STDMETHODIMP CStockMonitor::AddNewStock(BSTR ticker,
      float price, short propensityToRise)
{
      map<CComBSTR,float>::iterator iter;
      ObjectLock lock(this);
      iter=m_StockPriceList.find(ticker);
      if (iter==m_StockPriceList.end())
      {
        m_StockPriceList[ticker]=price;
        m_StockPropensityList[ticker]=propensityToRise;
        m_StockTickerList.push_back(ticker);
```

```
            Fire_MonitorInitiated(ticker,price);
            return S_OK;
        }
        else
            return E_STOCKALREADYMONITORED;
}
```

Notice that, in this C++ version of the AddNewStock function, I do not call the ATL Error function when I return with an error, which populates the error object. Instead I just return the HRESULT.

TABLE 7–8 *Source of data for .NET exception classes when there is no COM error object*

Where the Information Comes From	Exception Field
"Exception from HRESULT: [HRESULT in hex form]"	Message
The name of the Interop assembly that threw the exception, e.g., Interop.StockserverLib	Source
The top of the stack is the unmanaged code (COM) method that generated the error. The bottom of the stack is the managed code method that caught the error.	StackTrace
The name of the unmanaged code method that generated the exception	TargetSite
The HRESULT returned by the COM method	ErrorCode (available on **COMException** and other exception classes that derive from **System.Runtime.InteropServices.External-Exception**)
Null	InnerException
Null	HelpLink

The Message field in the Exception object will contain the string: "Exception from HRESULT: [HRESULT in hex form]" where [HRESULT in hex form] is the value of the HRESULT in hex e.g.,

```
Exception from HRESULT:  0x80040268
```

Notice that the StackTrace, TargetSite, and ErrorCode fields are populated exactly the same as they are populated when the unmanaged object sets an error object. The main difference is the contents of the HelpLink field, which can only be populated by a COM error object and therefore will be NULL if you do not create an error object.

Multithreading and COM Apartments

In a multithreaded environment, COM objects use Apartments to synchronize access to resources that may be shared by multiple threads. Managed code objects use synchronization regions and synchronization primitives like monitors, mutexes, and locks for the same purpose. Yes, you read that correctly. Assuming that you are not using COM Interop (or Windows Forms), your managed code does not use Apartments. For those of you who never quite grasped the concept of COM Apartments, this is probably cause for celebration.

Note I personally think that Microsoft dropping the Apartment concept in the .NET Framework is a tacit admission by them that the "fix"—COM Apartments—was worse than the original problem—the need to synchronize access to resources in a multithreaded environment.

But before you pop the champagne, keep in mind that, if you are reading this book, you probably want to use COM components in your managed code applications, and, unfortunately, if you do use COM components, your managed code application will use Apartments.

Before a thread can instantiate a COM object, it must enter an Apartment. The way I like to think of it is that entering an Apartment is just the thread's way of announcing to the world (or at least to the COM objects that it will subsequently create) one of two things: whether the thread is primarily an independent thread that will not need to share resources extensively with other threads running in the same process or it is one of a group of threads in a multithreaded environment. An independent thread should enter an STA by calling CoInitializeEx as follows:

```
CoInitializeEx(NULL,COINIT_APARTMENT_THREADED)
```

If the thread is one thread in a multithreaded environment, it should enter the MTA (there's only one in each process) by calling CoInitializeEx as follows:

```
CoInitializeEx(NULL,COINIT_MULTI_THREADED)
```

In-Process COM objects specify which type of threading environment they can operate in by adding a registry value called ThreadingModel beneath their InprocServer32 subkey. The object can specify one of the five values shown in Table 7-9.

Note Out-of-process (executable) servers do not use the ThreadingModel registry key because they do not interact directly with their client's threads because the client runs in a different process.

TABLE 7–9 *Threading models for COM objects*

Threading Model Value	Description
Single	Objects of this class are pathologically un-thread safe. Not only are the objects not thread safe, but the class factory for the class and the DllGetClassObject and DllCanUnloadNow functions for the server are also not thread safe. A single thread must call *all* of the code in this server.
Apartment	Objects of this class do not protect their per-instance state from multithreading problems. Access to each instance must be limited to a single thread. However, the per-class state for this class and the class factory and the DllGetClassObject and DllCanUnloadNow functions in the classes' server *are* thread safe.
Free	COM objects of this class protect their per-instance state and per-class state from multithreading problems using thread synchronization primitives, such as critical sections or mutexes. These objects are safe to use in a multithreaded environment.
Both	Object of this class will be instantiated in the same apartment as their client so they can, for maximum performance, execute on their caller's thread. Because they may run in a multi-threaded environment, these classes should protect their per-instance state and per-class state from multi-threading problems.
Neutral	Objects of this class will also execute on their caller's thread, but they will reside in their own apartment, the Thread Neutral Apartment (TNA), rather then residing in their caller's apartment. Because any thread (STA or MTA) in a process can enter the TNA at any time, objects marked as Neutral must either use thread-synchronization primitives internally to make themselves thread safe, or they can use the thread synchronization service provided by the COM+ runtime.

If a COM object was not designed to be thread safe, it will typically use the Apartment (STA) for its ThreadingModel. Some older objects use the more restrictive Single ThreadingModel. If the COM object was designed to be thread safe, it can use either the Free, Both, or Neutral values for its ThreadingModel. To some extent, Free is almost a legacy value because most objects that can run in an MTA can also run in an STA, so Both is usually used nowadays where Free might have been used in the past. The Neutral threading model is primarily useful for COM+ objects.

After a thread has specified what sort of environment it is a part of, that is, an single-threaded environment (STA) or one thread in a multithreaded environment (MTA) and an object has specified what sort of threading environment it can operate in by setting the ThreadingModel registry value, it is fairly easy for the COM runtime to ensure that COM objects are only instantiated in an environment that they can safely operate in. For instance, if you instantiate a COM object that has the Apartment ThreadingModel value, that is, the object can only be instantiated in an STA, and the creating thread is an MTA thread, the COM runtime will create an STA (and potentially another thread) for the object and set up a proxy that marshals method calls between the object's STA thread and the calling MTA thread. However, if the creating thread is an STA thread, the COM runtime recognizes that the object is compatible with its creating thread, and it allows the calling thread to call the object directly without going through a proxy.

A fairly large performance penalty is associated with cross-apartment marshaling; it's almost as bad as cross-process marshaling. Therefore, the basic goal when using COM is to avoid cross-apartment marshaling to the greatest extent possible. That means you should try to make sure that an object is instantiated by a compatible thread. Table 7–10 shows the compatibility matrix between COM Apartments and threading models.

TABLE 7–10 *Compatibility matrix between COM objects and threading models*

Threading Model	MTA	Primary STA	Other STA
Single	Marshaled	Direct	Marshaled
Apartment	Marshaled	Direct	Direct
Free	Direct	Marshaled	Marshaled
Both	Direct	Direct	Direct
Neutral	Marshaled	Marshaled	Marshaled

Marshaled means that cross-apartment marshaling is required. Direct means that no marshaling is required.

If you are using COM objects from a managed code application, you will want to make sure that the apartment that the CLR creates is compatible with the threading model of the COM object so that you avoid cross-apartment marshaling. The basic goals are simple and can be summarized as follows:

- If you are using STA COM object(s) (Apartment ThreadingModel), you want to make sure that your managed code thread enters an STA.
- If you are using MTA-only COM object(s) (Free ThreadingModel), you want to make sure that your managed code thread enters the MTA.

- If you are using COM object(s) that can exist in either type of Apartment (Both ThreadingModel) or objects that are thread neutral (Neutral ThreadingModel), your managed code thread can enter either type of Apartment.

You can control the Apartment that your object enters using the ApartmentState property on the **System.Threading.Thread** class. You can access the Apartment state of the current thread using the following code:

```
ApartmentState aptState;
aptState=Thread.CurrentThread.ApartmentState;
```

CurrentThread is a static, read-only property on the **System.Threading.Thread** class, which returns a Thread object that represents the currently running thread. The ApartmentState property is typed as **System.Threading.ApartmentState**, which is an enumeration that has three possible values:

- **MTA**—The thread will create and enter an MTA.
- **STA**—The thread will create and enter an STA.
- **Unknown**—The apartment state has not been set (the initial value).

Table 7–11 summarizes the calls that your managed thread will make to the CoInitializeEx COM Apartment initialization function based on the various settings of the ApartmentState property.

TABLE 7–11 *COM Apartment initialization for various ApartmentState values*

ApartmentState Enumeration Value	COM Apartment Initialization
MTA	CoInitializeEx(NULL,COINIT_MULTIHREADED)
STA	CoInitializeEx(NULL,APARTMENTTHREADED)
Unknown	CoInitializeEx(NULL,COINIT_MULTIHREADED)

Keep in mind that the current value in ApartmentState does not necessarily represent the current Apartment that the object resides in. Rather, it represents the Apartment that the thread will enter if you perform some operation that requires you to enter an Apartment, such as instantiating a COM object. When you create a managed thread (I will show you how to do this shortly), it starts out with an ApartmentState of Unknown. You can only set the ApartmentState when the thread is in the Running or Unstarted states, and you cannot change the value of the ApartmentState after a call has been made to a COM component because a thread can only enter an Apartment once. Any calls to set the ApartmentState are ignored after the thread's Apartment has been initialized. If you instantiate a COM object without explicitly setting the ApartmentState, the CLR will call CoInitializeEx(NULL,COINIT_MULTIHREADED) on the current thread to enter the MTA.

I decided to experiment with this a little, so I entered the following code into the form-load method of a Windows Form application:

```
private void Form1_Load(object sender,System.EventArgs e)
{
     IThreadView objThread;
     Type objType;
     objType=
       Type.GetTypeFromProgID("ThreadDemo.FreeThreaded");
     objThread=
       (IThreadView)Activator.CreateInstance(objType);
     lblAptState.Text=
        Thread.CurrentThread.ApartmentState.ToString();
}
```

The code here creates an instance of a COM class with the ProgID ThreadDemo.FreeThreaded by first calling GetTypeFromProgID on **System.Type** to fetch the Type object for the class, and then it calls CreateInstance on **System.Activator** to create an object. As you might have guessed already, the **ThreadDemo.FreeThreaded** COM class has a ThreadingModel of Free. The last line of the code fetches the ApartmentState of the current thread after instantiating the COM object and displays it in a label. The code here was designed to show you the Apartment that the current thread entered after you instantiated a COM object from managed code.

If you build the executable and then run it from Windows Explorer or a command prompt, or if you select Debug | Start Without Debugging in Visual Studio .NET, the ApartmentState comes out to be MTA. You will also see MTA if you run the executable from within the Visual Studio .NET debugger by selecting the Debug | Start. This is the expected behavior. If you do not specify otherwise, your thread will enter an MTA when it has to.

However, if I moved the exact same logic out of the form-load method and into the clicked handler for a button as follows:

```
private void cmdSetApartmentState_Click(object sender,
System.EventArgs e)
{
     IThreadView objThread;
     Type objType;
     objType=
     Type.GetTypeFromProgID("ThreadDemo.FreeThreaded");
     objThread=
     (IThreadView)Activator.CreateInstance(objType);
     lblAptState.Text=
       Thread.CurrentThread.ApartmentState.ToString();
}
```

The label shows STA if I run the executable directly and MTA if I ran it within the debugger.

Note The ApartmentState always seemed to show MTA when I ran within the debugger indicating that there is code in the debugger that causes the thread to enter the MTA before it executes your code.

I came to a two-part conclusion based on these findings. First, a Windows Forms application enters an STA somewhere between the Form Load method and the call to the first event handler in the form. Second, if you want to be sure to get a particular Apartment type, you need to choose the Apartment type explicitly using the ApartmentState property on your thread. You also need to make this choice early in the life of the thread. If you don't make the choice early, the CLR may enter the wrong Apartment (that is, one that would require cross-apartment marshaling) before your initialization code. Unfortunately, this is easier said than done. You might think that you can just put a call to set the apartment state in the Main or the Form Load method of your application. However, this may not work because any code that uses COM in your application will initialize the ApartmentState, and, after it is set, it cannot change. The only surefire way to get the correct Apartment type is to set the ApartmentState before any startup code in your application is executed. Fortunately, there are two attributes, System.MTAThreadAttribute and System.STAThreadAttribute, that you may use for precisely this purpose. The following code shows you how to use System.STAThreadAttribute:

```
[STAThread]
static void Main()
{
// The apartment state is STA
      Application.Run(new Form1());
}
```

If you use this attribute on the Main method of my application, you are guaranteed that the ApartmentState will always be STA. If you want to enter an MTA, use the following code instead:

```
[MTAThread]
static void Main()
{
// The apartment state is STA
      Application.Run(new Form1());
}
```

When you initially create a Windows Forms project, Visual Studio .NET adds the System.STAThreadAttribute to the main function of your application as shown here:

```
[STAThread]
static void Main()
{
      Application.Run(new Form1());
}
```

Keep this in mind. If you are using free-threaded COM objects in your application, you may want to change your managed client code to use [MTAThread].

Primary Interop Assemblies

There is a major complication associated with generating an Interop assembly for a COM component. The problem occurs when you attempt to import a type library that references other type libraries. A type library (type library A) references another type library (type library B) when the COM component associated with type library A uses types from type library B in its interface. For instance, I may want to define an upgraded version of my financial COM component that can also issue stock quotes. To provide this functionality, I could implement the IStockMonitor interface that I defined in the Stock Server earlier in this chapter. The GetPrice method in this interface will allow me to return stock quotes, and I could reuse the existing implementation in the StockServer through aggregation as shown in Figure 7–7.

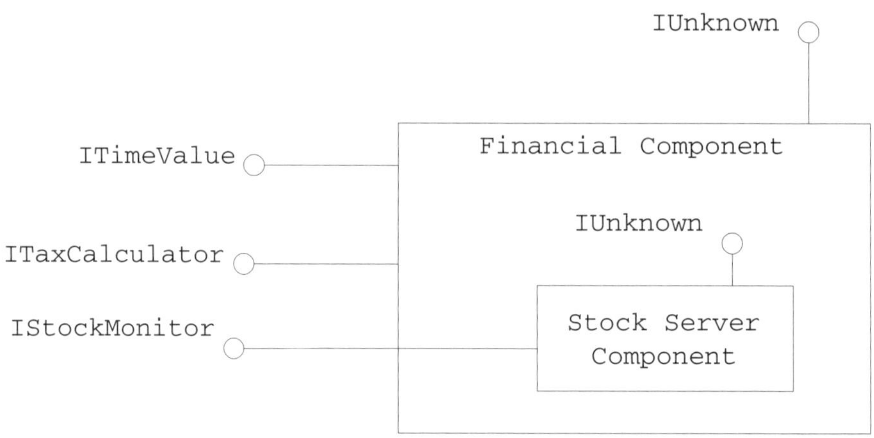

FIGURE 7–7 *An enhanced version of the financial component.*

The following code shows the IDL for my new financial component:

```
[
  uuid(EB47FA01-22EE-11D3-998A-E0EC08C10000),
  version(1.0),
  helpstring("financialcomponent 1.0 Type Library")
]
library FINANCIALCOMPONENTLib
```

```
{
  importlib("stdole32.tlb");
  importlib("stdole2.tlb");
  importlib("stockserver.tlb");
  [
  object,
  uuid(EB47FA0D-22EE-11D3-998A-E0EC08C10000),
  dual,
  helpstring("ITimeValue Interface"),
  pointer_default(unique)
  ]
  interface ITimeValue : IDispatch
  {
    [id(1)] HRESULT MonthlyPayment(
      [in] short numMonths,
      [in] double interestRate,
      [in] double loanAmt,
      [out,retval] double *result);
    [id(2)] HRESULT LoanAmount(
      [in] short numMonths,
      [in] double interestRate,
      [in] double monthlyPmt,
      [out,retval] double *result);
  };

  [
    object,
    uuid(1C208680-22F2-11d3-998A-E0EC08C10000),
    dual,
    helpstring("ITaxCalculator Interface"),
    pointer_default(unique)
  ]
  interface ITaxCalculator : IDispatch
  {
    [id(1)] HRESULT CalculateTax(
      [in] double earnings,
      [out,retval] double *tax);
  };

  [
    uuid(EB47FA0E-22EE-11D3-998A-E0EC08C10000),
    helpstring("Financial Class")
  ]
  coclass CFinancial
  {
    [default] interface ITimeValue;
    interface ITaxCalculator;
    interface IStockMonitor;
  };
};
```

Notice that, on line 10, I added a importlib statement for the stockserver's type library. This indicates that the financial component type library depends on types in the stockserver's type library. You can see the actual dependency on line 54 where I added the IStockMonitor interface to the list of interfaces that the **CFinancial** class implements.

When you use a COM component through Interop, the managed code client will need to have an Interop assembly for each COM component that the COM component you want to use depends on. Therefore, in my example, if I am using the enhanced Financial component from a managed client, I will need Interop assemblies for both the financial component and the stock server.

The usual behavior of the Type Library Importer (tlbimp.exe) and the Add reference... command in Visual Studio .NET is to generate a separate Interop assembly for each type library that the specified type library references. Therefore, if you run tlbimp on the modified financial component as follows:

```
tlbimp financialcomponent.dll /out:dotnetfinancial.dll
```

The type library importer will actually generate two assemblies: (1) an Interop assembly called **dotnetfinancial.dll** that contains managed equivalents of all the types declared in the financial component and (2) an interop assembly called **StockServerLib.dll** that contains the managed equivalents of the types in the stock server component. I did not have to explicitly tell tlbimp to generate this second assembly. It looked at the reference that the financial component's type library had to the stock server component and realized that it had to generate managed code equivalents for the types in the stock server type library in order for the financial component to be usable. When you build a managed code client that uses the financial component, you must reference both Interop assemblies in order to use it. If you reference only the financial component assembly, you will get the following compiler error:

```
Referenced class 'FINANCIALCOMPONENTLib.CFinancialClass'
has base class or interface 'STOCKSERVERLib.IStockMonitor'
defined in an assembly that is not referenced.  You must
add a reference to assembly 'STOCKSERVERLib'.
```

Unfortunately, the need to reference multiple assemblies is only one of the problems you will encounter if you attempt to use a COM component that is dependent on other COM components. Imagine that you had a second component (perhaps a business object that is used for calculating the value of investments) that also references the stock server; let's call it investmentcomponent.dll. If you run tlbimp on this component, it will generate two assemblies: (1) an interop assembly for **investmentcomponent.dll** and (2) an Interop assembly for the stock server. If you run tlbimp.exe on the investment component and the financial component, it will generate two different versions of the Stock Server Interop assembly as shown in Figure 7–8.

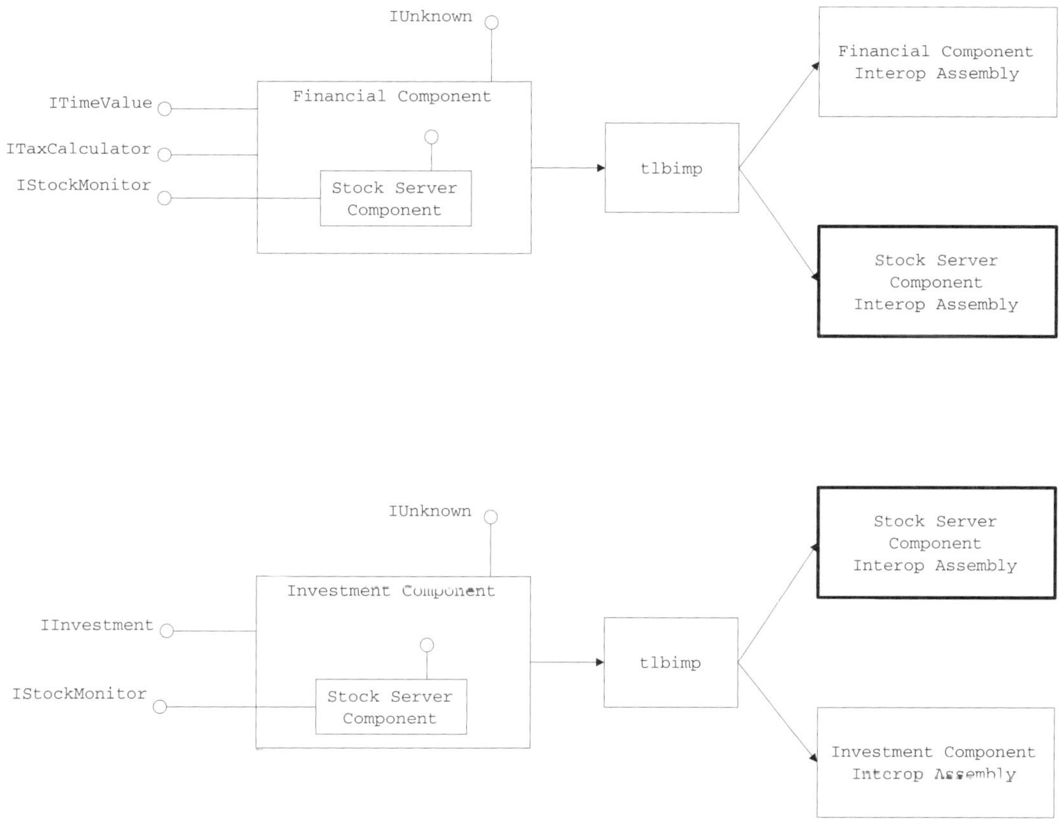

FIGURE 7–8 *Two versions of the stock server Interop assembly.*

This causes major problems because COM components have a completely different notion of identity than .NET components. Whether it's a class or an interface or a type library, a COM type has a unique identifier (a GUID) that identifies it. With .NET, a type's identity is assembly relative. Therefore, even if two types (two classes, for instance) have the same name and are structurally identical (that is, they have exactly the same members), they are considered to be two different types by the CLR if they reside in different assemblies. As long as you don't need to write a client application that uses both the enhanced financial component and the investment component, you're okay. However, as soon as you attempt to use both assemblies in the same application, you will have difficulties because each of these assemblies is dependent on its own version of an interop assembly for the stock server. Not only will you have the clutter associated with having multiple assemblies that contain structurally identical types with the same name, you also may have type mismatch errors in your code. The solution to this problem is Primary Interop Assemblies (PIAs).

A PIA is a digitally signed assembly that is installed in the GAC and contains a special attribute that identifies it as a PIA. When a type library references another type library, the Type Library Importer checks for a PIA before it generates a new Interop assembly for the referenced type library. If it finds a PIA, it does not generate an Interop assembly for the referenced type library. It assumes that all clients will share the PIA registered in the GAC.

To create a PIA, you must use tlbimp with the /primary parameter. A PIA must have a strong name, so you must use the /publickey, keyfile, or /keycontainer parameter on tlbimp to specify a strong name for the resulting assembly. You cannot use the Add Reference... command in Visual Studio .NET to generate a PIA. The following command will create a PIA for the Stock Server component:

```
tlbimp stockserver.exe /primary /keyfile:mykey.snk /
out:stockserver.dll
```

The type library importer searches for PIAs in the registry. When you generate an Interop Assembly, the Type Library Importer will look in the type library's entry in the registry for special entries that indicate that a PIA exists for the type library. You must add these registry entries before an Interop assembly will function as a PIA. It's easy to do this using the Assembly Registration Tool (regasm), which is a part of the .NET Framework SDK. Simply run the following command:

```
regasm stockserver.dll
```

Regasm will add the following value to the registry.

```
HKEY_CLASSES_ROOT\TypeLib\{LIBID}\Major.Minor\PrimaryIntero
pAssemblyName
```

Where {LIBID} is the GUID associated with the type library and Major.Minor is the major and minor version numbers of the assembly. The data at the PrimaryInteropAssemblyName value is just the full name of the PIA, as in the following example:

```
STOCKSERVERLib, Version=1.0.0.0, Culture=neutral,
PublicKeyToken=8a707be49fd7d8f4
```

If you do not want to install your PIA into the GAC, you can instead use regasm with the /codebase parameter and specify a path where the type library importer should search for the PIA. If you do this, regasm will add a second registry value at the following location.

```
HKEY_CLASSES_ROOT\TypeLib\{LIBID}\Major.Minor\PrimaryIntero
pAssemblyCodeBase
```

The data at this value will just be the path to the primary interop assembly, such as the following:

```
file:///C:/Alan/books/dotnetbook/demos/chapter7/
stockserver/server/stockserver.dll
```

After you have registered a PIA for a COM type library, the Type Library Importer will not generate a separate interop assembly for dependent type libraries. In other words, referring back to my example where the enhanced version of the financial COM component referenced the stock server COM component, if there is no PIA for the stock server, the Type Library Importer will generate two interop assemblies when I run it against the financial component: one for the financial component and one for the stock server component. If I register a PIA for the stock server component, the Type Library Importer will produce only one interop assembly, which is the one for the financial component. The generated interop assembly will reference the PIA.

If you are a vendor who produces COM components, you should create PIAs for your COM components. Not only will you save your customers a lot of grief with redundant Interop assemblies, but, in some cases, you may need to make small modifications to the Interop assembly that tlbimp generates for your COM component to make it easy to use from a COM client. By making these modifications in a PIA, you save your customers the grief of having to make these modifications themselves.

Advanced Interop Marshaling Considerations

When you use a COM object from a managed client or a managed object from a COM/Win32 client, the CLR must perform marshaling. For the purposes of this discussion, marshaling is just converting the parameters from managed types on the client to unmanaged types in the object and vice versa. What I am talking about here is different than COM marshaling. As I discussed earlier, if your managed thread has entered an MTA and you are calling a single-threaded (STA) object, cross-apartment marshaling will be used. Similarly, interprocess marshaling will be used if you use an object that is implemented in an out-of-process server. This marshaling is independent of the managed-to-unmanaged code marshaling that I am talking about here. What I am talking about here is the marshaling that occurs when I cross the managed code to unmanaged code boundary as shown in Figure 7–9.

For most objects with simple parameter lists and return values, the Interop Marshaler in the CLR handles this marshaling automatically. So far, all of the COM objects that I have examined have had very simple marshaling requirements. None of the methods or properties in these objects returned arrays or user-defined types or took arrays of user-defined types as parameters. In this section, I discuss how Interop marshaling works when your parameter lists and return values aren't so simple.

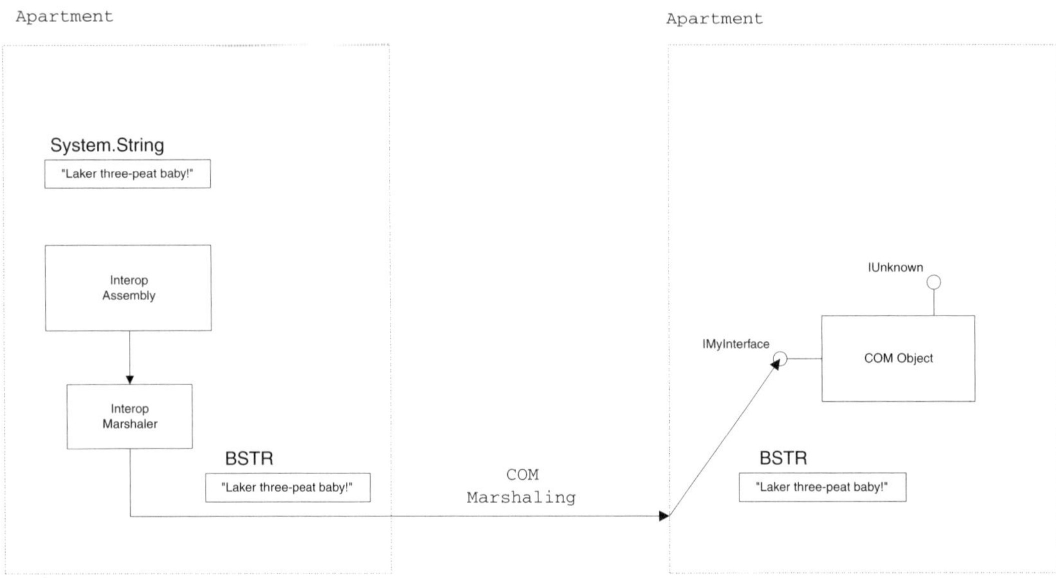

FIGURE 7–9 *Managed to unmanaged code marshaling.*

With most COM objects, a string is declared as a BSTR, but it may also be defined using one of several other string definitions, including a char *, an LPOLESTR, or a LPWSTR. In managed code, however, a string is always an instance of System.String. The Interop marshaler must be able to convert an instance of the managed type, System.String, to any of the unmanaged representations of a string. There are also times when the type library importer will effectively throw up its hands and decide that it cannot find a good managed type to map a parameter or return value of a COM object to. In these cases, you'll have to perform manual marshaling, that is, you will have to write the code to marshal parameters and return values from a managed type to an unmanaged type and vice versa. Arrays are another problem with COM Interop. Dealing with C-style arrays, which are usually expressed as a pointer to a type in unmanaged code, is especially difficult because it is hard for the Interop marshaler to tell if it is dealing with an array or a single instance. For instance, if I have a COM object whose IDL definition is as follows:

```
[id(3)] HRESULT Conformant1D([in] short arrlen,
     [in, size_is(arrlen)] short *arg);
```

It is difficult to tell whether the arg parameter is a pointer to a short or an array or an array of shorts. The size_is attribute actually does specify that the arg parameter is an array whose size is given by the first parameter arrlen.

However, this information is not present in a type library that I generate from this IDL code.

In the following subsections, I discuss the following aspects of interop marshaling: COM objects that use strings that are typed as something other than BSTR (for example, LPOLESTR) and arrays, including both safe arrays and c-style arrays. In the arrays section, I also discuss manual marshaling, that is, what to do when the interop marshaler throws up its hands and converts a parameter to a System.IntPtr in the Interop assembly.

String Parameters Other than BSTR

I decided to start this difficult section with the easiest subject to talk about: how the Interop Marshaler handles string parameters or return values that are expressed as something other than a BSTR. The transformation here is fairly simple. The type library importer will convert the parameter or return value to a System.String and use the MarshalAs attribute, which can be found in the System.Runtime.InteropServices namespace, to specify that the managed string should be converted to something other than a BSTR on the unmanaged side of the Interop boundary. Table 6–1 in Chapter 6 showed the default mapping of COM types to managed types. By default, the unmanaged equivalent of a System.String is a BSTR, but System.String can map to other unmanaged representations of a string. The Type Library Importer will use the MarshalAs attribute to specify which mapping should be used when a managed type can map to several unmanaged types as System.String does.

This is best illustrated with an example. Consider the following COM interface, which uses ANSI strings:

```
interface ISpellChecker : IUnknown
{
  HRESULT CheckSpelling([in,string] char *word,
          [out,retval] BOOL *isCorrect);
  HRESULT UseCustomDictionary(
          [in,string] char *filename);
}
```

This interface will convert to the following managed code equivalent:

```
public interface ISpellChecker
{
    public int32 CheckSpelling(
        [in] string  MarshalAs(lpstr) word);
    public void  UseCustomDictionary(
        [in] string  MarshalAs(lpstr) filename) ;
}
```

Notice the use of the MarshalAs attribute to convert the string to an lpstr. Now consider the following COM Interface, which uses wide character strings:

```
interface ISpellChecker : IUnknown
{
    HRESULT CheckSpelling([in] LPOLESTR word,
        [out,retval] VARIANT_BOOL *result);
    HRESULT UseCustomDictionary([in] LPOLESTR path);
};
```

This interface will map to the following managed code equivalent:

```
public interface ISpellChecker
{
    public bool CheckSpelling(
        [in] string  MarshalAs(lpwstr) word);
    public void  UseCustomDictionary(
        [in] string  MarshalAs(lpwstr) filename) ;
}
```

In this case the Interop assembly uses the MarshalAs attribute to convert the managed string to an lpwstr.

Arrays

I can guarantee that you won't be using COM Interop for very long before you will need to use a COM object that uses arrays in its interface. There are some difficulties associated with using Arrays, particularly c-style arrays, but, as long as you understand the concepts in this section, you won't have a problem.

SAFE ARRAYS

Safe arrays are a self-describing COM type that can be used to pass multidimensional arrays through a COM Interface. Safe arrays contain enough information for the receiver of the array to know exactly how many dimensions and elements there are in the array as well as the type of each element. The definition of the SafeArray data type looks as follows:

```
struct SAFEARRAY {
      WORD cDims;// The number of dimensions
      WORD fFeatures;    // A descriptive flag
      DWORD cbElements;// The size of each element in bytes
      DWORD cLocks;// A reference count for pvData
      void * pvData;// The data of the array
      [size_is(cDims)] SAFEARRAYBOUND rgsabound[];
}
```

The rgsabounds array contains an array of SAFEARRAYBOUND structures, which are defined as follows:

```
Struct SAFEARRAYBOUND {
       DWORD cElements; // The # of elements in this dimension
       LONG iLBound;    // The minimum index for this dimension
}
```

With C/C++, you can create and destroy safe arrays using the SafeArrayCreate and SafeArrayDestroy functions, respectively. You can access the individual elements in a SafeArray using the SafeArrayGetElement function. I won't go into a long discussion about how to use safe arrays. If you want to learn more about them, see the article entitled "The Safe OLE Way of Handling Arrays" in the Microsoft Developer Network (MSDN) libraries.

It's easy to create and use SafeArrays from VB. A dynamic array in VB is actually a SafeArray. To demonstrate safe arrays, I created a COM component that uses safe arrays in VB by creating an ActiveX DLL project and adding a class to the project with the following implementation:

```
Public Type udtEmployee
    ID As Integer
    Name As String
    Salary As Currency
End Type

Public Function TestSafeArrayOfStrings() As String()
//
// Implementation omitted…
//
End Function

Public Function TestSafeArrayOfIntegers() As Integer()
//
// Implementation omitted…
//
End Function

Public Function TestSafeArrayOfUDTs() As udtEmployee()
//
// Implementation omitted…
//
End Function

Public Sub TestSafeArrayAsParameter1(strs() As String)
//
// Implementation omitted…
//
End Sub

Public Sub TestSafeArrayAsParameter2(
```

```
Employees() As udtEmployee)
//
//  Implementation omitted...
End Sub
```

The first two methods, TestSafeArrayOfStrings and TestSafeArrayOfIntegers, return a safe array of strings and integers, respectively. The TestSafeArrayOfUDTs method returns a safe array of User-Defined Types (UDTs), and the fourth and fifth methods, TestSafeArrayAsParameter1 and TestSafeArrayAsParameter2, demonstrate methods that take a safe array of strings and UDTs as parameters, respectively. The IDL for this COM component is the following:

```
[
  uuid(9101979F-2B8C-4EA5-9FFC-DC588A07C6A9),
  version(5.0)
]
library TestProject
{
    [
      odl,
      uuid(D861E9BC-B4ED-47F0-926F-C6A4900BB5D5),
      version(1.0),
      hidden,
      dual,
      nonextensible,
      oleautomation
    ]
    interface _TestClass : IDispatch {
        [id(0x60030000)]
        HRESULT TestSafeArrayOfStrings(
            [out, retval] SAFEARRAY(BSTR)* );
        [id(0x60030001)]
        HRESULT TestSafeArrayOfIntegers(
            [out, retval] SAFEARRAY(short)* );
        [id(0x60030002)]
        HRESULT TestSafeArrayOfUDTs(
            [out, retval] SAFEARRAY(udtEmployee)* );
        [id(0x60030003)]
        HRESULT TestSafeArrayAsParameter1(
            [in, out] SAFEARRAY(BSTR)* strs);
        [id(0x60030004)]
        HRESULT TestSafeArrayAsParameter2(
            [in, out] SAFEARRAY(udtEmployee)* Employees);
    };

    [
      uuid(74A9A0C5-6589-4E41-9F0E-CF26DCDC0DC9),
      version(1.0)
    ]
```

```
    coclass TestClass {
        [default] interface _TestClass;
    };

    typedef [uuid(2063C9B0-4CC5-4271-BAE4-F56EC2EE0197),
          version(1.0)]
    struct tagudtEmployee {
        [helpstring("ID")]
        short ID;
        [helpstring("Name")]
        BSTR Name;
        [helpstring("Salary")]
        CURRENCY Salary;
    } udtEmployee;
};
```

I will use this COM component to demonstrate how the type library importer maps the SafeArrays in these methods to managed types. Before I show the mapping, I should mention that the tlbimp has two modes of operation, depending on whether you specify the sysarray parameter. If I run tlbimp on a COM server *without* using the sysarray argument, it will generate typed arrays in the Interop assembly for the SafeArray parameters and return values. If I use the sysarray parameter on tlbimp as follows:

```
tlbimp testproject.dll /sysarray
```

Then the Type Library Importer will convert the SafeArrays to instances of a class called **System.Array**. The **System.Array** class is the base class for all managed code arrays. For instance, the TestSafeArrayOfStrings method, which has the following definition in IDL:

```
[id(0x60030000)] HRESULT TestSafeArrayOfStrings(
       [out, retval] SAFEARRAY(BSTR)* );
```

will generate the following managed equivalent in the Interop assembly if I do *not* use the /sysarray parameter to tlbimp:

```
string[] [MarshalAs( safearray bstr)]
    TestSafeArrayOfStrings() { }
```

Notice that the return type is an array of System.Strings. You can call this code from a C# client using the following code:

```
int i;
string strName;
TestClass myClass = new TestClass();
string[] arr=myClass.TestSafeArrayOfStrings();
for (i=0;i<arr.Length;i++)
        strName=arr[i];
```

If I use the /sysarray parameter, tlbimp will generate the following managed code equivalent:

```
System.Array [MarshalAs( safearray bstr)]
    TestSafeArrayOfStrings() { }
```

This time the method returns an instance of System.Array. I can call this version of the method from a client as follows:

```
int i;
string strName;
TestClass myClass = new TestClass();
System.Array arr=myClass.TestSafeArrayOfStrings();
for (i=0;i<arr.Length;i++)
        strName=(string)arr.GetValue(i);
```

The client code is almost the same except that I have to cast the elements in the array to a string because the elements of System.Array are typed to System.Object. If you use Visual Studio .NET to generate the Interop assembly for a COM server by selecting the COM server from the COM tab of the Add Reference... dialog in the IDE, it will run the Type Library Importer with the /sysarray parameter. Therefore, if you want the default behavior, you will need to run the tlbimp manually and then reference the resulting Interop assembly using the .NET tab of the Add Reference... dialog.

Let's look at the other methods in the example SafeArray COM server. The TestSafeArrayOfIntegers method, which has the following IDL definition:

```
[id(0x60030001)] HRESULT TestSafeArrayOfIntegers(
      [out, retval] SAFEARRAY(short)* );
```

will generate the following managed code equivalent if you do not specify /sysarray:

```
int16[] [MarshalAs(safearray int16)]
        TestSafeArrayOfIntegers() { }
```

You can call this method from a managed code client using the following code:

```
int i;
short shtValue;
TestClass myClass = new TestClass();
short[] arr=myClass.TestSafeArrayOfIntegers();
for (i=0;i<arr.Length;i++)
        shtValue=arr[i];
```

If you use the /sysarray parameter, tlbimp will generate the following managed code equivalent for the TestSafeArrayOfIntegers method:

```
System.Array [MarshalAs(safearray int16)]
      TestSafeArrayOfIntegers() { }
```

You can call this method from a C# client using the following code:

```
int i;
short shtValue;
TestClass myClass = new TestClass();
System.Array arr=myClass.TestSafeArrayOfIntegers();
for (i=0;i<arr.Length;i++)
        shtValue=(short)arr.GetValue(i);
```

The TestSafeArrayOfUDTs is a little different than the first two methods because it returns a SafeArray of UDTs. In this case, the UDT is called udtEmployee. The IDL definition of this type is shown here:

```
typedef [uuid(2063C9B0-4CC5-4271-BAE4-F56EC2EE0197)]
struct tagudtEmployee {
    [helpstring("ID")] short ID;
    [helpstring("Name")] BSTR Name;
    [helpstring("Salary")] CURRENCY Salary;
} udtEmployee;
```

The IDL for the TestSafeArrayOfUDTs method itself is shown here:

```
[id(0x60030002)] HRESULT TestSafeArrayOfUDTs(
      [out, retval] SAFEARRAY(udtEmployee)* );
```

This method will generate the following managed code equivalent if you do not specify /sysarray when you run tlbimp:

```
testproject.udtEmployee[] [MarshalAs(safearray record)]
        TestSafeArrayOfUDTs () { }
```

The Employee UDT becomes a value type with the same name in the Interop assembly and the TestSafeArrayofUDTs method returns an array of these value types. You can call this method using the example code shown here:

```
int i;
string strName;
TestClass myClass = new TestClass();
udtEmployee[] arr=myClass.TestSafeArrayOfUDTs();
for (i=0;i<arr.Length;i++)
      strName=arr[i].Name;
```

If you do use the /sysarray parameter, the managed code equivalent of the TestSafeArrayofUDTs method will have the following prototype:

```
System.Array [MarshalAs(safearray record)]
        TestSafeArrayOfUDTs () { }
```

You can call this version of the method using the following code:

```
int i;
string strName;
```

```
udtEmployee emp;
TestClass myClass = new TestClass();
System.Array arr=myClass.TestSafeArrayOfUDTs();
for (i=0;i<arr.Length;i++)
{
      emp=(udtEmployee)arr.GetValue(i);
      strName=emp.Name;
}
```

In this case, the managed version of the method returns a System.Array that contains instances of the udtEmployee value type.

I'll next look at the TestSafeArrayAsParameter1 method; this method is declared as follows in the IDL for the COM object.

```
[id(0x60030003)] HRESULT TestSafeArrayAsParameter1(
      [in, out] SAFEARRAY(BSTR)* strs);
```

The parameter for this method is an array of strings, and it is a by-reference parameter, that is, the method accepts the parameter as input from its caller. However, it may also alter the array, and the client will see the method's updates. This is as opposed to a by-value parameter, which will have the IDL [in] attribute only, and any changes that the method makes to the parameter will be invisible to the client. Array parameters can only be by-reference in VB. If you attempt to create a by-value array parameter, you will receive the following compiler error:

```
Array argument must be ByRef
```

If I do *not* use the /sysarray parameter, the managed code equivalent of this method is as follows:

```
void  TestSafeArrayAsParameter1(
      [ref] string[] [MarshalAs(safearray bstr)] strs);
```

In this case, the parameter is declared in C# as a reference ([ref]) parameter; this is the way you declare in/out parameters in C#. You can call this version of the TestSafeArrayAsParameter1 method using the following code:

```
int i;
string strValue;
TestClass myClass = new TestClass();
string[] myStrs=new String[3];
myStrs[0]="Whatever";
myStrs[1]="It";
myStrs[2]="Takes";
myClass.TestSafeArrayAsParameter1(ref myStrs);
```

If the TestSafeArrayAsParameter1 method changed the contents of the array that was passed in, its caller will see the changes. If you use the /sysarray parameter, the Type Library Importer will generate the following managed code equivalent for the method.

```
void TestSafeArrayAsParameter1(
[ref] System.Array [MarshalAs(safearray bstr)] strs) { }
```

The final method is the TestSafeArrayAsParameter2 method, which is similar to TestSafeArrayAsParameter1 except it takes a SafeArray of udtEmployee objects instead of strings. If I do *not* use the /sysarray parameter, the managed code equivalent of this method is as follows:

```
void TestSafeArrayAsParameter2([ref] valuetype
testproject.udtEmployee[]
        [MarshalAs( safearray record)] Employees)  {  }
```

In this case, it converts the SafeArray of UDTs to an array of equivalent value types. The MarshalAs attribute will convert the array to a SafeArray of Records, which is how you represent a Safe Array of user-defined types. You can call this method from a C# client as follows:

```
int i;
string strName;
udtEmployee emp;
TestClass myClass = new TestClass();
udtEmployee[] empList=new udtEmployee[2];
empList[0].ID=10;
empList[0].Name="Alan Gordon";
empList[0].Salary=45;
empList[1].ID=20;
empList[1].Name="Bria Gordon";
empList[1].Salary=60;
myClass.TestSafeArrayAsParameter2(ref empList);
```

If I use the /sysarray parameter, the managed code equivalent of this method will be as follows:

```
void  TestSafeArrayAsParameter2(
[ref] System.Array
[MarshalAs(safearray record,"testproject.udtEmployee")]
Employees)  { }
```

Notice that tlbimp converts the parameter to an instance of System.Array, and, once again, the MarshalAs attribute specifies that the array should be converted to a SafeArray of udtEmployee instances. You can call this method from a C# client as follows:

```
int i;
string strName;
udtEmployee emp;
TestClass myClass = new TestClass();
udtEmployee[] empList=new udtEmployee[2];
```

```
empList[0].ID=10;
empList[0].Name="Alan Gordon";
empList[0].Salary=45;
empList[1].ID=20;
empList[1].Name="Bria Gordon";
empList[1].Salary=60;
System.Array arr=empList;
myClass.TestSafeArrayAsParameter2(ref arr);
```

C-STYLE ARRAYS

As I mentioned earlier, SafeArrays are easy to use from VB, so they are the preferred way to pass arrays across a COM Interface that is implemented in Visual Basic or will be called from a VB client. If you are implementing a COM object in C++ and the object will only be called from C++ clients, SafeArrays are cumbersome to work with. Fortunately, IDL supports the capability to use C-style arrays. These arrays are much easier to work with if both the COM client and server are implemented in C++. There are three types of C-style arrays: (1) fixed arrays, (2) conformant arrays, and (3) varying arrays. To illustrate the concepts in this section, I created another COM server using Visual C++ and ATL. The IDL for this server is the following:

```
import "oaidl.idl";
import "ocidl.idl";
[
object,
uuid(1A39EB1D-862F-4109-9E13-C6C8301F337A),
dual
]
interface ICStyleArrayTest : IDispatch
{
    [id(1)] HRESULT TestFixed(
    [in]  short  arg1[5], [in] short arg2[5][5]);
    [id(2)] HRESULT TestVarying1D(
        [in] short start,[in] short length,
        [in, first_is(start),length_is(length)]
        short arg[5]);
    [id(3)] HRESULT Conformant1D([in] short length,
        [in, size_is(length)] short *arg);
    [id(4)] HRESULT Conformant2D([in] short rows,
        [in] short columns,
        [in, size_is(rows,columns)] short **arg);
    [id(5)] HRESULT EmployeeTest1([in] short numEmps,
        [in,size_is(numEmps)] Employee *employees);
    [id(6)] HRESULT EmployeeTest2([in,out] short *numEmps,
        [out] Employee **employees);
};

[
    uuid(308E9B90-59E2-4D53-A56F-9E3BF40AF173),
```

```
    version(1.0)
]
library CSTYLEARRAYPROJECTLib
{
importlib("stdole32.tlb");
importlib("stdole2.tlb");
[
    uuid(ABD60198-74F7-4955-AC38-016F8ADA2D82)
]
coclass CStyleArrayTest
{
    [default] interface ICStyleArrayTest;
};
};
```

FIXED ARRAYS • The following IDL code shows an example of a method that takes a fixed array as a parameter:

```
[id(1)] HRESULT TestFixed([in]  short  arg1[5], [in] short
arg2[5][5]);
```

The managed code equivalent of this method looks as follows:

```
void TestFixed([in] int16[]  MarshalAs([5]) arg1,
                [in] int16[]  MarshalAs([25]) arg2);
```

In the managed code version of the method, the second argument, which is a 5×5 2D array, is converted to a 25 element, one-dimensional (1D) array in row-major order. The Interop Marshaler is not currently able to support fixed-length arrays with more than one dimension, so it flattens the 2D array into a 1D array. The following code shows how you would call the TestFixed method from managed code:

```
private void button3_Click(object sender,
   System.EventArgs e)
{
   short i, j, numRows, numCols;
   numRows=5;
   numCols=5;
   short[] arg1=new short[5];
   short[] arg2=new short[numRows*numCols];
   for (i=0;i<5;i++)
       arg1[i]=(short)(5*i);
   for (i=0;i<numRows;i++)
       for (j=0;j<numCols;j++)
       arg2[i* numCols+j]=(short)(2*i + 3*j);
   CStyleArrayTest obj=new CStyleArrayTest();
   obj.TestFixed(arg1,arg2);
}
```

On line 4, I declare several variables. On lines 5 through 8, I initialize the variables that store the number of rows and columns for the 2D arrays, and I also initialize the arrays that I will pass to the TestFixed method. On lines 9 and 10, I initialize the 1D array, and, on lines 11 through 13, I initialize the 2D array. On line 14, I create an instance of CStyleArrayTest, and, on line 15, I call the TestFixed method. Fixed arrays are by far the easiest c-style arrays to use. Let's look at conformant arrays, which are a little more difficult to work with from managed code.

CONFORMANT ARRAYS • A conformant array is one where the size of the array is specified at runtime. The following IDL code shows an example of a method that takes a 1D conformant array as its second parameter:

```
[id(3)] HRESULT Conformant1D([in] short arrlen,
      [in, size_is(arrlen)] short *arg);
```

Notice that I use the size_is attribute to specify that the size of the array is passed in the first parameter. The managed code equivalent of this method is shown here:

```
void  Conformant1D(int16 length,ref int16 arg);
```

You can see that the managed code version of the method is just plain wrong. The second parameter is not typed as an array, but is typed as a by-reference (ref) argument to a single, short instance. This will only work for a single-element array.

If you dig a little deeper, you can see that the tlbimp is not at fault. The real problem is the COM type library. Take a look at the definition of the Conformant1D method as it appears in the COM object's type library.

```
[id(0x00000003)] HRESULT Conformant1D(
      [in] short arrlen,[in] short* arg);
```

Notice that all of the size information for the second argument is lost. Because the Type Library Importer uses the type library as its input, it has no way of knowing if the second parameter is a pointer to a single instance (for example, a by-reference argument) or if it represents an array. Furthermore, the connection between the first and second parameter—that the first parameter specifies the length of the array that is passed in the second parameter—is also lost. The managed code declaration of the Conformant1D method in the Interop Assembly is only useful if you are passing an array that contains a single element. The only solution to this problem is to edit the method signature in the Interop assembly manually. The process for doing this is shown in Figure 7–10.

You start by using ILDASM to save the IL code for your Interop assembler into a text file. You then edit the code using your favorite text editor. You then reassemble the code back into an assembly—with the same name—

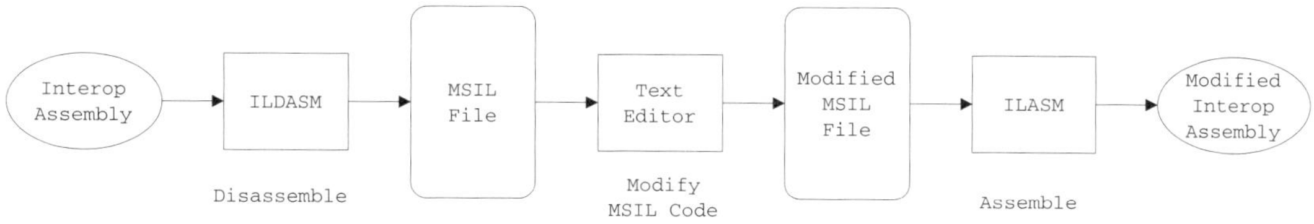

FIGURE 7–10 *The process for manually editing an Interop assembly.*

using the IL Assembler (ILASM). Both of these IL tools ship with the .NET Framework SDK.

Let's follow this example through and actually alter the Interop assembly so that the Conformant1D method will work properly. Earlier I created a COM object that contains all of the methods that I've talked about so far: Conformant1D, TestFixed, and so forth. I created an Interop assembly for this COM server by running the following command:

```
tlbimp cstylearrayproject.dll /out:dotnetcstylearray.dll
```

Note When I ran this command, the tlbimp generated several warnings with a message similar to the following: "Tlbimp warning: At least one of the arguments for '[MethodName]' can not be marshaled by the runtime marshaler. Such arguments will therefore be passed as a pointer and may require unsafe code to manipulate". Where "[MethodName]" is the name of a method in the type library. Whenever you run tlbimp and it encounters a parameter that it cannot convert to a managed code equivalent, it throws up its hands and converts it to a native pointer. A native pointer is an instance of System.IntPtr. System.IntPtr is a platform-specific type that is used to hold pointers and handles. The size of a System.IntPtr is the size of a memory address on the platform, that is, 32 bits on a 32-bit platform and 64 bits on a 64-bit platform. You then have to write your own code to marshal native pointer parameters correctly. I will show you how to do this shortly.

If you want to alter the generated Interop assembly, you will first need to open the assembly in ILDASM by running the following command:

```
ildasm dotnetcstylearray.dll
```

You can then save the MSIL code for the Interop assembly by performing the following steps:

1. Select File | Dump.
2. Accept the default Dump options by clicking OK. A File | SaveAs dialog will appear.
3. Select the location where you want to save the file to.
4. Click the Save button.

For this example, save the MSIL code to a file called **cstyleproject.il**. Now, find the Conformant1D method in the MSIL code; it should look like the following:

```
instance void  Conformant1D([in] int16 length,
                            [in] int16& arg)
```

Change this definition to look as follows:

```
instance void  Conformant1D([in] int16 length,
                        [in] int16[] marshal([+0]) arg)
```

Here I am using the marshal attribute with square brackets "[]" to specify that the second parameter is actually an array.

Note The marshal attribute in MSIL maps to the MarshalAs attribute in C#.

You can use the marshal attribute in two ways: (1) You can specify a fixed number of elements that the array will contain (tlbimp used this form of the marshal attribute for the TestFixed method), and (2) you can specify the zero-based index (reading from left to right) of the parameter that contains the size of the array. This is called a parameter index, and it is what I just used for the Conformat1D method. To specify a parameter index, you must preceed the index value with a "+" symbol. In this case, I specified that the length of the second parameter is contained in the first parameter.

You will need to alter the MSIL code in two places. First there is the Conformant1D method declaration in the ICStyleArrayTest interface and then there is the implementation of the method in the CStyleArrayTestClass class. Make sure that you save the MSIL file with the updated definition of the Conformant1D method. You can now recompile the MSIL using the MSIL Assembler by issuing the following command:

```
ilasm /OUT=dotnetcstylearray.dll cstyleproject.il /DLL
```

The assembly called **dotnetcstylearray.dll** will now contain the updated definition of the Interop assembly. Make sure you give this assembly the same name as the original assembly that it was built from. If you are not sure what this name should be, you can find it in the IL by looking for the assembly declaration near the top of the IL file.

```
.assembly dotnetcstylearray
{
   ...
}
```

You can now create a C# client, reference the new version of the assembly, and call the Conformant1D method using the following code:

```
private void btn1_Click(object sender, System.EventArgs e)
{
      CStyleArrayTest obj=new CStyleArrayTest();
      short[] arr=new short[5];
      short i;
      for (i=0;i<5;i++)
        arr[i]=i;
      obj.Conformant1D(5,arr);
}
```

Unfortunately, the modification that I made to the Conformant1D method will not work if the array parameter is an in/out argument, that is, an argument that the COM method may change and you want the managed client to see the changes. The following IDL code shows a version of the Conformant1D method where the second parameter is in/out:

```
[id(3)] HRESULT Conformant1D([in,out] short *length,
      [in, out, size_is(*length)] short **arg)
```

Notice that the second parameter is declared as a pointer to a pointer. If you run the type library importer on a type library that contains this updated version of the Conformant1D method, you get the following managed code equivalent in MSIL:

```
instance void  Conformant1D([in][out] int16& length,
                            [in][out] native int arg)
```

The C# equivalent of this managed code looks as follows:.

```
void Conformant1D(ref short length,
                  System.IntPtr arg);
```

Notice that the second parameter to the Conformant1D method is now a native pointer (System.IntPtr). A native pointer is a platform-specific type that is used to hold pointers to unmanaged memory and handles. The size of a native pointer is the size of a memory address on the platform, that is, 32 bits on a 32-bit platform or 64 bits on a 64-bit platform. The type library importer will convert a parameter or return value to a System.IntPtr whenever it is unable to figure out how to marshal the parameter or return value to a managed type. This is effectively the type library importer's way of saying: "I don't know what to do with this, you figure it out!" You will have to marshal the parameter or return value manually. Fortunately, the System.Runtime.InteropServices.Marshal class contains all the tools you need to marshal managed types to unmanaged types and vice versa. Before we can implement managed marshaling we have to fix a problem with the interop assembly however.

The problem is that the second parameter is declared as a pointer to a pointer in the original IDL code. The Type Library Importer has no way of knowing if the parameter is supposed to be a 2D array or a by-reference 1D array. Therefore, if it sees a pointer with more than onc level of indirection (short **arg), it converts it to a native pointer. It's up to you to know whether the parameter is a 2D array or a by-reference 1D array.

In this case, because you know that the parameter is a by-reference 1D array, you should convert the second parameter to a by-reference argument by adding an ampersand "&" to its MSIL declaration as follows:

```
instance void  Conformant1D([in][out] int16& length,
                            [in][out] native int& arg)
```

To make this change, you must follow the same steps that you performed earlier:

1. Load the assembly into ILDASM.
2. Select File | Dump to save the MSIL file.
3. Modify the Conformant1D method.
4. Compile the MSIL file into the assembly using ILASM.

The C# version of this method will now look as follows in the interop assembly:

```
void Conformant1D(ref short length,
                  ref System.IntPtr arg);
```

Notice that the native int second parameter is now passed by-reference. You will still have to manually marshal this parameter from an array of shorts (System.Int16) on the managed side to a physical pointer to an array of shorts on the unmanaged side. Because a managed array of shorts is a "blittable" type (see the sidebar on "blittable" types in this section), there are 2 ways that you can do this manual marshaling. The first way is to "pin" the managed array in memory and then obtain the physical address of the array and pass it to the Conformant1D method. When you "pin" a managed object in memory you prevent the garbage collector from changing the physical memory address of the object so it is safe to pass the address directly to an umanaged method that expects a pointer. This approach has the highest performance, because you don't have to copy any data from managed to unmanaged buffers, but it will only work if the managed array contains "blittable" types. The second approach is to allocate an unmanaged buffer and then copy the contents of the managed array into the unmanaged buffer. You can then pass the address of this unmanaged buffer in the second parameter to the Conformant1D method. This approach will always work regardless of the type of the managed data that you are passing to the method but it is slower.

Blittable Types

A type is blittable if it has a common representation in both managed and unmanaged memory. When it is doing the marshaling for you, the Interop Marshaler will pin instances of blittable types and pass the address directly to unmanaged methods instead of copying the type to unmanaged memory; this improves performance. You should take the same approach when you are forced to implement manual marshaling. A list of blittable types is shown below.

- System.Byte
- System.SByte
- System.Int16
- System.UInt16
- System.Int32
- System.UInt32
- System.Int64
- System.IntPtr
- System.UintPtr
- A value type that contains fields of blittable types
- A one dimensional array of blittable types

The array of shorts (System.Int16) that I pass as the second parameter to the Conformant1D method is blittable. The second parameter to this version of the Conformant1D method is also an in/out parameter. Therefore, it will populate data in the array on return and it may even allocate a new buffer for the array and re-dimension it. You also have 2 choices as to how to marshal the output of the Conformant1D method. Your first choice is to use the methods in the System.Runtime.InteropServices.Marshal class to read the elements directly from the unmanaged array. Your second choice is to copy the data in the unmanaged buffer to a managed array.

Let's look at some managed code that calls the Conformant1D method. Since the second parameter to this method is blittable, let's look at pinning the object first.

```
private void button1_Click(object sender,
      System.EventArgs e)
{
      short i, arrayLength, result;
      short[] arr=new short[5];
      GCHandle handle=
        GCHandle.Alloc(arr,GCHandleType.Pinned);
      IntPtr ptr=handle.AddrOfPinnedObject();
      try
      {
           arrayLength=5;
           for (i=0;i<5;i++)
               arr[i]=i;
```

```
14.             CStyleArrayTest obj=new CStyleArrayTest();
15.             obj.Conformant1D(ref arrayLength,ref ptr);
16.             int sz=Marshal.SizeOf(typeof(System.Int16));
17.             for (i=0;i<arrayLength;i++)
18.             result=Marshal.ReadInt16(ptr,i*sz);
19.         }
20.         finally
21.         {
22.           if (handle.IsAllocated)
23.             handle.Free();
24.         }
25. }
```

On lines 1 through 5 I have some pretty standard variable declarations. On line 5 I declare an array of 5 shorts (System.Int16); this is the variable that I will pass as the second parameter to the Conformant1D method. On lines 6 and 7 I declare and initialize an instance of the System.Runtime.InteropServices.GCHandle type. The GCHandle type, which is declared a value-type structure, is used to access a managed object from unmanaged memory. In this case, I initialize the GCHandle instance to provide unmanaged access to the managed array of shorts that I declared on line 5. Notice that the array is the first parameter to the GCHandle.Alloc method. The second parameter to this method indicates that I wish to "pin" the array in memory, which will prevent the garbage collector from changing the physical address of this variable if a garbage collection occurs. On line 8 I call the AddrOfPinnedObject method on the GCHandle object to get the physical address of the managed array. This value is stored in an IntPtr instance called ptr. On lines 11 through 13 I populate the managed array. On line 14 I create a CstyleArrayTest object and on line 15 I call the Conformant1D method on this object passing in the IntPtr variable that contains the address of the managed array as the second parameter. On line 16 I get the size of each element in the managed array, which is 2 bytes for a short, and then on lines 17 and 18 I use the ReadInt16 method on the System.Runtime.InteropServices.Marshal class to read the elements of the unmanaged array that the Conformant1D method returned. The first parameter to the ReadInt16 method is a pointer to the beginning of the unmanaged buffer. The second parameter is an offset that is added to the first parameter before reading.

Note The Marshal class contains a series of methods for reading data from an unmanaged buffer. In addition to the ReadInt16 method, there are also ReadByte, ReadInt32, ReadInt64, and ReadIntPtr methods. The Marshal class also contains a set of matching methods for writing to an unmanaged buffer. These methods have the name WriteByte, WriteInt16, etc.

Finally, on lines 22 and 23 I free the memory handle. Notice that I put this logic in a "finally" clause so that this code will run regardless of whether an exception was thrown.

Now lets look at code that calls the Conformant1D method by copying the managed, input array to an unmanaged buffer. This approach will work even with non-blittable types.

```
1.  private void button1_Click(object sender,
2.       System.EventArgs e)
3.  {
4.       short i, arrayLength, rslt;
5.       short[] arr=new short[5];
6.       IntPtr ptr=IntPtr.Zero;
7.       try
8.       {
9.         arrayLength=5;
10.        for (i=0;i<5;i++)
11.          arr[i]=i;
12.        ptr=Marshal.AllocCoTaskMem(
13.          Marshal.SizeOf(Type.GetType(
14.          "System.Int16"))*arrayLength);
15.        Marshal.Copy(arr,0,ptr,arrayLength);
16.        CStyleArrayTest obj=new CStyleArrayTest();
17.        obj.Conformant1D(ref arrayLength,ref ptr);
18.        arr=new short[arrayLength];
19.        Marshal.Copy(ptr,arr,0,arrayLength);
20.        for (i=0;i<5;i++)
21.          rslt=arr[i];
22.      }
23.      finally
24.      {
25.        Marshal.FreeCoTaskMem(ptr);
26.      }
27. }
```

Lines 4 through 6 contain variable declarations. Notice the declaration of a managed array called arr on line 5 and the declaration of a native pointer (System.IntPtr) called ptr on line 6. On line 10 and 11, I populate the array that I declared on line 5. On lines 12 through 14, I call the AllocCoTaskMem method on the **System.Runtime.InteropServices.Marshal** class to allocate unmanaged memory for the native pointer that I declared on line 6. The AllocCoTaskMem method is just a wrapper on the CoTaskMemAlloc method in the COM API. On line 15, I call the Copy method on the **System.Runtime.InteropServices.Marshal** class to copy the contents of the managed array to the unmanaged memory block that the native pointer references.

There are two sets of Copy methods in the **System.Runtime.InteropServices.Marshal** class for a total of 14 methods in all. Seven methods copy data from a managed array to an unmanaged memory buffer. These methods are declared as follows:

```
public static void Copy(short[] src,int startIndex,
      IntPtr dest,int length);
```

The only difference between these methods is the type of the source managed array. There are versions of this method that take byte, char, short (System.Int16), int (System.Int32), long (System.Int64), float (System.Single), and double (System.Double). The other seven Copy methods allow you to perform the reverse operation, that is, to copy from an unmanaged memory buffer to a managed array of any of the aforementioned types. An example of one of these methods is as follows:

```
public static void Copy(IntPtr src,short[] dest,
      int startIndex,int length);
```

On line 16 of the source code example, I instantiate a CstyleArrayTest object, and then, on line 17, I call the Conformat1D method passing in the ArrayLength variable that holds the size of the array and the ptr variable that holds the native pointer. Remember that the second argument is a in/out or ref parameter, and the Conformant1D method may change the size and contents of the array and pass the result back to its caller in the second parameter. On lines 18 and 19, I show how to marshal the modified array from the COM component back into a managed array on the client. On line 18, I allocate a new managed array using the arrayLength that is returned from the Conformant1D method. Remember that if the Conformant1D changes the size of the array, it is responsible for deallocating the memory for the unmanaged array that was passed in and allocating a new, unmanaged buffer for the re-dimensioned array. On line 19 I copy the contents of the ptr native pointer that is returned as an output parameter from the Conformant1D method to the managed array that I initialized on line 18. Keep in mind that I didn't have to copy the unmanaged data to an managed buffer. I could have used the ReadInt16 to read directly from the unmanaged buffer as I did previously. I only used this approach here for pedagogical reasons to demonstrate both ways of reading unmanaged memory. On lines 20 and 21, I loop through the contents of the array to verify that the contents were copied correctly; this code is obviously not strictly necessary. Finally, on line 25, I free the unmanaged buffer that was returned from the Conformant1D method using the FreeCoTaskMem on the **System.Runtime.InteropServices** class. The FreeCoTaskMem method maps to the CoTaskMemFree method in the COM API.

Let's now look at how a COM method with a 2D conformant array parameter gets mapped to managed code. The following IDL code shows an example of a method that takes a 2D conformant array as an input parameter:

```
[id(4)] HRESULT Conformant2D([in] short rows,
[in] short columns,
[in, size_is(rows,columns)] short **arg);
```

We specify the number of rows and columns in the array using the size_is parameters. The values passed to the size_is are specified in the first and second parameters of the method. Notice that the third parameter is a pointer to a pointer, which is the same as the by-reference 1D array. The following code shows the managed code equivalent of the Conformant2D method in MSIL code:

```
instance void  Conformant2D([in] int16 rows,
     [in] int16 columns,
     [in] native int arg)
```

Here is the same code in C#:

```
void  Conformant2D(short rows,
     short columns,
     System.IntPtr arg)
```

As I mentioned earlier, the Type Library Importer will always convert any pointers with two or more levels of indirection into a native pointer. The only difference between the way that this function works and the Conformant1D method is the way that you handle the third parameter. Notice that the array parameter in this method also gets converted into an IntPtr.

The .NET Framework SDK documentation says that, if you edit the IDL definition of your object to look as follows:

```
instance void  Conformant2D([in] int16 rows,
     [in] int16 columns,
     [in] int16[,] marshal([]) arg)
```

You should be able to pass a 2D managed array directly to the method as shown here.

```
private void button2_Click(object sender,System.EventArgs
e)
{
      short i, j, numRows, numCols;
      numRows=5;
      numCols=5;
      short[,] arr=new short[numRows,numCols];
      for (i=0;i<numRows;i++)
      for (j=0;j<numCols;j++)
        arr[i,j]=(short)(2*i + 3*j);
      CStyleArrayTest obj=new CStyleArrayTest();
      obj.Conformant2D(numRows,numCols,arr);
}
```

I was able to compile the Interop assembly with the altered definition, but, when I tried to call the Conformant2D method, I would always receive the following runtime error:

```
"Object reference not set to an instance of an object"
```

The error occurs when the COM object tried to access the array that the managed client passes to it, so I abandoned this approach. Using the original

Interop assembly generated by tlbimp, I was able to pass a 1D equivalent of a 2D array to the Conformant2D method using the logic shown here:

```
1.  private void button2_Click(object sender,
2.        System.EventArgs e)
3.  {
4.        short i, j, numRows, numCols;
5.        IntPtr ptr,ptr2ptr, ptrIter, ptr2ptrIter;
6.        numRows=5;
7.        numCols=5;
8.        short[] arr=new short[numRows*numCols];
9.        for (i=0;i<numRows;i++)
10.         for (j=0;j<numCols;j++)
11.             arr[i*numCols+j]=(short)(2*i+3*j);
12.       ptr2ptr=Marshal.AllocCoTaskMem(
13.         Marshal.SizeOf(
14.         Type.GetType("System.IntPtr"))*numRows);
15.       ptr=Marshal.AllocCoTaskMem(
16.         Marshal.SizeOf(
17.         Type.GetType("System.Int16"))*numCols*numRows);
18.       Marshal.Copy(arr,0,ptr,numRows*numCols);
19.       ptr2ptrIter=ptr2ptr;
20.       ptrIter=ptr;
21.       for (i=0;i<numRows;i++)
22.       {
23.         Marshal.StructureToPtr(
24.           ptrIter,ptr2ptrIter,false);
25.         ptr2ptrIter=(IntPtr)(
26.            (int)ptr2ptrIter+System.IntPtr.Size);
27.         ptrIter=(IntPtr)(
28.            (int)ptrIter+Marshal.SizeOf(
29.              Type.GetType("System.Int16"))*numCols);
30.       }
31.       CStyleArrayTest obj=new CStyleArrayTest();
32.       obj.Conformant2D(numRows,numCols,ptr2ptr);
33.       Marshal.FreeCoTaskMem(ptr2ptr);
34.       Marshal.FreeCoTaskMem(ptr);
35. }
```

Essentially, what I am doing here is converting a 1D managed array to the memory layout of a C/C++ 2D array. On lines 4 and 5, I declare variables. On lines 6 and 7, I initialize the variables that contain the number of rows and columns of the array. On line 8, I declare and initialize the 1D managed array that will be the managed equivalent of the 2D unmanaged array that I will pass to the COM object. On lines 9 through 11, I initialize the contents of the array. Notice how I use the expression i*numCols+j to index the array in row-major order. 2D arrays in C and C++ are arranged as an array of pointers to pointers with a length equal to the number of rows. Each element in the row array points to an array whose length equal to the number of columns. On lines 12 through 14, I allocate unmanaged memory for the row array of pointers to pointers. The elements of this array are native pointers, that is, System.IntPtr instances. On lines 15 through 17, I allocate unmanaged memory for all the data in the array. The size of this buffer is the number of rows times the number of columns times the size of each element, which is 2 bytes for a short. Rather than allocate a separate buffer for each row, I instead allocated a single buffer, and I'll point the pointers in the row array to the memory location that corresponds to the beginning of each row. On line 18, I copy the entire contents of the 1D managed array to the unmanaged buffer. All I need to do now is to point the row array of pointers to pointers at the right locations within this buffer. On lines 19 and 20, I initialize the variables that I will use to loop through the row and data buffers. On lines 21 through 30, I loop for each row and store the address of the beginning of each row into the elements of the row array of pointers to pointers. I use a method of the **Marshal** class called StructureToPtr to get these addresses. The StructureToPtr method has the following declaration in C#:

```
public static void StructureToPtr(object structure,
      IntPtr ptr,bool fDeleteOld);
```

This method is usually used to copy a structure to an unmanaged buffer. The first parameter is the structure, and the second parameter is a pointer to the unmanaged buffer. The third parameter is a Boolean that allows you to specify whether the StructureToPtr method should call the DestroyStructure method on the ptr variable before it sets its value equal to the contents of the structure that is passed in the first parameter. In this case, the structure is an instance of **System.IntPtr**. When you call the StructureToPtr method and pass in a **System.IntPtr**, you are assigning the pointer in the second parameter to the address contained in the first parameter, that is, you are essentially adding a level of indirection or creating a pointer to a pointer. On lines 25 through 29, I increment the row array pointer and the data array pointer so that I can set up the next row. You cannot perform pointer arithmetic directly on an instance of **System.IntPtr**, but the **System.IntPtr** class does support a type conversion to **System.Int**. Therefore, if you want to perform pointer arithmetic, you can cast the **System.IntPtr** to a **System.Int**, perform your arithmetic, and then cast the result back to a **System.IntPtr**. This is exactly what I did on lines 25 through 29. On line 31, I create an instance of the **CStyleArrayTest** class, and then, on line 32, I call the Conformant2D method passing in a **System.IntPtr** instance that points to the beginning of the row array of pointers to pointers. On lines 33 and 34, I free the memory allocated to these two buffers.

The last thing that I will look at before I leave the difficult subject of marshaling c-style arrays is marshaling an array of user-defined structures. Let's look at the EmployeeTest1 method in the COM object, which has the following IDL definition:

```
[id(5)] HRESULT EmployeeTest1([in] short numEmps,
[in,size_is(numEmps)] Employee *employees);
```

The second parameter to this method is an array of Employee structures. The Employee structure is defined in IDL as follows:

```
typedef struct tagEmployee {
      SHORT ID;
      BSTR Name;
      CURRENCY Salary;
} Employee;
```

The tlbimp will convert the Employee structure into a Value type called tagEmployee. The tlbimp will also generate the managed code equivalent of the EmployeeTest1 method shown here in MSIL:

```
instance void  EmployeeTest1([in] int16 numEmps,
      [in] valuetype
dotnetcstylearraynew.tagEmployee& employees)
```

This version of EmployeeTest1 has the same problem as the Conformant1D method earlier. The tlbimp cannot tell if the second parameter is a pointer to a single instance or an error, so it generates a managed code equivalent that assumes the parameter is a pointer to a single instance. As I did with the Conformant1D method, I have to change the definition of the method so that it is treated as an array. I need to follow the same procedure that I did for the Conformant1D method, that is, to change

```
ildasm dotnetcstylearray.dll
```

You can then save the MSIL code for the Interop assembly by performing the following steps:

1. Load the Interop assembly into the ILDASM by executing the following command: ildasm dotnetcstylearray.dll.
2. Select File | Dump.
3. Accept the default Dump options by clicking OK. A File | SaveAs dialog will appear.
4. Select the location where you want to save the file to.
5. Click the Save button.
6. Modify the EmployeeTest1 method to marshal the second parameter as an array in two places: (1) the **CStyleArrayTestClass** class and the (2) the ICStyleArrayTest interface.
7. Recompile the assembly by executing the following command: ilasm /OUT=dotnetcstylearray.dll cstyleproject.il /DLL.

You should have changed the EmployeeTest1 method to look as follows:

```
void  EmployeeTest1([in] int16 numEmps,
     [in] valuetype dotnetcstylearraynew.tagEmployee[]
     marshal([+0]) employees)
```

Now you can write the following client code to call the EmployeeTest1 method:

```
1.  private void TestEmp_Click(object sender,
2.       System.EventArgs e)
3.  {
4.       CStyleArrayTest obj=new CStyleArrayTest();
5.       tagEmployee[] employees=new tagEmployee[3];
6.       employees[0].ID=5;
7.       employees[0].Name="Alan Gordon";
8.       employees[0].Salary=2400;
9.       employees[1].ID=15;
10.      employees[1].Name="Tamber Gordon";
11.      employees[1].Salary=4800;
12.      employees[2].ID=25;
13.      employees[2].Name="Bria Gordon";
14.      employees[2].Salary=9600;
15.      obj.EmployeeTest1(3,employees);
16. }
```

The code here is pretty simple. On line 4, I create an instance of the **CstyleArrayTest** class. On line 5, I declare an array of tagEmployees with length 3. On lines 6 through 14, I populate the array, and, on line 15, I call the EmployeeTest1 method.

Now let's take a look now at a very common scenario with arrays, that is, a method that returns an array of user-defined structures as an output parameter. The IDL of just such a method, EmployeeTest2, is shown here:

```
[id(6)] HRESULT EmployeeTest2([in,out] short *numEmps,
      [out] Employee **employees);
```

The tlbimp converts this to the following managed code equivalent in MSIL:

```
instance void  EmployeeTest2([in][out] int16& numEmps,
                  [out] native int employees)
```

Currently, the managed code version of the EmployeeTest2 method will not work. Here, I have run into the problem that the tlbimp has in distinguishing between a by-reference 1D array (which is what I have here) and a 2D array. I have to change the second parameter to be a reference argument in the MSIL. I won't repeat the steps to do this because I have done it a few times now. However, you will need to edit the MSIL definition of the EmployeeTest2 method to look as follows and then recompile the code back into an assembly:

```
instance void  EmployeeTest2([in][out] int16& numEmps,
                    [out] native int& employees)
```

Don't forget to change the method definition in both the **CStyleArrayTestClass** class and the ICStyleArrayTest interface. You can now write the following client code to call this method:

```
1.  private void TestEmp_Click(object sender,
2.        System.EventArgs e)
3.  {
4.        short i, numEmps=4;
5.        IntPtr ptr; ptrIter
6.        int empSize;
7.        ptr=System.IntPtr.Zero;
8.        CStyleArrayTest obj=new CStyleArrayTest();
9.        obj.EmployeeTest2(ref numEmps,out ptr);
10.       tagEmployee[] outEmps=new tagEmployee[numEmps];
11.       empSize=Marshal.SizeOf(typeof(tagEmployee));
12.       ptrIter=ptr;
13.       for (i=0;i<numEmps;i++)
14.       {
15.         outEmps[i]=(tagEmployee)
16.           Marshal.PtrToStructure(
17.               ptrIter,typeof(tagEmployee));
18.         ptr=(IntPtr)((int)ptr+empSize);
19.       }
20.       Marshal.FreeCoTaskMem(ptr);
21. }
```

On lines 4 through 6, I have variable declarations. On line 4, I initialize the number of Employee objects that I would like to receive from the EmployeeTest2 method. On line 7, I initialize the unmanaged pointer that I will receive from the method to NULL (IntPtr.Zero). On line 8, I instantiate a CStyleArrayTest object, and, on line 9, I call the EmployeeTest2 method. On line 10, I instantiate a managed array of the tagEmployee value type that will hold the array that I receive from the method. On line 11, I calculate the size of each instance of tagEmployee. On line 12, I initialize an IntPtr variable that I will use to iterate through the unmanaged buffer that the EmployeeTest method returned. On lines 13 through 19, I fill the managed array with the contents of the buffer that is returned by the EmployeeTest2 method. On lines 15 through 17, I call the PtrToStructure method in the **System.Runtime.InteropServices.Marshal** class. This function takes two parameters: a native pointer that contains the unmanaged version of the structure and a System.Type object that contains the type object for the managed version of the structure. On line 18, I increment the native pointer so that it points to the next tagEmployee instance in the returned buffer. The calling is responsible for freeing the memory that is returned by output parameters on a COM method. On line 20, I free the memory buffer that the EmployeeTest2 function returned.

VARYING ARRAYS • COM (IDL really) varying arrays allow you to pass a dynamic slice of a fixed array. The following method, defined here in IDL, uses a varying array:

```
[id(2)] HRESULT TestVarying1D([in] short start,
[in] short length,
[in, first_is(start),length_is(length)] short arg[5]);
```

In this case, the first and second parameters to the method allow you to specify the starting index and the number of elements from that starting point that will be passed from the client to the server. You specify the starting index using first_is and the number of elements to copy over using length_is. You could instead use first_is and last_is to specify the starting and ending indexes to copy from the client to the server as follows:

```
[id(2)] HRESULT TestVarying1D([in] short start,
[in] short end,
[in, first is(start),last_is(end)] short arg[5]);
```

The tlbimp will convert either one of these IDL definitions to the following managed code equivalent:

```
instance void  TestVarying1D([in] int16 start,
[in] int16 length,[in] native int arg)
```

Notice that the third parameter is a native pointer. My own experiments showed that the tlbimp generates a native pointer for an array if you use the first_is, last_is, or length_is IDL attributes on the array. You can use the following logic in a C# client to call the method without making any changes to the Interop assembly:

```
1.  private void button3_Click(object sender,
2.        System.EventArgs e)
3.  {
4.        short i, start, length, arrSize=5;
5.        short[] arg1=new short[arrSize];
6.        System.IntPtr ptr, ptrStart;
7.        start=2;
8.        length=2;
9.        for (i=0;i<5;i++)
10.           arg1[i]=(short)(arrSize*i);
11.       ptr=Marshal.AllocCoTaskMem(
12.           Marshal.SizeOf(typeof(short))*arrSize);
13.       ptrStart=(IntPtr)
14.         ((int)ptr+start*Marshal.SizeOf(typeof(short)));
15.       Marshal.Copy(arg1,start,ptrStart,length);
16.       CStyleArrayTest obj=new CStyleArrayTest();
```

```
17.     obj.TestVarying1D(start,length,ptr);
18.     Marshal.FreeCoTaskMem(ptr);
19. }
```

On lines 4 through 6, I declare variables. On lines 7 and 8, I initialize the starting index and the length for the array that I will pass to the TestVarying1D method. On lines 9 and 10, I populate a 1D array. On lines 11 and 12, I allocate a buffer of unmanaged memory that is the same size as the array. On lines 13 and 14, I set the starting point in the unmanaged buffer. On line 15, I call the Copy method on the **System.Runtime.InteropServices.Marshal** class to copy the contents of the array to the unmanaged buffer. On line 16, I instantiate a CstyleArrayTest object, and then, on line 17, I call the TestVarying1D method. Finally, on line 18, I call FreeCoTaskMem to free the unmanaged buffer.

Using ActiveX Controls in Managed Code

ActiveX controls have always been one of the most misunderstood COM-based technologies. Microsoft didn't help the situation by changing the definition of what an ActiveX control is several times. The current definition of an ActiveX control is that it is a COM object that supports the IUnknown interface. ActiveX controls usually support many other interfaces, but all other interfaces should be viewed as optional and a container should not rely on these interfaces being supported.

However, to most people, an ActiveX control is a COM object that has a user interface and supports a special set of interfaces—IOleControl, IOleInPlaceObject, IDataObject, and so forth—that allow it to be hosted inside of (and displayed in-place within) an ActiveX control container. For the purposes of this discussion, I am going to use this second definition.

It's really not that difficult to understand how to use ActiveX controls from managed code if you understand how to use COM Interop in general. The coclasses, interfaces, and connection point events that ActiveX controls support are mapped to .NET classes, interfaces, and delegates in the same way as I discussed earlier in this chapter. The main difference is the way that you import an ActiveX control into your .NET projects. These differences are due to the fact that the ActiveX control has a user interface, so you must have a Windows Form wrapper for the control. You also need a way to add the ActiveX control to your toolbox in Visual Studio .NET.

You typically use an ActiveX control by dragging and dropping an icon that represents the control on to a form. You then set properties on the control that specify how the control will look and behave. Most ActiveX controls expose custom property pages that allow you to edit these properties in a convenient way. Most IDEs also support property browsers that you can use to edit the properties. Most ActiveX controls support source interfaces (that is, connection point events), and most ActiveX control-aware IDEs support a simple way to add handlers for events. Usually, you can add a handler by double-clicking a control and selecting the desired event from a list.

The .NET Framework supports Windows Forms controls, which are the managed code equivalent of ActiveX controls. Just like an ActiveX control, Windows Forms controls are displayed in place within a container, they have property pages, and they support events. You can probably guess then that the basic idea behind COM Interop for ActiveX controls is to make an ActiveX control appear as a Windows Forms control to a managed client. The .NET Framework SDK includes a tool called the Windows Forms ActiveX Control Importer (**aximp.exe**) that you can use to map an ActiveX control to a Windows Forms control. In addition to performing the same mapping that tlbimp does for the COM classes, interfaces, and source and event interfaces in the ActiveX control, this tool also generates a Windows Forms control that hosts the ActiveX control and exposes the ActiveX control's properties, methods, and events to managed code. The Windows Forms control that the ActiveX Control Importer generates derives from **System.Windows.Forms.AxHost**. This class, in turn, derives from **System.Windows.Forms.Control**.

You run the Windows Forms ActiveX Control Importer by entering the following command at a Visual Studio .NET command prompt:

```
aximp [options] {filename.ocx | filename.dll}
```

For example, the following command line will generate an Interop assembly and a Windows Forms control for an ActiveX control:

```
aximp hw2cntrl.ocx
```

This ActiveX control behaves like a rotary knob like the type you might see as the volume control on a stereo. Figure 7–11 shows what this control will look like in a client application. You can download the control from the Web site for this book, and I also included a document on the Web site that shows you how to build the control.

When you run **aximp.exe** on an ActiveX control, the ActiveX Control Importer will generate two assemblies:

- An Interop assembly with the name **[TypeLibName].ocx** that contains a very similar mapping of COM types to managed types as tlbimp.
- A second assembly that contains a Windows Forms control with the name **ax[TypeLibName].ocx**.

where **[TypeLibName]** is the name of the type library for the ActiveX control. In the case of the rotary knob control, the two assemblies will have the names **Hw2CntrlLib.dll** and **AxHw2CntrlLib.dll**. The ActiveX control that you run

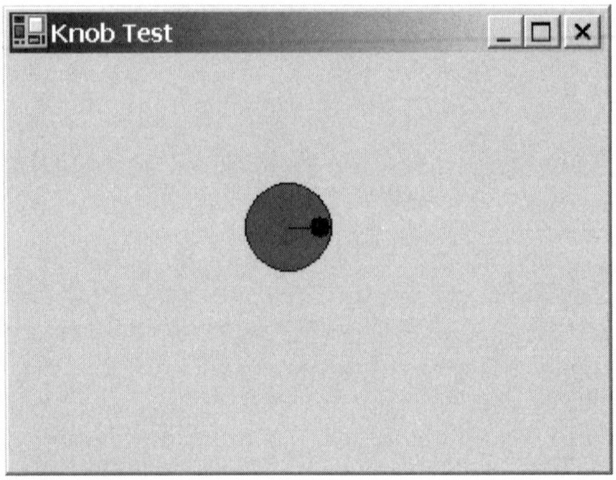

FIGURE 7–11 *The rotary knob control displayed within a client application.*

this command on can have either the .ocx (which is more typical) or .dll extension.

Table 7–12 lists the command-line options for the ActiveX Control Importer.

TABLE 7–12 *Available command-line parameters for the ActiveX Control Importer*

Parameter	Description
out	Specifies the file name of the assembly that aximp will generate.
publickey	Allows you to specify the file that contains the public key that should be used to delay-sign the Interop assembly.
keyfile	Allows you to specify the file that contains the key pair that should be used to sign the Interop assembly.
delaysign	Used to specify that the Interop assembly will be delay signed.
source	Generate C# code for the Windows Forms wrapper.
nologo	Prevents tlbimp from displaying the Microsoft logo.
silent	Suppresses all output except errors.
verbose	Display extra diagnostic output information.

You can also use the ActiveX Control Importer from within Visual Studio. To do this, perform the following steps:

1. Start Visual Studio .NET and create a C# Windows Forms project.
2. Move your mouse over the Toolbox in Visual Studio .NET.
3. The toolbox will slide right as shown in Figure 7–12.

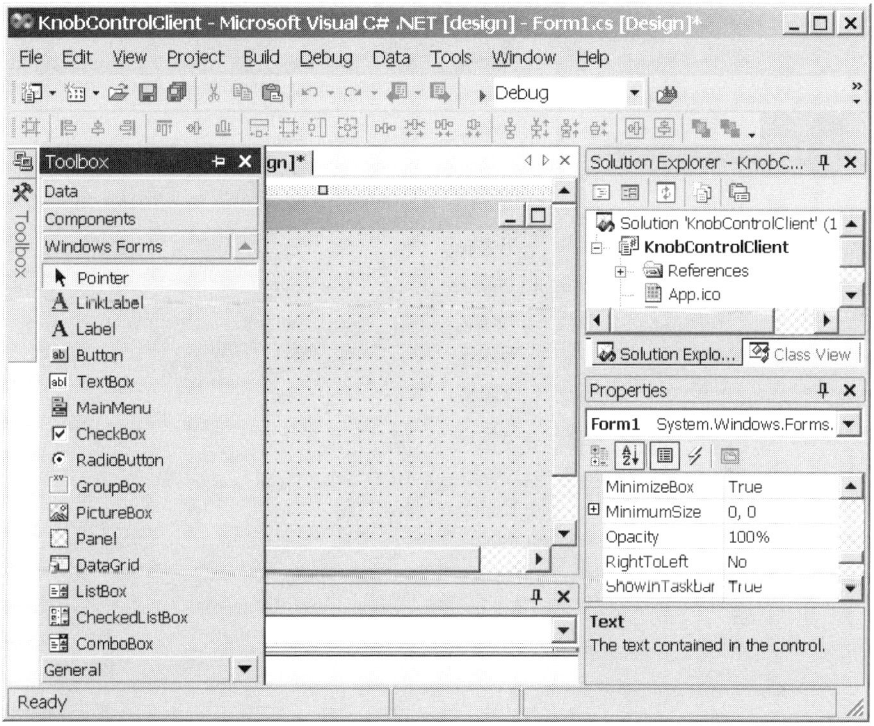

FIGURE 7–12 *The Visual Studio .NET toolbox.*

4. Right-click the toolbox and select Customize Toolbox... from the context menu. The Customize Toolbox dialog will appear as shown in Figure 7–13.
5. Click the COM Components tab.
6. Select the desired ActiveX control from the list of components by clicking the checkbox next to the component.
7. Click OK.

Visual Studio .NET will add an icon to your toolbox that represents the control. You can now drag and drop the icon onto a form to add an instance of the control to the form. After you add the control to a form, you can edit its properties using the property browser in Visual Studio .NET or the built-in custom property pages of the control. You can also add event handlers with a few mouse clicks.

Much like using COM Interop in general, using an ActiveX control from a managed code application is actually very simple to do. Understanding everything that's going on under the hood to make everything so simple is difficult to understand, however. Therefore, just as I did for generalized COM

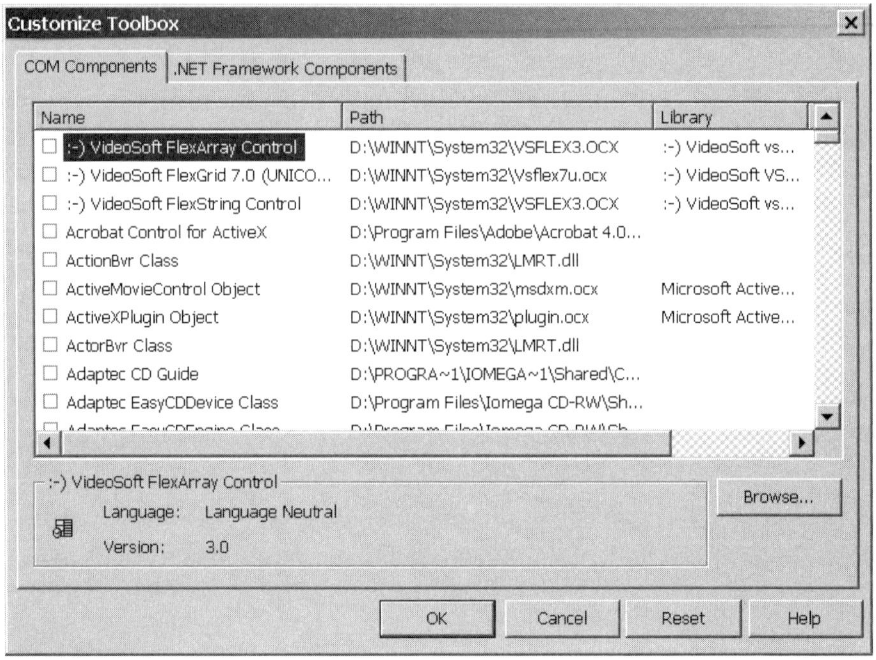

FIGURE 7–13 *The Customize Toolbox dialog.*

Interop, I will do a simple example that shows you how to use an ActiveX control from a managed code application. Then I'll go back and peer under the hood to see how it works.

For this example, I will use the rotary knob ActiveX Control that I used as a homework assignment for my COM class at UCLA Extension. The IDL for the rotary knob control is the following:

```
[
  uuid(D5ABDEA9-7D0A-11D0-818D-444553540000),
  version(1.0)
]
library HW2CNTRLLib
{
      importlib("stdole2.tlb");
    // Forward declare all types defined in this typelib
    dispinterface _DHw2cntrl;
    dispinterface _DHw2cntrlEvents;
    [
      uuid(D5ABDEAA-7D0A-11D0-818D-444553540000),
      hidden
    ]
    dispinterface _DHw2cntrl {
```

```
        properties:
          [id(0xfffffe0b), bindable, requestedit]
            OLE_COLOR BackColor;
          [id(0xfffffdff), bindable, requestedit]
            OLE_COLOR ForeColor;
          [id(0x00000001)]
            short Range;
          [id(0x00000002)]
            VARIANT_BOOL AmbientBackGround;
        methods:
            [id(0xfffffdd8)]
            void AboutBox();
    };

    [
      uuid(D5ABDEAB-7D0A-11D0-818D-444553540000)
    ]
    dispinterface _DHw2cntrlEvents {
        properties:
        methods:
            [id(0x00000001)]
            void SettingChanged(short value);
    };
    [
      uuid(D5ABDEAC-7D0A-11D0-818D-444553540000),
      control
    ]
    coclass Hw2cntrl {
        [default] dispinterface _DHw2cntrl;
        [default, source] dispinterface _DHw2cntrlEvents;
    };
};
```

This control has a default interface called _DHw2cntrl that contains BackColor, ForeColor, Range, and AmbientBackGround properties. BackColor and ForeColor are stock properties that affect the color of the rectangular area behind the control and the face of the knob respectively. Range is a custom property that controls the range of values that the knob sends to its client in the SettingChanged event as it moves through 360 degrees of rotation. Therefore, if you were using the knob to control an 8 bit color value, the Range property should be set to 255, because the color can take on any whole value between 0 and 255. The AmbientBackGround custom property allows you to specify that the control should always assume the background color of its container. The rotary knob control also has a default source interface called _DHw2cntrlEvents that contains an event called SettingChanged that the knob will fire as you turn it.

I will build the application shown in Figure 7–14, which uses three instances of the knob to control the RGB values of a color.

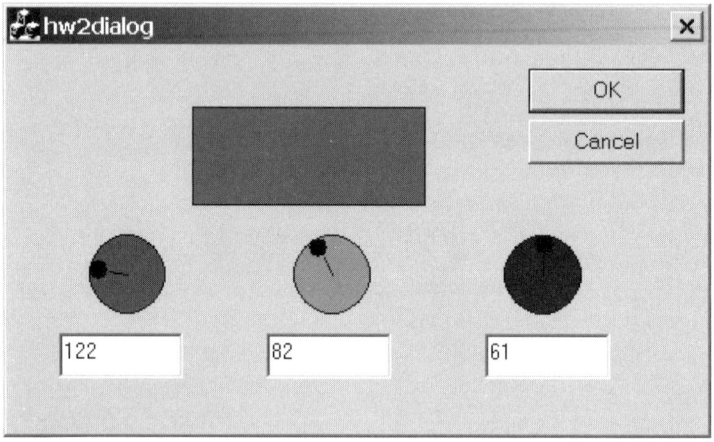

FIGURE 7–14 *A client that uses the knob control.*

You can download the control from the Web site for this book. Make sure that the control is registered using regsvr32 before you start this exercise. Start by performing the following steps:

1. Start Visual Studio .NET and create a C# Windows Forms project.
2. Move your mouse over the Toolbox in Visual Studio .NET.
3. The toolbox will slide right.
4. Right-click the toolbox and select Customize Toolbox… from the context menu. The Customize Toolbox dialog will appear.
5. Click the COM Components tab.
6. Select the item labeled Hw2cntrl Control.
7. Click OK.

Tip If you do not see the Hw2cntrl on the COM Components tab, you have not registered the ActiveX control. Use regsvr32 to register the control and then try again.

Visual Studio .NET will add an icon representing the control to the toolbox. The icon will look similar to the control itself. You can now drag and drop an instance of the control on to any of the forms in your project. When you do this, Visual Studio .NET will add a private member variable for the control to your form class, and it will add all the code needed to initialize the control (you will see this code shortly).

If you click on the ActiveX control that you dragged and dropped on to your form, you can see the properties for the control in the Visual Studio .NET property browser (see Figure 7–15).

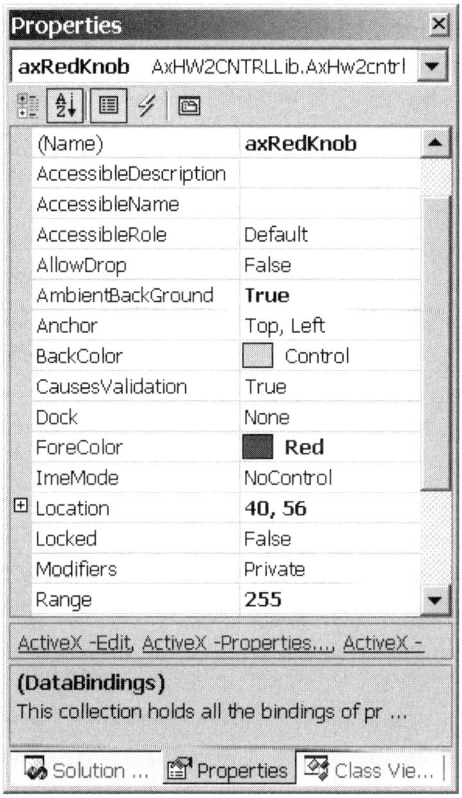

FIGURE 7–15 *The property browser.*

Notice that the AmbientBackGround and the Range properties display in this browser even though they are custom properties for this control. You can also edit the properties of the control by right-clicking on the control and selecting ActiveX–Properties... from the context menu. This will display the custom property pages for the control as shown in Figure 7–16.

For this example, add three instances of the knob control to the form. Call one axRed, one axGreen, and the other axBlue. Set the Range property on each of the controls to 255. Also add three text boxes to the form and give them the names txtRed, txtGreen, and txtBlue. Finally, add a Panel to the form. Your UI should look like Figure 7–14.

To add event handlers for the control, you can either double-click the control in Visual Studio .NET, which will add a handler for the default event of the control, which is the SettingChanged event. You can also click the Event tab on the property browser, which looks like a bolt of lightning (see Figure 7–17).

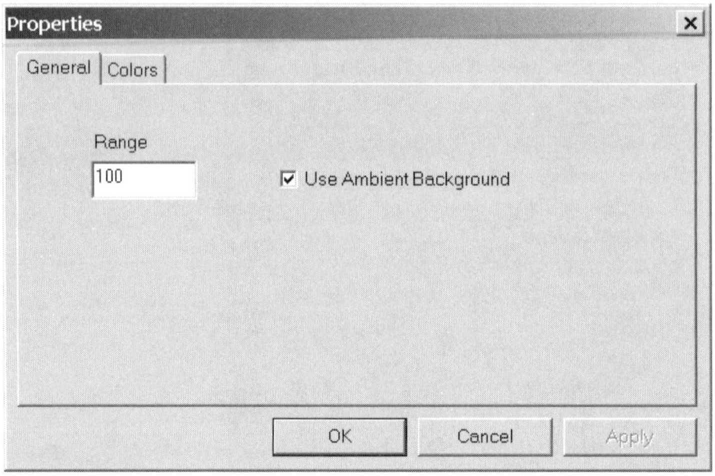

FIGURE 7–16 *The custom property pages for the knob control.*

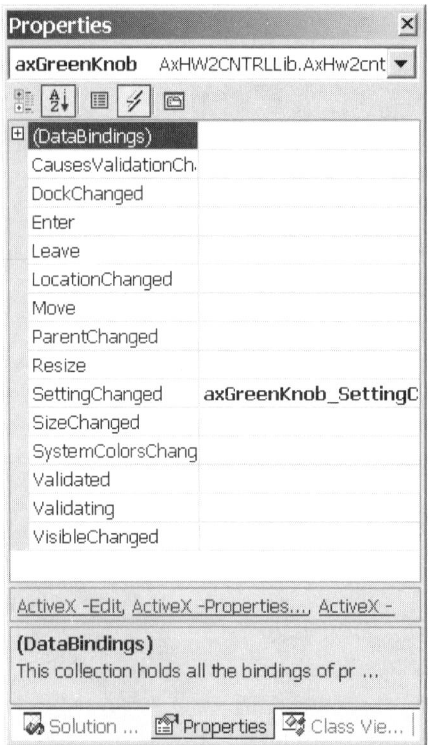

FIGURE 7–17 *The event browser.*

You can add a handler for an event by double-clicking the left column of the event browser. Doing this will insert the code in your form needed to catch the event (I will look at this code shortly). Add event handlers for all three knobs. Notice that the custom SettingChanged event appears on the browser as well as a number of other standard events like Enter, Leave, and Resize. These other events are provided for you by the ActiveX infrastructure.

To implement the UI for this example, I'll first add the following three private variables to the form class:

```
public class Form1 : System.Windows.Forms.Form
{
//code omitted...
      private short mRedValue=0;
      private short mGreenValue=0;
      private short mBlueValue=0;
// code omitted...
}
```

I'll then add the following code for the SettingChanged event handler on the red knob control:

```
private void axRedKnob_SettingChanged(object sender,
      AxHW2CNTRLLib._DHw2cntrlEvents_SettingChangedEvent e)
{
      txtRed.Text=e.value.ToString();
      mRedValue=e.value;
      SetPanelColor();
}
```

All of the parameters for an event will be exposed as public properties on the second parameter to the event. The Windows Forms ActiveX Control Importer will create a class that contains properties for each parameter of an event. In this case, the class is called **_DHw2cntrlEvents_ SettingChangedEvent**, and it has a property called value, which is the argument for the SettingChanged method. I convert this value to a string and then store its textual representation in the txtRed edit box. I then store the new red value in the mRedValue member variable and then call the SetPanelColor method to update the color of the panel on the main window. I will naturally repeat this implementation for both the blue and green knobs. Simply replace txtRed with txtGreen or txtBlue and replace mRedValue with mGreenValue or mBlueValue. The implementation of the SetPanelColor method follows:

```
private void SetPanelColor()
{
      panel1.BackColor=
Color.FromArgb(mRedValue,mGreenValue,mBlueValue);
}
```

The SetPanelColor method sets the color of a panel equal to the RGB color defined by the mRedValue, mGreenValue, and mBlueValue variables. Your code is now complete; you can run the application. It's a fun application to play with. Turn the knobs and watch how the color on the panel changes.

Now that you have seen how easy it is to use ActiveX controls from a managed code application, let's look behind the scenes to see how COM Interop with ActiveX controls works. When you add a knob control to a Windows Form, Visual Studio .NET will add code to the InitializeComponent method in your form. The form's constructor calls the InitializeComponent method to initialize the controls on the form. The following code listing highlights some of the code that Visual Studio .NET will add:

```
#region Windows Form Designer generated code
/// <summary>
/// Required method for Designer support-do not modify
/// the contents of this method with the code editor.
/// </summary>
private void InitializeComponent()
{
    System.Resources.ResourceManager resources = new
     System.Resources.ResourceManager(typeof(Form1));
    this.axRedKnob=new AxHW2CNTRLLib.AxHw2cntrl();
    this.axGreenKnob=new AxHW2CNTRLLib.AxHw2cntrl();
    this.axBlueKnob=new AxHW2CNTRLLib.AxHw2cntrl();
//
// Initialization for other controls omitted here…
//
    ((System.ComponentModel.ISupportInitialize)
      (this.axRedKnob)).BeginInit();
    ((System.ComponentModel.ISupportInitialize)
      (this.axGreenKnob)).BeginInit();
    ((System.ComponentModel.ISupportInitialize)
      (this.axBlueKnob)).BeginInit();
    this.SuspendLayout();
    //
    // axRedKnob (repeated for green and blue knob)
    //
    this.axRedKnob.Enabled = true;
    this.axRedKnob.Location =
        new System.Drawing.Point(40, 56);
    this.axRedKnob.Name = "axRedKnob";
    this.axRedKnob.OcxState =
        ((System.Windows.Forms.AxHost.State)
        (resources.GetObject("axRedKnob.OcxState")));
    this.axRedKnob.Size=new
        System.Drawing.Size(72, 50);
    this.axRedKnob.TabIndex = 0;
    this.axRedKnob.SettingChanged += new
    _DHw2cntrlEvents_SettingChangedEventHandler
        (this.axRedKnob_SettingChanged);
//
```

```
39. // End repeated section for green and blue knob
40. //
41.     ((System.ComponentModel.ISupportInitialize)
42.         (this.axRedKnob)).EndInit();
43.     ((System.ComponentModel.ISupportInitialize)
44.         (this.axGreenKnob)).EndInit();
45.     ((System.ComponentModel.ISupportInitialize)
46.         (this.axBlueKnob)).EndInit();
47.     this.ResumeLayout(false);
48. }
49. #endregion
```

Note The InitializeComponent method contains code that is generated by Visual Studio .NET's form designer. I did not write this code, and you should not ever change it because the form designer will likely overwrite your changes the next time it saves the code.

On lines 8 and 9, the InitializeComponent method instantiates a Resource-Manager object. The **ResourceManager** class provides access to the Resources (icons, bitmaps, and, most important for this example, the persisted state of the ActiveX controls) of an application. On lines 10 through 12, the generated code instantiates the three instances of the knob control—axRedKnob, axGreen-Knob, and axBlueKnob—that I dropped onto the form. I omitted the code that instantiates the other Windows Forms controls on the form (the edit boxes, panels, and so forth). Lines 16 through 21 call the BeginInit method on the ISupportInitialize interface for each control. The **System.Windows.Forms.AxHost** class (which is the base class for the **AxHW2CNTRLLib. AxHw2cntrl** class that the ActiveX Control Importer creates to represent my ActiveX control) implements the ISupportInitialize interface to allow a client to initialize the control from a persistently stored state. Among other things, the BeginInit method will call the CreateSink in the **AxHW2CNTRLLib. AxHw2cntrl** class (I'll explain this method more shortly). This will attach a connection point sink object that the **AxHW2CNTRLLib.AxHw2cntrl** class implements to the default source interface that the underlying ActiveX control implements. On line 22, the InitializeComponent method calls the SuspendLay-out method on the form, which will suppress multiple layout events while the InitializeComponent method positions and sizes all the controls on the form. A call to ResumeLayout near the end of the InitializeComponent method causes all these layout changes to take effect at once. Lines 26 through 37 show the code that sets the properties on the red knob. The InitializeComponent method contains similar logic for the Green and Blue knob, but I omitted this code because it's almost identical. Notice on lines 30 through 32 that the code fetches the persistently stored state of the ActiveX controls from the ResourceManager. Most ActiveX controls store the state of their properties into a container pro-vided by their host. In the case of a Windows form, that container is the resource area of the executable. The code to catch the SettingChanged event on the red knob is shown on lines 35 through 37. Here I instantiate an instance of the delegate that maps to the SettingChanged event (_DHw2cntrlEvents_SettingChangedEventHandler) passing in the name of the method in the form that will catch the event (axRedKnob_SettingChanged in this case). Then I assign this delegate to the SettingChanged event field on the ActiveX control wrapper. There is nothing unusual or ActiveX control specific about this code; it's the same code that you would write to catch any event on a managed class. Lines 41 through 46 contain a call to the ISupportInitialize.EndInit method on each control, which just signals the control that its container has completed initialization of the control. Line 47 contains the aforementioned call to the ResumeLayout method.

Code Regions

Notice the #region statement on line 1 and the corresponding #endregion statement on line 49 in the previous code listing. Code regions allow you to collapse and hide blocks of code so that you see an outline view of your source document. When a section of code is collapsed, you see a "+" symbol with a label next to it identifying the block of code as shown in Figure 7-18.

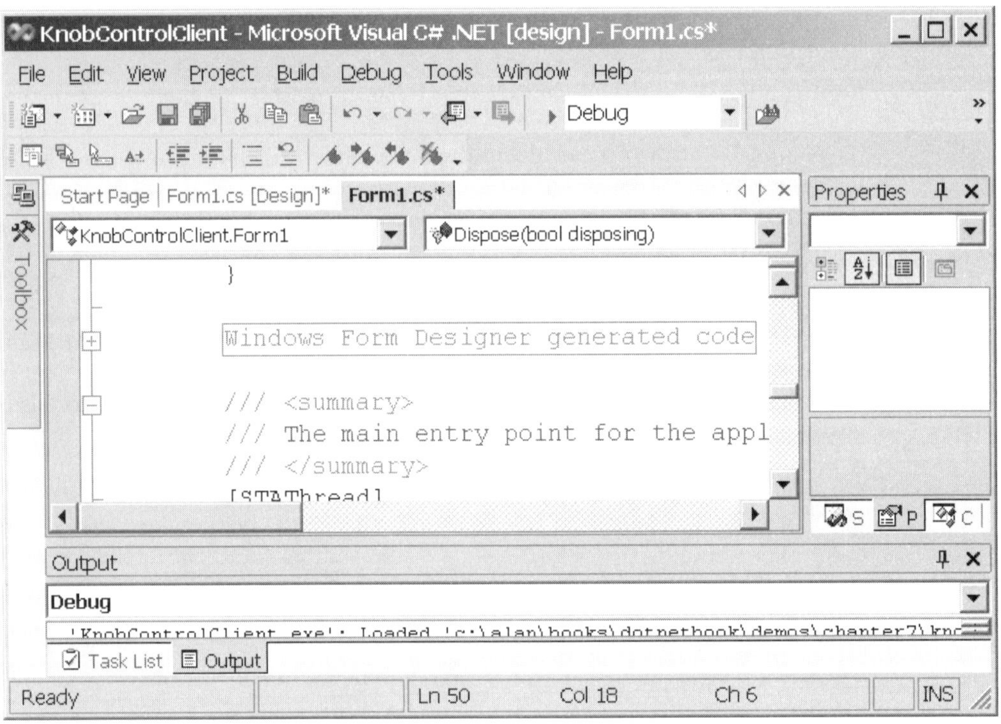

FIGURE 7-18 *Collapsed code in a region.*

You can click the "+" to expand the code as shown in Figure 7-19.

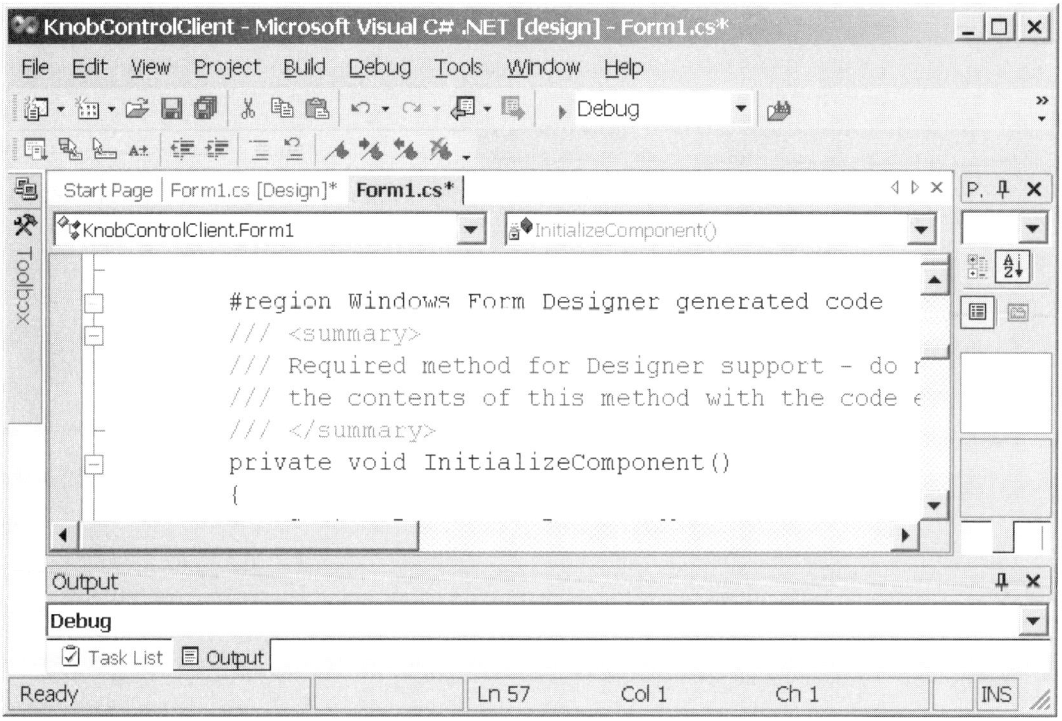

FIGURE 7–19 *Collapsed code in a region.*

You start one of these collapsible regions of code by using the #region and then specifying the text that should appear next to the "+" symbol when the code is collapsed. You end the region with a #endregion statement as shown here:

```
#region Windows Form Designer generated code
//
// code goes here…
//
#endregion
```

You can control Visual Studio .NET's outlining behavior using Outlining submenu on the Edit top-level menu. Visual Studio .NET uses #regions on its generated code, but you can use it in your own code also.

Table 7–10 showed the command-line parameters that you can pass to aximp.exe. One of the most interesting parameters is the source parameter. You can use this parameter to generate C# source code for the Windows Forms control that wraps your ActiveX control. It will write the source code to a file called **ax[TypeLibName].cs**. Now that you understand the code that a managed client uses to interact with an ActiveX control, let's take a look at the wrapper class that the Windows Forms ActiveX Control Importer generates for an ActiveX control. For our example ActiveX control, the file name is **axHw2cntrlLib.cs**. Some of the code generated by specifying the source parameter on the knob control follows:

```
namespace AxHW2CNTRLLib {
    [AxHost.ClsidAttribute
("{d5abdeac-7d0a-11d0-818d-444553540000}")]
    [DesignTimeVisibleAttribute(true)]
    [DefaultEvent("SettingChanged")]
    public class AxHw2cntrl : AxHost {

        private HW2CNTRLLib._DHw2cntrl ocx;

        private AxHw2cntrlEventMulticaster
      eventMulticaster;

        private AxHost.ConnectionPointCookie
    cookie;

        public AxHw2cntrl() :
                base
   ("d5abdeac-7d0a-11d0-818d-444553540000")
      {
            // …
        }
        [DispIdAttribute(2)]
        public virtual bool AmbientBackGround
      {
            get {
                if ((this.ocx == null)) {
                    throw new
      AxHost.InvalidActiveXStateException
    ("AmbientBackGround",
      AxHost.ActiveXInvokeKind.PropertyGet);
                }
                return this.ocx.AmbientBackGround;
            }
            set {
                if ((this.ocx == null)) {
                    throw new
    AxHost.InvalidActiveXStateException
    ("AmbientBackGround",
      AxHost.ActiveXInvokeKind.PropertySet);
                }
```

```
                this.ocx.AmbientBackGround = value;
            }
        }
        [DispIdAttribute(-513)]
        public override Color ForeColor
       {
            get {
                if (((this.ocx != null)
                  && (this.PropsValid() == true))) {
                    return GetColorFromOleColor
       (((UInt32)(this.ocx.ForeColor)));
                }
                else {
                    return base.ForeColor;
                }
            }
            set {
                base.ForeColor = value;
                if ((this.ocx != null)) {
                    this.ocx.ForeColor =
 ((UInt32)(GetOleColorFromColor(value)));
                }
            }
        }

        public event
    _DHw2cntrlEvents_SettingChangedEventHandler
    SettingChanged;

        protected override void CreateSink()
        {
            try {
                this.eventMulticaster=new
        AxHw2cntrlEventMulticaster(this);
                this.cookie=new
      AxHost.ConnectionPointCookie(this.ocx,
        this.eventMulticaster,
        typeof(_DHw2cntrlEvents));
            }
            catch (System.Exception ) {
            }
        }
        protected override void DetachSink()
      {
            try {
                this.cookie.Disconnect();
            }
            catch (System.Exception ) {
            }
        }
```

```

        internal void RaiseOnSettingChanged(
    object sender,
    _DHw2cntrlEvents_SettingChangedEvent e)
    {
            if ((this.SettingChanged != null)) {
                this.SettingChanged(sender, e);
            }
        }
    }

    public delegate void
    _DHw2cntrlEvents_SettingChangedEventHandler(
      object sender,
      _DHw2cntrlEvents_SettingChangedEvent e);

    public class _DHw2cntrlEvents_SettingChangedEvent {

        public short value;

        public _DHw2cntrlEvents_SettingChangedEvent(
        short value)
        {
            this.value = value;
        }
    }

    public class AxHw2cntrlEventMulticaster :
      _DHw2cntrlEvents
    {

        private AxHw2cntrl parent;

        public AxHw2cntrlEventMulticaster(
      AxHw2cntrl parent)
        {
            this.parent = parent;
        }

        public virtual void SettingChanged(short val)
        {
        _DHw2cntrlEvents_SettingChangedEvent
      settingchangedEvent=new
    _DHw2cntrlEvents_SettingChangedEvent(val);
            this.parent.RaiseOnSettingChanged
      (this.parent, settingchangedEvent);
        }
    }
}
```

I cleaned up the code and omitted some parts that were nonessential. Line 1 declares the namespace, AxHW2CNTRLLib, for the control, which is just the type library name, HW2CNTRLLib, with Ax prepended to it. Lines 2 through 6 contain the declaration of the class that will wrap the ActiveX control. In this case, the class is called **AxHw2cntrl**, which is just the class name of the ActiveX control with Ax prepended to it. Notice that this class derives from a class called **AxHost**, which resides in the System.Windows.Forms namespace and inherits from System.Windows.Forms.Control. Notice the attribute declarations on lines 2 through 5. The first attribute, AxHost.ClsidAttribute, contains the CLSID of the underlying ActiveX control. The next attribute, DesignTimeVisibleAttribute, indicates that the control should be visible at design time within a visual development environment. The last attribute, DefaultEvent, indicates which of the events should be treated as the default by a visual development environment. If you've used VB, you know that, when you double-click a button control, for instance, it will automatically add an event handler for the clicked event on the button. It does this because the clicked event is the default event for a button control. Similarly, the SettingChanged event is the default (and only) event for this control. Lines 7 through 15 contain the definition of three private fields in the **AxHw2cntrl** class. The first field is declared as follows:

```
private HW2CNTRLLib._DHw2cntrl ocx;
```

It contains the definition of an Interface reference called ocx. This field is typed as the default dispinterface in the ActiveX control, which is called **_DHw2cntrl**. The second field is typed as follows:

```
private AxHw2cntrlEventMulticaster eventMulticaster;
```

The **Multicaster** class is a connection point sink that implements the default source interface provided by the control and forwards the event to a .NET delegate. The last field is typed as follows:

```
private AxHost.ConnectionPointCookie cookie;
```

This field contains the cookie that represents a client's connection to a source interface. This cookie is returned by the Advise method in IConnectionPoint.

Lines 16 through 21 contain the definition of the constructor for the wrapper class. Notice that the constructor initializes the base class, **System.Windows.Forms.AxHost**, with the CLSID of the underlying ActiveX control. Lines 22 through 43 contain the wrapper for a custom property in the control. In this case, it's the AmbientBackGround property that determines whether the control uses the ambient background color, that is, the background color of its container. The get method for the property throws an exception of type, AxHost.InvalidActiveXStateException, if the internal field that represents the ActiveX control is null. If not, it just returns the value of the AmbientBackGround property. The set method does exactly the same null value check on the internal ActiveX control and throws the same error if the field is not set and sets the AmbientBackGround property on the ActiveX control otherwise. Notice that the dispid for this method is declared as an attribute on line 22. Lines 45 through 64 contain the wrappers for a stock property, ForeColor. These properties are handled slightly different because the base class of the wrapper control, **System.Windows.Forms.AxHost**, contains an implementation of these stock properties so there is no need to throw an exception. If the ocx field is non-null, the ForeColor property will return the value of the ForeColor property in the underlying ActiveX control after converting it from the OLE representation of a color to the .NET representation (System.Drawing.Color) using the GetColorFromOleColor method in the **System.Windows.Forms.AxHost** class. If the ocx field is null, the wrapper returns the ForeColor property from the base class, **System.Windows.Forms.AxHost**. You can find the declaration of a .NET event that is the managed code equivalent of the SettingChanged event in the ActiveX control on lines 66 through 68. On lines 70 through 82, you can see the definition of the CreateSink method, which is called to connect the **Multicaster** sink class that I described earlier with a connection point in the underlying ActiveX control. Lines 83 through 90 contain the definition of the DetachSink method, which is used to disconnect the Multicaster from the connection point. Lines 92 through 99 contain the definition of a method called RaiseOnSettingChanged that is called internally to send the SettingChanged event to the client. Lines 102 through 105 contain the definition of the delegate for the SettingChanged event. Like most event delegates, this delegate takes two parameters: (1) a sender, which contains the object that generated the event and (2) an object that contains the parameters for the event. The second parameter is typed as a **_DHw2cntrlEvents_SettingChangedEvent**, which is a class that is declared on lines 107 through 116. Unlike most event argument (EventArgs) classes, this class does not derive from **System.EventArgs**. This class contains a single public field, which is called value and typed as a short. This property maps to the value parameter passed in the SettingChanged event. Lines 118 through 138 contain the definition of the **Multicaster** class, which as I mentioned earlier, is just a connection point sink that implements the default source interface on the control, _DHw2cntrlEvents. This class is the connection point sink that will be passed to the Advise method of the IConnectionPoint implementation associated with the default source interface. Notice that the constructor for the **Multicaster** class takes a single parameter, which is an instance of the **AxHw2cntrl** class, which is the overall class that wraps the ActiveX control. The constructor stores this parameter in its private parent field. After you pass a Multicaster instance to the ActiveX control, the control will call the SettingChanged method in the **Multicaster** class whenever the SettingChanged event occurs. The SettingChanged method on the **Multicaster** class is defined on lines 130 through 137. This method will instantiate an instance of the event argument class for the SettingChanged event—_DHw2cntrlEvents_SettingChangedEvent (see lines 132 through 134)—and then, on lines 135 and 136, it will call the RaiseOnSettingChanged method (see lines 92 through 99) on the wrapper class through the parent field. It passes the parent object as the first parameter; this is the sender. It then passes the argument object that was instantiated on lines 132 through 134 as the event arguments parameter.

You can alter the source code for the wrapper control and recompile it if you need to. One case where you may want to do this is if your ActiveX control has more than one source (event) interface. The wrapper class generated by aximp maps only the events in default source interface to managed code equivalents. This is not as big a shortcoming as you might think because most ActiveX controls that I have seen only have a single source interface. If you happen to have an ActiveX control that has several source interfaces, you can modify the source code generated by running aximp with the /source parameter to map events in the non-default, source interfaces. A corollary to all of this is that, if you are creating an ActiveX control and you know ahead of time that you may need to use it through COM Interop, make sure that you only have a single source interface.

Performance Considerations

Perhaps the biggest problem with COM Interop is that it can be slow. There are approximately 50 instructions that get executed each time you cross the managed to unmanaged code boundary, and that does not include the time spent copying parameters from managed to unmanaged buffers. You should not, therefore, use COM Interop on chatty COM interfaces, that is, interfaces where you will have to make lots of method calls in order to use the interface. COM Interop is most useful for COM interfaces where method calls are not as frequent and where each method performs more functionality. For instance, if an object has four fields that make up its state, having a separate method to set the value in each field is a chatty interface. A single interface that has four parameters and that allows you to set all four fields with a single method call is preferred. If you have a COM object that has a chatty interface and you decide that you want to use it through Interop, you will probably be better off rewriting the object, especially for a time-critical application, or you can create another COM object that wraps the first object and makes the interface less chatty, that is, you call one method on this wrapper and it makes several calls on the underlying object. With this approach you only cross the managed to unmanaged code boundary once, so you do not incur as great a performance penalty. You will want to make sure that, if you use this approach, the wrapper COM object and the original COM object have compatible Apartments so that you avoid COM marshaling.

Advanced Aspects of PInvoke

Although it's not strictly a COM Interop topic, I wanted to end this chapter by discussing some advanced aspects of PInvoke. You learned in Chapter 6 that PInvoke is a technology that allows you to make calls to functions in non-COM, unmanaged DLLs. In this section we will look at the following advanced aspects of PInvoke: Pointers, Callback Functions and Structures.

Pointers

Win32 DLLs that use pointers typically use them in one of 2 ways: (1) to return or receive an array, or (2) to return or receive a structure. We'll start our discussion of pointers by looking at a pair of Win32 API functions that demonstrate each of these usages.

The fourth parameter to the CreateFile function API function takes a pointer to a security structure as shown here.

```
HANDLE CreateFile( LPCTSTR lpFileName,
    DWORD dwDesiredAccess, DWORD dwShareMode,
    LPSECURITY_ATTRIBUTES lpSecurityAttributes,
    DWORD dwCreationDisposition,DWORD dwFlagsAndAttributes,
      HANDLE hTemplateFile);
```

The second parameter to the ReadFile function is an output parameter that is typed as a pointer to a void array. This parameter contains the data read from the file. The fourth parameter to this function returns a pointer to a DWORD that contains the number of bytes read from the file.

```
BOOL ReadFile( HANDLE hFile, LPVOID lpBuffer,
    DWORD nNumberOfBytesToRead,
    LPDWORD lpNumberOfBytesRead,
      LPOVERLAPPED lpOverlapped );
```

Let's see how we would call these functions from managed code. The managed declaration for the CreateFile function looks as shown here.

```
[DllImport("Kernel32.dll", SetLastError=true)]
static extern int CreateFile(string filename,
    uint desiredAccess,uint shareMode,
    uint securityAttributes,
    uint creationDisposition,
    uint flagsAndAttributes,uint templateFile);
```

Remember that you will need to add a using statement for the System.Runtime.InteropServices namespace. Notice that the fourth parameter, which is typed as a pointer to a structure in the unmanaged declaration, is typed as an unsigned integer (uint) in the managed declaration. If an unmanaged function takes a pointer to a structure, as this function does, and you want to pass a null pointer to the function, you can simply declare it as a uint and then pass in a zero value. If you actually want to pass in a structure, you must declare an equivalent, managed structure and then create your managed declaration so that the managed structure is used wherever the equivalent unmanaged structure is called for. We'll explore how to pass a pointer to a structure later. For now, we'll look at how to pass a null value for a structure.

The managed code declaration for the ReadFile looks as shown here.

```
[DllImport("Kernel32.dll", SetLastError=true)]
static extern bool ReadFile(int hFile,byte[] buffer,
      int nBytes2Read,out int nBytesRead,int overlapped);
```

Notice that in this case the second parameter, which is declared as an LPVOID, is mapped to a byte array in the managed declaration. You can convert this byte array to a string using a System.Text.ASCIIEncoding or a System.Text.UnicodeEncoding object depending on the encoding used to write the file. The following code opens a file using the CreateFile function and then reads the first 256 bytes from the file using the ReadFile function.

```
using System;
using System.Runtime.InteropServices;
using System.Text;
const uint GENERIC_READ = 0x80000000;
const uint OPEN_EXISTING = 3;
[DllImport("Kernel32.dll", SetLastError=true)]
static extern int CreateFile(string filename,
    uint desiredAccess,uint shareMode,
    uint securityAttributes, uint creationDisposition,
    uint flagsAndAttributes, uint templateFile);
[DllImport("Kernel32.dll", SetLastError=true)]
static extern bool ReadFile(int hFile,byte[] buffer,
    int nBytes2Read,out int nBytesRead,int overlapped);
[DllImport("Kernel32.dll")]
static extern bool CloseHandle(int hFile);
private void cmdReadFile_Click(object sender,
    System.EventArgs e)
{
    int handle;
    int error;
    byte[] buffer;
    int nRead;
    bool bIsOkay;
    ASCIIEncoding encoding=new ASCIIEncoding();
    buffer=new Byte[256];
    handle=CreateFile(txtFileName.Text,GENERIC_READ,
```

```
30.          0,0,OPEN_EXISTING,0,0);
31.       error=Marshal.GetLastWin32Error();
32.       if (error != 0)
33.          System.Windows.Forms.MessageBox.Show(
34.          "The error number is: " + error.ToString());
35.       bIsOkay=ReadFile(handle,buffer,256,out nRead,0);
36.       if (bIsOkay)
37.         System.Windows.Forms.MessageBox.Show(
38.             "The number of bytes read is: " +
39.             nRead.ToString());
40.       else
41.       {
42.           error=Marshal.GetLastWin32Error();
43.           System.Windows.Forms.MessageBox.Show(
44.             "The error number is: " +
45.             error.ToString());
46.       }
47.       txtFileContents.Text=encoding.GetString(buffer);
48.       CloseHandle(handle);
49. }
```

On lines 1 through 3 I have a trio of "using" statements. The DllImport attribute resides in the System.Runtime.InteropServices namespace and the ASCIIEncoding class resides in the System.Text namespace. On lines 4 and 5 I declare a pair of constants that I will use in the CreateFile function on line 28. The managed equivalent of the CreateFile function is declared on lines 7 through 10. The managed equivalent of the ReadFile function is declared on lines 12 through 14. I declare a managed equivalent of the CloseHandle function on lines 16 and 17. I need the CloseHandle function to clean up the handle that I receive from the CreateFile function. On lines 22 through 26 I declare some variables. On lines 27 and 28 I declare an instantiate an ASCII-Encoding object and a byte array respectively. On lines 29 and 30 I call the CreateFile function. Notice that I pass zero for the fourth parameter to this function. Passing zero is how I pass in a NULL pointer. The CreateFile function returns a handle which I store in a variable of type int. On line 35 I call the ReadFile function passing in the handle that I received from the CreateFile function. The second parameter to ReadFile is the byte array that will contain the data from the file. The third parameter specifies that I will read at most 256 bytes. The fourth parameter is an output parameter that contains the number of bytes read from the file. Lines 40 through 46 contain error-handling code and on line 47 I use the ASCIIEncoding object to convert the byte array to a string. On line 48 I close the file handle. I won't go into C-style arrays or Safe Arrays because the procedure for handling them in PInvoke is exactly the same as that for COM Interop.

Callback Functions

There are a number of Win32 API functions that use callbacks. A good example is the EnumWindows function, which enumerates all the top-level windows on the screen. For each window the EnumWindows function will invoke a callback function that you define passing in a handle to each window. The unmanaged definition of the EnumWindows function is shown here.

```
BOOL EnumWindows(WNDENUMPROC lpEnumFunc,LPARAM lParam);
```

The first parameter to the EnumWindows function is a function pointer that points to a WNDENUMPROC, which has the following prototype.

```
BOOL CALLBACK EnumWindowsProc(HWND hwnd,LPARAM lParam);
```

The second parameter to the EnumWindows function is an application-specific value that is passed through to the EnumWindowsProc callback as its second parameter. The first parameter passed to the EnumWindowsProc callback is the handle for each window.

In order to call the EnumWindows function from managed code I have to first define a managed code delegate that is the equivalent of the EnumWindowsProc as shown here.

```
public delegate bool EnumCallBack(int hwnd, int lParam);
```

Next I have to create the usual managed code declaration for the EnumWindows function as shown here.

```
[DllImport("user32")]
public static extern int EnumWindows(
      EnumCallBack aCallBack, int data);
```

The following code shows how to use the EnumWindows function from managed code.

```
public delegate bool EnumCallBack(int hwnd,int lParam);
[DllImport("user32")]
public static extern int EnumWindows(
     EnumCallBack aCallBack, int data);
[DllImport("user32")]
public static extern void GetWindowText(int hwnd,
     StringBuilder x, int maxCount);

private void cmdEnumerateWindows_Click(object sender,
     System.EventArgs e)
{
     EnumCallBack aCallBack=new
          EnumCallBack(MyCallBack);
     lstWindows.Items.Clear();
     EnumWindows(aCallBack, 0);
}
private bool MyCallBack(int hWnd,int data)
```

```
18. {
19.     StringBuilder sbCaption=new StringBuilder(256);
20.     GetWindowText(hWnd,sbCaption,sbCaption.Capacity);
21.     if (sbCaption.Length > 0)
22.         lstWindows.Items.Add(sbCaption.ToString());
23.     else
24.         lstWindows.Items.Add(hWnd.ToString());
25.     return true;
26. }
```

On line 1 I declare the delegate that maps to the WNDENUMPROC call back function. The managed code declaration of the EnumWindows function can be found on lines 2 through 4. I also declare a managed code equivalent of the GetWindowText Win32 API function on lines 6 and 7. I will use this function to print out the caption of each window. Lines 9 through 16 contain some test code that calls EnumWindows. On lines 12 and 13 I create a new instance of the callback delegate that points to a method called MyCallBack. On line 14 I clear a listbox that holds the window captions and then on line 15 I call the EnumWindows function. The MyCallBack function is shown on lines 17 through 26; it simply adds the Window caption to a listbox or if there is no caption, it adds the value of the Windows handle to the listbox. On line 19 I declare and instantiate a StringBuilder object. Remember that we have to use the System.Text.StringBuilder class for output parameters that are strings, because the System.String class is immutable. On line 20 I call the GetWindowText function to retrieve the window caption into the StringBuilder. On lines 21 through 24 we add the caption to a list box. Don't forget that you will need "using" statements for the System.Runtime.InteropServices and System.Text namespaces in order to compile this code.

Structures

Many Win32 functions accept a structure or a pointer to a structure as an argument. In order to call these functions you have to create managed code equivalents of these structures. For instance, consider the GetSystemTime function, which is declared as follows.

```
VOID GetSystemTime(LPSYSTEMTIME lpSystemTime);
```

The return value of this function is a pointer to a SYSTEMTIME structure that is returned as an output parameter. The SYSTEMTIME structure is declared as shown here.

```
typedef struct _SYSTEMTIME {
    WORD wYear;
    WORD wMonth;
    WORD wDayOfWeek;
    WORD wDay;
    WORD wHour;
```

```
    WORD wMinute;
    WORD wSecond;
    WORD wMilliseconds;
} SYSTEMTIME, *PSYSTEMTIME;
```

In order to use this function from managed code, I start by creating a managed code equivalent of the SYSTEMTIME structure.

```
[StructLayout(LayoutKind.Sequential)]
public struct MySystemTime
{
    public ushort wYear;
    public ushort wMonth;
    public ushort wDayOfWeek;
    public ushort wDay;
    public ushort wHour;
    public ushort wMinute;
    public ushort wSecond;
    public ushort wMilliseconds;
}
```

I use the StructLayout attribute to specify how the fields in the structure should be layed out in memory. In this case, I specify that they should be laid out sequentially in the order in which they appear, just like a C structure.

Note Other possible values for the LayoutKind enumeration are: Auto (the default), which specifies that we want the runtime to choose an appropriate layout and Explicit, which allows you to explicitly specify the byte offset of each field in the structure.

Next I declare fields for the managed structure that match the type and size of the fields in the unmanaged, SYSTEMTIME structure. The managed, MySystemTime structure that I created has the same memory footprint as the unmanaged SYSTEMTIME structure. Finally, I add a managed code declaration for the GetSystemTime function that uses the managed code structure wherever the SYSTEMTIME structure is called for.

```
[DllImport("Kernel32.dll")]
public static extern void GetSystemTime(
      out MySystemTime st);
```

The following code shows how easy it is to call the GetSystemTime function from managed code once you have followed the preceding steps.

```
private void cmdGetDateTime_Click(object sender,
    System.EventArgs e)
{
    MySystemTime stm;
    GetSystemTime(out stm);
```

```
    txtDateTime.Text=stm.wDay.ToString() + "/" +
        stm.wMonth + "/" + stm.wYear;
}
```

Notice that I declare an instance of the MySystemTime managed structure and then I call the GetSystemTime method passing in the managed structure as an output parameter. After the method returns I can print out the contents of the managed structure

Summary

In this chapter, you learned about some of the advanced aspects of COM Interop from the perspective of a .NET client talking to a COM object. You learned about the object life cycle implications of COM Interop, that is, that a COM object when used through COM Interop will behave like a managed object because the RCW will hold a reference to the object until the RCW is garbage collected. If you want to destroy your COM object immediately after its use, you will need to call the ReleaseComObject method on the **System.Runtime.InteropServices.Marshal class**.

You next learned how COM events map to managed events. You learned that, even though this mapping is difficult to understand, it is trivial to use. I next turned my attention to how COM-rich error information is mapped to managed code exceptions. Then, I turned my attention to multithreading and COM Apartments. You learned that, even though managed code does not use COM Apartments by default, a managed thread will enter an Apartment if you use a COM object. For performance reasons, it is important that you make sure that this Apartment is compatible with the object that you are using. I showed you how to specify what type of Apartment your managed thread should enter. I next talked about primary Interop assemblies. You learned that, if you have created a COM object that you expect to be called from managed code, you should create a primary Interop assembly. By doing this, a client won't generate multiple versions of the Interop assembly for your COM object if the assembly is referenced by several other COM servers. Next I discussed Interop marshaling. You learned how COM Interop marshals strings that are declared by the COM object as something other than BSTR. I than spent a long time discussing arrays. I first talked about marshaling safe arrays, and then I talked about c-style arrays. I then talked about how to use ActiveX controls from managed clients. I then discussed the performance implications of COM Interop. I ended the chapter by discussing some advanced aspects of COM Interop.

In the next chapter, I will look at advanced aspects of COM to .NET Interop, that is, calling a managed code component from a COM/Win32 client.

E I G H T

Advanced COM to .NET Interop

In this chapter, I discuss advanced aspects of COM to .NET Interop, that is, using .NET components from a COM/Win32 client. Some of the issues that I discuss in this chapter include the following: techniques for creating objects without requiring registration, object life cycle implications, class interfaces, rich error information, using Windows Forms controls as ActiveX controls, managed events in unmanaged clients, and deployment. By the time you are done with this chapter, you will be ready to use COM to .NET Interop in most real-world scenarios.

Object Creation

In Chapter 6, I looked at using managed components from a COM/Win32 client at a very high level. In that chapter, you saw that, in order to use a .NET component from a COM/Win32 client, you had to insert registry entries for the .NET component that are similar to the entries required by a regular COM object. You also learned in Chapter 6 that, in order for a .NET object to be creatable from a COM client, it must have a default constructor, that is, a constructor that takes no arguments. The reason for this restriction is that the CoCreateInstance method—and the other object activation methods in the COM API--do not provide any means to pass initialization parameters to a COM object. Therefore, if an unmanaged client instantiates a managed object through CoCreateInstance, it has no way to pass parameters to the object's constructor. If you are willing to do a little extra work, you can get around both of these restrictions. In this section, you learn how to create a .NET object from an unmanaged client without having to register the .NET object first. You also learn how to create a .NET object and pass parameters to its constructor.

Creating Objects Without Registering Them First

The CLR execution engine (MSCOREE.DLL) exports a function called ClrCreateManagedInstance that you can use to create a COM object that has not been registered using the Assembly Registration Tool (regasm.exe). When you call CoCreateInstance (or a similar COM activation method), the COM runtime takes the CLSID that you pass to it and uses it to look up the path to the executable or DLL that implements the CLSID beneath the HKEY_CLASSES_ROOT\CLSID\{CLSIDForComponent} key in the registry. When you use the Assembly Registration Tool to register an assembly, it inserts an entry beneath HKEY_CLASSES_ROOT\CSLID\{CLSIDForComponent} that points to the CLR execution engine (MSCOREE.DLL) and then puts a value beneath that key that identifies the managed class that the CLR execution engine should load after it starts. The ClrCreateManagedInstance function takes an assembly name and the name of a class within the assembly to load. ClrCreateManagedInstance then loads the execution engine and uses the CLR's standard assembly search algorithm to find the assembly and load the specified class. Unfortunately, you cannot call the ClrCreateManagedInstance function from Visual Basic. To use the ClrCreateManagedInstance function, you must first reference the mscoree type library (mscoree.tlb) from a Visual C++ application using the #import keyword, which is part of the native COM support in Visual C++. You can find the mscoree type library at: **D:\WINNT\Microsoft.NET\Framework\v1.0.3705**. This is the correct version number for the release version of the .NET Framework, but your version number may vary. You can also use the mscoree include file (**mscoree.h**) or the mscoree IDL file (**mscoree.idl**) at **D:\Program Files\Microsoft Visual Studio .NET\FrameworkSDK\include**.

The following code shows Visual C++ logic that creates an instance of the .NET version of the financial component and calls the MonthlyPayment method. You do not need to register the assembly with the Assembly Registration Tool (regasm.exe) in order for this code to work.

```
void CTestClrCreateInstanceDlg::OnTestObjectButton()
{
      HRESULT hRes;
      DISPID dispid;
      float fltResult;
      CString strPayment;
      OLECHAR *methodName=L"MonthlyPayment";
      EXCEPINFO errorInfo;
      UINT intArg;
      VARIANT vntArgs[3], vntResult;
      DISPPARAMS param;
```

```
12.     param.cArgs=3;
13.     param.rgvarg=vntArgs;
14.     param.cNamedArgs=0;
15.     param.rgdispidNamedArgs=NULL;
16.     vntResult.vt=VT_R4;
17.     vntArgs[0].vt=VT_R4;
18.     vntArgs[0].fltVal=360000;
19.     vntArgs[1].vt=VT_R4;
20.     vntArgs[1].fltVal=6.75;
21.     vntArgs[2].vt=VT_I2;
22.     vntArgs[2].iVal=360;
23.     IDispatch *pObject;
24.
25.     hRes=::CoInitializeEx(NULL,COINIT_MULTITHREADED);
26.
27.     hRes=ClrCreateManagedInstance(
28.          L"DotNetFinancial.TimeValue,DotNetFinancial,
29.          Version=1.2.4.0,Culture=Neutral,
30.          PublicKeyToken=8a707be49fd7d8f4",
31.          IID_IDispatch,(void **)&pObject);
32.
33.     hRes=pObject->GetIDsOfNames(IID_NULL,&methodName,
34.           1,GetUserDefaultLCID(),&dispid);
35.
36.     hRes=pObject->Invoke(dispid,IID_NULL,
37.         GetUserDefaultLCID(),DISPATCH_METHOD,
38.         &param,&vntResult,&errorInfo,&intArg);
39.
40.     VarR4FromDec(&vntResult.decVal, &fltResult);
41.     strPayment.Format("$%.2f",fltResult);
42.     AfxMessageBox(strPayment);
43.
44.     if (pObject != NULL)
45.         pObject->Release();
46. }
```

In this code, you are late binding to the .NET Financial component using the IDispatch interface. Lines 3 through 11 are variable declarations. One of the most important of these declarations is on line 7 where you declare a string variable that contains the name of the method you plan to call (MonthlyPayment). Lines 12 through 22 initialize the DISPPARAMS structure that will hold the parameters that you will pass to the method. On line 25, you enter the MTA. So far, this code is identical to the code that you would write to access any COM component through the IDispatch interface. The most important lines of code in this example are lines 27 through 31. On these lines, you call the CLRCreateManagedInstance method to create an instance of the .NET Financial component. The CLRCreateManagedInstance method has three parameters. The first parameter contains the complete name of the class and the full name of the assembly where the class resides encoded as a string with the following format:

```
"Namespace.TypeName,[FullAssemblyName]"
```

The FullAssemblyName is the usual textual representation of a string name that includes the friendly name, version number, culture, and public key token of the assembly. The CLRCreateManagedInstance method will use the standard assembly search algorithm, so you don't need to register the assembly using regasm.exe. However, the assembly will either have to reside in the same directory as its client, or you will need to place it in the GAC. The remaining lines of code simply make a late-bound call to the MonthlyPayment method.

Remember that you need to include the header file for the runtime execution engine (mscoree.h) header file in order to compile the previous code. You also need to link with the link library for the execution library (mscoree.lib). If you are using Visual Studio .NET, you don't have to do any additional work to make all of this happen. The include and library directories for the .NET Framework SDK are included in the list of directories that Visual Studio .NET searches in for include and library files, respectively. If you are building your client with Visual Studio 6, you need to make some configuration changes before the previous code will compile.

First, you need to add the include directory for the .NET Framework SDK to the list of directories that Visual Studio 6 will search for include files. To do this, perform the following steps:

1. Select Tools | Options... and then click the Directory tab.
2. Select Include files from the Show directories for: drop-down list.
3. Click the New Entry button (the left-most button directly to the left of the red X).
4. Enter the location for the .NET Framework SDK include files. On my machine, it is **D:\PROGRAM FILES\MICROSOFT VISUAL STUDIO .NET\FRAMEWORKSDK\INCLUDE** (see Figure 8–1).

Also, make sure that you add the include file for the CLR execution engine to the top of your source file as shown here.

```
#include "mscoree.h"
```

Next, you need to add the .NET Framework SDKs library directory to the list of directories that Visual Studio 6 will search for libraries. To do this, perform the following steps:

1. Select Tools | Options... and then click the Directory tab.
2. Select Library files from the Show directories for: drop-down list.
3. Click the New Entry button.

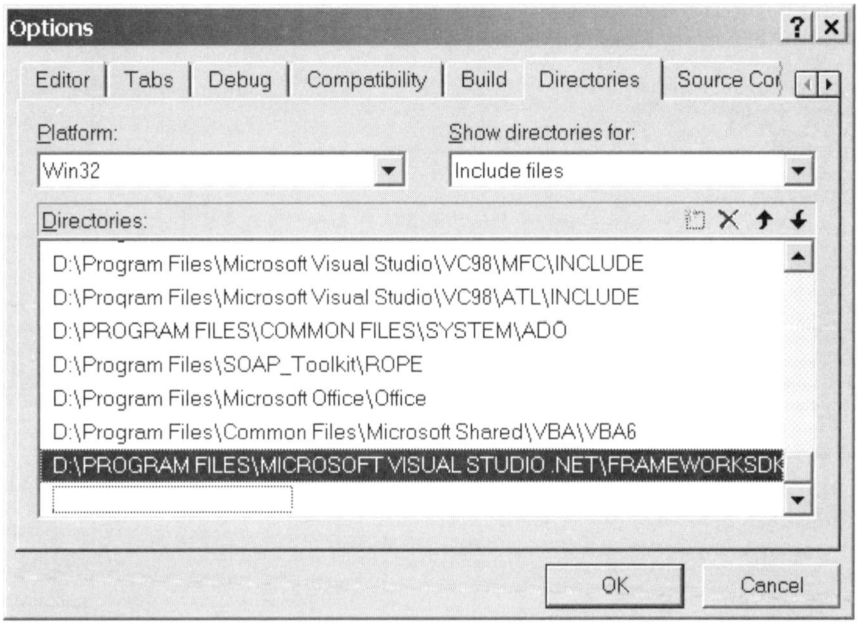

FIGURE 8–1 *Setting the Include directories on the Options dialog.*

4. Enter the location for the .NET Framework SDK library files. On my machine, it is **D:\PROGRAM FILES\MICROSOFT VISUAL STUDIO .NET\FRAMEWORKSDK\LIB** (see Figure 8–2).

Next you must add the link library for the CLR execution engine (mscorlib.lib) to the list of modules that the application will link with. To do this, perform the following steps:

1. Select Project | Settings. The Project Settings dialog will appear.
2. Click the Link tab and enter **mscoree.lib** in the Object/library modules: field (see Figure 8–3).

If you are using Visual Studio 6 and you want to use the CoInitializeEx method, you also need to add the following the following code to **stdafx.h**:

```
#define _WIN32_WINNT 0x0400
```

If you are using Visual Studio .NET, you do not need to perform this step. This last step has nothing to do with using .NET, but it is required to compile the code listing shown previously.

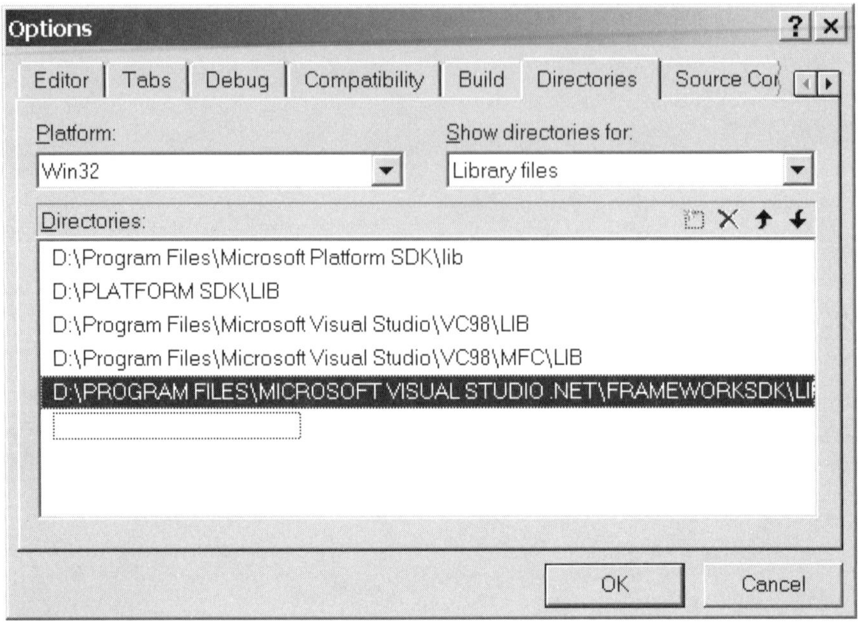

FIGURE 8–2 *Setting the Library directories on the Options dialog.*

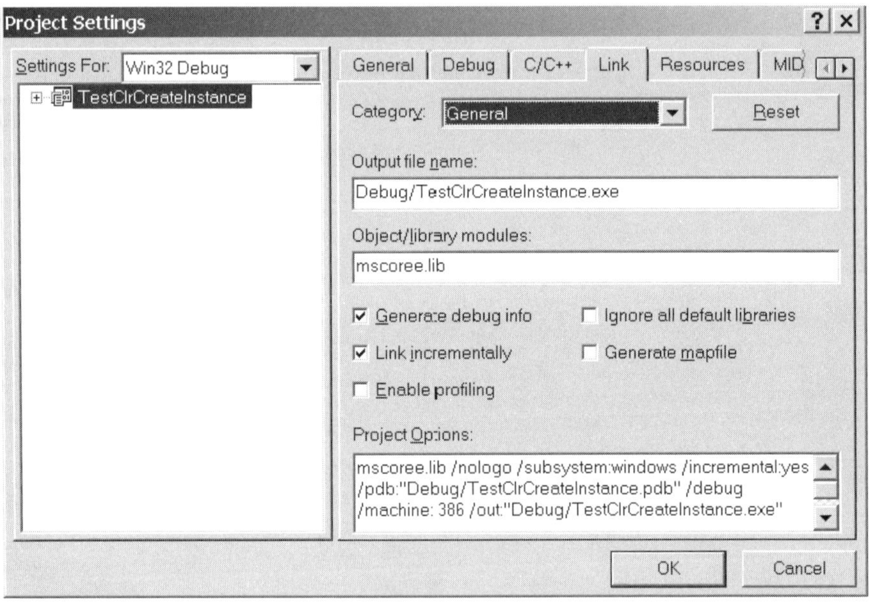

FIGURE 8–3 *Add the MsCoree library to the project settings.*

Hosting the CLR

Another way to access managed components from unmanaged code without having to register your assembly first is to host the CLR. The execution engine for the CLR is a DLL that can be hosted in any process. After you host the CLR, you can create application domains and load and run managed assemblies. You can find documentation on hosting the CLR at the following location: **[Visual Studio .NET Install Location]\FrameworkSDK\Tool Developers Guide\docs\Hosting Interfaces.doc**. On my machine, the exact location is: **D:\Program Files\Microsoft Visual Studio .NET\FrameworkSDK\Tool Developers Guide\docs\Hosting Interfaces.doc**.

One big advantage of hosting the CLR is that you can call nondefault constructors, that is, constructors that have arguments. The steps to hosting the CLR are as follows:

1. Create an instance of the **CorRuntimeHost** class.
2. Call the Start method on the object.
3. Create a new application domain (AppDomain object) or call GetDefault-Domain to get the default application domain.
4. Call the CreateInstance method on the **AppDomain** class to instantiate managed objects.
5. Call methods on the managed objects.
6. Call stop on the CorRuntimeHost instance when you are done.

You can host the CLR from a Visual Basic or a Visual C++ application. If you are using Visual Basic, you will need to reference the CLR execution engine 1.0 library (mscoree.tlb), which you can find at the following location: [.NET Framework SDK Install Dir]\v[Version#]\mscoree.tlb. On my machine, this file resides at **D:\WINNT\Microsoft.NET\Framework\v1.0.3705\mscoree.tlb**.

If you do not see an entry called Common Language Runtime Execution Engine 1.0 Library when you select Project | References..., just click the Browse... button and navigate to the location where the file resides on your machine. Because the CLR execution engine uses types from the CLR library, you also need to reference type library for the Common Language Runtime Library, which you can find at the following location: **[.NET Framework SDK Install Dir]\v[Version#]\mscorlibee.tlb**. This file resides at the following location on my machine: **D:\WINNT\Microsoft.NET\Framework\v1.0.3705\mscorlib.tlb**.

The following code shows how to host the CLR from a Visual Basic program:

```
Private Sub Command1_Click()
    Dim clr As CorRuntimeHost
    Dim domain As AppDomain
    Dim params(3) As Object
```

```
5.       Dim objFinancial As Object
6.       Dim fltResult As Single
7.       Set clr = New CorRuntimeHost
8.       clr.Start
9.       clr.GetDefaultDomain domain
10.      Set objFinancial = domain.CreateInstance(
11.         "DotNetFinancial,
12.         Version=1.2.4.0,Culture=Neutral,
13.         PublicKeyToken=8a707be49fd7d8f4",
14.           "DotNetFinancial.TimeValue").Unwrap
15.      fltResult = objFinancial.MonthlyPayment(
16.         360, 6.75, 360000)
17.      clr.Stop
18.      lblPayment.Caption = fltResult
19. End Sub
```

Lines 1 through 6 contain variable declarations; the most important of these is the declaration of a CorRuntimeHost reference on line 2. On line 7, you create an instance of the **CorRuntimeHost** class. On line 8, you call the Start method on this object. Even though the documentation on hosting the CLR states that calling Start and Stop on the CorRuntimeHost object is not strictly necessary, I found that, if you omitted the Start and Stop methods, the previous code would only work correctly if you ran it from within the Visual Basic 6 IDE. If you build the executable without the Start and Stop methods, you always get a Catastrophic failure error when you run the application from the ".exe" file. On line 9, you call the GetDefaultDomain method on the **CorRuntimeHost** class to fetch an AppDomain object that references the default domain. Notice that the domain is returned as an output parameter to this method. On line 10, you call the CreateInstance method on the AppDomain object to create an instance of the **TimeValue** class in the DotNetFinancial namespace. The first parameter to the CreateInstance method is the full name of the assembly that contains the class. You must specify a full name if the assembly resides in the GAC. If the assembly is private, you can load it with a partial name. If you were using a private assembly, you could replace lines 10 through 14 shown previously with the following code:

```
        Set objFinancial =
domain.CreateInstance("DotNetFinancial",
"DotNetFinancial.TimeValue").Unwrap
```

The only exception to this rule is the mscorlib assembly. You can create instances of classes in this library by specifying a partial name even though it resides in the GAC.

Regardless of whether you use a full or partial name to reference the type name, DotNetFinancial.TimeValue must be qualified with its namespace, and the type name is case sensitive. Notice that you call the Unwrap method on the return value of the Unwrap method. The CreateInstance method returns an object handle (an instance of the **Mscorlib.ObjectHandle** class). You must call the Unwrap method on this object in order to get a reference to a callable object.

If you are using Visual C++, you can use the CreateInstance_3 in the _AppDomain interface to instantiate an object that has a parameterized constructor.

Note CreateInstance_3 is actually the name for one of the overloads of the CreateInstance method on the AppDomain class. See the section in this chapter entitled "Overloaded Methods" for an explanation of why this has such an odd name.

In this case, you are using the CreateInstance_3 method to instantiate the **manager** class that you created in Chapter 3. (I repeated the definition of the class here for your convenience.)

```
namespace AssemblyDemo
{

        public class Manager : Employee
        {
          public Manager(int id,string name,
              decimal salary,decimal bonus) :
              base(id,name,salary)
          {
            this.mBonus=bonus;
          }
          public override decimal GetSalary()
          {
            return base.GetSalary()+mBonus;
          }
          private System.Object[] _array;
          private decimal mBonus;
        }
 }
```

You cannot call the Create_Instance_3 method from Visual Basic because it uses by-value array parameters, which Visual Basic does not support.

```
void CVcpphostclrDlg::OnTestmanagedclassButton()
{
    HRESULT hRes;
    ICorRuntimeHost *pRuntimeHost;
    IUnknown *pUnkAppDomain;
    _AppDomain *pAppDomain;
    _ObjectHandle *pHandle;
    OLECHAR *methodName=L"GetSalary";
    VARIANT vntResult;
```

```
    float fltVal;
    DISPID dispid;
    EXCEPINFO errorInfo;
    UINT intArg;
    DISPPARAMS param;
    BSTR bstrTypeName, bstrAssemblyName;
    SAFEARRAY *paramArray;
    VARIANT paramID, paramName;
    VARIANT paramSalary, paramBonus;
    LONG index;
    hRes=CoInitializeEx(NULL,COINIT_MULTITHREADED);
    if (FAILED(hRes))
        AfxMessageBox("Could not initialize COM");
    hRes=CoCreateInstance(CLSID_CorRuntimeHost,
        NULL,CLSCTX_INPROC_SERVER,
        IID_ICorRuntimeHost,
        (void **)&pRuntimeHost);
    if (FAILED(hRes))
        AfxMessageBox("Could not create host");
    hRes=pRuntimeHost->Start();
    hRes=pRuntimeHost->GetDefaultDomain(
        &pUnkAppDomain);
    if (FAILED(hRes))
        AfxMessageBox("Could not get Appdomain");
    hRes=pUnkAppDomain->QueryInterface(
        IID__AppDomain,(void **)&pAppDomain);
    if (FAILED(hRes))
        AfxMessageBox("Failed to get domain");
    if (pUnkAppDomain!=NULL)
        pUnkAppDomain->Release();
    bstrTypeName=SysAllocString(
        L"AssemblyDemo.Manager");
    bstrAssemblyName=SysAllocString(
        L"multifile3,Version=2.0.0.0,Culture=neutral,
          PublicKeyToken=8a707be49fd7d8f4");
    paramArray=SafeArrayCreateVector(VT_VARIANT,0,4);

    VariantInit(&paramID);
    paramID.vt=VT_I4;
    paramID.lVal=45;
    index=0;
    hRes=SafeArrayPutElement(paramArray,
        &index,&paramID);
    VariantInit(&paramName);
    paramName.vt=VT_BSTR;
    paramName.bstrVal=SysAllocString(L"Alan Gordon");
    index=1;
    hRes=SafeArrayPutElement(paramArray,
        &index,&paramName);
    VariantInit(&paramSalary);
```

```
    paramSalary.vt=VT_R4;
    paramSalary.fltVal=1000.0;
    VariantChangeType(&paramSalary,&paramSalary,
        0,VT_DECIMAL);
    index=2;
    hRes=SafeArrayPutElement(paramArray,
        &index,&paramSalary);
    VariantInit(&paramBonus);
    paramBonus.vt=VT_R4;
    paramBonus.fltVal=100.0;
    VariantChangeType(&paramBonus,&paramBonus,
        0,VT_DECIMAL);
    index=3;
    hRes=SafeArrayPutElement(paramArray,
        &index,&paramBonus);
    hRes=pAppDomain->CreateInstance_3(
        bstrAssemblyName,bstrTypeName,VARIANT_TRUE,
        BindingFlags_Default,NULL,paramArray,
        NULL,NULL,NULL,&pHandle);
    if (FAILED(hRes))
        AfxMessageBox("Could not create object");
    VARIANT vntObject;
    IDispatch *pObject;
    VariantInit(&vntObject);
    pHandle->Unwrap(&vntObject);
    vntObject.punkVal->QueryInterface(IID_IDispatch,
        (void **)&pObject);
    if (vntObject.punkVal!=NULL)
        vntObject.punkVal->Release();

    param.cArgs=0;
    param.rgvarg=NULL;
    param.cNamedArgs=0;
    param.rgdispidNamedArgs=NULL;
    VariantInit(&vntResult);
    hRes=pObject->GetIDsOfNames(IID_NULL,
        &methodName,1,GetUserDefaultLCID(),&dispid);
    hRes=pObject->Invoke(dispid,IID_NULL,
        GetUserDefaultLCID(),
        DISPATCH_METHOD,&param,&vntResult,
        &errorInfo,&intArg);
    if (SUCCEEDED(hRes))
    {
        vntResult.decVal;
        VarR4FromDec(&vntResult.decVal,&fltVal);
    }
    else
    {
    // Handle the error, code omitted…
    }
```

```
110.     if (pObject!=NULL)
111.         pObject->Release();
112.     if (pAppDomain!=NULL)
113.         pAppDomain->Release();
114.
115.     SysFreeString(bstrTypeName);
116.     SysFreeString(bstrAssemblyName);
117.     SafeArrayDestroy(paramArray);
118. }
```

Lines 3 through 19 contain variable declarations. On line 20, you enter the multithreaded apartment. Lines 23 through 26 create an instance of the **CorRuntimeHost** class and request the ICorRuntimeHost interface. On line 29, you call the start method, and, on line 30, you get the default appdomain. So far, the code that you have written is identical to the Visual Basic code that you wrote earlier to host the runtime. The difference starts on line 45 where you create a SafeArray of variants that will contain the parameters you will pass to the constructor. Lines 47 through 74 initialize each argument by first calling the VariantInit function and then initializing the fields of each variant. You then call the SafeArrayPutElement method to insert each parameter into the SafeArray. Lines 75 through 78 call the CreateInstance_3 method and pass in the full assembly name and the name of the type that you wish to instantiate for the first two parameters. The third, fourth, and fifth parameters are, respectively, as follows:

- Boolean specifying whether the type name is case sensitive or not
- Flag indicating whether to do a case-sensitive search for a constructor
- Binder object that affects how you bind, coerce and retrieve argument types

The sixth parameter is the array of parameters that you wish to pass to the method. The seventh, eighth, and ninth arguments are the culture, the activation attributes, and the security attributes. The tenth parameter is an output parameter that contains the return value for the method, which is an object handle. Lines 81 through 88 turn the object handle into an IDispatch pointer, and then, lines 90 through 100 make a late-bound call to the GetSalary method on the **Manager** class. Lines 101 through 105 process the return value into a floating-point variable, and lines 110 through 117 contain cleanup code.

Object Life-Cycle Implications

When you are using a managed code object from a COM/Win32 client, you face a mismatch between the life-cycle scheme that the client uses and expects and the life cycle that the underlying object uses. As you already learned in Chapter 6, the CCW exposes a managed object to unmanaged consumers so that it appears for all intents and purposes to be like any other COM object. The CCW synthesizes an implementation of system-level interfaces like IUnknown, IDispatch, and ISupportsErrorInfo. The CCW exposes COM equivalents of any managed interfaces that the managed class supports, and it may also expose a class interface that exposes all of the public methods implemented by the class. All of these interfaces exposed by the CCW support a reference counting, life-cycle management scheme through the AddRef and Release methods in the IUnknown interface. Under the covers though, the CCW is holding an internal reference to the underlying COM object as shown in Figure 8–4.

When you release all the COM interfaces that you are holding on the object, the CCW will remove its reference on the managed object. The managed object then becomes eligible for garbage collection, but it is not immediately destroyed. In fact, it won't be destroyed until the garbage collector runs, which, in many cases, won't be until the client application shuts down. This is the expected behavior for a managed class, but it's not the behavior that a COM/Win32 client is expecting. A COM/Win32 client will expect the object to destroy itself immediately after it makes its final Release call on the object.

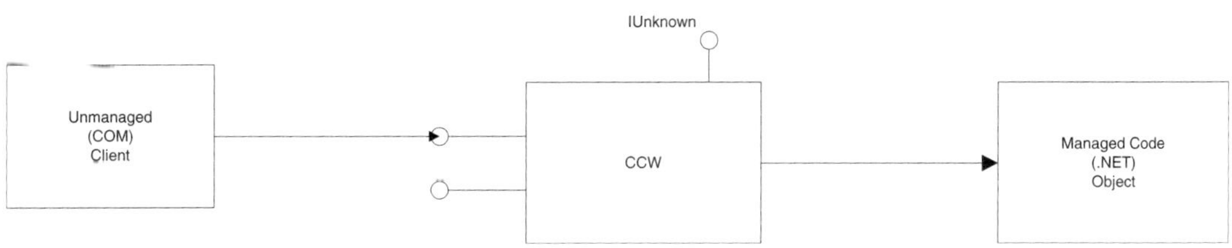

FIGURE 8–4 *The CCW holding a reference to a managed object.*

Using the IDisposable Interface from an Unmanaged Client

If the managed object holds time-critical resources and implements the IDisposable interface, the COM/Win32 client can get the IDisposable interface and call the Dispose method explicitly, just as a managed client would. How the client will call the Dispose method depends on whether the client is implemented in Visual Basic or Visual C++; it also depends on the class interface options you chose for your managed class. The following code shows how you would call the Dispose method from an unmanaged Visual C++ client:

```
1.  void CVcppclientDlg::OnCalculatePaymentButton()
2.  {
3.        HRESULT hRes;
4.        IDispatch *pDisp;
5.        IDisposable *pDisposable;
6.        CLSID clsID;
7.        hRes=CLSIDFromProgID(L"LifeCycleDemo.TestClass",
8.          &clsID);
9.        hRes=CoCreateInstance(clsID,NULL,CLSCTX_ALL,
10.         IID_IDispatch,(void**)&pDisp);
11.  // Use the object here…
12.       hRes=pDisp->QueryInterface(
13.         IID_IDisposable,(void **)&pDisposable);
14.       if (SUCCEEDED(hRes))
15.       {
16.         pDisposable->Dispose();
17.         pDisposable->Release();
18.       }
19.       pDisp->Release();
20. }
```

Lines 3 through 6 contain variable declarations. Line 7 calls the CLSIDFromProgID method to get the CLSID for the managed class. Lines 9 and 10 call the CoCreateInstance method and request the IDispatch interface. (You could also have requested IUnknown here.) Lines 12 and 13 run a QueryInterface for the IDisposable interface. Assuming the call to QueryInterface succeeds, lines 16 and 17 call the Dispose method on the IDisposable interface pointer and then release the interface. Line 19 releases the interface that you acquired on lines 9 and 10. As with all of my COM-related examples, I use less-than-perfect error handling for the sake of brevity.

In order to compile this code, you must reference the type library for the .NET Framework class library (mscorlib.tlb) using Visual C++'s native COM support as follows in **stdafx.h**:

```
#import "mscorlib.tlb" no_namespace named_guids
raw_interfaces_only exclude("IObjectHandle")
```

You will need to do this regardless of whether you are using Visual C++ 6 or Visual Studio .NET. This statement will include the definition of the IDisposable interface in the Visual C++ project as well as GUIDs, such as IID_IDisposable. Keep in mind that, by default, the CCW exposes an IDispatch interface that contains all of the methods and properties supported by the managed object, including the Dispose method if the object implements the IDisposable interface. Therefore, if you would prefer instead to take a late bound approach, you can also call the Dispose method using the following code:

```
1.  void CVcppclientDlg::OnCalculatePaymentButton()
2.  {
3.       HRESULT hRes;
4.       DISPID dispid;
5.       IDispatch *pDisp;
6.       OLECHAR *methodName;
7.       CLSID clsID;
8.       EXCEPINFO errorInfo;
9.       UINT intArg;
10.      DISPPARAMS param;
11.      param.cArgs=0;
12.      param.rgvarg=NULL;
13.      param.cNamedArgs=0;
14.      param.rgdispidNamedArgs=NULL;
15.
16.      hRes=CLSIDFromProgID(L"LifeCycleDemo.TestClass",
17.        &clsID);
18.      hRes=CoCreateInstance(clsID,NULL,CLSCTX_ALL,
19.        IID_IDispatch,(void**)&pDisp);
20. // Use the object here…
21.      methodName=L"Dispose";
22.      hRes=pDisp->GetIDsOfNames(IID_NULL,
23.           &methodName,1,GetUserDefaultLCID(),&dispid);
24.      hRes=pDisp->Invoke(dispid,IID_NULL,
25.        GetUserDefaultLCID(),
26.        DISPATCH_METHOD,&param,NULL,
27.        &errorInfo,&intArg);
28.
29.      pDisp->Release();
30. }
```

Lines 3 through 10 contain variable declarations. Lines 11 through 14 initialize the DISPPARAMs structure that will contain the parameters that you will pass to the Invoke method. Lines 16 through 19 call the CLSIDFromProgID method to get the CLSID of the managed class, and then they use the CoCreateInstance method to create an instance of the managed class. Lines 21 through 23 call the GetIDsOfNames method to get the ProgID of the Dispose method, and then, on lines 24 through 27, I call the Dispose method via the

Invoke method on IDispatch. Finally, I call the Release method on IDispatch on line 29.

Here is early-bound code showing you how to call the IDisposable.Dispose method from a Visual Basic client:

```
1.  Private Sub Command1_Click()
2.       Dim objLifeCycleDemo As Object
3.       Dim intfDisposable As IDisposable
4.       Set objLifeCycleDemo = CreateObject(
5.         "LifeCycleDemo.TestClass")
6.  ‘ Use the object here…
7.
8.       Set intfDisposable = objLifeCycleDemo
9.       intfDisposable.Dispose
10. End Sub
```

The code here is very simple. Lines 2 and 3 contain variable declarations for a late-bound object (objLifeCycleDemo) and an IDisposable interface pointer (intfDisposable). Lines 4 and 5 call the CreateObject method to create an instance of the managed class and then assign the object reference to the objLifeCycleDemo object variable. I then use the object and, on lines 8 and 9, get an IDisposable interface from the object reference and call the Dispose method. In order to compile this code, you must reference the type library called CLR Library using the Project | References... command in Visual Basic. Here is the late-bound equivalent of the Visual Basic code:

```
1.  Private Sub Command1_Click()
2.      Dim objLifeCycleDemo As Object
3.      Set objLifeCycleDemo = CreateObject(
4.       "LifeCycleDemo.TestClass")
5.  ' Use the object here…
6.
7.      objLifeCycleDemo.Dispose
8.  End Sub
```

Line 2 declares a late-bound object reference. Lines 3 and 4 instantiate an instance of the managed class. I can then use the object, and, finally, on line 7, I call Dispose through the late-bound class interface that the CCW exposes. With this code, you do not have to reference the CLR library.

Using CorExitProcess

In many cases, the garbage collector will not run until an application shuts down. If you create managed objects and use them from a managed client, the CLR will run the garbage collector and will faithfully call the Finalization method on every object that you instantiated before the application shuts down. Unfortunately, things don't work as well when you instantiate a managed object from an unmanaged client. The process termination steps are different for a managed executable as opposed to an unmanaged executable, and any managed objects that are still alive when you shut down an unmanaged application will not have their Finalization methods called. Fortunately, the CLR's runtime execution engine (**mscoree.dll**) exports a method called CorExitProcess that you may call from an unmanaged client that will force a Finalization method call on every managed object that the unmanaged process currently contains. You should place the call to CorExitProcess as near as possible to the end of your application. The CorExitProcess method is declared as follows in **mscoree.h**, where exitCode is just the integer value that the process will return when it shuts down.

```
void STDMETHODCALLTYPE CorExitProcess(int exitCode)
```

The bolded code that follows shows a call to CorExitProcess in the InitInstance method of an MFC dialog-based application:

```
BOOL CVcppclientApp::InitInstance()
{
    AfxEnableControlContainer();

    CVcppclientDlg dlg;
    m_pMainWnd = &dlg;
    int nResponse = dlg.DoModal();
    if (nResponse == IDOK)
    {
    // TODO: Place code here to handle when the dialog is
    //  dismissed with OK
    }
    else if (nResponse == IDCANCEL)
    {
    // TODO: Place code here to handle when the dialog is
    //  dismissed with Cancel
    }
    ::CorExitProcess(0);
    return FALSE;
}
```

In order to use this code, you need to include **mscoree.h** at the top of the file and link with **mscoree.lib**. Remember that, if you are using Visual Studio 6, you will need to add the path to the .NET Framework SDK include and library files on the Directories tab of the Tools | Options... dialog. If you are using Visual Studio .NET, no additional project configuration is necessary.

Overloaded Methods

A managed class can have overloaded methods. A single method name can have multiple argument lists and return values. Unfortunately, COM does not support overloaded methods. The CCW that .NET exposes to unmanaged clients handles this mismatch by exposing one unmanaged method that has the exact name as the overloaded method. It then exposes the other overloaded versions of the method with _N appended to the managed name where N starts at 2. For instance, given the following managed class, which has three different versions of a method called TestMethod:

```
using System;
using System.Runtime.InteropServices;
namespace TestOverload
{
    public class TestClass
    {
      public TestClass()
      {

      }
      public string TestMethod(int arg1)
      {
          return "TestMethod(int arg1)";
      }
      public string TestMethod(int arg1,string arg2)
      {
          return "TestMethod(int arg1,string arg2)";
      }
      public string TestMethod(string arg1,string arg2)
      {
          return "TestMethod(string arg1,string arg2)";
      }
    }
}
```

The CCW will expose the following methods from its automatically generated class interface (_TestClass):

```
[id(0x60020004)] HRESULT TestMethod(
        [in] long arg1,[out, retval] BSTR* pRetVal);
[id(0x60020005)] HRESULT TestMethod_2(
        [in] long arg1,[in] BSTR arg2,
        [out, retval] BSTR* pRetVal);
[id(0x60020006)] HRESULT TestMethod_3(
        [in] BSTR arg1,[in] BSTR arg2,
        [out, retval] BSTR* pRetVal);
```

Unless you use the ClassInterface attribute on the managed class and specify AutoDual for the ClassInterfaceType, these methods will not be exposed directly from the exposed class interface. The class interface instead looks as follows:

```
interface _TestClass : IDispatch
{
};
```

You will only be able to invoke the overloaded methods through the Invoke method of IDispatch. This presents a problem. If you have three overloads of a particular method, you know that the equivalent unmanaged method names will be MethodName, MethodName_2, and MethodName_3. However, if you only have a late-bound interface, you won't know which argument list corresponds to which unmanaged method name. For instance, you may know that you want to call the version of TestMethod method that takes two string arguments, but, unless you use the AutoDual attribute to generate the overloaded methods explicitly, how will you know that the version of the TestMethod method with two string arguments corresponds to TestMethod_3?

You can figure this out in two ways. The first way is to use the ClassInterface attribute (with AutoDual) to generate a late-bound interface temporarily, which will show the mapping of unmanaged method names to the various permutations of the overloaded managed method. In other words, if you add the following line to the TestClass

```
[ClassInterface(ClassInterfaceType.AutoDual)]
public class TestClass
{
// Implementation omitted…
}
```

The Assembly Registration Tool will generate the following class interface:

```
interface _TestClass : IDispatch
{
//… other methods omitted
    [id(0x60020004)] HRESULT TestMethod(
        [in] long arg1,[out, retval] BSTR* pRetVal);
    [id(0x60020005)] HRESULT TestMethod_2(
        [in] long arg1,[in] BSTR arg2,
        [out, retval] BSTR* pRetVal);
    [id(0x60020006)] HRESULT TestMethod_3(
        [in] BSTR arg1,[in] BSTR arg2,
        [out, retval] BSTR* pRetVal);
}
```

This interface clearly shows which overloaded argument list corresponds to each unmanaged method name. You don't have to keep the early-bindable version of the assembly around. As soon as you have figured out the mapping of the overloaded managed methods to the various permutations of the overloaded unmanaged methods, you can remove the ClassInterface attribute and go back to accessing your managed components through the late-bound interface. Another way to determine which overload corresponds to a particular unmanaged method is to use the IL Disassembler (ILDASM). Bring up ILDASM on your assembly and make sure that Sort by name and Show Public are the only items selected under the View menu and then view the list of methods for your class. The order in which the methods are displayed tells you which method corresponds to each unique unmanaged name. Using this example, the first method in the list will have the name TestMethod, and the next two will have the names TestMethod_2 and TestMethod_3.

COM Apartments

Whether you register a managed object using the Assembly Registration Tool (regasm) or you use one of the activation functions that do not require registration, like ClrCreateManagedInstance, a managed object behaves like a COM object with the Both threading model when called from an unmanaged client. In other words, the object will run on the same thread as its caller whether the calling thread resides within an STA or an MTA. The implication of this is that, if you are going to call a managed object from a multithreaded unmanaged client, you need to make sure that the managed object is thread safe. With COM, if you did not want to write thread synchronization code, you could simply specify that your object use an STA. With the .NET Framework, if multithreaded clients will use your managed class, you must write thread synchronization code using the **System.Threading.Monitor** or **System.Threading.Mutex** classes. You can also use the lock statement in C#, which simplifies the use of **System.Threading.Monitor**.

Using Types from the .NET Framework Class Library

The .NET Framework class library contains a rich set of classes, some of which have no analog in the various unmanaged class libraries that are available to programmers on Microsoft platforms, such as MFC, ATL, and the Visual Basic runtime. Unfortunately, many of these classes are invisible to COM.

Note I was disappointed to find that the very useful and well-designed regular expression classes in the System.Text.RegularExpression namespace are COM invisible. I really wanted to use them as my demonstration for this section.

For the classes that are visible, you have three ways to use them from an unmanaged application: (1) You can register the assembly that contains the class, (2) you can call the ClrCreateManagedInstance method to create an instance of the class without registering its assembly, or (3) you can host the CLR and call one of the object creation methods in the **CorRuntimeHost** class. The code you write if you use one of the last two options is almost identical to what you would write if you used a user-defined class with the ClrCreateManagedInstance method or by hosting the CLR. The main difference is that, if you are using the mscorlib library, you do not have to use the full assembly name even though it resides in the GAC.

If you use either of the first two choices, you can only instantiate managed classes that have constructors that take no parameters. Hosting the CLR is more complicated, but it's the only way that you can create instances of classes that have parameterized constructors using the CreateInstance_3 overload of the CreateInstance method on the **CorRuntimeHost** class. (Remember that you cannot call the method that takes parameterized constructors from Visual Basic.) Let's look briefly at each of these techniques for using the classes in the .NET Framework class library from unmanaged code.

Registering the Assembly

Checking the registry on my machine showed that only the types in the System.EnterpriseServices namespace (these classes wrap the COM+ Services) are pre-registered by the setup program for the .NET Framework SDK. If you want to use any of the other managed types in the .NET Framework class library from your unmanaged applications using standard COM Activation functions, you will need to add the prerequisite registry entries for those types using the Assembly Registration Tool (regasm.exe). In order to use the **Stack** class, I registered the core library assembly (**mscorlib.dll**) by navigating to the directory where the .NET Framework library files reside (**D:\WINNT\Microsoft.NET\Framework\v1.0.3705** on my machine) and then running the following command:

```
Regasm mscorlib.dll
```

I then wrote the following code in Visual Basic 6, which uses the **Stack** class. To compile this code, I also had to reference the type library for the core library assembly by selecting Project | References... | Common Language Runtime Library.

```
Private Sub Command1_Click()
    Dim aStack As Stack
    Set aStack = New Stack
    aStack.Push ("Shaquille ONeil")
    aStack.Push ("Kobe Bryant")
    aStack.Push ("Derek Fisher")
    aStack.Push ("Robert Horry")
```

```
8.      aStack.Push ("Rick Fox")
9.      MsgBox aStack.Count
10.     aStack.Pop
11.     MsgBox aStack.Pop
12. End Sub
```

Line 2 declares an instance of the **Stack** class from the .NET Framework class library. Line 3 creates an instance of this class, and then lines 4 through 8 push the names of the starting lineup for the Los Angeles Lakers onto the stack. Line 9 displays the number of items on the stack (5), and then lines 10 and 11 pop two items off the stack. If you neglected to register the **mscorlib.dll** assembly, you will get a runtime error when you attempt to instantiate the stack object. Notice that the class interface for the **Stack** class is an empty interface that does not contain any methods. You are actually calling these methods through the IDispatch interface, so the Push, Count, or Pop methods will not appear in Visual Basic's IntelliSense.

Calling the ClrCreateManagedInstance Method

Another way to use types from the .NET Framework class library is to use the ClrCreateManagedInstance method. By using this method, you avoid having to register any of the class assemblies. The code here is very similar to the code that you looked at earlier that used ClrCreateManagedInstance with a user-defined managed class. The main difference is that you don't have to use the full name of the mscorlib assembly even though it resides in the GAC. In this case, I will demonstrate using the **Stack** class (late bound) from a Visual C++ 6 application.

```
void CUsecollectionsvcppDlg::OnButton1()
{
      HRESULT hRes;
      DISPID dispid;
      BSTR bstrItem1, bstrItem2;
      CString strResult;
      OLECHAR *methodName=L"Push";
      EXCEPINFO errorInfo;
      UINT intArg;
      VARIANT vntArgs[1], vntResult;
      DISPPARAMS param;
      param.cArgs=1;
      param.rgvarg=vntArgs;
      param.cNamedArgs=0;
      param.rgdispidNamedArgs=NULL;
      vntResult.vt=VT_R4;
      vntArgs[0].vt=VT_BSTR;

      bstrItem1=SysAllocString(L"Alan Gordon");
      vntArgs[0].bstrVal=bstrItem1;
```

```
    IDispatch *pObject;

    hRes=::CoInitializeEx(NULL,COINIT_MULTITHREADED);

    hRes=ClrCreateManagedInstance(
      L"System.Collections.Stack,mscorlib",
      IID_IDispatch, (void **)&pObject);

    hRes=pObject->GetIDsOfNames(IID_NULL,&methodName,
        1,GetUserDefaultLCID(),&dispid);

    hRes=pObject->Invoke(dispid,IID_NULL,
        GetUserDefaultLCID(),DISPATCH_METHOD,
        &param,NULL,&errorInfo,&intArg);

    bstrItem2=SysAllocString(L"Tamber Gordon");
    vntArgs[0].bstrVal=bstrItem2;

    hRes=pObject->Invoke(dispid,IID_NULL,
        GetUserDefaultLCID(),DISPATCH_METHOD,
        &param,NULL,&errorInfo,&intArg);

    methodName=L"Count";
    hRes=pObject->GetIDsOfNames(IID_NULL,&methodName,
        1,GetUserDefaultLCID(),&dispid);
    param.cArgs=0;
    hRes=pObject->Invoke(dispid,IID_NULL,
        GetUserDefaultLCID(),DISPATCH_PROPERTYGET,
        &param,&vntResult,&errorInfo,&intArg);

    strResult.Format(
      "Stack contains %d items",
      vntResult.lVal);
    AfxMessageBox(strResult);

    methodName=L"Clear";
    hRes=pObject->GetIDsOfNames(IID_NULL,&methodName,
        1,GetUserDefaultLCID(),&dispid);
    param.cArgs=0;
    hRes=pObject->Invoke(dispid,IID_NULL,
        GetUserDefaultLCID(),DISPATCH_METHOD,
        &param,NULL,&errorInfo,&intArg);

    if (pObject != NULL)
      pObject->Release();

    SysFreeString(bstrItem1);
    SysFreeString(bstrItem2);
}
```

Lines 3 through 11 declare variables. Lines 12 through 20 initialize the DISPPARAMS structure that will contain the parameters that I will pass to the Push method. On line 23, I enter the MTA. Lines 25 through 27 are the key lines in this example. There I call the ClrCreateManagedInstance method. The first parameter contains the type name and the partial name of the assembly. (Remember you don't need a full name for mscorlib.) Lines 29 and 30 get the DISPID for the Push method. I then call the Push method twice on lines 32 through 34 and again on lines 39 through 41. Lines 47 through 49 call the Count method, and Lines 51 through 54 display the value. Lines 56 through 62 call the Clear method on the stack to remove all the items that I pushed onto it. Finally, lines 64 through 68 clean up.

Remember that you need to add the directory that contains the include files for the .NET Framework SDK to the list of directories that Visual C++ will search for include files. You also need to add the directory that contains the library files for the .NET Framework SDK to the list of directories that Visual C++ will search for library files. In addition, you need to add the CLR execution engine (mscoree.lib) to the list of libraries that the project will link with.

Hosting the CLR

The two techniques that you have seen so far for using System classes—that is, registering the classes or calling ClrCreateManagedInstance—have one fatal flaw. You cannot use classes unless they have a constructor that takes no arguments. Unfortunately, that eliminates many useful classes in the .NET Framework class library from consideration for use.

As you learned in Chapter 3 when I discussed MSIL, the capacity parameter allows you to specify how large the stack's internal storage is initially. It's important to make this parameter as large as you expect the stack to be because expanding the internal storage is an expensive operation. Because of this, most of the collections in the .NET Framework class library support a constructor that allows you to specify the initial size of its internal buffer. The only way to call a parameterized constructor from unmanaged code is by hosting the CLR and using the CreateInstance_3 method on the **AppDomain** class. The code to do this is no different than the example that I looked at earlier that uses the CreateInstance_3 method, so I won't show the listing here. The difference is that you don't have to use the full name for the mscorlib library.

Class Interfaces Revisited

You always interact with a COM object through the interface(s) that it implements. A managed object, however, is not required to implement any interfaces. Therefore, when you use a managed object from an unmanaged client, one of the first questions you must ask yourself is what COM interface should you use to talk to the managed object? In Chapter 6, you learned that, by default, the CCW will expose a late-bound (IDispatch) interface through which you can call all of the public methods that the managed object exports. You can either use this IDispatch interface to call the managed object's methods (by running a QueryInterface for IID_IDispatch in Visual C++ or declaring your object variable to be of type object in Visual Basic), or you can use an empty IDispatch-derived interface that regasm will generate for you. This interface is called a class interface. For instance, a managed class that is declared as shown here in C#:

```
namespace DotNetFinancial
{
    public class TimeValue
    {
      public TimeValue()
      {
}
      public decimal MonthlyPayment(
          short numMonths,
          double interestRate,
          decimal loanAmt)
      {
      //...
      }
      public decimal LoanAmount(
          short numMonths,
          double interestRate,
          decimal monthlyPmt)
      {
      //...
      }
    }
}
```

will produce the following interface and coclass when you generate a type library using the assembly registration tool:

```
   [
   odl,
   uuid(F00794BD-914A-3411-A633-6FABAD549E80),
   hidden,
   dual,
   oleautomation,
   custom({0F21F359-AB84-41E8-9A78-36D110E6D2F9},
   "DotNetFinancial.TimeValue")
]
interface _TimeValue : IDispatch {
};
```

```
[
   uuid(311F0CBD-FB08-3DB4-A87C-96EA3C30DA0D),
   version(1.0),
   custom({0F21F359-AB84-41E8-9A78-36D110E6D2F9},
   "DotNetFinancial.TimeValue")
]
coclass TimeValue {
   [default] interface _TimeValue;
   interface _Object;
};
```

The class interface is _TimeValue. Notice that this interface contains no methods. You call methods in this interface in a late-bound manner, that is, by calling the Invoke method on IDispatch. If you want an early-bound interface, you can get the CCW to expose a COM dual interface by adding the ClassInterface attribute to the TimeValue class and specifying AutoDual as shown here:

```
namespace DotNetFinancial
{
     [ClassInterface(ClassInterfaceType.AutoDual)]
     public class TimeValue
     {
       public TimeValue()
       {
}
       public decimal MonthlyPayment(
            short numMonths,
            double interestRate,
            decimal loanAmt)
       {
       //...
       }
       public decimal LoanAmount(
            short numMonths,
            double interestRate,
            decimal monthlyPmt)
       {
       //...
       }
     }
}
```

Doing this will yield the following interface when you use (regasm.exe):

```
[
       odl,
       uuid(8C14F750-B657-3ACA-B95D-14B9733A5F29),
       hidden,
       dual,
       nonextensible,
```

```
        oleautomation,
        custom({0F21F359-AB84-41E8-9A78-36D110E6D2F9},
            "DotNetFinancial.TimeValue")
]
    interface _TimeValue : IDispatch {
        [id(00000000), propget)]
        HRESULT ToString([out, retval] BSTR* pRetVal);
        [id(0x60020001)]
        HRESULT Equals([in] VARIANT obj,
                [out, retval] VARIANT_BOOL* pRetVal);
        [id(0x60020002)]
        HRESULT GetHashCode([out, retval] long* pRetVal);
        [id(0x60020003)]
        HRESULT GetType([out, retval] _Type** pRetVal);
        [id(0x60020004)]
        HRESULT MonthlyPayment([in] short numMonths,
                        [in] double interestRate,
                        [in] wchar_t loanAmt,
                        [out, retval] wchar_t* pRetVal);
        [id(0x60020005)]
        HRESULT LoanAmount([in] short numMonths,
                        [in] double interestRate,
                        [in] wchar_t monthlyPmt,
                        [out, retval] wchar_t* pRetVal);
    };
```

With this approach, you can either call the LoanAmount or MonthlyPayment methods directly on the _TimeValue interface, or you can still make late-bound calls through IDispatch.

Although both the AutoDispatch and AutoDual settings are interesting, there are major problems with each of these approaches. With AutoDispatch, the biggest problem is that you must use late binding. With unmanaged Visual Basic (that is, Visual Basic 6), the only thing you really give up is IntelliSense, but, with Visual C++, using the IDispatch interface is verbose, error prone, and complicated, as you have already seen with many of the code samples in this chapter. Using AutoDual has a different set of problems that are caused by the different approaches to versioning that .NET and COM use. With COM, published interfaces are immutable, that is, after you publish an interface, you are not allowed to change it. This is the way that COM handles the versioning problem. As long as the old interfaces that existing clients use are always supported, they should (in theory, at least) never break.

The .NET Framework takes a different approach to solving the versioning problem. It uses private assemblies and side-by-side execution. In most cases, an application should be deployed with its own private versions of the assemblies that it is dependent on. It's not a problem if two applications use different versions of an assembly because the CLR can load and execute the code in two different versions of the same assembly simultaneously. Even assemblies that are shared through the GAC don't require backward compatibility because the GAC can store multiple versions of the same assembly. Therefore, with .NET components, there is no compelling need to maintain backward compatibility when updating your components. If you want to change the signature of a method (thus changing an object's interface), you can do it, as long as you change the version number of the component. As long as you continue to deploy the old version on client machines, either as a private assembly or as a shared assembly in the GAC, existing clients will continue to work.

Although you are not required to maintain backward compatibility with your managed components, you will break COM clients who are using your components through COM Interop if you use the AutoDual ClassInterface setting and if clients early bind to the corresponding COM interface. Because of this and the aforementioned problems with the AutoDispatch setting, the recommended approach is to use the None setting on the ClassInterface attribute as follows:

```
[ClassInterface(ClassInterfaceType.None)]
public class TimeValue
{
    public TimeValue()
    {
    }
    public decimal MonthlyPayment(short numMonths,
          double interestRate, decimal loanAmt)
    {
    //...
    }

    public decimal LoanAmount(short numMonths,
          double interestRate, decimal monthlyPmt)
    {
    //...
    }
}
```

This will cause the CCW to expose only a generic IDispatch interface as opposed to the empty IDispatch-derived interface that you get when you use the ClassInterface attribute with the AutoDispatch setting. This yields the following definition of the TimeValue coclass in the type library if you used the assembly registration tool:

```
[
    uuid(57290E60-9265-359D-859E-B26FBB7861CE),
    version(1.0)
]
coclass TimeValue
{
```

```
    [default] interface _Object;
};
```

In this case, the TimeValue coclass supports a single interface called _Object that contains the ToString, GetHashCode, and GetType methods from the **System.Object** class. The _Object interface derives from IDispatch, so you can still call all of the **TimeValue** classes' methods using the Invoke method of IDispatch. If you want to support an early-bound interface, you must explicitly define and implement managed interfaces in your managed classes. These interfaces will be exposed as COM interfaces when you use COM Interop. Therefore, if I change the definition of the **TimeValue** class to look as follows:

```
public interface ITimeValue
{
    decimal MonthlyPayment(short numMonths,
          double interestRate, decimal loanAmt);
    decimal LoanAmount(short numMonths,
          double interestRate, decimal monthlyPmt);
}
[ClassInterface(ClassInterfaceType.None)]
public class TimeValue : ITimeValue
{
    public TimeValue()
    {
    }
    public decimal MonthlyPayment(short numMonths,
          double interestRate, decimal loanAmt)
    {
    // Implementation omitted…
    }

    public decimal LoanAmount(short numMonths,
          double interestRate, decimal monthlyPmt)
    {
    // Implementation omitted…
    }
}
```

the regasm-generated COM interface and the coclass in the type library will now look as follows:

```
   [
     odl,
     uuid(3B36FDAF-A541-3765-8853-1397B24BB95A),
     version(1.0),
     dual,
     oleautomation
   ]
   interface ITimeValue : IDispatch {
```

```
        [id(0x60020000)]
        HRESULT MonthlyPayment(
                        [in] short numMonths,
                        [in] double interestRate,
                        [in] wchar_t loanAmt,
                        [out, retval] wchar_t* pRetVal);
        [id(0x60020001)]
        HRESULT LoanAmount(
                        [in] short numMonths,
                        [in] double interestRate,
                        [in] wchar_t monthlyPmt,
                        [out, retval] wchar_t* pRetVal);
    };

    [
      uuid(57290E60-9265-359D-859E-B26FBB7861CE),
      version(1.0)
    ]
    coclass TimeValue {
        interface _Object;
        [default] interface ITimeValue;
    };
```

You can use this version of the managed **TimeValue** class from an unmanaged Visual C++ client as follows:

```
1.      HRESULT hRes;
2.      DECIMAL decLoanAmt,decMonthlyPmt;
3.      ITimeValue *pTimeValue;
4.
5.      CoInitializeEx(NULL,COINIT_MULTITHREADED);
6.      hRes=CoCreateInstance(CLSID_TimeValue,NULL,
7.        CLSCTX_ALL,IID_ITimeValue,
8.        (void **)&pTimeValue);
9.      VarDecFromR8(360000,&decLoanAmt);
10.     hRes=pTimeValue->MonthlyPayment(360,
11.       6.75,decLoanAmt,&decMonthlyPmt);
12.     pTimeValue->Release();
```

Notice how simple this code is compared to the late-bound code samples that you have looked at recently. Lines 1 through 3 have variable declarations. Line 5 enters the MTA. Lines 6 through 8 create an instance of the **TimeValue** class and request the ITimeValue interface. Line 9 converts the value 360,000 to a decimal, and lines 10 and 11 call the MonthlyPayment method. Line 12 releases the ITimeValue interface pointer. In order to write this code, you must add the following code to the **stdafx.h** file in your project:

```
#import "[path]\dotnetfinancial.tlb" no_namespace
named_guids raw_interfaces_only
```

where "[path]" is the path to the type library for your assembly.

By default, the ITimeValue interface will be exposed as a dual interface, but you can change this using the InterfaceType attribute. The following code shows how you would change the ITimeValue interface so that it will be exposed to COM clients as an IUnknown-derived interface:

```
[InterfaceType(ComInterfaceType.InterfaceIsIUnknown)]
public interface ITimeValue
{
    decimal MonthlyPayment(short numMonths,
          double interestRate, decimal loanAmt);
    decimal LoanAmount(short numMonths,
          double interestRate, decimal monthlyPmt);
}
```

Notice that I used the InterfaceType attribute to specify that the managed interface should have an IUnknown-derived COM equivalent. The InterfaceType attribute has the following three values:

- *InterfaceIsDual*—Indicates that the managed interface should be exposed to COM clients as a dual interface.
- *InterfaceIsDispatch*—Indicates that the managed interface should be exposed to COM clients as a dispatch interface.
- *InterfaceIsIUnknown*—Indicates that the managed interface should be exposed to COM clients as an IUnknown-derived interface.

After you make this change to the managed interface, regasm will now generate the following COM interface for unmanaged clients:

```
[
  odl,
  uuid(3B36FDAF-A541-3765-8853-1397B24BB95A),
  version(1.0),
  oleautomation
]
interface ITimeValue : IUnknown {
    HRESULT _stdcall MonthlyPayment(
            [in] short numMonths,
            [in] double interestRate,
            [in] wchar_t loanAmt,
            [out, retval] wchar_t* pRetVal);
    HRESULT _stdcall LoanAmount(
            [in] short numMonths,
            [in] double interestRate,
            [in] wchar_t monthlyPmt,
           [out, retval] wchar_t* pRetVal);
};
```

In some cases, you may also want to specify the Interface Identifier (IID) that regasm should generate for the unmanaged version of the interface.

You can do this using the GUID attribute in the System.Runtime.InteropServices namespace. The following code shows the ITimeValue managed interface declared in C# with a specified GUID:

```
[InterfaceType(ComInterfaceType.InterfaceIsIUnknown)]
[Guid("FB66D91D-7A53-490f-ABEB-A53486A516C2")]
public interface ITimeValue
{
    decimal MonthlyPayment(short numMonths,
          double interestRate, decimal loanAmt);
    decimal LoanAmount(short numMonths,
          double interestRate, decimal monthlyPmt);
}
```

This GUID will be used as the GUID for the ITimeValue interface in its COM equivalent.

Rich Error Information

Most COM programmers know that COM objects return a data structure called an HRESULT to indicate the status of a method call. If the method is successful, the COM object should return S_OK. If the method fails, the COM object can return any number of pre-defined HRESULTS, such as E_FAIL or E_INVALIDARG, or you can use the MAKE_HRESULT macro to create your own error HRESULTs. Although just returning an HRESULT is sufficient in some cases, in many cases, a client will want a textual description of the error, the name of the method that was the source of the error, and perhaps even a link to a help file that contains additional information about the error. A COM object can return this sort of rich error information to a client in two ways: (1) using the EXCEPINFO structure or (2) using COM error objects. The EXCEPINFO structure is used by late-bound clients and is an output parameter on the Invoke method of the IDispatch interface. The fields in this structure are shown in Table 8–1.

TABLE 8–1 *The mapping between fields in an EXCEPINFO structure and .NET exception*

EXCEPINFO Field	Value When Set from a .NET Exception
wCode	0
wReserved	0
bstrSource	Source property
bstrDescription	Message property

TABLE 8–1 *The mapping between fields in an EXCEPINFO structure and .NET exception (continued)*

EXCEPINFO Field	Value When Set from a .NET Exception
bstrHelpFile	HelpLink property
dwHelpContext	0
pvReserved	Null
PfnDeferredFillIn	Null
scode	HResult property (protected)

v-table-bound COM objects use COM error objects. A COM error object is an object that implements the IErrorInfo interface. The IErrorInfo interface is shown here:

```
interface IErrorInfo : IUnknown
{
    HRESULT GetGUID([out] GUID *pGuid);
    HRESULT GetSource([out] BSTR *pbstrSource);
    HRESULT GetDescription([out] BSTR *pbstrDescription );
    HRESULT GetHelpFile([out] BSTR *pbstrHelpFile);
    HRESULT GetHelpContext([out] DWORD *pdwHelpContext);
}
```

The COM runtime provides methods that you can use to create a COM error object and send it to a client. The COM API also includes other methods that you can use to fetch the COM error object that the COM has set.

Managed objects use managed exception objects (a class that derives from **System.Exception**) to return error information to managed clients. The CCW will catch the managed exception and convert it to an EXCEPINFO structure for a late-bound client and to an error object for a v-table-bound client. The mapping between the fields in the .NET exception object and a COM error object is shown in Table 8–2.

TABLE 8–2 *The mapping between fields in a COM error object and a .NET exception*

Field in the COM Error Object	Value When Set from a .NET Exception
IErrorInfo->GetDescription()	Message
IErrorInfo->GetSource()	Source
IErrorInfo->GetGUID()	GUID_NULL
IErrorInfo->GetHelpFile()	HelpLink
IErrorInfo->GetHelpContext()	0

To illustrate the concepts that you just learned, I defined the following exception class:

```
public class FinancialException : ApplicationException
{
    public FinancialException(string message,
      double rate,short nMonths) : base(message)
    {
      mNumMonths=nMonths;
      mInterestRate=rate;
    }
    public double InterestRate
    {
      get { return mInterestRate; }
    }
    public short NumMonths
    {
      get { return mNumMonths; }
    }
    private double mInterestRate;
    private short mNumMonths;
}
```

This exception class is used to throw errors that result from an improperly specified interest rate or term for a loan. This exception class derives from **System.ApplicationException** (which, in turn, derives from **System.Exception**).

> ***Note*** Non-fatal, application-specific exceptions that are thrown from managed applications should derive from System.ApplicationException. This class is provided to differentiate between exceptions defined by user programs versus exceptions defined by the system. When you derive from ApplicationException, you should pass a human-readable message describing the error to the base class constructor. The ApplicationException class uses the HRESULT COR_E_APPLICATION, which has the value 0x80131600.

Next, I added logic to the MonthlyPayment and LoanAmount methods to throw instances of this exception class when certain conditions occur. For instance, the MonthlyPayment method will throw a FinancialException if you specify a number of months for the loan that is less than zero as shown here:

```
public decimal MonthlyPayment(short numMonths,
    double interestRate, decimal loanAmt)
{
    double monthlyRate, tempVal;
    decimal unRoundedAmt;
    if (numMonths <= 0)
      throw new FinancialException(
```

```
            "Invalid number of months",
            interestRate,numMonths);
    if (interestRate <= 0.0 || interestRate >= 100.0)
      throw new FinancialException(
            "Invalid interest rate",
            interestRate,numMonths);
    monthlyRate=interestRate/1200;
    tempVal=Math.Pow((1+monthlyRate),(double)numMonths);
    unRoundedAmt=(decimal)((double)
      loanAmt*(monthlyRate*tempVal/(tempVal-1)));
    return decimal.Round(unRoundedAmt,2);
}
```

Visual Basic Client

Let's first look at using .NET exceptions from an unmanaged Visual Basic 6 client. Regardless of whether you are using late binding or early binding, the situation is the same.

```
Private Sub Command1_Click()
    On Error GoTo errHandler
    Dim obj As Object
    Dim rslt As Single
    Set obj = CreateObject("DotNetFinancial.TimeValue")
    rslt = obj.MonthlyPayment(-60, 7, 25000)
    Exit Sub
errHandler:
    Dim strMsg As String
    strMsg = "Source: " & Err.Source & vbCrLf & _
           " Description: " & Err.Description
    MsgBox strMsg
End Sub
```

To catch the managed exception, you use Visual Basic's familiar "on error goto" syntax. The source and description fields of the error object (err) will contain the source and description information from the managed exception object as shown in Table 8–2.

Unmanaged Visual C++ Client

The following code shows how you would catch the exception from a late-bound client that was built with Visual C++. Here you receive the error information from the EXCEPINFO structure that is returned by the Invoke method.

```
void CDotNetFinancialClientDlg::OnMonthlyPmtButton()
{
     DECIMAL decLoanAmt;
     IDispatch *pDispatch;
     HRESULT hRes;
```

```
6.      DISPID dispid;
7.      OLECHAR *methodName;
8.      EXCEPINFO errorInfo;
9.      UINT intArg;
10.     VARIANT vntArgs[3], vntResult;
11.     DISPPARAMS param;
12.
13.     UpdateData(TRUE);
14.
15.     VarDecFromR8(m_loanAmt,&decLoanAmt);
16.     methodName=L"MonthlyPayment";
17.     param.cArgs=3;
18.     param.rgvarg=vntArgs;
19.     param.cNamedArgs=0;
20.     param.rgdispidNamedArgs=NULL;
21.     vntResult.vt=VT_R4;
22.     vntArgs[0].vt=VT_R4;
23.     vntArgs[0].fltVal=360000;
24.     vntArgs[1].vt=VT_R4;
25.     vntArgs[1].fltVal=6.00;
26.     vntArgs[2].vt=VT_I2;
27.     vntArgs[2].iVal=-360;
28.
29.     CoInitializeEx(NULL,COINIT_MULTITHREADED);
30.     hRes=CoCreateInstance(CLSID_TimeValue,NULL,
31.       CLSCTX_ALL,IID_IDispatch,
32.       (void **)&pDispatch);
33.
34.     hRes=pDispatch->GetIDsOfNames(IID_NULL,
34.       &methodName,1,GetUserDefaultLCID(),&dispid);
35.     hRes=pDispatch->Invoke(dispid,IID_NULL,
36.       GetUserDefaultLCID(),DISPATCH_METHOD,
37.       &param,&vntResult,&errorInfo,&intArg);
38.     if (hRes==DISP_E_EXCEPTION)
39.     {
40.       CString strMsg;
41.       strMsg.Format("Source: %s \n Description: %s",
42.         CString(errorInfo.bstrSource),
43.         CString(errorInfo.bstrDescription));
44.       AfxMessageBox(strMsg);
45.     }
46.     m_monthlyPmt=vntResult.decVal;
47.     pDispatch->Release();
48.     UpdateData(FALSE);
49. }
```

I've gone through code like this so many times in this chapter that I won't go line by line through this code. The key lines of code are lines 35 through 37 where I call the Invoke method on IDispatch and lines 38 through 45 where I print the source and description of the error if the Invoke method returns an error. The contents of the EXCEPINFO structure are populated from the managed exception object that was thrown by the managed **TimeValue** class.

Here is equivalent code using v-table binding and COM error objects:

```
1.  void CDotNetClientDlg::OnBnClickedMonthlypayment()
2.  {
3.      HRESULT hRes;
4.      DECIMAL decLoanAmt,decMonthlyPmt;
5.      ITimeValue *pTimeValue;
6.      IErrorInfo *pErrorInfo;
7.      BSTR bstrSource, bstrDescription;
8.      CoInitializeEx(NULL,COINIT_MULTITHREADED);
9.      hRes=CoCreateInstance(CLSID_TimeValue,
10.       NULL,CLSCTX_ALL,IID_ITimeValue,
11.       (void **)&pTimeValue);
12.     VarDecFromR8(360000,&decLoanAmt);
13.     hRes=pTimeValue->MonthlyPayment(360,
14.       -6.75,decLoanAmt,&decMonthlyPmt);
15.     if (FAILED(hRes))
16.     {
17.        hRes=::GetErrorInfo(0,&pErrorInfo);
18.        pErrorInfo->GetSource(&bstrSource);
19.        pErrorInfo->GetDescription(&bstrDescription);
20.        CString strMsg;
21.        strMsg.Format("Source: %s \n Description: %s",
22.           CString(bstrSource),
23.         CString(bstrDescription));
24.        AfxMessageBox(strMsg);
25.        ::SysFreeString(bstrSource);
26.        ::SysFreeString(bstrDescription);
27.     }
28.     pTimeValue->Release();
29.     m_monthlyPmt=decMonthlyPmt;
30.     UpdateData(FALSE);
31.     }
```

The key lines of code here are lines 13 and 14 where I call the MonthlyPayment method on the TimeValue object and lines 15 through 27 where I handle errors returned from the method. Notice that lines 18 and 19 call the GetSource and GetDescription methods to retrieve the source and description from the managed exception object.

Using the _Exception Interface

If you use v-table binding to call a managed object from an unmanaged client, and the method raises a managed exception, the CLR will use the managed exception object as the COM error object. This means that the _Exception interface, which contains all of the methods in the **System.Exception** class, is available to unmanaged code. All you have to do is to QueryInterface on the COM error object for _Exception, and then you can access all of the members of the System.Exception class from your unmanaged code including the stack trace.

To use the _Exception interface from Visual C++, you must first import the type library for **mscorlib.dll** as follows in **stdafx.h**:

```
#import
"C:\WINNT\Microsoft.NET\Framework\v1.0.3705\mscorlib.tlb"
  no_namespace named_guids raw_interfaces_only
```

The following code shows you how to obtain the _Exception interface from a COM error object and how to use the interface:

```
void CDotNetClientDlg::OnBnClickedMonthlypayment()
{
    HRESULT hRes;
    DECIMAL decLoanAmt,decMonthlyPmt;
    ITimeValue *pTimeValue;
    _Exception *pException;
    IErrorInfo *pErrorInfo;
    BSTR bstrSource, bstrDescription, bstrStackTrace;
    CoInitializeEx(NULL,COINIT_MULTITHREADED);
    hRes=CoCreateInstance(CLSID_TimeValue,NULL,
      CLSCTX_ALL,IID_ITimeValue,
      (void **)&pTimeValue);
    VarDecFromR8(360000,&decLoanAmt);
    hRes=pTimeValue->MonthlyPayment(360,
      -6.75,decLoanAmt,&decMonthlyPmt);
    if (FAILED(hRes))
    {
        hRes=::GetErrorInfo(0,&pErrorInfo);
        pErrorInfo->GetSource(&bstrSource);
        pErrorInfo->GetDescription(&bstrDescription);
        pErrorInfo->QueryInterface(
          IID__Exception,(void **)&pException);
        pException->get_StackTrace(&bstrStackTrace);
        pException->Release();
        pErrorInfo->Release();
        CString strMsg;
        strMsg.Format(
          "Source: %s \n Description: %s \n Stack: %s",
        CString(bstrSource),
        CString(bstrDescription),
        CString(bstrStackTrace));
        AfxMessageBox(strMsg);
        ::SysFreeString(bstrSource);
              ::SysFreeString(bstrDescription);
              ::SysFreeString(bstrStackTrace);
```

```
36.         }
37.         pTimeValue->Release();
38.         m_monthlyPmt=decMonthlyPmt;
39.         UpdateData(FALSE);
40. }
```

The key lines of code here are lines 21 and 22 where I use QueryInterface for the _Exception interface and line 23 where I call the get_StackTrace method on the _Exception interface pointer to retrieve the stack trace. Of course, the stack trace only shows the managed code portion of the stack.

Note Because the Interface name for the System.Exception class is _Exception, the named IID for this interface is IID__Exception with two underscores.

Using Windows Forms Controls

With all the hype about ASP.NET and XML Web services, many people have completely neglected the fact that the .NET Framework is a full-featured development platform. The .NET Framework includes support for rich-user interfaces using Windows Forms. Most of the demos that you have built so far have been built using Windows Forms. The .NET Framework also includes tools for creating rich-user interface controls that are very similar in concept to ActiveX controls. These controls are called Windows Forms controls. Because the focus of this book is COM Interop, you are probably waiting for me to tell you that Windows Forms controls can be exposed as ActiveX controls to unmanaged clients. Unfortunately, it's not quite that simple. It turns out that there is such a wide variation in the implementation of ActiveX control containers that Microsoft was not willing to claim that Windows Forms controls can be hosted in any ActiveX control container. Officially, you can host Windows Forms controls—and use them as though they were ActiveX controls—in IE 6 (or greater) only. Unofficially, with a few incantations, you can host Windows Forms controls as ActiveX controls in many ActiveX control containers. Just keep in mind that, if you attempt to use a Windows Forms control as an ActiveX control in any container other than IE, you are on your own if anything goes wrong.

In this chapter, I give you a brief overview of Windows Forms controls. You then build a very simple Windows Forms control, and I show you how to host a Windows Form control in IE and in other ActiveX control containers.

An Introduction to Windows Forms Controls

If you understand ActiveX controls, understanding Windows Forms controls should be simple. An ActiveX control is a COM object that supports a specified set of interfaces that make it easy to use in a visual development environment. A Windows Forms control is a managed class in a .NET assembly that derives from a specified base class. It also supports properties and design-time attributes that make the control easy to use in a visual development environment. Windows Forms controls have a user interface that is displayed within its client window. They also have properties and events, and their state can persist to a container provided by their client, just like ActiveX controls.

An Example Windows Forms Control

The easiest way to understand Windows Forms controls is to build one. I will build a simple Windows Form control and then use it in IE and also in Visual Basic 6. The control that I will build is a simple digital alarm clock that looks as shown in Figure 8–5.

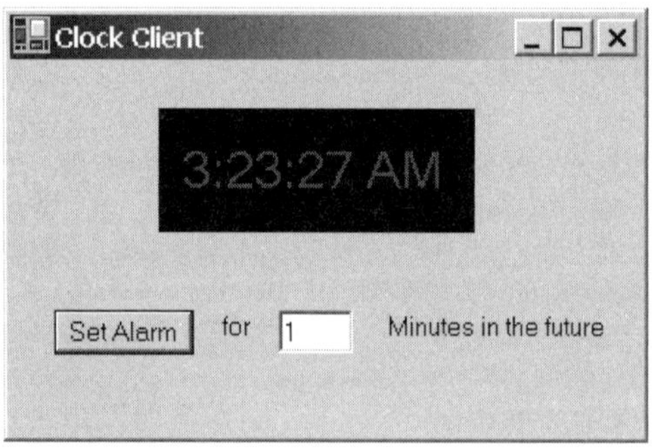

FIGURE 8–5 *The digital clock control.*

The digital clock control supports the custom properties and methods shown in Table 8–3.

TABLE 8–3 *The properties and methods of the digital clock control*

Member Names	Type of Member	Data Type	Description
DisplayFormat	Property (default)	Enumeration	Controls whether hours are shown in 12- or 24-hour format.
ShowSeconds	Property	Boolean	Specifies whether seconds are shown with the time.
SetAlarm	Method	N/A	Allows you to set the clock's alarm. The clock fires an event when its alarm goes off.
Alarm	Event	N/A	Fires when the alarm goes off.
AlarmHandler	Delegate	N/A	Is the delegate used by the Alarm event.

The DisplayFormat property allows you to control whether the digital clock uses 24-hour or 12-hour format for the time; the default is 12-hour format. The ShowSeconds property allows you to specify whether the clock shows seconds or not; the default is to show seconds. The SetAlarm method allows you to set the alarm on the digital clock. To use this method, pass a System.DateTime object to the SetAlarm method specifying the date and time that the alarm should go off. The digital clock fires an Alarm event back to its client at the specified time. The delegate for the Alarm event is called AlarmHandler. It is a standard event delegate that sends the object that generates the event (the sender) as the first parameter and an EventArgs object that contains the arguments for the event as the second parameter. A Windows Forms control automatically inherits support for a number of other stock properties, such as BackColor, ForeColor, and Font, from its base class: **System.Windows.Forms.UserControl**. Therefore, the list of properties that a consumer will see is far more complete than the list of members that I show in Table 8–3.

Let's build this control using Visual Studio .NET, and then you can use it to learn how to use Windows Forms control from IE and most other ActiveX control containers. A summary of the steps to build this control is as follows:

1. Create a Windows control library project in Visual Studio .NET.
2. Add the logic to draw the UI.
3. Add properties to the control.
4. Add the Alarm event.
5. Add design-time attributes.
6. Test.

CREATE A WINDOWS CONTROL LIBRARY PROJECT

Perform the following steps to create a Windows control library project:

1. Start Visual Studio .NET.
2. Select File | New | Project... . The New Project dialog will appear as shown in Figure 8–6.
3. Under Project Types, select Visual C# Projects and, under Templates, select Windows Control Library.
4. Change the name of the project to ClockControlLibrary.
5. Click OK.

Visual C# will create a project that contains a **UserControl** class that derives from **System.Windows.Forms.UserControl**. This base class contains most of the logic required to make your derived class behave like a Windows Forms control. All of the methods and interfaces that a Windows Forms control must implement in order to be hosted in a Windows Forms control container are contained in this base class, as well as the logic to allow the control to be hosted in an ActiveX control container. The only thing you need

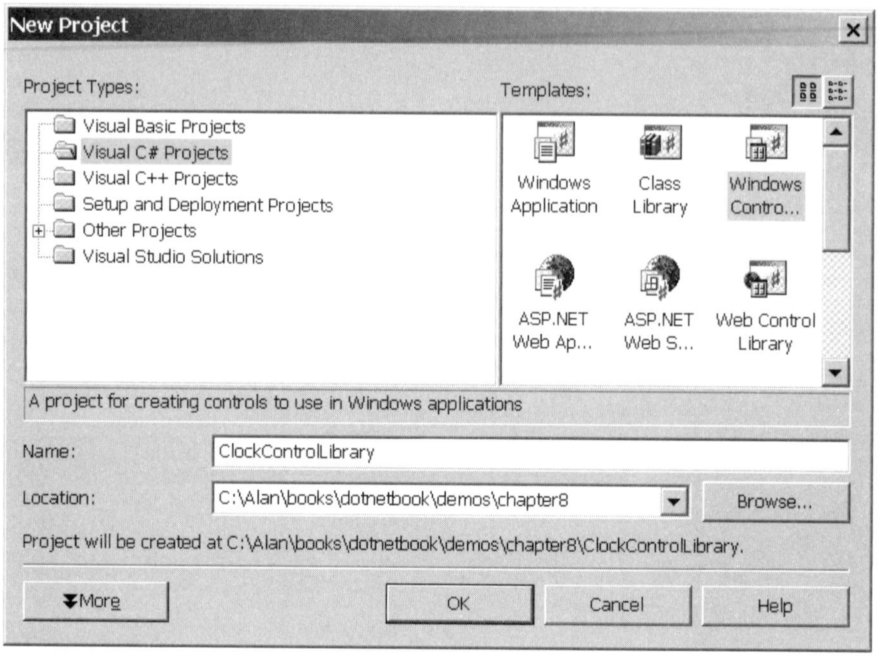

FIGURE 8–6 *The New Project dialog.*

to do is to fill in the code that is specific to your control. In many cases, you will have to draw the UI by overriding the OnPaint method in the **System.Windows.Forms.UserControl** class. If you create a composite control that is just a conglomerate of other controls, such as a text box, a label, and a checkbox, you don't need to do this. You can just draw your control using the Visual Studio .NET form designer. Let's look first at the code to draw the UI.

ADD THE LOGIC TO DRAW THE UI

You can implement the UI for a Windows Forms control in two ways:

- Override the System.Windows.Forms.UserControl.OnPaint method in your control class and use the GDI+ API to draw your UI.
- Drag and drop controls onto your control's form using the Visual Studio .NET form designer.

You could implement the digital clock control either way, but I decided to override the OnPaint method because I believe that you will learn more if I do it this way. To implement the OnPaint method, first change the name of the class. This is initially called **UserControl1**, but change it to **ClockControl**. In other words, go to the file called **UserControl1** and change the bolded code shown below:

```
namespace ClockControlLibrary
{
    public class UserControl1 :
        System.Windows.Forms.UserControl
    {
      public UserControl1()
      {
      // code omitted for clarity…
      }
    // code omitted for clarity…

    }
    // code omitted for clarity…

}
```

This is what the new code should look like:

```
namespace ClockControlLibrary
{
    public class ClockControl :
        System.Windows.Forms.UserControl
    {
      public ClockControl()
      {
      // code omitted for clarity…
      }
    // code omitted for clarity…

    }
    // code omitted for clarity…

}
```

Notice that you change both the name of the class and the name of its constructor. Next I'll add some member variables to the **ClockControl** class as shown in bold:

```
namespace ClockControlLibrary
{
    public enum TimeFormat { Hour12=0, Hour24=1 }
    public class ClockControl :
        System.Windows.Forms.UserControl
    {

      private System.ComponentModel.Container
        components = null;
      private TimeFormat mFormat;
      private Boolean mShowSeconds;

      public ClockControl()
```

```
        {
        //
// Code omitted for clarity…
//
          mFormat=TimeFormat.Hour12;
          mShowSeconds=true;
        }
      }
//
// code omitted for clarity…
//
}
```

The TimeFormat enumeration is used to specify whether the digital clock will show the hour portion of the time in 12-hour or 24-hour format. I could have used a Boolean, perhaps called Use12Hour (or something similar). However, I wanted to show you that, if you use an enumeration as the data type for a property in your Windows Forms controls, the property browser in your visual development environment will display the enumeration values in a dropdown list that you can choose from. The mShowSeconds property allows you to specify whether the digital clock will include seconds in the displayed time. Notice that, in the constructor for the control class, I initialize the time format to 12 hour and set the ShowSeconds property to true. Now I'll override the OnPaint method to draw the control. The OnPaint method on **System.Windows.Forms.Usercontrol** will be called whenever the control needs to redraw itself. Like most event handlers, the OnPaint method has a single argument that contains an instance of an **EventArgs**-derived class called **PaintEventArgs**. The properties of this derived class contain the arguments for the event. The **PaintEventArgs** class contains only two properties: (1) a clipping rectangle and (2) a graphics object that you use to paint the screen. The graphics object is an instance of the **System.Drawing.Graphics** class. This class encapsulates a GDI+ drawing surface. You can think of the **System.Drawing.Graphics** class as the managed code equivalent of a Device context. You call methods on this object to draw to the screen, a printer, or other graphics output devices. The code for the OnPaint method is as follows:

```
public class ClockControl : UserControl
{
//Code omitted for clarity…
    protected override void OnPaint(PaintEventArgs e)
    {
      String strTmFormat, strTm;
      if (mFormat==TimeFormat.Hour12)
        strTmFormat="hh:mm";
      else
        strTmFormat="HH:mm";
```

```
11.         if (mShowSeconds)
12.           strTmFormat+=":ss";
13.         if (mFormat==TimeFormat.Hour12)
14.           strTmFormat+=" tt";
15.         strTm=DateTime.Now.ToString(strTmFormat);
16.         SizeF txtSz=
17.           e.Graphics.MeasureString(strTm,Font);
18.         RectangleF rect = new RectangleF(
19.           (ClientRectangle.Width-txtSz.Width)/2,
20.           (ClientRectangle.Height-txtSz.Height)/2 ,
21.             txtSz.Width,
22.             txtSz.Height);
23.         Brush frClrBrush=new SolidBrush(ForeColor);
24.         e.Graphics.DrawString(
25.           strTm,Font,frClrBrush, rect);
26.       }
27. // Code omitted for clarity…
28. }
```

Line 6 declares two strings. The string strTmFormat will hold the format string for the time, and strTm will hold the time itself. Lines 7 through 10 determine the format for the hours and minutes portion of the time. The DateTime type contains an overload of the ToString method that takes a format string, which allows you to specify the format of the textual representation of the date. I won't give an exhaustive explanation of the contents of this format string; you can see the documentation for the **System.DateTimeFormatInfo** class in the .NET Framework SDK for that. I can tell you that hh means to show the hour of the time portion of the date in 12-hour format (that is, 5 o'clock in the afternoon is displayed as 5:00 PM). HH means to display the hour in 24-hour format (that is, 5 o' clock in the afternoon is displayed as 17:00). In both cases, single-digit hours will have a leading zero. The format specifier mm means that the minute portion of the time should be displayed with a leading zero for single-digit minutes. The format specifier ss means to display the seconds, and tt specifies that you want to display AM and PM with the time, which is only necessary if you are using 12-hour format. The default format string (12-hour format with seconds showing) is the following: hh:mm:ss tt. Lines 11 and 12 append the seconds designator ss to the format string if the ShowSeconds property is set to true. Lines 13 and 14 append the AM/PM designator only if the DisplayFormat property is set to show hours in 12-hour format. Line 15 calls the ToString method on the DateTime object that you get from the Now static method, which returns the current date and time. You pass the format statement that you constructed on lines 7 through 14 to the ToString method. Lines 16 and 17 call the MeasureString method on the **System.Drawing.Graphics** class. This method returns a System.Drawing.SizeF structure that will contain the rectangular region that the text will occupy when it is drawn in the specified font. Notice that the second parameter to the MeasureString is a property of the control called Font. This property is inherited from the **System.Windows.Forms.Usercontrol** class, and it contains the current value of the Font property for the control.

> ***Note*** The Font property is one of a number of stock properties (BackColor and ForeColor are two notable others) that are exposed, by default, on all Windows Forms controls. If you do not want to expose any of these properties, you can override the property in your user control class and provide a read-only implementation.

Lines 18 through 22 calculate a bounding rectangle for the time string that will center the string in the client area of the control. Line 23 creates a solid brush using the ForeColor property of the control. The ForeColor property contains the foreground color of the control. Lines 24 and 25 use this brush and the bounding rectangle that you calculated on lines 18 through 22 to draw the formatted time string. It draws the string in the center of the client area of the digital clock control using the currently selected foreground color.

Now that you understand how this code works, there's just one problem. As currently coded, it won't work properly. The time on the clock won't be updated unless you force the control to redraw itself every second. You can do this using a timer. With the .NET Framework, two types of timers are available:

- A Windows-based timer that uses the Windows message-pumping infrastructure. This timer is encapsulated in the **System.Windows.Forms.Timer** class.
- A server-based timer that is designed for use with worker threads in a multithreaded environment. This timer is not dependent on Windows messaging and is encapsulated in the **System.Timers.Timer** class.

Interestingly, I found that the Windows-based timer would work just fine when I used a Windows Forms client, but it would not update the window correctly when I used the control in IE. The server-based timer worked like a champ everywhere. Because of this, I used the server-based timer for the clock control. To add a server-based timer, you need to add the code shown in bold to the **ClockControl** class:

```
// other "using" statements omitted for clarity…
using System.Timers;
namespace ClockControlLibrary
{
     // Code omitted for clarity…
     public class ClockControl : UserControl
     {
       // Other private variable declarations omitted…
          private System.Timers.Timer mTimer;
          public ClockControl()
```

```
11.           {
12.         // Code omitted for clarity…
13.           mTimer=new System.Timers.Timer(1000);
14.           mTimer.Elapsed+=new
15.           ElapsedEventHandler(timer_Elapsed);
16.           mTimer.Enabled=true;
17.         }
18.         private void timer_Elapsed(object sender,
19.           System.Timers.ElapsedEventArgs e)
20.         {
21.           Refresh();
22.         }
23.         // Code omitted for clarity…
24.     }
25. }
```

Line 1 adds a using statement for the System.Timers namespace. Line 9 adds a private field to the ClockControl that will contain an instance of the **System.Timers.Timer** class. You add the code shown in lines 13 through 16 to the end of the constructor for the **ClockControl** class. Line 13 instantiates a new timer using an interval of 1,000 milliseconds (1 second). Lines 14 and 15 add a handler for the Elapsed event, which is fired at the end of each interval. Lines 18 through 22 show the handler for the Elapsed event. This method simply calls the Refresh method, which is implemented in the **System.Windows.Forms.UserControl** class and which invalidates the client area of the control and triggers a call to OnPaint for the control to redraw itself.

Note Actually the Refresh method is implemented in the System.Windows.Forms.Control class, which is a base class of System.Windows.Forms.UserControl.

Line 16 sets the Enabled property of the Timer object to true, which will cause it to start firing Elapsed events every second. The UI for the digital clock control is essentially complete. However, we still need to do a few more things to make the control easier to use. Even though the clock contains private fields that determine whether the clock will display seconds or the hour in 12- or 24-hour format, consumers of the control have no way to set these values in their visual design environment. In order for consumers to do this, you must add properties to the control.

ADD PROPERTIES TO THE CONTROL

I will add a ShowSeconds property to the control, which will specify whether the control will display seconds, and a DisplayFormat property, which will specify whether the control will show hours in 12- or 24-hour format. Add the following code to the **ClockControl** class to support the ShowSeconds and DisplayFormatProperties:

```
namespace ClockControlLibrary
{
        public class ClockControl : UserControl
        {
          //
          // The rest of the ClockControl code is omitted…
          //
          [Category("Appearance")]
          [Browsable(true)]
          public TimeFormat DisplayFormat
          {
            get
            {
              return mFormat;
            }
            set
            {
              mFormat=value;
            }
          }
          [Category("Appearance")]
          [Browsable(true)]
          public Boolean ShowSeconds
          {
            get
            {
              return mShowSeconds;
            }
            set
            {
              mShowSeconds=value;
            }
          }
        }
}
```

Most of the code here is actually not particularly interesting. It is the same code that you would write to expose properties from any class. The part that is interesting is the use of the Category and Browsable attributes. These two attributes, which you can find in the System.ComponentModel namespace, allow you to control if and how the property is displayed in the property browser of a visual development environment. The Browsable attribute allows you to specify whether an attribute should be visible at all in the property browser of a visual development environment. Set this attribute to true to make a property visible in a property browser at design time. If a property is not appropriate for design-time editing in the property browser of a visual development environment, set the Browsable attribute to false. The default is true, so, if you do not use the Browsable attribute on a property, the property will be visible. Most property browsers allow you to group the properties of a control by category or to sort them alphabetically. The Category attribute allows you to specify which category a property should be displayed in. Figure 8–7 shows the properties of the digital clock control sorted alphabetically. Figure 8–8 shows the properties of the digital clock control grouped by category. In the case of the digital clock control, I placed both the ShowSeconds and DisplayFormat properties in the Appearance category.

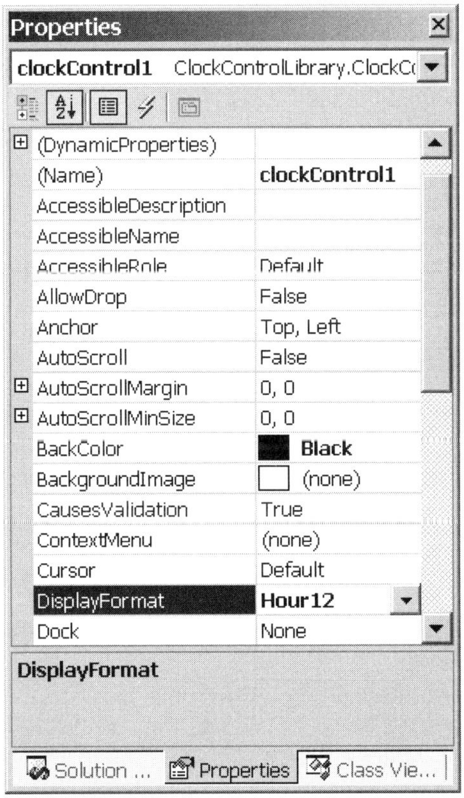

FIGURE 8–7 *The properties of the clock control sorted alphabetically.*

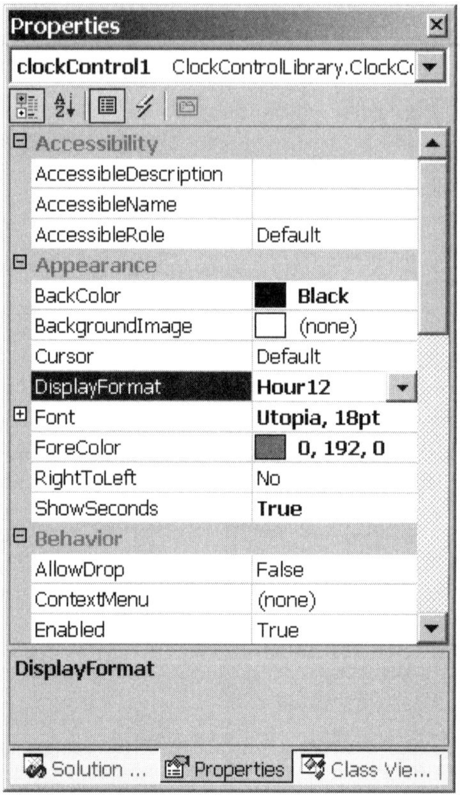

FIGURE 8–8 *The properties of the clock control grouped by category.*

ADD THE ALARM EVENT

Like ActiveX controls, most Windows Forms controls support at least one event. The digital clock control supports an event called Alarm. I will add a SetAlarm method to the digital clock control that allows you to specify the date and time when the alarm event should fire. When the alarm is set, you see a small circle in the upper left corner of the control. When the specified time is reached, the digital clock fires an Alarm event that the client can catch and provide some audible or visible alert to the user. In order to implement this functionality, add the code shown in bold to the **ClockControl** class:

```
namespace ClockControlLibrary
{
    public delegate void AlarmEventHandler
    (
      object sender,
      EventArgs e
    );
```

```
8.         // TimeFormat enumeration omitted…
9.         public class ClockControl : UserControl
10.        {
11.        // Other private fields omitted…
12.            private Boolean mbAlarmIsSet;
13.            private DateTime mAlarmTime;
14.            public event AlarmEventHandler Alarm;
15.            private void timer_Elapsed(object sender,
16.              System.Timers.ElapsedEventArgs e)
17.            {
18.              if (mbAlarmIsSet==true)
19.              {
20.                if (Alarm != null &&
21.                  DateTime.Now > mAlarmTime)
22.                {
23.                  mTimer.Enabled=false;
24.                  Alarm(this,EventArgs.Empty);
25.                  mbAlarmIsSet=false;
26.                    mTimer.Enabled=true;
27.                }
28.              }
29.              Refresh();
30.            }
31.          protected override void
32.            OnPaint(PaintEventArgs e)
33.          {
34.          // The rest of the implementation of
35.          // OnPaint is omitted…
36.            if (mbAlarmIsSet)
37.            {
38.              int diameter=
39.                ClientRectangle.Height/10;
40.              e.Graphics.FillEllipse(
41.                frClrBrush,5,5,
42.                diameter,diameter);
43.            }
44.          }
45.          public void SetAlarm(DateTime tm)
46.          {
47.            mbAlarmIsSet=true;
48.            mAlarmTime=tm;
49.          }
50.        }
51. }
```

Lines 3 through 7 declare a delegate for the Alarm event called AlarmEventHandler. This delegate has the standard, 2-parameter prototype for an event delegate. The first parameter is a System.Object instance that points to the object that generated the event, and the second parameter is an EventArgs-derived object that contains the parameters for the event. In this case, there are no event-specific parameters, so I am using the EventArgs class itself rather than deriving an event-specific **EventArgs** class. Line 12 declares a Boolean member variable called mbAlarmIsSet that is used to indicate if the alarm is set. Line 13 declares a System.DateTime instance that is used to store the date and time at which the alarm should fire. Line 14 declares an event called Alarm that uses the delegate that I declared on lines 3 through 7. Lines 18 through 28 contain the logic that I added to the timer_Elapsed method to fire the Alarm event when you reach the specified alarm time. Line 18 checks to see if the alarm is set. If it is set, lines 20 and 21 check if the client has added a callback handler and if the current time is greater than the alarm time. If both of these conditions are true, line 23 disables the timer to prevent timer events from accumulating while the client is responding to the Alarm event. Line 24 then fires the Alarm event. Line 25 turns off the alarm. (You may want to add the option to have a recurring alarm. I'll leave the implementation of this to the reader). Line 26 reenables the timer so that the control will continue to update itself. Lines 36 through 43 in the OnPaint method print a small circle in the upper left portion of the digital clock's client area if the alarm is set. Lines 45 through 49 show the implementation of the SetAlarm method, which the control's consumer can call to set the alarm. The implementation of this method is simple. You set the mbAlarmIsSet field to true so that the timer_Elapsed callback will start checking the alarm. You then store the specified alarm time in the mAlarmTime field.

ADD DESIGN-TIME ATTRIBUTES

The control is almost complete. The last step is to add a design-time attribute that specifies a default event for the control. If you have used Visual Basic, you know that, after you drag and drop a control onto a form, you can double-click the control. Visual Basic then automatically adds a callback for the most commonly used event on the control. For instance, if you drag and drop a command button onto a form, Visual Basic will add a callback for the Clicked event when you double-click the control. Visual Basic can do this only if the control specifies a default event, that is, the event that consumers will tend to handle most often. To define a default event, add the DefaultEvent attribute to the **ClockControl** class as shown in bold here:

```
[DefaultEvent("Alarm")]
public class ClockControl : UserControl
{
// Implementation of the ClockControl class omitted…
}
```

TEST

You are now ready to test the Windows Form control. The easiest way to test the control is to add a client project to the user control's solution. To do this, perform the following steps:

1. Right-click the ClockControlLibrary solution in Visual Studio .NET's Solution Explorer as shown in Figure 8–9.
2. From the context menu, select Add | New Project.... The Add New Project dialog will appear.
3. Under Project Types, select Visual C# Projects.
4. Under Templates, select Windows Application.
5. Enter ClockControlTester for the Name.
6. Click OK.

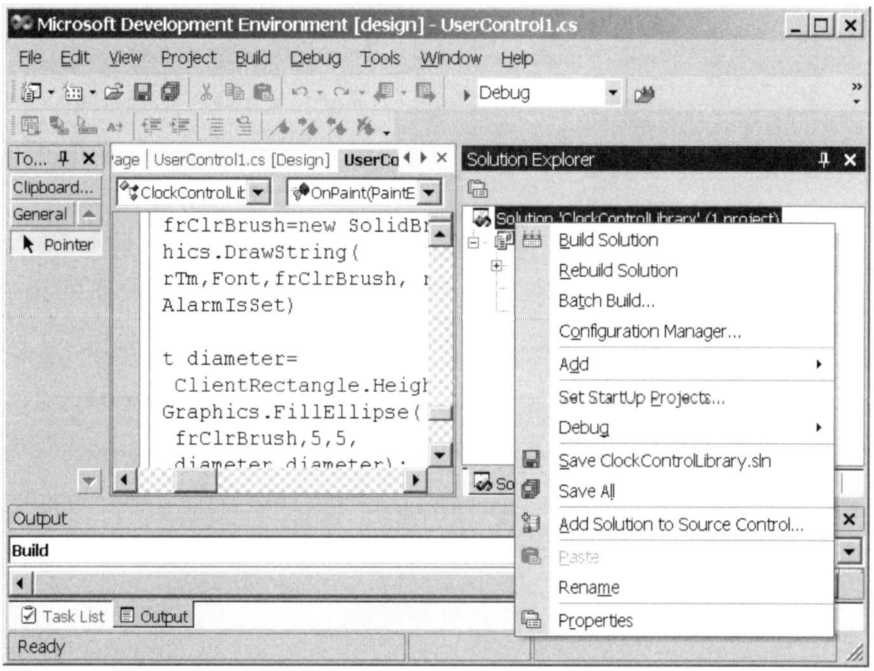

FIGURE 8–9 *Adding a second project to a solution.*

You should also set the new Windows Forms project as the startup project for the solution, that is, the project that will start running when you use the Debug | Start or Debug | Start without debugging. Perform the following steps to do this:

1. Right-click the ClockControlTester project beneath the current solution as shown in Figure 8–10.
2. From the context menu, select Set as Startup Project.

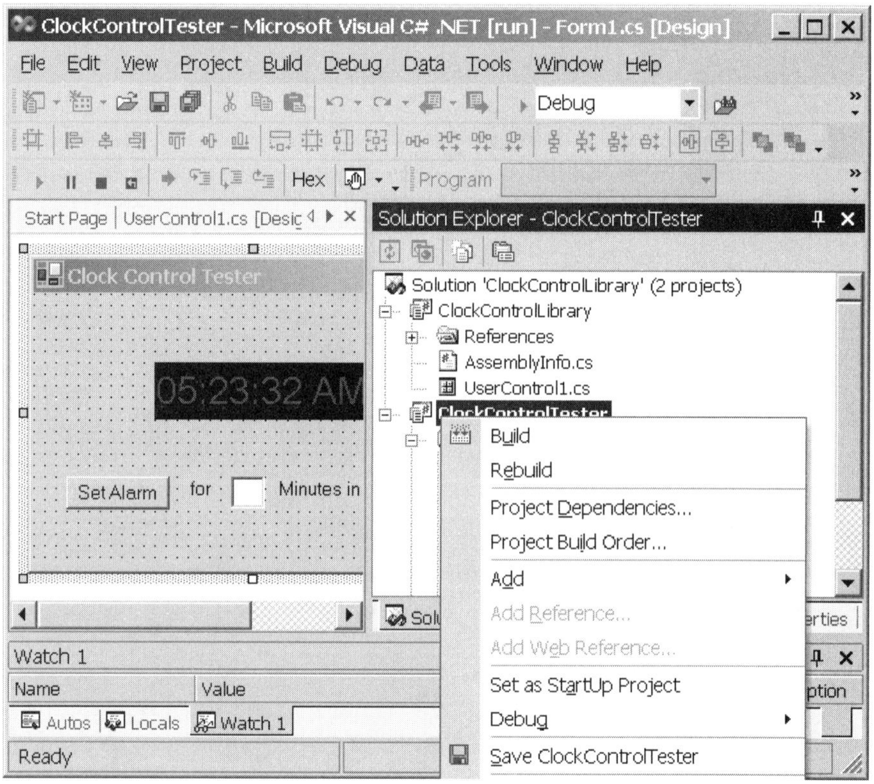

FIGURE 8–10 *Setting a project to be the startup project.*

Visual Studio .NET will create a project for you that contains a form. If you look at the toolbox, though, you'll notice that there is a special entry for the ClockControl as shown in Figure 8–11.

You do not have to reference the digital clock control explicitly from the client project. Visual Studio .NET will create a reference for you when you add a Windows Forms project to a solution that contains a Windows Forms control.

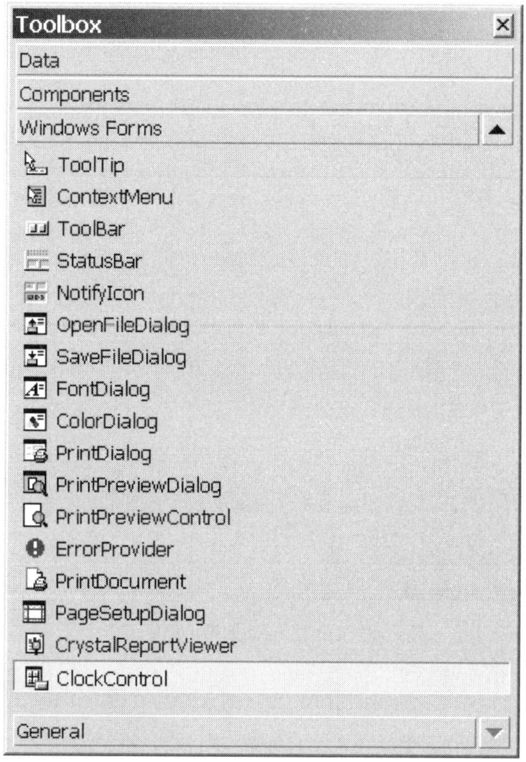

FIGURE 8–11 *The Clock Control displayed in the Visual Studio .NET toolbox.*

Drag and drop an instance of the digital clock control onto the form. Set the properties of the control as shown in Table 8–4.

TABLE 8–4 *The property values for the digital clock control*

Property	Value
BackColor	Black
ForeColor	Green
Font	Microsoft Sans Serif, 16.2pt
ShowSeconds	True
DisplayFormat	Hour12

Now add the controls shown in Figure 8–12 to the application.

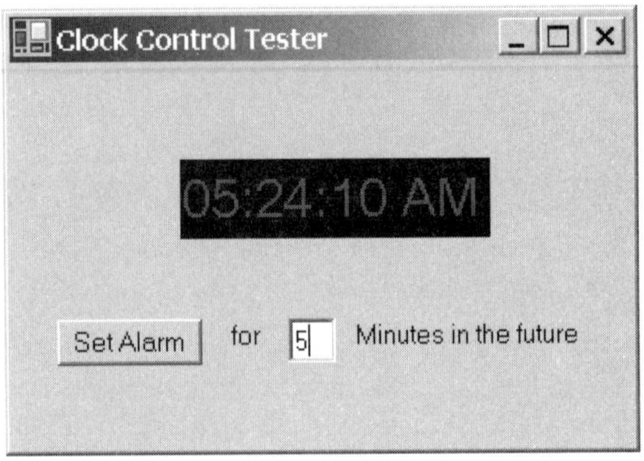

FIGURE 8–12 *The test application for the digital clock control.*

Name the controls as shown in Table 8–5.

TABLE 8–5 *The property values for the digital clock control*

Control Description	Name
Set Alarm button	cmdSetAlarm
Text box for entering minutes	txtNumMins

Now double-click the Set Alarm button to create a Clicked event handler and add the following code:

```
private void cmdSetAlarm_Click(object sender,
    System.EventArgs e)
{
    double dblNumMins;
    try
    {
      dblNumMins=double.Parse(txtNumMins.Text);
      clockControl1.SetAlarm(
          DateTime.Now.AddMinutes(dblNumMins));
    }
    catch(FormatException )
    {
      MessageBox.Show("Please enter a number");
    }
    catch(Exception ex)
    {
      MessageBox.Show("The following error occurred: "
        + ex.Message);
    }
}
```

Now double-click the digital clock control. This will add a handler for the Alarm event because you made this event the default event for the control. Add the following code for this handler:

```
private void clockControl1_Alarm(object sender,
      System.EventArgs e)
{
    System.Windows.Forms.MessageBox.Show(
          "The alarm went off");
}
```

Try the application out. Enter a number of minutes in the text box, and you should see a message box pop up when the number of minutes that you specified for the alarm elapses.

Hosting Controls in IE

The only ActiveX control container that can officially host Windows Forms controls is IE. The following file shows an example of an HTML file that uses the digital clock control:

```
<html>
<head>
<title>Test Clock Control</title>
</head>

<script language="VBScript">
<!--
Sub chkShowSeconds_OnClick()
        ClockControl1.ShowSeconds=chkShowSeconds.Checked
 end sub
-->
</script>

<body>
<table border="0" width="64%">
  <tr>
    <td width="100%" colspan="2">
      <p align="center">Testing the Digital Clock Control
</td>
  </tr>
  <tr>
    <td width="100%" align="center" colspan="2">
    <object classid=
"http:ClockControlLibrary.dll#ClockControlLibrary.ClockCont
rol" id="ClockControl1" width="168" height="64">
        <param name="BackColor" value="Black">
        <param name="ForeColor" value="Green">
        </object>
```

```
      </td>
    </tr>
    <tr>
      <td width="22%"></td>
      <td width="78%"><p><input type="checkbox"
name="chkShowSeconds" value="Show Seconds" checked>
    Show Seconds</p></td>
    </tr>
</table>
</body>
</html>
```

The syntax for using a Windows Forms control as an ActiveX Control is simple. You must first use the object tag as you would for a regular ActiveX control. The main difference is that, instead of putting a GUID for the classid parameter, you identify the Windows Forms control using the following syntax:

```
URL/AssemblyFileName#FullQualifiedClassName
```

The value that I used in this example for the classid parameter of the object tag is shown here:

```
"http:ClockControlLibrary.dll#ClockControlLibrary.ClockCont
rol"
```

In this case, I used the abbreviated syntax, *http:ClockControlLibrary.dll*, for the URL/AssemblyFileName combination, which indicates that the assembly resides in the same directory as the HTML file. If the assembly resides at some other URL, you need to specify the full path to the assembly. You can then use the param subtag with name/value pairs to specify properties for the control. Here I have set the BackColor to black and the ForeColor to green.

You will need to create an IIS virtual directory and add both the HTML file and the clock control assembly to the directory. Now, when you navigate to the HTML page in your browser, IE will download the ClockControlLibrary and cache it in the download cache. You can view the download cache in the download subfolder of the GAC. On my machine, the download cache is located at **D:\WINNT\assembly\Download**.

If you navigate to this folder, you will see all the assemblies that have been downloaded by IE from intranet or Internet sites. This folder uses the same shell viewer that you use to view the GAC. You can clear the download cache by executing the following command at a Visual Studio .NET command prompt:

```
gacutil /cdl
```

As you learned in Chapter 3 when I discussed code access security, when IE downloads an assembly, it will assign security privileges to the assembly based on evidence that it is able to collect. Part of that evidence is the zone where the assembly came from. An assembly that is downloaded from the Internet or your intranet obviously has fewer privileges than an assembly that is accessed directly from your hard drive. When you download an ActiveX control from the Internet or the intranet, it is allowed to run on your machine, but it is only partially trusted. If the Windows Forms control has a strong name, you must attach the AllowPartiallyTrustedCallers attribute to the control's assembly in order for it to be usable in the download scenario. You can do this by adding the following code to the **AssemblyInfo.cs** file:

```
[assembly: System.Security.AllowPartiallyTrustedCallers]
```

Keep in mind that this attribute, which is very poorly documented in the .NET Framework SDK, is only necessary if you assign a strong name to the assembly that contains your Windows Forms control.

Hosting Windows Forms Controls in Other Containers

Although it is not supported, you can host Windows Forms controls in other ActiveX control containers, such as Visual Basic 6. Using Windows Forms controls in any ActiveX control container was supported in beta versions of the .NET Framework. Unfortunately, there is so much difference in the implementation of the various ActiveX control containers that Microsoft eventually decided that it would be impossible to guarantee that Windows Forms controls would work in all ActiveX control containers. Therefore, Microsoft decided to officially drop support for all ActiveX control containers except IE. Unofficially, you can use Windows Forms controls in many ActiveX control containers. The fact that it's not supported just means that, if you run into any problems, Microsoft is not going to help you solve them.

A Windows Forms control already implements all of the COM interfaces required of an ActiveX control. The main things missing are a number of registry entries that are expected of an ActiveX control. You need to add the following subkeys beneath the control's entry under HKEY_CLASSES_ROOT\CLSID\{CLSIDForControl} where {CLSIDForControl} is the CLSID for the Clock control:

- *Control*—With no value
- *MiscStatus*—With value 131457
- *Version*—With value = Major.Minor where major and minor are the major and minor parts of the version number of the assembly
- *TypeLib*—With value = LIBID of the type library exported by regasm

The Control entry indicates that the COM class is an ActiveX control. See the documentation for the OLEMISC enumeration in the Platform SDK to understand the MiscStatus entry and what the value 131457 means. The Version subkey contains a two-part version number that you can construct from the major and minor versions of the assembly. The TypeLib entry contains the GUID (the LIBID) of the generated assembly. You will also need to add the following subkey under HKEY_CLASSES_ROOT\CLSID\{CLSIDForControl}\Implemented Categories:

{40FC6ED4-2438-11CF-A3DB-080036F12502}

This GUID is the CATID of the Component Category for ActiveX controls.

We need a way to easily insert these entries into the registry. The .NET Framework provides a mechanism that you can use to execute your own code when a user runs the Assembly Registration Tool (regasm.exe) to register an assembly for use by a COM client. You can use this mechanism to add the additional registry entries that you need to expose the Windows Forms control as an ActiveX control. To do this, perform the following steps:

1. Add ComRegister and Comunregister functions.
2. Register your assembly using the Assembly Registration Tool (regasm).

ADD COMREGISTER AND COMUNREGISTER FUNCTIONS

When a user runs regasm.exe to register a managed code assembly for use by a COM client, regasm.exe looks for a COM register function within the assembly. If such a function is present, regasm.exe executes it. This is your opportunity to exert some control of how your assembly is exposed to COM clients. To create a COM register function, add a static void function that accepts a System.Type parameter to your Windows Forms control's class and then mark it with the ComRegisterFunction attribute, which you can find in the System.Runtime.InteropServices namespace. The following code shows a COM register function for the clock control that adds the registry entries needed for the control to be visible to any ActiveX control container:

```
public class ClockControl : UserControl
{
// Implementation of the ClockControl class omitted…
    [ComRegisterFunction]
    private static void RegisterForCOM(Type aType)
    {
      String strCtrlKey, strVersion;
      Guid typeLibGUID;
      strCtrlKey="CLSID\\"+
          aType.GUID.ToString("B");
      RegistryKey key=
          Registry.ClassesRoot.OpenSubKey(
          strCtrlKey,true);
      key.CreateSubKey("Control");
      key.CreateSubKey("Implemented Categories\\{40FC6ED4-2438-11CF-A3D8-080036F12502}");
      key.CreateSubKey(
          "MiscStatus").SetValue("","131457");
      typeLibGUID=
          Marshal.GetTypeLibGuidForAssembly(
```

```
20.             aType.Assembly);
21.         key.CreateSubKey("TypeLib").SetValue(
22.             "",typeLibGUID.ToString("B"));
23.         Version asmVersion=
24.             aType.Assembly.GetName().Version;
25.         strVersion=asmVersion.Major.ToString()+
26.             "."+asmVersion.Minor.ToString();
27.         key.CreateSubKey(
28.             "Version").SetValue("",strVersion);
29.         key.Close();
30.     }
31. }
```

Lines 7 and 8 declare variables. Lines 9 through 13 use the **RegistryKey** class, which resides in the Microsoft.Win32 namespace to open the CLSID registry key for the clock control (HKEY_CLASSES_ROOT\CLSID\{CLSIDForControl}). The System.Type parameter that regasm will pass to the RegisterForCOM function contains the Type object for the class that is being registered. Line 10 uses the GUID property of this type object and converts it to a string. You then pass this GUID (after prepending CLSID\\ to it) to the OpenSubKey method of the ClassesRoot property, which returns a RegistryKey object that represents the HKEY_CLASSES_ROOT registry key.

Note Passing B to the ToString method on the GUID class indicates that you want the string representation of the GUID to be in registry format, that is 32 characters separated by hyphens and enclosed by brackets.

Line 14 adds the Control subkey. Line 15 adds a subkey that contains the CATID for ActiveX controls to the Implemented Categories' subkey for the Clock control. Lines 16 and 17 add the MiscStatus entry for the control. Lines 18 through 20 use the GetTypeLibGuidForAssembly method on the **System.Runtime.InteropServices.Marshal** class to retrieve the GUID (LIBID) that is assigned to a type library when it was exported from the specified assembly. Lines 21 and 22 add a TypeLib subkey that contains this value. Lines 23 through 26 generate a string that contains the major and minor versions of the assembly separated by a ".". Lines 27 and 28 add a Version subkey that contains this value. Finally, line 29 closes the CLSID key for the clock control.

Note Because the code shown previously uses the RegistryKey class, which resides in the Microsoft.Win32 namespace, you need to add the following using statement to compile this code: *using Microsoft.Win32;*.

You can also create a function that will be called when a user unregisters a managed assembly for use by unmanaged clients. This method has the same signature as the COM register function, but it is marked with the ComUnregisterFunction attribute. Add this function to the **ClockControl** class directly beneath the COM register function as shown in the following:

```
public class ClockControl : System.Windows.Forms.UserControl
{
// Implementation of the ClockControl class omitted...
    [ComRegisterFunction]
    private static void RegisterForCOM(Type aType)
    {
// Implementation of the RegisterForCOM method omitted...
    }
    [ComUnregisterFunction]
    private static void UnregisterForCOM(Type aType)
    {
      try
      {
         Registry.ClassesRoot.DeleteSubKeyTree(
        "CLSID\\"+aType.GUID.ToString("B"));
      }
      catch (ArgumentException)
      {

      }
    }
  }
}
```

The code here is fairly simple. You call the DeleteSubKeyTree method on the **Microsoft.Win32.RegistryKey** class to delete all the subkeys beneath the CLSID entry for the control.

ComVisible

You can specify which members of your classes will be visible to unmanaged (COM) clients using the ComVisible attribute, which resides in the System.Runtime.InteropServices namespace. To specify that a property or method should be visible to COM, set ComVisible to true as follows:

```
[ComVisible(true)]
public void DoSomething()
{
// Do something...
}
```

To specify that a property or method should not be visible to COM, set ComVisible to false as follows:

```
[ComVisible(false)]
public void DoSomething()
{
// Do something...
}
```

The ComVisible attribute can be applied to a class, structure, enumeration or an entire assembly. It can also be applied to any of the members of a type such as a method, property, field, interface or delegate. You can hide specific members of a type by setting the ComVisible attribute to false on that member. Public managed types in an assembly are visible (ComVisible=true) by default, so you don't have to do anything if you want all of your public managed types to be available to unmanaged consumers. Setting ComVisible to false on on an assembly hides all public types within the assembly. The ComVisible value applied to a specific type overrides the assembly setting, however. Therefore, you can expose only selected types from an assembly by setting the ComVisible attribute to false on the assembly and true on the types you want to expose. Only public types can be made visible. The ComVisible attribute cannot be used to make an internal or protected type visible to an unmanaged client.

Handling Managed Events from a COM Client

In Chapter 7, you saw how easy it is to handle COM connection point events from a managed client. Therefore, you are probably thinking that it is just as easy to handle events from a managed object in a COM client, right? Well, unfortunately, you will be disappointed. By default, events in a .NET object are not exposed to unmanaged clients at all. You must perform a few extra steps in order to expose your managed events to a COM client. These steps are quite easy, but, even after you perform these steps, you still may encounter some problems. This section shows you how to enable COM clients to handle events fired from your managed components and how to work around some of the problems this may cause.

Exposing Managed Events to Unmanaged Clients

A COM object that supports Connection Point events must publish a source (outgoing) interface in its type library. Although this interface appears in the COM object's type library, it is actually the object's client's responsibility to implement it. The client passes its implementation of the source interface to the object using the connection point interfaces (IConnectionPointContainer and IConnectionPoint), and then the COM object calls back on the source interface when it wants to fire the event.

Managed code objects that support .NET events do not fit into the connection point mechanism because—for a start—they do not expose a source interface. In order to support COM-style events, a managed code class needs to do three things:

- Expose a source interface that contains a method for each event that the object supports.
- Provide a mechanism to advertise that the class supports event notifications through the source interface.
- Implement the IConnectionPointContainer and IConnectionPoint interfaces to allow a client to pass its implementation of the source interface to instances of the class.

Fortunately, the System.Runtime.InteropServices namespace provides a pair of attributes that allow you to do all of this. If you want to expose .NET events to COM clients, you need to perform the following steps:

1. Define an interface, with members that correspond to each of the events that the managed class exports.
2. Mark the interface as a Dispatch interface using the Interface System.Runtime.InteropServices.InterfaceType attribute, specifying the following: `ComInterfaceType.InterfaceIsIDispatch.`
3. Mark the managed class that uses the source interface to fire events with the System.Runtime.InteropServices.ComSourceInterfaces attribute.

An example should make this clear. In Chapter 7, I demonstrated a COM StockMonitor object that fired PriceChange events to a managed client. These events showed the changing price on a number of stocks. In this chapter, I demonstrate the opposite scenario: a managed stock server object firing events to a COM client. The code for the managed stock server follows:

```
using System;
using System.Collections;
using System.Timers;
namespace DotNetStockServer
{
    public class PriceChangeEventArgs : EventArgs
    {
      private string mTicker;
      private float mOldPrice;
      private float mNewPrice;
      public PriceChangeEventArgs(string ticker,
        float newPrice,float oldPrice)
      {
        mTicker=ticker;
        mOldPrice=oldPrice;
```

```
      mNewPrice=newPrice;
    }
    public string Ticker
    {
      get
      {
        return mTicker;
      }
    }
    public float OldPrice
    {
      get
      {
        return mOldPrice;
      }
    }
    public float NewPrice
    {
      get
      {
        return mNewPrice;
      }
    }
  }
  public class MonitorInitiatedEventArgs :
    System.EventArgs
  {

    private string mTicker;
    private float mPrice;
    public MonitorInitiatedEventArgs(
      string ticker,float price)
    {
      mTicker=ticker;
      mPrice=price;
    }
    public float Price
    {
      get
      {
        return mPrice;
      }
    }
  }
  public delegate void PriceChangeEventHandler(
    object sender,PriceChangeEventArgs e);
  public delegate void MonitorInitiatedEventHandler
      (object sender,MonitorInitiatedEventArgs e);
  public class StockMonitor
  {
```

```
        private Hashtable mStockList;
        private ArrayList mTickerList;
        private Timer mTimer;
        public event PriceChangeEventHandler
          PriceChange;
        public event MonitorInitiatedEventHandler
          MonitorInitiated;
        public StockMonitor()
        {
          mStockList=new Hashtable(25);
          mTickerList=new ArrayList(25);
          AddNewStock("EMLX",(float)90.0);
          AddNewStock("IBM",(float)30.0);
          AddNewStock("MSFT",(float)49.0);
          mTimer=new Timer(5000);
          mTimer.Elapsed+=new
            ElapsedEventHandler(
            timer_Elapsed);
          mTimer.Enabled=true;
        }
        public void AddNewStock(
          string ticker,float price)
        {
          mTickerList.Add(ticker);
          mStockList.Add(ticker,price);
          OnMonitorInitiated(new
          MonitorInitiatedEventArgs(
            ticker,price));
        }
        public float GetPrice(string ticker)
        {
          return (float) mStockList[ticker];
        }
        private void timer_Elapsed(object sender,
            System.Timers.ElapsedEventArgs e)
          {

              if (mStockList.Count > 0)
              {
              Random randomizer=new Random();
              int index;
              float oldPrice, newPrice;
              String ticker;
              index=randomizer.Next(
              mStockList.Count);
              ticker=(string)mTickerList[index];
              oldPrice=(float)mStockList[ticker];
              newPrice=oldPrice+(float)0.1;
              mStockList[ticker]=newPrice;
              OnPriceChange(
```

```
                new PriceChangeEventArgs(
                ticker,newPrice,oldPrice));
                }
            }
            protected void OnPriceChange(
              PriceChangeEventArgs e)
            {
              PriceChange(this,e);
            }
            protected void OnMonitorInitiated(
              MonitorInitiatedEventArgs e)
            {
              MonitorInitiated(this,e);
            }
        }
}
```

The main class here is called **StockMonitor**, and it has two methods: (1) GetPrice, which takes a stock ticker as a parameter and returns the current price of the stock, and (2) AddNewStock, which allows you to specify the ticker and current price of a stock, which should be monitored. The StockMonitor class supports two events: (1) a MonitorInitiated event, which is fired when a client calls AddNewStock, and (2) PriceChanged, which is fired whenever the price of a monitored stock changes. In reality, the price changes are actually implemented by a timer (using the **Systems.Timers.Timer** class), which fires an event every 5 seconds and randomly picks a stock, raises its price by 10 cents, and then fires the PriceChange event. I won't walk through every line of code of this example, and I won't discuss in depth how to create a Visual Studio .NET project to build this assembly. The code is simple, and you've built projects similar to this many times already in this book.

Note I added a strong name to the DotNetStockServer assembly because you will install it into the GAC later.

I will quickly run through the event-related code in this class. Before I do that, however, I would like to quickly discuss the recommended design pattern for events as published in the .NET Framework SDK. That way you will understand why I structured this managed event as I did.

THE RECOMMENDED DESIGN PATTERN FOR EVENTS

If you want to expose an event called EventName, the .NET design guidelines for events recommends that you do the following:

"Declare an 'argument' class for the event, which is just a class called EventNameEventArgs. This class should derive from the System.EventArgs class and it should contain a property for each argument of the event.

Declare a delegate for the event called *EventName*EventHandler. This delegate should return void and have 2 parameters. The first parameter should be a System.Object that contains the object that fired the event; this argument should be called "sender". The second parameter is an instance of the "argument" class defined above; this parameter should be called "e". The sender should initialize this instance with the argument values that it is passing to the consumer of the event.

Declare the event as a public member of the "event firing" class and give it the name: EventName. Use the EventNameEventHandler delegate declared above for the event.

Add a protected method to the "event firing" class called OnEventName and fire the event from there. The reason for this is so derived classes can override the event behavior of the "event firing" class. By default, derived classes cannot directly raise events in their base classes."

Now, let's return the discussion to the StockMonitor class. In this example, the **StockMonitor** class is the event-firing class. Let's look at all the elements that make up the PriceChange event. If you refer back to the previous code listing, notice that you declared a **PriceChangeEventArgs** class on lines 6 through 39. This class has three read-only properties: Ticker, which contains the ticker name of the stock; old price, which contains the old price of the stock prior to the price change; and new price, which contains the price of the stock after the price change. I made these properties read-only because the event-firing class will use the parameterized constructor to initialize the underlying data for the class and the consumer of the event only needs to read the properties. Lines 60 and 61 declare the PriceChangeEventHandler delegate. Notice that the second parameter to this delegate is an instance of the **PriceChangeEventArgs** class. Lines 120 through 124 declare the protected OnPriceChange method, which raises the event to the client. The OnPriceChange method is called from the timer_Elapsed method on lines 115 through 117. The timer_Elapsed method is called every 5 seconds by the **StockMonitor** class' internal timer.

As it stands right now, a COM client cannot receive events from the **StockMonitor** class. Let's take a look at the changes you must make to allow a COM client to receive these events. First, you need to define a source interface that contains matching methods for each event. Let's add an interface called IStockMonitorEvents as follows:

```
[InterfaceType(ComInterfaceType.InterfaceIsIDispatch)]
public interface IStockMonitorEvents
```

```
{
      [DispId(1)] void PriceChange(
          object sender,PriceChangeEventArgs e);
      [DispId(2)] void MonitorInitiated(
          object sender,MonitorInitiatedEventArgs e);
}
```

The names and signatures of the methods in this interface must match up exactly with both the event names and the method signature of the managed classes' event delegates. Aside from that, this interface has nothing unusual or event specific. I declared it to be an IDispatch-only interface because that will make it accessible to the largest number of connection-point event consumers. I also explicitly declared DispIDs for the methods because that saves the CLR from having to call GetIDsOfNames to fetch the DispID for the method. I'll add the IStockMonitorEvents interface outside the declaration of the **StockMonitor** class, but inside the DotNetStockServer namespace. I'll also add a using Statement for System.Runtime.InteropServices as follows because the InterfaceType and DispId attributes reside in this namespace:

```
using System.Runtime.InteropServices;
```

Next, add the following attribute to the **StockMonitor** class:

```
[ComSourceInterfaces(typeof(IStockMonitorEvents))]
public class StockMonitor
{
// Implementation omitted...
}
```

This attribute, when applied to the **StockMonitor** class, indicates that the class uses the IStockMonitorEvents interface to fire connection point events to unmanaged clients. Finally, execute the following command to register the .NET **StockMonitor** for use by a COM client:

```
regasm DotNetStockServer.dll /tlb
```

Let's also execute the following commend to insert the stock server assembly into the GAC:

```
gacutil -i DotNetStockServer.dll
```

This last step isn't strictly necessary, but, if you don't do it, you will need to remember to deploy the assembly in the same directory as its unmanaged client.

Next, I built a client for the DotNetStockServer using Visual Basic 6. I first referenced the DotNetServer using the Project | References... as shown in Figure 8–13.

Notice, that, if I declare the StockMonitor object using the WithEvents keyword as shown here

```
Private WithEvents mStockServer As StockMonitor
```

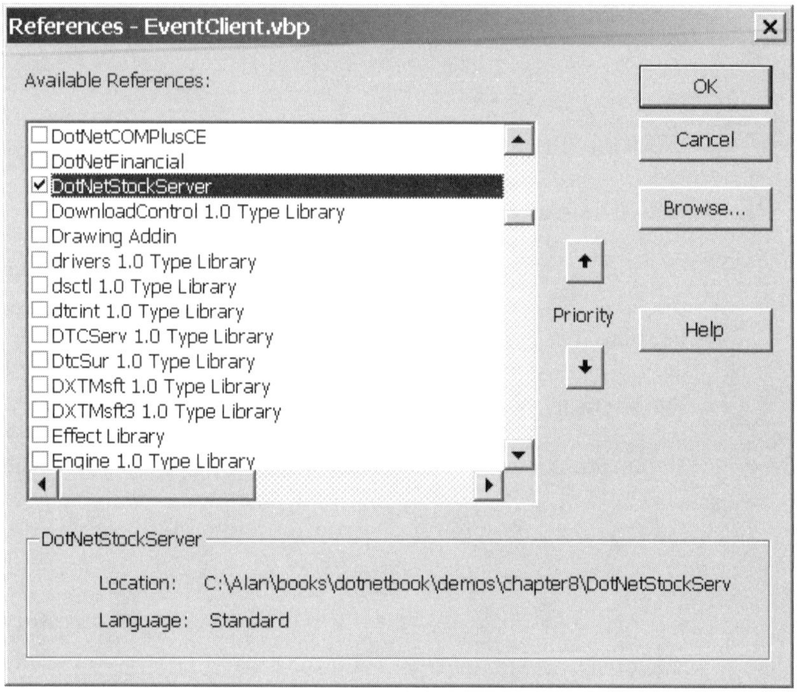

FIGURE 8–13 *Referencing the DotNetStockServer from a Visual Basic 6 client.*

I can now view the two events for the **StockMonitor** class in the events dropdown list in Visual Basic as shown in Figure 8–14.

The UI for my Visual Basic client looks as shown in Figure 8–15.

The code for this client is as follows:

```
Option Explicit
Private WithEvents mStockServer As StockMonitor

Private Sub cmdAdd_Click()
    On Error GoTo errHandler
    Call mStockServer.AddNewStock(
txtTicker.Text, txtPrice.Text)
    Exit Sub
errHandler:
    MsgBox (Err.Description)
End Sub

Private Sub Form_Load()
    On Error GoTo errHandler
    Set mStockServer = New StockMonitor
    Exit Sub
errHandler:
```

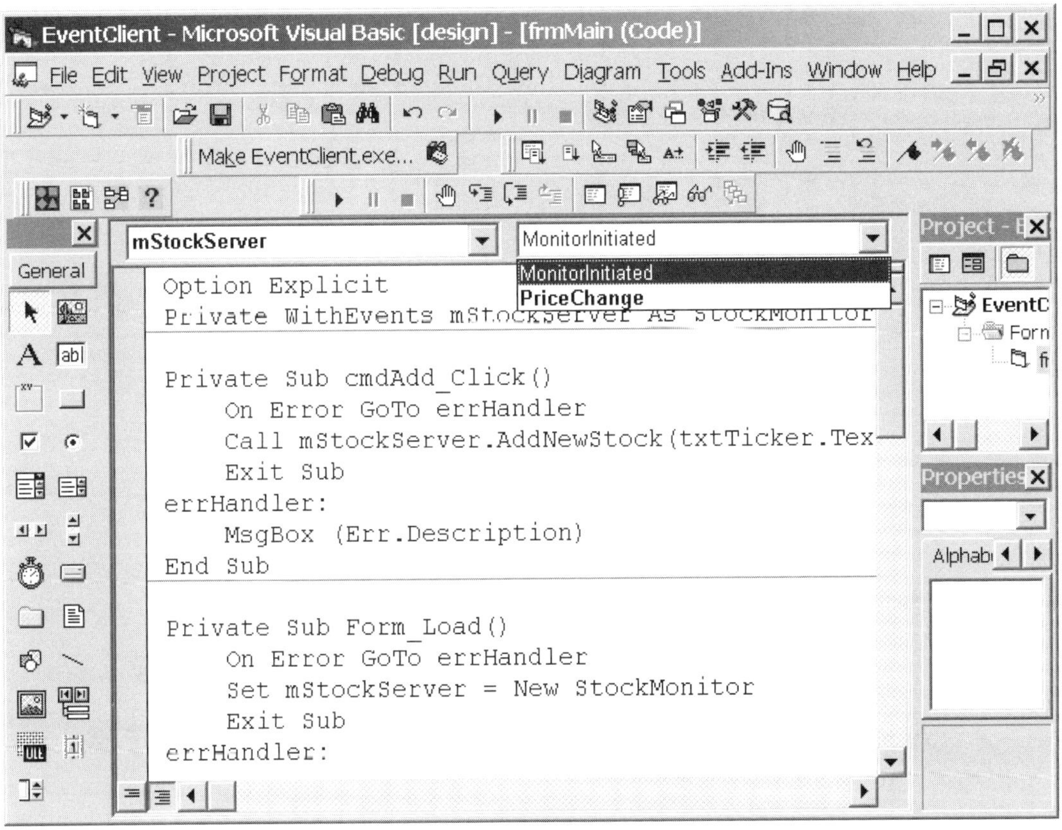

FIGURE 8–14 *The MonitorInitiated and PriceChange events viewed from Visual Basic 6.*

```
        MsgBox (Err.Description)
    End Sub

    Private Sub Form_Unload(Cancel As Integer)
        Set mStockServer = Nothing
    End Sub

    Private Sub mStockServer_MonitorInitiated(
    ByVal sender As Variant,
    ByVal e As DotNetStockServer.MonitorInitiatedEventArgs)
        Dim strMessage As String
        strMessage = "Monitor initiated for " & _
             e.ticker & vbCrLf & _
               "Current price $" & CStr(e.Price)
        Call MsgBox(strMessage, vbInformation,
             "Monitor Initiated")
    End Sub
```

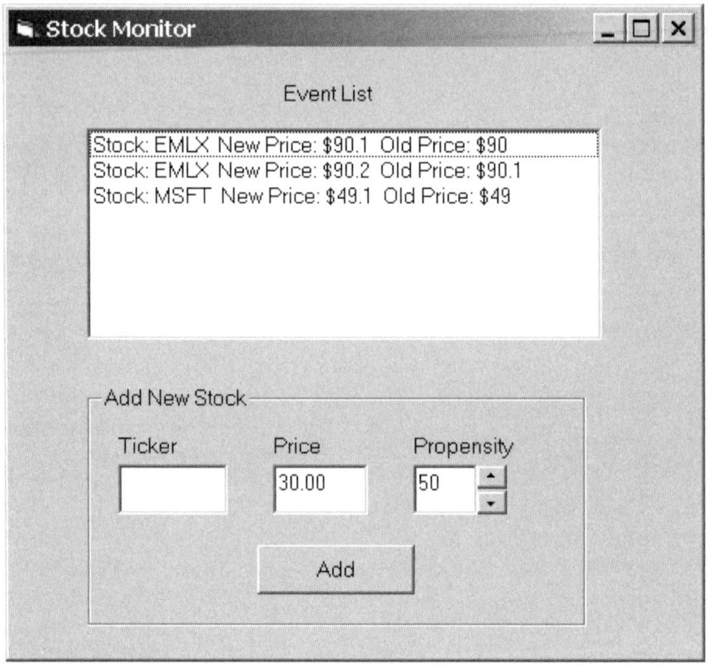

FIGURE 8–15 *The UI for the Visual Basic 6 stock monitor client.*

```
Private Sub mStockServer_PriceChange(
ByVal sender As Variant,
ByVal e As DotNetStockServer.PriceChangeEventArgs)
    Dim strMessage As String
    strMessage = "Stock: " & e.ticker & _
         "  New Price: $" & CStr(e.newPrice) & _
         "  Old Price: $" & CStr(e.oldPrice)
    lstEvents.AddItem strMessage
End Sub
```

I won't go line by line through this code because there really is nothing .NET–specific about it. It looks exactly like any code that you would write to use a COM object that supports connection point events.

Deploying COM/Win32 Applications That Use .NET Components

When you instantiate a .NET object from a COM client, the CLR must be able to locate the assembly that contains the .NET object's class. The CLR uses the same algorithm to locate the assembly that it would use if the object were instantiated from a managed client. The CLR first applies versioning policy to potentially change the requested version number of the assembly. The CLR then checks to see if the requested version of the assembly is already loaded into the current AppDomain. If the current version is not already loaded, the CLR searches the following in order: the GAC and then a specified CodeBase. Finally, it probes for the assembly beneath the unmanaged client application's root directory.

Note See the section entitled "How the Runtime Locates Assemblies" in Chapter 3 for complete details on how the CLR locates assemblies.

Therefore, when you attempt to use a managed code assembly from an unmanaged client, the managed code assembly must reside in one of three places: (1) the client application's root directory (or a subdirectory beneath this root), (2) the GAC, or (3) a specified codebase. At this point, you should be familiar with options 1 and 2. When you use the Assembly Registration Tool, you can specify a codebase for the assembly using the /codebase parameter to the tool. For instance, the following command registers the assembly called **myassembly.dll** for use by an unmanaged client, creates and registers a type library for the assembly, and sets the codebase for the assembly equal to the location where the assembly currently resides:

```
regasm myassembly.dll /codebase /tlb
```

The Assembly Registration Tool inserts the code base location into the registry entries that it creates for the assembly. Use the codebase during development or as a last resort. If you cannot install the assembly beneath the root directory of the unmanaged client application, you are better off using the GAC instead of specifying a codebase. The GAC supports versioning. This brings some performance benefits because the .NET runtime will verify the assembly when you install it into the GAC, and therefore the runtime does not have to verify the assembly each time an application loads it.

Summary

In this chapter, you learned some of the advanced aspects of using a managed object from an unmanaged client. You learned alternate ways of instantiating a managed object besides the standard COM CoCreateInstance function. Using these techniques, you can instantiate a managed object without having to register the object first or instantiate a managed object that has a parameterized constructor. You also learned how garbage collection complicates object life-cycle management and how to solve some of these problems. You also learned how to call overloaded methods and how to control the class interface that the CCW will expose. I also covered using COM apartments, rich-error information, and Windows Forms controls as ActiveX controls. In addition, I explained how to catch managed events in an unmanaged client. You are now ready to tackle most "real-word" problems associated with using a managed object from an unmanaged client.

NINE

Using COM+ (Enterprise Services)

In this chapter, I discuss how to use the COM+ Component Services from a managed application. COM+ was designed to facilitate the development of enterprise-class distributed applications. In support of this goal, COM+ provides the following services to middle-tier COM components:

- Fine-grained security.
- Distributed transactions.
- Thread synchronization.
- Load balancing.
- Asynchronous store and forward method invocation.
- Enhanced scalability through JIT activation, and pooling of objects and database connections.

These same services are accessible from the .NET Framework. In the .NET Framework, these services are referred to as the .NET Enterprise Services. It's best to think of the relationship between the .NET Enterprise Services and COM+ as one where the COM+ Component Services are used as the underlying implementation of the .NET Enterprise Services. In the future, it is likely that the .NET Enterprise Services will be built on an entirely managed foundation; it's also possible that these services will be implemented on non-Microsoft operating system platforms using other application server products like Transarc's Encina.

This chapter was not designed to be an exhaustive introduction to either COM+ or the .NET Enterprise Services. That would require an entire book. Because I've already written one (see *The COM and COM+ Programming Primer* [Prentice Hall]) I will direct you to that rather than rehash the same description of each of the services that is already contained there. In this chapter, my intention is to show you how to use the tools that the .NET Framework provides to make the COM+ Component Services available to managed applications. I also explain how the integration between the .NET Framework and the COM+ Component Services works.

A Couple of Big Caveats

Before I dive into the subject matter of this chapter, I would be remiss if I didn't start with a couple of big caveats. First of all, the current implementation of .NET Enterprise Services appears to be just a stop gap. It may change significantly when Microsoft implements Enterprise Services on an entirely managed-code foundation. I think it is significant that, even though Microsoft has released a significantly improved version of COM+ with Windows XP (version 1.5 of COM+ ships with Windows XP), it has hardly promoted it at all. In fact, few people that I have talked to even know that there is a new version of COM+ in Windows XP. To me this is a strong indication that Microsoft is probably moving in a different direction sometime in the near future.

Note See my article in the September 2000 edition of *Visual C++ Developers Journal* to learn about the new features that were implemented in version 1.5 of COM+, which shipped with Windows XP Professional and Windows .NET Server.

Second, think long and hard before you decide to use the .NET Enterprise Services. The current implementation uses a great deal of unmanaged code. As you learned in Chapter 6, there is a significant performance penalty to be paid when you cross the managed to unmanaged code boundary. Microsoft has worked hard to minimize this penalty for serviced components, but there is still a price to pay in terms of performance. In reality, this admonition was true even before .NET came along. COM+ has always had a significant amount of overhead associated with its use. The interception architecture that COM+ uses means that making method calls between objects in a COM+ application can be slow. Moreover, people often use the distributed transaction support in COM+ when they really don't need to. If your COM+ business objects access a single database, you don't need the Distributed Transaction Coordinator (DTC) transactions that COM+ provides. Distributed transactions are only required if you need to create a transaction that involves multiple resource managers, for example, two databases or a database and a message queue, and you want the operations to be done in an all or nothing manner. This means that both databases are updated or neither is updated, or a database is updated and a message is written to a message queue, or neither operation is performed. Unless you need this kind of functionality, using the transaction service in COM+/.NET Enterprise Services is overkill. You are better off using the Transaction class from your managed provider (**sqlTransaction** for the SQL Server Managed Provider and **OleDbTransaction** for the OLEDB Managed Provider) to create and commit your transactions manually.

Note There is an excellent white paper in the MSDN Library called "Performance Comparison: Transaction Control" by Priya Dhawan, which provides an in-depth performance comparison of DTC and manual transactions.

Creating a Serviced Component

A managed class that uses the .NET Enterprise Services is called a serviced component. To create a serviced component, you need to perform the following steps:

1. Derive your class either directly or indirectly from the **System.EnterpriseServices.ServicedComponent** base class.
2. Add attributes to your classes, methods, and interfaces that specify the services that you want to use.
3. Add assembly-level attributes that specify the type of COM+ application you would like to create: Library (in-process) or Server (out-of-process). You can also use assembly-level attributes to specify other things about your COM+ application, such as its name or GUID.
4. Use the **ContextUtil** and **SecurityCallContext** classes to interact with your classes' context if necessary.
5. Compile your classes into an assembly with a strong name.
6. Use the .NET Services Installation Tool (regsvcs.exe) to register and build a COM+ application for your assembly. You do not have to do this step explicitly because the .NET Framework supports Lazy Registration, but, in most cases, it is a good idea.
7. Insert your serviced component assembly into the GAC. This last step is optional for a serviced component hosted in a Library (in-process) COM+ application, but it is required for a serviced component that is hosted in a Server (out-of-process) COM+ application.

After you have performed all of these steps, you can call your serviced component from either a managed or an unmanaged client in the same way that you would call any other managed component. Let's examine each of these steps in greater detail.

The Serviced Component Base Class

The first step to creating a serviced component is to derive your class from the **ServicedComponent** class in the System.EnterpriseServices namespace as shown here:

```
using System;
using System.EnterpriseServices;
```

```
namespace BusObjectLibrary
{
        public class Book : ServicedComponent
        {
        // Implementation omitted...
        }
}
```

In order to inherit from the **ServicedComponent** class, you will first need to reference the System.EnterpriseServices assembly. In Visual Studio .NET, you can do this by selecting Project | Add Reference… and then selecting System.EnterpriseServices from the .NET tab as shown in Figure 9–1.

You then need to add a using statement for the System.EnterpriseServices namespace as shown in the previous code listing.

The **ServicedComponent** class contains most of the logic needed to interact with the COM+ infrastructure. Table 9–1 lists the methods in the **ServicedComponent** class.

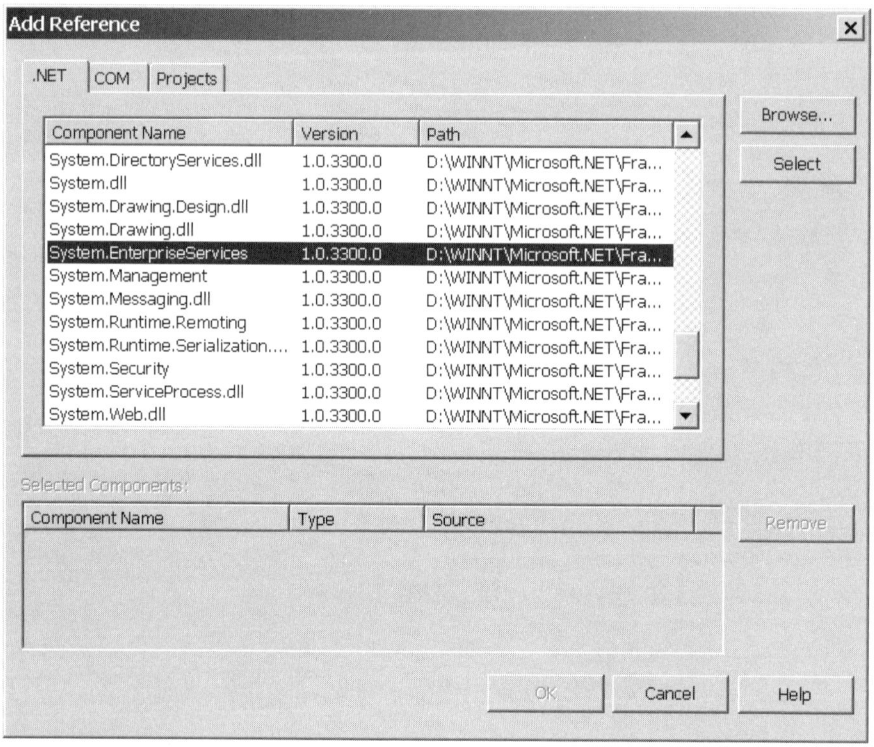

FIGURE 9–1 *Referencing the Enterprise Services assembly in Visual Studio .NET.*

TABLE 9–1 *The methods in the ServicedComponent class*

Method Name	Accessibility	Description
Activate	Protected	This method is called by the runtime when an object is created or activated from the object pool. Override this method to provide custom initialization logic. This method is equivalent to the Activate method in the IObjectControl interface from MTS/COM+.
Deactivate	Protected	This method is called by the runtime when an object is destroyed or returned to the object pool. Override this method to provide custom finalization logic. This method is equivalent to the Deactivate method in the IObjectControl interface from MTS/COM+.
CanBePooled	Protected	Override this method to indicate whether an object can be used with the COM+ object pooling service. Return true if the object can be pooled and false if it cannot be pooled.
Construct	Protected	This method is called by the runtime to give an object an opportunity to cache a construction string that is passed to it. Override this method if your class uses construction strings.
Dispose	Public	Call this method to free the managed and unmanaged resources associated with a serviced component.
Dispose(Boolean)	Protected	Call this method with the parameter set to true to release both managed and unmanaged resources. Passing in false for the parameter will release only unmanaged resources. You do not need to call this method directly. Calling the Dispose method with no parameters will call this Dispose method with the parameter set to true. The finalize destructor for the **ServicedComponent** class will call this method with the parameter set to false because the CLR will already have reclaimed the managed memory.

Perhaps the most important thing that the **ServicedComponent** base class does is to endow a derived class with the correct context and marshaling behavior. In order for an object to reside in a COM+ application and use the COM+ services, it must be a marshal by reference object, and it must be context bound.

MARSHAL BY REFERENCE

A marshal by reference object communicates across application domain (and process) boundaries using a proxy to send messages. This is in contrast to marshal by value objects (which the .NET Framework also supports) where the entire object's state is passed across application domain and process boundaries. A serviced component must be marshal by reference because it must execute within a COM+ application. It would not make sense to marshal the object's state over to a client and have it execute there. The **System.EnterpriseServices.ServicedComponent** class derives (indirectly) from the **System.MarshalByRefObject** class, which enforces the correct marshal by reference behavior.

CONTEXT-BOUND OBJECTS

Understanding what a ContextBound object is a little more difficult. A context-bound object is an object that resides in a context. A context is a runtime environment in which one or more compatible COM+ objects in a particular process execute. Contexts are created during object activation. When you instantiate a context-bound object, the new object is placed into an existing context or into a new context that is created for it. Whether the object goes into a new context or an existing one depends on whether the runtime requirements of the object (as identified by the attributes included in the metadata of the type) are compatible with the context of its creator. Context-bound classes are marked with context attributes that identify the services the object requires from its runtime environment. These services include thread synchronization, thread affinity, transactions, and so forth. If they are compatible, the object shares the context of its creator, and the creator can make direct calls on the object, assuming it is in the same AppDomain as its creator (see Figure 9–2).

If the object and its creator are incompatible, the runtime will place the object in a new context and set up a proxy between the object and its creator. The runtime also sets up the necessary interception logic to provide the services that the object needs (see Figure 9–3). The runtime determines what services the object needs by examining its metadata.

Any code that is executing outside of the object's context must access the object through a proxy, which will call an interception layer on creation of the object, before and after each method call on the object, and when the object is destroyed. This interception layer is actually just a chain of objects that are called in succession whenever a piece of code in another context activates, makes a method call on, or destroys a context-bound object. These service-providing objects are sometimes called policy objects. Any managed class that derives from **ContextBoundObject** (as the **ServicedComponent** class does) will be bound to a context, and the CLR will ensure that the require-

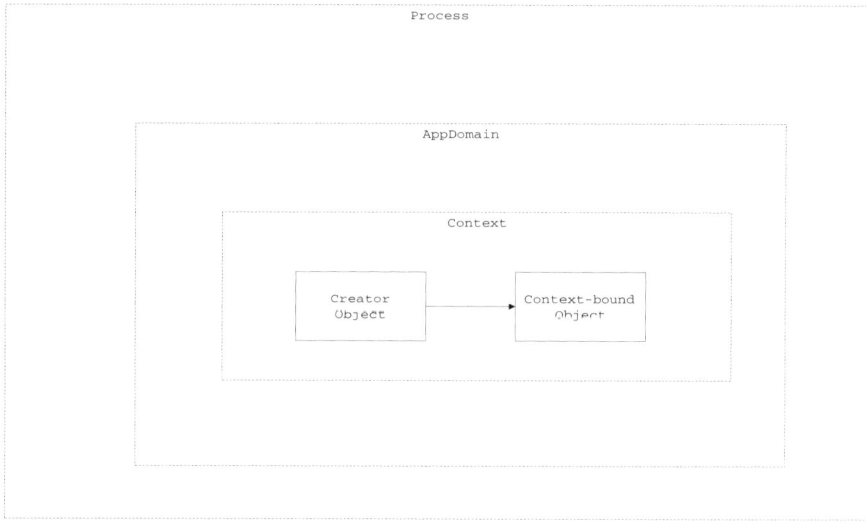

FIGURE 9–2 Two objects that share the same context.

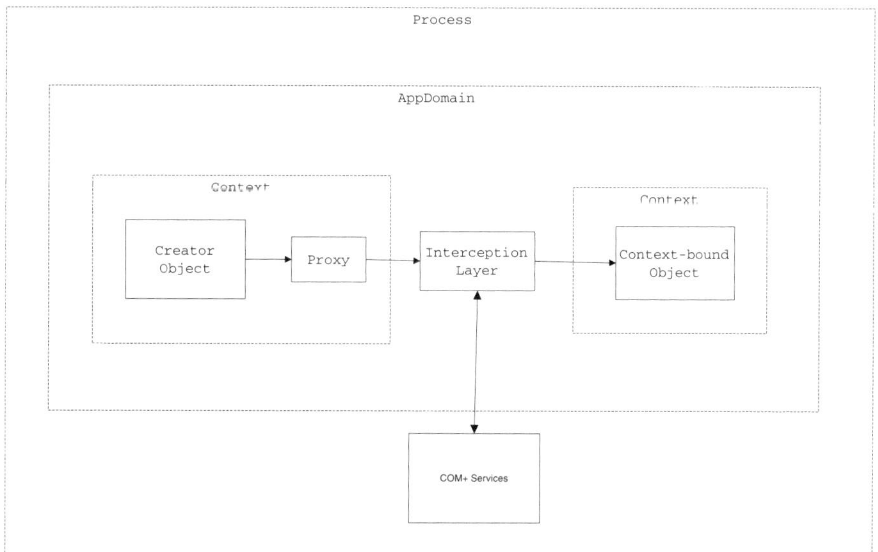

FIGURE 9–3 Two objects in different contexts.

ments of the classes' context (as identified by its context-related attributes) are enforced through interception. The CLR automatically places the object within a context, ensuring that only compatible objects share the same context, and sets up the proxy and interception layer.

Eventually, the .NET Framework will use this infrastructure to implement Enterprise Services entirely in managed code, but, for now, serviced components use the COM+ services, which are implemented in unmanaged code. At activation, instances of the **ServicedComponent** class insert a special object called a Serviced Component Proxy (SCP) into the chain of policy objects in the managed Interception layer. The serviced component class also sets up a COM+ context that reads the COM+ configuration of the object from the COM+ catalog. The SCP takes care of communicating with the COM+ context to provide the COM+ services that the serviced component requested. Figure 9–4 shows how this works for an in-process object, that is, an object that is configured to run in a Library COM+ Application.

In this case, the client object and the context-bound object reside in different contexts within the same AppDomain. The client object will access the context-bound object using a context-aware proxy that will call into the managed interception layer. The policy objects for the serviced components in the

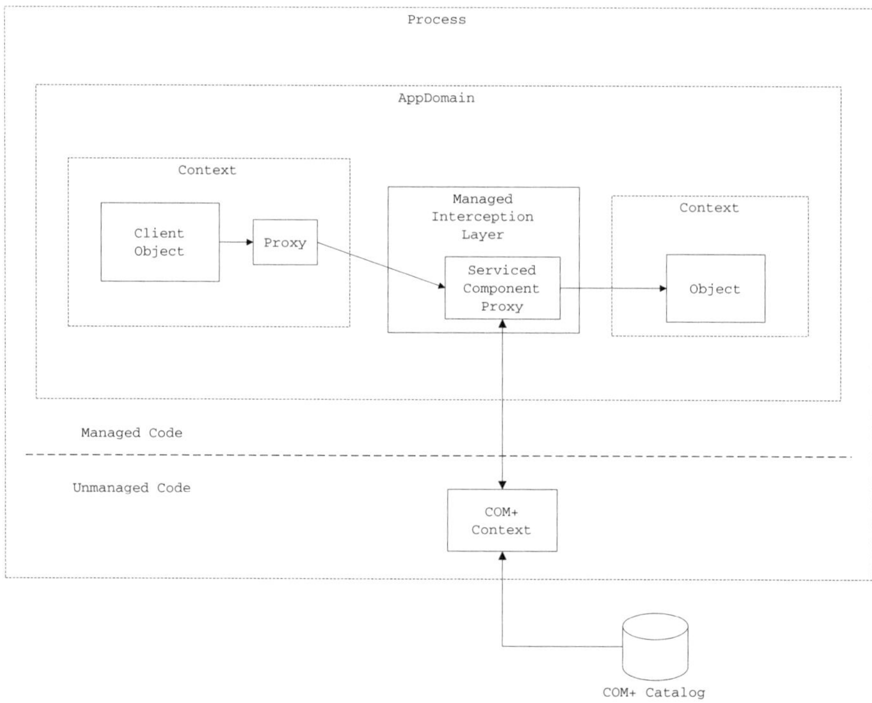

FIGURE 9–4 *Setting up the unmanaged context for an in-process object.*

Interception layer will call the SCP, which in turn will call the COM+ context to provide the COM+ services that the serviced component requested.

Figure 9–5 shows how this works for an out-of-process object, that is, an object that is configured to run in a Server COM+ application.

The situation here is obviously far more complicated. When you activate an object that resides in a server COM+ application, the CLR will setup a Remote Serviced Component Proxy (RSCP) in the client process. When you make a method call, the RSCP will use a RCW to call a DCOM proxy for the context-bound object. This proxy will talk to a stub in the process that hosts the serviced component (**dllhost.exe**). The server process will use a CCW to invoke a managed proxy, which will call into the managed Interception layer. At the managed Interception layer, there will be an SCP for the serviced component that will call a COM+ context to provide COM+ services for the object.

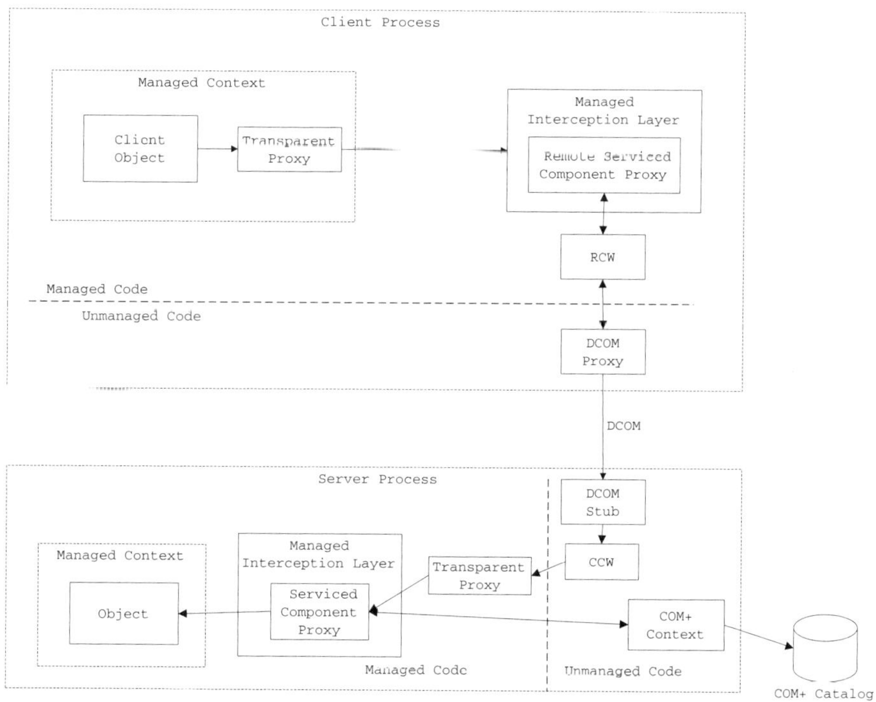

FIGURE 9–5 *Setting up the unmanaged context for an out-of-process object.*

Add Class, Interface, and Method Level Attributes

The next step to create a serviced component is to add class, interface, and method level attributes that specify the services that your component requires. You specify which services you want to use using the attributes in the System.EnterpriseServices namespace. Table 9–2 summarizes the available services and the attributes that relate to those services.

TABLE 9–2 *The .NET Enterprise Services attributes*

Attribute Name	Purpose	Applies to	Default Value When Not Applied
ApplicationName	Specifies the name of the COM+ application.	Assembly	The assembly name
ApplicationId	Specifies the COM+ application's GUID. The COM+ runtime generates a GUID for you if you don't specify a value for this attribute.	Assembly	A system-generated value
ApplicationActivation	Specifies whether the COM+ application will be a library application, which runs in its creator's process (ActivationOption.Library), or a server application, which runs in **dllhost.exe** (ActivationOption.Server).	Assembly	Library (in-process)
ApplicationAccessControl	Specifies the security configuration for your COM+ application. You can configure whether access control is turned on. You can also specify the authentication and impersonation levels.	Assembly	Enabled= false
Description	Allows you to specify a description for your COM+ application that will appear in the Component Services explorer.	Assembly, Class, Interface, Method	
Transaction	Specifies COM+ (distributed) transaction support. Possible values reside in the TransactionOption enumeration: Ignored, None, Required, RequiresNew, Supported.	Class	Disabled

TABLE 9–2 *The .NET Enterprise Services attributes (continued)*

Attribute Name	Purpose	Applies to	Default Value When Not Applied
Synchronization	Specifies COM+ concurrency support. Possible values reside in the SynchronizationOption enumeration: None, Required, RequiresNew, Supported.	Class	Disabled
JustInTimeActivation	Specifies JIT Activation support.	Class	False
ObjectPooling	Specifies support for object pooling. Properties on this attribute allow you to configure the minimum and maximum size of the pool and the creation timeout.	Class	Enabled=false
ConstructionEnabled	Specifies that a class supports construction strings. Use the default property of this attribute to specify an initial value for this construction string.	Class	Enabled=false
AutoComplete	Specifies that the transaction automatically calls SetComplete if the method call returns successfully. If the method call throws an exception, the transaction is aborted.	Method	False
MustRunInClientContext	Specifies that a class must run in the same context as its client.	Class	False
EventTrackingEnabled	Specifies that a class supports events and statistics.	Class	False
EventClass	Specifies that a class is a COM+ event class. Calls on the class are delivered to the classes event subscribers.	Class	False
LoadBalancingSupported	Specifies whether a component supports the Component Load Balancing service available in Microsoft Application Center Server.	Class	False
ComponentAccessControl	Specifies whether role-based security checks are performed at the component level.	Class	False
ApplicationQueuing	Enables queuing support for a COM+ application.	Assembly	Enabled=false

TABLE 9–2 *The .NET Enterprise Services attributes (continued)*

Attribute Name	Purpose	Applies to	Default Value When Not Applied
InterfaceQueuing	Specifies that calls on this interface will be queued using message queuing.	Interface, Class	Enabled = false
ExceptionClass	For queued components, allows you to specify a class that will receive exceptions.	Class	None
PrivateComponent	Specifies that a class can only be used by components in the same COM+ application.	Class	N/A If this attribute is not used, the class is public.
SecurityRole	Adds a role to a COM+ application and specifies that a class requires users to be in the role.	Assembly, Class, Interface, Method	No default roles are added.
SecureMethod	Specifies that role-based security will be used on an assembly, class or method and that you will configure role-based security administratively.	Assembly, Class, Method	

All of the attributes listed in Table 9–2 relate to a preexisting COM+ feature. These attributes are just a way to make these services available in a convenient way to allow managed components to use these services. Column 3 of Table 9–2 lists which entity (assembly, class, interface, or method) the attribute can apply to. In most cases, you will not apply all of these attributes to your components, so column 4 of Table 9–2 lists the value that your assembly, class, or method will assume for that attribute if you do not use the attribute.

The following code shows an example of a class that uses some of the most commonly used of these attributes:

```
using System;
using System.Messaging;
using System.Data;
using System.Data.SqlClient;
using System.EnterpriseServices;
namespace BusObjectLibrary
{
      [ConstructionEnabled(true,Default=
        "user id=sa;password=;initial
        catalog=DevDotNet;data source=localhost")]
      [Transaction(TransactionOption.Required,
        Isolation=
```

```
13.         TransactionIsolationLevel.RepeatableRead,
14.         Timeout=45)]
15.       [ObjectPooling(Enabled=true,MinPoolSize=2,
16.         MaxPoolSize=100,
17.         CreationTimeout=3000)]
18.       public class Book : ServicedComponent
19.       {
20.         private string mConnString;
21.         private const string
22.            m_strQueuePath=".\\private$\\devdotnet";
23.         public Book()
24.         {
25.         }
26.         protected override void Construct(string s)
27.         {
28.           mConnString=s;
29.         }
30.         [AutoComplete]
31          public DataSet GetBooksByTitle(
32.           string title)
33.         {
34.         // Implementation omitted...
35.         }
36.         [AutoComplete]
37.         public DataSet GetBooksByISBN(string isbn)
38.         {
39.         // Implementation omitted...
40.         }
41.         [AutoComplete]
42.         public int InsertOrder(DataSet dsOrderInfo)
43.         {
44.         // Implementation omitted...
45.         }
46.       }
47. }
```

Lines 8 through 17 use the attributes in the System.EnterpriseServices namespace to specify which of the COM+ services you would like the class to use. In this case, I am using construction strings, transactions, and object pooling. The construction string is configured on lines 8 through 10 and is used to specify the database connection string for the object. Lines 26 through 29 override the Construct method in the **System.EnterpriseServices** class to receive the construction string. You then cache the string that you receive in a private variable called mConnString that I declared on line 20. Lines 11 through 14 use the Transaction attribute to specify that all method calls on instances of this class will execute within a distributed transaction. I use the TransactionIsolation and Timeout properties of the Transaction attribute to specify that the transaction for the class will have the Repeatable Read isolation level and a timeout of 45 seconds. These two Transaction properties are new features of COM+ 1.5 and are only supported on the Windows XP family of operating systems. If you use these properties on Windows 2000, it will cause an error when you attempt to register the component. On Windows 2000, you should replace lines 11 through 14 with the following:

```
[Transaction(TransactionOption.Required)]
```

The Transaction attribute has an implicit dependency on the Synchronization and JustInTimeActivation attributes. In order to use automatic DTC transactions, an object must also be configured with the Synchronization attribute set to Required (if the Transaction attribute is set to Required or Supported) or Requires New (if the Transaction attribute is set to Requires New). The JustInTimeActivation attribute must also be set to True whenever you use transactions. If you set the Transaction attribute to Supported, Requires, or Requires New and you do not set the Synchronization and JustInTimeActivation attributes appropriately, the system will just ignore your Synchronization and JustInTimeActivation settings and set them to the appropriate value required by the Transaction attribute. In other words, the following attribute settings

```
[Transaction(TransactionOption.Required)]
public class Book : ServicedComponent
{
}
```

are equivalent to

```
[Transaction(TransactionOption.Required)]
[Synchronization(SynchronizationOption.Required)]
[JustInTimeActivation(true)]
public class Book : ServicedComponent
{
}
```

If you tried to configure the following settings

```
[Transaction(TransactionOption.Required)]
[Synchronization(SynchronizationOption.Disabled)]
[JustInTimeActivation(false)]
public class Book : ServicedComponent
{
}
```

the .NET Services Installation Tool (regsvcs.exe) will simply ignore your settings for the Synchronization and JustInTimeActivation attributes and configure these attributes as shown here:

```
[Transaction(TransactionOption.Required)]
[Synchronization(SynchronizationOption.Required)]
```

```
[JustInTimeActivation(true)]
public class Book : ServicedComponent
{
}
```

I did find one exception to this rule. If you attempt to set both the Transaction and Synchronization attributes to Supported, regsvcs.exe will fail and report the following error:

```
The following installation error occurred:
1: Errors occurred while configuring components.
    BusObjectLibrary.Book.Synchronization: One or more
property settings are either invalid or in conflict with
each other
```

Lines 15 through 17 in the previous code listing use the ObjectPooling attribute to specify that the class will use the object pooling service provided by COM+. I use the MinPoolSize property to specify the number of objects that the system should create initially and the MaxPoolSize property to specify the maximum number of objects that are allowed to exist before the system starts queuing further activation requests. Lines 30, 36, and 41 use the AutoComplete attribute on each method in the book class. This specifies that the object should call SetComplete automatically to commit the object's transaction if the method returns without error and SetAbort to roll back the transaction if the methods raises an error. If you register the class using the NET Services Installation Tool (I talk about this shortly), you will receive the following warning:

```
WARNING: The class 'BusObjectLibrary.Book' has no class
interface, which means that unmanaged late bound calls
cannot take advantage of AutoComplete methods.
```

The problem is that the AutoComplete attribute is a method-level attribute, but the **Book** class does not currently expose any early-bound methods. If you remember from Chapters 6 and 8, a managed object exposes a COM class interface to unmanaged consumers. By default, this interface is a late-bound interface. You can probably understand this better by looking at the **Book** class in the COM+ Component Services explorer after you have registered our assembly. Figure 9–6 shows the interfaces that the class exposes to COM consumers, after it is registered.

Notice that, in addition to the class interface for the managed **Book** class (_Book), there is a _Object interface, which explicitly exposes all the methods found in the **System.Object** class. The serviced component also exposes IDisposable, IManagedObject, and IServicedComponentInfo interfaces, but the key point is that the _Book interface contains no methods.

The end result of all of this is that the **Book** class, as written, is unsuitable for use with an unmanaged client. The AutoComplete attribute will not work when the **Book** class is called from an unmanaged client, and I have

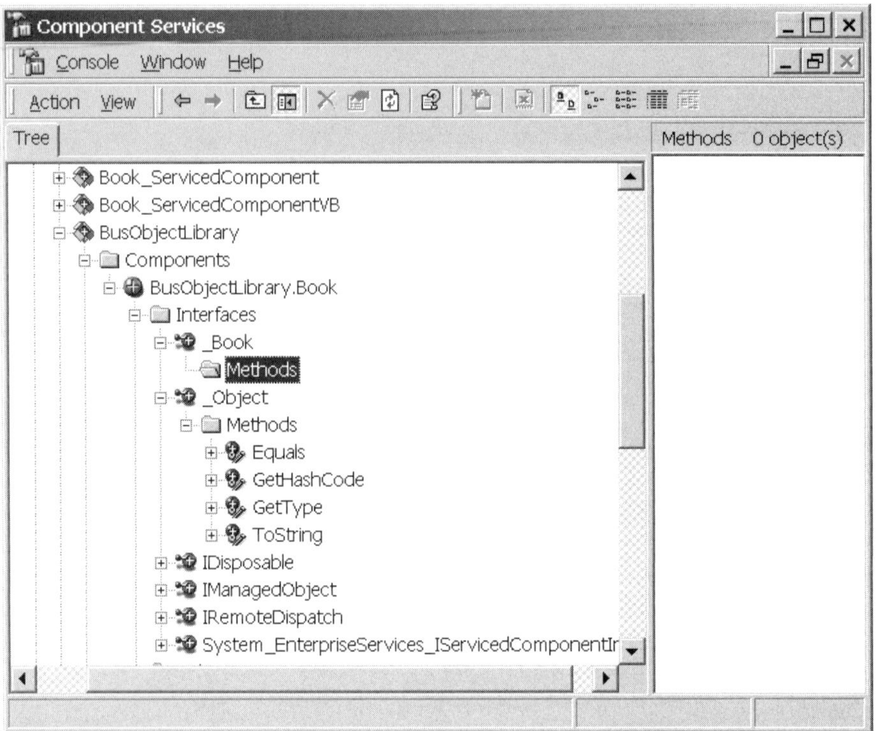

FIGURE 9–6 *The interfaces that the Book class exposes.*

not called SetComplete or SetAbort explicitly in the **Book** class' methods. A transactional managed object will not commit (or roll back) its transaction or free its resources until the object calls SetComplete or SetAbort either explicitly or by using the COM+ AutoComplete feature.

Remember that this is only a problem if you attempt to call the serviced component from an unmanaged client. The AutoComplete attribute does work correctly with a managed client.

You can make the **Book** class work with an unmanaged client in one of two ways. You can use the System.Runtime.InteropServices.ClassInterface attribute to create a dual interface for the **Book**, or you can declare and implement a managed interface that contains the class' methods.

Note You could also call the SetComplete/SetAbort methods on the System.EnterpriseServices.ContextUtil class explicitly instead of using the AutoComplete attribute, but I would be jumping ahead if I discussed this here. I will discuss this in the next section.

To use the first approach, change the definition of the **Book** class to look as follows:

```
using System;
using System.Messaging;
using System.Data;
using System.Data.SqlClient;
using System.EnterpriseServices;
using System.Runtime.InteropServices;
namespace BusObjectLibrary
{
     [ConstructionEnabled(true,Default=
      "user id=sa;password=;initial catalog=DevDotNet;
      data source=localhost")]
     [Transaction(TransactionOption.Required,
        Isolation=
        TransactionIsolationLevel.RepeatableRead,
        Timeout=45)]
      [ObjectPooling(Enabled=true,MinPoolSize=2,
        MaxPoolSize=100,
        CreationTimeout=3000)]
     [ClassInterface(ClassInterfaceType.AutoDual)]
     public class Book : ServicedComponent
     {
       private string mConnString;
       private const string m_strQueuePath=
         ".\\private$\\devdotnet";
       public Book()
       {

       }
       protected override void Construct(string s)
       {
         mConnString=s;
       }
       [AutoComplete]
            public DataSet GetBooksByTitle(
                 string title)
       {
         // Implementation omitted…
       }
       [AutoComplete]
       public DataSet GetBooksByISBN(string isbn)
       {
         // Implementation omitted…
       }
       [AutoComplete]
       public int InsertOrder(DataSet dsOrderInfo)
       {
         // Implementation omitted…
```

```
        }
    }
}
```

As I mentioned in Chapter 8, using the AutoDual class interface setting is problematic because managed class signatures are not subject to the same immutability rules as COM interfaces. If you expose an AutoDual class interface from a managed object, and a COM client early binds to it, and then you change the interface, the COM client may break. A better approach is to define a managed interface explicitly as follows. This will allow the AutoComplete attribute to work, as well as provide the most stable and easy-to-use interface for unmanaged clients.

```
public interface IBook
{
  DataSet GetBooksByTitle(string title);
  DataSet GetBooksByISBN(string isbn);
  int InsertOrder(DataSet dsOrderInfo);
}
[ConstructionEnabled(true,Default=
  "user id=sa;password=;
    initial catalog=DevDotNet;
  data source=localhost")]
[Transaction(TransactionOption.Required,
  Isolation=
  TransactionIsolationLevel.RepeatableRead,
  Timeout=45)]
 [ObjectPooling(Enabled=true,MinPoolSize=2,
   MaxPoolSize=100,
   CreationTimeout=3000)]
public class Book : ServicedComponent, IBook
{
  private string mConnString;
  private const string m_strQueuePath=
            ".\\private$\\devdotnet";
  public Book()
  {
  }
  protected override void Construct(string s)
  {
    mConnString=s;
  }
  [AutoComplete]
  public DataSet GetBooksByTitle(
          string title)
  {
    // Implementation omitted…
  }
  [AutoComplete]
  public DataSet GetBooksByISBN(string isbn)
```

```
38.         {
39.           // Implementation omitted…
40.         }
41.         [AutoComplete]
42.         public int InsertOrder(DataSet dsOrderInfo)
43.         {
44.           // Implementation omitted…
45.         }
46.     }
```

Lines 1 through 6 define an interface that contains the GetBooksByTitle, GetBooksByISBN, and InsertOrder methods from the **Book** class. I then implement the IBook interface on the **Book** class on line 18. You can then use the AutoComplete attribute on the three methods that you are implementing from the IBook interface. As long as an unmanaged client uses the IBook interface, the AutoComplete attribute will work as advertised.

Add Assembly-Level Attributes

You can compile the **Book** class into an assembly without applying any of the assembly-level attributes listed in Table 9–2. You can then register the assembly using the .NET Services Installation Tool (regsvcs.exe). Regsvcs.exe will create a COM+ Library application and install the class into the application. By default, it will give the COM+ application the same name as the assembly. It will generate a GUID for the application and configure all of the assembly-level attributes with their defaults as outlined in Table 9–2. In most cases, though, you will want to exercise more control over the properties of the COM+ application that regsvcs.exe will create. The assembly-level attributes in Table 9–2 provide this control. For instance, the ApplicationName attribute allows you to control the name that regsvcs.exe will assign to the COM+ application. The ApplicationActivation attribute allows you to control whether your serviced components will be hosted in a Library (in-process) or Server (out-of-process) COM+ application. The following code demonstrates how to use the ApplicationName and ApplicationActivation attributes.

```
[assembly: ApplicationName("DemoServicedComponent")]
[assembly: ApplicationActivation(ActivationOption.Server)]
```

If you add this code to the AssemblyInfo.cs file that Visual Studio .NET creates for your project, your COM+ application will have the name DemoServicedComponent, and it will be hosted in a COM+ Server application In order to use these attributes in your assembly info file, you will need to add a using statement for System.EnterpriseServices to the top of the assembly info file as shown here:

```
using System.EnterpriseServices;
```

The following code shows another example of assembly-level enterprise services attributes. Here I am using the ApplicationAccessControl and SecurityRole attributes to configure COM+ role-based security.

```
[assembly: ApplicationActivation(ActivationOption.Server)]
[assembly: ApplicationAccessControl(true,
AccessChecksLevel=
AccessChecksLevelOption.ApplicationComponent,
          Authentication=AuthenticationOption.Privacy,
          ImpersonationLevel=
ImpersonationLevelOption.Impersonate)]
[assembly: SecurityRole("Manager")]
[assembly: SecurityRole("Customer",true)]
```

Once again, you should add these attributes to your assembly info file. Setting these security settings will configure security for the component, as shown in Figure 9–7.

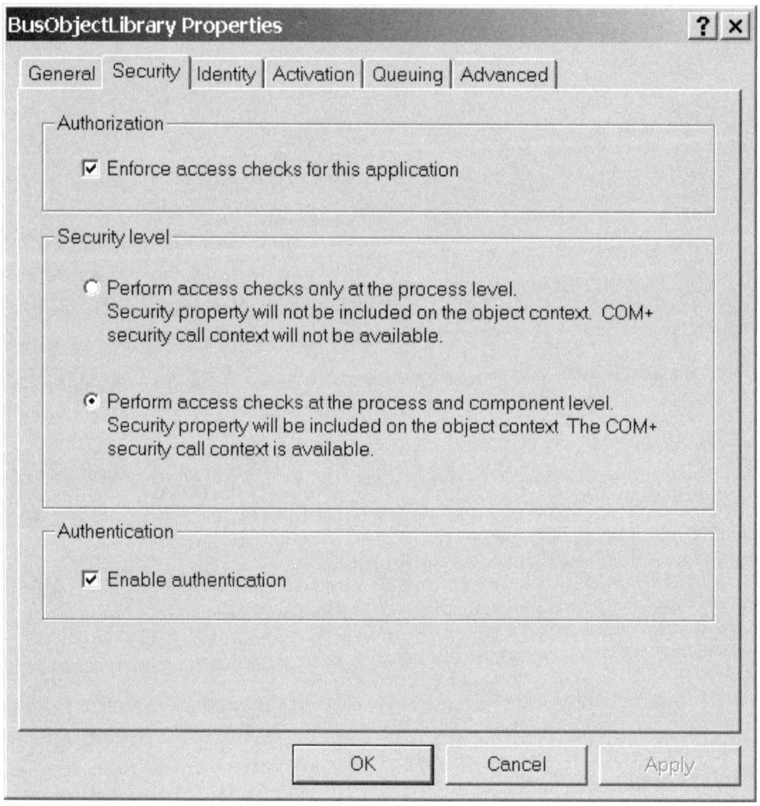

FIGURE 9–7 *The COM+ application configured using the settings shown in the previous code.*

In this case, I am specifying that the COM+ application should be an out-of-process (Server) application, and I also turn on Access Control at the component level and use the Privacy authentication level, which will encrypt communications between the client and the server. I also have added two roles—Manager and Customer—to the application. In the case of the Customer role, the second parameter (true) indicates that regsvcs.exe should add the Identity called Everyone to the customer role. In order to use these two roles, you have to attach them to a class, interface, or method. This indicates that membership in the role is required to use that class, interface, or method. For instance, if we attach the Customer role to the GetBooksByTitle and GetBooksByISBN methods and the Manager role to the InsertOrder method as follows

```
public interface IBook
{
  DataSet GetBooksByTitle(string title);
  DataSet GetBooksByISBN(string isbn);
  int InsertOrder(DataSet dsOrderInfo);
}
// Other attributes omitted…
[ComponentAccessControl(true)]
public class Book : ServicedComponent, IBook
{
  [SecurityRole("Customer")]
  [AutoComplete]
  public DataSet GetBooksByTitle(string title)
  {
  //…
  }
  [SecurityRole("Customer")]
  [AutoComplete]
  public DataSet GetBooksByISBN(string isbn)
  {
  //…
  }
  [SecurityRole("Manager")]
  [AutoComplete]
  public int InsertOrder(DataSet dsOrderInfo)
  {
  //…
  }
}
```

a user must be in the Customer role in order to call the GetBooksByTitle or GetBooksByISBN methods, and the user must be in the Manager role in order to call the InsertOrder method. If you assign a role to a method, regsvcs.exe will add an additional role called Marshaler to your COM+ application. Users must be added administratively to this role in order to call the methods.

Use the ContextUtil and SecurityCallContext Classes

In many cases, a serviced component will need to interact directly with its context. An object's context is divided into two objects that are accessed separately: a method-invariant context called an Object Context and a per-method context called a security call context. An object may need to call its object context directly to commit or abort a transaction (or at least to indicate that it is voting to commit or abort the transaction), to check if the current method is executing within a transaction, or to check if the caller is in a particular role. An object may need to access its call context to get the identity of the method's caller, to determine if security is enabled, or to determine the minimum authentication level in the current call chain. A serviced component can interact with its object context using the **System.EnterpriseServices.ContextUtil** class, and it can interact with its security call context using the **System.EnterpriseServices.SecurityCallContext** class. Table 9–3 lists the methods of the **ContextUtil** class.

TABLE 9–3 *The methods of the ContextUtil class*

Method Name	Description
SetComplete	Sets the transaction vote bit (also called the consistent bit) to commit and the done bit to true. An object calls this method to indicate that is has completed its work and is voting to commit the transaction. The DTC will commit the transaction as long as all of the other participants in the transaction also vote to commit.
SetAbort	Sets the transaction vote flag to abort and the done bit to true. An object calls this method to indicate that is has completed its work and is voting to roll back the transaction. The DTC will roll back this transaction regardless of how the other participants vote.
EnableCommit	Sets the transaction vote bit (also called the consistent bit) to commit and the done bit to false. An object calls this method to indicate that it is not done with its work, but, if the object is deactivated, the DTC can commit the transaction.
EnableCommit	Sets the transaction vote bit (also called the consistent bit) to abort and the done bit to false. An object calls this method to indicate that it is not done with its work, and, if the object is deactivated, the DTC should roll back the transaction.
IsCallerInRole	Is called to test if the caller is in a specified role.
GetNamedProperty	Returns a named property of the context.

Table 9–4 lists the properties of the **ContextUtil** class.

TABLE 9–4 *The properties of the ContextUtil class*

Property Name	Description
ActivityId	Returns the GUID of the activity of the current context or GUID_NULL if the context is not part of an activity.
ApplicationId	Returns the GUID of the object's COM+ application.
ApplicationInstanceId	Returns the GUID associated with the current instance of the object's COM+ application.
ContextId	Returns the GUID of the current context.
DeactivateOnReturn	Gets or sets the done bit of the current context.
IsInTransaction	Returns true if the current context is transaction and false otherwise.
IsSecurityEnabled	Returns true if role-based security is enabled.
MyTransactionVote	Gets or sets the transaction vote (consistent) bit in the COM+ context.
PartitionId	Returns the GUID of the current partition. Partitions are a COM+ 1.5 feature that is only supported on Windows .NET Server and the Windows XP family of operating systems.
Transaction	Returns an ITransaction interface that represents the current DTC transaction.
TransactionId	Returns the GUID of the current DTC transaction.

All of the methods and properties on the **ContextUtil** class are static. You do not need to create an instance of this class. The following code shows how you might use the **ContextUtil** class in a method of a serviced component:

```
public DataSet GetBooksByTitle(string title)
{
      DataSet ds;
      try
      {
        if (!ContextUtil.IsCallerInRole("Customer"))
          throw new UnauthorizedAccessException(
            "Caller must be in the Customer role");
        if (ContextUtil.IsInTransaction)
        {
        // Log the transaction ID
            System.Diagnostics.Trace.WriteLine(
               "Transaction ID=" +
               ContextUtil.TransactionId.ToString());
        }
```

```
16.         StoredProcParam[] spParameters=new
17.           StoredProcParam[1];
18.         spParameters[0]=new StoredProcParam(
19.             "@Title",SqlDbType.NVarChar,255,title);
20.         ds=GetDataSetFromStoredProc(
21.           "GetBooksByTitle",spParameters,"Titles");
22.         ContextUtil.SetComplete();
23.       }
24.       catch (Exception )
25.       {
26.         ContextUtil.SetAbort();
27.         throw;
28.       }
29.       return ds;
30. }
```

Line 6 calls the IsCallerInRole method to programmatically check if the caller is the customer role. Line 9 checks if the method is executing within a transaction. If it is, you log the transaction ID on lines 12 through 14. Lines 16 through 21 execute the business logic of this method. Don't worry if you don't understand this code; I will explain it shortly. Line 22 calls the SetComplete method on the **ContextUtil** class to indicate that you are voting to commit the transaction. If any of the logic in this method throws an exception, it will jump to the exception handler on lines 24 through 28, which will abort the transaction and rethrow the error.

You use the **SecurityCallContext** to access security information related to a particular call on an object. Just like the **ContextUtil** class, all the methods and properties of the **SecurityCallContext** class are static. Table 9–5 lists the methods of the **SecurityCallContext** class.

TABLE 9–5 *The methods of the SecurityCallContext class*

Method Name	Description
IsCallerInRole	Tests if the direct caller is a member of the specified role.
IsUserInRole	Tests if the specified user is a member of the specified role.

Table 9–6 lists the properties of the **SecurityCallContext** class.

TABLE 9–6 *The properties of the SecurityCallContext class*

Property Name	Description
Callers	Gets a SecurityCallers object that describes the callers of a method.
CurrentCall	Gets a SecurityCallContext object that describes the current method call.

TABLE 9–6 *The properties of the SecurityCallContext class (continued)*

Property Name	Description
DirectCaller	Gets a SecurityIdentity object that describes the direct caller of the current method.
IsSecurityEnabled	Returns true if role-based security is enabled in the current context.
MinAuthenticationLevel	Returns the lowest authentication level of all callers in the current call chain.
NumCallers	Returns the number of callers in the current chain of calls.
OriginalCaller	Gets a SecurityIdentity object that describes the caller that initiated the current call chain.

The following code demonstrates how you to use the **SecurityCallContext** class.

```
1.  [AutoComplete]
2.  public DataSet GetBooksByISBN(string isbn)
3.  {
4.        DataSet ds;
5.        string callerName=
6.          SecurityCallContext.CurrentCall.
7.          DirectCaller.AccountName;
8.        System.Diagnostics.Trace.WriteLine(
9.          "Caller=" + callerName);
10.       if (SecurityCallContext.CurrentCall.IsSecurityEnabled)
11.       System.Diagnostics.Trace.WriteLine(
12.         "Authentication level=" +
13.         SecurityCallContext.CurrentCall.
14.       MinAuthenticationLevel.ToString());
15.       StoredProcParam[] spParameters=new StoredProcParam[1];
16.       spParameters[0]=new StoredProcParam(
17.         "@ISBN",SqlDbType.NVarChar,13,isbn);
18.       ds=GetDataSetFromStoredProc(
19.         "GetBooksByISBN",spParameters,"Titles");
20.       return ds;
21. }
```

Lines 5 through 7 get the AccountName of the current caller. Line 10 checks if security is enabled, and, if it is, you write the minimum authentication level of the current call chain to the trace log on lines 13 and 14.

Compile Your Classes into an Assembly with a Strong Name

An assembly that contains serviced components must have a strong name. There are 3 reasons for this. (1) If an assembly does not have a strong name, the GUIDs that the .NET Services Installation Tool (regsvcs.exe) generates to expose the types in the assembly through COM/COM+ are not guaranteed to be unique. Because of this, regsvcs.exe will throw an error if you attempt to register a component that is not signed. (2) Another more subtle reason for requiring a strong name for serviced components is that even if you made a serviced component's assembly private, that is, each client had its own copy of the assembly beneath its directory tree, the COM+ configuration for each of these assemblies is shared. Thus, one application's version of the assembly can affect another application's version. It is best then to go ahead and make the assembly shared and place it in the GAC. If we want to put an assembly in the GAC it must have a strong name. (3) If the serviced component is hosted in a server (out-of-process) COM+ application, you cannot put the assembly underneath the directory tree of its client application. With a server application, the assembly will actually run within the dllhost process, which resides in your System32 directory. In order for dllhost to be able to load the assembly, you have to either place the assembly in the GAC or put it in the same directory as the dllhost executable. Putting application code in the System32 directory is obviously a bad idea. It makes more sense to just put the assembly in the GAC and hence you need a strong name.

Register Your Assembly Using Regsvcs.exe

You have already learned that, in order to use a .NET assembly from a COM client, you must create a type library and add the necessary entries to the registry to support the COM activation functions like CoCreateInstance. You need to perform these steps for a serviced component even if it will only be called by managed clients because the COM+ runtime only knows how to work with COM objects.

Note One positive side benefit of the need to create a type library and add registry entries for all serviced components is that serviced components are immediately callable from a COM client with no additional work.

In addition to registering the serviced component as a COM component, you must also create a COM+ application for the serviced component if one does not exist already. You must also add the serviced components to the COM+ applications and configure the components according to their attributes.

The .NET Framework SDK contains a tool called the .NET Services Installation Tool (regsvcs.exe) that performs all of these tasks. Execute the following command at a Visual Studio .NET command prompt to use regsvcs.exe:

```
regsvcs assemblyname.dll
```

Because the .NET Services Installation Tool accesses the COM+ catalog, you will need to have admin rights in order to run this command. Regsvcs.exe will perform the following steps:

1. Register the assembly in the registry, generating GUIDs as appropriate and adding an InprocServer32 entry that points to **mscoree.dll**.
2. Generate a COM type library for the assembly.
3. Register the type library.
4. Create a COM+ application for the component if one does not exist already using the assembly-level attributes in the serviced component's assembly.
5. Add each **ServicedComponent** derived class to the COM+ application and configure the class according to the class, interface, and method level attributes associated with each class.

Regsvcs will perform all of these updates within a transaction using the **RegistrationHelperTx** class. If any of the aforementioned steps fail, it will roll back the state of the registry and the COM+ catalog. You need to remove the type library manually, however. You can unregister a serviced component's assembly using the /u parameter to regsvcs.exe as shown here:

```
regsvcs /u assemblyname.dll
```

This command removes the COM+ application and the registry entries that regsvcs created for the assembly. You need to remove the assembly from the GAC manually if you added it. The full list of possible command-line arguments for regsvcs.exe is shown in Table 9–7.

TABLE 9–7 *Command-line arguments for regsvcs.exe*

Argument	Description
/appname:ApplicationName	Specifies the name of the COM+ application to either find or create.
/c	Creates the target COM+ application. This command will fail if the application already exists.
/componly	Configures classes only. This argument will cause regsvcs.exe to ignore methods and interfaces.
/exapp	Modifies an existing COM+ application. This command will fail if the application does not exist.
/extlb	Uses an existing type library.

TABLE 9–7 *Command-line arguments for regsvcs.exe (continued)*

Argument	Description
/fc	Uses an existing COM+ application if one exists already. Creates a new application if one does not exist.
/help	Displays help information for regsvcs.exe.
/noreconfig	If the COM+ application exists already, it will not alter the current settings even if the settings in the assembly are different than those currently configured in the assembly. (I could not get this setting to work for me as advertised. Regsvcs.exe would always behaved as though I was using the reconfig setting.)
/nologo	Suppresses the Microsoft logo when the tool runs.
/parname:Name	Specifies the name or ID of the COM+ application to either find or create.
/reconfig	If the COM+ application exists already and its settings are different than those in the assembly, it will alter the configuration of the COM+ application to match the attributes specified in the assembly (default).
/tlb:TypeLibraryFile	Specifies the type library to install.
/u	Uninstalls the target COM+ application.
/quiet	Suppresses both the Microsoft logo and the success message.
/?	Displays help information for regsvcs.exe

You can also install serviced components programmatically using the **System.EnterpriseServices.RegistrationHelper** class. This class has two methods: InstallAssembly and UninstallAssembly. The InstallAssembly method has the following prototype:

```
public void InstallAssembly(
   string assembly,
   ref string application,
   ref string tlb,
   InstallationFlags installFlags
);
```

The assembly argument is the name of the assembly that you want to register, application is the name of the COM+ application that you want to create, tlb is the name of the type library that the tool will output, and install-Flags allows you to control the installation process by passing a bitwise combination of values from the System.EnterpriseServices.InstallationFlags enumeration. This enumeration contains the values shown in Table 9–8.

TABLE 9–8 *Values for the InstallationFlags enumeration*

Enumeration Value	Description
ConfigureComponentsOnly	Configures classes only. This argument will cause regsvcs.exe to ignore methods and interfaces.
CreateTargetApplication	Creates the target COM+ application. This command will fail if the application already exists.
Default	Does the default installation, which does the configure, install, and register steps, and assumes that the application already exists.
ExpectExistingTypeLib	Modifies an existing COM+ application. This command will fail if the application does not exist.
FindOrCreateTargetApplication	Uses an existing COM+ application if one exists already. Creates a new application if one does not exist.
ReconfigureExistingApplication	If using an existing application, ensures that the properties on this application match those in the assembly.
ReportWarningsToConsole	Writes warnings and alerts to the console.

The values in this enumeration correspond almost exactly to the command-line arguments for the regsvcs.exe tool.

There is also a second version of this method InstallAssembly method that has the following prototype:

```
public void InstallAssembly(
   string assembly,
   ref string application,
   string partition,
   ref string tlb,
   InstallationFlags installFlags
);
```

This method adds an additional string parameter called partition, which allows you to specify the partition of your COM+ application.

Note Partitions are a COM+ 1.5 feature. See my article in the September 2000 edition of *Visual C++ Developers Journal*.

The UninstallAssembly method in the **RegistrationHelper** class has the following two overloads:

```
public void UninstallAssembly(
   string assembly,
   string application
);

public void UninstallAssembly(
   string assembly,
   string application,
   string partition
);
```

The first version of the method has two arguments, assembly and application, that allow you to specify the assembly name and the COM+ application name for the serviced component assembly that you want to remove. The second version also allows you to specify a partition.

In most cases, you will want to use the regsvcs.exe tool or the **RegistrationHelper** class to register your serviced component explicitly, but the .NET Framework also supports lazy registration. With lazy registration, the CLR (actually it's the Interception layer doing the work at Activation) will create the COM+ application, register the assembly, generate and register the type library, and configure the classes in the assembly (in other words, perform all the steps that regsvcs does) automatically the first time a client attempts to use a serviced component. Lazy registration has two major problems, however: (1) It does not work for server (out-of-process) COM+ applications, and (2) you must have admin privileges to edit the COM+ catalog. Therefore, lazy registration will fail if the user who first activates a serviced component is not an administrator. All things considered, you're better off running a script or batch file to configure your serviced components either using regsvcs.exe or the **RegistrationHelper** class.

Insert Your Assembly into the GAC

The final step to create a serviced component is to install the component's assembly into the GAC. Strictly speaking, this is not a requirement if you are using a Library (in-process) COM+ application. If you are using a library application, you can deploy the assembly that contains your serviced component into the same directory as the client, and everything will work. Remember, however, if you have two clients that use the same assembly, they will share the same COM+ configuration settings even if the each client has its own private copy of the assembly. Moreover, an assembly that contains serviced components in a server COM+ application must be installed into the GAC so that the dllhost process can load the assembly. You can install a serviced component into the GAC the same way that you would install any managed component into the GAC using gacutil.exe.

Creating a Client

Now that you have created a serviced component, you can use it in much the same way as you would use any other managed class. The following code shows how you would use the **Book** class.

```
1.  private void cmdGetData_Click(object sender,
2.  System.EventArgs e)
3.  {
4.       Book obj;
5.       IDisposable disp;
6.       DataSet ds;
7.       obj=new Book();
8.       ds=obj.GetBooksByTitle(txtTitle.Text);
9.       grid1.DataSource=ds.Tables["Titles"].DefaultView;
10.      disp=obj as IDisposable;
11.        disp.Dispose();
12. }
```

In this code, you instantiate an instance of the **Book** class on line 7. Line 8 calls the GetBooksByTitle, passing in the title of a book (or a portion of the title). This method will return an ADO.NET dataset (we'll talk more about ADO.NET and datasets shortly). Line 9 binds the default view of this dataset to a datagrid, which is a WinForms table control. Finally, lines 10 and 11 call the Dispose method on the object to free its resources immediately. It's a good idea to do this with serviced components. Calling Dispose will immediately free the unmanaged context that is associated with each serviced component.

The Implementation of the Serviced Component Methods

I did not want to clutter my explanation of serviced components by including the implementation of each method in the **Book** class. However, I would be remiss if I didn't discuss it before I concluded this chapter. Serviced components are primarily designed for Enterprise class applications. Enterprise applications use relational databases and often other resource managers like message queues. In fact, the transaction service in the .NET Enterprise Services (COM+) is designed for distributed applications involving two or more databases or other resource managers. I decided therefore to make the **Book** class an example of the kind of datacentric business object that .NET Enterprise Services was designed to help you build.

The **Book** class that I used throughout this chapter uses ADO.NET to retrieve data from and issue updates to a SQL 2000 database that contains information about .NET and COM-related books. The database also includes customer and order information.

Note I used this database in an article called "Integrate .NET Technologies" that I wrote in the Fall/Winter 2001 edition of *.NET Magazine*. In that article, I created an eCommerce application that modeled an online technical bookstore.

The **Book** class uses ADO.NET with the SQL client provider, which is optimized for SQL Server. The code uses Transact SQL (TSQL) stored procedures to retrieve data from and update the database. The following code shows the implementation of the GetBooksByTitle method in the **Book** class.

```
1.  public DataSet GetBooksByTitle(string title)
2.  {
3.        DataSet ds;
4.        StoredProcParam[] spParameters=
5.          new StoredProcParam[1];
6.        spParameters[0]=new StoredProcParam(
7.          "@Title",SqlDbType.NVarChar,255,title);
8.        ds=GetDataSetFromStoredProc(
9.          "GetBooksByTitle",spParameters,"Titles");
10.       return ds;
11. }
```

Lines 4 and 5 declare an array (with a single element) of StoredProcParam objects. This StoredProcParam is a class that I created that represents a parameter to a stored procedure. The array has one element because the stored procedure that I will use to fetch the data takes a single argument. Lines 6 and 7 initialize the lone element of the StoredProcParam array. The parameters that you pass to the constructor are (in order from left to right) the name of the stored procedure argument, the type of the stored procedure argument, the size in bytes of the stored procedure argument, and the variable that contains the value you will pass to the stored procedure. Lines 8 and 9 call the GetDataSetFromStoredProc method. GetDataSetFromStoredProc is a private method in the **Book** class, which does exactly as its name implies. It calls a stored procedure and returns the result as an ADO.NET dataset. The first parameter to this method is the name of the stored procedure. The second parameter is the StoredProcParam array that contains the arguments that you are passing to the stored procedure. The third parameter is the name that you want the method to assign to the data table of the dataset that it will return.

Here is the implementation of the **StoredProcParam** class.

```
struct StoredProcParam
{
  public StoredProcParam(string name,SqlDbType
      type,int size,object val)
  {
    this.mName=name;
    this.mType=type;
    this.mSize=size;
    this.mParamValue=val;
```

```
    }
    public SqlDbType Type
    {
      get
      {
        return mType;
      }
      set
      {
        mType=value;
      }
    }
    public int Size
    {
      get
      {
        return mSize;
      }
      set
      {
        mSize=value;
      }
    }
    public string Name
    {
      get
      {
        return mName;
      }
      set
      {
        mName=value;
      }
    }
    public object ParamValue
    {
      get
      {
        return mParamValue;
      }
      set
      {
        mParamValue=value;
      }
    }
    private SqlDbType mType;
    private int mSize;
    private string mName;
    private object mParamValue;
  }
```

This class is fairly simple, so I won't discuss it. The following code shows the implementation of the GetDataSetFromStoredProc method:

```
private DataSet GetDataSetFromStoredProc(
     string spName,StoredProcParam[] spparams,
     string dsTableName)
{
     int i, n;
     DataSet ds;
     ds = new DataSet();
     SqlCommand cmd;
     SqlDataAdapter dsAdapter;
     SqlParameter param;
     SqlConnection conn;
     StoredProcParam inputParam;
     conn=GetConnection();
     cmd=new SqlCommand(spName,conn);
     cmd.CommandType = CommandType.StoredProcedure;
// If parameters are passed, add them to the command
     if (spparams != null)
     {
       n=spparams.Length;
       for (i=0;i<n;i++)
       {
         inputParam=spparams[i];
         param=cmd.Parameters.Add(
             new SqlParameter(inputParam.Name,
             inputParam.Type ,
             inputParam.Size));
         param.Value=inputParam.ParamValue;
         param.Direction=
             ParameterDirection.Input;
       }
     }
     try
     {
// Open the connection and execute the Command
       conn.Open();
       dsAdapter =new SqlDataAdapter();
       dsAdapter.SelectCommand=cmd;
       dsAdapter.Fill(ds, dsTableName);
       return ds;
     }
     catch (Exception err)
     {
// An error occurred, pass the exception up
         throw err;
     }
     finally
     {
```

```
48. // Close the Connection
49.         if (conn.State == ConnectionState.Open)
50.           conn.Close();
51.     }
52. }
```

I highly recommend that you read the sidebar on ADO.NET before you read the following explanation of the code. Lines 6 and 7 declare and create a new instance of the **DataSet** class. Lines 8 through 11 declare instances of the ADO.NET **SqlCommand**, **SqlDataAdapter**, **SqlParameter**, and **SqlConnection** classes. These classes represent, respectively, a database command, a class for connecting a database command to a dataset, a parameter to a parameterized query or stored procedure, and a database connection. Line 13 connects to the database. Lines 14 and 15 initialize the command object using the connection and the stored procedure name that was passed in as the first parameter to the GetDataSetFromStoredProc method. Lines 17 through 31 add the contents of the StoredProcParam array that was passed to the method to the Parameter list of the command. Line 35 opens the connection. Line 36 creates an instance of the **SqlDataAdapter** class, and line 37 initializes the Select command for the **SqlDataAdapter** class to the SqlCommand that I initialized earlier. Line 38 calls the Fill command on the **SqlDataAdapter** to fill a dataset with the result of the command, and then, finally, line 39 returns the dataset to the caller.

A Sidebar on ADO.NET

ADO.NET is the first data access technology that was designed specifically for use with Web applications. To satisfy the unique needs of Web applications, ADO.NET has rich support for the disconnected database programming model. It also has integrated support for XML. With ADO.NET, it's easy to convert your data to an XML document that can be transported across the network using HTTP or any other Internet protocol. Let's explore both of these ideas further.

A classic client/server application connects to a data source and performs an operation to fetch data from its data source. It usually remains connected to its data source while it iterates through the returned data using a cursor. In many cases, the application will not disconnect from the data source until the user closes the application. The biggest problem with the connected programming model is that it does not scale very well. If 10,000 clients are using a server, there will be 10,000 open connections, even though only a small percentage of those clients will be making a request on the server at any moment in time.

With the disconnected database programming model, an application connects to its data source, fetches the data into a client-side data structure, and then immediately disconnects from the data source and releases its locks on the data. The client application then uses the client-side data structure to update, delete, insert, sort, and filter the data. These operations initially operate only on the client-side data structure. When the application wants to propagate its updates to the underlying data store, it reconnects to the data source and applies its updates to the server. The application has to handle conflict resolution if, for instance, another application has made updates to the data after the application has read it.

This approach is far more scalable than the connected database programming model and hence better suited to the Web. The only time your application holds a connection to the data store is when it is querying or updating data. If an application has 10,000 clients, it is likely that only a few hundred of those clients will be querying or updating data at any given moment in time.

The key to the disconnected database programming model support in ADO.NET is the **DataSet** class. A dataset is an in-memory collection of related data tables. You use DataAdapter and Command objects to fill a dataset. The **DataSet** class contains a rich set of functionality for operating on the data that it contains. You can read, sort, search, filter, and modify the data in a dataset.

The **DataSet** class is implemented in the System.Data namespace and is shared by all managed providers (if you're not sure what a managed provider is, see my high-level explanation of ADO.NET in Chapter 1). It includes a set of supporting classes. Figure 9–8 shows the relationship between the **DataSet** and its supporting classes and the rest of ADO.NET.

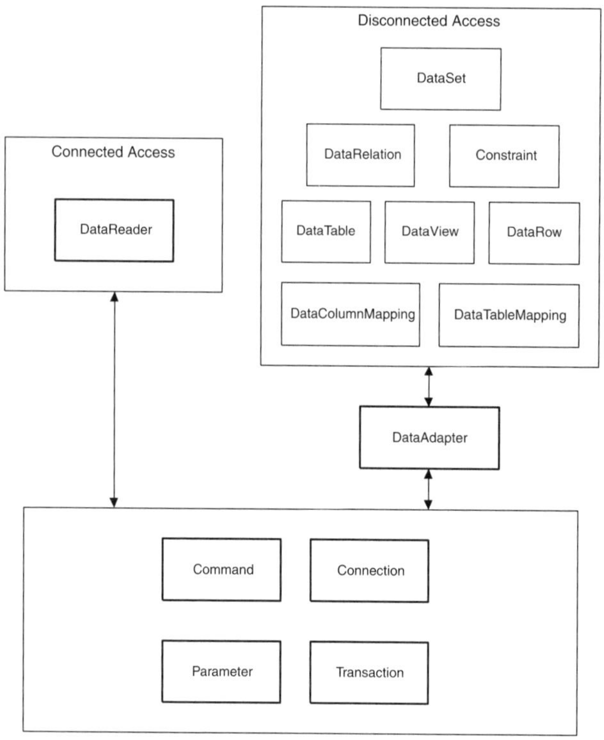

FIGURE 9–8 *The relationship between the DataSet class and the rest of the classes in ADO.NET.*

The **DataTable** and **DataRow** classes contain the tables and rows of the **DataSet** respectively. These **DataTables** may have the same schema as the data source that they were created from, or their schema may be completely different. The **DataTableMapping** and **DataColumnMapping** classes allow you to map tables and columns in your data source's schema to tables and columns in your dataset's schema. The **DataView** class allows you to maintain filtered or sorted views of the data in your dataset. The **Constraint** class allows you to enforce constraints in your dataset (an account balance cannot be negative, for instance). The **DataRelation** class allows you to maintain referential relationships within your data (an Employee must have a foreign key to a department).

If you have experience with ADO, it is tempting to think that a dataset is analogous to a recordset. Actually, an ADO recordset is analogous to a data table. A dataset is analogous to a collection of ADO recordsets.

You fill a dataset with data using a **DataAdapter** class that is implemented by each managed provider. The SqlClient managed provider has a class called **SqlDataAdapter**, and the OleDb managed provider has a class called **OleDbDataAdapter**. The following code shows how to fill a dataset using a select command:

```
public DataSet GetCustomers(
        string strCustID)
{
    DataSet ds=new DataSet();
    string strSQL="SELECT * FROM " +
  "CUSTOMERS WHERE CUSTOMERID " +
  "LIKE '%" + strCustID + "%'";
    SqlConnection conn =
       new SqlConnection(mConnString);
    SqlCommand cmdSelectCustomer=
      new SqlCommand(strSQL,conn);
    SqlDataAdapter daCustomer=
      new SqlDataAdapter();
    daCustomer.SelectCommand=
      cmdSelectCustomer;
    conn.Open();
    daCustomer.Fill(ds,"Customers");
    return ds;
}
```

Notice that I first create Connection and Command objects. Next I create a SqlDataAdapter and assign the Command object to the SelectCommand property of the SqlDataAdapter.

```
SqlDataAdapter daCustomer=
      new SqlDataAdapter();
daCustomer.SelectCommand=
      cmdSelectCustomer;
```

Then I call the Fill method on the SqlDataAdapter passing in the dataset and specifying a name for the data table in the dataset that will contain the data—Customers in this case.

```
conn.Open();
daCustomer.Fill(ds,"Customers");
```

Reading data from a dataset is just as easy as filling it. The following code shows how to read the Customer ID and Company Name of each row in the Customers table of the dataset:

```
string cstID;
string cstName;
DataTable tblCustomers=ds.Tables["Customers"];
foreach (DataRow cst in tblCustomers.Rows)
{
  cstID=(string)cst["CustomerID"];
  cstName=(string)cst["CompanyName"];
}
```

The following code shows how to populate a dataset with more than one table and how to set up a relationship between tables:

```
DataSet ds=new DataSet();
string strSQL="SELECT * FROM " +
    "CUSTOMERS WHERE CUSTOMERID " +
    "LIKE '%" + txtCustID.Text + "%'";
SqlConnection conn = new SqlConnection(mConnString);
SqlCommand cmdSelectCustomers=
    new SqlCommand(strSQL,conn);
strSQL="SELECT * FROM " +
    "ORDERS WHERE CUSTOMERID " +
    "LIKE '%" + txtCustID.Text + "%'";
SqlCommand cmdSelectOrders=
    new SqlCommand(strSQL,conn);
SqlDataAdapter daCustomer=
    new SqlDataAdapter();
SqlDataAdapter daOrder=
    new SqlDataAdapter();
daCustomer.SelectCommand=
    cmdSelectCustomers;
daOrder.SelectCommand=
    cmdSelectOrders;
conn.Open();
daCustomer.Fill(ds,"Customers");
daOrder.Fill(ds,"Orders");
ds.Relations.Add("CustomerOrders",
    ds.Tables["Customers"].Columns["CustomerID"],
    ds.Tables["Orders"].Columns["CustomerID"]);
grdCustomers.DataSource=ds.Tables["Customers"].DefaultView;
conn.Close();
```

In this case, I am querying from the Customers and Orders tables in the Northwind database and setting up a relationship that will allow you to find all the orders for a customer quickly. Notice that I create two DataAdapters, one for the Customers query and one for the Orders query. I then call the Fill method on each Adapter using different table names as follows:

```
daCustomer.Fill(ds,"Customers");
daOrder.Fill(ds,"Orders");
```

To add the relationship, I call the Add method on the Relationships collection of the dataset and specify a name for the relationship, the parent column, and the child column as follows:

```
ds.Relations.Add("CustomerOrders",
     ds.Tables["Customers"].
     Columns["CustomerID"],
     ds.Tables["Orders"].
     Columns["CustomerID"]);
```

The following code shows how to navigate the relationship from a row in the Customers table to get the orders associated with the customer:

```
string orderID;
DataSet ds;
// Populate the DataSet …
DataRow aCustomer=
ds.Tables["Customers"].Rows[0];
DataRow[] orderRows=
aCustomer.GetChildRows("CustomerOrders");
string customerID=
aCustomer["CustomerID"].ToString();
foreach (DataRow order in orderRows)
{
     orderID=
       order["OrderID"].ToString();
}
```

The .NET Windows Forms namespace also contains a DataGrid control that will navigate these relationships for you. If you set the data source for the grid to be the parent table, each row in the grid will automatically display a link that will allow you to navigate to its associated children as shown in Figure 9-1.

```
grdCustomers.DataSource=ds.Tables["Customers"].DefaultView;
```

If you are creating a read-only application, you only need to set the SelectCommand in the data adapter. If you plan to modify data, you must also assign a Command object to the InsertCommand, UpdateCommand, and DeleteCommand properties of your data adapter. You don't have to populate them all, but be aware the data adapter will throw an error if you pass a dataset to the data adapter that contains modified rows. It will also throw an error if you have not defined an Update command for the data adapter, if you pass in a dataset that contains deleted rows and you have not defined a Delete command, or if you pass in a dataset with new rows and you have not defined an Insert command. You can determine whether a dataset contains modified, inserted, or deleted rows using the GetChanges method as follows:

```
DataSet ds =
 (DataSet)(Session["Data"]);
DataSet dsDeletedRows =
 ds.GetChanges(DataRowState.Deleted);
```

The process for updating a dataset is simple. First, make your updates using methods on the **DataSet**, **DataRow**, and **DataTable** classes. The following code shows how to add a new row to a DataTable class:

```
DataSet ds;
// populate the DataSet …
DataTable custTable=
    ds.Tables["Customer"];
DataRow newRow=custTable.NewRow();
newRow["CustomerID"]=txtID.Text;
newRow["CompanyName"]=txtName.Text;
custTable.Rows.Add(newRow);
```

The following code shows how to modify an existing row:

```
DataSet ds;
// Populate the DataSet …
DataTable custTable=
ds.Tables["Customer"];
DataRow custRow=custTable.Rows[0];
custRow["CustomerID"]=txtID.Text;
custRow["CompanyName"]=txtName.Text;
```

The following code shows how to delete a row:

```
DataSet ds;
// Populate the DataSet …
DataTable custTable=
ds.Tables["Customer"];
custTable.Rows[0].Delete();
```

The dataset will store both the current and the original values of any data that you modify. You can call RejectChanges on a **DataRow**, **DataTable**, or **DataSet** to undo any changes you have made at that level. RejectChanges will set the current value of the data equal to the original. You can call AcceptChanges to commit changes to the dataset. AcceptChanges actually is more of a checkpoint than a commit because calling this method will not update the underlying data store. AcceptChanges just sets the original values equal to the current values. Your changes can therefore no longer be undone with a call to RejectChanges. When you are ready to commit your changes to the data store, you must first create a data adapter, set the necessary commands (Insert, Update, and Delete) and then call the Update method on the data adapter passing in either a dataset, a dataset and the name of a table, a data table, or an array of datarows as shown here:

```
daCustomer.Update(ds,"Customer");
```

If the select statement that you use to populate a dataset uses a single table, that is, there are no joins, you can let ADO.NET create the Insert, Update and Delete commands for you. The SqlClient managed provider contains a **SqlCommandBuilder** class, and the OleDB managed provider contains an **OleDdbCommandBuilder** class that can create all of the other commands given a Select command. To create all the necessary commands for your data adapter, set the Select Command property on the data adapter and then create an instance of the Sql/OleDbCommandBuilder, passing the data adapter as a parameter as follows:

```
string strSQL;
SqlCommand cmdSelectCustomer;
SqlCommandBuilder cbCustomer;
SqlConnection conn =
       new SqlConnection(mConnString);
private SqlDataAdapter daCustomer;
strSQL="SELECT * FROM CUSTOMERS " +
    "WHERE CUSTOMERID='" +
    strCustomerID + "'";
cmdSelectCustomer=new
    SqlCommand(strSQL,conn);
daCustomer=new SqlDataAdapter();
daCustomer.SelectCommand=
    cmdSelectCustomer;
cbCustomer=new
    SqlCommandBuilder(daCustomer);
daCustomer.Update(ds,"Customer");
```

One of the most powerful features of the ADO.NET dataset is its tight integration with XML. You can call the GetXml method to return an XML representation of a dataset. You can use the GetXmlSchema method to return the XML Schema Definition (XSD) schema that the dataset is using. You have complete control of the XML schema that your dataset will use. At the simplest level, you can use the ColumnMapping attribute of the **DataColumn** class to control whether a column is represented as an element or an attribute as shown here:

```
ds.Tables["Customers"].
Columns["CustomerID"].ColumnMapping=
MappingType.Attribute;
```

You can also explicitly set the XSD XML schema that the dataset uses with the ReadXmlSchema method. You can also use the ReadXml method to populate a dataset with XML data from a file, stream, TextReader, XMLTextReader, or XmlReader object. The WriteXml object allows you to write XML data to a file, stream, TextReader, or XMLText-ReaderXmlReader. With ReadXML and WriteXML, it's easy to roundtrip an XML document, that is, read it into a dataset, update it using the methods you learned in this sidebar, and save it back to disk. Datasets are also the best way to return tabular or hierarchical data from a Web service. Simply return a dataset from a method that is adorned with the WebMethod attribute. The ASP.NET runtime will send the XML representation of the dataset in the SOAP response from the method.

I have only just scratched the surface of ADO.NET. This sidebar has given you a good start, but there is a lot more to learn. Some important topics that I did not cover include transactions (ADO.NET supports them), typed datasets, and building a dataset in memory without a data source.

Summary

In this chapter, you learned how to create and deploy serviced components. Serviced components are the name for .NET classes that use COM+ services, which are now called Enterprise Services. To create a serviced component, you must inherit from the **System.EnterpriseServices.ServicedComponent** class. You must then add assembly attributes that you can use to configure the COM+ application that the component will be hosted with and class attributes that configure the serviced component within its application. You deploy serviced components using the .NET Services Installation Tool (regsvcs.exe).

The current implementation of serviced components uses a significant amount of unmanaged code. It's likely that this implementation will be replaced by a serviced component infrastructure that is based entirely on managed code.

In the next chapter, I discuss the quintessential technology in the .NET Framework: XML Web services.

TEN

XML Web Services

In this chapter, I discuss how to create and consume XML Web services. An XML Web service is a programmable application component that is accessible using standard Internet protocols, primarily HTTP. The .NET Framework and Visual Studio .NET have a substantial amount of technology that is designed to make it simple to create and consume XML Web services. This chapter gives you a high-level introduction to this technology. Given that the primary purpose of this book is to discuss interoperability and migration, I won't go in depth into Web services in this chapter. My main purpose in this chapter is to provide you with enough background of XML Web services for you to understand Chapter 12 when I discuss migration strategies. Many of these migration strategies involve using XML Web services.

Web Services: The Big Picture

Before I look at how the .NET Framework and Visual Studio .NET help you to develop Web services, let's look at the constituent elements of an XML Web service at a very generic level. Remember, XML Web services are not strictly a .NET technology. The .NET Framework and Visual Studio .NET were designed to make it easy to develop XML Web services, but you can build an XML Web service on any platform that supports HTTP and XML.

A Web service is composed of a SOAP/HTTP listener, one or more classes that implement the Web service's business logic, and a metafile for the Web service that you can write with WSDL (see Figure 10–1).

The SOAP/HTTP listener reads the SOAP requests sent through HTTP or some other standard Internet protocol. The listener can be an Active Server

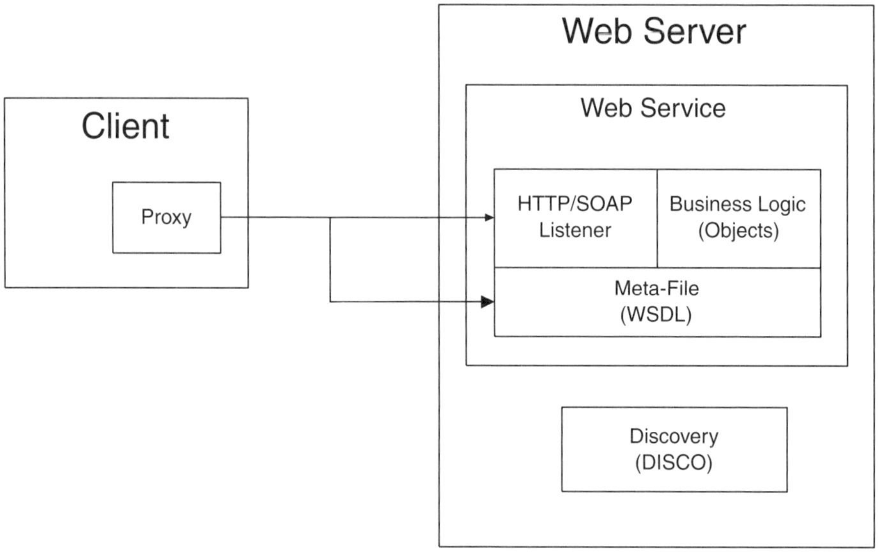

FIGURE 10–1 *An XML Web service.*

Page, an Internet Services API (ISAPI) DLL, or, in the case of .NET, an HTTP handler, which is the ASP.NET equivalent of an ISAPI DLL. The listener parses the XML-based SOAP request and makes the desired call on the object(s) that implement the Web service's business logic. These objects can be .NET components, COM objects, CORBA objects, or enterprise JavaBeans. In fact, you could implement the Web service's business logic directly in the listener.

The metafile contains a complete description of the methods that are supported by the Web service, including the name and type of each argument and the return value for each method. This metafile is encoded in an XML-based language called WSDL. The WSDL metafile associated with each XML Web Service allows users to determine the capability of a Web service. It also allows development tools to generate a proxy automatically to call the Web service. This prevents users from doing the grunt work of formatting an HTTP request and parsing the response in order to call the Web service.

You can think of WSDL as the Web service's equivalent of COM IDL. The WSDL metafile associated with a Web service is the equivalent of a COM type library. Visual Studio .NET uses the information in the WSDL file to generate a proxy, which makes it simple for clients to call a Web service. If you don't have Visual Studio .NET, the .NET Framework SDK contains a utility called the Web Services Description Language Tool (wsdl.exe), which can read a WSDL file and create a proxy. See the following URL for an excellent explanation of XML Web services, SOAP, WSDL, and UDDI: *msdn.microsoft.com/webservices/understanding/webservicebasics/default.asp.*

Microsoft has also defined a discovery mechanism (an XML schema and a search algorithm) called Web Services Discovery Tool (DISCO) that allows a user to discover the XML Web Services that are deployed at a particular URL. There is also an industry-wide movement afoot to create an online directory of Web services. These online directories will allow users to look up a Web service by company name (like the white pages in your telephone directory), by category (think of the yellow pages in your telephone directory), or by technical specification. These online directories are themselves Web services, which use a specification called UDDI. As with a phone directory, you can search for a company that offers the Web services you need, read about the Web service offered (including how you will be charged to use the service), and, if you so choose, immediately locate the Web service and start using it. You can find out more information about UDDI at *uddi.org/about.html.*

Note Both Microsoft and IBM currently have UDDI Repositories up and running. See the following URLs to learn more: *uddi.microsoft.com* and *www-3.ibm.com/services/uddi.* While writing this chapter, I went to the Microsoft UDDI repository and found several interesting XML Web services that, among other things, verify credit card numbers; perform currency conversions; provide stock quotes; track UPS packages online; and provide shopping cart, ordering, and order history functionality. My personal favorite, though, was an XML Web service that provides weather information (including temperature, humidity, wind direction and speed, and sunrise and sunset times) based on your ZIP code. You can find this Web service at *glkev.net innerhost.com/glkev_ws/WeatherFetcher.asmx.*

The ASP.NET Web Services Infrastructure

ASP.NET is completely rearchitectured from the ISAPI model for server-side programming using IIS and HTTP. The ISAPI model allowed you to create your own DLLs that would receive HTTP requests, could perform custom processing, and return a response. ASP (the predecessor to ASP.NET) was implemented as an ISAPI DLL that received requests from files with a .asp extension, compiled the script contained in these pages, and returned the result of the script, along with any surrounding HTML. The architecture of ASP.NET is far more flexible. It allows you all the power of ISAPI, with a much simpler programming model and the ability to support both Web Forms and Web services. At a high level, the ASP.NET architecture is as shown in Figure 10–2.

ASP.NET uses an extensible HTTP pipeline. When you first install ASP.NET, it adds a number of standard file extensions to the IIS metabase. Perform the following steps to view these file extensions on your machine:

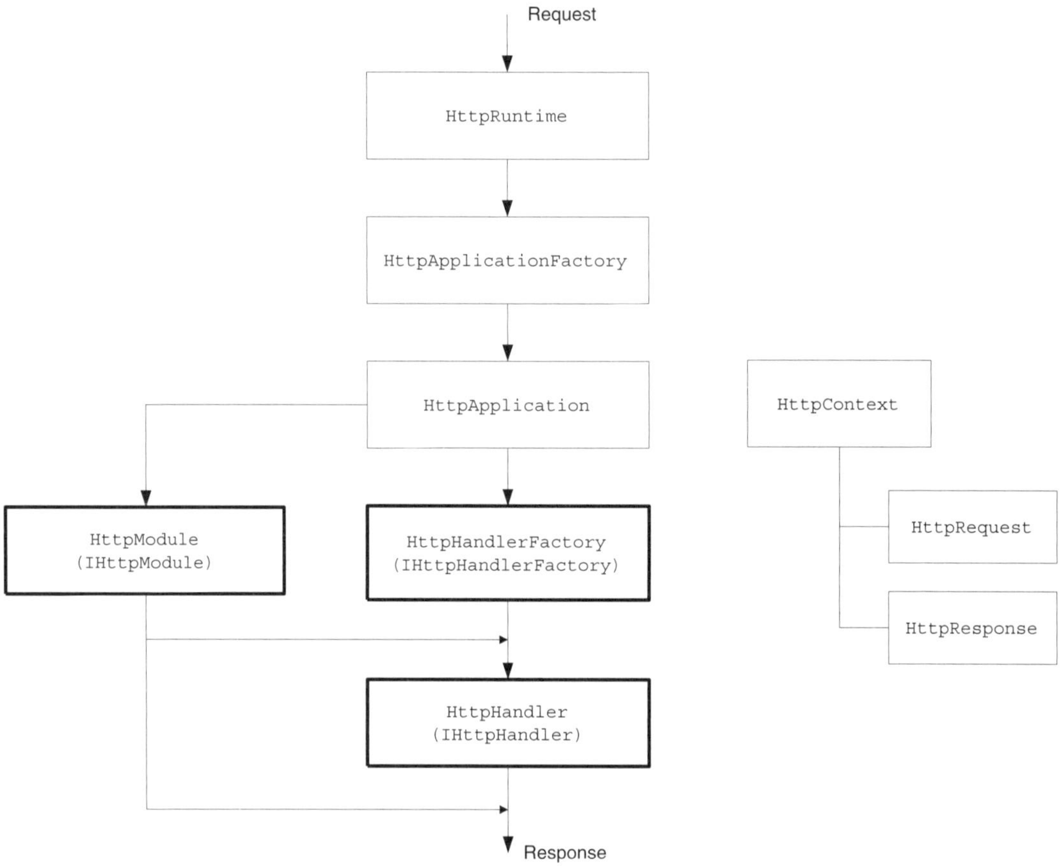

FIGURE 10–2 *The ASP.NET architecture.*

1. Select Programs | Administrative Tools | Computer Management from the Start menu. The Computer Management MMC snap-in appears.
2. Open the Default Web Site node in the tree under Services and Applications | Internet Information Services.
3. Right-click on a virtual directory beneath the Default Web Site node and select Properties... from the context menu. The IIS Application properties dialog appears.
4. On the Virtual Directory tab of the properties dialog, click the Configuration... button. The Application Configuration dialog appears as shown in Figure 10–3.

You can see that there are a number of familiar .NET file extensions, including .aspx, .config, .soap, .cs, and .vb. There are two new ones that are XML Web service related, .asmx and .ashx., which I talk about shortly and

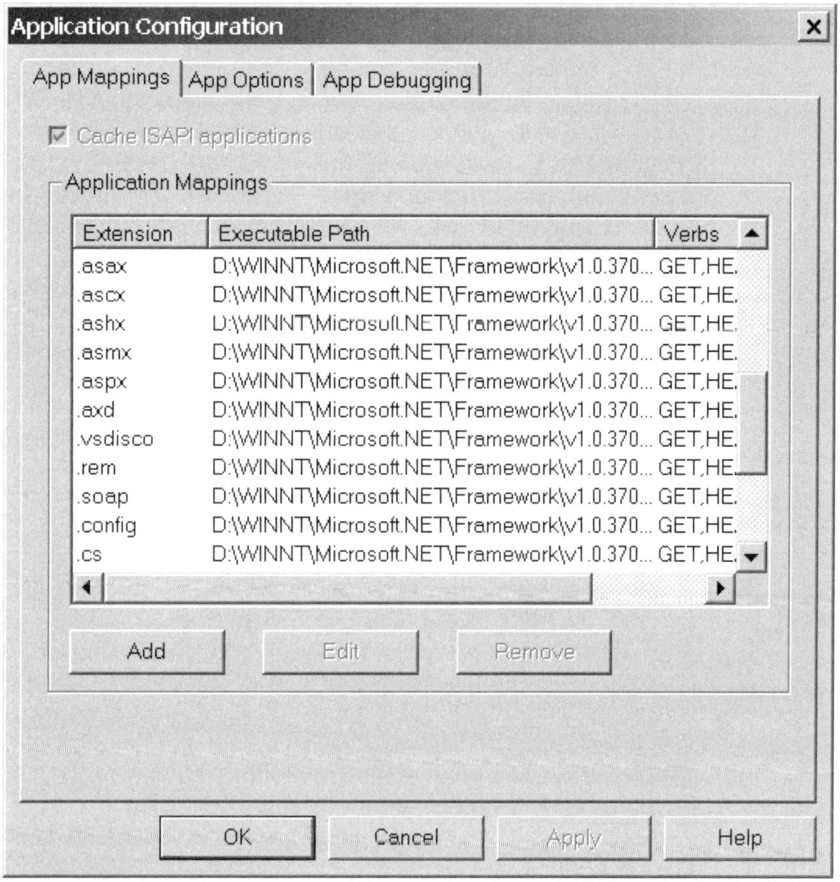

FIGURE 10–3 *The IIS Application Configuration dialog.*

which are mapped to the following executable: **D:\WINNT\Microsoft.NET\Framework\v1.0.3705\aspnet_isapi.dll**.

Note The .asp file extension still maps to the ASP runtime at D:\WINNT\System32\inetsrv\asp.dll.

When IIS receives an HTTP request for a file with one of these extensions, it funnels the request into the HTTP pipeline shown in Figure 10–2. The **aspnet_isapi.dll**, which—like all ISAPI DLLs—runs in the same process as the IIS service (inetinfo.exe), forwards the request using a named pipe to the ASP.NET worker process (aspnet_wp.exe). The HTTP pipeline runs in the ASP.NET worker process.

The request first goes to an HttpRuntime object, which examines the request and figures out which application it was sent to. The HttpRuntime then uses an HttpApplicationFactory object to create an HttpApplication object to handle the request. The HttpRuntime object also creates an HttpContext object that, among other things, contains the request (an instance of the **HttpRequest** class) and the response (an instance of the **HttpResponse** class) and passes it to the HttpApplication object. An HttpApplication object is created to handle each request, so the HttpApplicationFactory object pools HttpApplication objects to maintain optimal performance. An HttpApplication object holds a collection of HttpModules, and it also uses an HttpHandlerFactory object to create an HttpHandler object.

HttpHandlers are the endpoints of the ASP.NET HTTP pipeline. They will consume the request and produce a response. Like HttpApplication objects, one HttpHandler object is created for each request, and they are pooled for optimal performance. The HttpApplication object uses different HttpHandlers to process requests, depending on the file extension of the request. You can also create your own HttpHandlers by providing an implementation of the System.Web.IHttpHandler interface and then adding an entry to a configuration file to specify which file extensions the System.Web.IHttpHandler implementation should be used with.

HttpModules are filters that can examine and modify the contents of a request, but do not consume the request. They are the successor to ISAPI filters. Standard HttpModules are used to implement security and session management. You can also create your own modules by creating a class that implements the System.Web.IHttpModule interface. Let's take a more in-depth look at HTTP handlers and modules.

HTTP Handlers

ASP.NET comes out of the box with a set of standard HTTP handlers that implement both Web Forms and Web services. You can view the mapping of file extensions to HttpHandlers (actually, the mapping is to handler factories) by looking at the **machine.config** file, which you can find at **[WINNT_Directory]\Microsoft.NET\Framework\[Version]\CONFIG** where **[WINNT_Directory]** is the location of the **Winnt** directory on your machine and **[Version]** is the version number of .NET Framework. On my machine, the complete path is **D:\WINNT\Microsoft.NET\Framework\v1.0.3705\CONFIG**.

If you search for the HttpHandlers subelement in this configuration file, you will see the following:

```
<httpHandlers>
<add verb="*" path="trace.axd"
type="System.Web.Handlers.TraceHandler"/>
<add verb="*" path="*.aspx"
```

```
type="System.Web.UI.PageHandlerFactory"/>
<add verb="*" path="*.ashx"
type="System.Web.UI.SimpleHandlerFactory"/>
<add verb="*" path="*.asmx"
type="System.Web.Services.Protocols.WebServiceHandlerFactor
y,
System.Web.Services, Version=1.0.3300.0, Culture=neutral,
PublicKeyToken=b03f5f7f11d50a3a" validate="false"/>
<add verb="*" path="*.rem"
type="System.Runtime.Remoting.Channels.Http.HttpRemotingHan
dlerFactory,
System.Runtime.Remoting, Version=1.0.3300.0,
Culture=neutral,
PublicKeyToken=b77a5c561934e089" validate="false"/>
<add verb="*" path="*.soap"
type="System.Runtime.Remoting.Channels.Http.HttpRemotingHan
dlerFactory,
System.Runtime.Remoting, Version=1.0.3300.0,
Culture=neutral,
PublicKeyToken=b77a5c561934e089" validate="false"/>
<add verb="*" path="*.asax"
type="System.Web.HttpForbiddenHandler"/>
<add verb="*" path="*.ascx"
type="System.Web.HttpForbiddenHandler"/>
<add verb="*" path="*.config"
type="System.Web.HttpForbiddenHandler"/>
<add verb="*" path="*.cs"
type="System.Web.HttpForbiddenHandler"/>
<add verb="*" path="*.csproj"
type="System.Web.HttpForbiddenHandler"/>
<add verb="*" path="*.vb"
type="System.Web.HttpForbiddenHandler"/>
<add verb="*" path="*.vbproj"
type="System.Web.HttpForbiddenHandler"/>
<add verb="*" path="*.webinfo"
type="System.Web.HttpForbiddenHandler"/>
<add verb="*" path="*.asp"
type="System.Web.HttpForbiddenHandler"/>
<add verb="*" path="*.licx"
type="System.Web.HttpForbiddenHandler"/>
<add verb="*" path="*.resx"
type="System.Web.HttpForbiddenHandler"/>
<add verb="*" path="*.resources"
type="System.Web.HttpForbiddenHandler"/>
<add verb="GET,HEAD" path="*"
type="System.Web.StaticFileHandler"/>
<add verb="*" path="*"
type="System.Web.HttpMethodNotAllowedHandler"/>
</httpHandlers>
```

Notice the handlers for the .aspx and .asmx file extensions, which I have shown in bold. The entry for the .aspx extension shows that the ASP.NET Web Forms files are handled by a class called **System.Web.UI.PageHandlerFactory**. This class parses and compiles the aspx file (if it hasn't been compiled already) and renders the result as HTML. The handler for asmx files is the one that implements most of the ASP.NET Web services' functionality. The asmx files are handled by a class called **System.Web.Services.Protocols.WebServiceHandlerFactory**. The following code shows an example asmx file for a very simple Hello World XML Web service:

```
<%@ WebService Language="C#" class="Hello" %>
using System.Web.Services;
class Hello
{
    [WebMethod]
    public string HelloWorld()
    {
        return "Hello XML Web Service World!!!";
    }
}
```

Note You will soon see how to deploy and use an XML Web service.

The WebServiceHandlerFactory handler parses the asmx file. The WebService header at the top of the file tells the handler that the code for the Web service was written in C# and that the class that contains the business logic for the Web service is called **Hello**. In this case, the code for the **Hello** class is contained directly in the asmx file, but later you see how you can use the code-behind directive to put the business logic of the Web service into a separate file. The handler will invoke the C# compiler to compile the code for the Web service. It then caches the compiled assembly and uses reflection to find the method that the request is trying to invoke. All methods that will be exposed through the Web service must be marked with the System.Web.Services.WebMethod attribute as shown previously in the asmx file. The handler will then call the requested method, take the result, and send it to the client as an HTTP response.

Thanks to the ASP.NET infrastructure, your job as an XML Web service developer is incredibly easy. Simply create a file with the .asmx extension and then specify what language you are using and the name of the class that contains the implementation of the XML Web service. Define the business logic of your Web service as a class in your selected language, adding the System.Web.Services.WebMethod attribute to the methods that you want to expose through the Web service. You then create an IIS virtual directory for your Web service and add the asmx file to the virtual directory. Then add the assembly that contains the class that implements the business logic of the assembly to a **bin** directory beneath your virtual directory (or to the GAC).

The ASP.NET Web services infrastructure is fully extensible. If you don't like the handlers that ASP.NET provides out of the box, you can create your own by implementing the System.Web.IHttpHandler interface. The System.Web.IHttpHandler interface is defined as shown here:

```
interface IHttpHandler
{
        void ProcessRequest(HttpContext ctx);
        bool IsReusable { get; }
}
```

Let's define the Hello World Web service as a custom HTTP handler using the .ashx file extension. If you refer back to the **machine.config** file, you will see that there is an HTTP handler for files with the extension .ashx.

```
<add verb="*" path="*.ashx"
type="System.Web.UI.SimpleHandlerFactory"/>
```

The handler for this file extension compiles and calls an implementation of the IHttpHandler interface. Therefore, you can create a Web service by defining an implementation of the IhttpHandler interface as shown here and saving it in a file with the extension .ashx:

```
<%@ WebHandler Language="C#" class="Hello" %>
using System.Web;
class Hello : IHttpHandler
{
   public void ProcessRequest(HttpContext ctx)
   {
        ctx.Response.ContentType="text/xml";
        ctx.Response.Write("<Greeting>");
        ctx.Response.Write("Hello World");
        ctx.Response.Write("</Greeting>");
    }
    public bool IsReusable { get { return true; }}
}
```

You can then place the file in a virtual directory, navigate to it using Internet Explorer, and see the expected Hello World greeting. When you use an ashx file to create a Web service, you are using the ASP.NET HTTP pipeline at a lower level than when you use an asmx file. Instead of using the asmx handler that understands the WebMethod attribute and knows how to funnel an HTTP request to a method of a class, you are responding to the HTTP request directly by implementing the IHtpHandler interface.

HTTP Modules

HttpModules are filters that can examine and modify the contents of a request, but that do not consume the request. They are the successor to ISAPI filters. Standard HttpModules are used to implement security and session management. If you go back to the **machine.config** file and search for the HttpModules subelement, you will find the following entries:

```
<httpModules>
<add name="OutputCache"
type="System.Web.Caching.OutputCacheModule"/>
<add name="Session"
type="System.Web.SessionState.SessionStateModule"/>
<add name="WindowsAuthentication"
   type="System.Web.Security.WindowsAuthenticationModule"/>
<add name="FormsAuthentication"
type="System.Web.Security.FormsAuthenticationModule"/>
<add name="PassportAuthentication"
  type="System.Web.Security.PassportAuthenticationModule"/>
<add name="UrlAuthorization"
type="System.Web.Security.UrlAuthorizationModule"/>
<add name="FileAuthorization"
type="System.Web.Security.FileAuthorizationModule"/>
</httpModules>
```

Notice that HTTP modules handle output caching, session state, the three forms of authentication supported by ASP.NET (Windows, Forms, and Passport), and authorization based on URL or files.

Note Output caching is a performance optimization used by ASP.NET Web Forms that caches rendered HTML. If the same page is requested again with the same parameters, the ASP.NET runtime can simply return the prerendered HTML.

You can also create your own modules by creating a class that implements the System.Web.IHttpModule interface. The IHttpModule interface contains the following methods:

```
interface IHttpModule
{
        void Init(HttpApplication app);
        void Dispose();
}
```

The HttpApplication, which is passed to the Init method, defines a number of events. You define event handlers in your HttpModule to insert your own logic anywhere in the HTTP pipeline. Table 10–1 lists the HttpApplication events that you can respond to in an HttpModule.

TABLE 10–1 *HttpApplication events*

Event	When Called
BeginRequest	Before request processing starts
EndRequest	After request processing ends
AuthenticateClient	To authenticate client
AuthorizeClient	To check if the client has access rights to the requested resource
AcquireRequestState	To load session state
ReleaseRequestState	To store session state
ResolveRequestCache	To get a response from the cache
UpdateRequestCache	To update the response cache
PreRequestHandlerExecute	Before the request is sent to the handler
PostRequestHandlerExecute	After the request is sent to the handler
PreSendRequestHeaders	Before buffered response headers are sent
PreSendRequestContent	Before buffered response body is sent

In order to create a custom IHttpModule, you need to define event handlers for the events that you would like to respond to and then add these handlers to the events exposed by the HttpApplication. You then add an HTTPModule entry to the **web.config** file in the virtual directory of the applications that you would like to use the module. For instance, the following HttpModule calculates the processing time for each request and appends it as a header to the response. The module does this by calculating the elapsed time between the BeginRequest and EndRequest events.

```
using System;
using System.Web;
namespace TestModule
{
    public class ResponseTimeModule : IHttpModule
    {
      DateTime mStart;
      public void Init(HttpApplication app)
      {
        app.BeginRequest += new
          EventHandler(OnBeginRequest);
        app.EndRequest += new
          EventHandler(OnEndRequest);
      }
      public void Dispose() { }
      public void OnBeginRequest(object o,
        EventArgs args)
      {
```

```
19.             mStart=DateTime.Now;
20.         }
21.         public void OnEndRequest(object o,
22.           EventArgs args)
23.         {
24.           TimeSpan elapsed=DateTime.Now-mStart;
25.           HttpApplication app=
26.               (HttpApplication) o;
27.           HttpContext ctx=app.Context;
28.           ctx.Response.AppendHeader(
29.               "ResponseTime",
30.               elapsed.ToString());
31.         }
32.     }
33. }
```

In the Init method on lines 8 through 14, I add handlers for the BeginRequest and EndRequest events. The event handler for the BeginRequest event is shown on lines 16 through 20. Notice that all I do is to cache the start time in a member variable of the **HttpModule** class. The event handler for the EndRequest event is shown on lines 21 through 31. I calculate the elapsed time between the current time and the time that was cached when the BeginRequest event handler was called on line 24. I then cast the first parameter to an HttpApplication. Remember that the first parameter to an event handler should be the source of the event, which, in this case, is the HttpApplication object. I get the HttpContext object associated with this request on line 27, and, on lines 28 through 30, I use the HttpContext object to write the response time to a custom header. If you want to abort further processing of a request in your **HttpModule**, simply call CompleteRequest on the HttpApplication object.

I'll compile this class into an assembly called TestModule. To make an HTTP application use this HttpModule I only need to add the following entry to the **web.config** file of the HTTP application:

```
<httpModules>
    <add name="ResponseTime"
      type="TestModule.ResponseTimeModule,TestModule"/>
</httpModules>
```

Creating a Simple Web Service

Now that you have an understanding of the ASP.NET infrastructure, let's use it to create a simple Web service. Let's start by creating a simple Web service without the help of Visual Studio .NET so that you can understand all the constituent pieces of a Web service. The high-level steps are as follows:

1. Create an asmx file that contains the source code for the Web service.
2. Create an IIS virtual directory.
3. Test.
4. Create a client.

Create an asmx File for the Web Service

The following code shows the source for a very simple Web service. Save this code into a file called **arithmetic.asmx**.

```
1.  <%@ WebService Language="C#" class="Arithmctic" %>
2.  using System.Web.Services;
3.  class Arithmetic
4.  {
5.       [WebMethod]
6.       public float Add(float arg1,float arg2)
7.       {
8.         return arg1+arg2;
9.       }
10.      [WebMethod]
11.      public float Subtract(float arg1,float arg2)
12.      {
13.        return arg1-arg2;
14.      }
15.      [WebMethod]
16.      public float Multiply(float arg1,float arg2)
17.      {
18.        return arg1*arg2;
19.      }
20. }
```

Line 1 uses the WebService directive to specify that the Web service is implemented in C# and that the name of the class that provides the business logic for the Web service is called **Arithmetic**. In this case, the implementation of the **Arithmetic** class is contained directly in the asmx file. Line 2 has a using statement for the System.Web.Services namespace. I include this namespace primarily so that I have access to the WebMethod attribute. In order to expose a method using a Web service, you must mark the method with the WebMethod attribute as I have done with the three methods implemented in this web service.

Create an IIS Virtual Directory

To create an IIS virtual directory for your Web service, perform the following steps:

1. Select Programs | Administrative Tools | Computer Management from the Start menu. The Computer Management snap-in for the MMC appears.
2. Right-click Services and Applications | Internet Information Services | Default Web Site and select New |Virtual Directory from the context menu that appears. This starts the Virtual Directory Creation Wizard.
3. Click Next on the introductory window. This takes you to a window where you can enter the directory alias.
4. Enter "Arithmetic" for the directory alias.
5. Click Next. This takes you to a window where you can enter the physical directory for the Web content.
6. Click Browse... (a directory browser dialog appears). Navigate to the location where you saved the **arithmetic.asmx** file and click OK button on the directory browser.
7. Click Next. This takes you to a window where you can select access permissions.
8. Accept the defaults for the access permissions, click Next, and then click Finish on the final window.

You now have an IIS virtual directory that should correspond to the following URL: *localhost/Arithmetic/*.

Test

You can now test your Web service without having to build a client. You will see the help file shown in Figure 10–4 if you point your Web browser to the following URL: *localhost/Arithmetic/arithmetic.asmx*.

This help file is generated by a script called **DefaultWSdlHelpGenerator.aspx**, which you can find at **D:\WINNT\Microsoft.NET\Framework\v1.0.3705\CONFIG** (although your version number may vary). Using this help file, you can execute any of the three methods in the Web service. For instance, if you click the Add link shown in Figure 10–4, you see the Web page shown in Figure 10–5.

Although, in practice, most people will use SOAP, the .NET Framework's Web services infrastructure also supports HTTP Post and HTTP Get. In fact, the help page uses HTTP Get. If you scroll down in the page, it does show you how to submit a request to the Add method using each of these three protocols. If you enter a value for arg1 and arg2 and click the Invoke button (see Figure 10–5), you see the result shown in Figure 10–6.

Note If you receive an error that contains the description "Unable to generate a temporary class", you may need to give read/write privileges for the Temp folder to the ASPNET account. See the Knowledge Base article at *support.microsoft.com/default.aspx?scid=kb;en-us;Q322886*.

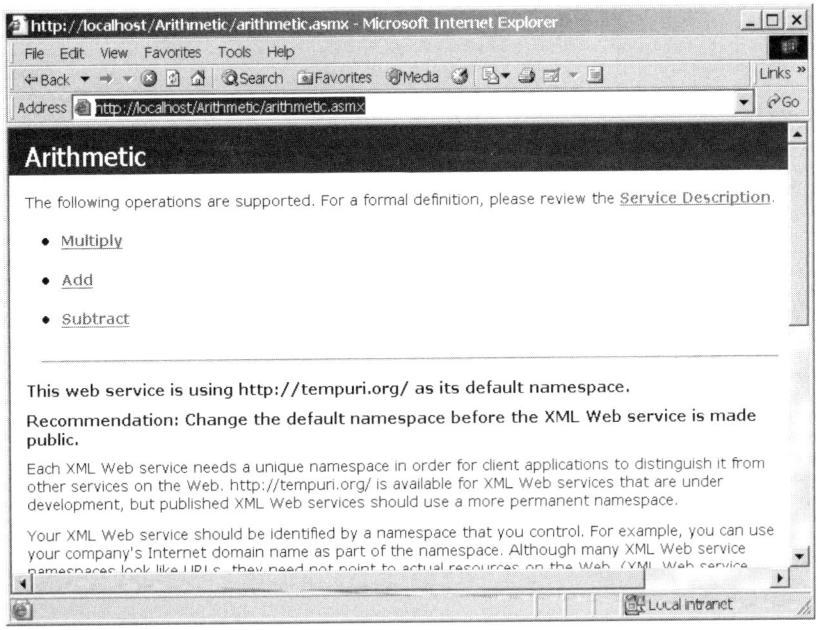

FIGURE 10–4 *The Web services help file.*

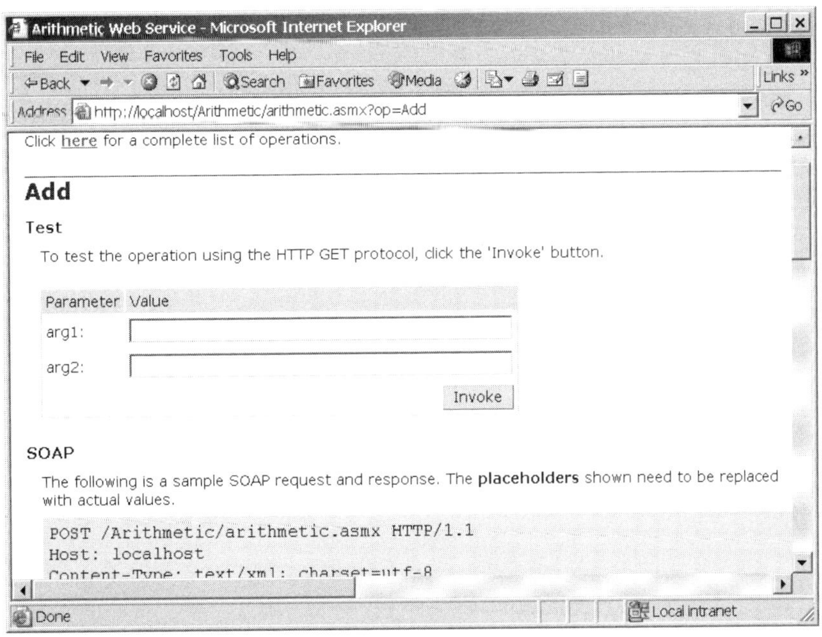

FIGURE 10–5 *The Web services help file.*

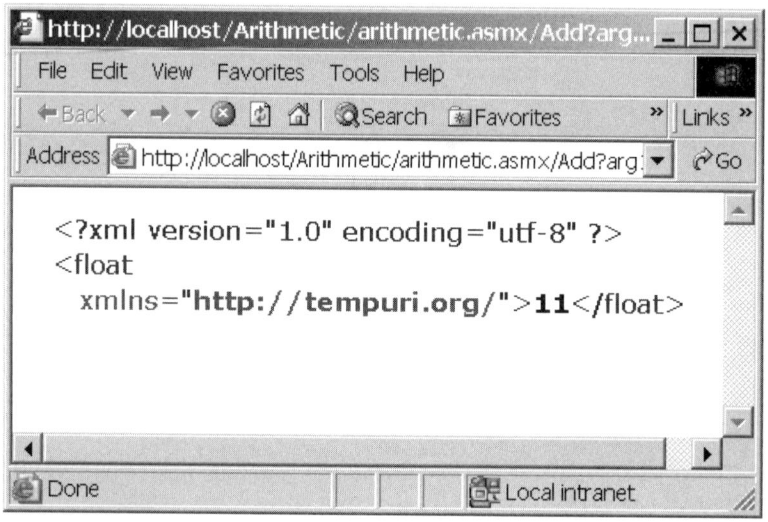

FIGURE 10–6 *The Web services help file.*

You can view the WSDL file for the Web service by clicking the Service Description link on the Web service help file (see Figure 10–4) or by entering this URL in your Web browser: *localhost/arithmetic/arithmetic.asmx?WSDL.*

You see the result shown in Figure 10–7.

Currently, a few things are wrong with this Web service that you should correct before you go any further. If you do not specify an XML namespace for your Web service, the system gives it the namespace *tempuri.org*. This temporary URI should only be used while your Web service is under development. The automatically generated help file warns you in excruciating and very clearly worded detail that you should change the namespace for your Web service before you release it for public consumption. The namespace that you choose for your Web service should be a unique name. Your company's Internet domain name is a good choice. You can change the namespace for your Web service using the System.Web.Services.WebService attribute as follows:

```
<%@ WebService Language="C#" class="Arithmetic" %>
using System.Web.Services;
[WebService(Namespace="http://gordon.com/webservice/")]
class Arithmetic
{
     [WebMethod]
     public float Add(float arg1,float arg2)
     {
       return arg1+arg2;
     }
```

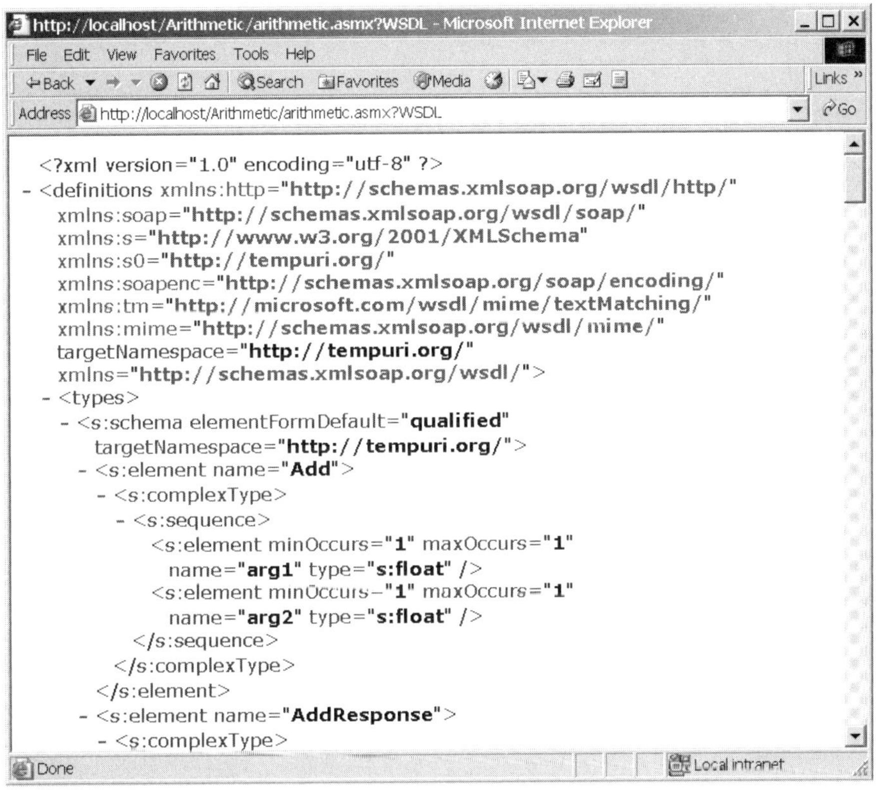

FIGURE 10–7 *The WSDL file for the Web service.*

```
      [WebMethod]
      public float Subtract(float arg1,float arg2)
      {
        return arg1-arg2;
      }
      [WebMethod]
      public float Multiply(float arg1,float arg2)
      {
        return arg1*arg2;
      }
}
```

After you make this change, if you navigate to *localhost/Arithmetic/arithmetic.asmx*, you will see that the rather verbose warning about the temporary URI has gone away.

The next problem has to do with the organization of the code. ASP.NET Web services support the code-behind attribute just like Web forms. Using code-behind allows you to precompile the source code for your Web service into an assembly, which you deploy in a **bin** directory beneath the IIS virtual directory. If you put the source code for your Web service in the asmx file, the ASP.NET runtime compiles this code into an assembly, which it caches at the following location: **D:\WINNT\Microsoft.NET\Framework\v1.0.3705\Temporary ASP.NET Files\arithmetic**\.

To use code-behind, change the asmx file to look as follows:

```
<%@ WebService Language="C#" Codebehind="Arithmetic.cs"
class="Arithmetic" %>
```

Then add the following code to a file called **Arithmetic.cs**:

```
using System.Web.Services;
[WebService(Namespace="http://gordon.com/webservices/")]
class Arithmetic
{
    [WebMethod]
    public float Add(float arg1,float arg2)
    {
      return arg1+arg2;
    }
    [WebMethod]
    public float Subtract(float arg1,float arg2)
    {
      return arg1-arg2;
    }
    [WebMethod]
    public float Multiply(float arg1,float arg2)
    {
      return arg1*arg2;
    }
}
```

Then compile this into an assembly by executing the following command at a Visual Studio .NET command prompt:

```
csc /t:library /out:arithmetic.dll arithmetic.cs
```

Finally, create a directory beneath the root directory of your virtual directory called **bin** and copy the **arithmetic.dll** assembly to this location.

Create a Client

So far, I have only used a Web browser and the **DefaultWSdlHelpGenerator.aspx** test page to execute the Web service. Let's build a Web Forms client. You can call the Web service using one of three protocols: HTTP GET, HTTP POST, or SOAP. In order to make this call, you need to format an HTTP request using one of these protocols, send the request to the URI for the Web service, and then parse the HTTP response that contains the result. Fortunately, the .NET Framework SDK provides a tool called the Web Services Description Language Tool (wsdl.exe) that generates a proxy that does all of the hard work for you. This proxy is a class that contains methods with the same argument list and return value as the Web service. To call a method in your Web service, you call the corresponding method on the proxy. The proxy turns your method call into a SOAP, HTTP GET, or HTTP POST message. (You decide which protocol the proxy will use when you generate it with wsdl.exe. It defaults to using SOAP, but you can change the protocol if you want). The proxy will then send the message to the Web service's URI. The proxy defaults to using the URI that you specified when you generated the proxy, but you can alter this by setting the URL property on the proxy. Finally, the proxy parses the response from the Web service and returns it to the caller as the return value from the method. The proxy even allows you to make method calls on the Web service either synchronously or asynchronously.

Let's generate a proxy for the arithmetic Web service. Create a separate directory to hold the client for the XML Web service and execute the following command at a Visual Studio .NET command prompt to generate the proxy:

```
wsdl http://localhost/arithmetic/arithmetic.asmx?wsdl /
language:CS /out:arithmeticproxy.cs
```

In this case, I have specified that the proxy should be generated using the C# code and that the result should be written to a file called **arithmeticproxy.cs**. The complete list of possible command-line parameters for wsdl.exe is shown in Table 10–2.

TABLE 10–2 *Command-line parameters for wsdl.exe*

Parameter	Description
urlkey	Specifies the XML element (key) in the configuration file from which to read the default URL for the Web service. If you do not use this parameter, the URL property defaults to the URL in the WSDL file.
baseurl	Specifies that the URL property should default to the concatenation of the value read from the /urlkey entry in the configuration file and the URL in the WSDL file. You must specify the /urlkey parameter with this option.
domain	Specifies the domain name to use when connecting to a computer that requires authentication.
language	Specifies the language to use for the generated proxy class. Possible values are CS (C#), VB (Visual Basic .NET), and JS (JavaScript).
namespace	Specifies the namespace to use for the generated proxy.
nologo	Suppresses the Microsoft banner.

TABLE 10–2 *Command-line parameters for wsdl.exe (continued)*

Parameter	Description
out	Specifies the file in which to save the generated proxy code.
password	Specifies the password to use when connecting to a server that requires authentication.
protocol	Specifies the protocol to implement. You can specify SOAP (default), HttpGet, HttpPost, or a custom protocol specified in the configuration file.
proxy	Specifies the URL of the proxy server to use for HTTP requests. The default is to use the system proxy setting.
proxydomain	Specifies the domain to use when connecting to a proxy server that requires authentication.
proxypassword	Specifies the password to use when connecting to a proxy server that requires authentication.
proxyusername	Specifies the user name to use when connecting to a proxy server that requires authentication.
server	Generates an abstract class for an XML Web service based on the contracts. The default is to generate client proxy classes.
username	Specifies to use only assemblies specified with /reference to resolve references.
?	Displays command syntax and options for the tool.

Note By default, wsdl.exe will write the source code for the proxy to a file with the same name as the asmx file, but with the correct file extension for the specified language (for example, .cs for C#). If you generate the source file for the proxy in the same directory as the asmx file, and you do not explicitly specify a name for your source file using the out parameter, wsdl.exe will overwrite (and it does so without warning) the asmx file. Obviously, you would only generate the proxy in the same directory as the asmx file in a pedagogical example like this one.

The source code that wsdl.exe generates follows. In this case, I'm only showing the generated methods for the Add method in the Web service because the Subtract and Multiply methods generate similar code.

```
using System.Diagnostics;
using System.Xml.Serialization;
using System;
using System.Web.Services.Protocols;
using System.ComponentModel;
using System.Web.Services;
[DebuggerStepThroughAttribute()]
[DesignerCategoryAttribute("code")]
```

```
[WebServiceBindingAttribute(
    Name="ArithmeticSoap",
    Namespace="http://gordon.com/webservices/")]
public class Arithmetic :
    [4]SoapHttpClientProtocol {
// Constructor
    public Arithmetic() {
      this.Url =
      "http://localhost/arithmetic/arithmetic.asmx";
    }
    [4] [SoapDocumentMethodAttribute(
    "http://gordon.com/webservices/Add",
    RequestNamespace="http://gordon.com/webservices/",
    ResponseNamespace="http://gordon.com/webservices/",
    [6].Description [SoapBindingUse.Literal,
    ParameterStyle=[4]SoapParameterStyle.Wrapped)]
    public System.Single Add(System.Single arg1,
        System.Single arg2)
    {
      object[] results = this.Invoke("Add",
      new object[] {arg1,arg2});
      return ((System.Single)(results[0]));
    }

    public System.IAsyncResult BeginAdd(
        System.Single arg1,
        System.Single arg2,
        System.AsyncCallback callback,
        object asyncState)
    {
      return this.BeginInvoke("Add", new object[] {
        arg1,arg2},callback,asyncState);
    }

    public System.Single EndAdd(
        System.IAsyncResult asyncResult)
    {
        object[] results = this.EndInvoke(asyncResult);
        return ((System.Single)(results[0]));
    }
    //
    // Similar methods for the Subtract and Multiply
    // methods are omitted…
    //
}
```

The generated proxy derives from a .NET Framework class called **SoapHttpClientProtocol**, which encapsulates the logic you need to call an XML Web service using SOAP. Notice the Hello Web service contains only one method called SayHello, but the proxy contains three methods: SayHello,

BeginSayHello, and EndSayHello. The last two methods allow you to call the Web service asynchronously. Notice the hard-coded URL for the Web service on lines 16 and 17. You can alter the URL that the proxy uses by setting the URL property on the proxy, but a better solution is to use the urlkey parameter to wsdl.exe, which inserts logic to read the URL from a key in the client's configuration file. If you use wsdl.exe with the following command line:

```
wsdl /urlkey:WebServiceURL
http://localhost/arithmetic/arithmetic.asmx?wsdl
/language:CS /out:arithmeticproxy.cs
```

Then wsdl.exe adds the following logic to the proxy:

```
string urlSetting =
System.Configuration.
ConfigurationSettings.AppSettings["WebServiceURL"];
if ((urlSetting != null))
    this.Url = urlSetting;
else
    this.Url =
       "http://localhost/TestWebService/Service1.asmx";
```

Notice that the logic will first try to read the URL from a configuration file, and, if no configuration file is specified, it defaults the URL to the original location of the Web service. This is a much better approach and is highly recommended.

You can compile the proxy into an assembly using the following command:

```
csc /t:library /out:arithmeticproxy.dll arithmeticproxy.cs
```

Because you've already built so many Windows Forms clients, let's build a client for this Web service using ASP.NET Web Forms. I'll use Visual Studio .NET to build the Web Forms client. The steps are as follows:

1. Create an ASP.NET Web Forms project.
2. Draw the UI.
3. Reference the proxy assembly.
4. Implement the UI.

CREATE AN ASP.NET WEB FORMS PROJECT

Start Visual Studio .NET and then execute the following steps:

1. Select File | New | Project.... The New Project dialog appears.
2. Under Project Types, select Visual C# Projects, and, under Templates, choose ASP.NET Web Application.
3. Change the location of the project to *localhost/ArithmeticClient*.
4. Click OK.

Visual Studio .NET creates a new virtual directory for the application at the location that I specified. The physical location of the virtual directory is [Inetpub]\wwwroot\ArithmeticClient where **[InetPub]** is the location of the **InetPub** directory on your machine. On my machine, this location is **D:\Inetpub**. Visual Studio .NET creates a project at this location that contains a single ASP.NET Web Form called **WebForm1.aspx**, which is the main window of your application.

DRAW THE UI

Using the toolbox in Visual Studio .NET, draw the UI shown in Figure 10–8 on your form.

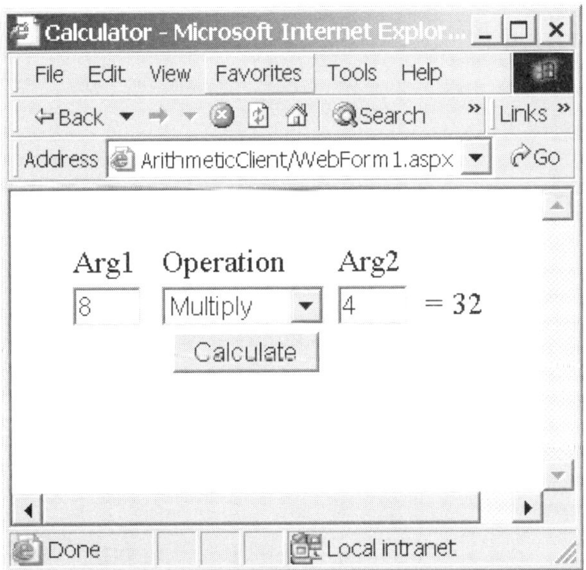

FIGURE 10–8 *The UI for the Arithmetic Web Forms client in Visual Studio .NET.*

Name the controls on the UI as shown in Table 10–3.

TABLE 10–3 *Control IDs for the Web Forms client*

Description	Control ID
Arg1 text box	txtArg1
Dropdown list of operations	dpdOperations
Arg2 text box	txtArg2
Result label	lblRslt
Calculate button	cmdCalculate

REFERENCE THE PROXY ASSEMBLY

In order to call the Web, you need to reference the proxy assembly that you built earlier. To do this, perform the following steps:

1. Select Project | Add Reference.... The Add Reference dialog appears).
2. Make sure you are on the .NET tab and click Browse. The Select Component dialog appears.
3. Navigate to where you built the proxy assembly.
4. Select the assembly and click Open.
5. Click OK button on the Add Reference dialog.

Note In the next section, you learn how to create a Web reference, which both creates the proxy and references it, using Visual Studio .NET.

IMPLEMENT THE UI

Here is the code for the Calculate button:

```
1.  private void cmdCalculate_Click(object sender,
       System.EventArgs e)
2.  {
3.       Arithmetic ws;
4.       float arg1, arg2, result=0;
5.       ws=new Arithmetic();
6.       arg1=float.Parse(txtArg1.Text);
7.       arg2=float.Parse(txtArg2.Text);
8.       switch (dpdOperations.SelectedIndex )
9.       {
10.      case 0:
11.        result=ws.Add(arg1,arg2);
12.        break;
13.      case 1:
14.        result=ws.Subtract(arg1,arg2);
15.        break;
16.      case 2:
17.        result=ws.Multiply(arg1,arg2);
18.        break;
19.      }
20.      lblRslt.Text=result.ToString();
21. }
```

Line 5 creates a new instance of the Arithmetic proxy, which calls the Arithmetic Web service. Lines 6 and 7 parse the contents of the two argument text boxes into two floating-point values. Lines 8 through 19 is a switch statement that calls the appropriate method on the Arithmetic Web service based on the operation that the user selected in the operations dropdown. Line 20 displays the result. Notice that the calls we make to the Web service on Lines 11, 14, and 17 are simple and straightforward. I don't have to worry about formatting a SOAP request or parsing a SOAP response; the proxy does all of that.

Creating and Consuming a Web Service with Visual Studio .NET

In the previous section you created an Arithmetic Web service without using any of the Web service development features in Visual Studio .NET. In this section, I explore some of the tools available in Visual Studio .NET for Web service development. I also look at returning and accepting more complex data from the Web service.

Visual Studio .NET includes a project template for creating an XML Web service. This project template will create an asmx file for the Web service using the code-behind directive. It also creates the corresponding source file for the asmx file and creates the IIS virtual directory for the XML Web service. To create a project using this template, perform the following steps:

1. Select File | New | Project…. The New Project dialog appears as shown in Figure 10–9.
2. Under Project Types, select Visual C# Projects.
3. Under Templates, select ASP.NET Web Service.

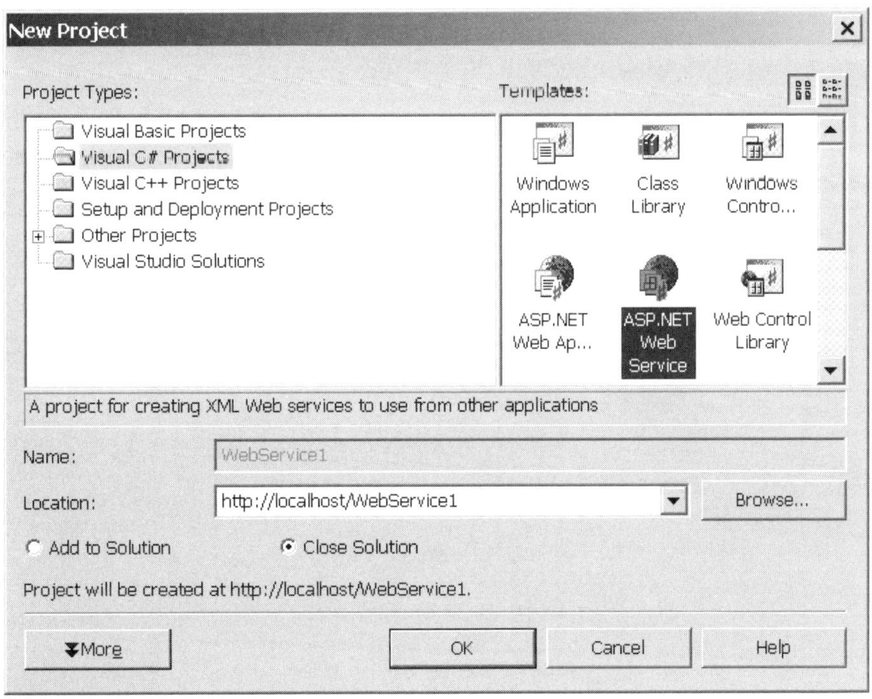

FIGURE 10–9 *The New Project dialog.*

4. Enter "http://localhost/FinancialWebService" in the Location field and click OK.

This creates a project on your machine beneath your **InetPub** directory at **wwwroot\FinancialWebService**. On my machine, the Web service resides at **D:\Inetpub\wwwroot\FinancialWebService**.

In this directory, Visual Studio .NET creates a project file with the extension .csproj. This file is actually an XML file. Try bringing it up in Notepad, and you can see how Visual Studio .NET stores all of the necessary information about a project. The project directory will also contain an asmx file called **Service1.asmx** (you can obviously change this name if you like). The contents of this file are as follows:

```
<%@ WebService Language="c#"
Codebehind="Service1.asmx.cs"
Class="FinancialWebService.Service1" %>
```

The contents of the code-behind file are as follows:

```
using System;
using System.Collections;
using System.ComponentModel;
using System.Data;
using System.Diagnostics;
using System.Web;
using System.Web.Services;
namespace FinancialWebService
{

    public class Service1 : System.Web.Services.WebService
    {
      public Service1()
      {
        InitializeComponent();
      }
      private IContainer components = null;
      private void InitializeComponent()
      {
      }
      protected override void Dispose( bool disposing )
      {
        if(disposing && components != null)
        {
          components.Dispose();
        }
        base.Dispose(disposing);
      }
//    [WebMethod]
//    public string HelloWorld()
//    {
```

```
//        return "Hello World";
//     }
    }
}
```

There is also a **Global.asax** file and a corresponding **Global.asax.cs** file. The contents of the **Global.asax** file are shown here:

```
<%@ Application Codebehind="Global.asax.cs"
 Inherits="FinancialWebService.Global" %>
```

Here are the contents of the **Global.asax.cs** file:

```
using System;
using System.Collections;
using System.ComponentModel;
using System.Web;
using System.Web.SessionState;
namespace FinancialWebService
{
    public class Global : System.Web.HttpApplication
    {
      public Global()
      {
        InitializeComponent();
      }
      protected void Application_Start(Object sender,
          EventArgs e)
      {

      }
      protected void Session_Start(Object sender,
          EventArgs e)
      {

      }
      protected void Application_BeginRequest(
          Object sender, EventArgs e)
      {

      }
      protected void Application_EndRequest(
          Object sender, EventArgs e)
      {

      }
      protected void Application_AuthenticateRequest(
          Object sender, EventArgs e)
      {

      }
```

```
        protected void Application_Error(
            Object sender, EventArgs e)
        {

        }
        protected void Session_End(Object sender,
            EventArgs e)
        {

        }
        protected void Application_End(Object sender,
            EventArgs e)
        {

        }
        private void InitializeComponent()
        {
        }
    }
}
```

These files contain an override of the **System.Web.HttpApplication** class. You can customize the behavior of your HttpApplication by adding logic to the empty event handlers shown in **global.asax.cs**. The project also contains an important file called **[ProjectName].csproj.webinfo**. For the project that I just created, the name of the file is **FinancialWebService.csproj.webinfo**. The contents of this file are as follows:

```
<VisualStudioUNCWeb>
  <Web URLPath =
"http://localhost/FinancialWebService/
FinancialWebService.csproj" />
</VisualStudioUNCWeb>
```

If you ever need to move your project to another virtual directory, you need to change the URLPath in this file to point to the new location.

To implement the financial Web service, you can go to the code for the Web service by right-clicking the **Service1.asmx** file in the solution explorer view of Visual Studio .NET as shown in Figure 10–10.

Change the name of the class from **Service1** to **LoanService** and add the MonthlyPayment and LoanAmount methods that follow:

```
public class LoanService :
    System.Web.Services.WebService
{
    public LoanService()
    {
      InitializeComponent();
    }

```

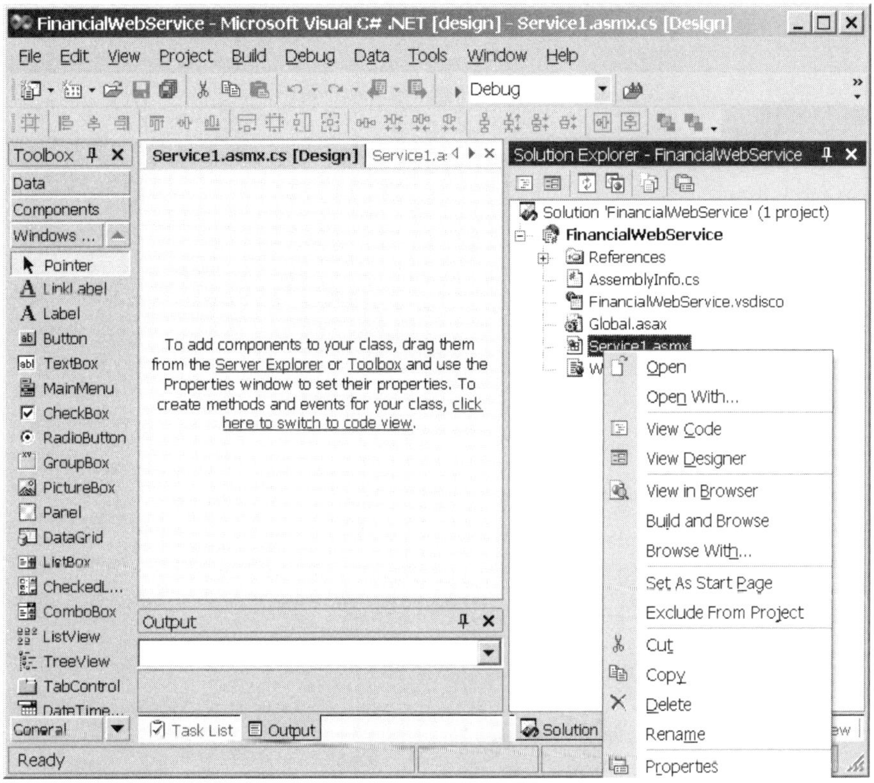

FIGURE 10–10 *Viewing the code for your Web service.*

```
      // The rest of the code is omitted for clarity…

      [WebMethod]
      public decimal MonthlyPayment(short numMonths,
        double interestRate, decimal loanAmt)
      {
        double monthlyRate, tempVal;
        decimal unRoundedAmt;
        monthlyRate=interestRate/1200;
        tempVal=Math.Pow((1+monthlyRate),
          (double)numMonths);
        unRoundedAmt=(decimal)((double)loanAmt*
          (monthlyRate*tempVal/(tempVal-1)));
        return decimal.Round(unRoundedAmt,2);
      }
      [WebMethod]
      public decimal LoanAmount(short numMonths,
        double interestRate, decimal monthlyPmt)
      {
        double monthlyRate, tempVal;
```

```
        decimal unRoundedAmt;
        monthlyRate=interestRate/1200;
        tempVal=Math.Pow((1+monthlyRate),
          (double)numMonths);
        unRoundedAmt=(decimal)((double)monthlyPmt*
          (tempVal-1)/(monthlyRate*tempVal));
        return decimal.Round(unRoundedAmt,2);
    }
}
```

The MonthlyPayment method takes a number of months, an annual percentage rate, and a loan amount, and it calculates the monthly payment needed to pay off the loan amount. The LoanAmount method takes a number of months, an annual percentage rate, and a monthly payment, and it calculates the loan amount that you can afford.

You can now test this Web service using the test HTML page by navigating to the following URL: *localhost/FinancialWebService/*. If you do this, you see the test page shown in Figure 10–11.

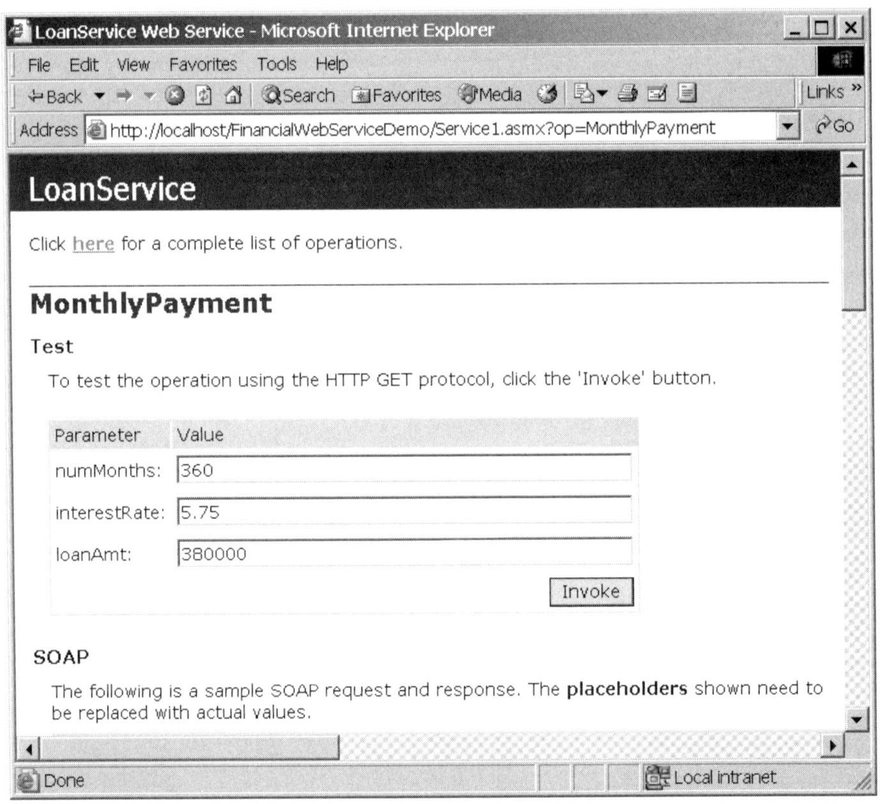

FIGURE 10–11 *Viewing the code for your Web service.*

Let's now look at a feature that Visual Studio .NET provides to automate the process of creating a client of a Web service. Let's create a Windows Forms-based client this time to show that you can call an XML Web service just as easily from either type of client. To create a Windows Forms client for the financial Web service, perform the following steps:

1. Select File | New | Project.... The New Project dialog appears as shown in Figure 10–12.
2. Under Project Types, select Visual C# Projects.
3. Under Templates, select Windows Applications.
4. Enter "FinancialWebServiceClient" in the name field.
5. Click OK.

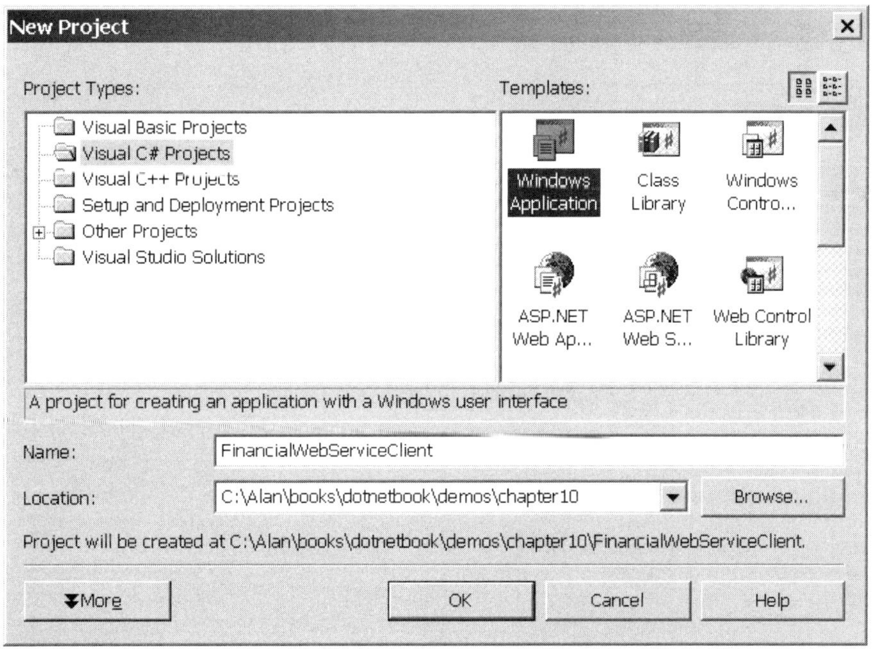

FIGURE 10–12 *The Add Web Reference dialog.*

Next, add a Web reference for the client. To do this, perform the following steps:

1. Select Project | Add Web Reference.... The Add Web Reference dialog appears as shown in Figure 10–13.
2. Enter the URI for the wsdl file for the Web service: "localhost/FinancialWebServiceDemo/Service1.asmx?WSDL". You can also enter the URI for the disco file: "localhost/FinancialWebServiceDemo/Service1.asmx?disco".
3. Click Add Reference.

Visual Studio adds a Web References folder to the solution view in your project as shown in Figure 10–14.

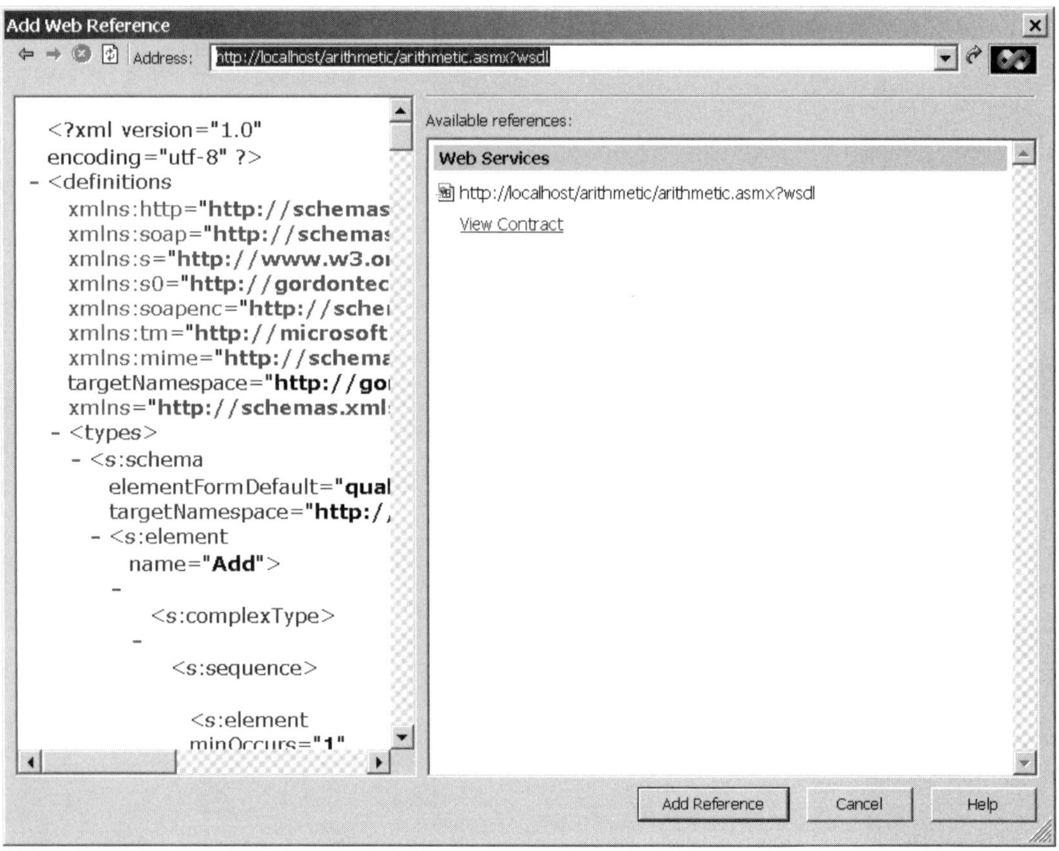

FIGURE 10–13 *The Add Web Reference dialog.*

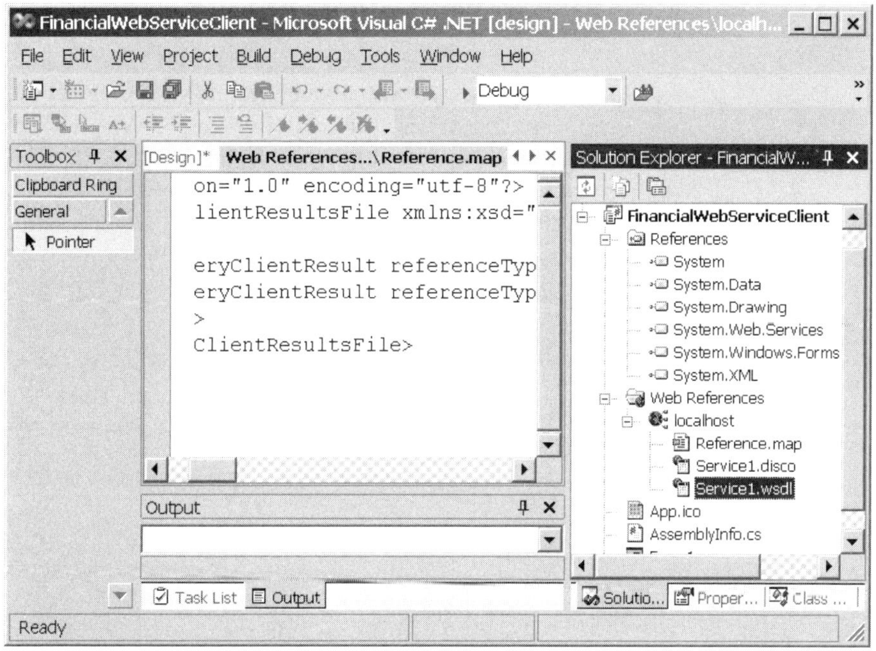

FIGURE 10–14 *The Web reference in Visual Studio .NET.*

This folder will contain the DISCO and WSDL files for the Web service as well as a map file that contains location information for the Web service. However, notice that there is no source file. If you go to the operating system folder for the project, you will see that the Add Web Reference command created a new directory with the name **Web References**. Beneath this directory is a directory called **localhost**. Beneath that directory you will see four files: (1) **reference.cs**, (2) **reference.map**, (3) **service1.disco**, and (4) **service1.wsdl**. The **reference.cs** file will contain the exact same proxy code that you generated earlier using wsdl.exe. Therefore, using the Add Web Reference command in Visual Studio .NET is equivalent to running WSDL to generate a proxy and then adding the source code for the proxy to your project. The **reference.map** and **service1.disco** files contain location information for the Web service, and **service1.wsdl** contains a copy of the WSDL file. After you compile the client, you should be able to type in loan amounts, an interest rate, and a number of months and calculate a monthly payment, or you can enter a monthly payment, interest, and a number of months and calculate a loan amount.

XML Web Services and Data

So far, there is nothing from a technological standpoint in this Web service that isn't like the previous Web service. Therefore, let's add another method to the Web service that will return an amortization table for a loan. An amortization table is a table with one entry for each payment on the loan. Each entry shows the amount of principal and interest in the payment and the remaining balance after the payment. You can return tabular data like this using a Web service in two ways: (1) using an ADO.NET dataset or (2) using a custom class.

Returning Data Using a Custom Class

Let's look first at returning the amortization table using a custom class. Here is a **Payment** class that you can use to hold each entry in the amortization table:

```
namespace FinancialWebService
{
     public class Payment
     {
          public Payment(short mnth,decimal amt,
        decimal prinAmt,decimal intrstAmt,
        decimal balance)
          {
               this.Month=mnth;
          this.Amount=amt;
          this.PrincipleAmount=prinAmt;
          this.InterestAmount=intrstAmt;
          this.Balance=balance;
          }
          public Payment() {}
          public short Month;
          public decimal Amount;
          public decimal PrincipleAmount;
          public decimal InterestAmount;
          public decimal Balance;
     }
}
```

This class has five member variables: a month, a payment amount, a principle amount, an interest amount, and a remaining balance. This is all the information you need for each entry in the amortization table. Here is a web service method that returns an Amortization table for a loan using the **Payment** class:

```
[WebMethod]
public Payment[] AmortizationTable(short numMonths,
     double interestRate, decimal loanAmt)
{
```

```
5.      short i, numLoops;
6.      double monthlyRate;
7.      decimal monthlyPmt, remainingBalance,
8.        principle, interest;
9.      Payment[] payments;
10.     payments=new Payment[numMonths];
11.     monthlyRate=interestRate/1200; // Convert A.P.R.
12.               //to decimal monthly rate
13.     monthlyPmt=MonthlyPayment(numMonths,
14.       interestRate,loanAmt);
15.     remainingBalance=loanAmt;
16.     numLoops=(short)(numMonths-1);
17.     for (i=0;i<numLoops;i++)
18.     {
19.       interest=decimal.Round(
20.         (decimal)monthlyRate*remainingBalance,2);
21.       principle=monthlyPmt-interest;
22.       remainingBalance=
23.          remainingBalance-principle;
24.       payments[i]=new Payment((short)(i+1),
25.       monthlyPmt,principle,interest,
26.       remainingBalance);
27.     }
28. // Calculate the final payment so the balance is zero;
29.     if (numMonths > 0)
30.     {
31.       interest=decimal.Round((decimal)
32.         monthlyRate*remainingBalance,2);
33.       principle=
34.         decimal.Round(remainingBalance,2);
35.       monthlyPmt=interest+principle;
36.       remainingBalance=(Decimal)0.0;
37.       payments[numMonths-1]=
38.         new Payment((short)(i+1),
39.              monthlyPmt,principle,
40.              interest,remainingBalance);
41.     }
42.     return payments;
43. }
```

I won't go into the details of the math for this method. The key lines for this discussion are lines 9 and 10, where I declare and instantiate an array of payment objects. I then populate the array with payment information for the loan on lines 11 through 41, and I return the array on line 42. I don't have to do anything special to return a complex type like this from a Web service. If you look at the WSDL file for the Web service, you will see that the Payment type appears there.

```
<s:complexType name="Payment">
  <s:attribute name="Month" type="s:short" />
```

```
        <s:attribute name="Amount" type="s:decimal" />
        <s:attribute name="Principle" type="s:decimal" />
        <s:attribute name="Interest" type="s:decimal" />
        <s:attribute name="Balance" type="s:decimal" />
      </s:complexType>
```

If you regenerate the proxy for the Web service, you will also see that the Payment type now appears in the wsdl.exe-generated source code.

```
    public class Payment {
        /// <remarks/>
        public short Month;
        /// <remarks/>
        public System.Decimal Amount;
        /// <remarks/>
        public System.Decimal PrincipleAmount;
        /// <remarks/>
        public System.Decimal InterestAmount;
        /// <remarks/>
        public System.Decimal Balance;
    }
}
```

An important point to mention here is that only the state of the **Payment** class is carried across to the WSDL file and the generated proxy class. If you added additional methods to the original implementation of the **Payment** class, those methods will not be reflected in the WSDL file or the proxy. An XML Web service can only transport data, not code. Here is an example of the XML response you will see when you call the Amortization method:

```
<?xml version="1.0" encoding="utf-8"?>
<ArrayOfPayment xmlns:xsd="http://www.w3.org/2001/
XMLSchema" xmlns:xsi="http://www.w3.org/2001/XMLSchema-
instance" xmlns="http://tempuri.org/">
  <Payment>
    <Month>1</Month>
    <Amount>2216.58</Amount>
    <PrincipleAmount>341.58</PrincipleAmount>
    <InterestAmount>1875</InterestAmount>
    <Balance>359658.42</Balance>
  </Payment>
  <Payment>
    <Month>2</Month>
    <Amount>2216.58</Amount>
    <PrincipleAmount>343.36</PrincipleAmount>
    <InterestAmount>1873.22</InterestAmount>
    <Balance>359315.06</Balance>
  </Payment>
  <Payment>
    <Month>3</Month>
```

```
    <Amount>2216.58</Amount>
    <PrincipleAmount>345.15</PrincipleAmount>
    <InterestAmount>1871.43</InterestAmount>
    <Balance>358969.91</Balance>
  </Payment>
…
</ArrayOfPayment>
```

Notice that the ASP.NET Web services infrastructure serialized the array of payment objects into an XML representation with an ArrayOf[ClassName] top-level element for the array and then one Payment subelement for each element of the array. Each member variable of the **Payment** class is a subelement of the Payment element. If you don't like the default XML representation that the ASP.NET runtime uses for the **Payment** class, you can change it. For instance, if I wanted to change the **Payment** class so that the member variables of the class appeared as attributes of the Payment element instead of subelements, I would only need to change the definition of the Payment class to the following:

```
namespace FinancialWebService
{
     using System.Xml.Serialization;
     [XmlRoot("Payment")]
     public class Payment
     {
       public Payment(short mnth,decimal amt,
         decimal prinAmt,decimal intrstAmt,
         decimal balance)
       {
         this.Month=mnth;
         this.Amount=amt;
         this.PrincipleAmount=prinAmt;
         this.InterestAmount=intrstAmt;
         this.Balance=balance;
       }
       public Payment() {}

       [XmlAttribute("Month")]
       public short Month;
       [XmlAttribute("Amount")]
       public decimal Amount;
       [XmlAttribute("Principle")]
       public decimal PrincipleAmount;
       [XmlAttribute("Interest")]
       public decimal InterestAmount;
       [XmlAttribute("Balance")]
       public decimal Balance;
     }
}
```

Using the XmlRoot, XmlAttribute, and XmlElement attributes, which can be found in the System.Xml.Serialization namespace, you can control how instances of the class are rendered as XML. In this case, I have specified that the member variables of the Payment class should be attributes of a root element called Payment. If I call the AmortizationTable method again, you can see that the generated XML will now look as follows:

```
<?xml version="1.0" encoding="utf-8"?>
<ArrayOfPayment xmlns:xsd="http://www.w3.org/2001/
XMLSchema" xmlns:xsi="http://www.w3.org/2001/XMLSchema-
instance" xmlns="http://tempuri.org/">
  <Payment Month="1" Amount="469.7" Principle="369.7"
      Interest="100" Balance="19630.3" />
  <Payment Month="2" Amount="469.7" Principle="371.55"
      Interest="98.15" Balance="19258.75" />
  <Payment Month="3" Amount="469.7" Principle="373.41"
      Interest="96.29" Balance="18885.34" />
  <Payment Month="4" Amount="469.7" Principle="375.27"
      Interest="94.43" Balance="18510.07" />
</ArrayOfPayment>
```

Notice that the member variables of the Payment class appear as attributes of the Payment, XML element.

Returning Data Using a Dataset

Another way to return tabular data from a Web service is to return it as an ADO.NET dataset. Just like ADO Recordsets, you can fabricate a dataset from in-memory data that does not come from a database. To understand how to do this, let's first look at the object model for ADO.NET datasets, which is shown in Figure 10–15.

As you can see, a dataset is a collection of data tables. A data table is actually the equivalent of an ADO Recordset; it contains columns and rows. To create a fabricated Dataset, you first need to add a data table to the dataset using the Add method on the Tables collection, which is a property of the dataset. You then add the columns to the table by calling the Add method of the Columns collection, which is a property of the **DataTable** class. The following code shows an implementation of the Amortization table method that returns a fabricated dataset:

```
[WebMethod]
public DataSet AmortizationTableDS(
     short numMonths,double interestRate,
     decimal  loanAmt)
{
```

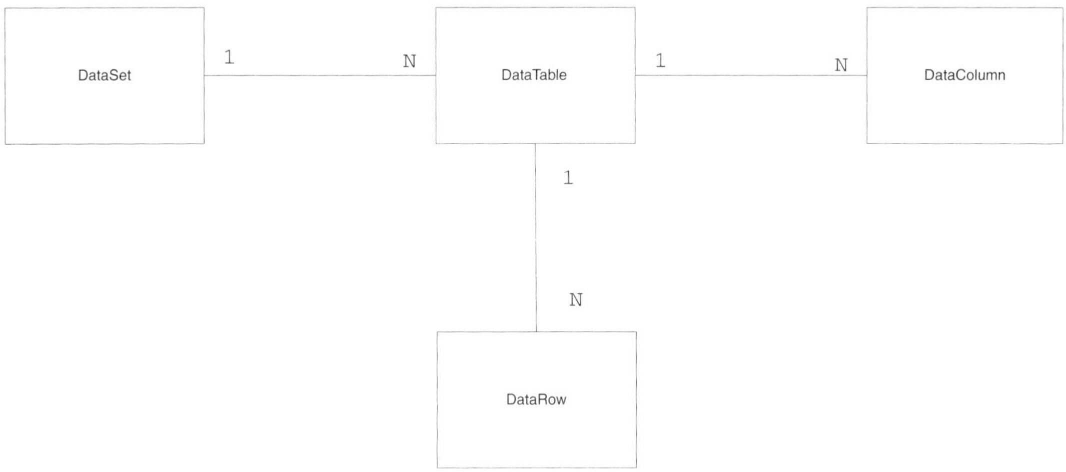

FIGURE 10-15 *The object model for ADO.NET datasets.*

```
      DataTablc dtPayments;
      DataRow rowPayment;
      short i, numLoops;
      double monthlyRate;
      decimal monthlyPmt, remainingBalance,
        principle, interest;
      DataSet ds=new DataSet();
      dtPayments=ds.Tables.Add("Payments");
      dtPayments.Columns.Add("Month",
        typeof(System.Int16));
      dtPayments.Columns.Add("Payment",
        typeof(System.Decimal));
      dtPayments.Columns.Add("Principle",
        typeof(System.Decimal));
      dtPayments.Columns.Add("Interest",
        typeof(System.Decimal));
      dtPayments.Columns.Add("Balance",
        typeof(System.Decimal));
      monthlyRate=interestRate/1200;
      monthlyPmt=MonthlyPayment(numMonths,
              InterestRate,loanAmt);
      remainingBalance=loanAmt;
      numLoops=(short)(numMonths-1);
      for (i=0;i<numLoops;i++)
      {
        interest=decimal.Round(
          (decimal)(monthlyRate*
          (double)remainingBalance),2);
        principle=monthlyPmt-interest;
        remainingBalance=
```

```
36.          remainingBalance-principle;
37.        rowPayment=dtPayments.NewRow();
38.        rowPayment["Month"]=i+1;
39.        rowPayment["Payment"]=monthlyPmt;
40.        rowPayment["Interest"]=interest;
41.        rowPayment["Principle"]=principle;
42.        rowPayment["Balance"]=remainingBalance;
43.        dtPayments.Rows.Add(rowPayment);
44.      }
45. // Calculate the final payment so the balance is zero;
46.      if (numMonths > 0)
47.      {
48.        interest=decimal.Round((decimal)
49.          (monthlyRate*
50.          (double)remainingBalance),2);
51.        principle=decimal.Round(
52.          remainingBalance,2);
53.        monthlyPmt=interest+principle;
54.        rowPayment=dtPayments.NewRow();
55.        rowPayment["Month"]=numMonths;
56.                  rowPayment["Interest"]=interest;
57.                  rowPayment["Principle"]=
58.                    remainingBalance;
59.        rowPayment["Payment"]=monthlyPmt;
60.        rowPayment["Balance"]=(decimal)0.0;
61.        dtPayments.Rows.Add(rowPayment);
62.      }
63.      return ds;
64. }
```

Line 12 creates an instance of the **DataSet** class. In order for this line to compile, you have to add a using statement for the System.Data namespace as shown here:

```
using System.Data
```

Line 13 adds a data table called Payments to the dataset. Lines 14 and 15 add a Month column to the Payments data table. Notice that we specify the name and type for the column. Lines 16 through 23 add Payment, Principle, Interest, and Balance columns to the data table. Lines 24 through 62 populate the data table with the amortization information for a loan. Line 37 calls the NewRow method on the Payments data table to get a new row. I then populate the row on lines 38 through 42, and line 43 calls the Add method on the Rows collection of the data table to add the new row to the table. Lines 45 through 62 repeat the same logic to calculate the final payment. Line 63 returns the data set normally. Here is the generated XML:

```
<?xml version="1.0" encoding="utf-8"?>
<DataSet xmlns="http://tempuri.org/">
  <xs:schema id="NewDataSet" xmlns="" xmlns:xs="http://
www.w3.org/2001/XMLSchema" xmlns:msdata="urn:schemas-
```

```
microsoft-com:xml-msdata">
    <xs:element name="NewDataSet" msdata:IsDataSet="true">
      <xs:complexType>
        <xs:choice maxOccurs="unbounded">
          <xs:element name="Payments">
            <xs:complexType>
              <xs:sequence>
                <xs:element name="Month" type="xs:short"
                 minOccurs="0" />
                <xs:element name="Payment"
                 type="xs:decimal" minOccurs="0" />
                <xs:element name="Principle"
                 type="xs:decimal" minOccurs="0" />
                <xs:element name="Interest"
                 type="xs:decimal" minOccurs="0" />
                <xs:element name="Balance"
                 type="xs:decimal" minOccurs="0" />
              </xs:sequence>
            </xs:complexType>
          </xs:element>
        </xs:choice>
      </xs:complexType>
    </xs:element>
  </xs:schema>
  <diffgr:diffgram xmlns:msdata="urn:schemas-microsoft-
com:xml-msdata" xmlns:diffgr="urn:schemas-microsoft-
com:xml-diffgram-v1">
    <NewDataSet xmlns="">
      <Payments diffgr:id="Payments1" msdata:rowOrder="0"
diffgr:hasChanges="inserted">
        <Month>1</Month>
        <Payment>2308.94</Payment>
        <Principle>355.82</Principle>
        <Interest>1953.12</Interest>
        <Balance>374644.18</Balance>
      </Payments>
      <Payments diffgr:id="Payments2" msdata:rowOrder="1"
diffgr:hasChanges="inserted">
        <Month>2</Month>
        <Payment>2308.94</Payment>
        <Principle>357.67</Principle>
        <Interest>1951.27</Interest>
        <Balance>374286.51</Balance>
      </Payments>
</Payments>
    </NewDataSet>
  </diffgr:diffgram>
</DataSet>
```

Here I am using the default XML schema for data sets, but remember you can change this by calling one of the many overloads of the ReadXMLSchema method and by passing in an XSD schema. The data set will now be rendered in XML using the XSD schema that you specified.

In some (many) cases, your XML Web service will actually return data from a database. In these cases, you can use ADO.NET from your Web service methods. The following code shows an example of an XML Web service method that returns data from a database:

```
[WebMethod]
public DataSet GetBookByTitle(string title)
{
    DataSet ds;
    SqlCommand cmd;
    SqlDataAdapter dsAdapter;
    SqlParameter param;
    SqlConnection conn;
    ds=new DataSet();
    conn=new SqlConnection(
        "user id=sa;password=;initial
        catalog=DevDotNet;data source=localhost");
    cmd=new SqlCommand("GetBooksByTitle",conn);
    cmd.CommandType = CommandType.StoredProcedure;
    param=cmd.Parameters.Add(new
      SqlParameter("@Title",SqlDbType.NVarChar,255));
    param.Value=title;
    param.Direction=ParameterDirection.Input;
    try
    {
    // Open the connection and execute the Command
      conn.Open();
      dsAdapter =new SqlDataAdapter();
      dsAdapter.SelectCommand =cmd;
      dsAdapter.Fill(ds,"Titles");
      return ds;
    }
    catch (Exception err)
    {
    // An error occurred, pass the exception up
      throw err;
    }
    finally
    {
    // Close the Connection
      if (conn.State == ConnectionState.Open)
        conn.Close();
    }
}
```

This code is no different than any managed code that you would write to access a database using ADO.NET. You do not have to do anything special in order to write this code from within an XML Web service, so I won't walk through all the code. In this case, I am using the SQLClient managed provider. Therefore, I need to reference the System.Data.dll assembly and add the following using statement to the code:

```
using System.Data.SqlClient;
```

The most important section of this code is on lines 21 through 25. Line 21 opens a connection to the database. Line 22 creates a data adapter. Line 23 defines a Select command for the adapter. Line 24 calls the Fill method on the data adapter to execute the command and fill a data set with the results. Line 25 returns the data set to the client. As before, the ASP.NET runtime will serialize the data set into its XML form and encode it into the response message without any additional work from you.

You can do other things with this ability to return XML data sets from Web services. For instance, if you currently have a COM/COM+-based business object that returns ADO Recordsets, you can turn it into Web service that returns ADO.NET Datasets using the following code:

```
1.  [WebMethod]
2.  public DataSet RetrieveByKeyword(string strKeyword)
3.  {
4.        PUBSBOSERVERLib.Book objBook=new
5.          PUBSBOSERVERLib.BookClass();
6.        ADODB.Recordset rs;
7.        DataSet ds=new DataSet();
8.        OleDbDataAdapter adapter=new
9.          OleDbDataAdapter();
10.       rs=objBook.RetrieveByKeyword(strKeyword);
11.       adapter.Fill(ds,rs,"Books");
12.       return ds;
13. }
```

Lines 4 and 5 create an instance of the COM/COM+ business object. I used the Add Reference command (the COM tab) in Visual Studio .NET to create an Interop assembly for the business object. Because the business object uses ADO, the Interop assembly will reference the PIA for ADO, and it will be referenced automatically when you reference the COM/COM+ business object. Line 6 creates an instance of an ADO Recordset. Line 7 creates a data set. Lines 8 and 9 create an instance of the OleDbDataAdapter. Here I am using the managed provider for OleDb. In order to compile this code, I need to add the following using statement:

```
using System.Data.OleDb
```

Line 10 calls the RetrieveByKeyword method of the business object. This method returns an ADO Recordset that contains a list of books with titles that contain the specified keyword. Line 11 is the key line in this listing. This line uses a special Fill method in the OleDbDataAdapter, which fills a data set with the contents of an ADO Recordset. Line 12 returns the data set normally from the method.

Unfortunately, there is a problem with this approach. If you implement your XML Web Service using an ASP.NET "asmx" file, you will always incur a thread switch when you call an STA COM object because ASP.NET worker threads are setup to enter an MTA by default. Web forms ("aspx" files) support an "aspcompat" attribute that will cause the worker thread to use an STA, but this functionality is not currently supported with Web Services.

Fortunately, on some platforms, there is a better way to expose an existing COM+ application as a Web service. If you are using any of the Windows XP family of operating systems, which includes XP Professional or Windows .NET Server, you can expose an existing COM+ application as an XML Web service by clicking a single checkbox. Microsoft refers to XML Web services that you create in this manner as COM+ Web services. Because this functionality is built on the .NET remoting infrastructure, I will defer discussion of it until Chapter 11, when I talk in depth about .NET remoting.

Transactions

The .NET Framework provides an integration between XML Web services and Microsoft DTC distributed transactions. You can cause a method that is exposed using the WebMethod attribute to start a DTC transaction using the Transaction property of the WebMethod attribute.

```
[WebMethod(TransactionOption=TransactionOption.Required)]
public DataSet GetBookByTitle(string title)
{
    DataSet ds;
    SqlCommand cmd;
    SqlDataAdapter dsCmd;
    SqlParameter param;
    SqlConnection conn;
    ds=new DataSet();
    conn=new SqlConnection(
        "user id=sa;password=;initial
        catalog=DevDotNet;data source=localhost");
    cmd=new SqlCommand("GetBooksByTitle",conn);
    cmd.CommandType=CommandType.StoredProcedure;
    param=cmd.Parameters.Add(new
        SqlParameter("@Title",SqlDbType.NVarChar,255));
    param.Value=title;
    param.Direction=ParameterDirection.Input;
    try
```

```
    {
    // Open the connection and execute the Command
        conn.Open();
        dsCmd=new SqlDataAdapter();
        dsCmd.SelectCommand =cmd;
        dsCmd.Fill(ds,"Titles");
        return ds;
    }
    catch (Exception err)
    {
    // An error occurred, pass the exception up
      throw err;
    }
    finally
    {
    // Close the Connection
        if (conn.State == ConnectionState.Open)
            conn.Close();
    }
}
```

Using transactions in this manner will only coordinate a transaction involving multiple resource managers (say a database and an MSMQ message queue) from a single Web service. Microsoft, IBM, and BEA Systems are currently working on a specification called Web Services Transaction (WS-Transaction) that will allow you to coordinate a transaction between multiple XML Web services. See the following URL for more information: *msdn.microsoft.com/library/default.asp?url=/library/en-us/dnglobspec/html/ws-transaction.asp.*

Summary

In this chapter, you got a brief introduction to XML Web services. You learned about the infrastructure that ASP.NET provides to create and execute XML Web services. You also saw how to create an XML Web service both with and without Visual Studio .NET. You learned how to call an XML Web service from a managed client using the WSDL tool, which is included with the .NET Framework SDK, or from Visual Studio .NET to generate a proxy. This proxy exposes the same methods as the Web service, and, when you call these methods from a client, it turns the method call into a SOAP request, processes the response, and returns it as the return value from the method.

In the next chapter, I explore the other mechanism that the .NET Framework provides to support distributed application development: .NET remoting. In Chapter 11, I also compare and contrast .NET remoting with XML Web services.

E L E V E N

.NET Remoting

In this chapter, I discuss .NET remoting. .NET remoting is a technology in the .NET Framework that allows you to make method calls across app domain, process, and machine boundaries. (From now on, I'll just say across app domains where the app domains can be in different processes or on different machines.) In some respects .NET remoting is similar to XML Web services, which also facilitate distributed application development. However, a key design goal of XML Web services is to allow cross-platform method calls in a heterogeneous environment. The focus of .NET remoting is on .NET clients talking to .NET servers (even though it can be used in some cross-platform and interop scenarios). .NET remoting offers higher performance by giving you the option to use a lower-level TCP network protocol instead of HTTP and binary data encoding on the network instead of XML. It also offers far better fidelity with the CTS than XML Web services, allowing you to access methods, properties, and even events across the wire.

You could think of .NET remoting as the replacement for DCOM in the .NET Framework, but that wouldn't do it justice. .NET remoting adds a number of significant improvements from DCOM. It is easier to use and to configure and gives you the flexibility to choose the network protocol and serialization format used to transmit your method calls across the wire. As you go through this chapter, keep in mind that there is some overlap between .NET remoting and XML Web services. You will see that you can create an XML Web service using .NET remoting. In this chapter, I give you an introduction to the fundamentals of .NET remoting. Again, the purpose is not to try to teach you everything there is to know about .NET remoting. That would take an entire book. The purpose here is to give you enough background so you can talk about how .NET remoting fits into an overall migration scheme.

Why Do We Need .NET Remoting?

There are two technologies in the .NET Framework for facilitating distributed application development: (1) XML Web services and (2) .NET remoting. The first question that people might ask when they find out that these two technologies exist is, why two technologies? After Microsoft adds security, transactions, and reliable messaging to its Web services infrastructure (as it is feverishly doing), one could argue there is no need for another distributed application development technology. So why are there two technologies? The answer in two words is flexibility and type fidelity.

Flexibility

At a fundamental level, .NET remoting is about making method calls across app domain (and process and machine) boundaries. In that respect, it is no different than XML Web services. However, .NET remoting gives you more choices as to how method calls are serialized into a network-transportable format. It also provides choices about which protocol is used to transport method calls from client app domain to server app domain. With .NET remoting, you can serialize your method calls using SOAP or a proprietary binary format, or you can define your own format. You can use HTTP or TCP as your network protocol, or you can create your own channel and choose other protocols. You can also define whether your remotable types (the classes that you expose using .NET remoting) are created by the server, as needed, to service requests or are client created with the client having a dedicated connection to a particular object with the object's lifetime controlled by a lease. With .NET remoting, you can either define your own host executable for your server, or you can use IIS as the host process for your server.

All of these choices give you an enormous amount of flexibility. If you use SOAP as your serialization format, use HTTP as your network protocol, specify server-created single-call objects, and host your process in IIS, you have effectively created an XML Web service that can be easily called from clients running on other platforms in a heterogeneous environment. If you're running in a pure .NET environment, you can choose a binary serialization format, use TCP as your network protocol, use client-created objects, and build your own server executable (perhaps with thread pooling provided by the **System.Threading.ThreadPool** class) to create a high-performance server that more closely approximates both the performance and functionality of DCOM. The true beauty of .NET remoting is that, if you build your client and your server properly (and I show you how to do that in this chapter), you can switch from one configuration to another without changing your source code. You only need to edit the entries in an XML configuration file.

Type Fidelity

One of the major design goals of XML Web services was to facilitate application integration in a heterogeneous environment. Unfortunately, this places some limitations on the types that you can expose through an XML Web service. The type system for XML Web services is the set of types that can be exposed through SOAP, which isn't nearly as rich as the CTS in the .NET Framework. For an example of this limitation, refer back to Chapter 10 when I used a **Payment** class to return the Amortization table information from the Financial Web service. Remember that the client could see all of the data (fields) in the **Payment** class, but custom methods that I added to the **Payment** class or interfaces that I implemented in the class were not visible to the client. With .NET remoting, you can get full CTS type fidelity across a network boundary as long as the client is also a .NET Framework-based application. In other words, a .NET (managed) client has access to all of the public members of the remote type including parameterized constructors, methods, interfaces, properties, public fields, events, and delegates. To get full CTS fidelity, you will have to use the binary serialization format and to reference the assembly that contains the remote types from the client, but it is still possible.

Therefore, to answer the original question posed at the beginning of this section, why should you use .NET remoting? The answer is that XML Web services implemented with ASP.NET give you maximum interoperability and ease of development. .NET remoting gives you maximum flexibility and performance as well as full CTS type fidelity, but it is intended for a homogenous .NET environment. The choice of which one to use depends on your needs and operating environment.

Note The choice between XML Web services and .NET remoting is not unlike the choice you have on the Java platform between CORBA (which is cross-platform) and Remote Method Invocation (RMI), which was designed for a Java-only environment.

.NET Remoting Architecture

The overall process of making a method call across process (or app domain) boundaries is, at a conceptual level, no different in .NET remoting than it is in DCOM or CORBA or even the Java programming language RMI for that matter. The key to making cross-process method calls is marshaling. The idea is that you have a piece of software called a proxy that runs in the client process and a piece of software, which is usually called a stub, that runs in the server process as shown in Figure 11–1.

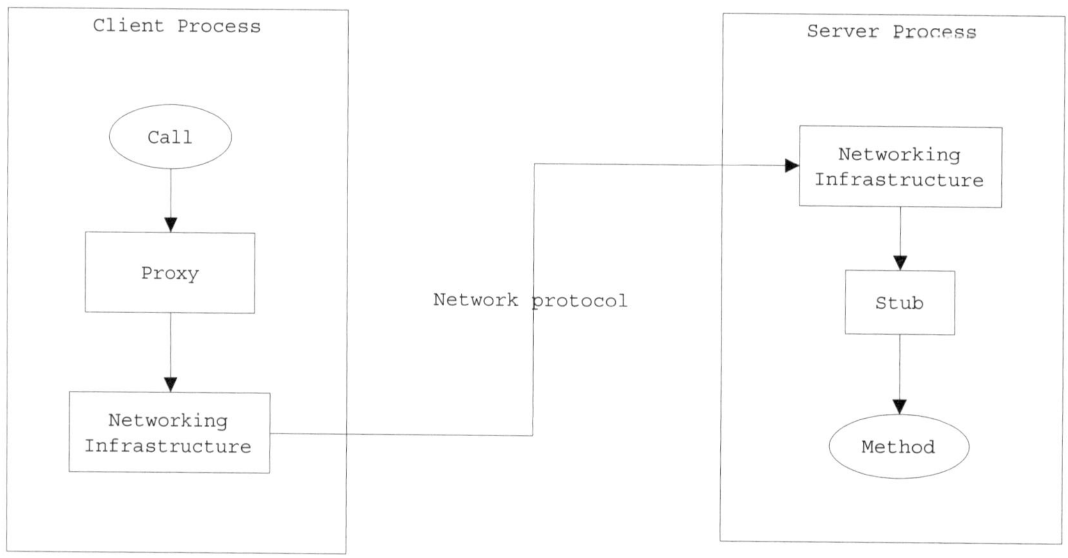

FIGURE 11–1 *Making a distributed method call.*

When you instantiate a remote object, the operating system runtime will return a transparent proxy to the client. This proxy looks exactly like the object that the client requested from the server. When the client calls methods on the proxy, the proxy will take the method call and turn it into a stream of bytes. Encoded in this stream of bytes is an identifier for the object that the client is making the method call on, the name of the method that the client wishes to call, and the parameters it is passing to the method. The networking infrastructure provided by the operating system will then send this stream across the network (using some network protocol) to a stub or dispatcher that runs on the server. This stub will interpret the message, dispatch the call to the requested method, and send the return value and output parameters back to the client.

.NET remoting is simply one implementation of this basic concept. Figure 11–2 shows a high level view of the .NET remoting architecture. The figure shows how method calls are made from a client to a marshal by reference object in a different app domain using .NET remoting.

Note Marshal by value objects behave differently. I discuss those later in this chapter.

When you instantiate a marshal by reference object, the CLR will return a proxy to the client. Although at a high level you can think of the proxy as a

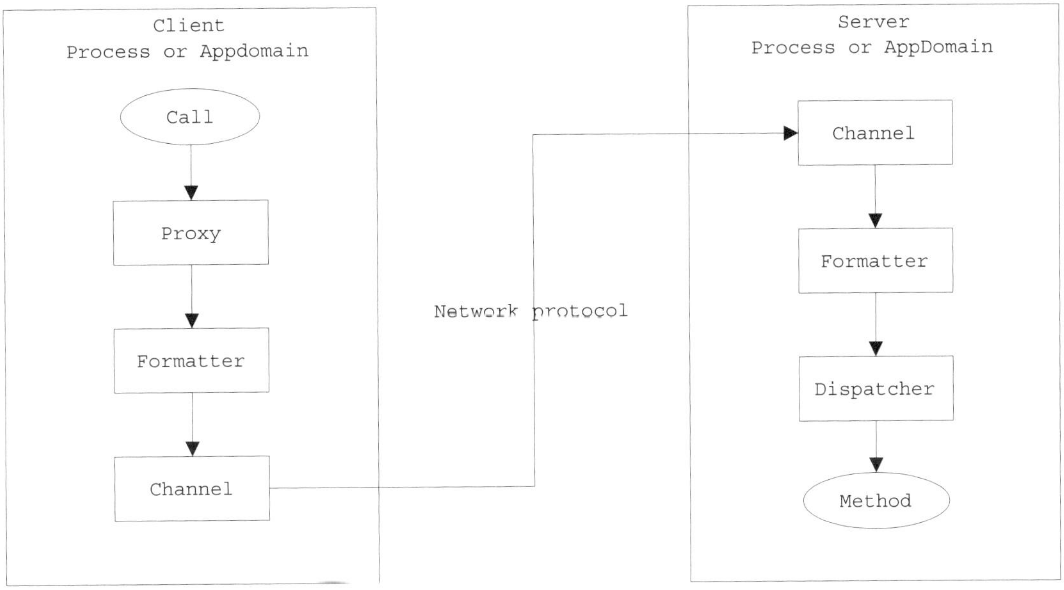

FIGURE 11–2 The .NET remoting architecture.

single object, with .NET remoting, it is actually composed of two objects: a transparent proxy, which is an instance of an undocumented class called **System.Runtime.Remoting.Proxies.__TransparentProxy**, and a real proxy, which is an instance of a documented class called **System.Runtime.Remoting.Proxies.RealProxy**. The client talks directly to the transparent proxy. The transparent proxy looks and behaves exactly like the remote object. It will have the same methods, properties, interfaces, and events. The transparent proxy contains a member variable with the name _rp, which contains the real proxy. The real proxy does most of the heavy lifting in making the cross-process app domain method call. When you make a call on the transparent proxy, it takes the method call and turns it into a call on the real proxy.

The proxy uses a formatter to turn the method call into a network transportable stream. The .NET Framework ships with two formatters: A SOAP formatter, which serializes the method call in SOAP 1.1 format, and a binary formatter, which serializes the method call in a compact binary format. You can also create your own formatters by implementing the System.Runtime.Remoting.Messaging.IRemotingFormatter.IRemotingFormatter and System.Runtime.Serialization.IFormatter interfaces. The proxy then sends the serialized method call to the server object using a channel. Channels are objects that transport messages between applications across remoting boundaries. The .NET Framework comes with two channels: an HTTP channel, which uses HTTP (see the **System.Runtime.Remoting.Channels.Http.**

HttpChannel class), and a TCP channel, which uses a lower-level TCP-based protocol (see the **System.Runtime.Remoting.Channels.Tcp.TcpChannel** class). You can also create your own channels by implementing the IChannel, IChannelReceiver, and IChannelSender interfaces from the System.Runtime.Remoting.Channels namespace. A channel actually has two halves: a sender channel, which runs on the client, and a receiver, which runs on the server (hence the two interfaces, IChannelSender and IChannelReceiver). You can create separate classes to do the sending and receiving, but the HTTP and TCP channels provided by the .NET Framework implement both interfaces. By default, the HTTP channel uses the SOAP formatter, and the TCP channel users the binary formatter. However, you can change this and use the HTTP channel with the binary formatter or the TCP channel with the SOAP formatter. The message is received by the server side of the channel, which reverses the process and passes the message to the formatter on the server, which decodes the method call and then sends the method call to a dispatcher, which calls the actual object. Any return values or output parameters are sent back to the client in the same manner.

Categories of Remotable Types

A type that is exposed through .NET remoting is called a remotable type. A remotable type can be either marshal by value, marshal by reference, or context bound. Let's explore how each of these remotable types behaves.

Marshal by Value

A marshal-by-value type is copied from the server app domain to the client app domain when it is first accessed from a client. After the object is copied to the client app domain, all further access on the object is direct, that is, it does not go through a proxy. Because marshal-by value-objects must be copied from one app domain to another through a channel, they must be serializable to a stream. A marshal-by-value object can be made serializable by implementing the ISerializable interface or by decorating its class with the System.Serializable attribute as shown here:

```
[Serializable]
public class Employee
{
...
}
```

When a marshal-by-value object is passed from one app domain to another, the .NET remoting infrastructure will copy it to the client app domain whether it is passed in as an input parameter, a return value, or an output parameter. When the object is called from a client that resides in the same app domain, no marshaling or copying of the object's state is performed.

Marshal by Reference

Marshal-by-reference objects are objects that always execute in their originating app domain. When you instantiate a marshal-by-reference object, the .NET remoting infrastructure will set up a proxy object in the client app domain. The client will make calls on the object through the proxy, and the proxy will marshal the method call to the host app domain for the object. To create a marshal-by-reference class, you need only to inherit from the **System.MarshalByRefObject** class as shown here:

```
public class Company : MarshalByRefObject
{
...
}
```

The .NET remoting infrastructure will return a proxy to the receiving app domain whenever you pass a marshal-by-reference object between app domains, whether it is passed in as an input parameter, a return value, or an output parameter. In some cases, the client may receive a proxy before the object actually exists in the server app domain. The object will only be created on the server when you make a method call through the proxy. This behavior depends on whether you are using client or server activation. I talk about activation modes shortly.

Context-Bound Objects

Context-bound objects are a special category of marshal-by-reference object. The difference is that the innermost boundary where a proxy is required is a context instead of an app domain. In other words, if a context-bound object and its client reside in different contexts, the client will only be able to access the object through a proxy, even if the client and object reside in the same app domain. A context is an environment in which objects with similar runtime requirements execute. Contexts are usually used to provide services, such as transactions or thread synchronization, for the objects that reside in them. Special interception code is used on a cross-context proxy to implement these system services.

Note Serviced components, that is, objects that use the .NET Enterprise Services, are the best example of a context-bound object. See the discussion of .NET Enterprise services and COM+ in Chapter 9 to learn more about contexts and interception.

Every app domain has a default context, and, unless you create context-bound objects (such as serviced components), all objects and clients in an app domain will reside in the default context.

To create context-bound object, you need only to inherit from **System.ContextBoundObject**, which itself inherits from **System.MarshalByRefObject** as shown here:

```
public class Company : ContextBoundObject
{
...
}
```

In most cases, though, the only context-bound object that you will create is a service component, which must inherit from the **System.EnterpriseServices.ServicedComponent** class (which inherits from **System.ContextBoundObject**) as shown here:

```
public class Company : ServicedComponent
{
...
}
```

The .NET remoting infrastructure will return a proxy to the receiving context whenever you pass a context-bound object between contexts, whether it is passed in as an input parameter, a return value, or an output parameter.

Now that you understand the three different types of remotable objects, you're probably wondering which one you should use in a particular situation. If you temporarily consider marshal-by-reference and context-bound objects to be a single category, because their behavior is similar, the real question becomes when should I use a marshal-by-value object and when should I use a marshal-by-reference object? The answer to this question depends on whether, for a given situation, it is better to bring the code to the data or the data to the code.

With a marshal-by-value object, you are essentially copying the state (the data) of your object to the client that is making the request on the object and then executing the code on the client, that is, you are bringing the data to the code. This works best for objects that have a small state or objects that do not have to run on a specific server for reasons of performance, security, or the availability of platform-specific services like COM+ or MSMQ. Objects that need to be called many times are also good candidates to be implemented as marshal-by-value objects. If you need to make many calls on an object, it's usually better to copy it to its client and access it from there rather than pay the price of a cross-app-domain (or context) hop each time you make a call. This is true even if the object has a large state. ADO Recordsets are a good example of a marshal-by-value object that potentially can be large.

Marshal-by-reference objects are most useful in situations where it is important for reasons of performance, security, or the availability of platform-specific services that the state (the data) of the object remains on a particular machine. In most cases, a marshal-by-reference object will execute either on the machine where the data that it uses resides or on a machine that is in close proximity to the machine that contains the data. So with a marshal-by-reference object you are taking the code to the data. If an object uses .NET Enterprise services or COM+, it must run on the machine where those services are available. If the object uses a large amount of data or if it is primarily a database object, it is always better for the object to execute in close proximity to its data. Another situation where a marshal-by-reference object makes sense is if an object requires a great deal of processing power. In this case, it is best to make sure that the object executes on a server class machine where you can be sure to have the available processing power.

The choice between a context-bound or a marshal-by-reference object is a little more subtle. Whether you need a context-bound object depends on whether you require runtime services like transactions or thread-synchronization for the object. If not, in most cases, you are better off just using a marshal-by-reference object.

Activation

.NET Remoting gives you a number of activation options when you use marshal-by-reference objects. You can specify two types of server activation or client activation for your objects.

SERVER ACTIVATION

With server activation, the client has no direct control over the life cycle of the objects that the server uses to service requests. The client makes a request on some well-known end point (either a URI or a TCP/IP port), and the server creates objects as needed to service these requests. Server-activated objects are also sometimes called well-known objects. A server-activated object can either be used to service only a single call, that is, the object is created when a request comes in, used to service the request, and then destroyed immediately. It can also be a Singleton, in which case a single instance is used to service all requests. If an instance exists, all client requests are serviced by that instance. If an instance does not exist, the server creates an instance, and all subsequent client requests will be serviced by that instance. Singleton objects have a lease-based lifetime associated with them, and they may be destroyed if their lease expires and they are not renewed by a sponsor.

When a client creates an instance of a server-activated object, the .NET remoting infrastructure returns a proxy to the client, but it will not actually create the object on the server. The server application domain will create the object when the client makes a method call on the object. This saves a network round trip, but it does mean that only default constructors are allowed for server-activated types because the server cannot specify a particular constructor when it creates the object. If you try to instantiate an object that is configured to use server activation, and you use a nondefault constructor, you will get a system.runtime.remoting error with the following message:

```
Cannot run a non-default constructor when connecting to
well-known objects
```

CLIENT ACTIVATION

Client-activated objects are objects with lifetimes that are controlled by their client. The client explicitly creates a new instance of an object using the new operator or the CreateInstance method on the **System.Activator** class. With client activation, a client proxy is created, and a network round trip to the server occurs to create the object immediately at activation time. The object will remain extant until its lease expires. Client-activated objects support nondefault constructors. Client activation more closely mimics the functionality of DCOM because it allows you to create stateful objects. The .NET Framework uses lease-based life cycle management for client-activated objects.

Lease-Based Life Cycle Management

In a distributed environment, the client proxy and the server object reside on different machines and thus use different instances of the CLR. Therefore, their life cycles must be managed separately. If no object pointers reference the proxy object on the client, it may be garbage-collected, but that doesn't automatically mean that the server object will be garbage-collected also. Ideally, when the proxy is garbage-collected on the client, it should send a message to the runtime on the server machine that it may release its reference to the remote object, which should eventually cause the remote object to be garbage-collected. Unfortunately, this approach is not sufficient. If you used only this scheme for life cycle management of remote objects and the client application crashed before it sent its release notification to the remote object, the remote object could continue to live on the server indefinitely.

The .NET Framework uses leased-based life cycle management to solve this problem. The .NET remoting infrastructure associates a lease with each remote object. A lease is an object that implements the System.Runtime.Remoting.Lifetime.ILease interface. The ILease interface has the members in Table 11–1.

TABLE 11-1 *The members of the ILease interface*

Property	Description	Default
InitialLeaseTime	The amount of time initially assigned to the lease.	5 minutes (zero=indefinite)
CurrentLeaseTime	The amount of time remaining on the lease.	N/A
CurrentState	The current state of the lease. Possible values are Active, Expired, Initial, Null, and Renewing.	N/A
RenewOnCallTime	The amount of time to add to the current lease time after each method call on the remote object.	2 minutes
SponsorshipTimeout	The amount of time to wait for a sponsor to renew the lease.	2 minutes
Register	A method that you can call to register a sponsor for the lease.	N/A
Unregister	A method that you can call to unregister one of a lease's sponsors.	N/A
Renew	A method that you can call to renew a lease.	N/A

Another important lease-related property is the LeaseManagerPollTime, which is the amount of time that the lease manager will sleep after checking for expired leases.

Each lease starts with an initial time as specified in the InitialLeaseTime property. Periodically, a piece of software in the .NET remoting infrastructure called a lease manager will check to see if there are any expired leases. The lease manager will use the LeaseManagerPollTime property to determine how often to check for expired leases. If a lease has expired, the lease manager will either cancel the lease by removing its reference to the lease, or it will renew the lease by calling one of the lease's sponsors. A lease can also be renewed each time a method is called on the object that the lease is associated with, or a client can renew a lease explicitly. If the lease manager cancels a lease, it will also remove all of its reference to the object associated with the lease, which will make the object eligible for garbage collection.

You can configure lease-related properties in two ways: (1) You can override the MarshalByRefObject.InitializeLifetimeService method in your marshal-by-reference object, or (2) you can specify lease-related properties in the <lifetime> element in the application or machine configuration file. You will see examples of how to do both in the examples that I do in this chapter.

A Simple .NET Remoting Client and Server

Let's build a very simple .NET remoting client and server. The use of .NET remoting is intended for .NET clients and servers, so, unlike COM or CORBA, you don't have to deal with IDL. You define the types that you will use remotely using the same .NET languages that you use to implement the types. The application will therefore be composed of three separate assemblies: (1) a shared library that contains the remotable types, (2) a console application that will be the server application, and (3) a console application that will be the client application.

The Shared Library

The server will contain two types: a marshal-by-reference class called **Company** and a marshal-by-value class called **Employee**. The **Company** class contains the members shown in Table 11–2.

TABLE 11–2 *The members of the Company class*

Member Name	Member Type	Description
Company	Constructor	There are two constructors: (1) a default constructor, which sets the name of the company to "Alans Company" and (2) a constructor that takes a string argument that contains the name of the company.
CreateEmployee	Public method	Creates a marshal-by-value Employee object and adds it to the company's internal Employee collection and returns it to the client. This method implements the factory design pattern.
GetEmployee	Public method	Looks up and returns an employee given the employee's ID.
CompanyName	Public property	Returns the name of the company.
mName	Private field	Is a private field that contains the company name. This field is exposed using the CompanyName property.
mEmployees	Private field	A private hash table field that contains all the employees of the company indexed by the employees' IDs.

The implementation of the **Company** class is shown in the following code:

```
using System;
using System.Collections;
namespace SharedLibrary
{
     public class Company : MarshalByRefObject
     {
       public Company()
       {
         Console.WriteLine(
              "Company created with no name");
         mName="Alan's company";
         mEmployees=new Hashtable();
```

```
13.       }
14.       public Company(string aName)
15.       {
16.         Console.WriteLine(
17.             "Company created with name: {0}",
18.             aName);
19.         mName=aName;
20.         mEmployees=new Hashtable();
21.       }
22.       public Employee CreateEmployee(
23.         int empID,string fstName,
24.         string lstName,decimal sal)
25.       {
26.         Console.WriteLine(
27.           "Called CreateEmployee with empID={0}",
28.         empID);
29.         Employee emp=new Employee(
30.           empID,fstName,lstName,
31.           DateTime.Now,sal);
32.         mEmployees.Add(empID,emp);
33.         return emp;
34.       }
35.       public Employee GetEmployee(int empID)
36.       {
37.         Console.WriteLine(
38.          "Called GetEmployee with empID={0}",
39.          empID);
40.         if (!mEmployees.ContainsKey(empID))
41.           throw new ApplicationException(
42.             "Key: " +
43.             empID.ToString() +
44.             " does not exist.");
45.         return (Employee)mEmployees[empID];
46.       }
47.       public string CompanyName
48.       {
49.         get { return mName; }
50.         set { mName=value; }
51.       }
52.       private string mName;
53.       private Hashtable mEmployees;
54.     }
55. }
```

Line 5 declares the **Company** class. Notice that it inherits from the **System.MarshalByRefObject** class. Lines 7 through 13 declare a default constructor. Remember that you need a default constructor if you wish to configure the class for server activation. The key line of this method is line 12, where I create a System.Collections.Hashtable object to hold the list of employees for this company. Notice that line 9 writes diagnostic output to the console so that you can see when a client creates an instance of the **Company** class. Lines 14 through 21 declare a parameterized constructor that allows you to pass a name for the company. I also write diagnostic output to the console and create a hash table in this method also. Lines 22 through 34 declare a CreateEmployee method. This method takes an employee ID, a first name, a last name, and a salary and will create an Employee marshal-by-value object and return it to the caller. Lines 35 through 46 declare a GetEmployee method that will look up an employee by ID in the Company object's internal hash table of employees. If the employee does not exist, this method raises an error. Since the list of Employees is stored in an in-memory data structure and not a database, the GetEmployee method will only work if the CreateEmployee and GetEmployee method are called on the same instance. I will actually make use of this fact to do some experiments with lease-based life cycle management shortly. Lines 47 through 51 declare a CompanyName property that I can use to get or set the name of the company. Lines 52 and 53 declare private fields that will hold the company name and the list of employees, respectively.

The CreateEmployee and GetEmployee methods return an instance of the **Employee** class. The **Employee** class is the marshal-by-value class that will hold information about the employees who work for a company. The code for this class is shown here:

```
using System
namespace SharedLibrary
{
    [Serializable]
    public class Employee
    {
        public Employee()
        {
          Console.WriteLine(
          "Called default Employee constructor");
        }
        public Employee(int aID,
          string aFirst,string aLast,
          DateTime aDate,decimal aSalary)
        {
          mID=aID;
          mFirstName=aFirst;
          mLastName=aLast;
          mHireDate=aDate;
          mSalary=aSalary;
          Console.WriteLine(
          "Called parameterized Employee constructor");
          Console.WriteLine(
          "ID={0},FirstName={1},LastName={2}",
          mID,mFirstName,mLastName);
```

```
26.         }
27.         public int ID
28.         {
29.           get { return mID; }
30.           set { mID=value; }
31.         }
32.         public DateTime HireDate
33.         {
34.           get { return mHireDate; }
35.           set { mHireDate=value; }
36.         }
37.         public string LastName
38.         {
39.           get { return mLastName; }
40.           set { mLastName=value; }
41.         }
42.         public string FirstName
43.         {
44.           get {      Console.WriteLine(
45.           "Calling get for FirstName property");
46.           return mFirstName; }
47.           set { Console.WriteLine(
48.           "Calling set for FirstName property");
49.           mFirstName=value; }
50.         }
51.         public decimal Salary
52.         {
53.           get { return mSalary; }
54.           set { mSalary=value; }
55.         }
56.         private int mID;
57.         private DateTime mHireDate;
58.         private string mLastName;
59.         private string mFirstName;
60.         private decimal mSalary;
61.     }
62. }
```

I won't explain this code; it's pretty straightforward. The only thing new is the use of the System.Serializable attribute on line 4, which makes this class a marshal-by-value class.

I compiled both the **Company** and the **Employee** class into a library (DLL) assembly called sharedlibrary. I won't go through the detailed steps for doing this because you have created Visual Studio .NET projects a number of times already in this book. Just remember that the sharedlibrary assembly should include all the code from the last two code listings.

The Server

The next thing you need to do is to create the server application. In this case, I use a Visual Studio .NET console application. The code for the server follows:

```
1.  using System;
2.  using SharedLibrary;
3.  using System.Runtime.Remoting;
4.  using System.Runtime.Remoting.Channels;
5.  using System.Runtime.Remoting.Channels.Http;
6.  namespace CompanyServer
7.  {
8.    public class CompanyServer
9.    {
10.     static void Main(string[] args)
11.     {
12.       HttpChannel chnl=new HttpChannel(8080);
13.       ChannelServices.RegisterChannel(chnl);
14.       RemotingConfiguration.
15.         RegisterWellKnownServiceType(
16.         typeof(Company),
17.         "Company.soap",
18.         WellKnownObjectMode.Singleton);
19.       Console.WriteLine(
20.         "Company server started!!!");
21.       Console.ReadLine();
22.     }
23.   }
24. }
```

Line 2 contains a using statement for the sharedlibrary assembly. I need this because I use the **SharedLibrary.Company** class on line 16. Lines 3 through 5 contain using statements for three remoting-related namespaces. Lines 10 through 22 declare the main method for this application. Line 12 creates an HTTP channel on port 8080. Line 13 calls the RegisterChannel method on the **System.Runtime.Remoting.Channels.ChannelServices** class to register this channel. Lines 14 through 18 call the RegisterWellKnownServiceType method on the **System.Runtime.Remoting.RemotingConfiguration** class to register the type with the .NET remoting infrastructure. The parameters to this method are a System.Type object for the type that I am exposing, the Uniform Resource Identifier (URI) for the object and the mode, that is, whether it's Singleton or SingleCall. The complete URI that you would need to access a remote object from a client is the following:

```
[protocol]://[servername]:[port]/[specified URI]
```

Where [SpecifiedURI] is the URI that I passed as the second parameter to the RegisterWellKnownServiceType method. Therefore, given that I have specified company.soap for the URI of the company object, the full URI to access the company object from an HTTP channel on port 8080 of the localhost machine is the following:

```
http://localhost:8080/company.soap
```

The following URI will access an object from a TCP channel on port 2400 on a server called gordon1.

```
tcp://gordon1:2400/company.soap
```

Lines 19 and 20 write a message to the console to show that the server process has started, and line 21 calls Console.ReadLine to force the server process remain alive until you press a key on the keyboard. Notice that I don't associate the Channel directly with the object that I am exposing. An object can be accessed through multiple channels, and a channel can provide access to multiple objects. A channel object provides access to all the types that are exposed by its host process.

I compiled the code shown previously into a console executable assembly called CompanyServer using Visual Studio .NET. The server project should reference the SharedLibrary assembly. Once again, I won't go into this in detail because I have built projects with Visual Studio .NET a number of times in this book.

The Client

The client will also use the Company and Employee types from the shared library. I will also build the client using a Visual Studio .NET console application. The code for the client application is the following:

```
using System;
using System.Runtime.Remoting.Channels;
using System.Runtime.Remoting.Channels.Http;
using SharedLibrary;
namespace CompanyClient
{
  class Class1
  {
      [STAThread]
      static void Main(string[] args)
      {
        HttpChannel chnl=new HttpChannel();
        ChannelServices.RegisterChannel(chnl);
        int empID;
        Employee emp1, emp2;
        Company obj=(Company)Activator.GetObject(
            typeof(Company),
            "http://localhost:8080/Company.soap");
        Console.WriteLine("Enter an Employee ID");
```

```
20.           empID=int.Parse(Console.ReadLine());
21.           Console.WriteLine("Enter a first name");
22.           string strFirstName=Console.ReadLine();
23.           Console.WriteLine("Enter a last name");
                string strLastName=Console.ReadLine();
25.           emp1=obj.CreateEmployee(empID,
26.           strFirstName,strLastName,1000);
27.           Console.WriteLine(
28.             "Enter the key of an Employee");
29.         empID=int.Parse(Console.ReadLine());
30.         emp2=obj.GetEmployee(empID);
31.         Console.WriteLine(
32.           "Employee first name is: " +
33.           emp2.FirstName);
34.         }
35.     }
36. }
```

Lines 2 and 3 contain using statements for two remoting-related namespaces. Line 4 has the using statement for the SharedLibrary assembly that contains the Company and Employee types. Lines 10 through 34 define the Main method for the client application. Lines 12 and 13 define and register an HTTP channel for the client. Notice that I don't have to define the port for this channel. I specify the port in the URI that I use to access the object. Lines 16 through 18 use the GetObject method on the **System.Activator** class to create an instance of the **Company** class in the server process.

Note Later on you will see how to use the new operator to create an instance of a remote object. I prefer to use the Activator.GetObject method in most cases because I prefer to specify explicitly where the object should be created. When you use the new operator, it can be difficult to tell whether the object resides on the client or the server.

Notice that I specify the protocol, the server name, and the port for the channel as well as the same URI that I specified in the RegisterWellKnownServiceType method on the server. Lines 19 through 24 prompt for and read the ID, first name, and last name for an employee. Line 25 calls the CreateEmployee method on the Company object to create and return a marshal-by-value employee instance called emp1. Lines 27 through 29 prompt for and read the ID of an Employee object to look up. Line 30 calls the GetEmployee method on the Company object to look up the requested employee. Lines 31 through 33 write the first name of the employee that you find.

I compiled the client into a console application using Visual Studio .NET. The client application should reference the SharedLibrary assembly.

To run this example program, start the server first by running the executable in a Visual Studio .NET command prompt. It should display a text string that says "Company Server Started!!!". Now start the client in a different Visual Studio .NET prompt. Enter an ID, first name, and last name when prompted. After entering this information, you will see output coming from the server's command prompt. The output is being written to the console from the constructor of the **Employee** class. This output shows that the Employee object is running in the server's app domain. The client will then prompt you for the ID of an employee. Type in the same ID that you specified initially, and the code will look up and display the name of the matching employee.

Configuration

In the previous example, I hard-coded the remoting configuration of both the client and server into the source code. I configured the server using the RegisterWellKnownServiceType method, and I configured the client using the RegisterChannel method and by specifying a URI in the GetObject method of the **System.Activator** class. If you want to change the type of channel that you are using (HTTP to TCP for instance), the port number, or the activation mode of the server object, you need to recompile the code. The .NET Framework supports a feature that allows you to configure your .NET applications using an XML configuration file. If you take advantage of this feature, you can easily change the .NET remoting configuration of both your client and server without having to change your source code.

Server

On the server, the types that you are exposing, the type of channel you are using, and the port number that you are listening on is specified in the source code by the following lines of code:

```
HttpChannel chnl=new HttpChannel(8080);
ChannelServices.RegisterChannel(chnl);
RemotingConfiguration.RegisterWellKnownServiceType(
      typeof(Company),"Company.soap",
      WellKnownObjectMode.Singleton);
```

The .NET Framework defines an XML schema that you can use to configure your client and server applications using XML configuration files. You can read the file and set your .NET remoting configuration to that which is specified in the configuration file by calling the RemotingConfiguration.Configure method. For instance, the following configuration file will configure your server exactly the same as the call to RegisterWellKnownServiceType in the previous example:

```
<configuration>
<system.runtime.remoting>
          <application>
            <channels>
              <channel ref="http" port="8080" />
            </channels>
          <service>
            <wellknown mode="Singleton"
type="SharedLibrary.Company,SharedLibrary"
objectUri="Company.soap" />
          </service>
          </application>
</system.runtime.remoting>
</configuration>
```

I use the channel element to specify both the protocol of the channel that the server will listen on (http in this case) and the port that the channel will use (8080). I use the wellknown sub-element of the service element to specify that the server should use server activation in Singleton mode. The type attribute in this sub-element contains the fully qualified type name of the type that I am exposing and the assembly name for the type in the following form: "typename,assemblyname".

In order to use this file, you need to save it and give it a name—**CompanyServer.exe.config**, for instance—and change your server code to use the configuration file as follows:

```
using System;
using SharedLibrary;
using System.Runtime.Remoting;
namespace CompanyServer
{
public class CompanyServer : MarshalByRefObject
{
      static void Main(string[] args)
      {
        RemotingConfiguration.Configure(
            "CompanyServer.exe.config");
        Console.WriteLine(
            "Company server started!!!");
        Console.ReadLine();
      }
}
}
```

Notice that I call the Configure method on the **System.Runtime.Remoting.RemotingConfiguration** class and specify the name of the file from which to read the remoting configuration settings. The advantage of using the configuration file is that you can now change the configuration of your server to use different channels, formatters, or ports just by changing the configuration file.

Client

The RemotingConfiguration.Configure method works just as well on the .NET remoting client. To use it from a client, create the following configuration file and save it in a file called **CompanyClient.exe.config**:

```
<configuration>
<system.runtime.remoting>
      <application>
        <client>
<wellknown type="SharedLibrary.Company,SharedLibrary"
url="http://localhost:8080/Company.soap" />
        </client>
      </application>
    </system.runtime.remoting>
</configuration>
```

Now change the source code for your client to look as follows. Notice that, once again, you simply call the Configure method on the **System.Runtime.Remoting.RemotingConfiguration** class and specify the name of the configuration file.

```
using System;
using System.Runtime.Remoting;
using SharedLibrary;
namespace CompanyClient
{
  class Class1
  {
    [STAThread]
    static void Main(string[] args)
    {
      Employee emp1, emp2;
      int empID;
      RemotingConfiguration.Configure(
          "CompanyClient.exe.config");
      Company obj=new Company();
      Console.WriteLine("Enter an Employee ID");
      empID=int.Parse(Console.ReadLine());
      Console.WriteLine("Enter a first name");
      string strFirstName=Console.ReadLine();
      Console.WriteLine("Enter a last name");
      string strLastName=Console.ReadLine();
      emp1=obj.CreateEmployee(empID,
      strFirstName,strLastName,1000);
      Console.WriteLine(
```

```
            "Enter the key of an Employee");
          empID=int.Parse(Console.ReadLine());
          emp2=obj.GetEmployee(empID);
          Console.WriteLine(
            "Employee first name is: " +
            emp2.FirstName);
        }
      }
}
```

Notice that, in this source code, I also use the new operator instead of the Activator.GetObject method. The wellknown element in the XML configuration file specifies that any attempt to instantiate the type SharedLibrary.Company in the SharedLibrary assembly should be instantiated on the remote server identified by the objectURI property.

The XML schema for a remoting configuration file is shown in Figure 11–3. In Figure 11–3, rectangles represent XML elements, and ovals represent attributes of the XML element that points to them. The Service element is only relevant on a server configuration file, and the Client element is only relevant on a client configuration file. For instance, the following configuration file, when used on the server, will add a TCP channel to the server with a port number of 2400:

```
<configuration>
    <system.runtime.remoting>
        <application>
            <channels>
            <channel ref="tcp" port="2400" />
            <channel ref="http" port="8080" />
        </channels>
        <service>
            <wellknown mode="Singleton"
      type="SharedLibrary.Company,SharedLibrary"
                objectUri="Company.soap" />
        </service>
        </application>
    </system.runtime.remoting>
</configuration>
```

A server application running with the previous configuration file can now be accessed from a client using a TCP channel on port 2400 or on a HTTP channel on port 8080. The following configuration file allows a client to talk to the server through the TCP channel on port 2400:

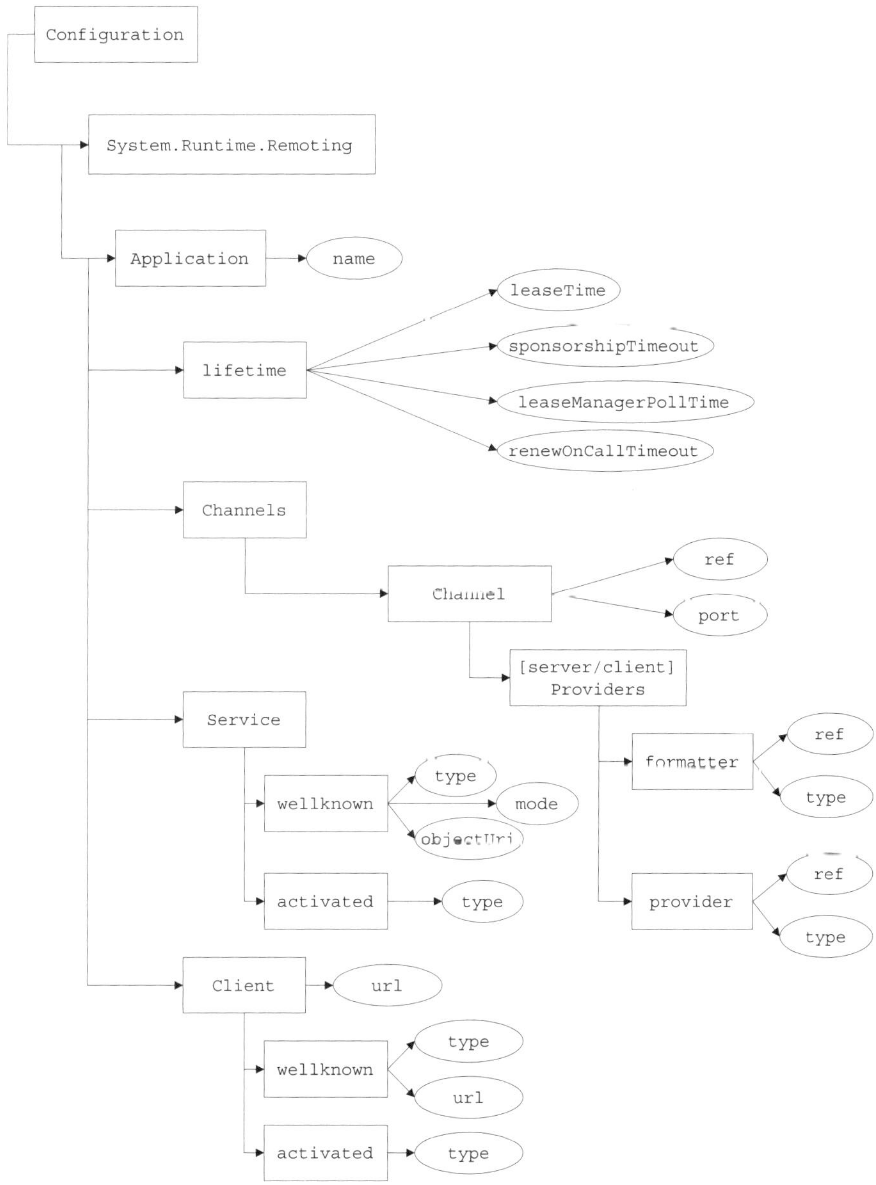

FIGURE 11–3 *The XML schema for a remoting configuration file.*

```
<configuration>
    <system.runtime.remoting>
      <application>
        <client>
```

```
            <wellknown
 type="SharedLibrary.Company,SharedLibrary"
 url="tcp://localhost:2400/Company.soap" />
         </client>
      </application>
   </system.runtime.remoting>
</configuration>
```

I'll leave it as an exercise for you to figure out how to access the server via HTTP on port 8080.

You can also configure leasing-related parameters using a configuration file. The following configuration file specifies that the initial lease time granted to the object is 10 seconds (see the leaseTime attribute on the lifetime element). The life of the object will be renewed for 100 milliseconds (one-tenth of a second) each time that you make a function call (see the renewOnCallTime attribute on the lifetime element), and the lease manager will poll every one-tenth of a second for expired leases (see the leaseManagerPollTime attribute on the lifetime element).

```
<configuration>
  <system.runtime.remoting>
    <application>
      <lifetime leaseTime="10S"
        renewOnCallTime="100MS"
        leaseManagerPollTime="100MS" />
      <channels>
        <channel ref="tcp" port="2400" />
        <channel ref="http" port="8080" />
      </channels>
      <service>
        <wellknown mode="Singleton"
      type="SharedLibrary.Company,SharedLibrary"
      objectUri="Company.soap" />
      </service>
    </application>
  </system.runtime.remoting>
</configuration>
```

You can specify entries in this file using time units of milliseconds (MS), seconds (S), minutes (M), hours (H), and days (D). If no time unit is specified, the unit defaults to seconds. After you change the server configuration file to look as shown previously, try running the client again. If you run the server with this new configuration file and then run the client, you'll see that, if you create an employee and then immediately type in the ID of the employee to look up, everything will work correctly. The server will look up and find the employee that you just entered. However, if you enter the ID and name of an employee and then pause for more than 10 seconds, when you enter the ID of the employee to look up and press Enter, you will get an exception. Do you understand why? The list of employees that I have created using a Company object is stored in a collection within the Company object. After the Company object dies, its collection of Employees dies with it. In this case, the Company object has an initial life of 10 seconds, and it will only be renewed for one-tenth of a second after each method call. This means that the object will be destroyed approximately 10 seconds after it was created. Therefore, if you wait more than 10 seconds after you create an employee to search for the employee, the application will behave as though the employee never existed because its Company will have died. This demonstrates the precise control that .NET remoting gives you over the lifetime of your objects. You can also control the life cycle of your objects by overriding the System.MarshalByRefObject.InitializeLifetimeService method in your remote object as shown in the following code:

```
public override object InitializeLifetimeService()
{
     ILease myLease=
          (ILease)base.InitializeLifetimeService();
     if (myLease.CurrentState == LeaseState.Initial)
     {
       myLease.InitialLeaseTime=
         TimeSpan.FromSeconds(10);
       myLease.RenewOnCallTime=
         TimeSpan.FromMilliseconds(50);
       myLease.SponsorshipTimeout=
         TimeSpan.FromMilliseconds(100);
     }
     return myLease;
}
```

Adding this code to the **Company** class will have the same effect as the preceding configuration file.

So far I have used the Singleton life cycle mode for the Company object. You can make the Company object a SingleCall object using the following server configuration file:

```
<configuration>
<system.runtime.remoting>
     <application>
       <channels>
         <channel ref="tcp" port="2400" />
         <channel ref="http" port="8080" />
       </channels>
       <service>
         <wellknown mode="SingleCall"
type="SharedLibrary.Company,
SharedLibrary" objectUri="Company.soap" />
       </service>
     </application>
```

```
</system.runtime.remoting>
</configuration>
```

If you run the server with this configuration file and then connect with the client, the lookup will always fail. The reason, of course, is that a new object is created to service each call. Therefore, the object that you call the GetEmployee method on to look up an employee is not the same object as the one that you called CreateEmployee on to create the employee. Because the company object stores its list of employees in memory in an internal hash table, the GetEmployee method always reports that the employee could not be found.

I can configure the server to support both server activation and client activation using the following configuration file:

```
<configuration>
  <system.runtime.remoting>
    <application name="Company" >
      <channels>
        <channel ref="tcp" port="2400" />
        <channel ref="http" port="8080" />
      </channels>
      <service>
        <wellknown
        mode="SingleCall"
      type="SharedLibrary.Company,SharedLibrary"
        objectUri="Company.soap" />
        <activated
          type="SharedLibrary.Company,
          SharedLibrary" />
      </service>
    </application>
  </system.runtime.remoting>
</configuration>
```

The activated sub-element within the service element configures client activation for the Company type. Notice that we only need to specify a type attribute within the activated element that contains the fully qualified type name of the Company type and the assembly that it resides in.

A client that wants to use the object as a client-activated object should use the following configuration file:

```
<configuration>
<system.runtime.remoting>
        <application>
         <client url="http://localhost:8080/Company/" >
        <activated type=
          "SharedLibrary.Company, SharedLibrary"  />
         </client>
        </application>
```

```
    </system.runtime.remoting>
</configuration>
```

A client that wants to use the object as a server-activated object should use the configuration file that follows:

```
<configuration>
<system.runtime.remoting>
      <application>
        <client>
          <wellknown type=
        "SharedLibrary.Company,SharedLibrary"
        url="http://localhost:8080/Company.soap" />
        </client>
      </application>
</system.runtime.remoting>
</configuration>
```

Before I leave the subject of configuration files entirely, let's take a look at how to configure a channel to use a nondefault formatter. In other words, let's look at how to configure the HTTP channel to use the binary formatter or the TCP channel to use the SOAP formatter. The following server configuration file shows how you would configure the TCP channel and the HTTP channel to use their nondefault formatter:

```
<configuration>
  <system.runtime.remoting>
    <application name="Company" >
      <channels>
        <channel ref="tcp" port="2400" >
          <serverProviders>
            <formatter ref="soap" />
          </serverProviders>
        </channel>
        <channel ref="http" port="8080" >
          <serverProviders>
            <formatter ref="binary" />
          </serverProviders>
        </channel>
      </channels>
      <service>
        <wellknown mode="Singleton"
        type="SharedLibrary.Company,SharedLibrary"
        objectUri="Company.soap" />
        <activated type="SharedLibrary.Company,
          SharedLibrary" />
      </service>
    </application>
  </system.runtime.remoting>
</configuration>
```

In order to use the HTTP channel with the binary formatter, you would use the following client configuration file:

```
<configuration>
  <system.runtime.remoting>
    <application>
      <channels>
        <channel ref="http" >
          <clientProviders>
            <formatter ref="binary" />
          </clientProviders>
        </channel>
      </channels>
      <client>
      <wellknown type="SharedLibrary.Company,SharedLibrary"
        url="http://localhost:8080/Company.soap" />
      </client>
    </application>
  </system.runtime.remoting>
</configuration>
```

The following configuration file will configure a client to use the tcp channel with the SOAP formatter.

```
<configuration>
  <system.runtime.remoting>
    <application>
      <channels>
        <channel ref="tcp" >
          <clientProviders>
            <formatter ref="soap" />
          </clientProviders>
        </channel>
      </channels>
      <client>
      <wellknown type="SharedLibrary.Company,SharedLibrary"
        url="tcp://localhost:2400/Company.soap" />
      </client>
    </application>
  </system.runtime.remoting>
</configuration>
```

Code Organization

In the examples that I have looked at so far, I have distributed the assembly that contains the remotable types to both the client and the server. In many cases, you will not want to do this. Another approach is to expose only an ICompany interface that contains the same methods as the **Company** class. To do this, you remove the **Company** class from the SharedLibrary assembly and then add the following interface to the assembly. Therefore, the complete contents of the SharedLibrary assembly will be as follows:

```
using System;
using System.Collections;
using System.Runtime.Remoting.Lifetime;
namespace SharedLibrary
{
    [Serializable]
    public class Employee
    {
      private int mID;
      private DateTime mHireDate;
      private string mLastName;
      private string mFirstName;
      private decimal mSalary;
      public Employee()
      {
        Console.WriteLine(
      "Called default Employee constructor");
      }
      public Employee(int aID,string aFirst,
        string aLast,DateTime aDate,
        decimal aSalary)
      {
        mID=aID;
        mFirstName=aFirst;
        mLastName=aLast;
        mHireDate=aDate;
        mSalary=aSalary;
        Console.WriteLine(
          "Called parameterized
          Employee constructor");
        Console.WriteLine(
          "ID={0},FirstName={1},
          LastName={2}",
          mID,mFirstName,mLastName);
      }
      public int ID
      {
        get { return mID; }
```

```
39.         set { mID=value; }
40.       }
41.       public DateTime HireDate
42.       {
43.         get { return mHireDate; }
44.         set { mHireDate=value; }
45.       }
46.       public string LastName
47.       {
48.         get { return mLastName; }
49.         set { mLastName=value; }
50.       }
51.       public string FirstName
52.       {
53.         get {
54.         Console.WriteLine(
55.       "Calling get for FirstName property");
56.           return mFirstName; }
57.         set {
58.         Console.WriteLine(
59.       "Calling set for FirstName property");
60.           mFirstName=value; }
61.       }
62.       public decimal Salary
63.       {
64.         get { return mSalary; }
65.         set { mSalary=value; }
66.       }
67.     }
68.     public interface ICompany
69.     {
70.       Employee CreateEmployee(int empID,
71.         string fstName,string lstName,
72.         decimal sal);
73.       Employee GetEmployee(int empID);
74.       string CompanyName
75.       { get; set; }
76.     }
77. }
```

The SharedLibrary assembly will contain 2 types: (1) an Employee, marshal by value type, and (2) an interface called ICompany. The **Employee** class, which is defined on lines 6 through 67, was not changed. Lines 68 through 76 declare the ICompany interface, which has CreateEmployee and GetEmployee methods and a CompanyName read/write property. I moved the Company type to the same assembly as its server executable, so it is hidden from the client.

In addition to moving the **Company** class to the server application's assembly, you need to change the **Company** class so that it implements the ICompany interface from the shared library as shown here:

```
using System;
using System.Collections;
using SharedLibrary;
namespace CompanyServer
{
    public class Company :
      MarshalByRefObject, ICompany
    {
      public Company()
      {
        Console.WriteLine(
        "Company created with default name");
          mName="Alan's company";
        mEmployees=new Hashtable();
      }
      public Company(string aName)
      {
        Console.WriteLine(
          "Company created with name: {0}",
          aName);
        mName=aName;
        mEmployees=new Hashtable();
      }
      public Employee CreateEmployee(int empID,
        string fstName,string lstName,
        decimal sal)
      {
        Console.WriteLine(
          "Called CreateEmployee with empID={0}",
          empID);
        Employee emp=new Employee(
          empID,fstName,lstName,
          DateTime.Now,sal);
        mEmployees.Add(empID,emp);
        return emp;
      }
      public Employee GetEmployee(int empID)
      {
        Console.WriteLine(
           "Called GetEmployee: empID={0}",
          empID);
        if (!mEmployees.ContainsKey(empID))
          throw new ApplicationException(
          "Key: " + empID.ToString() +
          " does not exist.");
        return (Employee)mEmployees[empID];
```

```
47.        }
48.        public string CompanyName
49.        {
50.          get { return mName; }
51.          set { mName=value; }
52.        }
53.        private string mName;
54.        private Hashtable mEmployees;
55.      }
56. }
```

Line 3 has a using statement for the SharedLibrary namespace that contains the ICompany interface. On line 7, you can see the major change that I made to the definition of the **Company** class. Now, in addition to extending System.MarshalByRefObject, the **Company** class also implements the ICompany interface. The implementation of the CreateEmployee and GetEmployee methods and the CompanyName property on lines 24 through 52 are the same as I had before I implemented the interface. Now I need to change the server configuration file so that it looks as follows:

```
<configuration>
    <system.runtime.remoting>
      <application>
        <channels>
          <channel ref="http" />
        </channels>
        <client>
          <wellknown
 type="SharedLibrary.ICompany,SharedLibrary"
url="http://localhost:8080/Company.soap" />
        </client>
      </application>
    </system.runtime.remoting>
</configuration>
```

Notice that I changed the type attribute of the wellknown to reference the SharedLibrary.ICompany interface instead of the **Company** class. Finally, change the source code on the client to look as follows:

```
using System;
using System.Runtime.Remoting;
using SharedLibrary;
namespace CompanyClient
{
    class Class1
    {
      [STAThread]
      static void Main(string[] args)
      {
        int empID;
```

```
12.            Employee emp1, emp2;
13.            RemotingConfiguration.Configure(
14.              "CompanyClient.exe.config");
15.            ICompany obj=(ICompany)
16.                 Activator.GetObject(
17.                typeof(ICompany),
18.                 "http://localhost:8080/Company.soap");
19.            Console.WriteLine(
20.              "Enter an Employee ID");
21.            empID=int.Parse(
22.              Console.ReadLine());
23.            Console.WriteLine(
24.              "Enter a first name");
25.            string strFirstName=
26.              Console.ReadLine();
27.            Console.WriteLine(
28.              "Enter a last name");
29.            string strLastName=
30.              Console.ReadLine();
31.            emp1=obj.CreateEmployee(
32.              empID,strFirstName,
33.              strLastName,1000);
34.            Console.WriteLine(
35.             "Enter the key of an Employee to lookup");
36.            empID=int.Parse(Console.ReadLine());
37.            emp2=obj.GetEmployee(empID);
38.            Console.WriteLine(
39.              "Employee first name is: " +
40.              emp2.FirstName);
41.          }
42.      }
43. }
```

The only changed code is on lines 15 through 18. Notice that, on these lines, I specify the ICompany interface as the remote interface instead of the **Company** class in the call to the GetObject method on the **System.Activator** class. You cannot use the new operator because the new operator only works with classes. Organizing the code this way is functionally equivalent to the code I wrote earlier. The difference is that the implementation of **Company** marshal-by-reference class is hidden. You only need to share the ICompany interface and the marshal-by-value classes in the shared library. This is the recommended way to share types between .NET remoting clients and servers. It minimizes the amount of code that you need to share with the object's clients. Using interfaces is also a good way to minimize the coupling between the components in a component-based system because it allows you to change the implementation of a component completely without recompiling all of the code that uses the component. This is as true with .NET as it was with COM.

Soapsuds

If you don't want to have a shared assembly at all, you can also use the soapsuds tool to generate metadata for your .NET remoting clients to use. Soapsuds is a command-line utility that is included with the .NET Framework SDK. It generates metadata that allow a client to call a .NET remoting server, even if the authors of the server did not create a shared library that contains the types that the server exposes. You can run soapsuds against a URL or directly against the assembly that contains the types that will be exposed through .NET remoting. Use the url parameter to generate your metadata from a URL as shown here:

```
soapsuds -url:[SchemaURL] -oa:[AssemblyName]
```

The URL that you specify is the URL for the schema file for the server, or you can run soapsuds against an assembly using the types parameter as shown here:

```
soapsuds -type:[type1,assemblyname][;type2,assemblyname]
    -oa:[AssemblyName]
```

Here, type1 and type2 are types that you want to generate metadata for, and assemblyname is the name of the assembly that contains these types.

You can run the following command to generate metadata for our server using its URL:

```
soapsuds -url:http://localhost:8080/company.soap?wsdl
    -oa:companyassembly.dll
```

You can also use the following command to generate metadata using the assembly that contains the remotable types:

```
soapsuds -types:SharedLibrary.Company,SharedLibrary
    -oa:CompanyServer.dll
```

You have your choice of two kinds of proxies. The previous commands will create a wrapped proxy, which has the URL of the server embedded into it and can only use SOAP channels. You can call soapsuds with the nowp parameter (as shown in the following) to generate a proxy that will work with any channel and that will work with configuration files:

```
Soapsuds -url:http://localhost:8080/company.soap?wsdl -nowp
    -oa:companyassembly.dll
```

Running the soapsuds command generates an assembly that contains metadata for the ICompany interface and the **Company** and **Employee** classes. You can now reference the soapsuds-generated assembly from your client and write the same code that you did before.

```
using System;
using System.Runtime.Remoting;
```

```
using CompanyServer;
namespace CompanyClient
{
    class Class1
    {
      [STAThread]
      static void Main(string[] args)
      {
        RemotingConfiguration.Configure(
        "CompanyClient.exe.config");
        Company obj=new Company();
        Console.WriteLine("Company name=",
          obj.CompanyName);
      }
    }
}
```

Unfortunately, if you attempt to use the **Employee** class, you get an XML serialization error. You can see the problem by looking at the (cleaned up) definition of the Employee class in the soapsuds-generated assembly:

```
class public serializable Employee
         extends System.Object
{
    .field public int32 mID
    .field public valuetype System.DateTime mHireDate
    .field public string mLastName
    .field public string mFirstName
    .field public valuetype System.Decimal mSalary
    .method public hidebysig specialname rtspecialname
            instance void  .ctor() cil managed
    {
      [...]
    }
}
```

Notice that this class looks nothing like the original definition of the **Employee** class. Soapsuds simply does not work well with marshal-by-value classes.

You can solve this problem by using soapsuds to generate source code instead of an assembly. You can then build your own assembly that contains only the marshal-by-reference types and interfaces, and clients can reference this assembly. You still have to require developers to ship a shared DLL for marshal-by-value classes. You can instruct soapsuds to generate source code by using the -gc parameter to soapsuds. Running the following command generates source code for the server:

```
soapsuds -url:http://localhost:8080/company.soap?wsdl -gc -
nowp
```

Soapsuds generates one source file for each namespace that the server contains. You can compile the marshal-by-reference classes and interfaces directly into the client and then put any marshal-by-value classes, which must be present on both the client and server, in a shared assembly that can be referenced from both the client and the server. Keep in mind that my recommendation is still to put your interfaces and marshal-by-value classes in a shared assembly and keep the implementation of your marshal-by-reference classes private to your server. If you use this approach, you do not need soapsuds.

Hosting Your Server in IIS

Creating your own server executable is an interesting exercise, but the reality is that, unless you have the time to build the proper thread-pooling and security support, you will be much better off hosting your .NET remoting server in IIS. Fortunately, it is easy to do this. To host the .NET remoting server in IIS, you have to perform the following steps:

1. Create a virtual directory.
2. Create a bin directory beneath the virtual directory and copy the server assembly and shared assembly to the bin directory.
3. Edit the server configuration file.
4. Edit the client configuration file.

Create a Virtual Directory

I won't go in depth into the steps to create a virtual directory because I have done this many times already in this book. Call your virtual directory MyCompany and make sure anonymous access is allowed. The requirement for anonymous access is motivated by a need for simplicity in my example, not an inherent need of .NET remoting.

Add a Bin Directory

You need to add a bin directory directly beneath your virtual directory to hold the implementation assembly for your .NET remoting server and the shared library assembly. The ASP.NET runtime looks for assemblies there. Copy the SharedLibrary assembly to the bin directory and also copy the assembly that contains the **Company** marshal-by-reference class to the bin directory.

Edit the Server Configuration File

You will need to make a number of edits to the server configuration file in order to make it work with IIS. First, you need to change the name of the configuration file to **web.config**, which is the name of the configuration file that the ASP.NET runtime looks for. Next, you need to remove all port numbers from the configuration file because specifying port numbers in the configuration file will interfere with IIS' connection handling. Finally, you need to make sure that you use a .soap or .rem extension for the object URI. To understand the reason for this, refer back to Chapter 10 where I talked about XML Web services and the ASP.NET runtime infrastructure. Remember I said that ASP.NET maps file extensions to HTTP handlers, which know how to process the contents of files with that extension. If you examine the default **machine.config** file at **[WINNT]\Microsoft.NET\Framework\v1.0.3705\CONFIG**, you see the following entries in the HttpHandlers tag.

```
<httpHandlers>
  ...
    <add verb="*" path="*.rem"
    type="System.Runtime.Remoting.Channels.Http.Http
RemotingHandlerFactory,
    System.Runtime.Remoting, Version=1.0.3300.0,
    Culture=neutral,
    PublicKeyToken=b77a5c561934e089" validate="false"/>

  <add verb="*" path="*.soap"
  type="System.Runtime.Remoting.Channels.Http.HttpRemoting
HandlerFactory,
  System.Runtime.Remoting, Version=1.0.3300.0,
  Culture=neutral,
  PublicKeyToken=b77a5c561934e089" validate="false"/>
...
</httpHandlers>
```

These entries indicate that files with an extension of .soap or .rem are mapped to a handler called System.Runtime.Remoting.Channels.Http.HttpRemotingHandlerFactory, which knows how to process IIS-hosted .NET remoting servers. I have actually been using the .soap extension all along, but it was not a requirement that you use this extension when you build your own host process. It is a requirement that you use the .soap or .rem extension if you use IIS. The new configuration file for the server is the following:

```
<configuration>
  <system.runtime.remoting>
    <application>
      <service>
        <wellknown mode="Singleton"
        type="SharedLibrary.Company, SharedLibrary"
        objectUri="Company.soap" />
      </service>
    </application>
  </system.runtime.remoting>
</configuration>
```

Edit the Client Configuration File

In the client configuration file, you only need to make sure that the URL references the new virtual directory and that you remove any port numbers. The configuration file to access the IIS-hosted server looks as follows:

```
<configuration>
  <system.runtime.remoting>
    <application>
      <client>
        <wellknown
        type="SharedLibrary.Company,SharedLibrary"
        url="http://localhost/MyCompany/Company.soap" />
      </client>
    </application>
  </system.runtime.remoting>
</configuration>
```

Try running the client again, and you will notice that it works exactly as it did before. However, it will be more scalable now because it runs in IIS.

Interoperation Between COM+ and Web Services

If you are using any of the Windows XP family of operating systems, which includes XP Professional or Windows .NET Server, you can expose an existing COM+ application as an XML Web service by clicking a single checkbox. This effectively allows you to substitute the SOAP protocol for the DCOM protocol. Microsoft calls this feature COM+ Web services. Although this functionality exposes an XML Web service, it actually uses the .NET remoting infrastructure. The best part about this functionality is that you can use it from either a .NET client or an unmanaged client.

Exposing a COM+ Application as an XML Web Service

I'll walk through a quick example to show you how to expose a COM+ application as an COM+ Web service. I'll use an unmanaged version of the financial component that I built in Chapter 7 of *The COM and COM+ Programming Primer.* (I included the source code for this component in this book). A COM object diagram for this financial component is shown in Figure 11–4. The component consists of a single COM class with progID of FinancialComponent.TimeValue.1, which implements two interface: ITimeValue(the default) and ITaxCalculator.

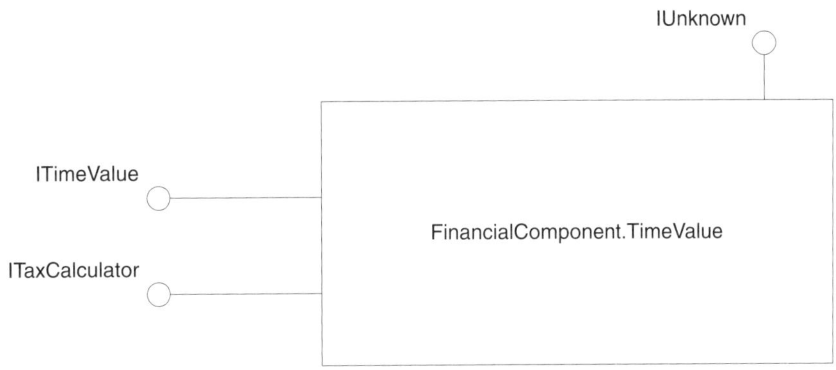

FIGURE 11–4 A COM object diagram for the financial component.

You will need to create a server (out of process) COM+ application and add the financial component to it. Now perform the following steps to expose this COM+ application as an XML Web service:

1. Right-click the COM+ application in the Component Services Explorer and select Properties… from the context menu as shown in Figure 11–5.

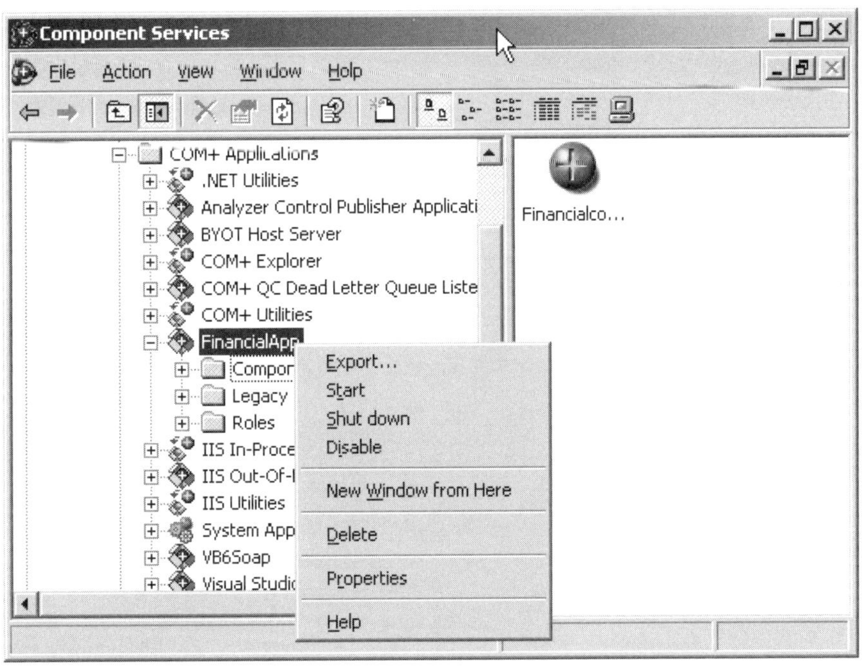

FIGURE 11–5 The Context menu for a COM+ application.

2. The properties dialog appears. Select the Activation tab of this dialog as shown in Figure 11–6.
3. Click the Uses SOAP checkbox and enter "FinancialWebService" (or whatever you like) for the SOAP VRoot.
4. Click OK.

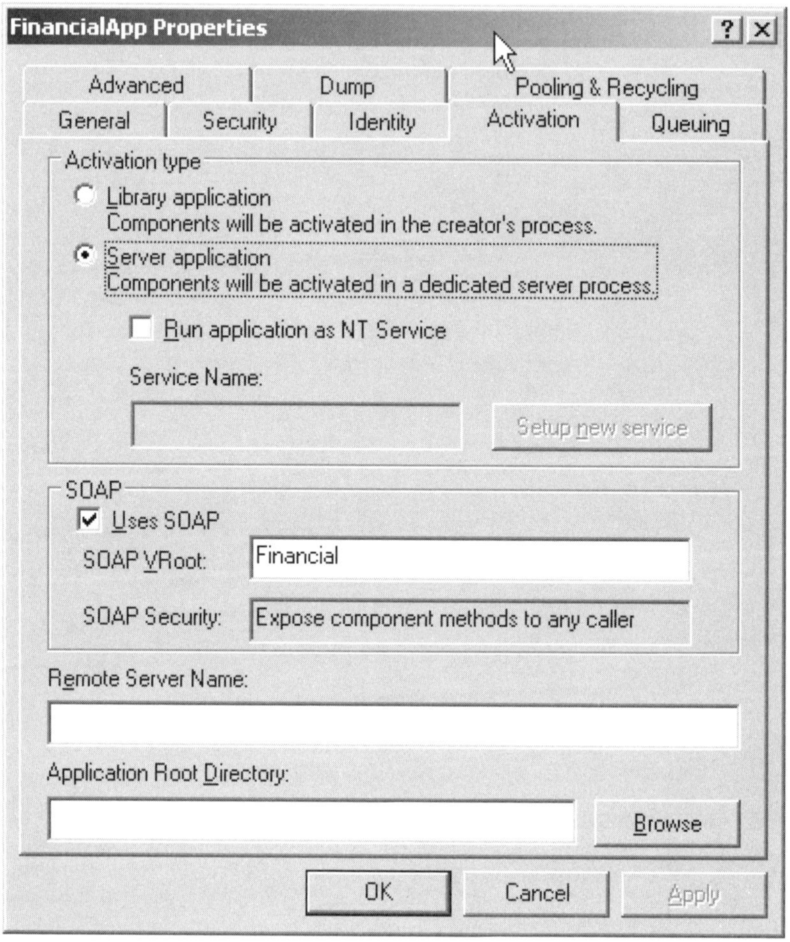

FIGURE 11–6 *The Activation tab of the COM+ application properties dialog.*

Note If you do not see the Uses SOAP checkbox on the Activation tab, you are probably not on a supported platform. Remember that this functionality is currently only available on Windows XP Professional and Windows .NET Server. If the Uses SOAP checkbox appears on the Activation tab, but it's disabled, check that your COM+ application is a server application and not a library application.

When you click OK, the COM+ runtime creates a new virtual directory called FinancialWebService (or whatever name you specified), and it adds the files shown in Table 11–3 to this virtual directory.

TABLE 11–3 *The files in a SOAP VRoot*

File Name	Description
web.config	This is a remoting configuration file for the VRoot. This file can be edited to tune the performance and security of the Web service.
default.disco	This allows you to use the Add Reference… command in Visual Studio .NET to create a managed code proxy.
Default.aspx	This is an ASP.NET file that displays each component as a hyperlink.

The most important of these files, and the one you are most likely to edit, is the **web.config** file. The content of this file is shown below.

```
<?xml version="1.0" encoding="utf-8"?>
<configuration>
  <system.runtime.remoting>
    <application>
      <service>
        <wellknown mode="SingleCall"
      type="FINANCIALCOMPONENTLib.TimeValueClass,
      FINANCIALCOMPONENTLib, Version=1.0.0.0,
      Culture=neutral, PublicKeyToken=a59f5f36bc9d34c0"
      objectUri="Financialcomponent.TimeValue.1.soap" />
        <activated
      type="FINANCIALCOMPONENTLib.TimeValueClass,
      FINANCIALCOMPONENTLib" />
      </service>
    </application>
  </system.runtime.remoting>
</configuration>
```

The key information is contained in the service subelement. By now the contents of this file should be familiar to you. Notice that this configuration file specifies that the server supports server activation in single call mode (see the wellknown subelement beneath the service subelement). It also supports client activation (see the activated subelement beneath the service subelement). Given that the Web service supports both server and client activation, the choice of which one to use is determined by the client. You will see how to make this choice when I show you how to create a client for the COM+ Web service.

You can change the server-activated mode to Singleton by altering the **web.config** file as follows:

```
<?xml version="1.0" encoding="utf-8"?>
<configuration>
```

```
  <system.runtime.remoting>
    <application>
      <service>
        <wellknown mode="Singleton"
      type="FINANCIALCOMPONENTLib.TimeValueClass,
      FINANCIALCOMPONENTLib, Version=1.0.0.0,
      Culture=neutral, PublicKeyToken=a59f5f36bc9d34c0"
      objectUri="Financialcomponent.TimeValue.1.soap" />
        <activated
      type="FINANCIALCOMPONENTLib.TimeValueClass,
      FINANCIALCOMPONENTLib" />
      </service>
    </application>
  </system.runtime.remoting>
</configuration>
```

You can control the life cycle of client-activated object using the Lifetime subelement exactly as I showed you before. For instance, add the following bolded text to the **web.config** file:

```
<?xml version="1.0" encoding="utf-8"?>
<configuration>
  <system.runtime.remoting>
    <application>
      <service>
        <wellknown mode="SingleCall"
      type="FINANCIALCOMPONENTLib.TimeValueClass,
      FINANCIALCOMPONENTLib, Version=1.0.0.0,
      Culture=neutral,PublicKeyToken=a59f5f36bc9d34c0"
      objectUri="Financialcomponent.TimeValue.1.soap" />
        <activated
      type="FINANCIALCOMPONENTLib.TimeValueClass,
      FINANCIALCOMPONENTLib" />
      </service>
      <lifetime leaseTime="45S" renewOnCallTime="45s" />
    </application>
  </system.runtime.remoting>
</configuration>
```

Adding that bolded text causes the initial lifetime of a client-activated object to be 45 seconds. The renewOnCallTime attribute specifies that the life cycle will be extended 45 seconds each time a call is made on the object.

The COM+ runtime will create the **web.config**, **default.aspx**, and **default.disco** files in the following physical directory: **[System32]\com\SoapVRoots\[vrootname]** where **[System32]** is the system directory for your machine, and **vrootname** is the name you entered for the SOAP VRoot (FinancialWebService for this example). On my machine, the complete, physical path for the Web service is **C:\WINNT\system32\com\SoapVRoots\FinancialWebService**.

Your COM+ Web service will have the following URL: *[servername]/[vrootname]/*.

If you followed the directions spelled out earlier, the URL for the FinancialWebService should be *//localhost/FinancialWebService/*.

If you navigate to this URL, you will see the page shown in Figure 11–7. This page is generated from the **default.aspx** and will contain one entry for each COM class that is exposed by the COM+ application or Web service. Each entry is a hyperlink to the WSDL file that corresponds to that class.

The URI for each WSDL file is *//[Servername]/[vrootname]/[ProgID].soap?WSDL*.

In this case, there is only one class. This has a ProgID of FinancialComponent.TimeValue.1, so the URI to retrieve the WSDL file for the Web service is *//localhost/FinancialWebService/FinancialComponent.TimeValue.1?WSDL*.

If you navigate to this URL using Internet Explorer, you will see the WSDL file shown in Figure 11–8.

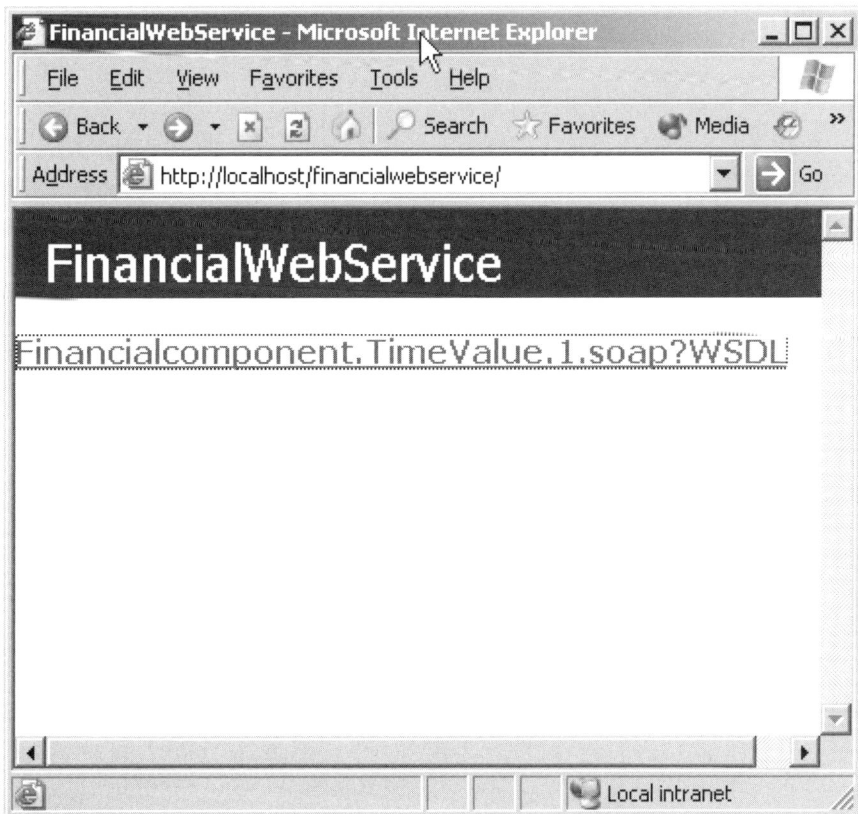

FIGURE 11–7 *The default Web page.*

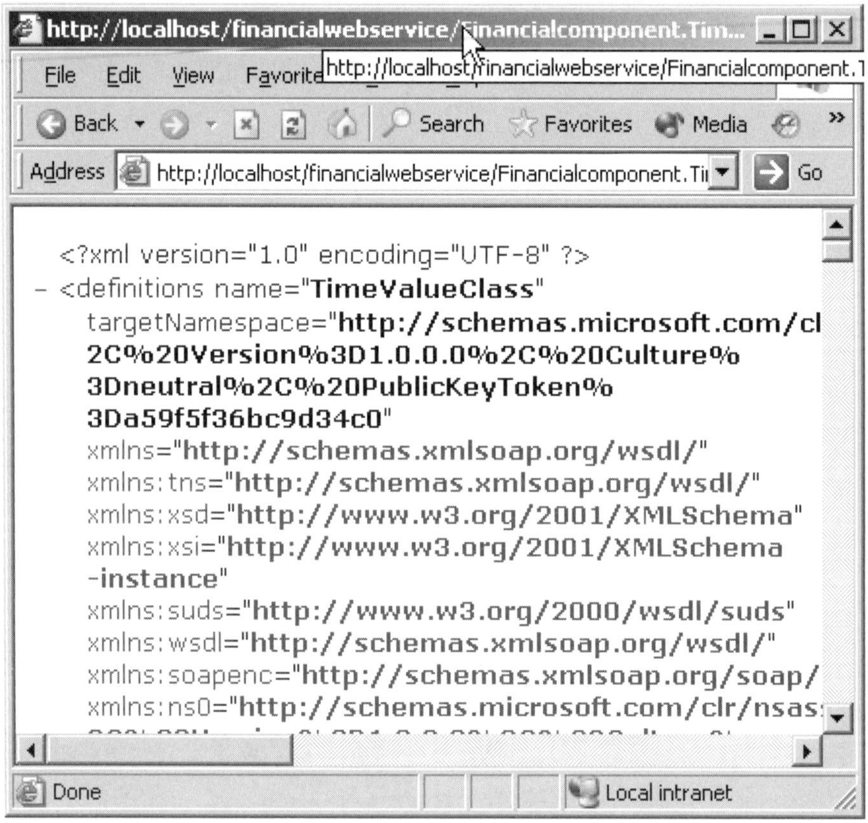

FIGURE 11–8 The WSDL file for the Web service.

Let's look at building a client for the COM+ Web service.

Building a Client for a COM+ Web Service

Now that you have exposed the COM+ application as a Web service, you can access it from managed code or unmanaged code.

CREATING A MANAGED CODE CLIENT

You can use the Web service from managed code the same way that you would use any other Web service. Simply use the Add Web Reference… command in Visual Studio .NET the same way that you would use it for any other Web service. Enter the URI for the WSDL file in the Address field of the Add Web Reference as shown in Figure 11–9.

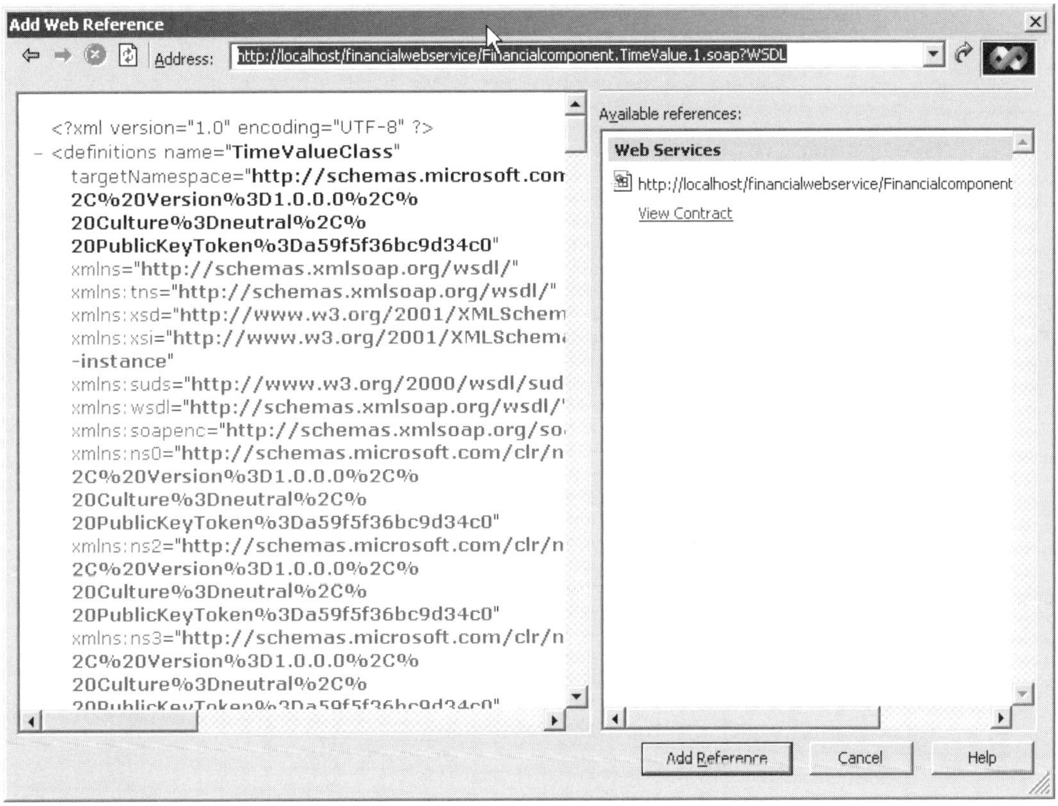

FIGURE 11–9 Using a COM+ Web service from a managed client.

The generated proxy for the COM+ Web service will contain the types shown in Table 11–4.

TABLE 11–4 *The types in a proxy for a COM+ Web service*

File Name	Description
ITimeValueBinding	Maps to the ITimeValue interface.
ITaxCalculatorBinding	Maps to the ITaxCalculator interface.
TimeValueClassBinding	A class that contains all of the methods implemented by the **TimeValue** coclass.
TimeValueBinding	A class that maps directly to the TimeValue coclass and hence contains no methods because the TimeValue coclass only implements interfaces, it has no methods defined directly on it.

The following code shows client code that calls the COM+ Web service through the generated proxy:

```
1.  private void cmdGetPayment_Click(object sender,
2.        System.EventArgs e)
3.  {
4.        double result;
5.        localhost.TimeValueClassBinding obj=
6.            new localhost.TimeValueClassBinding();
7.        result=obj.MonthlyPayment(
8.            short.Parse(txtNumMonths.Text),
9.            double.Parse(txtRate.Text),
10.           double.Parse(txtLoanAmt.Text));
11.       lblMonthlyPayment.Text=result.ToString();
12. }
```

Lines 5 and 6 create an instance of the **TimeValueClassBinding** class. Lines 7 through 10 call the MonthlyPayment method, and line 11 displays the result in a text box. This code will use server activation. You will see how to use client activation shortly.

CREATING AN UNMANAGED CODE CLIENT

Windows XP Professional and Windows .NET Server contain COM monikers that make it easy to call an XML Web service from an unmanaged client application.

Note If your client platform is something other than Windows XP Professional or .NET Server (Windows 2000), you can use the SOAP Toolkit to call an XML Web Service from unmanaged code. The SOAP toolkit is freely available at *//msdn.microsoft.com/*; search for SOAP Toolkit.

Even though I'm showing you how to use these Monikers in the context of demonstrating a COM+ Web service, you can actually use these Monikers to call any XML Web service. Using these Monikers, you can call a Web service using Well Known Object (WKO) mode or Client-Activated Object (CAO) mode, assuming that the Web service supports both modes.

What Is a Moniker?

In most cases, you instantiate a COM object using the CoCreateInstance(Ex) functions. If you knew ahead of time that you would need to instantiate many objects, you might instead call CoGetClassFactory to get an IClassFactory interface pointer and then call CreateInstance on this interface pointer to create each instance quicker. In some cases, though, the process for creating a COM object is more complicated than just creating a new instance of an object. The state of an object may be stored persistently in a file or database, and you want to reconstitute the object from the information in that file or database. In this case, the activation procedure is to create the object, open the file or connect to the database, locate the data that contains the state of the object, read the state information, and then pass it to an initialization method that the object supports. If the object is an ActiveX control that resides at an Internet URL, the activation process is that the client machine should download the DLL that contains the ActiveX control to the local machine, install and register it, instantiate the object, and then load the state information for the ActiveX control from properties that appear as subelements of the Object tag on the HTML page that contains the ActiveX control. Rather than requiring developers to remember a complicated sequence of activation steps, it is much easier to encapsulate all of the logic required in these scenarios into a special activation object. Then, when you want to instantiate an object using this activation logic, you simply create an instance of the activation object and then call a method on it to instantiate the object that you want. In the COM world, these special activation objects are called Monikers.

A Moniker is a COM component that implements the IMoniker interface. You can think of a Moniker as an object that allows you to locate and activate other objects. The business logic associated with locating and activating an object is unique to each particular type of Moniker. The most important method in the IMoniker interface is the BindToObject method, which will execute the activation logic of the Moniker and return the requested interface on the new object; this is called binding. The prototype of the BindToObject method is shown here:

```
HRESULT BindToObject(
IBindCtx *pbc, //Pointer to a bind context object
IMoniker *pmkToLeft, // For composite monikers, a
           // pointer to the moniker that
                // precedes this one
REFIID riidResult, //IID of the requested interface
void **ppvResult   // The requested interface pointer
);
```

There are a number of standard Monikers that are provided for you by COM, such as the file Moniker, which will create an object and initialize its state with the contents of a file, and you can also create your own Monikers. Most Monikers have a Create function. The COM API contains a CreateFileMoniker function for instance. However, the easiest and most flexible way to create a Moniker is using the MkParseDisplayName function. MkParseDisplayName is defined as shown here:

```
HRESULT MkParseDisplayName(
IBindCtx *pbc, //Pointer to a bind context object
     LPCOLESTR strDisplayName, // The display name
     ULONG *pEaten, // For composite monikers, a count
                    // of the number of characters
           // that have been eaten (used) by
           // previous Monikers
IMoniker **pMoniker);  // The requested Moniker
```

The MkParseDisplayName function creates a Moniker using a user-friendly string called a Display Name. The general format of a Display Name is as follows:

```
MonikerType:MonikerSpecificInformation
```

For example, the display name for a file moniker is constructed as follows:

```
File:Path
```

To use the MkParseDisplayName function, you must first create a bind context using the CreateBindCtx function. You then pass this bind context to the MkParseDisplayName function to get a moniker and call the BindToObject method on this moniker to bind an object. Therefore, you could have created and bound a file Moniker using the following call to MkParseDisplayName instead of using the CreateFileMoniker function:

```
    HRESULT hRes;
    IBindCtx *pBindCtx;
    IMoniker *pMoniker;
    IDispatch *pDispatch;
    ULONG lEaten;

    hRes=CreateBindCtx(0,&pBindCtx);
    hRes=MkParseDisplayName(pBindCtx,
L"file:c:\\alan\\filemonikertest.doc",
     &lEaten,&pMoniker);
    hRes=pMoniker->BindToObject(pBindCtx,
NULL,IID_IDispatch,
     (void **)&pDispatch);
```

Microsoft has even a provided an API function called CoGetObject that encapsulates the preceding logic. CoGetObject is defined as follows:

```
HRESULT CoGetObject(LPCWSTR strDisplayName,BIND_OPTS
*pBindOpts,REFIID riid,void **ppv);
```

CoGetObject creates a BindContext, calls MkParseDisplay, and then calls BindToObject on the Moniker to create a COM object. The following listing shows how you would use CoGetObject to implement the same logic shown in the previous listing:

```
HRESULT hRes;
IDispatch *pDispatch;
hRes=CoGetObject(L"c:\\alan\\filemonikertest.doc",NULL,
    IID_IDispatch,(void **)&pDispatch);
```

Notice how much simpler this code is.

You're now probably wondering how MkParseDisplayName (and hence CoGetObject) works. It's actually quite simple. When MkParseDisplayName receives a Display Name, like file:c:\alan\filemonikertest.doc, it looks beneath the HKEY_CLASSES_ROOT\ key in the registry for a key with the same name as the string to the left of the colon in the Display Name (file in this case). The CLSID for the Moniker associated with the Display Name is stored beneath a registry key with this name. Figure 11-10 shows the Registry key and the CLSID for the file Moniker.

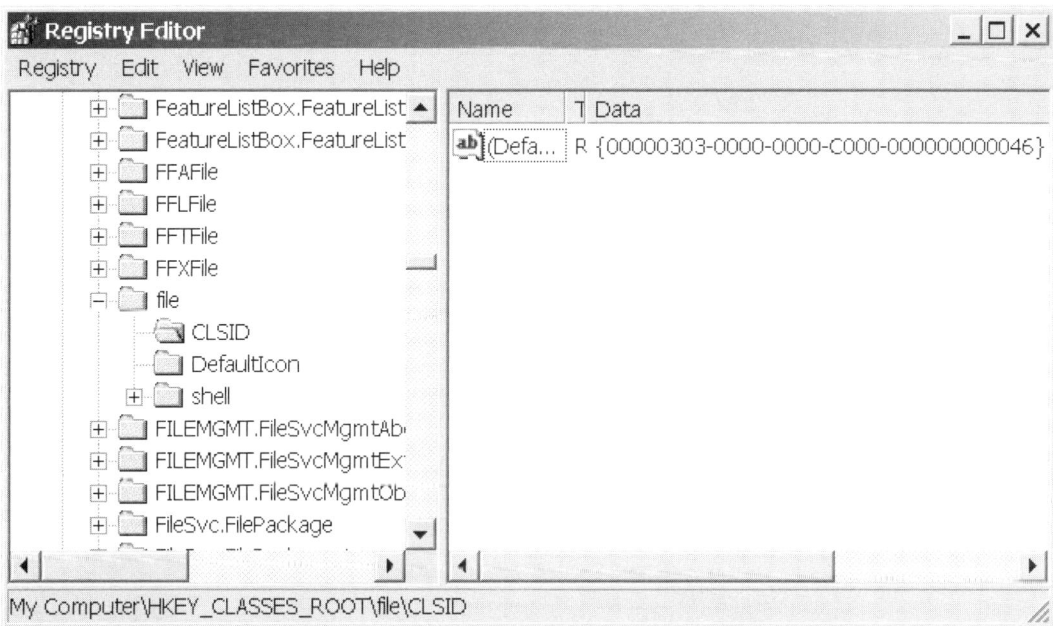

FIGURE 11-10 *Using a COM+ Web service from a managed client.*

MkParseDisplayName instantiates the COM class identified by this CLSID and requests the IMoniker interface. Then it creates a bind context and uses the bind context to pass the information on the right side of the colon to the BindToObject function of the Moniker. This is the additional information that the Moniker needs to do its work. Windows XP Professional and Windows .NET Server include a SOAP Moniker that allows you to bind to a COM+ Web service in much the same way that you would a COM object. Figure 11-11 shows this Moniker in the registry editor.

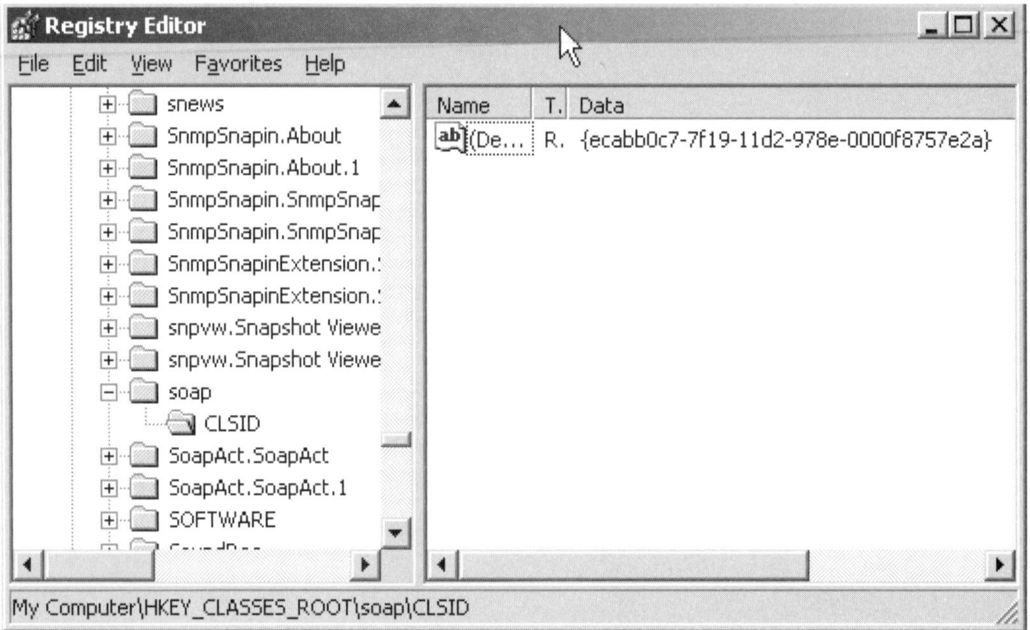

FIGURE 11-11 *The SOAP Moniker.*

The following code shows how you would use the SOAP Moniker in server-activated mode to access a Web service from an unmanaged Visual Basic client:

```
Set obj = GetObject(
    "soap:wsdl=http://[server]/[vroot]/[progID].soap?WSDL")
result = obj.Method(parameters…)
```

Notice that I use the GetObject API method with the SOAP Moniker (see the sidebar in this chapter about Monikers). The soap: at the beginning of the display name that I pass to GetObject indicates that I am using the SOAP Moniker. [Server] is the name of the server, [vroot] is the virtual root for the Web service on that server, and [progID] is the ProgID for the COM component. The following code shows example code for the financial COM+ Web service:

```
Private Sub Command1_Click()
    Dim obj As Object
    Dim result As Double
    Set obj = GetObject(
"soap:wsdl=http://localhost/financialwebservice/
Financialcomponent.TimeValue.1.soap?WSDL")
    result = obj.MonthlyPayment(360, 5.75, 360000)
End Sub
```

CLIENT-ACTIVATED OBJECT (CAO) MODE

In order to use a COM+ Web service in CAO mode, you have to export the SOAP-enabled COM+ application from your server in proxy mode and then import the application into the client from which you want to access the COM+ application as an XML Web service. After you have done this, you can instantiate the application's components in the same way that you would instantiate a local object or a DCOM object, using GetObject and CoCreateInstance for instance. To export a COM+ application from your server, first make sure that you have selected the Uses SOAP checkbox on the Activation tab of the property page for your COM+ application in the Component Services Explorer (see Figure 11–6) and then perform the following steps:

1. Right-click the COM+ application and select Export... from the context menu as shown in Figure 11–12. The welcome page of the Export Wizard appears.
2. Click Next on the welcome page. The main page of the Export Wizard appears as shown in Figure 11–13.

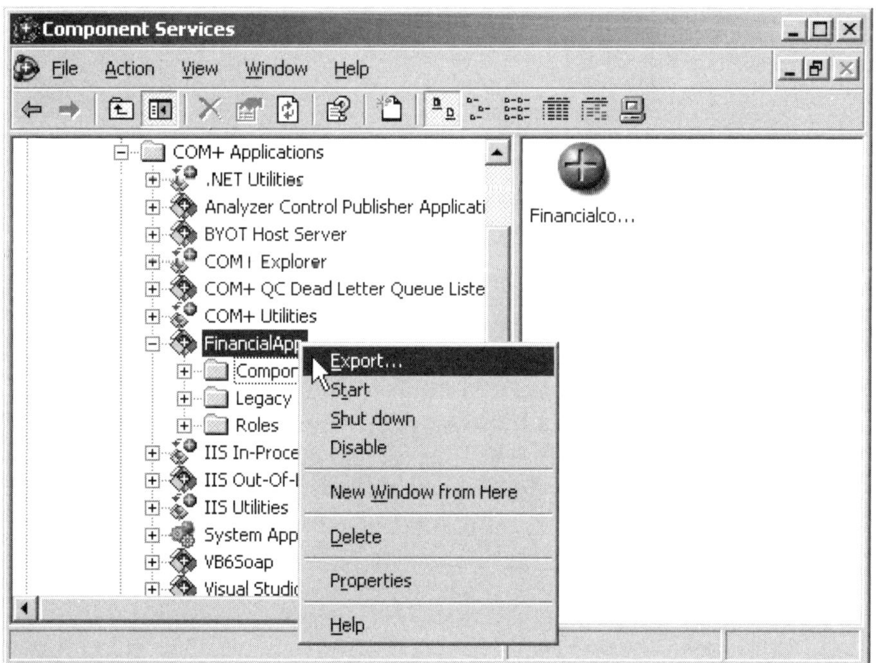

FIGURE 11–12 *Exporting a COM+ application.*

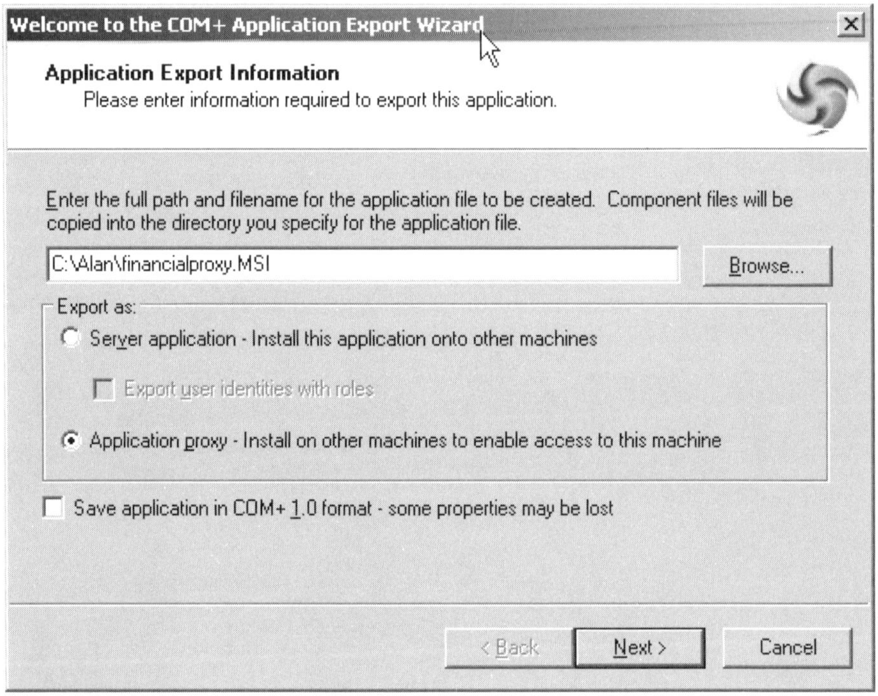

FIGURE 11–13 *The Export Application Wizard.*

3. In the Export Wizard, enter a location where you want the MSI file (that you will run on the client) to be created and under the Export As options, select Application Proxy. Click Next.
4. Click Finish on the last page of the Export Wizard.

You can now take the MSI file that the Export Wizard generated and run it on a remote client computer. On that computer, you can now use GetObject or CoCreateInstance to use the objects that are exposed through SOAP. For instance, the following code will work on a remote client:

```
Private Sub Command1_Click()
    Dim obj As Object
    Dim result As Double
    Set obj = CreateObject("Financialcomponent.TimeValue")
    result = obj.MonthlyPayment(360, 5.75, 360000)
End Sub
```

If you installed the SOAP-enabled proxy on a client, the client will communicate with the Web service using SOAP; if you have not done this, it will use DCOM. This last point is an important one to emphasize. Just because you have configured a COM+ application to use SOAP does not mean you are limited only to using SOAP. You can still access the COM+ application using DCOM if you would like to. You can also use a COM+ Web service in CAO mode using the type name and assembly moniker as shown here (this is another Moniker supported by Windows XP and Windows .NET Server):

```
Private Sub Command1_Click()
    Dim obj As Object
    Dim result As Double
    Set obj = GetObject(
        "soap:typename=Financialcomponent.TimeValue,
        assembly=Financialcomponent")
    result = obj.MonthlyPayment(360, 5.75, 360000)
End Sub
```

Remember that the main advantage of CAO activation is that you can have a stateful persistent connection to the server much like what you have with DCOM.

Summary

In this chapter, you received an introduction to .NET remoting. Remoting is a technology in the .NET Framework that allows you to make method calls across app domain, process, and machine boundaries. .NET remoting is a key enabling technology for writing distributed applications on the .NET platform. .NET remoting is intended primarily for .NET clients talking to .NET servers, unlike XML Web services, which are designed for heterogeneous environments. .NET Remoting has great flexibility and allows you to choose between SOAP or a binary format for serializing message streams and HTTP or TCP as the network protocol. In the next (and final) chapter, I discuss migration strategies.

TWELVE

Migration and Interop Strategies

So far in this book, I have explained most of the nuts and bolts of COM interoperability and given you an introduction to the .NET Framework. What I have not discussed is when to use COM interoperability. In other words, when does it make sense to use COM Interop to call your existing COM components from a .NET client, and when does it make more sense just to rewrite the component as a managed component? In this chapter, I discuss these issues and show you how to develop an overall strategy for migrating your existing unmanaged code to .NET. I define the notion of horizontal and vertical migration and discuss how you can determine which approach is best for your software.

Migration versus Interop

For the purposes of this chapter, migration is the process of taking unmanaged code that was written using the various technologies in Windows DNA, such as COM, MTS, COM+, ADO, ASP, or Win32, and converting that code to use managed code and the technologies in the .NET Framework, such as XML Web services, .NET remoting, serviced components, ADO.NET, and ASP.NET. Interop means using the various Interop technologies provided by the .NET Framework (primarily COM Interop and P/Invoke) to call existing COM or COM+ components and unmanaged APIs. Using migration and Interop are not mutually exclusive; in fact, they complement each other. Most software development organizations cannot afford to migrate their entire application to the .NET Framework in a single release. Because of this, many organizations will instead perform an incremental migration of their software system, migrating more and more portions of their application from unmanaged code to managed code with each release. Those portions that have been migrated to .NET in a given release will need to talk to the unmanaged portions of the application that have not been migrated using Interop. Similarly, if you do migrate certain parts of your application to .NET, there is the possibility that unmanaged portions of the application will need to interact with portions of the code that have been migrated, which means that they will also need to use Interop to call the unmanaged code from .NET.

Although an incremental migration is the only practical approach for most organizations, the problem with this gradual migration approach is that you could be left with an application that performs poorly until the application is fully migrated. A call from managed to unmanaged code or vice versa uses approximately 50 instructions, independent of marshaling. If your object contains a large number of parameters, particularly nonblittable types, marshaling Interop calls between managed and unmanaged code will burn a significant amount of time. In addition, if your current application uses ADO Recordsets to communicate between tiers, which many applications built with the Windows DNA do, migrating portions of your application to managed code may require you to perform expensive translations between ADO Recordsets and ADO .NET datasets. You have to do this, in particular, if you decide to use ASP.NET data binding. Another significant problem is that ASP and ASP.NET pages cannot share data through the session or application. Therefore, if your existing ASP application makes extensive use of the session object, you will not be able to access that session information from your ASP.NET code. These and other problems make performing an incremental migration a process fraught with peril. The rest of this chapter is devoted to providing ideas for navigating around this peril. I won't be providing new nuts and bolts information in this chapter, but rather will be showing you how best to use the Interop concepts that you learned in this book as part of an overall incremental migration strategy.

An Introduction to Migration Strategies

Microsoft recommends that you use a three-tiered logical design when you build your applications using its platforms as shown in Figure 12–1.

Note A three-tiered logical design means that the three tiers have well-defined interfaces between them. It does not mean that the three tiers must run in separate processes or on separate hosts.

This is as true with .NET as it was with the Windows DNA. The three tiers are the data tier, which is typically a database; the business tier, which is

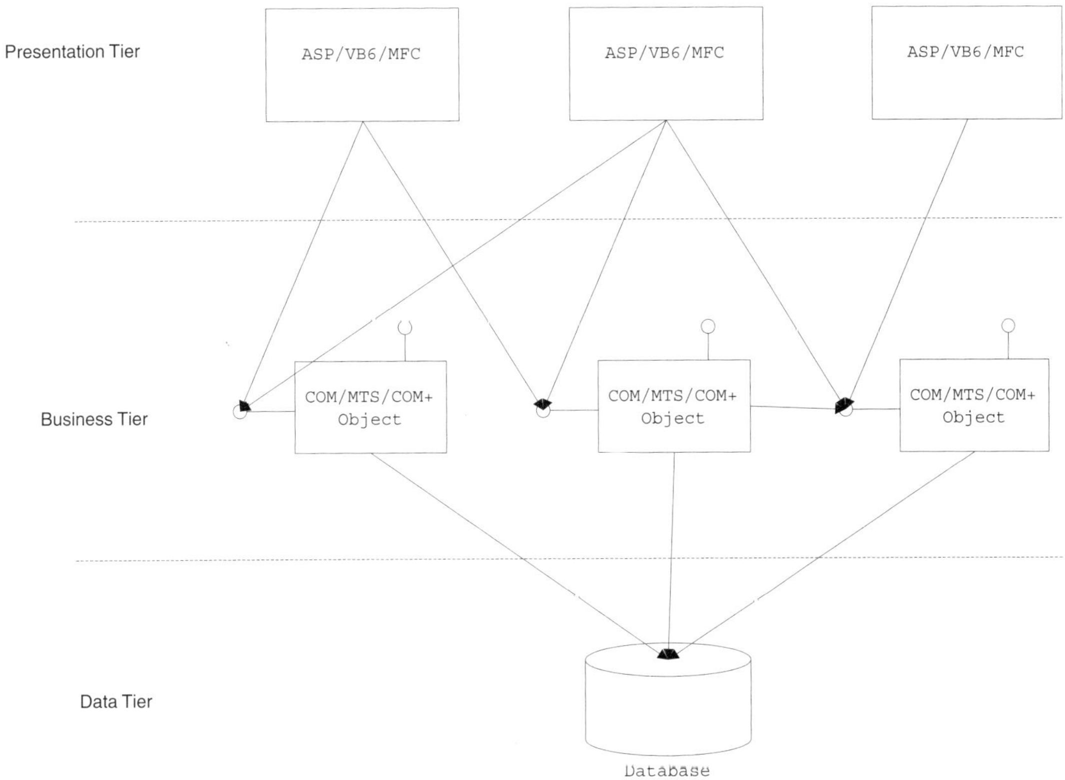

FIGURE 12–1 *The canonical three-tiered architecture.*

usually composed of a set of COM, MTS, or COM+ business objects that implement the business logic of the application; and the presentation tier, which typically consists of ASP clients and, in many cases, rich clients that are implemented using Visual Basic or MFC.

When examining the tiers of a well-written business application, you have two choices as to how to migrate your code. You can either use a vertical migration or a horizontal migration.

In a vertical migration, you migrate an entire functional slice of your application as shown in Figure 12–2. In other words, you reimplement the portion of your client associated with a particular functionality by converting your ASP client to ASP.NET. If your application has a rich client implemented with Visual Basic or MFC, you may instead migrate it to Windows Forms using C# or Visual Basic .NET. You will also reimplement the business objects for this functionality. If your objects are implemented as regular COM objects that are accessed from your ASP pages, you will rewrite them as managed objects hosted in a DLL assembly. If your business objects were hosted in MTS or

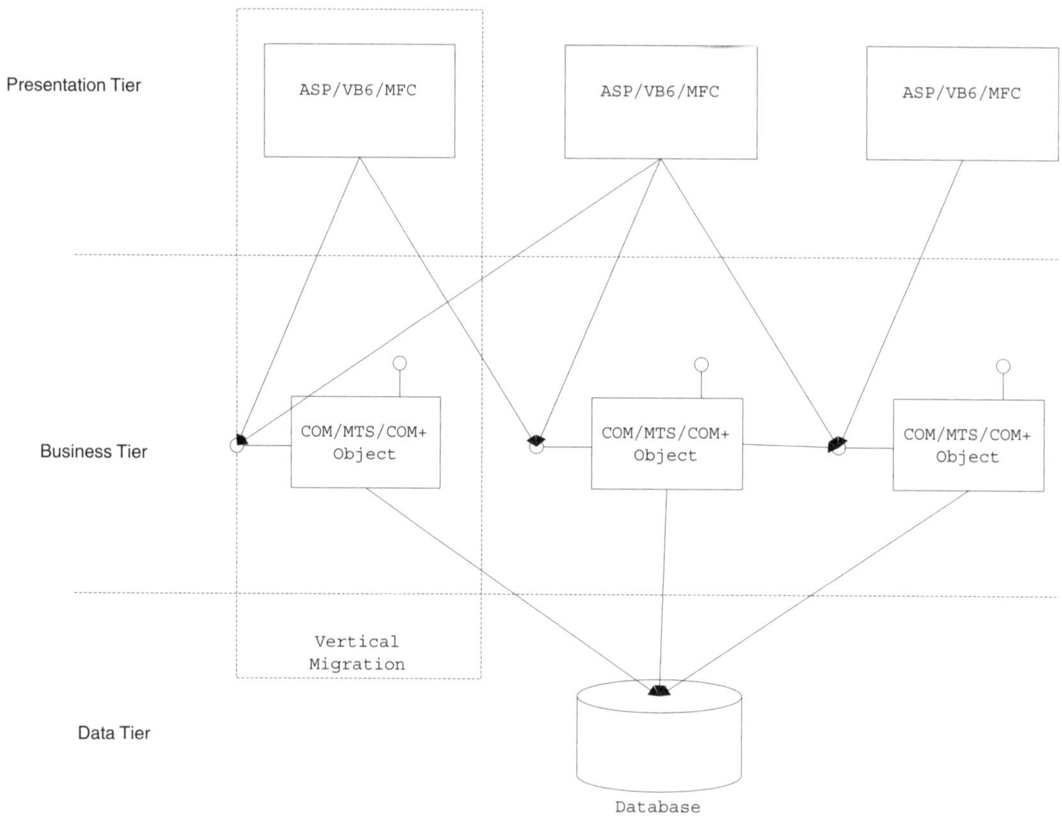

FIGURE 12–2 *Vertical migration.*

COM+, you may instead choose to reimplement them as serviced components, a Web service, or a .NET remoting server. In most cases, the data tier will be unaffected regardless of whether you choose to use a vertical or horizontal migration.

In a horizontal migration, you migrate an entire tier of your application as shown in Figure 12–3. With this approach, you may choose to rewrite the entire presentation tier of your application using ASP.NET or Windows Forms and leave your middle tier unmodified, or you may instead choose to rewrite your middle tier using XML Web services, .NET remoting, serviced components, or just plain vanilla .NET assemblies. However, you will continue to use an unmanaged client.

The choice of which migration strategy to use is a difficult one that depends on the characteristics of the application that you are migrating. A general rule of thumb is that you should minimize the number of Interop boundaries that your application must cross when executing its most common-use

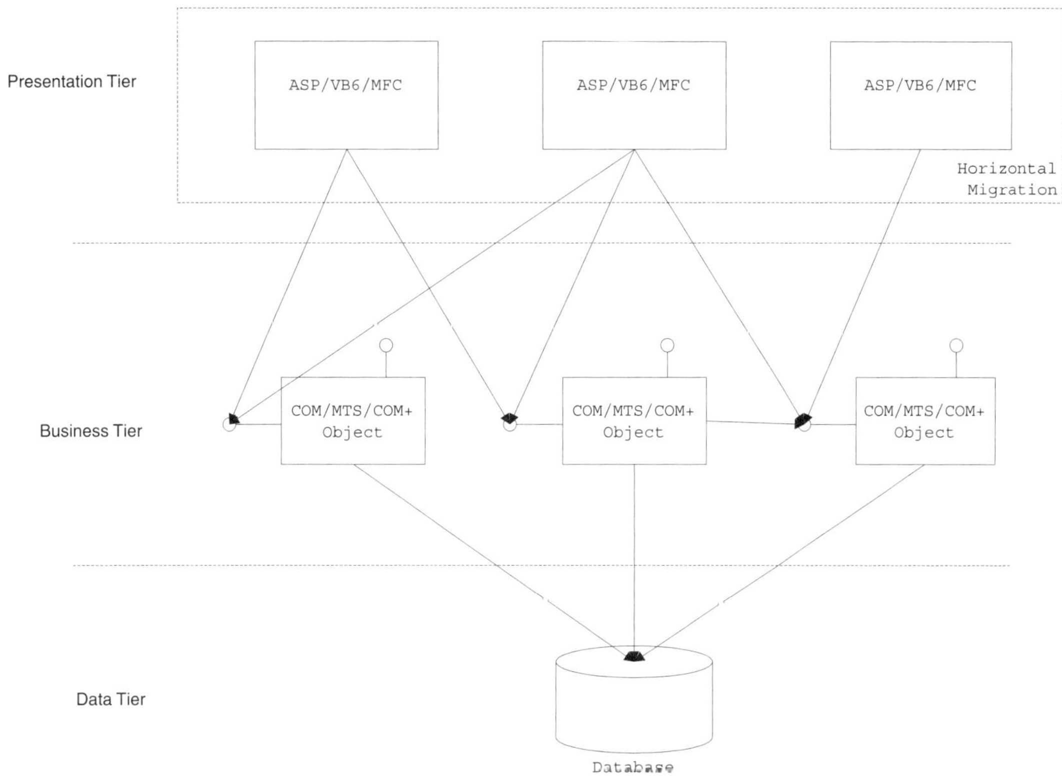

FIGURE 12–3 *Horizontal migration.*

cases (code paths). However, following this rule of thumb alone is not sufficient to make a good decision. Some applications are not amenable to a vertical migration because, in order to perform a vertical migration, you must be able to isolate a functional slice of your application. With some applications, this is not easy. Similarly, if your unmanaged application makes heavy use of ADO Recordsets to pass data back and forth between the presentation and middle tiers, doing a horizontal migration may cause unacceptable performance degradation because you will need to do lots of translation between ADO.NET datasets and ADO Recordsets and vice versa.

Let's look more in depth at each of these approaches and explore how each type of migration is done and the things you need to consider before deciding to perform a horizontal or vertical migration.

Vertical Migration

The most important thing you need in order to have a successful vertical migration is an application where it is easy to isolate the implementation of a functional slice of your application. Figure 12–4 shows a typical vertical migration.

Notice that, in this case, I have rewritten the client using ASP.NET or .NET Windows Forms. I have also reimplemented the business objects associated with that particular functionality as a managed object using an XML Web service or .NET remoting. You can immediately see the potential problems with this approach by looking at Figure 12–5.

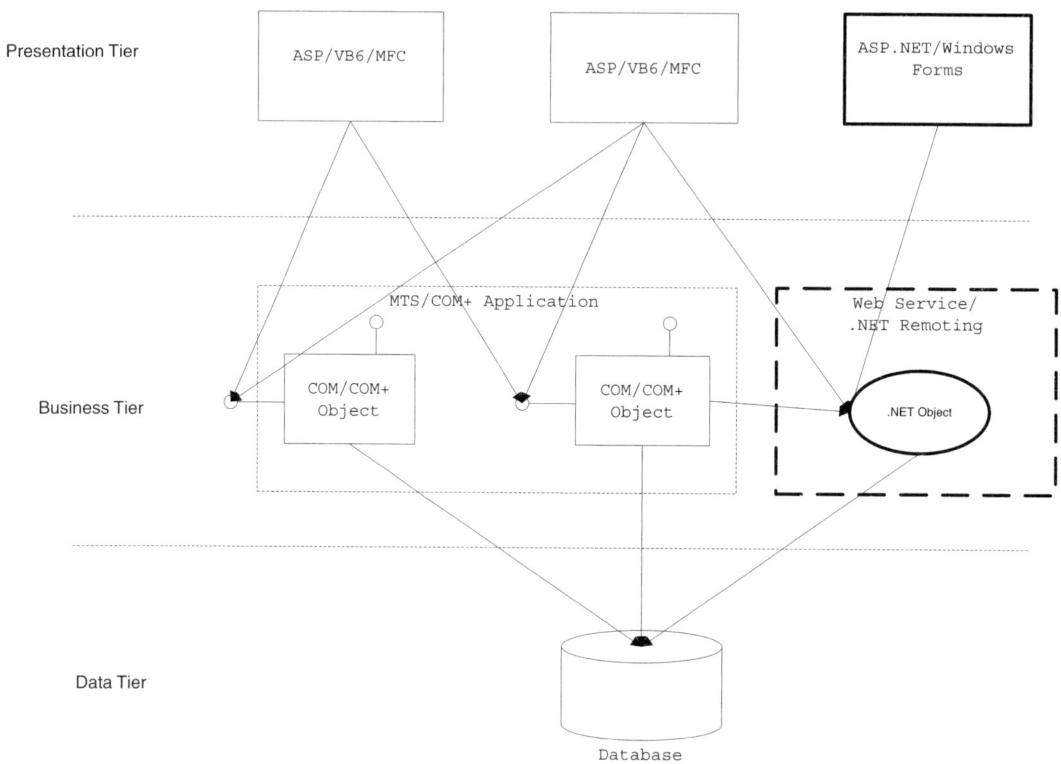

FIGURE 12–4 *A detailed look at a vertical migration.*

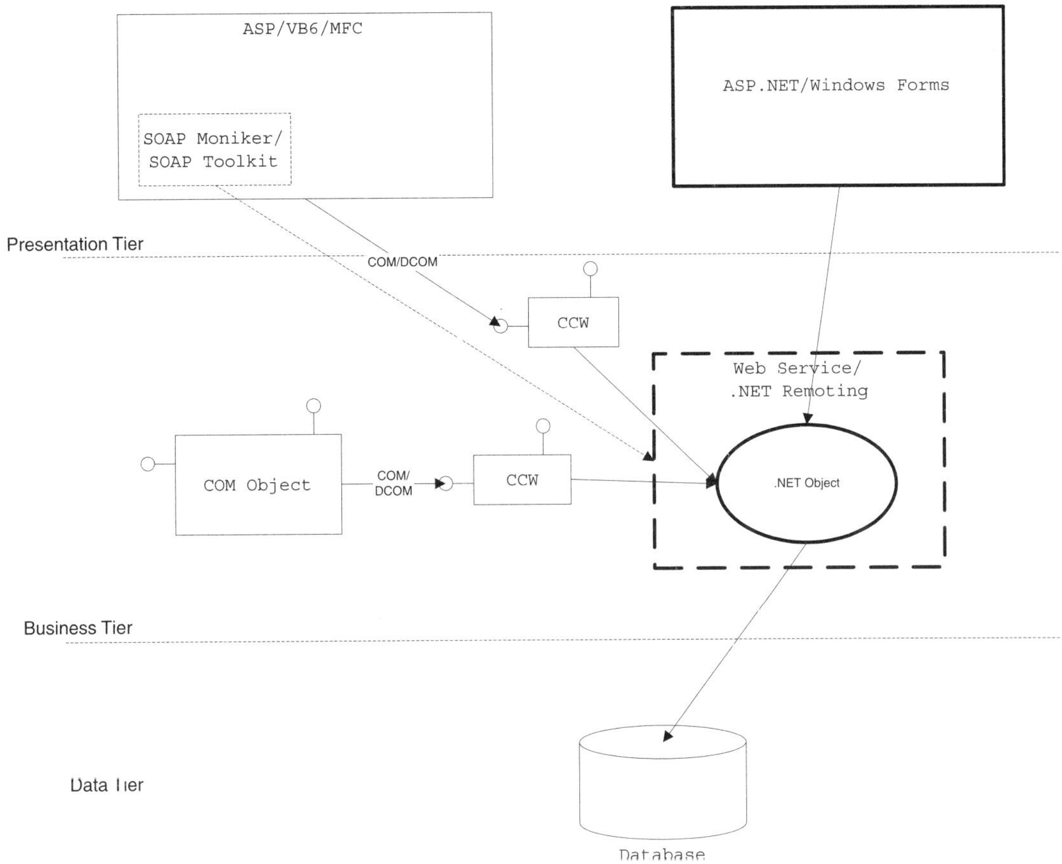

FIGURE 12–5 *A detailed look at a vertical migration.*

If the middle-tier objects are accessed by any other portions of the application, such as a UI or an unmanaged business object for another module, you need to change those applications and/or use Interop to talk to the new managed object from the unmanaged portions of the application. This adversely affects performance, depending on how many calls you need to make to the managed object. In this example, the business object that I just migrated is accessed by other parts of the application besides the portion that I am migrating. These other parts of the application will have to access the managed object using Interop. As I show with the dotted lines on Figure 12–5, if the business object is migrated to an XML Web service using ASP.NET asmx files or .NET remoting, you have the option of using either the SOAP moniker (if the client is using Windows XP or .NET Server) or the SOAP Toolkit to access the object from an unmanaged client. You can also access the object directly using CCW.

A good reason to use a vertical migration is if your existing unmanaged application uses ADO Recordsets to communicate between the presentation and business tiers. If you do a horizontal migration and use ADO.NET datasets on the managed tier, you will have to convert back and forth between the Recordsets used by the unmanaged tier and the datasets used by the managed tier. However, with a vertical migration, you will migrate the presentation and business tiers at the same time, so you can write both to use datasets. The only time that you will have to convert datasets to Recordsets (or vice versa) is if the vertically migrated portion of your application needs to use unmanaged portions of the application.

Another problem with a vertical migration is the inability to share data in the session and application objects between ASP and ASP.NET code. ASP.NET made substantial improvements to the implementation of the session and application objects. You now, for instance, have the option of storing your session data in SQL Server, but a downside of these changes is that ASP and ASP.NET code cannot share information through the session object. Information that your ASP pages save to the session and application objects will not be available to your ASP.NET pages and vice versa. If your application makes heavy use of the ASP session and application objects and you still want to perform a vertical migration, you will need to remove your application's dependence on the session and application objects. You can do this by using hidden form fields, by encoding the session within your URL strings (URL munging), or by writing your own logic to store and retrieve session from a database. You can also use cookies, but, because many people disable them on their Web browser, this is typically not a good idea.

It is absolutely critical when using vertical migration that you find a portion of the application that is well isolated. You might want to perform code path analysis to see which portions of your code are the most isolated from other parts. An ideal candidate for vertical migration would be a module like that shown in Figure 12–6.

Because no unmanaged code needs to talk with the new managed object, no Interop boundaries need to be crossed. Unfortunately, many software systems do not have an ideal subsystem like this that immediately lends itself to a vertical migration. In most cases, identifying a candidate module for vertical migration will take some searching, and you will likely have some cross-talk between the newly migrated managed code and your unmanaged code.

The best way to find a good vertical migration candidate is using code path analysis. One of the easiest ways to perform code path analysis is to use a debugger. By stepping though the code for your most popular use cases, you will get a good idea of which portions of the code are isolated enough to make them good candidates for a vertical migration.

One perfect candidate for a vertical migration is a new piece of functionality. A perfectly valid migration strategy is to leave your existing code as

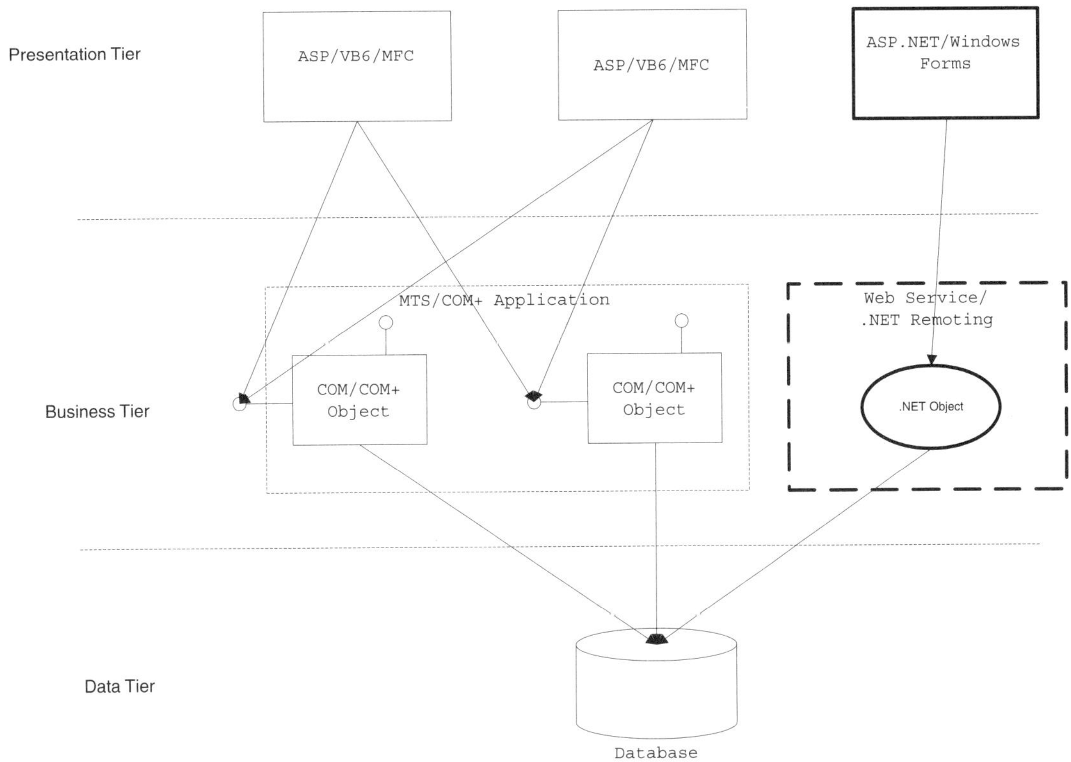

FIGURE 12–6 *An ideal candidate for a vertical migration.*

is and use the .NET Framework for all of the tiers of any new functionality you develop, using Interop as necessary to leverage your existing functionality. With this approach, you can actually design for isolation up front and can even duplicate functionality, if necessary, in order to maintain isolation.

When to Use

You should use a vertical migration in the following scenarios:

- If it is easy to identify an isolated portion of the application that you can migrate all at once.
- If your unmanaged application makes extensive use of ADO Recordsets to pass data back and forth between the presentation tier and the middle tier. Because you are migrating the presentation and UI tiers all at once, you won't have to convert between ADO Recordsets and ADO.NET datasets except where there is cross-talk with the unmanaged portions of the application.

- If your application does not make heavy use of the ASP session or application objects. Both ASP and ASP.NET have session and application objects that behave very similarly. However, the session and application objects are implemented differently, and you cannot share data.

Horizontal Migration

If you decide to do a horizontal migration, the first choice you need to make is whether to migrate the presentation tier or the business tier first. Depending on which tier you choose to migrate, you will have a very different set of tasks to do, and pros and cons are associated with the decision. Let's look first at migrating the presentation tier.

Migrating the Presentation Tier

A horizontal migration of the presentation tier means to take all of your existing ASP code and convert it to use ASP.NET and/or to take all of your Visual Basic or MFC-rich clients and convert them to use Windows Forms as shown in Figure 12–7. In this migration scenario, the business tier remains as COM, MTS, or COM+ business objects. The client may communicate with the server using an RCW that will then communicate with the object through COM if the presentation layer and business layer reside on the same machine or through DCOM if they do not. If you do not want to use DCOM as your remoting technology, you have two choices:

- If your business objects are hosted in a COM+ application and you are able to use Windows XP or Windows .NET Server as your server host, you can use COM+ Web services (as explained in Chapter 11) to expose your business objects as an XML Web service. You can then create a proxy using the Add Web Reference command in Visual Studio .NET or the Web Services Description Language Tool (wsdl.exe) in the .NET Framework SDK.
- You can build a custom managed wrapper for the COM component implemented within a .NET remoting server as shown in Figure 12–8. With this approach, you can both move the remoting boundary so that you use .NET remoting (with all of its flexibility and ease-of-configuration advantages) as your networking infrastructure and create a more natural interface for your managed client. You can convert a chatty interface (one with lots of property sets and gets, for instance) to a more chunky one (one that requires fewer method calls to get anything done). A chunky interface will have less network traffic than

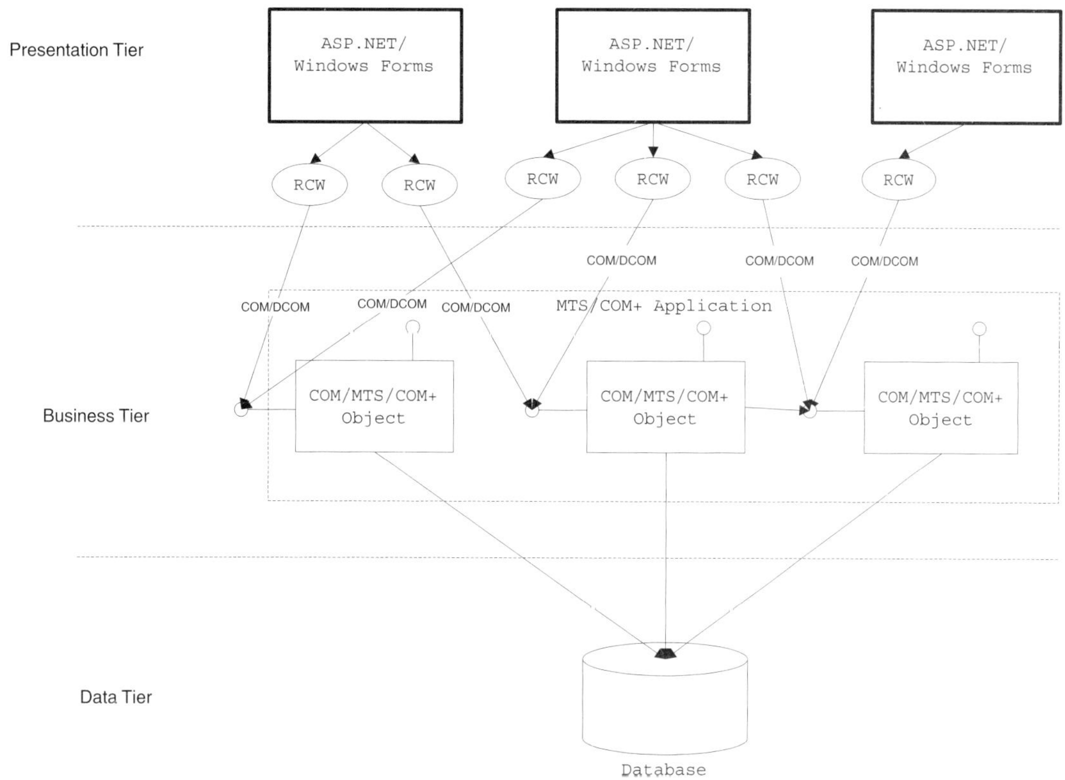

FIGURE 12–7 *A horizontal migration of the presentation tier.*

a chatty interface. You can also use implementation inheritance where appropriate. Creating a custom managed wrapper for your business tier is not the same as migrating the business tier because you do not need to reimplement any of the business rules in the business tier. Your wrapper will delegate all of its business-related work to the existing unmanaged business objects.

One of the major reasons why people may choose a horizontal migration of the presentation tier is so that they can use ASP.NET, which has substantial improvements over ASP in terms of functionality, administration, ease of development, and code maintainability. One of the biggest benefits of using ASP.NET is that you can use data binding. Unfortunately, in order to use data binding, you need to convert tabular data that is returned from the middle tier to ADO.NET datasets. In most cases, this data will be returned from your unmanaged middle tier as ADO Recordsets. Therefore, you need to write code to convert ADO Recordsets to ADO.NET datasets and vice versa. As you saw in Chapter 10, the OLEDB managed provider contains a Fill method that

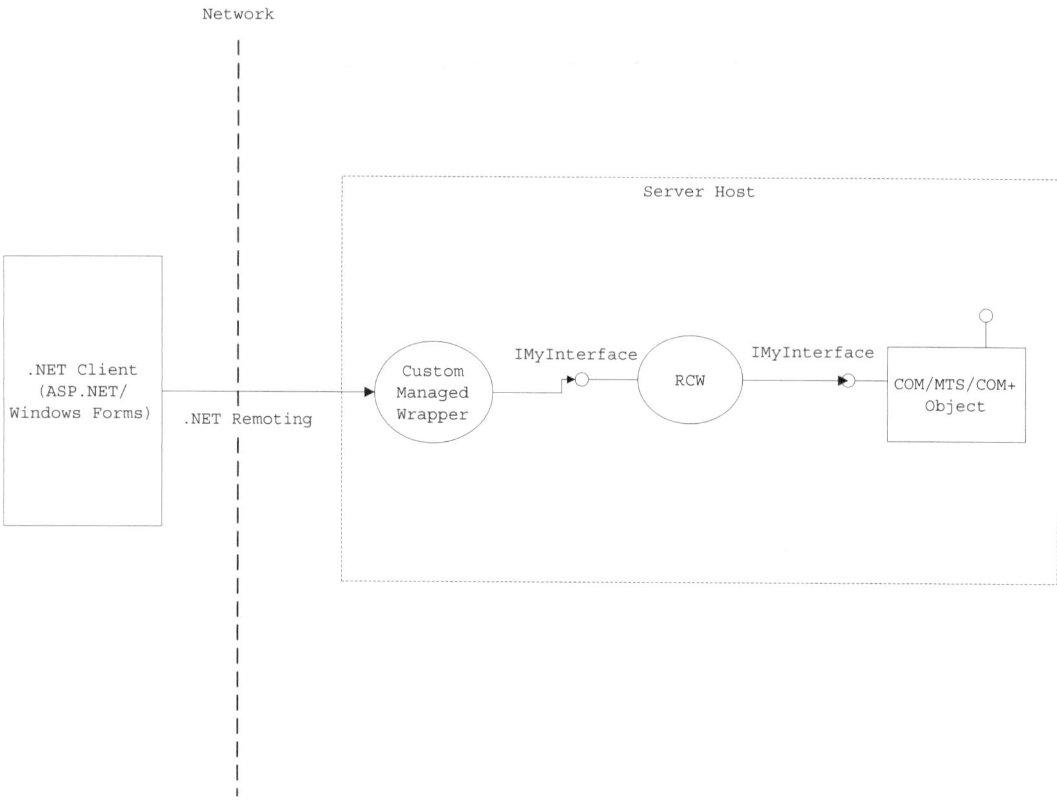

FIGURE 12–8 *Using .NET remoting through a custom managed wrapper.*

converts an ADO Recordset to a dataset, but there is no mechanism for converting a dataset back to a Recordset. You have a number of choices as to how to tackle this problem:

- Perform a brute force translation, that is, create a new ADO Recordset, add columns to the Recordset, and then iterate over the records in the dataset by adding new rows to the Recordset and populating it with the values from the dataset.
- Leave the dataset as XML and then use XSLT to convert the XML to the ADO Recordset schema and then load the XML into the Recordset.
- Write custom marshaling code that translates ADO.NET datasets to Recordsets. This topic is outside the scope of this book, see the documentation for the ICustomMarshaler interface in the .NET Framework SDK.

If you are using ASP.NET, your UI (the HTML pages generated from the ASP.NET pages) is actually generated on the server, and you may be able to access your business objects using COM Interop. If you use this approach, you need to be aware of an issue related to threading models. Managed code, like an ASP.NET page, does not enter a COM Apartment until you call COM code. By default, it enters an MTA. If you are using an STA object, you incur a thread switch through an interapartment proxy.

Note All business objects built with Visual Basic 6 are STA objects.

You can force your ASP.NET page to enter an STA by using the aspcompat attribute in your page as shown in the following:

```
<%@ Page language="c#" aspcompat="true"
Codebehind="WebForm1.aspx.cs" AutoEventWireup="false"
Inherits="ArithmeticClient.WebForm1" %>
```

If the middle tier is implemented as a COM+ server (out-of-process) application and your server platform is Windows XP or .NET Server, you may instead choose to use COM+ Web services to expose your middle tier using SOAP. Unfortunately, as I showed you in Chapter 11, this functionality will not work if your COM+ application returns ADO Recordsets. One solution to this problem is to create an XML Web service or .NET remoting server manually and convert the ADO Recordset returned by the unmanaged business object to an ADO.NET dataset yourself. Unfortunately, this, too, is problematic because of threading issues. If you implement your XML Web service using an ASP.NET asmx file, you will always incur a thread switch when you call an STA object because asmx files do not support an aspcompat attribute like Web Forms and will always enter an MTA.

When to Use

You should use a horizontal migration of the presentation tier in the following scenarios:

- If you want to make maximum use of the functionality, ease of development, and deployment advantages of ASP.NET.
- If your application does not make heavy use of ADO Recordsets to transmit data between the application and business tiers.
- If your existing application makes heavy use of the ASP session or application objects.
- If your existing application does not use STA COM objects, it is much more efficient to use this approach (although there are workarounds). In most cases, your managed client enters an MTA prior to calling your COM objects, so a thread switch will be required.

Migrating the Business Tier

A horizontal migration of the business tier means to take all of your existing COM, MTS, or COM+ objects and rewrite them as managed types. You may choose to use plain vanilla assemblies or serviced components or to expose your types as an XML Web service or as a .NET remoting server as shown in Figure 12–9.

You have a variety of ways that you can access your managed code business objects from your unmanaged client. If your managed code objects are implemented in an XML Web service or a .NET remoting server, you can use COM Interop to call a managed proxy that you generated using wsdl.exe, soapsuds, or the Add Web Reference command in Visual Studio .NET. The proxy will reside on your client, and you will use SOAP (or possibly TCP/binary remoting) as your communication protocol. Another way to use SOAP from an unmanaged client is through the SOAP moniker or the SOAP Toolkit.

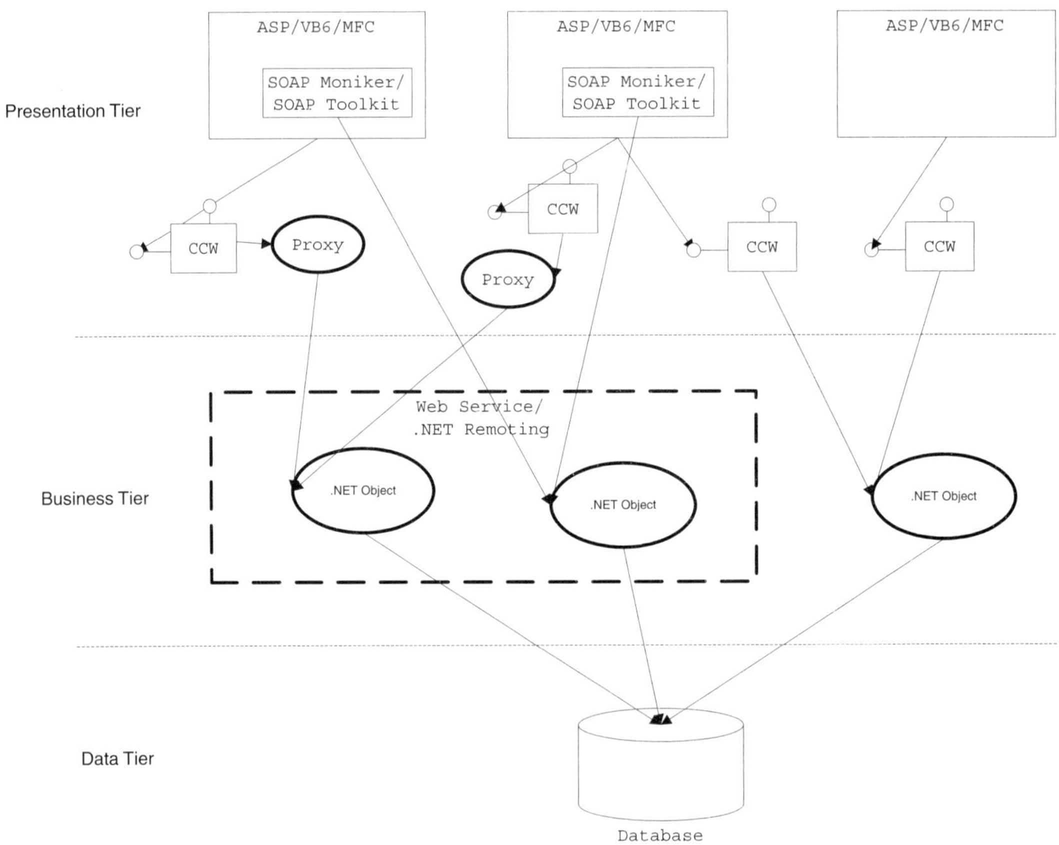

FIGURE 12–9 *A horizontal migration of the presentation tier.*

If your migrated business objects are implemented as plain vanilla assemblies or serviced components, you can generate an Interop assembly using tlbimp or the Add Reference command in Visual Studio .NET. In this case, you will be using DCOM as your communication protocol.

A horizontal migration of the business tier is a good approach to use if you have a complex object hierarchy with many method calls occurring between the various objects within the business tier. If you do have a complex object hierarchy and you do not migrate the entire business tier at one time, you may have to make many calls across the managed to unmanaged code boundary.

If your current business tier makes extensive use of ADO Recordsets, a horizontal migration of the business tier suffers from the same problem with ADO.NET dataset to ADO Recordset conversion as when migrating the presentation tier, although the problem is slightly mitigated. The UI is likely to access most of the data in the Recordset in order to display the interface, which generates a lot of Interop calls. That's why, in general, it's not practical to continue to use ADO Recordsets on a managed client. In many cases, though, a managed business object may execute a query and then immediately return the results to the client without iterating through the data. In a case like this, no significant performance penalty is associated with just returning the ADO Recordset to the unmanaged client. When going the other way, such as when the unmanaged client passes an ADO Recordset to the managed business object, the business object can simply use ADO through Interop to persist the Recordset to the database. If it needs to operate on the data, it can use the Fill method on the **OledbDataAdapter** class to convert the Recordset to a dataset.

When to Use

You should use a horizontal migration of the business tier in the following scenarios:

- If you want to immediately leverage the cross-platform potential and firewall friendliness of XML Web services.
- If your application has a complex object hierarchy. The .NET Framework supports implementation inheritance, which makes it easier to handle complex object hierarchies in your business tier. Moreover, a vertical migration will be inefficient if your object hierarchy is complex because there will be a significant amount of Interop calls.
- If you want to get started with a .NET migration, but a vertical migration of your application is difficult because your application makes extensive use of the ASP session or application objects and/or makes extensive use of ADO Recordsets to communicate between the presentation and business tiers. Many Windows DNA applications fit this profile.

- If your application requires a rich client, that is, you must use Windows Forms, and if you must support Windows 95 as a client, a horizontal migration of the business tier may be your only option because the .NET Framework will not run on Windows 95.

Summary

This chapter summarized when and how to apply the Interop techniques that you learned earlier in the book as part of an incremental .NET migration strategy. One of the key goals is to perform your migration in a way that will minimize the amount of Interop that is necessary. It may sound a little odd to write an entire book about Interop and then write a concluding chapter showing you how to minimize the extent to which you use it, but, in this case, it makes perfect sense. If your organization can make it work from a business standpoint, the ideal migration path is if you can rewrite your entire Windows DNA application as a .NET application in a single release. For most organizations, this is neither practical or possible, so you must use Interop. However, use it carefully and as part of an overall migration strategy. Using Interop is not free. It does exact a performance penalty.

You have learned in this book that Interop is easy to use, that it is possible to call almost any unmanaged component from a managed application, and that you can call any managed component from unmanaged code. Hopefully, with the knowledge that you have gained in this book, you are ready to start migrating your Windows DNA applications to managed code.

INDEX

Note: Page numbers ending in "f" refer to figures. Page numbers ending in "t" refer to tables.

A

D

E

N

O

P

Q

R

S

T

.NS

www.objectinnovations.com

TRAINING

.NNOVATIONS offers training course materials in fundamental software technologies used in .g applications in modern computing environments. We emphasize object-oriented techniques, with a .n Microsoft® technologies, XML, Java™, and Linux®. Our courses have been used by businesses, .ing companies, and universities throughout North America. End clients include Microsoft, IBM®, .P®, Dell®, Compaq®, FedEx®, UPS®, AOL®, U.S. Bank®, Mellon Bank®, and NASA. Our courses are frequently updated to reflect feedback from classroom use. We aggressively track new technologies and endeavor to keep our courseware up-to-date.

Founded in 1993, Object Innovations has a long record of firsts in courseware. Our Visual C++ course was released before Microsoft's, we introduced one of the first courses in JavaServer Pages, and our Linux Internals 2.4 kernel course came out several months before Red Hat's course. Now we are leading the development of comprehensive developer training in Microsoft's .NET technology.

.NET DEVELOPER TRAINING

OBJECT INNOVATIONS is writing the premier book series on .NET for Prentice Hall PTR. These authoritative books are the foundation of our curriculum and are an ideal supplement to .NET training courses. We provide both comprehensive 5-day courses and also shorter courses focused on specific aspects of .NET technology. Our curriculum is evolving, so please check our Web site *www.objectinnovations.com* for current information. The following is a representative list of our courses.

401 Introduction to .NET for Developers (1 day)
402 .NET Overview (1 day)
410 Object Oriented Programming in C# (5 days)
411 C# Essentials (2 days)
414 Application Development Using C# and .NET (5 days)
415 .NET Framework Using C# (3 days)
416 ASP.NET Using C# (3 days)
420 Introduction to Programming Visual Basic Using .NET (5 days)
421 VB.NET Essentials (2 days)
424 Application Development Using Visual Basic and .NET (5 days)
425 .NET Framework Using VB.NET (3 days)
426 ASP.NET Using VB.NET (3 days)
434 .NET Architecture and Programming Using Visual C++ (5 days)
451 Web Services Using Microsoft .NET and C# (5 days)

See our .NET Web site for complete course listings: www.objectinnovations.com/dotnet.htm

MICROSOFT DEVELOPER TRAINING

Our Microsoft curriculum is very extensive, with introductory and advanced courses on MFC, C(
DCOM, OLE, COM+, and advanced topics in Visual Basic™. Selected courses include:

- 123 Programming COM and DCOM Using ATL (5 days)
- 127 Programming COM and OLE Using MFC (5 days)
- 149 Distributed COM+ Programming (5 days)
- 133 Distributed COM+ Programming Using Visual Basic (5 days)
- 145 MFC Windows Programming for C++ Programmers (5 days)

XML AND WEB SERVICES DEVELOPER TRAINING

Our XML curriculum covers the broad range of XML technology. We offer courses in "pure" XML—all discussions and exercises based entirely on W3C recommended standards—as well as training in the use of XML through today's dominant enterprise platforms, .NET and Java. We offer Web services training using both .NET and Java. Selected courses include:

- 511 XML for the Enterprise (5 days)
- 514 Powering Web Sites Using XML (4 days)
- 542 XML Programming Using Java (3 days)
- 562 Fundamentals of Java Web-Service Development (3 days)
- 451 Web Services Using Microsoft .NET and C# (5 days)

JAVA DEVELOPER TRAINING

Java training courses span the spectrum from beginning to advanced and provide extensive coverage of both client-side and server-side technologies. We emphasize distributed application development using Java. Selected courses include:

- 103 Java Programming (5 days)
- 105 Using and Developing JavaBeans (4 days)
- 106 CORBA Architecture and Programming Using Java (4 days)
- 109 JavaServer Pages (2 days)
- 163 Enterprise JavaBeans (4 days)
- 172 Java Foundation Classes (5 days)

LINUX AND PERL COURSES

Linux courses range from fundamentals and system administration to advanced courses in internals, device drivers and networking. We offer introductory and advanced courses in Perl. Selected courses include:

- 135 Fundamentals of Linux (4 days)
- 310 Linux Internals (5 days)
- 314 Linux Network Drivers Development (3 days)
- 158 Programming in Perl (5 days)
- 159 Advanced Perl Programming (4 days)

See our Web site for complete course listings: www.objectinnovations.com

Object Innovations .NET Training and Consulting Partners

For information about .NET consulting and training using OBJECT INNOVATIONS courseware, please check with our .NET Training and Consulting Partners.

ANEW TECHNOLOGY CORPORATION — www.Anew.net

Specialized in IT consulting, training, mentoring, and development, Anew Technology has been serving many satisfied clients. Our business mission is threefold: to stay at the forefront of IT technologies, to satisfy client needs by applying these technologies, and to provide the best service in our industry. Anew Technology is a business partner with Object Innovations in operations and courseware development.

COMPUTER HORIZONS — www.ComputerHorizons.com/Training

For over sixteen years Computer Horizons Education Division (CHED) has been providing on-site, instructor-led IT training and customized workshops for organizations nationwide. We have developed extensive curriculum offerings in Web Technologies, Relational Databases, Reporting Tools, Process Improvement, UNIX® and LINUX®, Client/Server, Mainframe & Legacy Systems, Windows® 2000, and much more. CHED will design, develop and deliver a training solution tailored to each client's training requirements.

CUSTOM TRAINING INSTITUTE — www.CustomTraining.com

Custom Training Institute is a provider of high quality High-End training since 1989. Along with our full line of "off-the-shelf" classes, we excel at providing customized Solutions—from technical needs assessment through course development and delivery. We specialize in Legacy Skill Transformation, Oracle, UNIX, C++, Java™ and other subjects for computer professionals.

COMPUWORKS SYSTEMS, INC. — www.CompuWorks.com

CompuWorks Systems, Inc. is an IT solutions company whose aim is to provide our clients with customized training, support and development services. We are committed to building long term partnerships with our clients in an effort to meet their individual needs. Cutting-edge solutions are our specialty.

DB BASICS — www.DBBasics.com

DBBasics, founded in 1988 as a Microsoft® solution development company, has developed and delivered Microsoft technology training since its inception. DBBasics specializes in delivering database and developer technology training to corporate customers. Our vast development experience, coupled with the requirement for instructors to consistently provide hands-on consulting to our customers, enables DBBasics to provide best of breed instruction in the classroom. In addition to instructor-led training, DBBasics also develops customized eLearning solutions and provides database technology consulting.

DEVCOM — www.dev-cominc.com

Devcom Corporation offers a full line of courses and seminars for software developers and engineers. Currently Devcom provides technical courses and seminars around the country for Hewlett-Packard®, Compaq® Computer, Informix® Software, Silicon Graphics®, Quantum/Maxtor® and Gateway® Inc. Our senior .NET/C# instructor is currently working in conjunction with Microsoft to provide .NET training to their internal technical staff.

FOCAL POINT — www.FocalPoint-Inc.com

Focal Point specializes in providing optimum instructor-led Information Technology training for our corporate clients on either an onsite basis, or in regional public courses. All of our course curricula is either developed by our staff of "World Class Instructors" or upon careful evaluation and scrutiny is adopted and acquired from our training partners who are similarly focused. Our course offerings pay special attention to Real World issues. Our classes are targeted toward topical areas that will ensure immediate productivity upon course completion.